Research on Human Behavior

A Systematic Guide to Method

Research on Human Behavior

A Systematic Guide to Method

PHILIP J. RUNKEL
University of Oregon

JOSEPH E. McGRATH
University of Illinois

HOLT, RINEHART AND WINSTON, INC.
New York Chicago San Francisco Atlanta
Dallas Montreal Toronto London Sydney

Library of Congress Catalog Card Number: 76-171521
ISBN: 0-03-078695-9
Printed in the United States of America
890 038 09876543

Preface

Experience brings knowledge. More exactly, people interpret their experience; they come to conclusions about it. Research systematizes the process and enables the researcher to be explicit about the parts of his observations (experience) he pieces together in coming to his conclusions. This systematic explicitness enables others to make very similar observations (undergo very similar experiences) and judge for themselves whether they, too, would adopt the same conclusions. This book examines the ways researchers can organize their experiences about the world of human behavior so as to be explicit and systematic in reporting their experiences, their conclusions, and their logic to others.

It is a recurring theme of this book that research proceeds through a series of choice points, at each of which the investigator chooses one among several available strategies. Each course of action opens up new sets of alternatives and puts other sets out of reach. Each alternative offers advantages and disadvantages; there is no magical path to "good" research. There is never an unquestionably best method. Choices must be made to suit the investigator's purpose—the questions he is trying to answer.

We describe in this book what seem to us the major choice points. At each point, we offer a rationale (sometimes even a theory) for conceiving alternatives among which to choose, and we describe at least some of the advantages and disadvantages of choosing each alternative. A recurring theme of the book is that the researcher buys advantages by accepting disadvantages. You will find no "right answers" in this book. At least, we hope we have not let any slip in. What you will find are advantages and disadvantages of various strategies for various purposes.

This is not a book for the technician. You cannot learn here how to delineate, in practice, the subsystems of a living system. No exercises are offered in hypothesis writing. The technicalities of using balanced incomplete block designs for experimental treatments are omitted. We give no instructions for computing a chi square or a factor analysis. What you will find here, instead, is a systematic display of the sorts of choices every researcher makes, whether or not he wishes to do so. You will find statements of what you pay and what you get when you make one choice or another. Of course, many technical procedures are described briefly, and examples are given, because we must give some picture of the procedures that are available. But we leave the task of imparting skill in these procedures to the books that have been written for that purpose.

We have written this book primarily for the almost-beginner. We hope the reader will have had a couple of undergraduate courses in which he spent some time talking with others (not just sitting quietly before a lecturer) about empirical research. We hope he has spent some time visualizing the process of research, or even trying it, and comparing his ideas with those of others. We hope he can say a few things in the language of elementary algebra. We do not think a course in statistics, however, is necessary for the reader to grasp the important concepts in this book. The concepts and an interim version of the manuscript have been presented to college juniors, seniors, and graduate students; the quickness of the student to grasp the argument did not seem strongly related to the number of his credit hours in psychology or statistics.

Although this book is introductory in the way we have described, it is advanced in the sense that its systematic treatment makes use of recent and advanced thinking about the logic and facets of research. It should serve as a textbook for introductory and advanced courses in research methods in a variety of scientific behavioral disciplines, such as social psychology, education, sociology, and political science, and in a number of interdisciplinary areas, such as industrial relations, organizational studies, and communications research. It can also serve as background reading for students engaged in dissertation research or other empirical research projects in these fields.

If we have one hope more poignant than others, it is that we have embedded our descriptions of research methods in a way of thinking about research that the reader can use to absorb new methods easily into his planning. It is too much to hope that our systematization contains cubbyholes for all the new ideas that will be coming on the scene, and it is too much to hope that our way of thinking about things will be compatible with all the temperaments found among researchers in social science. We do hope, however, that our organization of research choices will find wide enough use so that others will find the scheme worth improving.

In the body of each chapter, we have tried to keep references to supplementary writings to a minimum. At the end of each chapter (except the last), we have included a section headed "Further Reading," in which we describe briefly some literature that will expand and illuminate what we have written. Much of this literature is technical and will not be easily deciphered by the beginner. We include these sections primarily for the advanced student and the instructor.

Philip J. Runkel
Joseph E. McGrath

Acknowledgments

Many generous people have helped us with this work. Many, such as the students in our methods classes over the years, must go unnamed, but we can name our more recent benefactors. We are grateful to those who read various drafts of the manuscript, or parts of it, and made suggestions: James H. Abrams, Chris Argyris, Hagopjan Arslanian, James F. Azumano, David Bakan, Matilde C. Batista, Marilynn Brewer, Walter Buckley, Donald T. Campbell, Curtis R. Chamberlain, Clyde H. Coombs, Lee J. Cronbach, Robyn Mason Dawes, Uriel G. Foa, Catherine K. Fullbright, J. Richard Hackman, Dale B. Harris, James G. Kelly, Fred N. Kerlinger, Tim F. Kral, Daniel Langmeyer (who also used some chapters in his teaching), Charles A. Lindley, James C. Lingoes, Matthew B. Miles, William R. McCluskey, Theodore Newcomb, and Albert H. Yee. We thank Louis Guttman for his encouragement of an early paper that contributed to Chapter 2. We hope these people approve the use we have made of some of their suggestions; we hope they do not feel the suggestions we ignored were vital.

Credit is also due to the following for permission to reprint or adapt material:

Excerpts from J. G. Miller, Living systems: Basic concepts, *Behavioral Science*, 1965, **10** (3), 193–237, are reprinted by permission of James G. Miller, M.D., Ph.D., Editor.

Excerpts from G. Sjoberg and R. Nett, *A methodology for social research* (1968), are reprinted by permission of Harper & Row, Publishers.

Excerpts from G. A. Kelly, The language of hypothesis: Man's psychological instrument, *Journal of Individual Psychology*, 1964, **20**, 137–152, are reprinted by permission of the *Journal of Individual Psychology*.

Excerpts from M. J. Slonim, Sampling in a nutshell, *Journal of the American Statistical Association*, 1957, **52**, 143–161, are reprinted by permission of the author and the American Statistical Association.

Figure 5-2 is reprinted from F. Attneave and M. D. Arnoult, The quantitative study of shape and pattern perception, *Psychological Bulletin*, 1956, **53**, 452–471, by permission of the author and the American Psychological Association.

Excerpts from H. H. Remmers, N. L. Gage, and J. F. Rummel, *A practical introduction to measurement and evaluation* (1960), are reprinted by permission of Harper & Row, Publishers.

Figures 7-1 and 7-2 are adapted from and excerpts are reprinted from C. H. Coombs, *A theory of data* (1964), by permission of John Wiley & Sons, Inc.

Excerpts from P. Horst, *Psychological measurement and prediction,* © 1966 by Wadsworth Publishing Company, Inc., Belmont, California 94002, are reprinted by permission of the publisher, Brooks/Cole Publishing Company.

Table 11-4 is reprinted from W. L. Hays, *Quantification in psychology,* © 1966 by Wadsworth Publishing Company, Inc., Belmont, California 94002, by permission of the publisher, Brooks/Cole Publishing Company.

Excerpts from W. S. Torgerson, *Theory and method of scaling* (1958), are reprinted by permission of John Wiley & Sons, Inc.

Figures 12–5 and 12–6 and accompanying text excerpts are reprinted from R. M. Dawes, Social selection based on multidimensional criteria, *Journal of Abnormal and Social Psychology,* 1964, **68,** 104–109, by permission of the author and the American Psychological Association.

Figure 12-8 and excerpts are reprinted from A. R. Baggaley, *Intermediate correlation methods* (1964), by permission of John Wiley & Sons, Inc.

Figure 12-12 is adapted from and excerpts are reprinted from L. Guttman, The structure of interrelations among intelligence tests, in C. W. Harris, ed., *Proceedings of the 1964 invitational conference on testing problems* (1965), by permission of the author.

Tables 13–17, 13–18, and 13–19 are adapted from U. G. Foa, Three kinds of behavioral changes, *Psychological Bulletin,* 1968, **70,** 460–473, by permission of the author and the American Psychological Association.

Excerpts from R. N. Shepard and J. D. Carroll, Parametric representation of nonlinear data structures, in P. R. Krishnaiah, ed., *Multivariate analysis: International symposium on multivariate analysis* (1966), are reprinted by permission of the authors and the Academic Press, Inc.

Tables 13-14, 13-15, and 13-16 are adapted by permission of Prentice-Hall, Inc., from James S. Coleman, *Models of change and response uncertainty,* © 1964, pp. 2, 4, 5.

Figure 13-15 is reprinted from D. T. Campbell and J. C. Stanley, Experimental and quasi-experimental designs for research on teaching, in N. L. Gage, ed., *Handbook of research on teaching* (1963), by permission of the American Educational Research Association.

Excerpts from U. Bronfenbrenner, Socialization and social class through time and space, in E. E. Maccoby, T. M. Newcomb, and E. L. Hartley, eds., *Readings in social psychology* (1958), are reprinted by permission of Holt, Rinehart and Winston, Inc.

Contents

Research on Human Behavior

A Systematic Guide to Method

CHAPTER 1
Introduction

Every day, every one of us distills information about human behavior from our experiences with other humans. This is both ordinary and vital. Insofar as it is ordinary, we are usually unaware of the exact processes by which we come to conclusions about other humans and ourselves. We have observed others (and ourselves in interaction with them) all our lives, and we usually act in an intuitive and unexamined manner when we turn our eyes to some particular event and ponder on what we see. But insofar as information about ourselves and others is vital, we want our conclusions to be accurate and describable to others, and insofar as our conclusions are intuitive and unexamined, we cannot ascertain their accuracy. It is true that we can get much information about human behavior from books and much, too, from the memories of individual humans. But if the words in books or the words uttered by other persons are accurate in what they say about human behavior, then they must have sprung from someone's actual observations of humans acting, however long ago. It is the process of moving from observations of actual behavior to descriptions or conclusions with which this book is concerned.

When we want to check the degree to which our information is accurate and transmissible, we then begin to examine the process or method by which we extract information from observations of humans in action. In making explicit the *method* of moving from observation to conclusion, we shift from intuitive information-getting to scientific information-getting. In simplest terms, a social scientist is a man who tells you not only what he believes about human behavior but also what he observed and how his observations give rise to his beliefs. This book sets forth the major steps by which the systematic (or scientific) inquirer can make explicit his methods of observation and the connection between his observations and his conclusions.

Competent scientific research—that is, systematic inquiry—can be a complicated and difficult process. But there is no magic in it. The competent researcher need have no particular heritage aside from moderately good physical and mental health, nor does he need to acquire mysterious abilities from some dark source inaccessible to the rest of us. However, competent research does require diligence, logical reasoning, and painstaking observation. Effective research requires scholarship—mastery of what is already known about the subject of study. In most cases, competent research in the behavioral or social sciences requires skill in stating hypotheses, designing samples, choosing observations, constructing scales, and in other techniques. But all of these can be learned.

At heart, research consists of systematically asking questions. The answers derived depend very heavily on what questions are asked and how they are asked. It is our premise that the research process involves a *series of choice points,* each of which poses alternative ways in which a general question can be given more specific shape. The meaning of research results is always contingent on the particular series of choices made in the process of the research. The main aims of this book, therefore, are to lay out the major choice points involved in research in behavioral science, to indicate the several alternative paths available at each choice point, and to discuss the consequences, favorable and unfavorable, that follow from each potential choice. In a sense, we will try to present the major outlines of a "theory of method" (or, more precisely, a metatheory about method) to serve as a guide or map of the research process.

The analogy with a map is useful in making several further points. First, as on any map, some paths are better charted than others. Some will be more difficult to traverse, and some will provide more interesting and rewarding experiences along the way. Second, there is no right path, or best path, for all journeys. The best road to take depends on where you want to go and the resources (time, money, manpower) you can invest in the trip. Finally, the map analogy is useful for describing the general organization of the book. We shall begin by presenting in this chapter a large-scale map laying out the entire domain of concern. In Chapter 2 we shall describe several important sets of concepts that will provide language for later parts of the book. Succeeding parts of the book offer small-scale maps of particular portions or phases of the research process (problem formulation, study design, and other topics) arranged in an oversimplified chronological sequence. The final chapter contains a recapitulation of the general problems that characterize the process of behavioral research and some extended discussion of the ways those problems affect the conclusions one can draw.

1-1. The Research Process as an Open System

Research is a continuous process made up of highly interdependent activities. Slicing the process into neat, ordered steps must be arbitrary and an oversimplification. Nevertheless, in this book we shall arbitrarily slice the research process into eight ordered phases (see Figure 1-1); we have found these phases useful in organizing our thinking in this book and we hope they will also be useful to readers. Professional researchers do not work in the neat, strictly ordered succession of logical steps suggested by our diagram. Often they work on some "later" steps before they complete "earlier" ones. Furthermore, their plans many times go awry, or their educated guesses turn

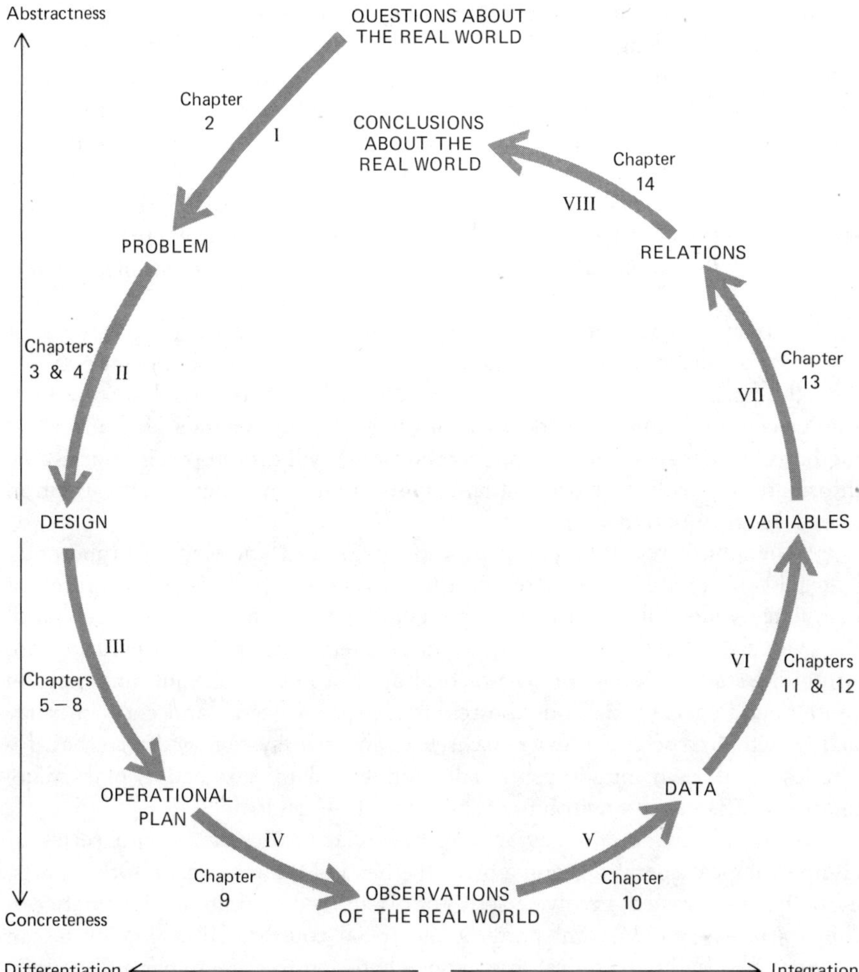

Figure 1-1. The cycle of empirical research and the plan of the book.

out to be wrong, requiring them to recycle through the earlier steps. The research process is not chaotic, however. Above all, it has a *directionality* to it: from question to plan to evidence to understanding. It is literally impossible—as well as absurd—to analyze your data before you have gathered it or to use an instrument or procedure before you have selected or developed it. It is largely the recycling, both to correct mistakes and to take advantage of new insights, that makes the research process seem disorderly in its flow. But this aspect of research is simply the operation of feedback loops by which problems and insights encountered at any stage of the process are "fed back" to be used in reworking some earlier stages.

Research is never done wholly in isolation, and the research process should not be viewed as an autonomous, closed system of activities. Research is always embedded in social and technological contexts. In the first place, the instigation to investigate a given research problem comes from *outside* the research process itself, from its embedding context. Ultimately, it comes from the real world; the instigation often comes from the groups, communities, and traditions in which the investigator moves. One source of research is the theory, knowledge, and lore of a field of science which serves as a repository of prior research on related phenomena. Another source of a research problem is the individual researcher himself; the selection of a research problem, as well as the style of its investigation, reflects his knowledge, interests, and circumstances.

If today's world were not riven with racial strife, much of today's research on race relations, intergroup conflict, and stereotypy would not be undertaken. And the particular way each researcher feels affected by racial strife affects the aspects of it that he chooses to investigate. His feelings also affect the methods he chooses—for example, methods that will give imprecise but usable information quickly or methods that will give precise and detailed information after a lengthy period.

The aim of research is to gain knowledge, and knowledge is inherently a social commodity to be shared and used. A research study is therefore not complete—indeed it does not even exist as an increment of knowledge—until the evidence it develops and some form of interpretation of that evidence are communicated by report or by practical application to relevant audiences in the embedding context. Thus the research process begins and ends in interaction with its social context. Research is an open system with internal dynamics of its own, but is continually influenced by interaction with many aspects of the social environment in which it is conducted.

Certain parts of the research process can be described as a series of complex logical operations going on in the head of the researcher. Other parts, as we have suggested, involve a series of disciplined communications between the researcher and relevant parts of the social context. Still other parts can be viewed as highly technical interactions between the researcher and various tools or technical aids—computers, statistical tests, measuring devices, observational aids, and the like. We should also note that the term *researcher* is a somewhat misleading label, since today few research studies in the social sciences are carried out by a single person but more often involve an organization or a team of researchers. Effectively organizing the research team is also important to the success of research.

1-2. The Research Process as a Network of Interdependent Choices

The research process has directionality, but it is not a single direct path from start to end. It is more like a network of intersecting paths. Each intersection is a choice point where the investigator must decide which of a number of alternative steps he will take to get to the next point on his journey. If we consider each path as a set of operations or procedures to accomplish a given task, then the paths that are available at any given intersection often differ greatly both in how far they will take you and where and in how costly and risky they are to travel. Some paths are very efficient and easy to travel, but may not take you where you want to go. In some places there are no paths from point X to point Y, and the researcher must either cut one for himself, go by a roundabout route, or change his destination.

Parenthetically, there is a temptation to select a path (a method) because it exists and is efficient even though it does not take you where you want to go. This is analogous to taking a freeway that goes to Philadelphia when you really want to get to Dodge City. Many new and efficient technical aids such as factor analysis, computer programs for certain statistical tests, or a particular test or questionnaire have lured many travelers to Philadelphia, so to speak. There is much interesting territory remaining unexplored because no easy roads lead there.

In this analogy of branching paths, the research phases presented in Figure 1-1 are like zones. Each zone has many points of entry, various paths within, and several different points of exit. But each must be crossed, somehow, to complete the journey. For example, it is not possible to bypass making a study design. You can be careless about your design, or let it take shape as you go along, but your study will inevitably have some kind of design, suitable or otherwise, when it is finished. In fact, every choice you make affects the set of alternate paths you will face later on, and some choices early in the process will virtually preclude a safe journey in later parts of the trip.

1-3. Phases and Choice Points

Figure 1-1 depicts the research process divided into eight phases. Each phase represents a bundle of choices or questions to be dealt with before subsequent phases can be undertaken. Note that each phase builds on the one before it and that the whole process is a closed loop that starts with questions drawn from the real world of empirical events and finishes with conclusions bearing on the portion of the real world about which the original questions were asked. These conclusions spur new questions and the cycle is repeated. The first several phases require moving from a universe of possibilities considered abstractly—that is, in thought—to a general notion of a limited problem, thence to differentiation of the aspects of the problem within a detailed study design, and eventually to a specific operational plan for making observations of concrete events. The later stages require integrating specific observations and data into larger patterns of relations among variables. Thus the cycle swings between the abstract and the concrete and between differentiation and integration.

Each phase poses a series of questions or choice points for the investigator.

We give below some of the major questions within each phase along with an indication of the parts of the book that deal with those questions. Some of the questions may well be unclear at this stage, but we hope this preview will give the reader a general sense of the progression of topics in the chapters to follow.

Phase I. Formulating the Problem. If he is to be systematic in his research, the investigator must fix upon a fairly restricted problem from among all the rather general questions he may have about the real world. And he will help himself immensely if he phrases his problem to be as sharp a guide as possible. To get started on sharpening up a problem he might ask himself questions such as the following: What kind of gain from my study will be most important to me? What thing or system do I want to make the chief object of my study? What is the effective environment of this kind of thing or system? What are the actors, behaviors, and contexts in this domain? What are the features of the systems or the environment by which I can tell when I am no longer looking at things that belong within the domain of my study? (Chapter 2)

Phase II. Designing. By designing, we mean choosing the actors, behaviors, and contexts to be selected for observation, the partitions to be made among them, and the comparisons to be made among observations. How can I distinguish between differences that are important and differences that are mere error? How can I arrange matters so that I can be confident that one difference I observe has some meaningful connection with something else I observe rather than with something I will not have observed? How can I get information about the effects my observations are having on the persons or groups I observe? Can I gain more of the kind of information I want from the natural setting, from an experiment in the laboratory, or from some other approach? (Chapters 3 and 4)

Phase III. Making an Operational Plan. When I study persons or groups of a particular sort and there are too many to observe all of them, how can I be confident that I will learn something about those persons or groups that I shall not have observed? If I want to study a property of persons or groups but the property is not directly observable—such as a need for companionship or *esprit de corps*—how can I set about obtaining a measurement of it? And how can I check on whether I succeeded in obtaining a measure of the intangible property? What kinds of things are there to observe that might serve as indicators of that intangible property? What comparisons might I ask persons to make among objects that would indicate to me the properties of the persons or the subjects? What are the advantages of selecting persons to observe who already have a certain characteristic as compared with producing that characteristic, perhaps by training? (Chapters 5–8)

Phase IV. Carrying Out the Operational Plan. What can I do to increase the probability that persons and groups will allow themselves to be observed? What can I do to insure that the behavior I observe will remain substantially "natural"? How can I anticipate possible harm to the people I am observing and protect them from it? (Chapter 9)

Phase V. Mapping Observations into Data. The behavior of a person or group can be interpreted as showing certain types of relations between the person (or group) and the objects toward which he is behaving. Counting the instances in which relations of different types occur or noting the combinations in which certain relations occur can enable us to make quantitative comparisons among sets of observations. When I interpret behavior as relations, what types of relations will best suit my purpose? When I convert observations into *data* in this way, what assumptions must I make about the people or groups? (Chapter 10)

Phase VI. Mapping Data into Variables. Data can accumulate into a vast collection. How can I simplify a mountain of data into a comprehensible array? Should I try to form the data into a scale? What kinds of evidence in the data should I seek if I want to test whether the data can form a scale? Would a unidimensional scale or a multidimensional scale be more suitable for my purpose? What are the advantages and disadvantages of the many different ways (models) in which to construct a scale, unidimensional or multidimensional? (Chapters 11 and 12)

Phase VII. Exploring Relations. Everything happens at some *rate.* When a rate of occurrence of one characteristic in a population changes concomitantly with the rate of occurrence of another characteristic, the concurrence is called a relation. What kinds of scales enable which kinds of relations to be ascertained? What kinds of relations are useful for which purposes? How can we describe relations with time? How can we confidently distinguish change from random variability? How can relations among more than two variables be described? How can patterns of change among more than two variables be distinguished? (Chapter 13)

Phase VIII. Drawing Conclusions. What assumptions will I have made about persons or groups that, if wrong, can be alternative explanations for my findings? What comparisons remain to be made to increase my confidence in my results? How likely is it that my results occurred by chance? What biases on the part of the persons I shall observe might help or hinder confident conclusions about their behavior? How can my results be put together with the results of studies by other investigators to our mutual benefit? (Chapters 13 and 14)

1-4. Further Reading

As in any other field of human endeavor, researchers in the field of human behavior differ somewhat in their views of what is important. For views somewhat different from ours, supplementary when not actually disagreeing, see Agnew and Pyke (1969), Anderson (1966), Bachrach (1962), Bruyn (1966),

Doby and others (1966), Fairweather (1967), Frohock (1967), Gephart and Ingle (1969), Glaser and Strauss (1967), Hyman (1964), Kaufmann (1968), Madge (1965), Phillips (1966), Plutchik (1968), Scott and Wertheimer (1962), Simon (1968), Sjoberg and Nett (1968), and Travers (1964). For discussions of the logical problems of research and the philosophy of science, see Hanson (1958), Kaplan (1964), Kuhn (1962), Nagle (1961), Popper (1959), Wolman and Nagle (1965), and Zetterberg (1963). For some personal histories in research, see Hammond (1964). For strategies in studying the future of human behavior, see Helmer (1966).

CHAPTER 2

Formulating a Problem for Empirical Research

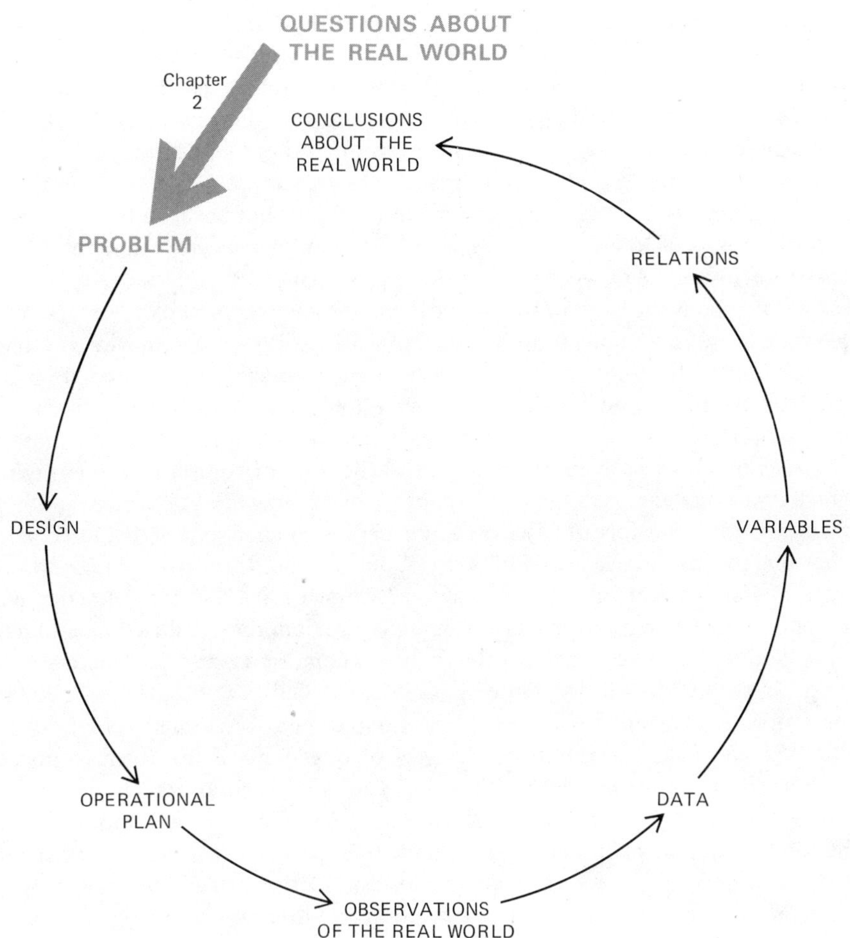

In one sense, finding a form into which to cast a question for research is no trick at all. Every one of us does this daily. Where is the bottle opener? Does she want to go to the movies? How hard do I have to scold him to get him to brush his teeth? Such questions serve us daily as guides to inquiry, and they often serve well enough. The reason that books are written about formulating a research question is that it is not always easy to form a research question that helps us in the way we want to be helped. This is especially true when we get interested in behavioral realms for which our culture has given us no everyday questions to serve as guides.

Take our first everyday example: "Where is the bottle opener?" This question may serve me well a good many times, but one day I may hunt high and low without success. I turn to my wife: "I can't find the bottle opener!" And it turns out that my question was bootless, because my wife threw the opener in the trash three days ago. "And how then am I to drink my beer?" And now I learn that I don't even need a bottle opener, for the beer bottle has a twist-off top! The moral here is that the original question assumed a world of unduly restricted alternatives. It implied that there *was* a bottle opener somewhere in the house. Furthermore, it implied that I could not achieve my goal without a bottle opener. The result was frustration—not because there was any objective obstacle between me and my goal but because I had framed my question so as to demand an answer within an over-narrow domain. I had frustrated myself. And so we often do as scientists.

Does she want to go to the movies? Maybe she wants to please me, going if I want to go and not going if I do not wish to do so. Or maybe she has no opinion on the matter. How hard do I have to scold him to get him to brush his teeth? Maybe he will brush his teeth if I *stop* scolding him. Or maybe he will not brush his teeth as long as I betray any interest in the matter whatsoever. This last example brings us to the kind of complex problem with which professional researchers try to cope. As we follow one guess after another unsuccessfully, the form of the question begins to change. We begin to ask, what are the useful ways of thinking about a child's teeth-brushing? What are the effective features of the situation? Chances are that what is effective for one child or at one time is not effective for another child or at another time. And if this is so, what are the features, conditions, and parameters that are good possibilities to look into? In George A. Kelly's (1955) term, what are some useful ways in which we can *construe* the teeth-brushing problem?

We can next ask ourselves a series of questions of the form, suppose the persons surrounding this child were to act as if such-and-such were true; how would this child act then? Such a question, of course, has the shape of the kind of query (or tentative statement) that we call a *hypothesis*. The spirit of a hypothesis is to act as if some description the researcher makes of a piece of the world were a relevant description and then see, by acting according to that description, what happens. We shall say more about hypotheses later in this chapter.

In our homely illustrations thus far, we have, first, implied that there were some interesting things to be studied: a bottle opener, she who might want to go to the movies, the nonbrushing child. An important topic of this chapter will be the question of what kind of "thing" the researcher can choose to study. We have limited this book to human behavior, and we shall therefore confine our discussion largely to the study of entities that are humans or entities in which humans are involved. Section 2-3 will discuss these living systems as objects of study.

Second, we use our illustrations to say that a useful question asks us to try out some features, conditions, parameters—*facets* of the problem—that help us to construe a perplexing situation in new ways. We discuss facets in section 2-4; in that same section we point out some of the ways we have used various general facets of human interaction to organize this book. The discussion of the facets of a research problem leads us into some brief remarks about theory in section 2-6. Before then we shall mention, as some of the facets of behavior, *actors* (living systems) *behaving toward objects* in a *context;* this topic will comprise section 2-5. The third topic raised by our illustrations was the rhetoric of hypotheses; we shall go into this matter in section 2-7. Before beginning on this list of topics, however, let us clear away some possible stumbling blocks—namely, the researcher's personal motivations and preferences.

2-1. Motivations

Most readers of this book will be students at some college, and a good portion of them will be either graduate students or undergraduates intending to undertake graduate study. Students undergo a socialization process. They are subject to interactions—some of them very persuasive interactions—with social scientists having certain values for which they demand a good deal of deference from their students. One value widely shared among social scientists is an admiration for scientific method and for people who carry out projects using scientific methods of highly systematic and specifiable sorts. So widespread and so strong is this admiration of scientific research that a college student can hardly be exposed to it for very long without succumbing to it to some degree. It is easy for the student to come to view skill in scientific work as valuable in itself rather than as a means to an end. The adulation of science is common in the United States and it is especially severe on campuses. We think it worthwhile, therefore, to say clearly that in this book we confine ourselves to a pragmatic orientation.

Different people have different objectives for their research, and misunderstandings regularly occur when a man doing research for one particular reason talks to a man doing research for a different reason. For convenience, let us divide motivations for research into *intrinsic* and *extrinsic.* The researcher is intrinsically motivated who seeks the sheer joy of the work itself, quite apart from any benefits the outcome of the research might bring. Extrinsic benefits, in contrast, exist outside the research project, or beyond it; they lie in salary, prestige, and in gaining information not known before. When the primary purpose of the researcher is to learn something about the real world, he guides his actions, above all else, by the thought of how he can best learn what he wants to learn. If he can obtain the information he wants by rough-and-ready methods, he uses them. If the problem seems likely to yield only to very subtle and sophisticated techniques, he uses those. This researcher prefers methods yielding results that are prey to a minimum of doubts, but if he discovers that findings of this kind will take an inordinately long time to obtain, he may undertake a project yielding weak but quick results that will give him information enabling him to decide whether to invest in a more penetrating sort of project.

Our orientation is this: we value research procedures primarily for the information they will bring. We shall try to evaluate procedures on this basis and describe advantages and disadvantages of alternatives on the basis of their efficiency in producing desired information. We urge the reader to put minimal weight on the matter of whether a technique is currently fashionable or on what kinds of analyses editors are favoring this year. We shall certainly insist that there are not any generally "better" research methods and "worse" methods; some methods are better for some purposes and some for others. Our orientation is that we are describing a set of tools useful in extracting information from nature. We do not deny that many of these tools can give pleasure in the very using of them. We grant that research in social science is a nice way to make a living. We admit that using some tools will bring more prestige than using others. We emphasize, however, that we are trying to keep constantly in mind the goal of getting valid information from nature with minimal trouble and expense.

2-2. Personal Flavor

Every human act is an interaction between person and environment. This is as true of a researcher (or a team of researchers) as it is of other persons in other roles. In consequence, every scientific study has a personal uniqueness and is to that extent a work of art. It is true that the scientist tries hard to be *objective;* he conducts his research and keeps his records in such a way as to make his procedures maximally understandable and able to be replicated by other investigators. He wants the description of what he did to become public knowledge. More than this, the scientific researcher wants what he *did* to become part of the repertoire of action available to his colleagues and to society at large. He wants anyone else who so wishes to be able to repeat what he did—either as a substantial replication or as a variant.

When we say that one researcher might want to do what another did as a *substantial replication,* we mean that the second study would duplicate the first closely enough in its relevant aspects to give us no confidence that the outcome of the second would differ from the outcome of the first. The phrases *relevant aspects* and *different outcomes* are vague, however. They admit that no act can ever thoroughly duplicate another; in final detail, every event is unique. These phrases also admit that we never intend to study every conceivable aspect of the subject we are studying; some aspects[1] are more rele-

[1]In later chapters we shall use the term *dimension* or *variable* more often than "aspect," but synonymously.

vant to our interests than others. Finally, quantities are always measured with some error. The array of the ages of the actors in one study, for example, will inevitably differ, no matter how little, from the array in a preceding study.

But especially, no matter how objectively a researcher may carry out his study and record it for others, his choice of a question (or hypothesis) to guide his research must always be to a large extent his own idiosyncratic, arbitrary, personal question. There is nothing in the nature of scientific method that requires one man to study clustering in human crowds and another to study oxygenation in cuttlefish. Nothing scientific presses one man to study social conformity in relation to sex and another to study social conformity in relation to occupational status. These are matters of preference and of the researcher's intuition about what will best lead him where he wants to go.

The initial choice of a research question is an interaction among three sources of conceptualization. One source, of course, is the set of ideas already available from the mind of the researcher. A second source is the body of assertions comprising the current state of knowledge in the relevant sciences. Some of this knowledge is available in print and some is to be obtained through personal communications, written or oral. Finally, the actual world of observable events[2] yields ideas to the researcher when he interacts directly with it as a human being, quite aside from any other work he does with the procedures of science. All of these sources of conceptualization interact when the researcher is seeking a formulation for his curiosity that will be a good guide to him in research. He begins with his own previous ways of thinking about things; he seeks help in organizing his perplexities from literature and colleagues; finally, he is inevitably affected by his own personal experience as he interacts with the real world.[3] Any research project is shaped to some extent by every one of these sources of conceptualization.

2-3. Living Systems

The life sciences, as disciplines or professions, seem to be divided, roughly, by the inclusiveness of the living units studied. Cystology focuses primarily on processes within cells; histology focuses on tissues, which are built of cells; other branches of physiology study organs, composed of tissues; portions of psychology and ethology deal with the individual organism, an organized composite of organs; branches of psychology, social psychology, and political science deal with relatively small groups of organisms; sociology, political science, and economics study relatively large organizations and societies; and so forth. There are other disciplines devoted to types of living units classified by other schemes. There are researchers devoted to armies, families,

[2]Later in this chapter, we shall prefer the phrase *concrete systems*.

[3]For a discussion of the interaction between the ideology of the researcher and his research, see Chapter 9 of Sjoberg and Nett (1968), especially pages 233–237.

and schools. We mention these focuses of scientific effort as evidence that students of life have perceived, now and again, some advantages in choosing domains of study that seem to be also natural delimitable entities in the world of living things. They have sought to comprehend certain "complexly organized accumulations of matter-energy" (J. G. Miller's phrase, 1965, p. 213) that exhibit a "functional unity" (Helen Peak's phrase, 1953, p. 248) in their behavior. In this book, we shall accept this point of view without serious question, drawing chiefly upon the formulation of *living systems* by James G. Miller (1965).[4]

Whenever behavior is observed, it is *always* manifested by some living system such as an individual human, a more-or-less organized group, an organization such as a business firm, a town, a nation, or the like. Behavior can be observed *only* by looking at the interaction of some living system with its environment. It is almost never possible for the observer to understand the behavior of one component of a system without knowing a good deal about the rest of the system. It is also usually impossible to understand a single arbitrary aspect of a system (such as motion in a certain direction) without knowing a good deal about other aspects and functions of the system. To be scientifically productive, it is not enough that a question lend itself to research; it must promise to lead us to new knowledge about some "complexly organized accumulation of matter-energy." Any other way of asking questions can only lead us to a hodgepodge collection of factual bric-a-brac. Let us turn to a few examples.

As one example, we might ask, "What is the correlation between the phases of the moon and the menstruation of women?" This is clearly a question that can be researched; it presents no serious difficulty. As a matter of fact, people noted a strong correlation between these two variables many millennia ago. This correlation had some practical value, but it was a dead end as far as learning anything that would help explain further either the phases of the moon or menstruation (or, at least, it seems so at our present stage of knowledge). Although this is a good example of a question that lends itself to research, it is not an example of a scientifically *productive* question.

As another example, we might ask about the association between social class and permissiveness in child rearing. In looking at studies of permissiveness in child rearing by families in the middle and lower classes in many sections of the United States between 1930 and 1955, we might notice that sometimes lower class parents seemed to behave more permissively toward their children than middle class parents and sometimes less. We might conclude, as some researchers did during that period, that there was no over-all relation between social class and permissiveness in child rearing. However, if we were to order the data from the studies according to the year to which they applied, we could find a clear pattern among them. Indeed, Bronfenbrenner (1958) carried out such an analysis of trend and discovered that lower class

[4]For a less technical, more general, and more elementary introduction to general systems theory, see the first few chapters of Boulding's (1961) book, *The Image*.

parents were generally more permissive than middle class parents near 1930, but the relation gradually reversed itself over the years until the middle class parents were generally the more permissive by 1955. Bronfenbrenner believed that the change was produced largely by communication from the leaders of opinion concerning child rearing. Since middle class parents were more susceptible to verbal influence than lower class parents, the middle class parents responded more quickly to the exhortations of the experts toward greater permissiveness and overtook the lower class parents between 1940 and 1945. As originally hypothesized, there was indeed a relation between social class and child rearing, but the question had been asked too simply and an important process underlying the relation had been obscured. Obviously, differential influences on child rearing in different social classes are to be understood only in terms of processes in the total society; yet for many years we omitted from our thinking an essential process regulating family standards in child rearing, namely, communication from legitimized arbiters affecting both social classes, but affecting them at different rates.

For still another example, let us turn to what Barker (1963, 1965; see also Barker and Barker, 1961) calls the *behavior setting.* Using one of Barker's examples, suppose we take a camera to a baseball game and narrow the field of the camera until it "sees" a picture just large enough to hold one man. Let us keep the camera focused upon the second baseman throughout the game. Let us then give the film to someone who has never seen a game of baseball nor heard it described; let him observe the film as closely and as often as he likes, and let us ask him to account for the behavior of the man in the picture. For example, we might ask, "What is the nature of the man's orientation toward that white patch (the base) on the ground?" If that question seems too vague, we could ask something more specific, such as, "What circumstances are associated with the man having his foot on the white patch?" We would let our investigator see and hear everything that goes on in the frame of the picture—people running in and out, a ball flying in and flying out, the cheering and other crowd noises, our man sitting on a bench, swinging a wooden club, running, and so forth. Without a doubt, the investigator's report would have an odd ring to anyone acquainted with the game of baseball.

To magnify the point a final degree, we can be fairly sure that any biologist would think it foolish to measure the temperature of John and check the concentration of some hormone in the blood of Mary, perform a series of pairs of such assessments, and compute the correlation. He would say that to try to find a relation between variables of subsystems located in two *different systems* is a very poor bet—unless the two systems in every instance happen to be functionally related in a suprasystem such as a family or a love affair.

Miller (1965) notes that three kinds of systems have been useful: conceptual, abstracted, and concrete systems. Describing concrete systems, he says,

> Confusion of abstracted and concrete systems has resulted in the contention that the concept of system is logically empty because one cannot think

> of anything or any collection of things which could not be regarded as a system. . . . What is *not* a concrete system? Any set of subsystems or components in space-time which do not interact or coact, which do not have relationships in terms of the variables under consideration, is not a concrete system. Physicists call it a *heap.* My heart and your stomach, together, are not a concrete system; the arrangements of cells in your fingernails and in your brown felt hat are not a concrete system; the light streaming through my study window and the music floating out from my phonograph are not a concrete system. All the coal miners in Wales were not a concrete system until they were organized into an intercommunicating, coacting trade union. Sherlock Holmes assumed red-haired men in general were not a concrete system, but when he got evidence that some of them were interacting he deduced the existence of an organized Red-Headed League (pp. 206–207).

The word *system* is used in many ways in our language. In this book, we shall always mean a concrete, living system when we say *system,* unless we expressly note differently.

An important distinction in the structure of a living system is the distinction between *subsystem* and *component.* Miller (1965) says:

> In every system it is possible to identify one sort of unit, each of which carries out a distinct and separate process, and another sort of unit, each of which is a discrete, separate structure. The totality of all the structures in a system which carry out a particular process is a *subsystem.* A subsystem, thus, is identified by the process it carries out. It exists in one or more identifiable structural units of the system. These specific, local, distinguishable structural units are called *components* or *members* or *parts* (p. 218).

This distinction is especially important in the study of social systems, where human individuals are always components, but each subsystem is usually composed of a number of humans, with one component-human often serving as a part of more than one subsystem and with subsystems having rotating components. In a business firm or in a school, components rotate from day to day as different members are absent or on vacation. But the subsystems for bringing in supplies, for distributing them, for keeping records, for making decisions—these continue to appear daily and to operate.

There is some formal evidence that relations among variables are easier to discern within a living system and harder to discern when one variable is manifested inside that system and the other is manifested outside the system. McGrath and Altman (1966) examined a large number of studies of variables manifested in individuals, groups, and the social environments of groups. They discovered that researchers had found considerably more significant relations among variables when the two variables studied both showed themselves within the same system (the same individual, the same group, or the same social environment) than when the researchers had tried to find a relation between one variable in one system and another variable in another.

2-4. Facets

Facet *design* is a way of laying out a domain for research. Although it systematizes the generation of hypotheses, its special power resides in the fact that it enables one to specify the boundaries and structure of the entire domain of relevance within which one may wish to experiment. Facet *analysis* then enables one to test the validity of one's assessment of the entire domain before he invests great time and money in experiments upon portions of the domain. But these are rather abstract phrases. Let us put things in more customary terms.

In designing an experiment, one of the most nagging problems is whether we have chosen (1) relevant variables to be allowed to vary and (2) relevant variables to be controlled.[5] That is, our hypotheses typically take this form: under what conditions will values of a certain (dependent) variable be higher and under what conditions will the values be lower? For example, we might ask under what conditions teachers will stay longer in a school and under what conditions teachers will cut short their stay. We might believe that the amount of communication of some certain kind within the faculty is related to length of service—and we might, therefore, produce or look for schools in which there are conditions of low, medium, and high communication. For purposes of economy in research, we might want to rule out the effects of other conditions that we believe also have an effect on length of service. We might think that salary levels are related to length of service, but if we are primarily interested in the effects of communication, we either let salary levels vary randomly among our subjects or we examine length of service within groups of teachers having salary levels substantially the same. The point is that we pay attention in one way or another *both* to communication levels and salary levels (as well as to other variables we think might be relevant) and the conclusions we draw from our study are necessarily circumscribed by these relevant variables. It is not easy to ascertain which variables have their interaction with other variables predominantly within the "boundaries" of the living system we want to study. Only one of the difficulties is the ever-present bias on the part of the experimenter in favor of his own particular ways of looking at the world. Selecting variables to be examined, to be left to vary randomly, and to be held constant typically becomes a matter of intuition instead of a systematic sequence of deliberate decisions.[6]

The beginning logic of facet design is extremely simple; it is simply that of the Cartesian coordinates one uses when drawing graphs. The chief differences are that (1) we do not always deal in the social sciences with numerical quantities along the coordinates, and (2) we typically deal with many more coordinates than we can neatly draw on a graph on paper.[7] To return to our

---

[5]Chapter 3 discusses this topic in detail.

[6]Technicalities in selecting variables to be examined, randomized, and held constant are discussed in Chapter 3.

[7]For a brief introduction to the logic of facets, but expressed with the concept of *sets*, see Chapter 5 of Kerlinger (1964), especially pages 73–78.

Levels of Salary

Levels of Communication	s_1	s_2	s_3	s_4
c_1				
c_2				
c_3				
c_4				

earlier example, we might list levels of communication up the left side of the page and levels of salary across the top of the page. Then, separating the various levels by horizontal and vertical lines, we would obtain a grid of cells. Each cell would be designated by a particular level of communication and a particular level of salary. In any particular cell we could enter observations of length of service on the part of those teachers who are characterized by that particular salary level and that particular amount of communication in their schools. Comparisons of length of service in relation to level of communication, with salary held constant, could then be made up and down a column of the diagram. Comparisons of length of service in relation to salary levels, with amount of communication held constant, could be made left and right along the rows of the diagram. Comparisons taking into account both communication and salary would be made diagonally. In this example, communication is one facet and the various levels of communication are the *elements* of that facet. Salary is the other facet. The variable of length of service is, of course, the dependent variable. Note that length of service remains a variable within each cell of the table; teachers classified within any one cell can still differ one from another in length of service.

Taking this example a little farther, let us suppose for the sake of illustration that we predict that length of service will be longer where levels of communication are higher and also where salaries are higher. We would then expect that the average length of service would increase in the cells reading from left to right along a row and would also increase in the cells running from bottom to top in a column. Furthermore, we would predict that the average length of service in any particular cell would be higher than in cells to the south and west of it. On the other hand, we would not be able to predict the relative magnitudes to be found in cells to the northwest or southeast because the elements corresponding to those cells would be lower in one facet but higher in the other and therefore incomparable. Facet design does not lay out predictions about all possible comparisons among the sets of conditions specified by the facets.

There is another important feature to be observed in this example. Since the values for length of service increase along a row, a value in one cell is more similar to a value in an adjacent cell than it is to a cell farther away.

The same kind of pattern will be true in a column and it will also be true diagonally across the diagram. This pattern reflects what Foa (1958, 1965) calls the *principle of contiguity*—the principle that the similarities posited among the elements of the facets should predict similarities in the levels of the dependent variable when it is measured in the various cells specified by the crossed facets. Foa (1965, p. 264) states the principle this way: ". . . variables which are more similar in their facet structure will also be more related empirically." This principle is part of the basic logic of facet *analysis*.[8]

SOME REQUIREMENTS

We do not have space here for a general treatment of the logic of classification; we leave the more subtle questions to other authors (for example, Altman, 1968). But certain principles of classification in choosing facets and elements within facets are vital in constructing a maximally useful facet design. The list below follows McGrath (1967).

1. Objects should be classified by *all* the properties or facets that the investigator has chosen as relevant to his study. Any "object"—be it a concept, event, person, or whatever—has more than one property in common with others. A facet design will be more comprehensive and serviceable if a facet applicable to any object is applicable to all.
2. Each facet should be divided into an *exhaustive* set of categories or elements; that is, every object must be classifiable in one of the elements.
3. The elements of each facet should be *mutually exclusive;* that is, each object must be classifiable in *only* one of the elements.
4. The logical *relation among the elements* of a facet should be specified. A facet design is more powerful if the elements can be at least ordered.
5. The logical *relations among facets* should be specified. Ideally, the act of classifying an object within one facet should put no constraint on its classification within another.
6. The facets, collectively, should *exhaust the domain of interest.*

More detail on the structure of facets can be found in McGrath (1967) as well as in the references cited in the preceding section. Many researchers have made use of the logic of facet design without calling it by that name. Some comparatively early examples of explicitness in this regard can be found

[8]Foa and Guttman often use the term *variable* to mean the dependent variable as it is measured in a *single one* of the cells specified by the crossed facets. In the sentence of Foa's (1965) quoted above, for example, the plural term *variables* means the dependent variable as it appears in one cell, in another cell, in another, and so on.

Let us also note here a key distinction between facet analysis and factor analysis (for which see section 12-4), since the two labels are sometimes confused. In factor analysis, factors are typically "extracted" *after* the data are collected. Quite the contrary is true of facet design. The facets must be chosen *before* data are collected.

in Brunswik (1956) and Stephenson (1953).The situation is similar to that of the character in the play *Le Bourgeois Gentilhomme* by Molière, who learned one day that "For more than forty years I have been speaking prose without knowing it!" We feel, however, that the advantages of the logic of facets will be more readily available to researchers now that systematic technology and terminology have entered the literature.

FACETS OF THIS BOOK

We have made conscious use of facet design in writing this book. In Chapter 1, we set forth the idea that the cycle of every project in empirical research turns within a space of two facets: the cycle runs from abstractness to concreteness and back, and also from differentiation to integration and back (see Figure 1-1). Visualizing the cycle in this way helped us choose the boundaries for the chapters and reminded us of some of the connections we wanted to point out among the several phases. In the next section, we shall describe the three facets (1) actor, (2) behavior-toward-an-object, and (3) context. In section 3-3 we shall present modes for treatment of variables within a faceted logic; see especially Tables 3-3 and 3-4 and Figure 3-4. In Chapter 4, we shall compare research strategies by using two facets: (1) obtrusive versus unobtrusive research operations and (2) abstract versus concrete behavior systems. This logic leads to a circular or "circumplex" classification; see Figure 4-1.

Campbell and Fiske (1959) have presented a logic for observation that focuses upon the two facets of (1) the characteristics or traits being observed and (2) the methods being used to observe them; we shall present this logic in the discussion of the multitrait-multimethod paradigm in section 6-4. The *searchingness structure* is the name given by Coombs (1964) to a way of classifying the combinations of choices or comparisons a researcher can ask an actor to make; we shall present this logical structure and its facets in section 7-2. We could go on listing the use of facets in the remaining chapters of this book, but the point is only that the logic of facets enables the researcher to systematize not only the content or "stuff" that he wants to study but also the methods he uses to study it. We shall point out both sorts of uses in later chapters.

SUMMARY

Facet design is a way of laying out a domain for research; it specifies the limits of the domain and the presumed ordering of its subparts. It systematizes the researcher's planning and his communication with colleagues. To achieve the maximum power of a facet design, the facets and their elements should conform to certain rules of classification. Given facets and elements chosen according to these rules, a facet design constitutes a theory or metatheory within which more specialized content theories can be elaborated. The overarching theory or metatheory of the facets can be tested by the use of the principle of contiguity and by recently developed computer programs that apply the principle of contiguity to very complex configurations. Facet design is also useful in nonempirical undertakings such as organizing this book.

2-5. Actor, Behavior, Context

We shall be discussing human behavior in this book as (1) actor or actors engaging in (2) behavior-toward-an-object in (3) a setting or context. These three aspects of behavior are themselves facets. Each of these facets can contain categories or elements. These facets become important early in the planning of research because one can go a long way toward specifying the domain of one's investigation by carefully specifying the elements of these facets as one conceives them and by then pointing to the particular elements one intends to include in his research. No study can encompass all conceivable actors, behaviors, and contexts, for this would be to claim the universe of events related to living systems. A single study might, for example, limit itself to (1) individual humans (2) exchanging oral messages about their common task (3) within the walls of a newspaper's editorial office. It is very important for the researcher to specify elements of these facets as precisely as possible so that other researchers will know what "things" he was studying and therefore where his domain of investigation overlaps their own. Because of the importance of precision at this stage, we shall say more about choosing elements for these facets.

To begin with the first facet, actors can be individual humans, small groups such as an airplane crew, an organization such as the students and faculty of a school, a community such as a small town, and so forth. Or the researcher may choose to classify actors in some other way, depending on his judgment about what strategy will lead most quickly to information about the questions he has in mind. In some particular context, for example, a researcher might choose to divide his actors into those that have a technology that can communicate beyond earshot and those that do not have such a technology. If a researcher chooses to study only one "level" of actor, such as the individual, he may find it convenient, nevertheless, to make subclassifications (elements) among the actors; examples of actor facets within individuals would be sex, occupation, region of residence, and so forth.

It must be clear that neither facets nor elements of facets are given by nature. Facets and elements are chosen arbitrarily by the researcher. It is true, of course, that certain facets sometimes become very widely used and are then accepted as the basis for *taxonomies* and *conceptual frameworks*. Nevertheless, even widely used intellectual structures such as the periodic table of the chemical elements or the evolutionary taxonomies of organisms are revised from time to time as more meaningful ways are found to choose the elements (categories) within the facets and as additional important facets are added. As ways are worked out to order the elements within facets more clearly, the logical structure of the scheme comes closer to what we ordinarily mean by *theory*—a logical arrangement of concepts that parallels in some specifiable way some experiences that can occur during our observations of the real world.

The second facet mentioned above—behavior-toward-an-object—illustrates the arbitrary nature of facets and elements very well. We could have made one facet out of types of behaviors and another out of types of objects. We prefer to take the view, however, that behaviors and objects are inextricably intertwined in action. A screwdriver in one context is a device for implanting or removing screws. In another context it is a paperweight. In a third, when thrust forcibly into another human's flesh, it becomes a weapon. The behavior shares in "defining" the object and the object shares in "defining" the behavior; the interaction between human and object is a joint product. And again, the manner in which the researcher chooses elements of this facet will reflect his theoretical ideas about how acts carry functions in the living system.

Large segments of psychological thought have been devoted to the manner of choosing behaviors, objects, and their interaction. One way to describe the contribution of Freud is that he conceived a new realm of action for humans; namely, the unconscious, in which "behavior" consists largely of coming to terms with conflicts among one's impulses and in which many of the "objects" have their full meaning only within those unconscious struggles. The chief legacy of Watson can be said to be an argument about the best strategy for empirically defining actor, behavior, and object. Similar remarks can be made about the contributions to this puzzle by the phenomenologists, the gestalt psychologists, the practitioners of factor analysis, and others.

The third facet of our schema—context—refers to the time-place-thing setting within which behavior takes place. Again, the arbitrary nature of these facets is apparent; we might have combined objects and contexts in the third facet as easily as we combined behavior and objects in the second.

Actors, behaviors, and objects exist in contexts. The term *situation* is a synonym for context that stresses the aspect of meaning to the subject. The term *occasion* is a synonym for context that stresses the temporal aspect. The terms *environment* and *milieu* are synonyms for context with special connotations of physical place and condition. Other somewhat synonymous terms are *behavior settings, embedding system, surround.*

Relatively little systematic work has been done by behavioral scientists either to conceptualize or to sample contexts. Most empirical work has been conceived in terms of objects or stimuli and little in terms of larger settings or contexts. One major exception is the work of Barker and his colleagues (see, for example, Barker and Wright, 1955; Barker and Gump, 1964), who have applied elaborate and comprehensive procedures to identifying and classifying behavior settings (to use their term). They have, indeed, attempted to enumerate and classify *all* of the nonhousehold behavior settings that existed in an entire rural community for an entire year (Barker and Wright, 1955) and to do the same with all of the nonclassroom behavior settings that existed in a high school during an entire school year. This work stands as a monumental exception to the behavioral scientists' lack of concern with contexts.

Most studies—field or laboratory—while they have used multiple actors and multiple behaviors, have worked within only one context or, at most, have compared two or a few contexts. Perhaps this prevalent use of one or a few contexts, combined with a tendency to select contexts on pragmatic grounds, has allowed researchers to accept unanalytically the contexts chosen. A classification of various kinds of settings from the viewpoint of research strategy, and the consequences of using one or another of them, are discussed in Chapter 4. Some aspects of sampling contexts are discussed in Chapter 5.

2-6. Theory

In simplest terms, a theory is a guide to tell you where to look for what you want to observe. For example, a theoretical statement about the rate of falling bodies tells you that if you want to predict how fast a freely falling body will be moving through space (in feet per second, say) you must observe how long it has been freely falling. As another example, a theoretical statement about meteorology might specify the set of atmospheric conditions that must be observed to predict the change in temperature at a given place and time. Laying out a theory can become very complicated. Indeed, how to find the best strategies for building theories in behavioral science is still very much a matter of argument.[9] We shall not undertake any argument about theory in this book, because our topic is method, not theory. We mention theory from time to time, however, and it may be helpful to say a few words about our understanding of the term and some sections of the book where relevant matters arise.

Different social scientists use the term *theory* to refer to different degrees of comprehensiveness in thinking about human behavior, and this variation in usage does not help to clarify discussion of the uses of theory.[10] In addition to using the term differently in denoting scope and strategy, social scientists also give different connotations of prestige to theory. Our own view of the latter matter is that precision of meaning is not helped by burdening the term *theory* with a dimension of prestige or respectability. The eventual value of a piece of theorizing is not easy to forecast. It sometimes turns out that a single proposition is worth more in advancing scientific thought than a million words of fine-spun elaborations, but this cannot often be ascertained, one way or the other, in the same week the proposition or the "theory" is published. As to scope and strategy, our view is close to that of Sjoberg and Nett (1968):

> In a broad sense, scientific theory serves to link apparently discrete observations. More specifically, it refers to a set of logically interrelated

[9]For some varying points of view on theory building in social science and some historical origins, concisely presented, see Sjoberg and Nett (1968), Chapters 3 and 9.

[10]For various uses of the term *theory* in sociology, see Sjoberg and Nett (1968), pages 29–32.

"propositions" or "statements" that are "empirically meaningful," as well as to the assumptions the researcher makes about his method and his data. Thus, there are three dimensions to theory in science: (1) the broad logical structure, or the form; (2) the generalizations or propositions concerning the patterning of the empirical world (the specific content); and (3) the assumptions regarding the scientific method and the nature of the data (p. 30).

Theory construction is too complex a matter for extended treatment in this book. However, a number of topics in this book bear upon one or another of the three dimensions mentioned by Sjoberg and Nett. Some considerations helpful in thinking about the logical structure of theory are to be found in most sections of this chapter and in Chapters 3, 6, 13, and 14. Matters relevant to forming propositions about the empirical world (about specific content) are mentioned in sections 2-3 (living systems) and 2-7 (hypotheses) of this chapter, in Chapter 3, and in parts of Chapters 13 and 14. Actual and imaginary examples of theoretical propositions are scattered throughout the book for illustrative purposes, though no logically interconnected sequences of propositions are displayed. Discussions of aspects of scientific method and the nature of data are to be found in every chapter of the book.

2-7. Hypotheses

It is one thing to say how a hypothesis should sound when one presents it at a seminar, at a colloquium, or in a report and quite another to say how one goes about constructing the statement and getting it ready for public view. The implications of one's ideas can be conveyed the more clearly to one's colleagues if the hypothesis can be stated precisely and concisely and if it can be shown to follow with tight logic from a well-known body of theoretical statement. But hypotheses are rarely generated by logical process. Researchers mostly produce them in very sweaty ways.

THE INVITATIONAL MOOD

A hypothesis is a piece of a theory; it a theoretical statement. It tells us where to look if we want to find some particular sort of experience. In Kelly's (1964) phrase, a hypothesis is "a human device for anticipating the events that are about to happen to us" (p. 138).[11] A hypothesis has the general form: "If *this* happens, then one will (with some probability) find himself observing *that*." An equivalent form is: "Suppose I were to do *this;* what would ensue? Would *that* perhaps occur?" The important thing about this mode of expression is that it is tentative and exploratory. The chief idea is not to "prove" that an idea is "true," but to open oneself to new possibilities and contingencies. Kelly

[11]Most of the ideas in this section are taken from Kelly (1964, 1965).

(1964) calls this point of view the *invitational mood.* "Suppose we regard the floor as if it were hard," Kelly begins. Then:

> The invitational mood . . . would have the effect of orienting one to the future, not merely to the present or to the past. It would set the stage for prediction of what is to ensue. It suggests that the floor is open to a variety of interpretations or constructions. It invites the listener to cope with his circumstances—in this case the floor—in new ways. But more than this, it suggests that the view of the floor as something hard is one that is not imposed upon us from without, nor is it isolated from external evidence, as a phenomenological proposition would be, but is one that can be pursued, tested, abandoned, or reconsidered at a later time (pp. 138–139).
>
> Suppose . . . we say, in effect, "To be sure the floor may be regarded as hard, and we know something of what ensues when we cope with it in the light of such an assumption. Not bad! But now let us see what happens when we regard it as soft." Out of this further exploration may come, not so much confirmation that it really is hard or that it really is soft—as Descartes would have reasoned—but a sequence of fresh experiences that invite the formulation of new hypotheses. For example, one may come up with a notion of relativism, that is to say, the floor is harder than some things and softer than others. Or he may come up with a notion of properties, the hardness aspect of the floor and its softness aspect. Or he may come to regard hardness not as anything that inheres in the floor, but as a dimension of appraisal useful in understanding floors. From this position he may launch out and contrive the notions of resilience and plasticity to account for what happened when he treated the floor as if it were soft (pp. 149–150).

We join Kelly in urging every researcher to think of his work as exploration—an opportunity to climb a new mountain, or at least a flank of one, and see the world from a new perspective. We agree with Kelly that this new perspective will have no claim on "truth"; but it will bring us new vistas and open possibilities hard to imagine earlier. It will enlarge our potentialities. These views are expanded in Chapter 14.

TECHNICALITIES

It is customary, these days, to use the indicative mood in stating hypotheses. An example (taken from Turk, 1961) is "The more highly task-identified a rater is, the higher will be the association between his ratings of the personal attractiveness of peers and his judgments of their task-proficiency." Following Kelly, this could be read, "Suppose we view people as being more or less task-identified. What new views would we obtain of the ways people rate their co-workers? Might it turn out, as an instance, that the workers who 'identify' more closely with the task find co-workers more personally attractive when the co-workers are more proficient at their tasks?" The researcher could sharpen his conclusions, too, by listing a few other possible and reasonable outcomes.

If he then picked in advance the outcome that did occur, his prediction would be the more impressive. Of course, there are always technicalities. For one thing, a hypothesis is more useful as a guide to observation if it tells *what to look at.* For example, Turk's hypothesis tells us that we must look at task identification, raters, associations, ratings, personal attractiveness, peers, judgments, and task proficiency. And if we do not know how to look at some of these things, Turk must tell us how to do so in terms that do *not* keep asking, "But how do I do *that?*"[12] In other words, if an hypothesis is to be a useful guide to empirical research, it must connect ideas about how to *conceive* the behavioral world (theory) to reasonably simple things you and I can *do* to see how those theoretical ideas work out. This idea will be carried further in later chapters, especially 3, 7, and 8.

Another technicality has to do with the fact that chance events are always with us. In tossing coins with an acquaintance, we might form the hypothesis that the coin is biased and heads are more likely to come up than tails. And if heads appear on the next toss, we might feel vindicated. But, of course, the chance of getting a head from a coin that operates entirely by chance is 50-50, and that is not a small probability. The appearance of the head of the coin, in brief, is not very convincing evidence that the coin is biased. We must come upon a much rarer event—rarer by chance, that is—before we can be ready to put high confidence in our idea that the coin is biased. For example, it would indeed be rare for the coin, by chance, to turn up heads 20 times in a row. If that event should occur, we would be well justified in looking askance at our acquaintance.

If one's observations are to be compared with the possibility of a chance event, the hypothesis must be stated so that there is a clear distinction between the event (or events) the researcher is interested in seeing and the event (or events) that chance would presumably bring. (In our example, chance would presumably bring heads half the time.) Many researchers first state a *hypothesis* in a way that makes it clear what they feel exploratory about and then state it again in a way that makes it clear what they think is likely to happen in contrast to the events that chance might bring. The latter form is sometimes called a *prediction*. We shall say more about chance and statistical considerations in section 14-13.

If a hypothesis is to be stated in a manner to draw a comparison with chance events, it must assert a particular set of events as alternatives to the chance events. The indicative, declarative form is convenient. For example,

> The proportion of tosses with this coin resulting in heads is different from 50 percent.
>
> The proportion of voters favoring fluoridation is larger than 60 percent.

[12]As indeed he does tell us in his article, if we presume that the reader is acquainted with some commonly used techniques of research. An article in a professional journal must make this presumption.

The difference in the mean ratings made by the two groups is larger than 1.6 but smaller than 2.3.

Each of these statements specifies precisely a certain subset of all possible events. Given certain assumptions about the probabilities of chance events, then the probability of the occurrence by chance of the hypothesized subset can be computed. If the probability is sufficiently small, we can decline to give the chance explanation credence, giving our confidence instead to the theory by which we predicted this outcome. For further explanation of this probabilistic thinking, see any book on applied statistics such as that by Hays (1963).

TYPES OF HYPOTHESES

Let us consider three particular ways in which questions (hypotheses) susceptible to empirical research can differ. These three facets will enable us to make a table that will, in turn, facilitate discussion of certain types of hypotheses. First, consider the facet of the *single case* versus a *population* of cases. When we are interested in a single actor (or object), we have questions such as

How tall is *Mary?*

How many people live in *Burned Bridges, Illinois?*[13]

(We are taking Mary as the actor in the first example and the town of Burned Bridges as the actor in the second.) When we are interested in a population, we have questions such as

What percentage of *people in Minnesota* give first preference to Glop Toothpaste?[14]

Can *eight-year-olds* run faster than *six-year-olds?*

When a population is large, it can become very difficult to assess the characteristic that interests us in every individual member, and we often adopt the technique of *sampling.* The sample enables us to make an *estimate* of the occurrence of the characteristic in the population (see Chapter 5).

Returning to the necessity of comparing the results we are looking for

---

[13]In a more invitational mood, these questions would become:

Suppose I look at the height aspect of Mary; what might I find?

Suppose I think of Burned Bridges as constituted of a certain number of people; what possible outcomes of counting them are conceivable?

[14]We chose this example to remind ourselves and the reader that all classifications of real-world events are arbitrary, including Burned Bridges and Minnesota. If we do not interpret the people of Minnesota as a *population,* but instead interpret the living *system* (if it might be) of Minnesota as an actor, then a hypothesis about Minnesota would illustrate the single case, not the population. Examples of arbitrary choices demanded of the researcher will occur repeatedly in later chapters.

with what might occur by chance, we find that it is convenient to phrase the hypotheses as follows:

> The percentage of people in Minnesota giving first preference to Glop Toothpaste is greater than 53 percent.
>
> The number of people maintaining residence in Burned Bridges, Illinois, is greater than 3870 and smaller than 3930.
>
> In races matching eight-year-olds with six-year-olds, more eight-year-olds win than six-year-olds.

Now consider a second facet describing a *characteristic* of a case or a population versus describing a *relation* between two or more variables. When we describe a case or a population, we have questions or hypotheses of this sort:

> *How tall* is Mary?
>
> *How many people* live in Burned Bridges, Illinois?
>
> *What percentage of people* in Minnesota give first preference to Glop Toothpaste?
>
> *How many cigarette smokers* ride the crosstown subway on a typical Saturday?

When we describe a relation, we have questions or hypotheses of this sort:

> Can eight-year-olds *run faster* than six-year-olds?
>
> Might it be true that *60 percent of eight-year-olds* can run faster than X miles per hour, while *only 40 percent of six-year-olds* can run faster than that?
>
> *A larger percentage of people who ride on subways* more than ten hours a week *contract cancer before the age of 40* than do people who ride subways ten hours or fewer.

These two aspects of research questions can be put together in a six-celled table, as shown in Table 2-1. Note that the table is written for cases where change from time to time is not a consideration. Research problems falling in the different cells call for different varieties of experimental and analytic procedures.

Problems in cell 1 require only measurement; that is, they require only obtaining a value on some selected variable by using some preselected measuring device. It is true that doubt can arise about the accuracy of the measurement taken on a single case, and repeated measurements assessed for reliability by statistical techniques can be used to increase the accuracy of the measurement. But the collection of observations in cell 1 and the analysis of the resulting data stop short of turning to other variables or estimating the proba-

Table 2-1. *Types of Measurement and Analyses Required for Various Hypotheses Concerning One Occasion*

	SINGLE CASE	POPULATION CENSUS	SAMPLED POPULATION
Description (evaluation on one variable)	1. Measurement of only one variable on the one case	2. Measurement of one variable and descriptive summaries only	3. Measurement and statistical inference concerning one variable
Relations (association among values on two or more variables)	4. Listing of measurements on two or more variables taken on the single case	5. Measurement of relations among two or more variables with descriptive summaries only	6. Measurement and statistical inference concerning relations

bility that the conclusion obtained applies to some population of cases. Similarly, in cell 4, measurement and analysis consist merely of assessing the values of two or more variables and listing them.

The researcher working in cell 2 applies his measuring technique to all cases (individuals, for example) in the population. If he then wishes to describe the distribution of the values he obtained, he employs descriptive statistics. Probability concepts and statistical inference are not required. When a sample is taken, even though only one variable is of interest, as in cell 3, the probabilistic relation of the sample to the population becomes important. This calls for new experimental procedures (such as random selection of subjects) and new analytic procedures; namely, those of statistical inference (estimating a population parameter such as the mean or testing the hypothesis that the population parameter exceeds some particular value). The conception of a sample implies that the hypothesis is meant to apply not only to cases that will be observed but to cases that will not be. (In different words, this is the choice of whether the hypothesis is meant to have only internal validity or both internal and external validity; see section 3-1 and Chapters 5 and 6.) In cell 6 the same operations are necessary as in cell 3; however, more than one measure is applied to each case, and the statistical inference concerns relations or associations among the variables. Relations also may be studied in cell 5, but no statistical inference is necessary; the entire population has been measured on all the variables.

We now turn to the third facet—that of *one occasion* of measurement versus *two or more occasions.* When we consider measuring cases on one or more variables at two or more times, we can make a new table, more complex than the first one. In Table 2-2, we are always considering a relation, if only between one variable characterizing the actor and *time.*

In cell 1 of Table 2-2, we have hypotheses that consider the change of

***Table 2-2.** Types of Measurement and Analyses Required for Various Hypotheses Concerning Two or More Occasions*

	SINGLE CASE	POPULATION CENSUS	SAMPLED POPULATION
Description (evaluation on one variable)	1. Relation of a variable with time, measured within a single case	2. Relation between distributions of a variable and time within a population: descriptive summaries	3. Relation between distributions of a variable and time within a population: statistical inference
Relations among two or more variables	4. Relations among two or more variables over time, within a single case	5. Change in relation over time among two or more variables: descriptive summaries	6. Change in relation over time among two or more variables: statistical inference

a single case on a single variable with time. This requires only listing the value of the variable at two or more times. A hypothesis would take the form: Mary gets more crotchety as time goes by.

A hypothesis in cell 2 might take the form: The distribution of variable x at time 2 will have a tail stretching toward the positive compared to time 1. A diagram of the two distributions might look like that in Figure 2-1.

A hypothesis in cell 4 might take the form: As the power of the prime minister increases or decreases, so will his arrogance. A hypothesis in cell 5 might read: The relation between family income and years of education reached by the children becomes less strong from one decade to another. Showing the distribution of families over the two variables by an oval enclosing the bulk of the points representing families, we can diagram this form of hypothesis as in Figure 2-2. (Types of relations, including this one, are discussed in Chapter 13.)

Cells 3 and 6 produce the same forms of hypotheses as cells 2 and 5, respectively, but inferences are necessary from the sample to the population.

These twelve types of hypotheses arise from the three facets we have presented, and any hypothesis a researcher states will be more precisely understood by others if he is clear where his hypothesis stands on these three facets. But the hypothesis must go beyond these three facets if it is to state unequivocally the domain to which it applies. As we said in section 2-5, it

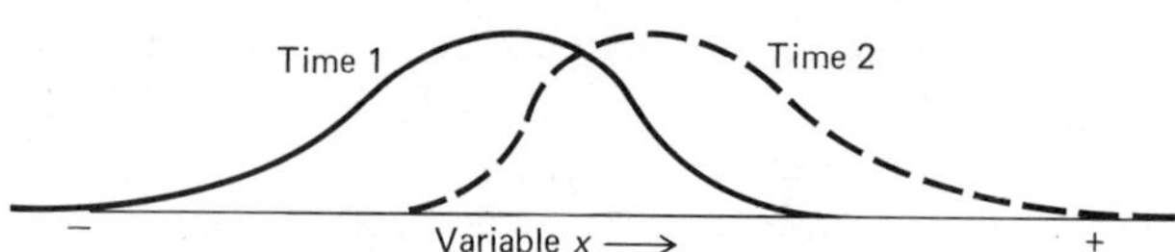

Figure 2-1. Example of a relation between distributions of a variable and time.

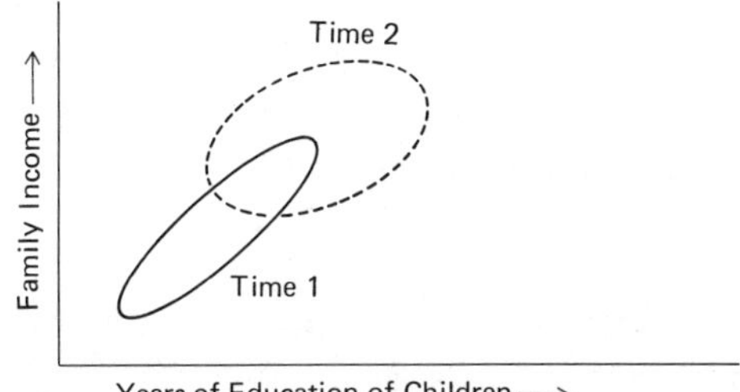

Figure 2-2. Example of a change in relation over time between two variables.

is helpful if the hypothesis is specific about the actors, behaviors, objects, and contexts with which it deals (see also Chapter 5). Further, the hypothesis might be explicit about whether it restricts itself to a limited subset of comparisons among variables or whether, like a facet design, it deals with an entire family of comparisons in one sweep. In Chapters 11 and 12 we shall discuss hypotheses about arrays and patterns of data, such as the hypothesis that some particular batch of data can be arrayed (without violating ordinary logic) in a unidimensional order, as opposed to a multidimensional order. In Chapter 13 we shall discuss hypotheses that ask about what kinds of relations among variables can occur and also what relations among relations can occur. In doing so, we shall again have occasion to mention facet design.

Although we have listed a few ways in which hypotheses can differ and have presented three of them as the facets of Tables 2-1 and 2-2, we have certainly not put forward a thoroughgoing set of facets to guide researchers in constructing hypotheses. Such a set of facets would be a great help in designing studies. At the very least, the set of facets of hypotheses would offer the researcher a checklist; at best, the facets would serve as explicit points of comparison between studies. An example of this latter virtue is the finding by McGrath and Altman (1966) that studies of small groups showed significant relations between variables much more often when the variables were manifested by living systems at the same level than when they were manifested at different levels (see section 2-3). The work of these authors shows, too, how difficult it can be to construct a serviceable set of facets for hypotheses even within a limited domain of living systems. We hope others are giving thought to this problem.

In the meantime, many facets show themselves implicitly to the careful reader of hypotheses, and the reader can usually find further facets explicitly stated in the section of the researcher's report where he describes his theory and the manner in which his thinking led him to his explicit hypotheses. There is no end to listing features of the research about which a hypothesis might deal. We can only urge that the researcher be systematic where he cannot be exhaustive—that he be specific about the facets of actor, behavior, and context within which he conceives himself to be working, and that he treat the actor as a living system and be as explicit as he can about its boundaries.

2-8. Summary

Near the beginning of this chapter, we said that researchers have both extrinsic and intrinsic reasons for wanting to do research. We honored motives of both sorts, but said we were writing this book strictly for those projects in which the researcher feels primarily motivated by wanting to learn something about the world of behavior that he can learn only by empirical research. We noted that many of the choices the researcher makes, especially in the early stages of study design, must be arbitrary and idiosyncratic. A choice of question for research is an interaction among three sources of conceptualization: the mind of the researcher, the current state of knowledge in the relevant sciences, and the actual, directly experienced world of observable events.

We next turned to an exposition of the concept of living systems, a concept growing out of general systems theory. We urged the researcher to pick, as a "thing" to study, a functional unity with a "boundary" to its functioning. As examples of living systems having this sort of functional unity, we mentioned individual humans, work groups, organizations such as schools and factories, communities, and so forth. We argued for the superiority of the research strategy focusing upon concrete, living systems.

We turned next to facet design as a way of specifying the domain of actor, behavior-toward-object, and context to be studied. Facet design enables the researcher (1) to be systematic about specifying the variables, actors, behaviors-toward-objects, and contexts he considers relevant to the domain he wishes to study, (2) to construct an interrelated family of hypotheses to be investigated in this or future studies, and (3) to check at the first round of data analysis whether he chose properly the ordering of elements in the facets.[15] One way to describe the effect of a facet design on a plan for a study is that it widens the alternatives toward which the researcher agrees to direct his attention. In section 2-7, we quoted Kelly's (1964) view that stating hypotheses is "a human device for anticipating the events that are about to happen to us." A facet design invites the researcher to say to himself, "Suppose we regard these facets as being ways that members of this family of events can be similar and not similar one to another; what family of similar and dissimilar events can we anticipate?" As part of the section on facets, we included some rules for composing them. Finally, we included among the illustrations some uses of facets in writing this book.

Three features of behavioral phenomena—actor, behavior, and context—are implicit or explicit facets in every study of behavior, and the specification of their elements immediately yields the beginning of a theory about the domain of study. We devoted some space to the arbitrary nature of facets and elements and to the ways their choice contributes to the structure of behavioral theory. In the section on theory, we began by saying that a theory

[15]For examples to support this last claim, see Chapter 12.

is a guide to tell you where to look for what you want to find. Because a discussion of how to build theory can get very complicated and we did not have the space to delve very far into the matter, we limited ourselves to a few remarks about the use of the term *theory* and then went on to the matter of formulating hypotheses.

We made considerable use of the idea of the "invitational mood"—the idea that, as researchers, we can invite ourselves and one another to act *as if* something is true, tentatively, to see what we learn from doing so. After that, we went into some technicalities in stating hypotheses. First, if the hypothesis says we should look at *this* to find *that*, the researcher should make clear either in the hypothesis itself or in supplementary statements just how one goes about looking at *this*. Second, it is convenient if the hypothesis is stated so that it is easy to compare certain predicted events with presumably chance events; the possibility that it was chance, not our cleverness, that produced what we observed is the ever-present alternative hypothesis. Finally, we mentioned some ways in which hypotheses can differ and said we would discuss some of them in later chapters.

When a hypothesis asks us to compare one set of events with another, or one set of actors with another, and asks us to observe some characteristics rather than others, we must follow the directions carefully as we turn to the real world. It is not usually a simple matter to carry out empirical observations so that they carry out the implications in the hypothesis. One must divide one's observations of the reality in the same ways the corresponding ideas were divided in the statement of the hypothesis. Chapter 3 discusses some of the complexities of making these necessary divisions or "partitions" among our observations of the real world and examines some further problems in developing a logically sound plan of study.

2-9. Further Reading

A repository, always up-to-date, of current thought about systems is *General Systems: The Yearbook of the Society for General Systems Research.* Recent comprehensive writings are those of Buckley (1967, 1968) and J. G. Miller (1965). Other useful writings on the nature of systems include those of Ashby (1962), Cooper, Leavitt, and Shelly (1964), Handy and Kurtz (1963), Marien (1970), Rapoport (1966), Toda (1967), and Toda and Shuford (1965). Sells (1964, p. 515) says, "In its fullest development the taxonomic approach should conform to the general systems approach; in any case, the two are compatible, and perhaps the salient strengths of each may contribute to the goals of the other." Instructive applications of the systems concept to problems in social science have been described by French (1963), Holmberg and others (1965), Katz and Kahn (1966), and McGrath and Altman (1966).

As this book is being written, a systematic exposition of facet design and analysis is still not available. As introductions to the literature, we suggest the brief and severely formal outline by Guttman (1959a), along with the instructive applications by Foa (1958, 1965, 1966) to interpersonal perceptions and behavior and by Guttman (1959b) to intergroup beliefs and action. Applications of facet design and analysis are increasing in number. In addition to the examples already given and those to be given in Chapter 12, Becker and Krug (1964) have applied facets to the study of social behavior in children, Laumann and Guttman (1966) to the perception of similarities among occupations, Elizur (1969) to reactions to the installation of computers in organizations, Foa, Triandis, and Katz (1966) to cross-cultural comparisons of familial roles, Mori (1965) to motivations for becoming a teacher, Robinson and Hefner (1968) to the perception of similarities among nations of the world, Wish (1965) to similarities of Morse code, and Yee and Runkel (1969) to pupils' attitudes toward teachers. Lingoes (1966b, 1968b) has discussed the use of computer programs in analyzing relations among cells.

Among introductions to formal theory construction, Woodger (1939) remains exemplary. Blalock (1969) gives much more attention than Woodger to patterns of interaction among variables. Both writings require some sophistication in mathematical notation. Most books on methods contain sections on the uses of theory and on the formulation of hypotheses; we have found Phillips (1966) and Sjoberg and Nett (1968) especially felicitous. Some further writings on various aspects of the logical form of theory are those of Feyerabend and Maxwell (1965), Hanson (1958), Kaplan (1964), Kuhn (1962), Madge (1962), Maslow (1966), Popper (1959), and Turner (1965).

CHAPTER 3

Planning a Study. The Logic of Study Design

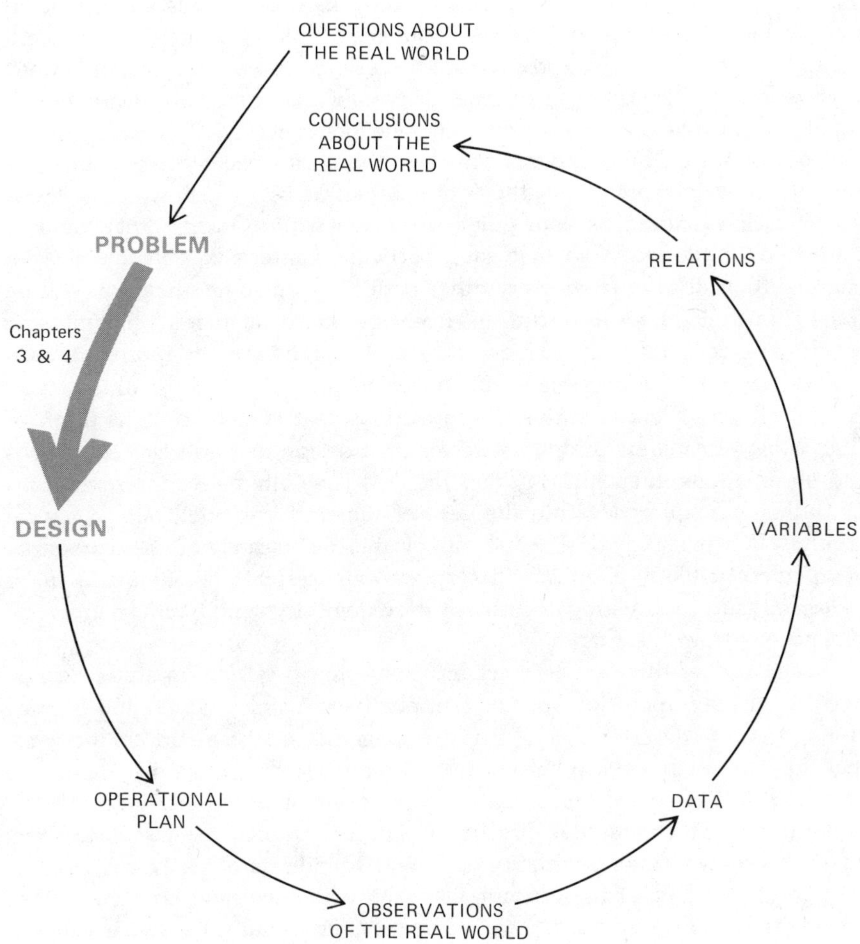

In the previous chapter we talked about formulating a question (or set of questions) on which a study will focus. In Chapters 3 through 8, we shall set forth a series of important choices the researcher must make to build an operational plan for his empirical work. We touch in this chapter and the next on the more fateful of the choices that put a "design" on the study; that is, the choices by which the researcher makes his major "slices of reality" and determines the chief groupings of his observations[1] so as to make possible the comparisons his hypotheses require.

3-1. Drawing Valid Conclusions: Macro-Design

Why do you need a study design? Mainly, you need it as a plan by which you will be able to reason, step by step, from the observations you intend to make to logically sound conclusions about the problems or questions you are trying to resolve. Your purpose in study design, always, is to arrange your observations and conditions so that each possible pattern of observations you might get will logically have one and only one interpretation. If a certain pattern of observations that might occur can logically be satisfied by two or three or more different interpretations, then you will not be able to tell which of those interpretations should be your guide to further work. On the other hand, if your study is designed so that each particular pattern of outcome has an interpretation distinct from every other pattern of outcome, then you will be able to draw unequivocal conclusions from your study no matter what outcome occurs. This, of course, is an ideal; all study designs remain approximations to it. It is probably impossible to rule out in advance (by the logic of the study design) all possible alternative interpretations that someone might think of later. Most researchers pride themselves on a design that arranges conditions and observations in such a way that the *most likely* alternative interpretations can either be explored within the data of the study or ruled out on logical grounds. When a study design does not permit the researcher either to explore or to rule out likely alternative interpretations, results are often said to be *confounded,* and the investigator cannot draw logically sound and unequivocal conclusions from his study.

The rest of this section considers some big problems in study design, drawing heavily upon the work of Campbell and Stanley (1963) and Stanley (1966). First, we describe several study designs that are "standard" in the sense that they are often used in behavioral science research. In this discussion, we point out certain weaknesses in each of them—that is, alternative interpretations to which results from that design are especially vulnerable. Then, we consider two kinds of validity or logical soundness of study conclusions: (1) internal validity, or the unambiguity with which we can draw conclusions about the set of observations in a particular study; and (2) external validity, or the degree to which we can generalize those conclusions beyond the specific conditions and observations of the particular study. But first we sound a note

[1] We use the term *observation* in this book in the most general way. We use it to indicate any way of sensing the real world or getting empirical information from it, whether by the most casual and direct use of the senses or by the most subtle of indirect techniques. In books on research methods, the word is often used in a technical sense to denote agents of the investigator watching actors and recording their behavior according to some scheme previously worked out. When we use the term in this latter sense, we shall call attention to the fact that we are doing so.

of warning. For convenience of presentation, we write in this chapter as if all studies were laboratory experiments in which some specific experimental condition is being manipulated (altered at will) by the investigator. However, it should be kept in mind that the same logical considerations apply to *any* study—in field or laboratory, in natural or contrived setting, with one, several, or no variables being deliberately manipulated—given only that observations are made under conditions at least partially known to the investigator and that he hopes to draw some logically sound conclusions about the patterns of those observations. The reader may profit from imagining applications of these principles beyond those our language immediately suggests to him.

THE PROBLEM OF DRAWING VALID CONCLUSIONS

Research always starts with a question—sometimes precisely stated, sometimes only vaguely put. For example, suppose you want to know whether a new method of teaching is better than present methods. The obvious thing to do is get a class, try the method on it, and see how much the students learn. Let us assume that we have some way to observe or measure how much a given collection of students know after they have taken a given class. (Developing such measures is a major part of the research process and will be discussed in Chapters 6, 7, and 11.) Let us symbolize the teaching method as X and the set of observations as O. We can diagram the study design involved as follows.

Design 1: One-shot design. $X\ O$

Let time flow from left to right; the diagram means that a given sample of people received treatment X (the new teaching method) and their performance was observed or measured (O) at a later time.

Suppose all the students knew a lot about the subject when you observed their performance (O). What can you conclude about the value of teaching method X? Virtually nothing! Maybe they would have learned as much, or more, from the usual old-fashioned methods. Maybe they all knew the subject matter already. (If you gave fifth grade arithmetic problems to a college math class as a part of the final exam and everyone got correct answers, you could scarcely claim to be using effective teaching methods!)

Knowledge is knowledge of differences. To find out about X, we need some kind of comparison—a comparison between our measures or observations (O) when the actors have been exposed to X and the same measures when the actors have not been exposed to X. We could achieve this sort of comparison in either of two ways, neither of which, unfortunately, solves all our problems. Consider first the following.

Design 2: One-group pretest-posttest design. $O_1\ X\ O_2$

The diagram of design 2 indicates a design in which a group of subjects is observed *before* being exposed to experimental treatment X (the teaching method, say) and then again *after* having treatment X. Here we could infer the effectiveness of X by noting improvement in performance from O_1 (before the treatment) to O_2 (afterward). While this is far better than the first design, there are still several weaknesses in design 2 that prevent us from drawing strong conclusions from our results.

First, other things that have nothing to do with teaching method X could have happened to this group between observation times 1 and 2. For example, the students could all have received especially good instruction in some other related course. Such effects of *history* are not taken into account in design 2. Second, if there were a long time between first and second measurements, the sheer *maturation* of the students during that time could have produced the improved performance, quite aside from any effects of treatment X. For example, maturation might produce improvements in reading skill among six-year-olds. We use the term *history* to label events in the environment of the actor that might affect the outcome of the study as well as the treatment X; we use the term *maturation* to label processes or developments that occur *within* the actor because of the nature of the actor, regardless of what we do in our experiment. Growing up in a family whose members do a lot of reading is a historical effect; reaching an age when bodily processes allow the individual to concentrate longer on a quiet task such as reading a printed page is an effect of maturation.

A third weakness of design 2 is that it does not enable effects of the *testing* itself to be detected. Many of the questionnaires, tests, and other techniques of data collection used by social scientists have the effect of increasing the alertness of the actor to the kind of phenomenon the investigator is asking the actor about. This very alertness often affects the outcome of the experiment. For example, a teacher might want to study the effects of his teaching and might give a test at the opening of the term (a *pretest*) to discover the level of knowledge of the class of students before he begins to teach them. But the experience of taking the test might alert the students to the way the teacher thinks about the subject matter, and this improved focus might in itself help them to do better on the final examination than they would have done had they not had the pretest. A fourth factor that weakens the conclusions we can draw from design 2 is *instrument decay*. We include under this heading obvious instances such as a mechanical defect occurring in a timer. But we also use the term for any change in a measuring technique that alters its functioning. For example, suppose observers are rating salesmen on how intently they listen to what customers say. Differences in ratings from first to second observation might be due to the observers having learned their observation tasks better or having become bored with their jobs or having made later observations under different conditions that altered the way they carried out their tasks. Certainly if we used different observers for the "before" and "after" measurements we might well question the comparability of their data. This would be another example of an effect due to instrument changes or "decay"—to use the term broadly.

A fifth factor that could go undetected in design 2 is *regression.* This concept is easier to illustrate than define. Suppose, as O_1, we give a performance test to ten actors. Perhaps the scores range as follows:

19
18
16
15
12
11
11
10
8
5

Now suppose we administer this test again to the same ten persons without having tried in the meantime to affect their performance in any way. We would not, of course, obtain identically the same scores as before. Even aside from the effect of "practice" on the first administration of the test, there would be differences the second time. No one ever gets out of a chair twice in exactly the same way or inhales twice in exactly the same way or answers a test (if it has a reasonable degree of complexity) twice in exactly the same way. Many of the ten individuals would exhibit different scores the second time. And for reasons we shall not discuss here, it is usually the case that persons with high scores on the first administration get lower scores on the second, while persons low on the first administration usually go higher on the second.[2] We repeat below the illustrative pretest scores given above:

PERSON		PRETEST	POSTTEST
1		19	18
2		18	17
3		16	16
4		15	15
5		12	10
	Mean	16	15.2
6		11	14
7		11	11
8		10	10
9		8	8
10		5	6
	Mean	9	9.8

[2] As a hint of what is at work here, consider the case of an individual who obtained the top possible score at first testing. The *only* way he could get a different score the second time would be to get a lower one. For further explanation of "regression toward the mean," see any text on statistics in the social sciences, such as that by Hays (1963).

Beside them are given the posttest scores, which, though imaginary, differ from the pretest scores by proportions that often appear in real data. We also show the upper and lower five persons at pretest and the same clusters of individuals at posttest—though not all of those having one of the five highest scores at pretest still have one at posttest, nor do all those with one of the five lowest scores at pretest have one at posttest.[3] This pattern of scores shifting or "regressing" toward the middle of the array is typical when the scores are taken from instruments such as the "tests" used in social science. The shift is not due to the nature of the actors nor to any experimental influence upon them; some shift toward the middle will occur solely because of the nature of this sort of measuring technique. But—and this, now, is the case where the regression effect is especially troublesome—suppose the researcher happened to select actors who scored in the upper (or lower) ranges of his pretest. Design 2 would give him no way of knowing whether the decrease (or increase) in the mean were due at least partly to the treatment X or solely to the regression effect.

Finally, design 2 could also be affected by selective *mortality.* Often subjects who start out in a study do not continue to the end of it. If students who drop out tend to be the poorer ones academically, for example, then an average improvement in scholastic achievement at O_2 might be misinterpreted as being attributable to treatment X.

We presented design 2 as a way of obtaining two measures, one taken without the influence of treatment X and the other with its influence. A second way of obtaining this arrangement is to use two separate groups of actors. In the diagram below (as well as in later diagrams in this section), each line represents a separate group of actors treated or measured differently from the others.

Design 3: Static group comparison. X O_1 (Group 1)
O_2 (Group 2)

In design 3, one group is measured after exposure to X and a different group is measured without having been exposed to X. This design avoids the confounding factors discussed for design 2, but is vulnerable to other confounding factors. First, we have no assurance that the two groups started (before group 1 got its treatment) from equivalent levels. If entry into either group is voluntary or is affected by administrative or logistic convenience, then one group might attract members that give it a "head start" over the other. Any biases in *selection*—whether intentional or not, and whether the investigator is

[3]It may seem at first thought that continued repeated testing would end with all actors obtaining scores at the mean, but this is not so. The actors who had the five highest scores at pretest and a mean of 16 have dropped to a mean of 15.2 at posttest, it is true, but the actors with the five highest scores at posttest (now actors 1, 2, 3, 4, and 6) still have a mean of 16. Whenever a distribution of scores is peaked in the middle, a retest will see more of the persons in the upper half moving downward than upward, but enough actors will move upward so that the *new* upper half will have about the same mean as the old upper half.

aware of them or not—invalidate conclusions about the effect of X on performance as measured by the subsequent observations, O. A second possible problem in design 3 is that the treatment X might affect the *mortality* from the study, or conversely. For example, actors who do not like the treatment X might be more likely to drop out of the experimental group than actors who like the treatment. Such differential mortality, *interacting* with X, might account for an observed difference in the measure of performance.

Campbell and Stanley (1963) have called all three of these designs "pre-experimental designs." It is not until the fourth design that we reach what they call a "true experimental design."

Design 4: Pretest-posttest control group design. $R\begin{cases} O_1 \ X \ O_2 \\ O_3 \quad\ O_4 \end{cases}$

This design indicates that one group (top line) was tested before and after being exposed to X, while another group (second line) was tested at the same two times, but was not exposed to X in the interim. Notice also the additional symbol, R, to the left of the diagram. *R stands for randomization* and indicates that subjects in both experimental and control groups *were selected from a common pool of subjects and were assigned to one or the other group on a random basis.* Random, here, does not mean haphazard, but has a very precise meaning. Random assignment (or random selection in general, as in sampling for polls and surveys) means a method of assignment by which *each member of the pool in question has an equal chance of being in either (experimental or control) group.* One way to do this, in our example, would be to take each potential subject and flip a coin, putting him in the experimental group if a head comes up and in the control group if a tail. Although there are some minor technical problems even here (as insuring that the coin is unbiased), such a random procedure for assigning subjects to conditions is one major way to answer the crucial question of comparability of the different groups at the time the study begins. *Random assignment is a necessary condition for a "true experiment,"* in the phrase of Campbell and Stanley (1963).

It is important to note that random assignment does not insure that the two groups will be equivalent. When each subject has a 50-50 chance of getting into one group or the other, there is also the 50-50 chance that his characteristics and abilities will enhance one group rather than the other. There are two conclusions one can draw under randomization. One is that the likelihood that one group will contain more of one type of subject than the other group is exactly equal to the likelihood that the other will contain more of that type than the first. We call this being *unbiased.* The other is that the likelihood of the two groups being *very* different is very small. (We shall have more to say about randomization in assignment of cases to conditions in a later section of this chapter.)

Given randomization of assignment of subjects to groups, design 4 copes with many of the factors we have discussed. *History* (that is, events other than X that occur between pretest and posttest) would be detectable because differences due to history from O_1 to O_2 would also show up as differences between O_3 and O_4. Similarly for *maturation* and for *instrument decay.* Design 4 is unbiased in respect to *regression, selection,* and *mortality* because of the random initial assignment of subjects to groups. If mortality interacts with X (as in our example under design 3), we could detect it by various comparisons of the four sets of observations (pretests with posttests across experimental and control groups).

Testing effects as such will not confound results in design 4 insofar as we are comparing the experimental with the control group at posttest, since both groups were given the same pretest. However, if testing *interacts* with X, the interaction would not be detectable. It could occur, for example, that testing alone did not "sensitize" the subject, and treatment X alone did not do so, but that the combination of testing followed by the experimental treatment did sensitize him. An example would be an experiment using a propaganda movie to produce attitude change. The control group given pretest and posttest of attitude might or might not show change. The experimental group in design 4, given an attitude measure and then shown the propaganda movie, might then say to themselves: "Aha, now I see what all those questions were for on that test yesterday." This might well lead to posttest changes in attitude—either to please the experimenter or to thwart him—which would not occur for a group of subjects who saw the movie without having been sensitized by prior attitude testing.

There are two ways to handle the one major flaw of design 4—that is, the flaw occurring when prior testing interacts with X to produce sensitization of subjects. The first of these ways is expressed in design 5.

Design 5: Posttest only control group design. $R\begin{cases} X & O_1 \\ & O_2 \end{cases}$

Design 5 meets all of the criteria that design 4 satisfies, assuming randomization of assignment to conditions before the occurrence of X. In addition, while it does not measure effects of testing or of interactions between testing and X, it does away with the possibility of these effects by doing away with pretesting.

Design 6 combines the features of designs 4 and 5; the result is a design that not only removes the threat of misinterpretation because of the factors listed earlier but enables us actually to measure the effects of history, maturation, testing, and interactions of testing with X.[4]

Design 6: The Solomon four-group design. $R\begin{cases} O_1 & X & O_2 \\ O_3 & & O_4 \\ & X & O_5 \\ & & O_6 \end{cases}$

[4] Design 6 is called the *Solomon four-group design,* following Campbell and Stanley's (1963) usage, in honor of the researcher who first pointed out the need for the four-comparison design.

The two X's in this diagram stand for the same treatment. The social scientist, however, often wants to test the effects of more than one treatment (X) at a time or of more than one level of one sort of treatment. He may also want to test the effects of X at several subsequent times—such as in investigations of trends and "sleeper effects." If the investigator uses design 6 as a basic paradigm, he must add additional groups to his design for each new treatment, each new level of treatment, or each subsequent time of measurement. If he adds only one group for each new condition, he will be unable to rule out some of the confounding factors because some of the groups needed for comparison will be missing. Clearly, investigating complex questions through empirical methods while maintaining defenses against the alternative hypotheses of history, maturation, testing, and the rest can become a large and expensive undertaking. However, design 6 is not the only paradigm available for investigating change or levels of treatment. We shall discuss some other paradigms in section 13-3. In the meantime, Tables 3-1 and 3-2 summa-

Table 3-1. *Some Classes of Factors That Confound Experimental Results*

History:	The performance of actors can be affected by other events occurring between premeasure and postmeasure as well as by experimental treatment X.
Maturation:	Changes within actors that occur with the passage of time and are independent of treatment X can affect the actors' performance.
Testing:	Changes can occur in the performance of an actor because a measurement of it sensitizes him to his own performance.
Instrument decay:	A later measurement can differ from an earlier one because of changes in the instruments or conditions—such as wear of parts for physical instruments or such as learning, boredom, or fatigue for human observers.
Regression:	If groups of actors are selected according to their performance on a given measure (O_1), the imperfections (unreliability) of that measure can produce systematic shifts toward the middle when scores are taken later from the same measures.
Selection:	If actors are assigned to different groups in any other way than randomly from a common pool, systematic differences between groups will result that may have direct effects on performance or that may interact with treatment X in having effects on performance.
Mortality:	If some of the actors observed at the first measurement drop out of the experiment before the final measurement, the distribution of characteristics in the several groups in the experiment will no longer be the same, and these differences may have direct effects on final performance or may interact with treatment X in doing so.
Interactive effects:	Any of several of the above factors may interact with experimental treatment X and produce confounding effects. For example, pretesting may sensitize the actor only when it is followed by treatment X. Or the types of actors dropping out of a study (mortality) may differ between the group receiving treatment X and the group not getting X.

Table 3-2. *Some Types of Research Design*

Design	Diagram	Comments
No. 1: The one-shot design:	$X \; O$	Vulnerable to history, maturation, instrument decay, selection
No. 2: One-group pretest-posttest design:	$O_1 \; X \; O_2$	Vulnerable to history, maturation, testing, instrument decay, regression, mortality
No. 3: Static group comparison:	$X \; O_1$ $ \; O_2$	Vulnerable to selection, regression, interaction of mortality with X
No. 4: Pretest-posttest control group design:	$R\begin{cases} O_1 \; X \; O_2 \\ O_3 \quad\; O_4 \end{cases}$	Vulnerable to interaction of testing and X
No. 5: Posttest only control group design:	$R\begin{cases} X \; O_1 \\ \quad\; O_2 \end{cases}$	Provides comparison group for preventing history, maturation, testing, or some combination of these from having effects, but it cannot assess these separately
No. 6: Solomon four-group design:	$R\begin{cases} O_1 \; X \; O_2 \\ O_3 \quad\; O_4 \\ \quad\; X \; O_5 \\ \qquad\; O_6 \end{cases}$	Combines features of designs 4 and 5. Detects and measures effects of history, maturation, testing, and interaction of testing with X

rize the six "basic" types of design we have discussed in this section along with their major weaknesses and a listing of the types of confounding factors we have mentioned.[5]

INTERNAL AND EXTERNAL VALIDITY

There are two fundamental problems in drawing conclusions from experimental studies. The first has to do with what kinds of statements we can logically make about the observations within the study itself. We are often interested in making statements about the effects of some experimental treat-

[5] See Campbell and Stanley (1963) for further discussion of these six designs and their relation to the confounding factors; Campbell and Stanley also describe some "quasi-experimental" designs for obtaining a limited degree of internal validity. This same line of logic is explored further by Campbell (1962, 1963, 1969), Stanley (1966), and Solomon and Lessac (1968). Argyris (1968) has described some threats to validity that can arise from the role relations between the experimenter and the humans he is studying; we shall deal with these questions in Chapter 9. There is also an extensive literature generally known under the label "experimental design," stemming from the logic of research in genetics and agriculture and oriented toward the complexities of statistical analysis. Many books have been published applying this logic to social research; see, for example, Lindquist (1953) and Edwards (1960).

ment we have introduced. Many of the confounding factors previously discussed can prevent us from making valid conclusions about the effects of treatment X. For example, if we use design 2, it would be risky to conclude that a change from pretest to posttest is due to X—it might just as well be due to something else that happens in that time interval or to maturation of subjects or to still other factors. The factors that affect what we can conclude about the effects of our experimental treatment X on the subjects in our study are those that limit the *internal validity* of the study.

But there is another kind of problem with which we must deal. Even when we find differences related to the experimental treatment X, and even when we have eliminated various extraneous factors (history, maturation, and so on) and thus can come to an internally valid conclusion about the effect of X in our study, there remains the further question of whether that effect is general—or, rather, how general it is. If the observed effect of X holds only for the particular subjects we observed in the study or only for the particular testing room we used or only for the particular time of day at which we made our observations, then we have not learned very much from our study that can be useful to other people at other times or other places. As an example, suppose we have investigated the effects of using a certain teaching method with social studies materials and fifth grade "gifted" children. Assume that we have used all the proper design features so that we can make valid conclusions about the effects of the method within our study, eliminating effects of factors such as history, maturation, and so on. Suppose, further, that we find a substantial effect attributable to the experimental treatment. Can we now conclude that this experimental teaching method will have salutary effects for "normal" children of fifth grade or for either normal or gifted children of other grade levels or for children of any age or ability level with general science, mathematics, or English courses? We most certainly cannot make any of these inferential leaps—or at least we are not logically justified in doing so on the basis of the results of this study of fifth grade gifted children taught social studies by a particular method, however well designed and however internally valid the study may be. The problem raised here is the question of the *external validity* of the study—that is, the extent to which the results can be *generalized* beyond the data of the specific study.

We must concern ourselves with generalizability of three forms. First, there is the generality of experimental treatment X over variation in the particulars of treatment. For example, can the new teaching method be used by many teachers (with training, of course), or is the effect due in part to the "magic" of the particular teacher in our study? Does the effect depend on particular instructions? Is the effect limited to the particular content material on which we used it (say fifth grade social science) and inapplicable to other subjects or even to other levels of the same subject? If treatment X is to have any future beyond this first study, we must discover how flexible we can be in adapting it to new situations.

Second, we must concern ourselves with the generality of results with respect to our methods of measurement or observation. If the effect disappears when we assess results with questions having a slightly different wording, or when we use a six-point scale instead of a nine-point scale, then the effect we obtained is not very "hardy"—it is going to be too difficult to be sure the effect is there at all. We can consider an effect general only if it holds for a variety of specific alternative forms of measurement.

Finally, we must be concerned with the generality of results with respect to actors: with the range of people over which the effect will hold. Using the example again of appraising a teaching method, we can readily think of dozens of reasonable teaching methods which might work well for children in primary school but which would fail pitifully in the college classroom, and conversely. Thus, while results of a study may be internally valid for the sample of persons studied, those results can be generalized only to that population of which the study sample is a representative sample. A study with high external validity requires random selection of actors to be included in the study in the first place as well as random assignment of actors to conditions once they have been taken into the study. Since it is only to that population from which you have randomly sampled that you may feel free to generalize results of your study, many critics of current research into human psychology have held that we are building a "psychology of the college sophomore" rather than a "psychology of man."

When we think of these three domains of generalizability, we remind ourselves again that the science of behavior deals with actors behaving with objects in a context. Consequently, when we conduct any investigation, we want to know what our findings can say to us (1) about actors other than (but similar to) those we actually observed, (2) about behaviors in response to treatments other than (but similar to) the behaviors in response to the exact treatment we used in this case, and (3) about contexts other than (but similar to) the exact contexts we had for this particular investigation. To check thoroughly the extent to which an effect penetrates each of the three domains requires a network of comparisons. Campbell and Fiske (1959) have worked out the prototype for this kind of network; we shall describe their paradigm in section 6-4.

How does one establish external validity? Any single study, even the most grandly planned, can yield only a very limited degree of external validity. If, in an initial study, we obtain a substantial and interesting finding within an internally valid experiment, we can be proud of having composed a hypothesis that predicted the fall of the data. However, our finding cannot have any practical influence on the wider world until this first study is followed by other studies that explore the range of treatment (X's), measurements (O's), and actors over which the obtained results will hold. (This point is elaborated further in section 14-14.) Only after we have demonstrated that the effect holds over a range of variations in treatments, observations, and actors can we begin to have confidence that it will hold in other cases under conditions not yet tested. And even then, we cannot know with certainty that it will hold under any given set of not-yet-tested conditions. *We can never gain logical certainty through induction.* All we can do is increase the probability that a given effect will hold in the next as-yet-unobserved case. We can strive to increase the probability of an effect to very near 1.00 (that is, certainty), but we can never reach certainty. This line of thinking brings us to the point that every empirical statement is a *contingent* statement and a *probabilistic* statement. (This is true of *all* sciences, the physical sciences as well as the behavioral.) Empirical statements are contingent statements because they *hold only under the complex of conditions under which the supporting evidence was gathered* or under "new" conditions not substantially different from these. Empirical statements are probabilistic statements because they are based on induction—that is, generalization from a collection of particulars—and while the probability of a particular not yet observed may approach certainty, it never reaches it.

Results obtained from a study are useful only if they are internally valid in terms of the design of the study. Results of an internally valid study have wider importance only to the degree that their generality over conditions—sampling of treatment, measurement, and actor—is established empirically by subsequent studies, each of which meets the criteria of internal validity as well. We do not advance a science—old or young—by conducting sloppy, internally invalid studies or by making inferential leaps that overgeneralize our conclusions beyond the conditions under which we have explored the phenomena.

3-2. Replication and Partitioning: Micro-Design

The previous section dealt with the first major chunks of study design, treating study design as a logical plan by which the investigator can eliminate, in advance, some of the major classes of confounding factors that are likely to threaten the validity (especially the internal validity) of his study. The present section will carry on the concern with study design as a logical plan to assure internal validity, but will deal with the finer detail. Any observation has three referents: actor, behavior toward object, and context. As soon as the investigator gathers (or plans to gather) more than one observation, he is faced with a set of decisions as to which observations are to be treated as alike (hence as *replications* of each other) and which are to be treated as different from each other (hence *partitioned* into subsets).

REPLICATION

Strictly speaking, no two observations can be exactly alike. Even such a simple observation as "John hits Henry," recorded on two occasions, does not refer to absolutely identical events. Not only do the occasions differ in a temporal sense but the behavior referent "hits" is likely to differ in intensity, motor movements involved, point of impact, and so on. It is also true, of course, that neither John nor Henry is in every respect the identical actor on those two occasions.

But, for a variety of reasons to be noted later, the researcher often will want to act *as if* certain sets of observations are alike in one or more of the facets of actor, behavior, and context. Which facets of his observations he treats as alike and which as different will depend on his purposes. For example, he may want to treat all "hits"—of all intensities, points of impact, and other features—as alike for his purposes and may also include acts of verbal abuse as like the hits, because his interest is in a category of "aggressive acts." At the same time, he may want to keep separate counts of the aggressive acts of John, Henry, and George, treating them as "different" sets of events because he wishes to study the frequency of aggressive acts by different actors. Similarly, he may have reason to distinguish "hits" according to place; he may wish to keep separate—as "different" from one another—aggressive acts on the playground, in the classroom, and in the home; or in the morning and in the evening; or toward persons present and persons not present. However, in saying that the researcher will often want to act as if certain sets of observations are alike, we do not mean that the researcher should do this if he wants to be respectable. We mean that it is inevitably so. We reiterate that our purpose in describing this sort of choice faced by the researcher is to help him become aware of a choice he will make willy-nilly; our purpose is not to say or imply that one choice is more welcome to the gods than another.

It is crucial to recognize that decisions about what will be considered the same and what different are for the most part arbitrary. That is, they are not dictated by the content or form of the observations. Instead, they are within the scope of decision of the investigator and need to be made with two considerations in mind:

1. The purposes for which the investigator has gathered the observations
2. The likelihood that observations differing in one aspect will show concomitant differences in other aspects.

These two considerations will become clearer with an example. Imagine that you are going to get 100 parallel observations, each about an individual actor (a voter) exhibiting a particular behavior (expressing a preference) in a particular context (being asked about his voting preference by an interviewer). Suppose, further, that your interest is in trying to establish the relative frequency with which voters express preference for a particular candidate. In this case, you might wish to treat all actors as the same and all the observed contexts (for example, regardless of different times of interviewing) as the same. You would probably then divide or "partition" the observed behaviors into two classes: those that were instances of the particular category you wished to study (choosing candidate A, say) and those that were instances of some other category of behavior. Here, you would be treating the 100 actors as *replications* of each other. That is, you would be ignoring all the various ways in which some of those individuals differ from each other, considering them not relevant *for your purposes.* You would also be treating all occasions as alike for your purposes—despite the fact that you may have collected some particular observations before you collected others, or that there may have been other minor differences in the conditions under which you gathered various observations. In our example, furthermore, you would be considering all choices of *any other* candidate than A as same for your purposes; and you would be considering all choices of candidate A to be the same even though various actors may have made the choice for different reasons, with different degrees of confidence, with different latencies of response, and with other differences. The point here is that a set of observations potentially can differ in a myriad of ways within each of the three facets of actor, behavior, and context, and the investigator must choose which of these potential differences he will attend to and consider worth study and which he will overlook as not relevant for his purposes. (There are some middle-ground alternatives, too, as we shall discuss later.)

Instead of studying voters as a uniform bunch, let us suppose the investigator is interested in studying—with the same set of observations—whether one kind of voter or another shows a higher relative frequency of choosing candidate A. For example, the investigator might believe that candidate A would be chosen in larger proportion by males, or by the younger voters, or by those higher in intelligence, or by those more extroverted. He might therefore divide his set of observations according to two or more classes of actors; let us say he divides his observations into two parts—those taken from voters of high intelligence and those taken from low. (He can, of course, divide his observations into a maximum of n classes, if n is the total number of actors.) He would then determine the relative frequency of choosing candidate A separately for each of these classes of actors and then compare those frequencies to see if there is a relation between being high in intelligence and exhibiting the particular behavior choice being studied. Note here that the researcher is still treating all the contexts of his observations as alike, ignoring temporal and other differences that might have occurred. He is still treating all other candidates as alike and treating all instances of choice of candidate A as the same, regardless of reason, speed, or other aspects of choice. Furthermore, although he is now making one major differentiation among actors—high versus low intelligence—he is still treating all actors as essentially alike in *all other respects.* The reader can easily imagine still further examples, perhaps instances in which different "kinds" of contexts are differentiated—for example, early versus late in sequence of observations; or with a male versus a female interviewer; or at mealtime or not. The reader can also extend the argument to cases where actors are differentiated into multiple classes on two or more facets—for example, sex and intelligence—still leaving, of course, many other potential differences among actors which are overlooked as not relevant for the investigator's purposes.

Thus, there is no such thing as a literal replication. Rather, the investigator chooses to *attend to* certain differences and overlook others. Observations are partitioned into classes or types on the bases[6] chosen by the investigator. All other possible bases for differentiating among observations are ignored; and observations that differ in any of those respects but do *not* differ on the chosen bases for typing are treated *as if* they were alike in all respects. Note, also, that the bases chosen for differentiating observations into types must be known *independently of the primary observations themselves.* Thus the observation that a particular actor chose candidate A does not *in itself* tell us the sex of the actor, his intelligence, the temporal locus of the occasion, conditions occurring for that context, and so on. All of these factors must be observed independently of observing the actor choosing the candidate. Each is a different property or variable that has its own actor-behavior-context designation. Note, also, that the facets to be investigated must be determined by the investigator in advance of gathering and analyzing the observation, or at any rate, independently of these steps. This is not to say that the investigator must decide in advance that he will divide his actor population in terms of sex or intelligence or some other property when he *analyzes* his observations. He can partly hold that decision until later. What he must do beforehand, though, is collect appropriate information in case he needs it for later analysis; he cannot decide later to split his choosers of candidate A according to other attitudes they held at the time of choice unless he arranges to gather that information beforehand.

One research principle that can be extracted from this discussion is that the researcher should plan to make observations on all variables (actor properties, behavior properties, context properties) that he *might* want to use later to partition his set of observations. He can later choose not to use some information he has available, but he cannot later choose to use information he does not have available. Sometimes it is possible to run back and collect previously neglected information; more often, the chance once lost is lost forever. Still, this principle cannot be followed to the limit; it is never feasible to observe every conceivable property that might later be of interest. The more realistic use of the principle is to plan in advance to make observations of all the variables (properties of actors, behaviors, and contexts) one expects to be important and are not prohibitively expensive. Thus, if one has reason to believe that the phenomena of interest do *not* vary as a function of sex of actor, but *do* vary as a function of intelligence, he should get some measure of intelligence on each actor and relinquish sex. (Actually, of course, the cost in time and effort of information about sex of actors is usually so low that the investigator would be foolish not to get the information, just in case he might need it later.) Some sort of compromise must always be reached between the cost of obtaining information about a variable and its importance to the study.

[6]One can partition things at a certain "value" and also on a certain "basis." One can divide a bunch of marbles into two or more parts on the basis (or by the criteria) of size, color, weight, roundness, and so on. On the basis of size, to take one basis or criterion as an example, one can partition the marbles at 5 millimeters, at 7, or at any arbitrary value (amount, degree, quantity, and so on). We shall use the terms *basis, criterion, attribute,* and the like, on the one hand, and *value, degree, cutting point,* and the like, on the other hand, in these two distinct senses.

Note that some variables mentioned in previous examples are not determined by observation; they are created or controlled by the investigator. For example, the problems actors are posed with, the alternatives they can choose, the alternative the investigator will treat as the positive response—all these may be built into the situation by the investigator. This is, in fact, usually the case for experiments in laboratories. In studies done in natural situations, though, the investigator must take such things as they come; there he can observe and record but can rarely create or control. These considerations suggest several modes of dealing with a particular variable within the study. (1) The investigator can deliberately control a variable—that is, hold it as nearly constant as he can for all cases (for example, he can select only males for his study). (2) He can deliberately *manipulate* it—subject the variable to his own management—holding it constant at a particular value for one subset of cases and holding it constant at a different value[7] for another subset (using, for example, only males in one subset and only females in another). (3) He can observe or *measure* what value of the variable occurs for each case (but make no attempt to control or modify that value). (4) He can *ignore* the variable—act as if cases did not differ on it, or as if such differences were not related to the phenomenon of interest. Such modes of dealing with a variable and their implications for study design will be discussed systematically in section 3-3, and two more modes will be added.

PARTITIONING

Knowledge is knowledge of differences. If we know something about men and women, it is because we know something about how men and women *differ.* That is, we can divide people into two nonoverlapping classes, men and women, and look to see how the people in one class differ from the people in the other. If we know something about children as children, it is because we know something about how they differ from adults. Or perhaps, on the basis of age, we might divide people into classes to be called infants, young children, older children, adolescents, adults, and senescents and examine the differences from one class to another. Research into the real world always requires dividing the observables in the real world into parts. We begin by dividing all possible observables into those we are going to pay some attention and those we are going to ignore forthwith. Then we proceed to more subtle divisions. We shall introduce the elementary sorts of divisions in this section and define, especially, two sorts: those established beforehand by *design* and those left to be *observed.* We shall use the term *partitioning* to mean dividing any set of elements into two or more mutually exclusive, exhaustive classes.

If we have multiple observations we wish to treat as a set from which we want to learn something, we must partition them in respect to *at least one*

---

[7] By *value* we wish to denote a category, level, type, numerical value, or any other form in which a property can vary.

aspect or variable within at least one of the facets of actor, behavior, or context. In the first example dealing with the choice of a certain candidate in the discussion of replication in section 3-2, the only partition was on the basis of whether the behavior was or was not the choice of candidate A. At the other extreme, though we may employ a large number of partitions, we can feasibly partition a set of observations into only a limited number of categories and only in respect to a limited number of properties or variables. Therefore, we must treat observations as replications indistinguishable with respect to *all other* variables beyond those we are using as criteria for partitioning. For example, we might want to study the number of children produced in families in relation to the number they already have, the family income, the extroversion of the husband, the mean number of children per family among the friends of the family, and so on. At some point, however, this list of independent variables must stop; and when it does, observations of further families will be considered observations of replicated families, since they will be counted as equivalent to the observation of some family already observed.

Now let us turn to more complicated possibilities. Returning to the example of the choice of candidate, let us suppose that we partition our observations of the behaviors-toward-objects according to sex of *actor* (male and female); that we make a single partition of *behavior* (the choice of candidate A rather than some other candidate); and that we recognize two classes of *context* (central city or suburban residence). Suppose, further, that we *control* by selection the number of males and females we observe (perhaps 50 each), and we also decide beforehand to observe some actors from central city residence and some from suburban residence (again perhaps 50 each, and, for convenience, observing equal numbers of males and females from each sort of residence). We, of course, do *not* control which actors make choice A rather than some other choice—this is what we are trying to find out.

We could then consider this set of observations as deliberately partitioned into four classes—sexes of actor crossed with two contexts. (We chose equal numbers of cases in each class in the example, but that was merely for convenience of discussion. Partitions need not divide sets of observations into equal parts.) Within each of the four classes, we would next be asking *how the observations are partitioned on the behavior*—how many cases exhibited the behavior of choosing candidate A and how many did not exhibit that behavior. The final observed partition is the locus of the "new information" in these observations. We did not make it happen, as we did with the actor sexes and contexts. Each case was presumably free to result in a choice of A or not—in the sense that it was not forced to be one or the other or prevented from being one or the other by some condition of the study. Therefore, the numbers of instances within the four categories (males and females in central city and suburban residences) exhibiting choice A is *information* that we can gain from our observations. We cannot gain information about partitionings that we made occur. For example, if we put 50 males and 50 females into our study, we cannot then "learn" that there were 50 of each sex in it. To learn something *new* from a study, we must arrange circumstances so that at least one property of each case is free to occur or not (or to occur at different values), so that what actually *does* occur for each case on that property *did not have to occur.* We learn something new only when something happens that was not a certainty beforehand.

We shall refer to partitions of observations that are predetermined by the investigator as *design partitions* (for example, the male-female division of actors, the central-city–suburban partition of contexts). We shall refer to the partitions of observations that occur outside the control of the investigator—and that contain potential information for him—as *observed partitions.*

There is *always at least one observed partition*—that is, at least one property of the set of observations that is free to vary outside the control of the investigator. If there is only one observed partition and *no* design partitions, then the only sort of information we can get is the distribution of the observed property in the population we have chosen. If we are observing a dichotomy (that is, if the partition yields only two classes), then we obtain a frequency count of the presence of some property, such as choosing candidate A or having curly hair. If we are observing an intensity or degree of some property (that is, if the partition yields classes having numerical values), then we can compute the average value and the variation of values around that average among the population of actors-behaviors-contexts on which observations are based.[8]

RELATING TWO PARTITIONS

Investigators in the behavioral sciences often use one or more design partitions along with one or more observed partitions. When an investigator uses two or more observed partitions but no design partitions, he usually intends to ask about the joint distribution of cases on the two (or more) observed partitions. For example, he might want to ask about the occurrence of central-city residence along with the occurrence of voting for candidate A. Further, suppose the investigator limits his interest to voters in the central city and in the suburbs and to the behavior of voting either for or against candidate A (excluding nonvoting persons). The investigator could now tally each voter in one of four categories, ending with four counts—namely, the number of voters:

1. Residing in the central city and choosing candidate A
2. Residing in the central city but choosing some other candidate
3. Residing in a suburb and choosing candidate A
4. Residing in a suburb but choosing some other candidate.

From the four frequencies (that is, counts), one can go on to assess the degree of association between the two observed partitions. If most of the cases fall

[8]The idea of partitioning is parallel to the idea of facets. Elements of a facet identify possible bases for classes or subsets into which observations may be partitioned, either beforehand by the experimenter (design partitions) or by empirical outcomes (observed partitions).

into the two classes (1) and (4), we say the two are *associated* or *related.* We may, if we wish, arbitrarily call this the positive direction and say that the two conditions (facets, variables) are *positively* associated or related. We would then declare a *negative* association or relation if most of the cases were to fall in the classes (2) and (3). If the proportions of voters choosing candidate A among central city dwellers turned out to be about the same as the proportion among suburbanites, we would say there was no association between the two variables—or that the association was one of zero degree.

The two properties might also be observed in nondichotomous terms; this would permit recording a number of degrees or values of each property (for example, scores on a test; number of items produced in an hour; weight in pounds; or number of times out of ten trials that A is chosen rather than something else). In this case, the joint distribution of values of the two properties could be plotted with the possible range of values of one property along a horizontal axis and the possible range of values of the other property along a vertical axis, and a point plotted to represent each case. There are numerous ways of quantifying the degree of association or relation between the two properties, the most common of which is the correlation coefficient. (See section 13-2 for descriptions of other kinds of relations.)

In the case of obtaining numerical scores from a test or other device, notice that we partition observations not merely into two or three types but into one type for each different score. And it should be clear that dichotomous partitioning on a property is a special case of nondichotomous partitioning or quantitative scoring on a property. We could readily reclassify each of two quantitative (many-valued) partitions into dichotomous ones by splitting each array of scores at the middle score and grouping all cases above that as replicated "highs" and all below as replicated "lows." We could then proceed to examine the relation of the two properties as in the earlier example by counting the cases that are high-high, high-low, low-high, and low-low.

DESIGN PARTITIONS

A frequent procedure is to partition a set of observations on one or more *predetermined* properties (such as type of actor or context) and assess some behavioral property within each resulting subset. For example, an investigator might observe the relative frequency with which behavior x occurs for each of two subsets of actors, one of which contains males and the other females.[9] Or the researcher might compute the average value on behavior y for all males and compare it to the average value on behavior y for all females. He could thus explore the *relation* between sex and occurrence of behavior y or the average *difference* in degree of behavior y for males and females.

[9] Sex, here, is considered a design partition. The investigator does not literally *make* certain cases male and others female, of course. Rather, he selects males for certain observation cases and females for others. See section 8-2 on selection and intervention.

A property (characteristic, dimension, aspect, attribute) can be used as a design partition in a number of ways that vary in the complexity of the relations among the subsets produced by the partition. The most elementary type of partition is a partition into two mutually exclusive nominal classes: one subset has property P, the other does not. (For example, one subset has smallpox while the other does not.) Only slightly more complex would be a partition into three or more mutually exclusive subsets such as teachers, students, and parents as actors in a school. Another level of complexity produces two or more subsets[10] that are *ordered* on a property; for example, children high in intelligence, children intermediate in intelligence, and children low in intelligence. Such partitions are like the partitions into nominal classes in that they yield mutually exclusive and collectively exhaustive subsets, but they differ in that the subsets are themselves *related by their order on the partitioning property.* (In the example, subsets are ordered on the property "intelligence of actor.")

The next extension of complexity of partitioning is the division of classes into subsets that not only have an order relation but can be "located" as some point (or region) on a quantitative continuum (either on an interval scale or a ratio scale); for example, 10-year-olds, 11-year-olds, 12-year-olds, and so on. Actually, the investigator may interpret such classes in any of four ways, involving increasingly strong assumptions:

1. That $10 \neq 11 \neq 12$ merely; that is, a set of *nominal* classes
2. That $10 < 11 < 12$; that is, a set of *ordered* classes
3. That the difference between 10 and 11 is equal to the difference between 11 and 12, and so on; 10, 11, and 12 are points on an *interval* scale
4. That the difference between 10 and 12 is one-fifth the difference between 0 and 10; 0, 10, and 12 are points on a *ratio* scale.[11]

With a property like age, time, weight, or number of members, any of these four assumptions is reasonable. But for high, middle, or low intelligence or strong, weak, or no incentive or similarly qualitative properties, either of the last two assumptions would obviously be very dubious.

So far, we have talked about complexity of a design partition in terms of number of classes and relation among classes. It is possible, of course, to use two or more properties as design partitions for the same set of cases. Each one can have two or more classes and nominal, ordered, interval, or ratio-scale relations among the classes. As only one example among many, a set of observations could be partitioned by design into five ordered classes of age *and* two nominal-scale classes of sex. This would yield 2 times 5, or 10 joint classes or subsets. One could then go on to examine the relation between *each*

[10] Though in most applications it is trivial to speak of only two things as ordered.

[11] For further elaboration on scales of measurement, see Coombs, Raiffa, and Thrall (1954) or Stevens (1951).

of those design-partition variables and some third observed-partition property (such as choice of candidate A) and also between the two design-partition properties *jointly* (or interactively) and the third observed partition.

In many cases in the behavioral sciences, a design-partition property cannot be made to occur at each of a wide range of values of that property, and the behavioral scientist finds it necessary to work with design partitions having two, three, or some relatively small number of categories or values. Often, too, these are only nominal categories, without a quantifiable relation to one another on some single known dimension. With a small number of categories and, of course, with unordered categories, sophisticated methods of assessing a co-varying relation are not applicable. Consequently, in many cases, design partitions are used in that special way of exploring a relation called *difference testing.* Relations and differences will be discussed again in Chapter 13.

The use of design-partition properties has some limitations, as we have seen, but it also has some advantages in comparison to using observed partitions only. One advantage of design partitions is that they allow you to explore systematically the effects on behavior (in the observed partitions) of various degrees or values of each of several properties; and they do so in a way that permits you to identify the effects of each property separately and of two or more simultaneously. This can be done by using several variables of interest as design partitions, making certain quantitative assumptions about how variables combine in their effects, and ascertaining by statistical analysis the effects of these design partitions on an observed partition.

We take time out here for a note on terminology. Many writers use the term *independent variable* to label the partition the investigator chooses to select or produce and *dependent variable* to label the observed partition. For example, an investigator might change the method of recruiting clients for welfare services to see whether the new method would be followed by a rise in the percentage of welfare clients subsequently enrolling in school. The method of recruitment would be called the independent variable, with the welfare clients partitioned by their method of recruitment. The rate of enrollment in school would be called the dependent variable, since the investigator lets it depend on the mode of recruitment; we call it here an observed partition.

Some writers urge the use of both *independent* and *dependent* even in a correlational study, where both partitions are observed and neither is established independently by the investigator. Consequently, what we call a design partition others would never call a dependent variable, but what we call an observed partition others sometimes call an independent variable and sometimes a dependent.

Another advantage of the design partition is available to the researcher who produces by his own intervention some particular difference among actors, behaviors, or contexts; namely, the researcher can be sure that the events in the observed partition did not produce the differences in the design partition. If the researcher *selects* cases for his design partition, however, and does not produce them before making the observations for his observed partition, he runs the risk that the events of his observed partition *did* cause those of the design partition. A researcher with the hypothesis that alcoholism produces certain personality characteristics might select 50 alcoholics and 50 non-alcoholics as a design partition to study the associated personality traits as observed partitions. But if personality traits in fact cause alcoholism, selecting the alcoholics would select the personality traits along with the alcoholics who had been produced by those traits, and the researcher would come to the wrong conclusion. The way to avoid this possibility is to choose persons randomly, divide them randomly into two groups, turn one group into alcoholics, and see whether the hypothesized changes in personality occur. Such a design is morally objectionable when humans are the subjects, and experimenters therefore often turn to rats and other animals for experiments of this sort. It is true, of course, that the researcher who has produced a design partition still does not know that the variable of that partition *caused* the differences in the observed partition. But this is still an advantage over the case of a relation between two observed partitions, where the researcher cannot rule out either direction of causality.

Being able to impose a number of design partitions on a set of observations is not an unmixed blessing. When you partition a set of observations on two or more variables at the same time, you have partitioned that set into as many subclasses as the number of categories or values of one property *multiplied* by the number of values of the other property—multiplied by the number of values of a third property, and so on. When you wish to test differences between combinations of conditions[12] in average values or relative frequency (proportions), it is necessary to have *a number of replicated cases within each joint condition* on which to base that average or proportion. The larger the number of cases within each joint condition (the more cases treated alike), the more stable will be the average value or the proportion estimated for that joint condition. On the other hand, the more properties used to partition a set of observations, and the more categories or values used in partitioning on each property, the more comprehensive will be the information extracted from that set of observations. Given any fixed total number of observations, however, the more partitioning properties and the more values of each, the more joint conditions and, hence, the fewer replications of cases within each joint condition. Obviously, there is a conflict here. Both stability of averages or proportions (based on replication of cases) and comprehensiveness of partitioning (in both number of partitioning properties used and number of categories of each) are desirable. But to maximize one is to minimize the other

[12]By this phrase we mean to point to differences to be seen by comparing the values of an observed partition (such as choice or nonchoice of candidate A) that occur in two or more of the conditions formed by the design partitions (conditions such as being male and between 20 and 30 years of age versus being male and between 30 and 40 years of age). As a synonym for *combinations of conditions,* we shall often use *joint conditions;* another synonym we have used is the term *cell,* as in discussing cells in facet designs in Chapter 2.

within any fixed total number of observations. There is no final solution to this dilemma. Given some total number of cases, the trick is to partition as much as you can (picking the most important variables, of course, and the most important degrees of differences within each to use as partitions) while still retaining enough replication of cases within each joint condition to provide stable averages or proportions. The other option is to add more observations to the total set. There are no precise rules for striking the proper balance in any given instance, but there are some guides that will help you make these decisions.

SOME GUIDES FOR PARTITIONING

First, you must partition—by design or by observation—in respect to those properties about which you wish to draw conclusions. Thus, the first guide lies in your own study purposes. If you are interested in how a certain personality characteristic is related to some behavior, you must obtain information that will let you establish either a design partition (that is, by setting up types or degrees of that characteristic) or an observed partition (that is, by measuring the degree of that characteristic for every case) and relate that partition to the behavioral property you are interested in studying. Second, you must be concerned with *any* variable that you have reason to believe may significantly influence the property of the observed partition. You can cope with a relevant variable by (1) building that property into your study plan as a design partition (which, of course, multiplies the number of joint conditions you have) or by (2) taking steps to control the variable (hold it at a single value for all cases in all conditions) or by (3) planning to deal with it as an observed partition. If you do none of these but ignore the variable, then it may confound the information you extract about relations between the design partitions and the observed partitions of your study. These basic modes of treating variables were mentioned earlier and will be discussed systematically in the next section.

The more important the property is—that is, the more influence it is likely to have on the other properties being studied—the less you can afford to ignore it in your study plan. Note, here, that it does not matter whether the variable is as interesting to you as the variables with which you began; what matters is whether, or to what degree, the variable is likely to influence the behavioral phenomena you wish to study. If that likelihood is high, you must do *something* about the variable or run the risk of concluding that the proverbial elephant is shaped like a snake. (The "somethings" you can do are treated in the next section.)

How can you know in advance whether a variable is likely to affect the behavior you are studying? You cannot know in any clear-cut sense; you must make an estimate. But there are several ways you can proceed to try to get a good estimate. First, you can draw upon existing theory relating to the problem you are studying and use the propositions and hypotheses of that theory to alert yourself to variables likely to influence the behavior to be studied. Second, you can study the literature for the empirical results of prior research. Third, you can ask the question empirically by means of a small-scale or pilot study prior to your main study, in which the variable whose effect you are trying to estimate is used as a design partition and the behavior in which you are interested is used as an observed partition. Such a pilot study can tell you whether the property *does* have substantial effects when studied in isolation from other properties; it cannot tell you whether the property will still have major effects when studied in interaction with other variables. Conversely, if the property shows *no* effect in your pilot study, it does *not* follow that it would have no effect in interaction with other variables. Nevertheless, although a pilot study cannot answer the question with certainty, it will usually permit you to make a better guess than you could make without having done the study.

Both the literature search and the pilot study can also help you decide how many values and which values of a property are best for you to use in a design partition. For example, results of a pilot study could indicate that while a certain property x partitioned into five levels had a large total effect on a behavior y, most of that effect came from the cases in the highest level of x in comparison with any of the other four levels, with differences between the other four values making little or no difference in y. You would then be in a position to be confident that (1) the property does have a substantial effect, and (2) it is most important to distinguish very high values of the property versus all other values if you use that property as a design partition in your study.

A pilot study lets you improve your best guess about effects of a property. A literature search lets you find out if someone else has already done the equivalent of the pilot study; if so, you can improve your best guess about the effects of the variable at a lower cost than by conducting a pilot study yourself. And drawing upon established theory lets you take advantage of the systematically considered best guesses of others—also at a lower cost than conducting a pilot study. Ultimately, of course, you must decide whether to include any given variable as a design partition on the basis of the best informed guess you can achieve.

The next section presents a systematic discussion of four specific modes for treating a given variable and offers some techniques for dealing with effects of all other variables not explicitly handled by the four specific modes.

3-3. Modes for Treatment of Variables in a Research Design

Research in behavioral science attempts to extract information about relations within behavior systems by analyzing systematic observations of behavior of actors toward objects within contexts. And whenever we set out to make observations of behavior systems—whether in contrived laboratory settings or in naturally occurring field settings—there is a large number of properties of those behavior systems (of actors, of behaviors, of contexts) that are *potentially relevant* to the behavioral phenomena of interest. We stated this point in the last section, but it is worth reviewing in connection with direct, indirect, and potential relevance of variables, and it is worth restating as an introduction to a systematic presentation of the four specific modes of treating variables.

A property or variable is *relevant* to the research if it varies with the behavior under primary study either directly or indirectly. A variable of actor, of behavior, or of context is *directly relevant* to a behavioral phenomenon of interest if a change in the phenomenon (or at least in some range of it) accompanies a change in the variable. For example, if we are studying a certain behavior y (perhaps the effectiveness of performing some task), we would say that a certain property x (perhaps the intelligence of the actors) is relevant if the value of y is high when the value of x is high and low when x is low. We would say that x is *potentially relevant* if we have reason to believe that it might have such a relation to the behavioral phenomena of interest.

In other ways, a property can be *indirectly relevant.* If a variable x_1 is related to a behavioral variable y, then another variable x_2 is relevant to our study of y if any of the following conditions hold:

1. If x_2 is related to x_1 and hence indirectly related to y (example: Manner of rearing is related to intelligence and therefore indirectly to effectiveness of performing task T)
2. If the relation between x_1 and y holds only when certain values of x_2 are present (example: Intelligence is related only to performing complex tasks, not simple tasks; consequently, complexity of task [x_2] is indirectly relevant to x_1 and y)
3. If the relation between x_1 and y is intensified or diminished when certain values of x_2 are present (example: Among actors working alone, the relation between intelligence of actor and performance on task T is stronger than it is among actors working as members of groups of mixed intelligences).[13]

So, if a property is itself related to the behavioral phenomenon being studied, or if it is related to some other property that affects the phenomenon, or if it interacts with other properties in affecting the phenomenon, then that property (variable, dimension, aspect, characteristic) is *relevant.* If we have reason to suspect that it might have any of these direct or indirect relations, then we must treat the variable as *potentially relevant.* (Strictly speaking, it is logical to hold a property as potentially relevant if we do *not* have adequate evidence that it is *not* related. But, of course, we can never have final evidence that it is *not* relevant—only that it has not as yet been shown to be relevant.)

In any behavioral problem, it is likely that there will be a rather large

[13] Actually, (2) is a special case of (3).

number of properties which, in the absence of evidence to the contrary, must be treated as potentially relevant. One of the fundamental dilemmas of behavioral research is that the investigator must reckon in some manner with every potentially relevant property or variable; but at the same time, for practical reasons, he cannot possibly deal with every potentially relevant variable directly and explicitly. (The reason he must reckon with every relevant variable in some way is that the variable is unavoidably a part of the behavioral system he is studying, and it will have whatever effects it has whether he deals with it explicitly or ignores it.) If a potentially relevant variable is ignored, its effects will add either systematic error (bias in comparisons of partitioned subsets) or random error (variation among cases treated alike) or both; and this will tend to distort or obscure the information that can be extracted from the observations.

The reason the researcher cannot possibly reckon with every potentially relevant variable in a direct and explicit way is twofold. First, there is a limit of feasibility to the number of variables that can be handled explicitly in any given study—not a fixed limit but a limit in terms of time and cost of the study. Second, it is not logically possible to anticipate in advance all possible variables that might later turn out to have been relevant. The researcher could anticipate all of them only if he already knew everything significant about the behavior system under study—and if that were true, he would not be doing research on it. There is a partial solution to this dilemma—that the investigator must reckon in some way with every potentially relevant variable, but that he cannot do so in direct, explicit ways for all such variables—because there is a technique that forestalls much of the harm of error-producing variables not explicitly treated. This technique, called *randomization,* was mentioned previously and will be discussed in detail in a later section of this chapter.

There are four basic modes for explicit treatment of a specific variable and dozens of techniques by which each of these modes can be applied. The four modes have already been suggested. They will be formally presented in the next section; the techniques for applying them are discussed in Chapters 7 and 8. In addition to the four specific modes, there remain two nonspecific ways of treating variables: randomize them or ignore them. These two nonspecific modes will be discussed later in this chapter.

THE FOUR SPECIFIC MODES

The first of the four basic ways of dealing specifically with a variable is to control it so that it occurs at some known value that is the same for *all* cases. When we use this kind of control, we shall speak of using the variable (which now is kept from varying) as a *design constant;* we shall give this treatment of the variable the arbitrary label K for brevity. A second mode is to control the variable so that it occurs at a particular known value for all cases within one subset, but at a different particular value for all cases within another subset. This is using the variable as a *design partition;* we have already discussed this mode at some length; we shall now give it the additional label X. A third mode is to measure the variable and then assign cases so that the *average* value on that variable (or the distribution of values) is the same for subsets that are partitioned on some other variable, although the values within each subset (the cases treated alike) vary. This is using the variable as a *matching* property; we shall call this mode M. The fourth specific mode for treatment of a variable is simply to measure the variable as it occurs, recording the value of the variable for each case. This is using the variable as an *observed partition;* we shall give it the additional label Y.

These four specific modes are related to one another in several ways, two of which are shown in Table 3-3. Modes K and X are alike in that each controls the variable in such a way that all cases treated alike are alike on *that* property. They differ in that the X mode partitions the observations into subsets such that the property in question, while kept at the same value (or substantially so) within each subset, takes on different values from subset to subset; mode K maintains the same value within and between subsets. Modes K and M are alike in that both insure that different subsets (partitioned on some other property) do not differ (on the average) on the property in question. These two modes differ in that K insures that cases treated alike are substantially alike, while M virtually insures that cases treated alike will differ in respect to the property in question. Modes X and Y are alike in that both permit variation on the property between subsets. They differ in two ways: Y also permits variation within subsets, while X does not; and mode X determines or influences what value will occur for each case, while mode Y merely observes and records what *does* occur for each case. Modes M and Y have a further relation that is worth noting. Both modes require measuring the property in question and both permit variation among cases treated alike; but Y permits variation between subsets, whereas M is designed to prevent such variation.

Mode X can later be converted into K if it turns out that the differences in the property in question between subsets are *not* directly or indirectly related to other properties of interest (that is, to the observed partitions). If the differences between subsets do not affect the dependent variable y, in other words, we can merely pretend they are not differences. Similarly, M can be converted to K if it turns out (or is decided by the investigator) that the variations among cases treated alike are of no consequence. Conversely, mode M—or the measurement underlying M—can be converted to a special form of Y, to be related

Table 3-3. *The Four Specific Modes for Treatment of Variables*

VALUES OF THE PROPERTY AMONG CASES WITHIN EACH SUBSET	AVERAGE VALUE OF THE PROPERTY BETWEEN CASES IN DIFFERENT SUBSETS	
	Same	*Different*
Same	K	X
Different	M	Y

to other observed partitions *within* subsets only (since putting mode M into effect has removed any variation between subsets). Mode Y can be converted into either X or M by regrouping cases after data are collected. A measurement of a certain property, originally intended as an observed partition, can later be used to group cases into subsets such that all cases within a subset have approximately equal values, while subsets differ in values of that property (mode X). On the other hand, an observed partition can also be used to group cases into "nominal" subsets that are matched in average values (and variation around the average) but show a range of values within each subset (mode M). You might want to create such matched subsamples, for example, to test some hypothesis on half your observations and then repeat the same test on the other half. Finally, mode Y can be converted into K if it turns out (or is decided) that variation on the observed partition, both within and between subsets, is absent or of no consequence.

AN ILLUSTRATION OF THE FOUR MODES

Let us, for convenience, recapitulate the names and symbols we have given to the four modes:

K: a design constant[14]
X: a design partition
M: a matching property
Y: an observed partition

Let us also take time to illustrate these modes with an actual study. Myers (1962) conducted a study to find out about the effects of interteam competition and success on the cohesiveness of groups.[15] He created two sets of leagues that engaged in tournaments in rifle marksmanship; each set of leagues contained two leagues and each league contained six three-man teams. Myers used two main design partitions (mode X). The first (X_1) was interteam competition versus noncompetition. In one set of leagues (the competitive condition) each team competed against each other team in its league in a round robin fashion several times round. Each team fired an hour once a week for five weeks. The team with the best score (the least scatter in three-shot volleys, each man firing one such volley in turn) won each match. The team with the most such victories in its league won the league tournament and received a marksmanship trophy. In the other league (the noncompetitive condition) he arranged conditions so that each team competed against performance standards, not against another team. If the team had a better score than the standard (less scatter in its three-shot volleys), it won that turn or trial. Every team in the league having

[14] Other writers use the term *controlled variable* to cover what we call a design constant; but in addition to applying to a design constant, the term *controlled* is also applied to other ways of ascertaining the effects of an independent variable.

[15] What follows is a highly simplified description of Myers' (1962) study.

a certain number of victories by the end of the tournament received a marksmanship trophy.

The second design partition (X_2) was also dichotomous and had to do with success or failure. Myers did *not* try to predetermine whether a team would be successful (win matches), although there are several ways in which an investigator might attempt to do so (for example, by falsifying reports of match outcomes). Instead, Myers divided teams within each league into the half with the most victories and the half with the least, waiting until *after* the tournament and using its outcome to establish this second design partition.

Myers' main observed partition (mode Y) was derived from a questionnaire administered to each participant at the end of each day's rifle matches. Myers interpreted different answers to certain questions on that instrument as indicating different degrees of attraction on the part of the individual member to his rifle team and interpreted the sum of such scores for all three members of a team as an index of cohesiveness in the team. (Much more is said about designing, scoring, and interpreting such measures in Chapters 6, 7, 10, 11, and 12.)

Myers used many design constants (mode K) in his study. All participants were male college students in the ROTC program who had volunteered for the study. The same indoor rifle range was used for all matches of all teams. Because there is evidence that immediate knowledge of results affects performance, Myers attempted to keep this feedback as nearly constant as possible by preventing participants from seeing their shot patterns on the target and by reporting only the outcomes of each trial (which team won in the competitive league; whether or not a given team beat the standard in the noncompetitive league), not the actual individual or team scores. Thus knowledge of results was also a design constant.

Myers realized that there are wide individual differences in rifle marksmanship skill and experience. To take the variable of prior level of ability into account, he chose to *match* the leagues on this property. To do so, he conducted a series of individual warm-up trials on the first day of the study. Each man received safety instructions and then fired several volleys for practice. Scores obtained from these practice trials served to index each individual's marksmanship. Men with relatively good scores were used as a pool from which two high-level leagues (one competitive, one noncompetitive) were formed by random assignment of each man in that high-level pool to one or the other condition (one or the other league), then to one of the six teams within that league. Individuals with relatively poor scores on the practice trials were similarly placed in a low-level pool, and each of them was randomly assigned to a competitive or noncompetitive condition and to a team. The procedures involving practice trials and assignment accomplished several things from the point of view of design. For one thing, the practice itself could serve to reduce, even if only to a small degree, effects of learning that otherwise would introduce variation in marksmanship performance of each participant from trial to trial and day to day; presumably, learning has the greatest effects on improving marksmanship per trial during the earliest trials. Second, the practice session provided a pilot study in which the researchers could make sure of their safety measures and details of other procedures and revise them prior to the first session of the tournament. Most important in the present context is the fact that the practice trials provided a means for measuring initial ability and using it as a *matching* variable (mode *M*). Myers ended with a high-level league and a low-level league within each condition of competitiveness. Thus he could compare a high competitive league with a high noncompetitive league, with assurance that members of the two leagues were about equal *on the average* in initial ability (treatment *M* for ability), though the members of each league varied quite a bit among themselves in initial ability. (He could also have used the difference between high-level and low-level leagues as a design partition later, if he had chosen to do so.) The within-league homogeneity of level resulting from the matching procedure used in this case had the additional advantage of putting each person into competition with others roughly of equal initial ability. Finally, the procedures just described incorporated the randomization (mode *R*) that is necessary for a "true experiment" and thus improved the odds that the two leagues began the tournament very nearly equal in average ability. The role of random assignment is discussed in detail in the next section.

THE NONSPECIFIC MODES

In addition to the four modes for dealing with specific variables, there are two other modes by which the investigator can deal with all the rest of the set of potentially relevant variables. These do not control or manipulate any particular variable, nor do they involve observation or measurement of any particular variable. The first of these is the technique called *randomization,* or random assignment of cases to conditions; we shall label this mode *R.* The other —really a "nonmode"—is to *ignore* all the variables not specifically treated on the assumptions (1) that subsets of cases will not differ systematically on any of the ignored variables, and (2) that cases within a subset will not differ substantially on any of the ignored variables. We shall label this mode *Z.* Using mode *Z* is always risky design. Doing so requires extremely strong assumptions about all the variables not specifically treated while generating no information that would permit testing those assumptions. But it is also true that a single study cannot possibly treat all potentially relevant variables by one of the four specific techniques *K, X, M,* or *Y.* This is true both because of feasibility and because of the logical limitation that it is not possible to know, in advance, what all the potentially relevant variables may be. So, since there are always some variables that cannot be handled by the modes *K, X, M,* and *Y,* and since handling them by mode *Z* is really *not* handling them at all, the use of mode *R*—randomizing the assignment of cases to subsets—is *always* a necessary feature of a thoroughly rational design. It is in this sense that Campbell and Stanley (1963) assert that randomization is a necessary condition for a "true experiment," as noted earlier.

Randomization is a technique by which the investigator assigns cases from a single common pool to each of his conditions on a random basis. (By cases we mean actor-behavior-context instances that the researcher plans to include in his observations. By conditions we mean subsets of cases designated so by the one or more design partitions.) *Random,* as the term is used here, does not mean whimsical or accidental, but has a precise technical meaning. A random assignment procedure is one by which every case in the pool has an equal chance of being assigned to any particular condition. (Techniques for actually carrying out a random assignment are like techniques for random selection or sampling and will be dealt with in Chapter 5. Our concern here is with the logic of random assignment and with its consequences.)

Perhaps the notion can be clarified by illustration. Suppose you wished to test the effectiveness of a new method for teaching third grade reading. Suppose, to obtain two groups of third grade pupils, you were to choose Miss Jones's class for the new method and Mrs. Brown's class as a control. Then your comparison of results would be contaminated by—that is, confounded with—effects of all the variables associated with:

1. The particular sets of actors in these two classes—students and teachers—and their interactive patterns
2. The total context of the two third grade classes as behavior systems.

Regardless of outcome, you would not be able to reach clear conclusions about effects of the teaching method. This would be an example of Campbell and Stanley's design 3—static group comparison—which is *not* a "true experiment," as noted earlier. Instead, suppose you randomly selected 25 students to be the experimental class and another 25 to be the control class out of the total pool of third graders in that school. Suppose you also randomly selected a teacher for each class out of some pool of third grade teachers. (It would be better, of course, to have several teachers and classes in each condition, so that you could gain some information about the stability of effects of the method for different teachers.) Such a procedure would yield design 6, a "true experiment."[16] Using this technique for establishing a design partition of classes to be taught or not taught by the new method—that is, by drawing actors randomly from a pool—yields groups that are as likely to get pupils with special capacities into one group as the other and are as likely to show emergent group characteristics helpful or obstructive to the new teaching method in one group as the other.

Design 6 does not erase all uncertainties and potential troubles. Students

[16] The results of this experiment would be *generalizable* over all classes that could be constructed from the pool of third-graders and the pool of teachers. By generalizable over a certain population, we mean that you would have no logical reason to expect that the results of a study of the same design performed on some other sample from that population would be significantly different from the results of the study you performed on the sample you drew. But this point foreshadows Chapter 5.

within each class would still differ in abilities, prior levels of reading skill, personality, and so on. Also the classes might show a difference in average level on one or more of these properties; the classes were not matched on any of these variables. Nevertheless, the random assignment of actors to classes makes less likely than by any other method of assignment a *disproportionate* distribution of reading skill or sex or emotional disturbance *or any particular variable* between the two conditions.

While randomization makes it *less likely* that any variable will be disproportionately distributed, it does *not* guarantee that no variable will be disproportionately distributed. And, given a truly random assignment procedure, the probability of getting proportional distribution depends solely on the number of cases involved. Thus, random assignment of a single teacher to each condition does not really help much—it would be better to "match" the teachers somehow. Random assignment of 25 students to each class is a lot more help, simply because 25 is a larger sample than one, and a mean value based on 25 cases is much more stable than a mean represented by a single case; but random assignment is still no guarantee of equivalent distributions on any relevant variable. When random assignment is used to make sure that each observation is equally likely to fall in any one of the subsets formed by the design partitions, two outcomes are guaranteed. First, any one subset is no more likely to contain observations of one sort than of another; the shorthand way of saying this is that selection of cases for subsets is *unbiased*. Second, the *most* likely outcome is that the means of the subsets on the design partitions will be equal, though there is still a good probability that they will not be equal.

Note, also, that while randomization prevents bias in the sense of uneven distribution of relevant properties *between* conditions (subsets of observations), it virtually guarantees that there will be a *lot* of variation on a lot of potentially relevant properties among the cases *within* each of the subsets (that is, among replications). So, even though randomization will *tend* to remove systematic error (but not guarantee to do so) on all properties that are not explicitly handled by one of the specific modes *K*, *X*, *M*, or *Y*, it will tend to increase, or at least will not reduce, "random error" within the subsets established by these modes. Thus, randomization is both a weakened form of mode *M* and a broadened form of it. It provides a quasi-matching *between* conditions permitting variation *within* conditions. It differs from *M* in that (1) it does not deal with any particular property; (2) it therefore does not involve any measurement or influencing of any particular property; (3) it does not provide for a precise equating of the subsets on average values or distribution of values on any property; and, therefore, (4) it does not give the investigator any information about any properties.

Randomization generates a kind of hidden "background noise," out of which the information "signal" involved in the variables treated by the specific modes must be extracted. In this respect, it is like mode *Z* (ignoring the variable). Randomization is also like *Z* in the way it is broader than *M*; namely, it deals with all remaining variables at once, but not with any particular one separately. *R* is like *Z* also because it does not involve any measurement and because the investigator cannot get any information from its use about values of individual cases or subsets on any variables. But mode *R* differs from *Z* in one very crucial aspect: it reduces the probability that properties of the behavior system not explicitly dealt with in the study design will operate so as to distort—bias systematically—the comparisons between subsets. So randomization is a very broad, weak, and only partially effective technique for treatment of potentially relevant variables; but it is a treatment that *must* be employed in any true experiment because the only alternative is to ignore (mode *Z*) at least some potentially relevant variables.

We must now sound a note of caution. We are using the phrase *true experiment* as a technical term in the same sense that Campbell and Stanley (1963) use it. We use it to signify a design in which some precise statements can be made about bias and selection. Perhaps *thoroughly rational* would be a more descriptive term, signifying that no assignment of actor-behavior-context within the experiment is arbitrary or negligent, but that even those variables left to vary with their values unknown are protected from the whim of the experimenter so that they will vary in full response to the laws of probability. We do not use the term *true experiment* in any magical sense signifying respectability or any other kind of freedom from sin. Not all "true experiments" are worth doing; many worthwhile questions can be investigated only through other designs. Furthermore, "true experiments," in the sense of studies with internally valid design as the term is used here, do not all take place in laboratory settings by any means. (The settings for research, and their strengths and weaknesses, are discussed in the next chapter.)

The relation of modes *R* and *Z* to each other and to the four specific modes is shown in Table 3-4. In the table, the four specific modes of Table 3-3 are now placed in the left column and the two nonspecific modes—*R* and *Z*—in the right column. The columns are designated to emphasize one additional distinction between the four specific modes and the nonspecific modes. In the specific modes the investigator ends by knowing the specific value of the given property that occurs for each case—in *K* and *X* because he made it occur, in *M* and *Y* because he measured it. In the nonspecific modes, the investigator ends without specific knowledge of the values of any cases on any properties—nor even knowledge of the properties thus treated.

The relations between *R* and *M* have already been noted. Table 3-4 suggests, also, a relation between *Y* and *Z*: both do *not* influence the value of any property for any case; both permit variation within and between subsets. But *Y* differs from *Z* in one very crucial aspect. Mode *Y* involves observing the value of the property that does occur for each case; hence, it permits information to be gained from the set of observations. Only mode *Z* ignores a set of variables; hence, it can yield no information. Furthermore, *Z* permits potential confounding (distortion and obscuring) of information in the observations.

Table 3-4. *Comparison of Modes for Treatment of Variables*

WHAT DOES THE INVESTIGATOR DO ABOUT THE VARIABLE?	WHAT DOES THE INVESTIGATOR LATER KNOW ABOUT THE VARIABLE? *Knows Values for Each Case*	*Does Not Know Values*
Makes it constant within subset *and* between subsets	Mode *K*: design constant	(Unknown sampling constraint)
Makes it constant within subset, but lets it vary between subsets	Mode *X*: design partition	(Unknown sampling bias)
Lets it vary within subset, but makes it constant between subsets	Mode *M*: matched groups	Mode *R*: randomization[a]
Lets it vary within and between subsets	Mode *Y*: observed partition	Mode *Z*: ignoring the variable

[a]Randomization does not guarantee equivalent distributions between subsets, as does *M*, but makes them the most probable outcome of the assignment of cases to subsets.

Note, also, that the structure of Table 3-4 suggests two additional nonspecific techniques that so far we have not labeled or discussed. One is an unwitting control of a variable at a constant value for all cases—called "unknown sampling constraint" in the table. This "mode" can easily occur. For example, if all actors in a study are college sophomores, then the investigator will have brought a number of variables, unknown as well as known, into the condition of being substantial constants for that population by this sampling constraint. All cases will be within a narrow age range; a fairly narrow range of high intelligence and perhaps a restricted range on a number of socioeconomic, personality, regional, and other properties. This has the same effect as treatment *K*, except that the investigator does not know precisely what properties are involved or at what values they are "controlled." Such unwitting sampling constraints place limits on the generality of results. This is also true of mode *K*, but in the case of the unknown sampling constraint the nature of the limits is not explicit.

Note, further, that such a sampling restriction applies to variables of behavior and context as well as to properties of the actor. For example, if all observations have to do with performance on a single specific task, results have reference only to *that task*, or at best to a class of tasks of which that task has already been demonstrated to be an instance. This is an unwitting sampling constraint for all properties on which tasks can vary. Behavioral scientists have been much more aware of such sampling constraints with respect to properties of actors than with respect to behavioral or contextual properties. Other questions of sampling from populations are discussed in Chapter 5.

The other previously unmentioned nonspecific mode is labeled "unknown sampling bias" in the table. This amounts to an unwitting treatment of an unknown set of properties in a manner similar to mode X—that is, in a manner such that subsets of cases may differ on one or more properties even though cases within a subset are alike. An example would be the earlier illustration in which an entire intact class was taken as the experimental group (one subset), another intact class as the control group (another subset), and where groups or subsets were distinguished on the design partition of teaching method. Any properties on which the two intact classes differed would partition the observations into the *same* two subsets as did the design partition, although the investigator would not know what those variables were nor what values held in each of the subsets. Hence, any behavioral differences observed between the two subsets could as logically be attributed to any one (or combination) of those properties that were unknown sampling biases as to the deliberate design partition *X* (the teaching method). It is exactly this kind of sampling bias between subsets on unknown properties that the randomization treatment *R* is designed to eliminate.

These different modes of disposition of variables differ in what they can gain for the investigator in information and in what they cost him in reduction of scope and in confounding. The particular gains and costs of each treatment will be discussed in the next section after a more thorough examination of what we mean by gaining research information, by reducing study scope, and by confounding information.

3-4. Research Information and the Treatment of Variables

INFORMATION GAIN

The only way to gain empirical information is to let two or more alternative values of some property be free to happen and then find out which one of those values *does* happen. This is another way of saying that mode *Y* (observed partition) is a necessary condition if a study is to produce information. In mode *Y*, any value of the property is free to happen for each case in the sense that the investigator does nothing to try to influence the value of that property; and the investigator finds (by observation and measurement) what value of the property does occur for each case.

When the investigator *makes* a property take a certain value in a given case (as in modes *K* and *X*) or makes a set of cases have a certain average value on that property (as in mode *M*), he does not learn anything through those operations that he does not already know. (Sometimes, it is true, one must check up on whether an attempted *X* treatment was successful; see Chapter 8.) On the other hand, if one lets a set of cases vary freely on a property but fails to find out what values of that property occur among the cases or sets of cases (as in mode *Z*), then, of course, one learns nothing in this instance, either, about outcomes. Nor can one learn about a property he has not measured but has influenced only by randomization. In mode *R*, one partially influences the distribution of a set of variables, but fails to measure the actual values that occur.

Given mode *Y*, an observed partition in which a property is free to vary with its values being observed as they occur, we can have either of two outcomes: all cases can have the same value of the property or cases can differ in value on the property. The first level of information to be obtained, then, is whether—and to what extent—a property varies within a set of observations. When a property does *not* vary within a set of observations, we can then establish what value all cases had on that property. In a sense, we are then establishing a norm, or expected value, on that property for the population of cases of which the observed cases are a sample (actually, we should say the population for which we have a *random* sample; this will be discussed in Chapter 5). It is very rare, of course, that all cases turn out to have the same value, even substantially the same. When a property of an observed partition *does* vary within a set of observations, we can establish several things about that property or dimension (for the population sampled). We can establish:

1. The *average* value (or some other index of central tendency such as the median value)
2. The *amount of dispersion* around that average or central value
3. The *shape of the distribution* of values, including the degree to which cases spread out evenly or bunch together (kurtosis) and the degree to which they are nonsymmetrical around the average (skewness).

Thus, from the measurement or observation (mode *Y*) of a single property we can get a descriptive picture (a profile, so to speak) of the property for our set of cases and can make predictions about what values on that property are *likely* to occur for the next case or set of cases sampled from the same population. But this is a relatively low degree of information. We are often interested in finding out *why* cases vary on the property. Another way to put this question is to ask: What *else* is true of cases that were high on the observed property, but not true of cases low on that property? And this "what else" question implies that the *same* cases have been measured or observed (mode *Y*) or divided on a design partition (mode *X*) on *some other* property or properties.

The next level of information, then, is to find out about the *relation* between two (or more) properties, at least one of which is free to vary and is measured (mode *Y*), while the other is either deliberately manipulated (mode *X*) or measured (mode *Y*). Whereas descriptive information about a property requires only the observations we call mode *Y*, information about a relation between a pair (or more) of properties requires either a *Y* to *Y* or an *X* to *Y* relation.

Treatment by mode *K* can never yield information about relations because cases treated this way do not vary and hence cannot co-vary with some other property; one cannot gain descriptive information about the value that cases take when subjected to mode *K*, because mode *K* causes them to take a single value. Mode *K*, however, yields research information in an indirect way. If one obtains a relation between a property treated by mode *X* and a property treated by mode *Y* within a set of cases all of which had a certain value on a third property treated by mode *K*, then that relation is potentially contingent on, limited to, instances where that *particular* value of the *K*-treated property holds. That is, the obtained *X* to *Y* relation may actually be an interaction of the *X*-treated property and a particular level of the third, *K*-treated property with the observed values of the *Y*-treated property. One would test whether the relation between *X* and *Y* would hold for further values of the *K*-treated property by conducting another study in which the former *K*-treated property is used in the *X* mode (that is, by selecting two or more values of the property as a design partition in the next study) or as *M* (matching pairs of cases by design) or as *R* (randomizing the cases on this property) or as *Y* (letting cases vary at will on this property but measuring them on the property as they occur). Such an iterative process, conducting a later study of the *X* to *Y* relation where previously controlled variables are now freed to vary or made to vary, is the typical process by which researchers determine the conditions under which the relation between *X* and *Y* does and does not hold.

To illustrate this iteration, suppose you discover a strong relation between intelligence of actors and their preference for complex paintings rather than simple ones. Suppose that the more intelligent respondents much more often chose the more complex paintings than did the less intelligent respondents. Suppose, further, that all of your actors are six-year-old boys, both sex and age having been treated as design constants (*X*) by sample selection. It may well be that the relation between intelligence and preference for complexity in paintings does *not* hold for adults—or even reverses in direction. It is also obvious that, if you were to test younger and younger children, the relation would probably diminish in degree or disappear at some age, since very young infants cannot even give the responses you would wish to observe.

This example points up a further concern as well. Note that the original *X* to *Y* relation not only was contingent on particular levels at which properties of actors had been controlled (age and sex, for example) but was also contingent on the particular operations used to determine complexity preference (that is, the paintings presented to the actor for choice, the kind of response observed to determine the choice—such as pointing, buying, or whatever—the instructions given to the respondent about what he was to do, and the like). Further, it was contingent on the operations used to assess intelligence such as the nature of the test and its instructions. Before you can make general statements about intelligence and preference for complexity in paintings, even among six-year-old boys (or even among *these* six-year-old boys), you must either (1) find out to what extent your testing operations and the operations you accept as responses are valid indicators of some more general concepts of intelligence and of preference for paintings—by further studies of the relation between *X* and *Y*, using other operations for *X* and *Y*—or else (2) assume without further evidence the validity of your operations. Validity of measures and related questions are discussed in Chapter 6.

We now recapitulate the sorts of information available from the various modes for treatment of variables. Mode *K* does not add information to the study. Furthermore, it reduces the number of *combinations of values of the set of properties* that can occur; hence, it reduces the generalizability of the results of the study. (Hereafter we shall use the term *scope* to refer to the combinations of values of the set of properties that can occur.) The advantages of mode *K* are that it can be used to reduce the variation within and between subsets and can often do this economically. Matching (*M*) as such cannot yield empirical information. When using mode *M*, the researcher himself produces an approximate equivalence of average values on some property between subsets (partitioned on some other property) and sometimes also an equivalence of variation around that average. Hence, the occurrence of equal average values on that property does not tell him anything he does not already know. But mode *M* is built after first obtaining an observed partition (mode *Y*) of the variable. Hence, *M* is convertible to *Y*, because the values originally observed can always be used in their original form. An *M*-treated variable can also be converted into a design partition (*X*) *within subsets* and used to assess its relation to some *Y*-treated property. Thus, mode *M* as such adds no information and does somewhat restrict the scope of the study. It also eliminates potential distortion, as we will see later in this section.

Mode *R* does not give the researcher information about any property nor about relations, because through it the researcher does not obtain knowledge of the values of any property. *R* does not tend to restrict scope in the same way that modes *M* or *K* do; it does not reduce the number of possible combinations of values of properties that can occur. But it tends partially to restrict the distributions of combinations of values between subsets of cases defined by one or more design partition properties. Mode *Z*, of course, neither adds information nor restricts scope, since no observation is obtained and no constraint on values of properties is imposed. It has, however, the undesirable effect of permitting confounding of potential information in the study.

RESTRICTION OF POTENTIAL INFORMATION

Let us suppose there is a research problem that involves ten properties or variables. Let us further suppose, for simplicity, that each of the properties can take on any of ten values (for example, ten meaningfully different age levels, ten levels of intelligence, ten alternative choices or solutions on some task, and so on). Let u be the number of values of a variable and v the number of variables. Then ten variables with ten values each would offer us $u^v = 10^{10}$, or ten billion possible combinations of values of the ten variables. The ten billion combinations comprise the total possible alternative outcomes (combinations of one value from each property). The ten billion combinations are an index of *total information* in the problem.

Suppose, now, that we decide to hold one of the properties at a particular constant value for all cases (that is, use it as a design constant, mode *K*). The number of possible alternative outcomes is now reduced from ten billion to one billion ($u = 10$; $v = 10 - 1 = 9$; $u^v = 1{,}000{,}000{,}000$). We now have just as many joint combinations of the other nine variables (10^9), but each of them can now occur in combination with *only one* value of the tenth property because our *K* treatment of that property has made it so. By reducing the possible values of one of the ten properties from ten alternatives to one alternative, we have removed 10 percent of the total potential information from our study. Any treatment that restricts the range of alternative values of a property that can occur within a set of observations reduces the informational scope of the study. Mode *K*, of course, provides the most drastic reduction—from *u* values to one value for a given property. Mode X also may restrict the range of alternative values—to as few as two alternative values in many cases—but in other cases it may not restrict the alternative values at all; the property may be manipulated so that one subset has each of the possible values of a variable. The fewer the subsets into which an X-treated property partitions the observations, the more restricted will be the potential information and hence the more reduced will be the informational scope of the study.

Mode *Y* does not restrict the potential information at all, in principle, because it is a treatment that permits all possible alternative values of the variable to occur. In practice, however, the actual observations may not be sufficiently sensitive to distinguish between some of the alternative values of the property. For example, if we are trying to measure attitude toward the British, we might use an instrument (a set of questions) that permits us to differentiate only between "favorable" and "unfavorable," not allowing us to differentiate among degrees of favorableness or unfavorableness. Thus, we would be grouping together *as alike* some behaviors (attitudes, in this case) that are not alike. This kind of limitation can lead to a restriction of potential information in an observed partition in the same way that a design partition can restrict potential information when it divides cases only into "high" and "low" on some property.The questions of sensitivity and reliability of observations are discussed in Chapter 6.

Mode *M* does not restrict the number of possible alternative values of a property that can occur (except insofar as its underlying *Y* treatment is too gross, as just mentioned). But mode *M* does restrict the *distribution* of values of the property with respect to subsets (the subsets, in turn, being defined by a partition on some other property). That is, mode *M* does not reduce the range of values of the property that can occur among the observations that will be used to construct the matches between subsets; but it restricts the distribution of values finally used to the same range in each of the subsets involved. Thus, treatment *M* does not reduce the potential information in the study by reducing the number of combinations of values of all properties that can occur but rather by constraining the *distribution* of cases within each set of observations; it reduces the frequency with which a case can assume any one of those potential combinations of values.

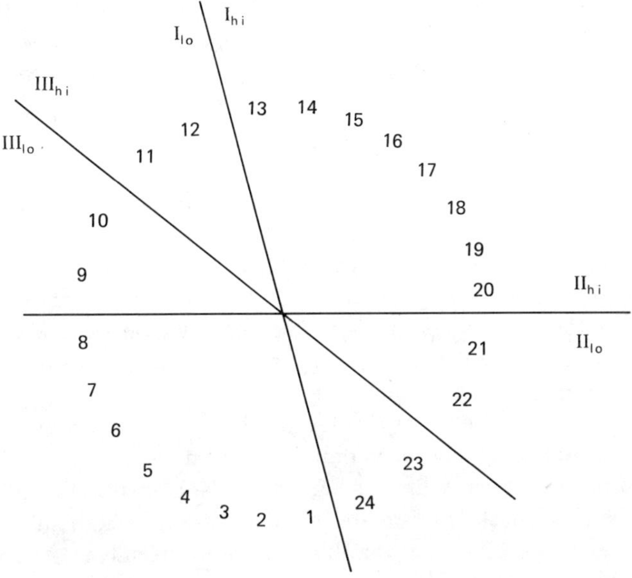

Figure 3-1. Regions showing stronger relations between variables I and III and between II and III but weaker between I and II.

Mode *R* is somewhat like mode *M* in restricting information. Mode *R* does not preclude the occurrence of any value of any property. Neither does it restrict the distribution of combinations of values with respect to any one property. Thus, while it does not lead to information gain, it does not reduce potential information and, as we shall see below, it helps to reduce confounding of potential information. Mode *Z* also does not restrict potential information and does not lead to information gain; but, unlike *R*, mode *Z* does not reduce confounding of potential information in the observations.

CONFOUNDING OF POTENTIAL INFORMATION

Some actual clustering of symbols on paper will illustrate how confounding can actually take place. We shall present three examples. To draw the diagrams we need some symbols. Suppose we use one variable for a design partition; call this variable II. Let the variable used as the observed partition be called variable I. Suppose an experimenter carries out a study in which he makes deliberate treatment only of these two variables. But, at the same time, suppose there is a third variable III that has effects on the other variables, but which the experimenter ignores. The illustrations that follow show some ways in which the third variable can have effects.

In Figure 3-1[17] we see a ring or cloud of events—let us call them actors—thrown upon the paper. The experimenter's design partition is repre-

[17] The reader who prefers Venn diagrams will find Figures 3-1 through 3-3 easily convertible.

sented by the horizontal line; it divides the actors high on variable II (namely, actors 9 through 20) from those low on that variable. Now the experimenter performs the experiment and observes that actors 13 through 24 come out high on the observed partition I while the other actors come out low; this is shown by the line I_{hi} on the east side and I_{lo} on the west. The experimenter might now properly conclude that there exists a *positive* relation between II and I, since most of the actors (eight of them) high on II are also high on I; only four of the actors high on II were *not* high on I. In other words, an actor high on II is also more likely to be high on I than low. Beyond this conclusion, however, the experimenter might be tempted to conclude—or at least to adopt the hypothesis for further research—that being high on II *leads on* to being high on I, or *causes* it. But, before he leaps to such a conclusion, he should beware of a variable such as variable III.

Variable III is one the experimenter decided to ignore. But let us suppose that the actors high and low on variable III, unknown to the experimenter, are those partitioned by the line in Figure 3-1 labeled III_{hi} to the northeast and III_{lo} to the southwest. If this were the distribution of high and low values of variable III, it would mean that variable III is more strongly related to variable I than is variable II, since, of the twelve actors high on variable I, ten are also high on III, whereas only eight of them are high on II. Thus there exists a variable III, unknown to the experimenter, that is more strongly related to his observed partition than the variable he used as his design partition. And variable III is at least as reasonable a candidate for the *cause* of different values in I as is II. We can also note in Figure 3-1 that II and III are very highly related. It might be that a high value of III is the cause (or one of many significant causes) of high values in *both* I and II.

As an example, consider black and white families as the design partition (II) and relative dominance of the wife as the observed variable (I). A number of investigators have found the wife to be relatively more dominant in black families than in white. Mack (1971) conducted a study, however, which suggests that the previous studies investigated samples of families in which social class (III) was more strongly associated with dominance by the wife than was race, and race was associated with social class in those samples. Where social class was supposedly controlled in the previous investigations, Mack argues (p. 86) that inappropriate measures were applied.

An investigator always risks the effects of an ignored variable such as III when he assigns cases to a design partition (II) systematically instead of randomly. If a design partition is made on the basis of a preexisting property, the risk is always there that an invisible property such as III, associated with the property used for the design partition, is actually doing the work. This risk is ever-present, for example, in studies using only observed partitions—often called *correlational studies*. Random assignment in a design partition before establishing the high and low conditions of the variable II reduces the risk that an effect will be observed because of some ignored variable and not because of the design partition. (We discussed this point in another way

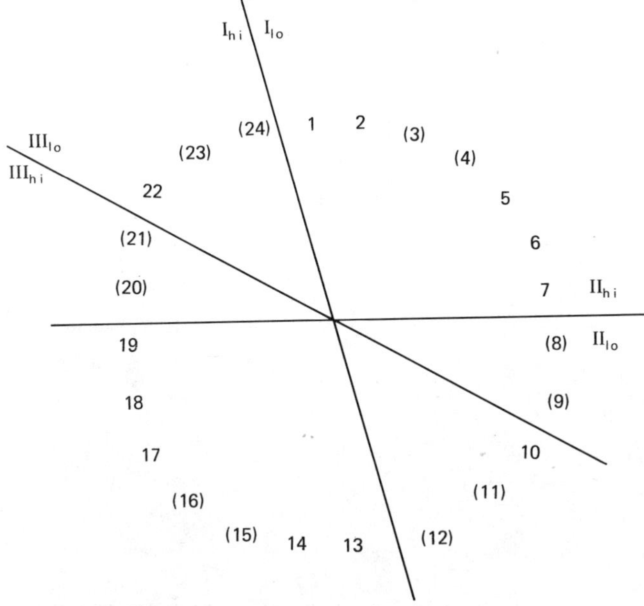

Figure 3-2. Regions showing a positive relation in the sample between variables I and II where the population relation is negative, with sample and population relations both positive between I and III and both negative between II and III. Parentheses indicate the sampled elements.

in our introductory discussion of design partitions in section 3-2 and shall return to it in section 8-2.)

In Figure 3-2, the experimenter's design partition is again represented by the horizontal line; the observed partition is again made with variable I, and the ignored variable is III. Unlike the previous figure, this illustration is one in which the experimenter has taken a sample (those numerals enclosed in parentheses) from a population (all 24 numerals). Looking at the relation between variables I and II as shown by the actors sampled (in parentheses), we see that of the six actors high on II (namely, 3, 4, 20, 21, 23, and 24), four turn out to be high on I (to the west of the partitioning line this time). From these observations the experimenter should conclude that a positive relation exists between I and II. In the population as a whole, however, a *negative* relation exists between I and II; of 12 actors high on II, only five (20 through 24) are high on I. Here is a case where the sample does not deliver the same proportions as exist in the population.

But the sample does not distort the positive relation between III and I. Of the twelve actors in the population high on III, six were sampled, and the majority (15, 16, 20, and 21) was likewise found high on I. Similarly, the relation between III and II is the same in population and sample, though negative. The sample has mirrored the population adequately for the experimenter except,

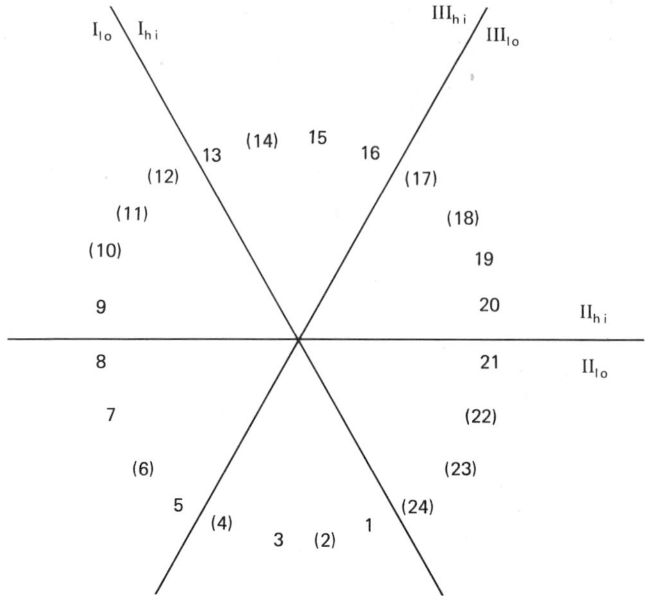

Figure 3-3. Regions showing a relation close to zero in the sample between variables I and II where the relation in the population is positive, with sample and population relations both negative between I and III and both positive between II and III. Parentheses indicate the sampled elements.

unfortunately, in the case of the relation between II and I—the only relation visible to the experimenter.

What function might variable III (*Z*) have in this picture? The relation between III (*Z*) and II (*X*) is strong and negative. Because of this relation, when the experimenter selects actors for the design partition based on variable II, he simultaneously partitions the actors in respect to variable III, though in the direction opposite to II. Now the relation between III (*Z*) and I (*Y*) is strong and positive; and if this relation were causal, then cases low on III would more often than not bring with them low values of I (namely, the cases 3, 4, 8, and 9 in the figure, in contrast to cases 23 and 24). Again, if the high and low values of II were established after the actors were assigned randomly to the conditions of the design partition, the values of III associated with the values of II would be distributed in the partition in an unbiased manner, leaving any effect of II on I to act unconfounded by III.

Our final illustration is shown in Figure 3-3. Here we see in the sample a relation close to zero, neither positive nor negative, between variables II and I; of six sampled actors high on II, just three (14, 17, 18) turn out also to be high on I. But in the population, there is clearly a positive relation between variables II and I; of the twelve actors high on II, eight are also high on I.[18]

---

[18]Note in both Figures 3-2 and 3-3 that it is not necessary to work out freakish samples to produce an important degree of disproportionality between sample and population in some segment of the population.

At the same time, variable III is related negatively to variable I in both sample and population. If these relations from variable III to the other two are causal, systematic selection of a sample could well produce a mixture of actors among which some embody a positive relation between I and II but some embody a negative relation between the same variables, resulting in a net relation between I and II close to zero, as in the figure. Again random assignment in the design partition could reduce the likelihood of this kind of distortion.

When a potentially relevant property is allowed to vary but the property's values are not observed, it is possible for the information in the observations actually made to be confounded in unknown ways; we have just illustrated some ways in which confounding can occur. Random assignment of cases to partitions reduces this danger.

ADVANTAGES AND WEAKNESSES OF THE MODES

Each of the specific modes for the treatment of variables offers its own advantages and disadvantages, as does the nonspecific mode, randomization. It is not accurate, however, to say this about the unwitting sampling constraints and biases or about mode *Z* (we displayed these terms in Table 3-4). These three modes offer *no* advantages; researchers let these modes occur only when they find the specific modes and randomization beyond their resources, but still prefer information with unknown unreliabilities to no information at all. We turn now to the four specific modes and to randomization to summarize their relative advantages and disadvantages. We include mode *Z* for purposes of comparison. Table 3-5 compares these six modes on a number of characteristics important to study design. Since we have discussed almost all of these matters at one point or another, we shall let the table stand without further discussion of it.

The minimum condition for information about a property is an observed partition, *Y*, on that property. The minimum conditions for fully rational

Table 3-5. *Some Advantages and Disadvantages of Modes for Treatment of Variables*

			REDUCTION OF VARIABILITY OR YIELD OF KNOWLEDGE ABOUT IT	
MODE	INFORMATION GAIN	RETENTION OF INFORMATIONAL SCOPE	*Within Subsets*	*Between Subsets*
Y	High	High	High	High
X	Moderate	Moderate	High	High
M	High	High	Moderate	High
K	None	Low	High	High
R	None	High	None	Moderate
Z	None	High	None	None

information about the relation between two or more properties is:

1. An observed partition, *Y*, on at least one property
2. Either an observed partition, *Y*, or a design partition, *X*, on at least one other property
3. Randomization, *R*, to handle partially the potentially confounding effects of all other variables.

Normally, a study will also include one or more other variables treated as design constants, *K*, or as unwitting sampling constraints. It may include more than one design partition, *X*, and more than one observed partition, *Y*. Design partitions and observed partitions may broaden (or at least not reduce) the scope and potential information gain of the study; a design constant increases the precision (eliminates confounding) but narrows the scope of the study. All three (*K*, *X*, and *Y*) reduce the burden placed upon the necessary randomization treatment.

The value of application of any of these modes to any given variable depends, of course, upon the purposes of one's study, upon the place of that variable in one's problem, and upon the nature of the variable—for example, how costly and obtrusive (see section 7-1) it would be to manipulate that particular variable. The usefulness and the ease of application of these modes also depend in part upon the total setting and strategy of the study. The range of general strategies or settings and their relations to these modes for treatment of variables is the topic of the next chapter.

3-5. Further Reading

As this is being written, the most compact sources of conceptualization about partitioning and other ways of treating variables are the writings of D. T. Campbell and J. C. Stanley. The following are representative and important: Campbell (1962, 1967, 1969), Campbell and Stanley (1963), and Stanley (1966).

More elaborate comparisons and combinations of treatments *X*, *M*, *R*, and *Y* can become very complicated. For methods of coping with some of the complications, see, for example, Kirk (1968), McGuigan (1968), Peng (1967), Stanley (1967), and Wiggins (1968).

CHAPTER 4

Planning a Study: Settings and Strategies for Research

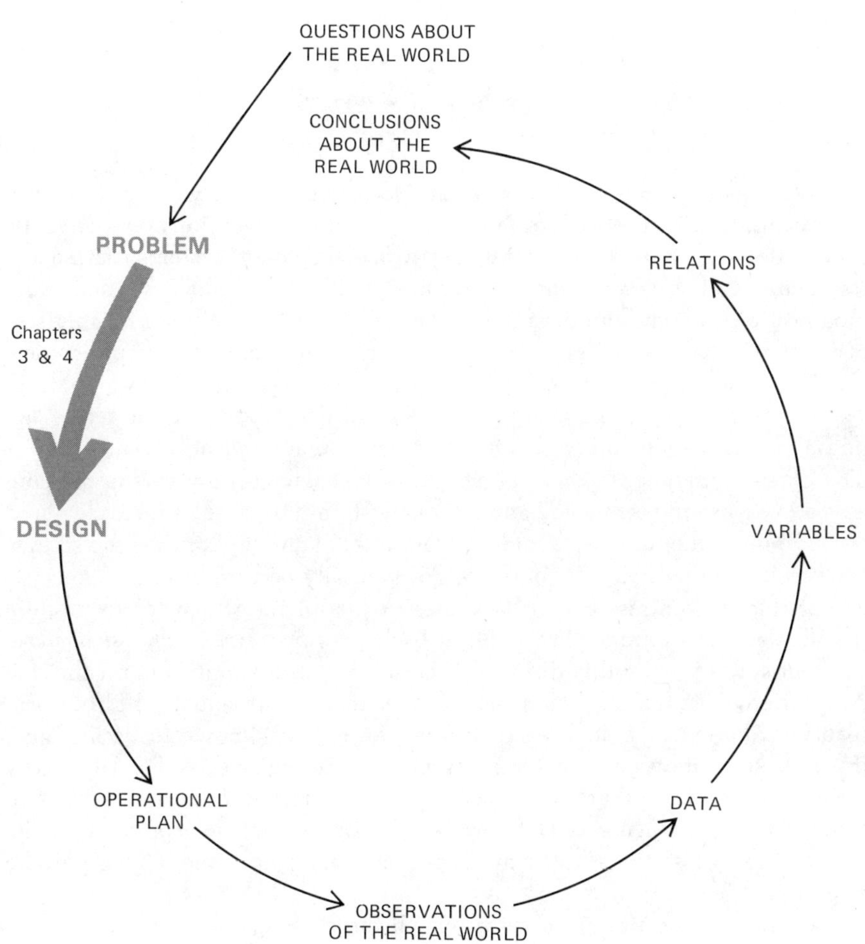

Much of the discussion in Chapter 2 stated or implied that behavioral research takes place in behavior settings that are actual parts of the real world of living systems. On the other hand, discussions in Chapter 3 carried the strong implication that research is done in laboratory-like situations over which the investigator exercises considerable control. These two orientations are not so much contradictory as they are complementary. Actually, behavioral research is carried out within a wide range of settings and with the use of a variety of strategies varying in control, precision of measurement, realism of situation, and a number of other characteristics. This chapter considers the spectrum of research strategies that have been used in the behavioral sciences, the characteristic strengths and weaknesses of each, and how they can be made to complement one another. We shall tie this chapter to the previous one by considering how the various strategies use the specific and nonspecific modes for treatment of variables.

4-1. A Framework for Comparing Some Major Research Strategies

Research in behavioral science can be carried out in a variety of settings and by means of a variety of strategies. Some studies rely entirely on systematic observation of phenomena within real-world behavior systems. These are frequently called *field studies*. Sometimes field studies include deliberate modification of some important property of the behavioral system; this sort of study we shall call a *field experiment*. On the other hand, some studies deal with behavior within settings that are deliberately created for the research itself. These are often called *laboratory experiments*. Incidentally, while the terms *field* and *laboratory* seem to imply *outdoor* versus *indoor*, that implication is misleading. The crucial difference is that of the natural behavior setting versus the contrived.[1] We use the terms *field* and *laboratory* simply because of their currency.

Some studies attempt a middle ground. Though they contrive the setting, they seek one that *simulates* some class of naturally occurring setting as nearly as possible, as contrasted with laboratory experiments which try to create a *generic* class of settings. We shall call the former *experimental simulations*. Another way to make this distinction is to say that a simulation, on the one hand, tries to emulate a behavioral system that might actually be found in reality to the extent that the actuality is well enough known to be imitated; thus, the simulation must to some degree be a particular case. The laboratory experiment, on the other hand, typically tries to represent an entire class of settings by reproducing only those characteristics that are common to the "population" of settings; thus, the experiment must to some degree partake of a *universal* setting.

Still other studies are done in which the investigator conceives the behavior as bearing no close connection to the setting in which it is assessed. For example, behavioral scientists often ask people about their opinions or attitudes toward political candidates or TV programs or some controversial issue. They might ask such questions by going door to door or by telephoning or by gathering those people into a meeting room. In many of these cases, the behaviors being observed—basically, self-reports of orientations toward

[1] For a discussion of the functional meaning of a behavior setting, see Barker (1963, 1965).

some sets of objects—can reasonably be presumed to have little or no intrinsic relation to the particular, concrete setting in which the observations are made. The recorded observations refer to a hypothetical class of behavior settings, or a variety of them, within which the respondent might find himself from time to time. We are talking here about studies in which the investigator conceives there to be characteristics associated with actors and conceives them to be ascertainable quite independently of the real-world setting in which the investigator finds the actor. Obvious examples are sex and, let us say, ability to quote phrases from the Constitution of the United States of America. Although there would be exceptional circumstances in which some particular male would behave like a female or forget every phrase he ever knew from the Constitution, it is reasonable to presume that these characteristics remain relatively stable over great ranges of behavior settings. Other examples would ascertain whether the actor can distinguish red from green, Republicans from Democrats, vertical from a 15-degree inclination, Rembrandt from Delacroix.

Studies such as those we have been describing are usually conducted by one of two strategies. In one strategy the researcher goes out and finds a certain type of actor whose opinion or judgment the researcher wishes to obtain. Whether the desired type of actor is to be found scattered over the world or the nation or a professional association or an industrial organization or a Boy Scout troop or whatever, we want to draw attention here to the sort of case in which the researcher does not believe it crucial to design a special setting in which to collect data from the actor, but does believe it crucial to find certain actors rather than others from whom to collect the data.[2] In the other strategy, the researcher invites the actors to a location where it is convenient for the researcher to pose for the actors the kind of task or judgment he has in mind. In this strategy, the researcher does not believe it crucial to corral a special list of actors, but does believe it crucial to control carefully the context of his observations.[3] Because researchers using the first strategy often call their studies *sample surveys,* we shall use that term to indicate studies in which the investigator seeks a specified partition or random sampling of actors to render judgments the investigator believes to be relatively uninfluenced by context.[4] Because researchers using the second strategy often label the activities they ask the actors to engage in as *judgment tasks,* we shall use that term to indicate studies in which the investigator establishes carefully controlled conditions within

[2]Wide use of study designs resting on this view has led to the growth of a sophisticated technology of sampling actors; this technology will be discussed in Chapter 5.

[3]Long use of study designs resting on this view has led to a sophisticated body of lore and technology, most notably exemplified in the study of *psychophysics;* see, for example, Stevens (1951).

[4]This is not to say that every study labeled a sample survey in the literature satisfies the description given here. Nor is it to say that every investigator who conducts a study such as we have described would be happy to call it a sample survey. Neither is it to say that a sample survey cannot be used as a part of a study of mixed and complex design. We use the term as a label because we believe the description we have given fits well the kind of study that comes into the minds of most researchers when they hear the phrase *sample survey.* Similar remarks apply to the labels we use in this chapter for the other seven strategies we discuss.

which actors whom the investigator believes to be relatively uninfluenced by their origins or backgrounds will render the judgments the investigator seeks. Obviously, we have been describing "pure types" and any actual study may show a mixture of several strategies. But no study, we believe, turns out to be a composite equally balanced among all available strategies.

There are two additional strategies often used in behavioral science research which differ from the others in that they do not gain any new information at all but rather process information put in by the investigator. *Computer simulation* is one of these; it is similar to the strategy of experimental simulation noted above in creating an imitation of some concrete, real system. The computer simulation, however, is an artificially complete, closed system and therein differs from the experimental simulation, which is an open system because the behavior of human actors is observed within the simulated context.[5] The other nonbehavioral strategy is that of *formal theory*. Here, the investigator constructs an abstract, logical model of a behavior system—usually a generic class of behavior systems—and performs logical (including mathematical) manipulations to adduce new insights (hypotheses, proofs of theorems, and so on). These two strategies are not empirical research; they do not extract new information about behavior from the real world, although they use prior empirical knowledge in their constructions. What they do is rearrange existing information into new forms to make it more useful.

Readers accustomed to recent literature in the social sciences may be startled to find us applying the label *research* to activities limited to processing information either in the computer or in the human mind. This use of the term, however, is quite common in other fields. In mathematics, of course, the term has no other meaning. The point we want to emphasize is that social science, in our opinion, will be most effectively carried on if it uses in complementary ways all available strategies of gathering information and organizing it. The human mind and the computer are two tools for organizing information. Studies using only these tools are important in making empirical knowledge comprehensible and useful. Every strategy of research has its own kind of usefulness, these two as well as the others.

Each of these eight strategies is described more fully in subsequent sections of this chapter. First, we shall discuss some major differences and similarities among the strategies. We believe that the differences and similarities among these eight types of activities imply a circular relation[6] among them, as shown in Figure 4-1. The strategies are highly interrelated in a variety of ways, and the figure displays some of those interconnections.

The two strategies on the right-hand side of Figure 4-1 deal with naturally occurring behavior systems. Field studies take the systems as they are, intruding

---

[5]The reader who wishes a more precise distinction between open and closed systems may consult the references given in section 2-3.

[6]The circular pattern implied by interrelations such as these is called circumplex; see section 12-6 for further description of this pattern.

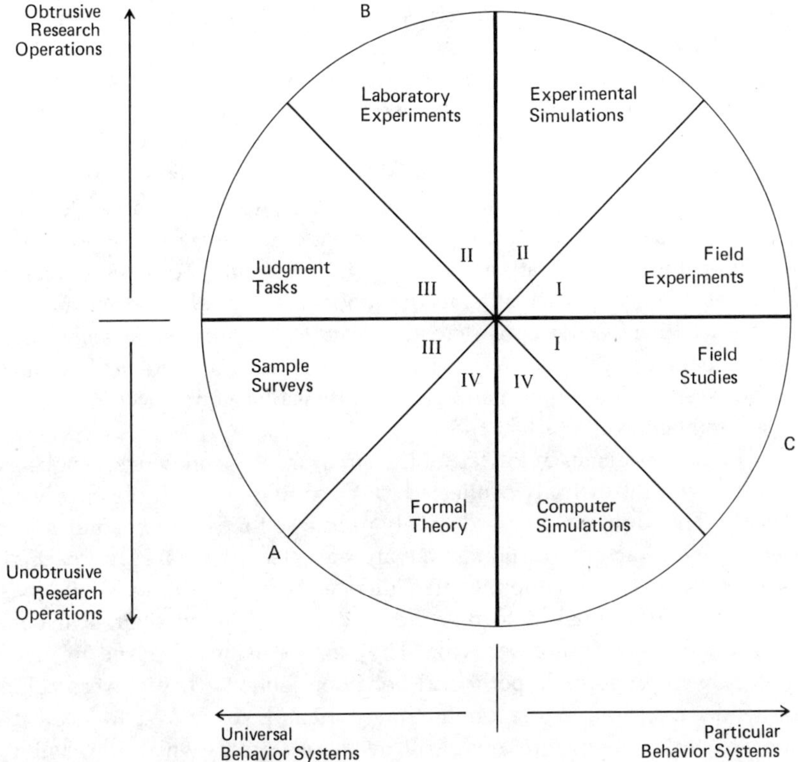

I. Settings in natural systems.
II. Contrived and created settings.
III. Behavior not setting dependent.
IV. No observation of behavior required.

A. Point of maximum concern with generality over actors.
B. Point of maximum concern with precision of measurement of behavior.
C. Point of maximum concern with system character of context.

Figure 4-1. Research strategies.

into them only to the extent of making systematic observations of one or more properties. An example is watching the functioning of an insurance company without interfering in its operation.[7] Field experiments also work with naturally occurring systems, but are one step more interventionist; they deliberately manipulate (mode *X*, design partition[8]) one or more properties as well as observe (mode *Y*, observed partition) one or more properties.

The two strategies at the top of the circle in Figure 4-1 carry obtrusiveness

[7] The crudeness or subtlety of the method of watching is irrelevant to the question of classifying the strategy of research.

[8] See Chapter 3 for explanations of modes of dealing with variables.

one stage further. By *laboratory experiments* and *experimental simulations* we mean studies in which the researcher not only manipulates the variables of chief interest but also creates the behavior setting within which the observed behavior is to take place. In the one case, experimental simulation, there is an attempt to recreate—or at least simulate—the features of some particular class of concrete, naturally occurring behavior system. An example is asking a collection of strangers to carry out a task as if they were a supervisor and a work crew; the experimenter would try to make the task and the roles as realistic as possible within the limitation that this setting would be a temporary and isolated one for the participants. In the other case, the laboratory experiment, there is a deliberate attempt to create the crucial conditions of some generic class of behavior systems—but not the conditions of any particular concrete behavior system. The experimental simulation is like a greenhouse; the laboratory experiment is like a test tube.

The two strategies at the left of the circle are those in which the observed behavior is not intrinsically connected to the setting in which the observations are made. The sample survey, so widely used in public opinion studies, is one example. Here, actors (respondents) are sampled; they are approached in whatever settings the sampling plan dictates (often at home, sometimes at work); and they are asked to respond to questions about their own beliefs, feelings, or past or future behavior. They are occasionally asked to respond *as if* they were in some hypothetical behavior context: "If you were going to buy a new car,. . . ." More often, they are implicitly asked to make their responses with reference to any or all behavior settings which they might be in, or in which they might have the attitude in question: "How do you feel about. . . ."

The other nonsetting strategy, the judgment tasks, produces similar observations—reports by respondents not directly connected to the behavior setting—but in a situation involving more manipulation and control of properties. Often, the reports are obtained in "laboratories," but we prefer to save the term *laboratory experiment* to apply to studies in which not only the actors and the objects being judged are deliberately changed from trial to trial, as in sample surveys and judgment tasks, but in which the contexts or behavioral environments are deliberately changed also. In a sample survey, a respondent might be asked, "People often speak of colors and designs as 'loud' or 'quiet.' I'm going to show you some samples of dress materials. Please tell me in each case whether you would describe the sample as loud, medium, or quiet." We would be more likely to call this task a judgment task in the sense of this chapter if the instructions were as follows: "This dial causes the sound of the trumpet you are hearing to become louder or softer. When I show you each sample of dress material, please turn the dial to the point you believe best matches the feeling the dress sample gives you." And we would call the study a laboratory experiment if some actors were given these instructions after they had watched their spouses respond and some were given the instructions without having watched anyone else respond.

Note that the apparatus producing the trumpet sound could be carried to the doorstep of the respondent, and the interviewer could exert some control over the context by refraining from asking the question if other musical sounds were present in the house at the time. The differences among laboratory experiments, judgment tasks, and sample surveys that we think instructive are the differences in the ways the context of behavior is handled. When the effects of the context are studied along with the behavior of chief interest and the variations in the context are treated by mode *X*, *M*, or *Y*, we label the study a laboratory experiment. When the context is made less obtrusive by holding it constant (mode *K*), we call the study a judgment task. When even the obtrusiveness of controlling the environment is relinquished and the respondent is studied in a relatively natural setting—but one the experimenter believes will not influence the main behavior to be observed—we call the study a sample survey. And when the researcher refrains even from observing any actors, we call his conclusions theorizing.

The two strategies at the bottom of the circle in Figure 4-1 do not involve actual behavior in setting. Like the two strategies at the top of the circle, the two strategies at the bottom of the circle also involve concern with behavior in created settings, but in this case the settings are symbolic ones. The two strategies at the bottom do not involve *actual* behavior. One of these two strategies, computer simulation, involves the attempt to create a symbolic replica of a concrete class of behavior systems. The other, formal theory, also involves the attempt to create a symbolic replica, but of a generic class of abstract behavior systems rather than concrete ones. Computer simulation is related to formal theory just as experimental simulation is related to the laboratory experiment.

The vertical line in Figure 4-1—from north to south, so to speak—divides the strategies into the left-hand subset, dealing with universal generic behavior systems, and the right-hand subset, dealing with particular or concrete behavior systems. For example, sample surveys and field studies differ (as do the other left-right pairs) in that the former selects actors without regard to their occurrence in intact behavior systems, while the latter selects behavior systems without regard for the particular actors that inhabit them. While investigators using experimental simulation or computer simulation typically seek to create a faithful replica of a concrete class of systems, investigators using either of the pair to the left (laboratory experiments and formal theory) create abstract, generic systems. Researchers using the pair of strategies at the far right (field experiments and field studies) work within naturally created concrete systems; those using the pair at the far left (judgment tasks and sample surveys) deal with behavior not intrinsic to the setting. The horizontal line in the figure—from west to east—divides the strategies into the top subset, involving relatively more obtrusive strategies, and the bottom subset, dealing with the less so. The two strategies at the bottom of the diagram are least obtrusive, since they do not even make observations. Both strategies next above, sample surveys and field studies, are intrusive only because they require observational procedures.

The next are more intrusive, since they involve manipulation and control of variables. The top two are the most obtrusive, since they create the entire behavior system within which the actor is behaving.

Note, also, the symbols A, B, and C, referring to actor, behavior, and context, in Figure 4-1. Concern with actors, and particularly with generalizability with respect to actors, is maximum at the southwest point of the circle through general theory or through broad sampling. Concern with behavior, and particularly with rigorous and comprehensive measurement of behavior, is maximized in the laboratory experiment, and only slightly less so on either side of it in the diagram. Concern with context, especially with the realism of the behavior setting, is maximized in the field study, and only a little less so on either side of it.

If we start at C in field studies and proceed counterclockwise around the circle, we come to the strategies in which the researcher's operations have more and more influence on outcomes. By the end of the circling at formal theory and computer simulation, the investigator determines *all* of his data; there is no actual behavior. Again starting at C, if we go around the circle in *either* direction, we reach strategies that are less and less concrete; we give up concreteness for rigor of measurement in the top half and give up concreteness for generality of the population in the bottom half.

From point A, if we proceed around the circle in either direction, we get less and less generality of the population; but we gain rigor in the clockwise direction and concreteness in the counterclockwise direction. If we start at B in the laboratory experiment and proceed in either direction, we get less and less rigor and comprehensiveness of measurement of behavior; we compensate by gaining concreteness in the clockwise direction and by gaining generality in the counterclockwise direction.

The purpose of the framework presented here is to show how various strategies are related to one another and, hence, the relative advantages and disadvantages of their use. It is true, of course, that all of these strategies are useful and should be employed in a programmatic fashion, since they tend to compensate for one another's weak points. But in any given study, the investigator almost always has to choose one strategy rather than the others. The choice of strategies is important because the strategies differ considerably in terms of:

1. The kinds of information they can yield
2. How much information can be gained from them
3. How "pure" or "unconfounded" that adduced information can be—that is, how well the investigator can make strong inferences about the nature of relations in his data
4. What the investigator must know, or assume he knows, about the problem before he begins his study
5. How generalizable the study results will be beyond the specific events

included in the study (that is, how much the investigator can say about events he did not observe)

6. How much and what kinds of resources are required for their use.

The choice of strategy in the behavioral sciences is too often made on the basis of the investigator's prior habits, experience, and prejudices. Investigators often become specialists, so to speak, in one or another of the strategies and use these strategies no matter what problem they are studying (or, perhaps, they select and formulate only problems that are amenable to their favorite strategies).

The choice among the strategies should be made with an eye to their respective advantages and weaknesses and on the basis of (1) the nature of the problem the investigator wants to study, (2) the state of prior knowledge about this problem, and (3) the amount and kinds of resources available to the investigator. We cannot emphasize too strongly our belief that none of these strategies has any natural or scientific claim to greater respect from researchers than any other. A researcher may find one strategy more comfortable than another for temperamental reasons, or he may find that his colleagues admire him for using one rather than another. From the point of view of the grand strategy of science, however, all of these methods are complementary; each serves the others.

In the next sections of this chapter we shall discuss, in turn, each of the strategies as potential vehicles for behavioral science research. We shall be interested in their strengths and weaknesses—what they let us gain and what they cost us. We shall frame this discussion of strategies in terms of their relative use of the several modes for treating variables (as set forth in Chapter 3), and hence in terms of their relative capacities for informational scope, reduction of confounding, and potential information gain.

But a note before we begin. We have presented the classification of Figure 4-1 not to say that any study any researcher conceives can be dropped neatly into one of the eight pockets. Rather, we are saying that there are many kinds of strategies for developing knowledge about behavior, and the strategies differ in their advantages and disadvantages. Two of the ways in which strategies differ are their obtrusiveness and their particularity. While many actual studies use mixed strategies, we have tried to help the reader understand our intent by labeling the eight octants in Figure 4-1 with some familiar names. We think that many studies to which researchers give these names do show the relative degrees of obtrusiveness and particularity we have described. In brief, we are trying to adopt the invitational mood (see section 2-7), asking the reader and ourselves, "Suppose we think of research strategies as varying in obtrusiveness and particularity? How might this help us think about fitting various research strategies to research questions?" This chapter is a response to such an invitation.

4-2. Field Studies

Some research consists entirely of systematic observation of behavior within actual behavioral systems in being. The investigator's intent is to disturb the behavioral system he is studying as little as possible so that the behavior observed is "true" or "natural" and is not behavior influenced by the research procedures themselves. We call this kind of research the *field study*. Barker (1965) refers to this strategy as one in which the investigator is only a "transducer." He recommends it as superior to other strategies in which the investigator is "operator" (that is, one who controls and manipulates the systems he is studying) as well as transducer. Much research in the fields of anthropology and sociology has utilized the field study strategy.

There is a principle in the physical sciences called the principle of uncertainty which suggests that there is always uncertainty in scientific information because the processes by which the scientist tries to measure a phenomenon always disturb or change that phenomenon.[9] For example, to measure the position of a subatomic particle it is necessary to use methods that alter its velocity. There is, in our view, an analogue of that principle of uncertainty that operates in the behavioral sciences, and the basic limitations of the field study exemplify it well. The very intent of the field study researcher—to study the behavior system "as it is"—means that he will forgo some of the more powerful modes for gaining information. For example, by definition a field study does not use mode X, design partition, because that treatment of variables requires the investigator to intrude into and disrupt the behavior system—he becomes an "operator-transducer" in Barker's terms. Thus, in seeking to observe only what is naturally there without disturbing it, the investigator leaves himself with a weaker sort of information; he must be satisfied with a correlational study[10] or, at best, with a study of trend—and can study a trend only if he repeats his observations over time, with a corresponding increase in the probability that he will, after all, influence the observed system by his methods of collecting data. But, conversely, using a stronger design such as 4 or 6[11] must to some degree leave the system different from its state before the researcher intruded. Thus, the researcher faces an ever-present dilemma: whether to learn something with relatively low confidence about the existing system or to learn something with relatively high confidence about a system that is now different from what it was when the researcher gathered information from it.

---

[9] For a lucid and nontechnical account, see Gamow (1958).

[10] Less familiarly but more accurately, "correlational" studies could be called studies of *joint distribution*. We discussed some advantages and disadvantages of this kind of study in section 3-2 in our discussion of relating two partitions. We used the term *correlational study* in section 3-4. This kind of study can be greatly strengthened if it is embedded in an interlocked series to show a trend; see section 13-3, "Inferring Cause of Change in One Variable," for a discussion of this latter strategy.

[11] These designs contain design partitions; they were described in section 3-1, "The Problem of Drawing Valid Conclusions."

Suppose we observe an organization composed of a large number of operating units, almost all of them performing complex tasks. Suppose we observe that some of the operating groups make their decisions concerning their tasks by using a group problem-solving method that draws out the resources of each individual, while other groups use a hierarchical and authoritarian mode of decision-making that causes members to keep their information and capacities hidden until they can be used competitively to gain advantage over others in the group. We note, let us say, that the former groups take somewhat longer to reach decisions, but that their decisions more often turn out to be productive than do the decisions made in the authoritarian groups. Furthermore, employees stay longer, on the average, with the resource-seeking groups than with the authoritarian groups. We could conclude that the authoritarian groups would make better decisions and increase the survival rates of their personnel if they would learn the group problem-solving techniques used by the other groups. But we could not be highly confident of this conclusion. The groups with the resource-using style might be responding not so much to the pleasures of their own way of working within their group as to a sense of competition with the authoritarian groups. And the higher survival (staying) rate in the resource-using groups might come about because, with such self-effacing teamwork, individuals cannot show prospective employers records of individual achievements. Thinking of possibilities like these, we might worry that training the authoritarian work groups to function like the resource-using groups would cause the effectiveness of both subsets of groups to decline. The only way to resolve the question is to train the groups and see what happens.

Suppose, then, that we train the erstwhile authoritarian work groups in the resource-using, problem-solving skill. And suppose we discover, then, that the effectiveness of decisions rises considerably in the newly trained groups and drops a little in the old resource-using groups. Another finding is that the mean turnover rate in the newly trained groups falls to a point even lower than the mean rate in the other groups. Where are we now? First, we have resolved the question of whether the training would improve effectiveness, over-all, or hurt it. We have gained information by using a direct intervention (mode X) that we could not have obtained from the field study using only mode Y. Now, however, we are faced with an organization having characteristics the old one did not have. Should we give further training to bring both sets of groups up to the level previously shown by the original resource-using groups? Or should we just wait and let time do it? Or, in time, will the organization fall back into its earlier pattern? We cannot use the same reasoning on the organization now that we used earlier *because the organization now has new dynamics.* If we apply training in the hope of raising the levels of resource-use in the groups, we would not now be applying training to groups (1) to whom the training was new and (2) who are undertaking to give up a tradition of being different from the other groups and to become like them. *Neither* subset of groups now fits this description, and it was the groups that *did* fit this description who responded favorably to the training. And these may be important variables. In brief, the training answered our earlier question with much more certainty than we had before the training, but our certainty concerns a system that *did* exist, not one that exists now.

To answer the new questions that spring to mind, we must seize one of the horns of the same dilemma: do we sit inconspicuously and watch, leaving the organization relatively unaffected but accepting relatively low confidence in our conclusions, or do we use mode X and learn something with greater confidence about this new organization—which will then have ceased to exist?

There is no neat answer to this dilemma, so far as we know. One way to go is to apply the findings of the intervention to *other* organizations that are like this one was before the intervention. This strategy runs into the difficulties of knowing how "like" this one the other organization has to be for our findings to apply. Another strategy is to keep trying the training in various ways in the same organization until the trends in effectiveness settle down. This seems a pretty good solution (1) if you have enough time and money and (2) if the trends do indeed settle down. Every research strategy has certain advantages, and every one has certain disadvantages. No single one outweighs all others in its benefits.

Although the strategy we have termed the field study does not in prototype include a design partition (X), the investigator using a field study can and often does convert observed partitions (Y) into design partitions when he is processing the data from his observations. For example, he might note whether he observed actors to be supervisors or workers. He might list other characteristics (Y) he observed about supervisors on one page and those characteristics as they applied to workers on another page and then compare the two arrays. But this is a weak form of treatment X precisely because the operator does not *cause* each subset of cases to have a certain value on the property, but rather aggregates them into homogeneous subsets on whatever values they turn out to have. He cannot then be sure that X is a determinant or prior condition for Y—it could very well be the other way around. Hence, he loses the fundamental and only advantage of mode X over mode Y; namely, that of gaining information about direction of a relation. Moreover, he incurs all the disadvantages of X vis-à-vis Y such as reduction of scope of information, to name only one. We also considered this point in our discussion of design partitions in section 3-2.

The investigator in a field study gives up deliberate control of variables (K). In his sampling of behavior systems for study, and of actors, behaviors, and contexts within them, he is likely to have unknown sampling biases. The possibility of unknown sampling biases is not unique to this method, of course, but the hazard is much greater here than in other strategies because the field study cannot employ the randomization treatment (R), or at least it cannot do so in the conventional form of random assignment of *actors* to conditions. The actors are already in the behavior systems being studied; indeed, in a field study there are no subsets defined by a design partition over which the random assignment could be made. Mode M also cannot be used, because it also requires assigning actors to conditions. Actually, in a field study the investigator often takes an observed partition (Y) on a property, then later *finds out* whether subsets within his observations were approximately equal on this property. If they were, he can then consider the property as having been treated by mode M even though he did not intervene. But if they were not equal, then he must either accept that property as a design partition made afterward or treat it as an observed partition.

Thus, the whole burden of the field study is placed on mode Y, observation of properties free to vary. Y is, of course, the most flexible mode. It has high information gain, does not reduce scope of information, and prevents confounding. Furthermore, it can be converted into a quasi-X mode or a quasi-M mode or a K mode if the information in the data warrants.

Useful though mode Y may be, however, the cost of mode Y mounts disproportionally as properties to be observed are added to the study. This happens because as we add properties we begin to need additional resources—for example, more observers and more different times of observation—and bringing in these new resources also brings in some *new properties* (for example, interobserver differences, occasion-to-occasion differences, and so on) which themselves must be taken into account by X, M, or Y treatments of these potential variables that have arisen as artifacts of our research operations. Thus, the "management costs" for gaining information about each additional substantive property and for keeping that information unconfounded by artifacts of research operations tend to increase rapidly with the number of variables to be measured.

It must also be clear that systematic observation (Y) itself is always, to some extent, an *intervention* or *intrusion* into the existing behavior system. Techniques for observation and measurement vary enormously in the degree to which they intrude upon or disrupt the behavior systems to which we apply them. Webb and his colleagues (1966) have written a very helpful book about this very point—about the *obtrusiveness* or *reactivity* of measuring techniques, to use their terms. Obtrusive or reactive measures produce confounding effects; we discussed these effects from the point of view of partitioning in section 3-1. Aside from the methods of macro-design, however, these effects can also be reduced by choosing unobtrusive measures. In their book, Webb and others have described many sorts of unobtrusive measures; we shall review them in section 7-1. All methods of measurement are potentially obtrusive, some more than others. In general, there seems to be an inevitable trade-off between obtrusiveness and precision of measurement. To gain an increase in precision of measurement (sensitivity, reliability) one must increase the degree of intrusion upon the behavior process. There are exceptions to this relation (indeed, Webb and others suggest some of them), but we believe the principle holds over a wide range of types of measurement and observational techniques. In brief, the investigator in a field study who gives up using K, X, M, and R treatments as antithetical to his strategy oftens finds himself forced either to give up precision of observation or to let the observational process itself intrude upon and disrupt the "naturalness" of the behavior system.

Then, too, the researcher using a field study cannot possibly measure (Y) *all* potentially relevant variables. He does not wish to use modes K, X, or R because they would interfere with the natural system. Hence, he frequently ends by treating all other potentially relevant variables (besides those he can measure) by treatment Z. He ignores all the variables he does not measure, and they confound his observations with unknown error. Thus, in the field study there is much potential information to be gained by assessing many variables as behavior goes on, and little, if any, reduction in scope; but the potential information is likely to be highly confounded with unknown error, leaving the investigator usually more or less uncertain of the meaning of his data. We might summarize our discussion by saying that, with the field study strategy, the investigator ends learning a lot about complex and meaningful behavior systems, but he does not know with high confidence just what he has learned. For those who wish to use a more rigorous strategy such as a laboratory experiment to dissect what happens naturally, a field study can be a matchless way of learning the variables, their ranges and combinations, that might reward study by the more rigorous strategy.

4-3. Field Experiments

We use the term *field experiment* when, as in the field study, the investigator relies mainly on systematic observation (Y) within naturally occurring behavior systems, but also intrudes to the extent of making a deliberate manipulation (mode X) of one or more variables. Usually a property of presumably major influence, or a cluster of them, is chosen for the manipulation, and the experimenter tries to produce two or three substantially different values of the property. The more important the variable being manipulated, however, the more those research operations will intrude upon and disrupt the naturalness of the situation.

Mode Y has the same status in field experiments that it has in field studies. It is the primary tool for gaining information about properties and relations between properties, and by conversion it is the main tool for seeking out, after the data are in, design partitions, matched subsets, and design constants, if any. Mode K also has the same status in field experiments as in field studies. But in field experiments, the investigator often *selects* the systems that are going to receive different levels of the experimental treatment so that they match on one or more properties (mode M), or he randomly assigns behavior systems to experimental treatments (a form of mode R). Still, though the experimenter often succeeds in carrying out this sort of intrusiveness in the natural setting, we must remember that reaching the natural setting is often expensive, and people working in the natural setting are not always willing to accept the sort of experimental treatment the experimenter would like to assign them. Because of the expense and the frequent reluctance of actors, the experimenter can rarely include more than a very few behavior systems (actors, objects, or contexts) in each experimental treatment. Consequently, the number of cases involved in this randomization of systems to conditions is usually so small that the randomization would probably do little to decrease the probability of biases between conditions. In such a case, the researcher is sometimes willing to turn to matching on some key variables, the systems to be assigned to different conditions so as to reduce bias on the key variables even if this permits bias in other unobserved variables. Moreover, it is usually the case in the natural setting that the investigator cannot (or does not wish to) assign actors to behavioral systems on a random basis. Rather, he takes each behavioral system in his study *as he finds it* (except for the property used for the experimental manipulation), even though he might attempt to match, or randomize, systems over conditions. So, when the investigator does this, the probability of systematic bias between experimental treatments in terms of variables associated with *actors* remains very high.

The main difference between field experiments and field studies is in the use of mode X, the design partition, for one major variable or more. This permits information on relations, including a better basis for inference about causal directionality, between manipulated variables and any observed partition (mode Y). The same advantages and limitations indicated for field studies hold for field experiments, except that the naturalness is lessened by the intrusion of a research manipulation. The investigator may be able to reduce confounding somewhat between systems, though not necessarily between actors, by the use of M and R.

There are some ways to reduce the expense of field experiments. One way is through the use of the *natural experiment*. This term is used when an event occurs "naturally" that the researcher wants to study and might otherwise have to go to the expense of producing himself. For example, Deutsch and Collins (1951) were able to study the effects of interracial housing without having to establish interracial residences at their own expense, recruit the residents, and so on. Festinger, Reicken, and Schachter (1956) studied the effects on a group who believed the world would end on a given date when they discovered that the world did not end. The literature contains many other examples.

Studies can sometimes be cheaply done in the field if the actions of interest to the investigator are those that naturally take place publically and with sufficient frequency so that the observer can collect instances from places of easy access and in a reasonable period of time. For example, Lefkowitz, Blake, and Mouton (1955) arranged to watch pedestrians at a crossing where signals alternately instructed the pedestrians "walk" and "don't walk." They counted the number of pedestrians who violated the "don't walk" signal when they had seen someone else do it and when they had not. Milgram (1969) surveyed the readiness to take helpful actions toward certain groups of others by dropping, as if lost, letters addressed to different groups. In one study, Milgram dropped letters in various electoral wards of Boston; the envelopes were addressed in four different ways: Committee to Elect Goldwater, Committee to Defeat Goldwater, Committee to Elect Johnson, and Committee to Defeat Johnson. This lost-letter technique correctly predicted the outcome of the election in each of the wards.

4-4. Experimental Simulations

The strategy of experimental simulation is another large step beyond the field experiment in departing from the study of naturally occurring, undisturbed behavior settings. An experimental simulation not only requires intrusion by measurement and by manipulation of a major property of the system but it also involves the deliberate attempt to construct a behavior setting—one that will mirror or typify some particular class of naturally occurring system. The experimental simulation is not a new strategy within the behavioral sciences, but it seems new because it is only in fairly recent times that behavioral scientists have begun to use it widely and have clearly distinguished between this strategy and two related strategies—computer simulation and laboratory experiments.

Guetzkow (1962) presented one of the earliest and still one of the most explicit discussions of the experimental simulation. He used the term "man-computer simulation" for what we are calling experimental simulation and the term "all-computer simulation" for what we are calling computer simulation. Experimental simulation is distinguished from computer simulation because it involves the empirical study of one or more behavior processes (involving mode *Y*) within a complex, artifically created behavior setting, whereas in the computer simulation *all* the processes of the system are represented symbolically and there are no actors behaving in context. Experimental simulation is distinguished from laboratory experiments insofar as the behavioral processes being studied are occurring while embedded in a total, intact (albeit artificially created), concrete behavior system; we use the label laboratory experiment, on the other hand, when the behavioral processes have been deliberately abstracted and isolated from any concrete embedding behavioral system and are studied within a highly controlled behavior system created by the investigator and intended to reflect a generic rather than a concrete class of behavior systems.

Note that the key issue differentiating experimental simulations from laboratory experiments, field experiments, and field studies is *not* the question of the approximation to reality of the behavior settings involved. All behavior settings are real, at least in the sense that they have real effects. Rather, the difference lies in the sort of approximation to the living system the researcher seeks.[12] One part of the distinction lies with the reasons the behavioral system exists and the actors are in it. In the field study and field experiment, the behavior setting exists prior to the research study, and independently of it, and actors are in it because it is part of their lives. In the experimental simulation and laboratory experiment, the setting exists *for purposes of the research study* and has no prior existence independent of the investigator's purposes. Actors are in the setting *to participate in the study* (and occasionally for training pur-

[12]The nature of systems was discussed briefly in section 2-3.

poses). This in turn implies a different basis of motivation for the actors' behavior—not necessarily lessened or increased motivation, but different. Whether they came to the study for money, class credit, love of science, "kicks," or any other possible reason, it is *not* a naturally occurring part of their lives. The context is different. In this way, the experimental simulation gives up "realism" in the sense that the actors bear a different relation to the setting. It may also give up realism to the extent that the simulation created by the investigator fails to reflect the important properties and dynamics (that is, changes and sequences as the behavior goes on) of the class of systems one ultimately desires to simulate. This latter, of course, is always the investigator's nagging fear.

The other part of the distinction is heightened in the difference between experimental simulation and laboratory experiment. It is not that the former is real and the latter artificial. Both are artificial in the sense that they are created by the investigator, but both are real in the sense that they affect behavior. The difference is that the former is created to be *like* some class of naturally occurring behavior system; the laboratory experiment, on the other hand, is deliberately created *not* to be like any particular naturally occurring class of systems, but rather to have the properties common to some generic or abstract class of systems. There are, of course, instances of studies that seem to lie between the experimental simulation and the laboratory experiment. Guetzkow's "internation simulation" (Guetzkow and others, 1963) is a case in point. It is intended to be an experimental simulation, because the underlying processes of the simulated system mirror those of real-life international relations pretty faithfully. On the other hand, the superficial or phenotypical properties of the real system are represented in the simulation in quite abstract and symbolic terms. For example, the "countries" involved are called Algo, Inga, and the like, rather than Spain, Russia, Britain, and so forth. Thus, it is both more general than the "classic" experimental simulation, but more oriented to a concrete class of systems than the "classic" laboratory esperiment. The vast array of available "management games" also yield instances of experimental simulation, and they vary widely in the degree to which they attempt faithfully to simulate particular systems rather than to represent more generic system processes.

Perhaps this point about particular versus general systems needs elaboration by illustration. No one would want to build a simulation of Mrs. Johnson's third grade class in New York PS 963 in 1970. That is too particularistic. But an investigator might well want to build a simulation of the typical third grade in a New York public school, or, even more broadly, a typical third grade, urban, U.S. classroom. On the other hand, one might wish to study learning behavior of children (or some particular aspect of it), using an experimental strategy in the laboratory. One might also wish to study learning behavior of children in the classroom by simulating a generic classroom rather than any particular one. Here, we would be at the boundary between laboratory experiment and experimental simulation.

There is another difference between experimental simulation and laboratory experiment. In the laboratory experiment, the investigator usually exerts rigorous control over the content and timing of stimulus inputs. To do so, the investigator in the laboratory often puts a temporal structure on the behavior that can be called a "stimulus-response" pattern. He can break the total action into segments or trials, or in some other way manage the temporal flow of events to allow making certain observations following certain prescribed inputs to the actor. In the experimental simulation, on the other hand, the temporal flow of behavior is regulated by (1) the dynamics built into the simulation and (2) the behavior of the actors. The stimulus inputs vary with the actors' behavior. An example of this would be a simulation of an aircraft or automobile. The visual pattern presented to the "pilot" keeps changing, not to follow some preordained sequence of stimulus events as in the laboratory experiment, but as a consequence of the prior actions of the "pilot" as they affect the dynamics of the simulated system. Thus, in the experimental simulation, the investigator cannot predetermine a fixed sequence of stimulus events to which observed behaviors can be attributed. The behaviors are reactions to stimulus events which themselves are system-reactions to prior behavior. This interactive feature has both advantages and disadvantages, as we shall see. It also clarifies some of the variants that seem to lie between laboratory experiment and experimental simulation. In Guetzkow's international game, for example, the behavior of participants is interdependent with the dynamics of the system; both for this reason and for others we have mentioned, the game fits more comfortably into our category of experimental simulation than into that of laboratory experiment.

In an experimental simulation, the investigator exercises substantial control over variables by selecting design constants (mode *K*) for the study. He also has the ability to manipulate systematically a large number of system variables. But this manipulation takes a special form. In an experimental simulation, we can consider the set of relevant variables to be divided into two subsets: (1) those to be built into the simulated system and (2) those that are free to vary with the behaving participants. The latter set are generally considered as variables to be observed (mode *Y*), though some of them (such as traits of actors) could be design partitions (*X*) by selection. In working with the variables to be built into the simulation, the investigator *constructs* the relations that will hold between participants' behavior on the one side and the set of simulated variables on the other. This process can be described as follows:

Step 1: The simulated system "presents itself" to participants in some system state
Step 2: The participants react
Step 3: That reaction modifies the system state in ways determined by the structure of the simulated system
Step 4: Whereupon a new state of the system is presented to the participants
Step 5: The participants react again, and so forth, either for a fixed time or until some specified subset of events occurs.

Steps 1, 3, and 4 are all predetermined by the investigator. Hence, he gains no "new information" from the fact that they occur. Steps 2 and 5 are not predetermined by the investigator; they contain all of the potential information in the study.

The investigator does not vary every one of the variables he has built into the simulation. Rather, he lets them occur at a number of values, but fixes the relation among them by constraining the combination of values of a number of crisscrossing X-treatments that he allows to occur. Further, the researcher fixes the effects running from the actors' behavior to the simulated portion of the system—that is, the causal connection from the Y partition to the X partition (steps 1 and 3 above). The investigator does not, however, determine the reaction of the actors to the stimulus situation—that is, the causal connection running from the X partition to the Y partition (steps 2 and 5 above). The point here is that the researcher cannot learn anything about the relation between any one variable (taken singly) in his system and the participants' behavior, because the simulated variables are not varied independently of one another but rather as a set, or interdependent system, of variables. This is equivalent to saying that while a large number of potential variables are incorporated into the simulated system, information about relations in the study has to do with all of them as a package in relation to an observed partition. The researcher using this kind of design does not have groups of actors receiving separate treatments that will show the effects of each variable singly. Of course, in a program of research, the investigator can conduct successive simulation studies, changing one variable to a new value at each new run of the simulation.

RANDOM VARIABLES

An experimental simulation often contains another feature (one that is also a part of computer simulations) that adds further complexity to the picture just described. That feature is the introduction of random (stochastic or probabilistic) variables into the simulation. An example would be the introduction of gusts of wind—random in direction, intensity, and time of occurrence—into an experimental simulation of an aircraft flight system. These are related to the simulated system dynamics in ways predetermined by the investigator, but their occurrence is independent of the rest of the simulated system state and independent of the prior behavior of the participants. Another example would be the chance cards that are made a part of many research and commercial games—"Go directly to jail"; "Do not pass go"; "Do not collect $200." These serve to add complexity and a kind of realism to the simulation, because there are usually important chance factors involved in the context within which many complex performance situations are embedded. These devices for introducing chance also serve the more research-related purpose of being a randomization process—in this case, random assignment of events to occasions.

The introduction of random variables into an experimental simulation is also related to the design partitions or X mode of treating variables and to the matching or *M* treatment of variables. Introducing a random variable is not mode *X* as such because it does not yield predetermined subsets of cases with preknown values of the property the same within subsets and different between subsets. But it is analogous to treatment *X* because, although the investigator does not know which values of the property will occur for any given occasion, he does know the approximate distribution of values that will occur for the subset of occasions in a given "run." (A "run" of a simulation simply means one operation of the simulated system from some starting point determined by the investigator until the system reaches some end point also determined by the investigator. The latter might be a certain specified system state—for example, safe landing or a crash for an aircraft flight system—or it might be a specified time duration.) The experimenter thus can *change this distribution* from one run to the next (an *X* treatment, but a complex form of it), or he can use the same distribution on all runs (thus approximating mode *M* with respect to that property).

The use of a random variable analogously to mode *X* or mode *M* is suitable only for comparisons between runs of a simulation. Within a single run, one mode feasible with a random variable is mode *R*; that is, at specified occasions the experimenter can let the variable take on a random value. This treatment will give unknown but unbiased variation among occasions during a run. Another mode useful within a run is an approximation to mode *Y*; in this treatment, the experimenter determines in advance the complete list of values of the variable that will occur during a run, but lets the values vary freely among the preselected values at any one occasion.[13]

The set of properties designed into the simulated system will, of course, contain none in mode *Z*. All modes will be *K* (or unknown design constants), *X* (or, more precisely, a global *X* property which is the combination of all variable properties in the simulation), or random variables giving the effect of *X* or *M* between subsets or the effect of *R* or *Y* within subsets. The subset of variables that are part of the participants' behavior and not part of the simulated system can, of course, be treated either as observed partitions (*Y*) or ignored (*Z*).

REALISM

The realism of an experimental simulation depends on two aspects: (1) the extent to which the dynamics of the simulated portion of the system accurately mirror the dynamics of the concrete system being simulated and (2) the extent to which the participants' relation to the simulated system mirrors that of

---

[13]This conversion of a random variable into a quasiobserved partition (*Y*) is similar to the conversion of a matching property (*M*) into mode *Y* for studying its relation to other *Y*-treated variables within a *subset* of actor-behavior-context events. In the case of mode *M*, no one event has a predetermined value, but the *subset* of events has a mean and, if desired, a variance predetermined by selective assignment. In the case of the random variable, no one event has a predetermined value, but the events in a *subset* (that is, in a run) approximate a distribution of values predetermined by the investigator.

comparable actors in naturally occurring systems so that typical motivational patterns underlie their behavior. For example, the realism of a simulated aircraft falters to the extent that the "pilot" of a simulated aircraft knows he will not die if he "crashes"—no matter how accurately flight dynamics are incorporated into the simulation. Again, "realism" turns out to be the extent to which the experimenter is successful in reproducing the system nature of the setting in which he is ultimately interested.

GENERALITY

The generality of an experimental simulation depends on the population from which actors are sampled for performance in the simulation and the process by which they are sampled. It also depends on the relation between those actors and the populations of actors who actually inhabit the naturally occurring behavior systems which are being simulated. The latter point is a particular weakness of many uses of experimental simulation by behavioral scientists. Often management games or political games or military strategy games are used with college sophomores as participants. This must certainly alter the degree to which the results of the simulation mirror results of the operation of naturally occurring systems containing managers, politicians, and generals.

SCOPE OF INFORMATION

The extent to which an experimental simulation limits the amount of potential information in a study depends on how many properties are treated as variables rather than constants (*K*) in the simulated portions, how widely they vary, and how fixed (rather than probabilistic) are the relations among the simulated variables. The extent to which an experimental simulation avoids confounding depends on how many of the properties of the participants' behavior are measured (*Y*) rather than ignored (*Z*). The extent to which the experimental simulation provides information gain also depends on the extent to which properties of the participants' behavior are measured (*Y*) rather than ignored (*Z*) and, in addition, upon the extent to which random variables are given *X* treatments rather than *M* treatments between subsets as well as upon the extent to which random variables are used in mode *Y* (measured) rather than in mode *R* (randomly assigned but not measured) within subsets.

THE RUN AS SINGLE OBSERVATION

There is one additional aspect of the strategy of experimental simulation that needs discussion. Recall that the set of variables in the simulation have predetermined interdependencies, so that they represent one overall "design partition" on a cluster of properties rather than a set of design partitions on each of a set of independently occurring properties. Recall also that the systemic state is interdependent with the participants' behavior, so that a single run does not provide a basis for partitioning into independent "trials" or "tasks" within the run, because the conditions for each occasion depend on responses to prior occasions. Thus, a single run of a simulation, for an actor or a set of actors, extending to some time limit or to some criterial state of the system or set of events, really provides only a *single observation*—although it is a very complex observation. To establish a number of replicated "cases" requires a number of separate runs—with same or similar actors, conditions, starting points of the system, and whatever other parameters are relevant. To establish subsets of partitioned cases varying in some design property of interest, the study design requires such a *set* of runs for each partitioned subset. Thus, many runs of the simulation are required to obtain a number of replicated cases in each of several conditions so that a relation between differences in conditions (X) and in observed behavior (Y) can be assessed. Experimental simulations are often very costly to set up and run—the more so the more they attempt "realistic" simulation of complex behavior. Moreover, they frequently have to be run in "real time," or at least take considerable time per run. For example, the internation game of Guetzkow and others (1963) usually takes some 15 hours per participant for *each* of 10 to 20 participants, all for a single run of the simulation. (Computer simulations, in contrast, usually can be run in a small fraction of "real time;" hence, very many repeated runs are possible in a reasonable length of time.) All of these features add up to a very high cost level for experimental simulation—both for initial set-up and for cost per additional case.

When high costs are involved, most experimental simulations in the behavioral sciences are used with very few runs per study and hence yield limited information per study. This is in contrast to both laboratory experiments and computer simulations, both of which generally have greatly diminishing costs per case, although the latter has very high initial costs. As a matter of fact, the strategy of experimental simulation in the behavioral sciences has been much more accepted as a training vehicle than as a strategy for research—by which we mean, of course, gaining new empirical information about behavioral properties and relations.

Experimental simulations are not always elaborate and expensive, however. A number of games that can serve various purposes of experimental simulations, that are inexpensive to purchase, and that can be run through in less than a half a day are described in the compendium by Zuckerman and Horn (1970).

4-5. Disclaimers

We have seen that different strategies of research deliver different sorts of information about the world, make different demands on the investigator, and incur different costs. It is therefore useful to the researcher to have a sort of catalog or taxonomy by which he can anticipate the advantages and difficulties he will encounter when he chooses a strategy that can be described by the facets of Figure 4-1.

In the course of laying out Figure 4-1, it seemed to us that the distinguishable strategies not only fit into a circle but also that each octant is typically represented by a recognizable kind of work in social science that already has a name. Using these names, of course, is both a help and a hindrance. The reader familiar with the names in the octants immediately possesses an imagery that connects him with the world of experience, and this is a help. But the world of the reader's experience cannot be exactly the world of our (the authors') experience, and this is a hindrance. We have no wish to argue about what a field experiment, for example, "really is." We only offer the possibility that the circle in Figure 4-1, along with the two facets we have labeled there, will be helpful to researchers in thinking about their choices. If the reader feels that other labels for the octants are more appropriate, we urge him to enter them in place of ours.

A second disclaimer is important. It should not be inferred that studies typically restrict themselves to only one of the strategies we have named here, or that there would be any faulty logic in combining several strategies in one study. Many studies do, in fact, employ two or three strategies in one design. Moreover, programs of research often consist of a series of studies in which some use primarily (though not necessarily exclusively) one strategy and others use others. Since every strategy has its own advantages or disadvantages, this last programmatic scheme enables each sort of study to buttress every other by contributing its own sort of complementary strength. Because the different methods draw out different sorts of knowledge, the programmatic policy seems to us most promising in achieving a comprehensive understanding of natural events.

Finally, we do not claim that "truth" is laid out according to Figure 4-1. The figure is intended to make it easier for researchers to think about their work and the relation of their work to the work of others. Our hope is that the reader, upon studying the circle, will see how a more helpful set of relations can be drawn and will replace those in the figure with his own.

4-6. Laboratory Experiments

The laboratory experiment—the study of one or more behavioral processes under conditions highly controlled by the investigator—has long been the classic research strategy in the behavioral sciences as well as in many of the physical and biological sciences. At the same time, it has been a controversial strategy for behavioral science, and justly so. The laboratory experiment as a strategy for research in the behavioral sciences has been well described in a number of sources (for example, Festinger and Katz, 1953; Lindzey,

1968; McGrath, 1964) and does not need detailed description here. Most previous discussions of the weaknesses of the laboratory experiment, however, have compared the laboratory experiment chiefly with the field study and have mentioned the other strategies distinguished here as minor variants, if at all. The discussion here will focus on those features by which we can contrast the laboratory experiment with the other strategies; we shall also describe its strengths and weaknesses in terms of information scope, confounding, and gain.

In a laboratory experiment, the investigator deliberately creates a behavior setting not to mirror some naturally occurring behavioral system but rather to highlight selected behavioral processes and certain conditions related to those processes. Rather than display an instance of a behavioral system, the experimenter typically intends a laboratory experiment to exemplify generically or prototypically a cluster of *processes,* quite apart from the settings or systems in which those processes are found naturally. The orientation of the laboratory experiment is toward behavioral *processes,* in contrast to the orientation of the field study toward the concrete behavioral *system.*

ARGUMENTS FOR AND AGAINST

Many of the behavioral scientists who question the use of laboratory experimentation oppose the strategy on the grounds that it studies behavior under "unreal" conditions; they point out that the results, therefore, do not pertain to behavior in "real" behavior systems. In our view, a more subtle and telling portrayal of the weakness of the laboratory method is revealed in Barker's (1965) contrast between operator and transducer. Behavior in the laboratory, Barker says, is behavior caused by activities of the investigator himself, or at least strongly influenced by him, and to this extent is not the kind of behavior that ought to be the primary interest of a science of behavior.

Both of these arguments question the external validity or generalizability of laboratory experiments. And it is indeed true that the laboratory experiment puts maximum emphasis on internal validity, necessarily at some cost in external validity. The emphasis on internal validity has its own cogency, since any study, however externally valid or generalizable it might have been, is worthless if it does not permit internally valid conclusions—that is, logically sound attribution of obtained effects to sources. Proponents of the laboratory experiment as a research strategy often point out that it provides the opportunity to maximize precision of measurement, rigor of control of extraneous variables, and, above all, deliberate manipulation (mode *X*) of variables of interest, so that some information about causal direction is contained in the findings concerning relations. These gains, of course, are purchased at a cost in the scope of information deliverable by some of the variables, this cost being extracted by modes *K* and *X*; and also at the cost of realism, this cost being extracted by the high level of intervention characterizing modes *K, X, M,* and *R.*

The analogy to physics—to the study of bodies falling in a vacuum, for example—is often used as an argument in support of the laboratory method. No one would expect the physicist to study bodies falling in a vacuum under naturally occurring conditions—at least not before rocket flights outside the earth's atmosphere became a reality. It is precisely the absence of effects of "extraneous" conditions, an absence enforced by rigorous control of variables, that makes the study of bodies falling in a vacuum worthwhile. The physicist is concerned with understanding and predicting an underlying process and he does not expect objects falling through unstable gases to behave as they do in his laboratory vacuum. But without a precise knowledge of the underlying *process* (bodies falling in a vacuum), the physicist could predict rates of fall in actual circumstances only poorly, or very cumbersomely, or both.

What is not said in this line of argument, of course, is that there are vast differences between the physical and the behavioral sciences that make the analogy an inadequate guide. One difference rests on the fact (or what we take to be a fact) that phenomena always occur within some sort of system, and this includes phenomena observed in a laboratory. As we said before, an important determinant of generalizability is the extent to which the system in the laboratory reproduces the system in which one is interested outside the laboratory. In laboratories of physics and chemistry, expecially, the system often duplicates very closely the system of interest outside the laboratory. In fact, relations elucidated in the laboratory are often used to produce laboratory-like events in the field. A study of the various substances in petroleum leads not so much to a study of the behavior of oil shales as to the erection of huge laboratory-like devices called refineries. When a magnet being rotated in a coil of wire is seen to produce an electrical current, this leads not so much to a study of rotating bodies as to the construction of larger versions of the laboratory device, versions we now call dynamos or electrical generators. The early theorizing about gravity led first to further thoughts about astrononomical bodies—truly bodies falling in a vacuum. Only later did the theory of gravity combine with the theory of fluid dynamics to produce a field of aerodynamics. The physical sciences, in brief, seem to move the laboratory into the natural world as often as vice versa.

The spectacular result of the scientific study of the growth of chickens has not been the greater predictability of the growth of chickens running a free range. Rather, it has been the development of highly controlled environments for raising chickens. Like the oil refineries, the new chicken "ranches" are essentially greatly enlarged laboratories. Some writers have spoken of man as a domesticated animal, one who domesticates himself. Aldous Huxley carried the analogy with the chicken ranch to its logical conclusion in his *Brave New World*. We feel uncertain whether the empirical study of man now taking place in Western society will seek to understand human behavior on the free range, so to speak, or whether it will seek to construct enlarged laboratories in which man can live a highly controllable (and restricted) life.

For each kind of problem, no doubt there is an optimum balance between moving the world into the laboratory or moving the laboratory into the world. A notable example of compromise between laboratory and real world—an example dealing with interpersonal communication in the face-to-face group—is the "laboratory method" developed by many investigators of group dynamics but made available chiefly through the training activities of the National Training Laboratories (now NTL-Institute for Applied Behavioral Science). See, for example, Miles (1959); Bradford, Gibb, and Benne (1964); and *Psychology Today* for December 1967.

The social sciences only rarely dare to move laboratory conditions into the real world, or vice versa. The reason is not far to seek. It lies in the ethical reasons for not treating people as if they were inanimate objects. The social scientist cannot establish social conditions in whatever way might suit his experimental rules while ignoring moral rules. The result is that the laboratory becomes a very special social system in itself with an explicit or implicit agreement between actor and researcher that neither is going to behave "naturally." Worse, the *particular* differences between laboratory behavior and natural behavior are usually left unspecified.

An even more critical difference between the physical and social sciences lies in the uncertainty principle, mentioned earlier. In physics, the disturbance given to the position or velocity of a particle by the act of observing it (such as by bouncing light off it) does not amount to an important interference with the results of an experiment until one turns to studying very small particles—until one enters the micro-world. As long as one stays in the macro-world and studies cannon balls, flowing water, and flying birds, the uncertainty principle can be ignored with little detriment. Consequently, physics was enabled to erect the magnificent theoretical structure that culminated in Newton before having to revise its very philosophy in the light of the puzzles of atomic physics. In the behavioral sciences, however, the analogy to the uncertainty principle has always been with us at every turn and no doubt always will be. We must always work under conditions that make it likely that the effect of the sheer act of getting information from the actor can easily change his orientation or his direction of action more than the experimental influence we feel it morally permissible to establish in the laboratory. The research setting, including the observational procedures of the investigator, becomes a "small world" in its own right. In short, the behavioral scientist can, literally, produce behavior that is indigenous only to the laboratory.

THE COSTS OF KNOWING WHAT YOU ARE DOING

In terms of modes for treatment of variables, the laboratory method trades precision and rigor of measurement for scope of information and realism of the behavioral system. The hallmark of the laboratory experiment is the deliberate manipulation of one or more crucial variables (mode *X*) and deliberate control of many others (mode *K*), accompanied by precise measurement (mode *Y*) of one or more variables characterizing the behavioral processes of interest. Part of the rigor of the laboratory experiment also derives from the potential use of randomization (*R*) to eliminate systematic confounding of information by all other variables not assigned to modes *K*, *X*, *M*, or *Y*. Since the laboratory situation is created, and since actors have no prior roles or interpersonal relations in the setting because the setting has never existed in their lives before, the experimenter can assign them to conditions randomly. Moreover, he has everything to gain and nothing to lose by doing so.[14] The experimenter may also choose to match (*M*) sets of actors assigned to different conditions on one or more properties. Since he can use randomization for all other variables, he need have no mode *Z* in his study.

The laboratory experiment, then, reduces potential confounding at a high cost in reduction of potential information—or, as we like to call it, in reduction in *scope* (see "Restriction of Potential Information" in section 3-4) of the information in the study. At the same time, the laboratory experiment wrings a very high gain in information from the potential information remaining in the scope of the study. Thus, in the laboratory experiment, in contrast with field studies, the investigator learns a great deal about a very narrow scope, and he knows what he has learned when he finishes. Nevertheless, he himself has caused to happen a lot of what does happen; he learns more about his own operations and less about behavioral processes than he would like.

RULING OUT ALTERNATIVE HYPOTHESES

As noted before, the laboratory experiment is a strategy designed to maximize internal validity; and, if it is designed properly, all the potentially confounding factors discussed in the previous chapter can be ruled out or explored within the resulting data. Rather elaborate designs are needed to rule out the alternative hypotheses that one's observed effects were produced by conditions in which one is *not* interested. And these designs involve high degrees of intrusiveness of research operations—literally creating a setting, assigning actors to it, controlling and manipulating the occurrence and sequencing of conditions and events, as well as intruding with measurement operations. These many activities create two pervasive problems for the laboratory experiment—problems that are the focus of complaints against it: (1) the relation of the actors to the artificially created behavior setting and the consequent difference in their motivations in the laboratory as compared to their everyday lives; and (2) the reactive or sensitizing effects (also called testing effects in section 3-1) of manipulative, control, and measurement operations on the behavioral processes being studied.

The laboratory experiment has a relatively low set-up cost; only judgment tasks and theory writing cost as little or less to stage. Furthermore, the laboratory experiment has a diminishing cost per case in contrast to the field study, field experiment, and experimental simulation. Therefore, greater complexity of design partitioning and larger numbers of replications within subsets are feasible in the laboratory experiment. This gives it a great potential for inter-

[14] The relative advantages and disadvantages of the modes are summarized in Table 3-5.

nally valid, reliable information about relations over all combinations of conditions of multiple design partitions simultaneously; that is, it yields information in considerable depth and detail, although at a sacrifice in scope of information.

The laboratory experiment maximizes rigor of control and precision of measurement at a cost in system realism and in generalizability to behavior in other settings. It maximizes information gain and minimizes confounding of potential information at a cost in reduction of the informational scope of the study. Finally, it maximizes opportunity for internal validity, but runs the risk of low external validity or generalizability.

4-7. Sample Surveys and Judgment Tasks

These two kinds of research activity are strategies, but not settings. More precisely, they are strategies for gathering observations in behavior settings where the behavior observed is not intrinsically connected to the setting. Both sample surveys and judgment tasks require eliciting subjective reports from actors (often called respondents or judges in these contexts) about themselves or about their opinions, attitudes, or beliefs regarding some aspect of the world. The behavior to be observed takes the form of responses generated by the investigator's questions and instructions; that behavior is not a response to properties of the concrete behavior setting in which it takes place. These strategies are opposite to the field study and field experiment in the sense that the behavior setting is intended to be *nonintrusive* and the research operations (questions, instructions) *all determining,* rather than the reverse, as in the field study.[15]

The strategies of the sample survey and judgment task are treated together here because of the features just cited that they have in common. Moreover, some research activities appear to be blends of the two strategies. On the other hand, they are distinguished in the framework of this chapter (Figure 4-1) because of several crucial differences. First, they differ in the way stimulus presentations are organized and in the nature of the response alternatives permitted. The sample survey prefers to use forms natural to the respondents for presenting stimuli (questions) and for laying out possible responses. Questions take such forms as, "For which candidates would you vote?" and, "Which product do you prefer?" Frames for responses include such familiar forms as preference for one object over another and agreement (or disagreement) with a statement. In contrast, stimuli used in judgment tasks are often complex, unfamiliar, and even esoteric; response forms, too, are often strange. Stimuli in a judgment task might be complex, irregular visual figures or pure-frequency sounds; responses required might include forms such as, "Which two of these three are most alike?" and, "What degree of confidence do you have in your answer to the previous question?" Furthermore, the sample survey presents comparatively few stimuli during an interview; the judgment

[15] Like most distinctions in this chapter, this is a matter of degree.

task presents relatively many during a sitting. In keeping with these differences, the strategy of the judgment task is more intrusive than the sample survey because it involves more rigorous control and manipulation or properties of the stimulus conditions and of the behavior.

A second difference is that sample surveys are generally concerned with generalizability over actors and focus on sound sampling of respondents from the populations to which results are intended to be generalized (for example, the electorate, housewives in midwestern cities, television set owners). In contrast, the judgment-task strategy is concerned with generalizability over stimuli and focuses on sound selection of stimuli (often using systematic rather than random sampling; see Chapter 5) in terms of the set of stimulus properties that are of concern. Judgment-task studies pay little attention to sampling of actors; in the early or classical tradition of psychophysics, for example, one actor is interchangeable with another, and multiple judges are used in the interest of replication and reliability (that is, eliminating judgment error by averaging over judges) rather than in the interest of generalizability over respondents.

Sample surveys are usually done in settings to which the respondents are indigenous. The investigator elicits information by going to the respondent in his home, his place of work, and the like. But the behaviors involved are not particularly relevant to that setting. In the judgment-task strategy, on the contrary, the investigator usually creates a setting and brings respondents to it, even though the behavior to be observed is not intrinsically connected to *that* setting. We might say that, in keeping with their respective emphases on actor-properties and stimulus conditions as reflected in their sampling methods, sample surveys are done in settings to which the actors are indigenous but the stimuli are not, while judgment-task studies are done in settings to which the stimuli are indigenous but the actors are not.

The two strategies contrast with the four strategies previously discussed because they do not deal with behavior emitted in response to a behavior setting—either naturally occurring or created for the study—but rather deal with behavior elicited in response to stimuli (questions or presentations and instructions) within behavior settings whose effects are intended to be muted or neutralized (by being natural in the sample survey, by being unobtrusive background in the judgment task), but which in any case are considered to be irrelevant to the behaviors being observed. For example, one's preference for one political candidate over another presumably has nothing to do with the fact that one is answering a question about it in his living room or at his doorstep.[16] Similarly, one's judgments of the relative degrees of curvature of

[16]Often, in sample surveys, the investigator finds that the setting or context does, in fact, affect the respondent's responses; whites interviewing blacks about racial matters get different answers from those obtained by black interviewers. The point is that these effects are typically conceived not as integral parts of the hypotheses or purposes of the study, but rather as interferences—as distortions of the "true" opinion of the respondent. The classic model of the sample survey calls for interviewing in places, by persons, and with techniques all of which have no effect on getting "accurate" answers.

two lines or one's responses about his own pain threshold presumably have nothing to do with the setting of the laboratory or the classroom in which they are obtained—although, of course, some features of that setting may distract or distort one's responses. The setting may have effects—deliberate or unwitting distortion of a response due to social pressures or judgment errors due to physical distractions—but investigators using these strategies typically conceive the effects of context or setting to be *extraneous to* the behaviors being studied rather than being important determinants of that behavior.

The strategy of the judgment task uses modes *K* and *X* heavily and usually uses mode *R* when assigning stimulus events to occasions (rather than actors to conditions). It can use mode *M*, and often does so to match subsets of stimuli. It is highly intrusive, but entails relatively low cost per observation. It maximizes rigor of manipulation and control of stimulus properties along with high precision of measurement, but does so at a cost in generality over actors and in realism and concreteness of behavioral system. It has high potential for information gain and can reduce confounding to a minimum, especially since its low cost per case makes it feasible to accumulate many replications within each subset of cases. But these gains are bought at the cost of a substantial reduction in potential information, or in scope of the study.

Many studies that actually use the judgment-task strategy are called laboratory experiments. The two are alike in many respects (as reflected by their proximity in Figure 4-1). Both emphasize rigor of control, manipulation, and measurement; both bring actors to settings that are not natural for them; both thereby permit intrusiveness and sacrifice naturalness of behavioral systems. But the fact that both often take place in rooms called laboratories is irrelevant to our concern here. The strategy of the laboratory experiment can be used indoors or out, with or without "instruments," and with or without the investigator appearing in a white smock. And studies using the judgment task can be done anywhere. The crucial difference between these two strategies is the extent to which the behavior of interest is affected by the behavior setting in which it is observed—affected either presumably or actually.

The sample survey relies most heavily on observation *Y*; it uses mode *K* primarily to specify the populations to be sampled and to standardize instructions and phrasing of questions. Sample surveys sometimes use mode *X* for methodological studies of question forms and the like, but more often to select (by systematic sampling) subsets of actors differentiated on one or more properties of substantive interest such as preferences among candidates on the part of voters registered as Democrats, Republicans, or Independents; or television program choices by subsets of respondents differing in levels of education. In surveys, the randomization technique *R* always should be used in sampling respondents to be included, at least when a listing of the population can be made.[17] If there are partitioned subsets on some design partition other than actor properties, one can then assign respondents to subsets randomly.

[17]See Chapter 5 for more detail on random selection of actors, objects, and contexts.

Sample surveys tend to be less intrusive than judgment tasks, but they exercise thereby less control and manipulation of stimulus conditions. This cost in rigor and the simultaneous cost in reduction of concreteness of behavior systems is in the interest of a large gain in generalizability over respondents. Sample surveys contain a lot of potential information with little reduction in scope of information delivered and can avoid systematic confounding by good sampling design. But the information obtained is often lacking in depth and detail (largely because of limited access to the time of respondents) and, as in the field study, the causal direction of obtained relations is moot.

It should be noted that both sample surveys and judgment-task studies can contain observations of behavior other than conscious self-report. Projective techniques intended to reflect attitudes or personality traits of which the respondent may not be aware have been utilized in door-to-door surveys as well as in judgment-task studies in indoor settings. And measures of such properties as latency of response or symptoms of tension (stammering, fidgeting, blushing) have also been utilized in both these strategies, although they are harder to use in the sample survey. The key attribute of these two strategies is that the behavior of interest is elicited in response to predetermined stimulus inputs controlled by the investigator; and that the investigator seeks responses unrelated to the concrete setting and, therefore, generalizable over a wide range of behavior settings.

Activities that might be classified as surveys or judgment tasks are often superimposed on studies using any of the four strategies previously discussed. In field studies, for example, actors (or a sample of them) are often asked to respond to a series of questions about their own attributes, events of the past, or estimates of the future. In laboratory experiments, it is common practice to obtain biographical information, personality measures, and measures of abilities such as general intelligence by judgment-task methods just prior to the experiment proper or just afterward. Such measures are then frequently used to establish design partitions after the data are in. But many studies are purely sample surveys, and quite a few are fairly pure examples of the judgment-task strategy; we feel it useful, therefore, to specify these two as separate strategies.

4-8. The Nonempirical Strategies: Formal Theory and Computer Simulations

These two strategies are not really strategies for gaining empirical information: they contain none. Rather, they are strategies for systematically processing information and extrapolating it. We include them in this chapter for completeness and because they represent very important strategies that complement the empirical strategies of behavioral science research. The complementary relation is important. Neither theory nor computer simulation can be useful for long if not backed by investigations using other methods. Conversely, the empirical researches soon become mere entries in a catalog or compendium unless they are organized in a meaningful way by theory and logical analysis. One kind of logical analysis is the logical simulation possible with the modern computer.

Both formal theory and computer simulation are strategies relying on specification and manipulation of symbolic representations of variables pertinent to behavioral processes in behavioral systems. They differ from the empirical strategies in that they do not entail any actual behavior by actors. The investigator puts into the symbolic representation the properties of the behavioral systems of concern, the properties of the behavior in these systems, and the relations among the properties of behavior and system. None of the "data" of the symbolic system come from actual behavior of actors in a concrete behavioral system. It is important, of course, that both formal theory and computer simulations draw upon relevant empirical evidence (collected in prior studies by one or another of the empirical strategies) as the source of their "inputs" to the symbolic system.

These two strategies differ in much the same ways that experimental simulations differ from laboratory experiments. The computer simulation intends to be a symbolic system whose properties and interrelation mirror the properties and dynamics of some class of concrete behavior system. Formal theories, on the other hand, generally are attempts to model generic behavior processes that hold over a wide range of classes of concrete systems.

When we speak of formal theory, we mean a symbolic system that contains a set of connected statements of primitive terms, assumptions, and postulates, in rigorous, logical (but not necessarily mathematical) form, and then proceeds by deductive logic to explicate a series of interconnected consequences derived from these basic assertions; see also section 2-6. Formal theories in the behavioral sciences have thus far more often relied on verbal rather than mathematical formulations and have varied in the degree to which they have met the criteria of explicit rigor and deductive derivations. In general, the more rigorous the theory in the behavioral sciences, the narrower it is in scope; this is not so much inevitable as it is a consequence of the relatively underdeveloped stage of behavioral science theory.

When we speak of computer simulation here, we mean to indicate those symbolic systems that model the properties and dynamics of some concrete class of behavior system, whether it actually involves the use of a computer or not. However, since most behavior systems are complex, and since they often involve stochastic (random) processes, this class of symbolic system frequently needs the processing capacity of a computer to be "run." Computer simulations are relatively new in the behavioral sciences, and the more complex forms that depend on sizable computer capacities have naturally been developed only since the recent advance in computer technology. But the central *ideas* of the computer simulation go far back in the history of behavioral science.

A computer simulation is really a formal theory about a concrete system stated in mathematical form and usually containing stochastic (probabilistic or random) processes. As in the experimental simulation, the properties of the system, the range of their values, and the relations among these are all predetermined by the investigator. Furthermore, and unlike the experimental simulation, relations between the set of system variables on the one hand and the behavior variables of interest on the other are also predetermined. These predeterminations may be in either of two forms: (1) fixed or deterministic or (2) probabilistic. In the former, any given system state (that is, any combination of values of system properties) implies one particular value of a given behavioral property. In probabilistic relations, a given system state implies a particular distribution of potential values of a given behavioral property, and the particular value that occurs in a given instance is determined on a chance basis. Such random variables were discussed in section 4-4 in regard to experimental simulation. Thus, while the behavioral outcome is not predetermined in any given instance, the distribution of outcomes for a number of cases is predetermined by the structure of the model.

The investigator does not gain any new empirical information from the strategy of computer simulation or formal theory because no empirical observations (mode *Y*) are made. All variables are employed in modes *K* or *X* or in a modified version of *R* (namely, the random variables described above). But computer simulations can be very valuable tools for the behavioral scientists for several reasons. First, they permit the investigator to "run out" all of the consequences and ramifications of his model or theory and discover its full implications, even though the system involves very complex interdependencies and random processes. He could not possibly do this in his head, nor could he do it effectively with a formal model stated in verbal terms. Second, the "behavior" of the simulation (that is, its consequences) can be compared to the behavior of the concrete system being simulated to gain insights about both the concrete system and the simulation. Third, the consequences of extreme or unlikely states of the system, or even system states that have never occurred in the natural system being modeled, can be drawn out by manipulation of appropriate system variables in the simulation. If such extreme system conditions turn out to have desirable consequences in the simulation, they can (if ethical considerations permit) be tried on concrete systems. In other words, variables can often be "manipulated" more readily and over a greater range in the simulation than is possible or feasible in the concrete systems the simulation represents. Finally, it is possible to generate multiple runs of the simulation that systematically vary values of all system properties in all combinations, and to have replications within each combination of values. Thus, it is possible to explore the system dynamics systematically (or even randomly, if desired) and thoroughly to a degree that is not possible with any of the empirical strategies. It is often feasible to amass large numbers of runs with a computer simulation because, while it has a very high set-up cost, it has a very rapidly decreasing cost per case; and, unlike the experimental simulation, each run of a computer simulation can take place in a tiny fraction of real time.

But the computer simulation stands or falls on the basis of the adequacy with which it represents the key properties of the natural systems being simulated and the strength and form of relations among those properties. And, since all of this is put into the computer simulation by the investigator, he learns only the implications of what he already knew. Operating the simulation tells him, in detail, what he presumed about the system when he built the simulation.

Much of what we have said about computer simulation also holds for the strategy of formal theory. Formal theories, stated in mathematical form, often differ from computer simulations in dealing with general behavioral processes rather than with particular concrete behavioral systems. Thus, we might have a formal theory of the learning process, but we would be more likely to have a computer simulation of *classroom* learning. Formal theories stated in verbal rather than mathematical terms also deal with more general behavior processes, but do so in less precise symbolic forms and hence often lose much of the power and rigor of deductive logic. Nevertheless, though we think this is a fair description of the present state of affairs, it need not forever be so; theories can be written for living systems: for the small group, for the family, and so on. This has been done in some cases already (for example, in theories of the firm), but most theories so far written have been theories of process (such as theories of learning, of suicide, of action, and so on). Examples of such theories will come to the mind of the reader who has read some of the literature.

Formal theory bears the same relation to laboratory experiments that computer simulation bears to experimental simulation. Indeed, explication of formal theory is often a prelude to conduct of laboratory experiments to test the theory, as well as the result of inference from prior experiments. In fact, it is necessary to have a theory (whether explicit or not) before one can do a laboratory experiment. In a similar way, it is necessary to have a theory of the system in question before one can set up either a computer simulation or experimental simulation of the system. The two nonempirical strategies, then, play an important role in behavioral sciences as complements to one or another of the empirical research strategies.

4-9. Comparison of Strategies

Having presented a framework for comparing the various research strategies and having discussed each strategy in terms of its potential and its weaknesses, it is now in order to make more direct comparisons among the strategies. We shall make comparisons in respect to three desirable features of a study design: concreteness of behavioral systems, precision of control and measurement, and generality of the conclusions over actors.

The field study maximizes realism and concreteness of the behavior system. The field experiment represents one step in the direction of intrusiveness, hence one step away from the naturally occurring behavioral system. Experimental simulation goes one long step further in intrusiveness; the laboratory experiment abandons any attempt to map a concrete, naturally occurring behavioral system. The judgment task and the sample survey deal with behavior not intrinsically connected with any behavior setting. The two nonempirical strategies, formal theory and computer simulation, do not deal with actual behavior, but the latter represents a return to concreteness of the behavioral system being represented.

The attraction of dealing with real and concrete systems is that the results of a study can be readily generalized to similar real-world systems; that is, the study has external validity with respect to its class of system. The investigator may wish to adopt a strategy that departs somewhat from that desirable condition for either of two reasons: (1) to obtain greater precision of control, manipulation, and measurement (in which case he can move from field study to field experiment to laboratory experiment to judgment task) or (2) to obtain greater generality with respect to actors (in which case he can move from field study to computer simulation to formal theory to sample survey). Sadly, these are desirable but not simultaneously attainable; all three—realism, precision, and generality—*cannot* be maximized at the same time.

The laboratory experiment maximizes precision of control, manipulation, and measurement of variables. Leaving the laboratory experiment and going to the judgment task, the sample survey, and formal theory may be desirable to achieve generality of results with respect to actors. Departure from the laboratory experiment in the direction of experimental simulation, field experiment, and field study means giving up control and manipulation in the interest of realism and concreteness of the behavioral system being studied.

The sample survey and the formal theory are the strategies with greatest potential for generality over actors. Departing from them toward the judgment task and laboratory experiment means giving up generality for precision. Departing in the direction of computer simulation and field study means giving up generality for concreteness of the system.

This trinity of desirable conditions—concreteness of behavioral systems, precision of control and measurement, and generality over actors—poses a constant three-horned dilemma to the investigator of behavior. All are desirable, indeed mandatory. Yet the investigator cannot maximize all of them in any one study. And a shift in strategy to increase any one will automatically decrease one or both of the others. Furthermore, most strategies that are balanced compromises between two of these tend to *minimize* the third. For example, the strategy of the judgment task, which is a compromise between generality and precision, achieves the least realism of all the strategies. Nevertheless, although the investigator's choice among strategies is never an entirely satisfactory one, choose he must. While it is possible to add judgment-task activities or sample survey operations in piggyback style to a study using another strategy, and while it is profitable to use formal theory or computer simulations in conjunction with one or another of the empirical strategies, it still remains necessary to choose one among the strategies as the main focus of any given study.

The investigator must decide:

1. Whether he is going to deal with empirical information (formal theory and computer simulation versus the other six). If yes, then:
2. Whether he is interested in behavior in setting (sample survey and judgment task versus the other four empirical strategies)
3. Whether he will *find* the behavioral systems of interest or *create* them (field study and field experiment versus experimental simulation and laboratory experiment).

The investigator also must decide how much he is willing to give up in concreteness of system for precision or generality. In short, he must weigh the three conflicting desiderata against his problem—what is already known about it and what he is interested in finding out about it. Too often in behavioral science the choice of strategy is made first, based on the investigator's previous experience, preferences, and resources, and then the problem is chosen and formulated to fit the selected strategy, rather than the other way around.

The investigator must reckon also with the fact that strategies differ in their relative costs and in the kinds of resources they require. Strategies vary in initial set-up costs—that is, in the time and resources needed to plan and initiate the study. They also vary in the cost per case for additional cases. These costs, as well as special resource needs of the various strategies, are indicated in Table 4-1. It is clear from this cost picture why some strategies have been more popular than others. For example, laboratory experiments and judgment tasks are relatively low in both set-up cost and costs per case, and the special resources they require are the stock-in-trade of the laboratory-oriented behavioral scientist. Formal theory, while low in cost in the general sense, requires a very special and rare kind of resource—creative insight—that cannot be bought in cash or time. It is also easy to see, from the costs per case, why certain strategies (for example, field studies, field experiments, experimental simulations) are seldom used to generate a large number of replicated cases within subsets, even though replication is crucial for both internal and external validity. The cost picture also suggests why certain strategies (field studies, field experiments, and especially sample surveys) tend to be carried out by relatively large research organizations, rather than by single investigators with few or no assistants. Finally, the requirement for vast computation facilities, especially "on-line" computer facilities, suggests the reason that computer simulation and experimental simulation have become available alternatives only in recent years and the reason it is likely they will be employed more often in the future. Thus, some of the preferences for strategies that are prevalent in the behavioral sciences, and that often seem to dictate the formulation of

Table 4-1. Costs of Research Strategies

STRATEGY	TYPICAL INITIAL SET-UP COST	TYPICAL COST PER ADDITIONAL CASE	SPECIAL RESOURCE NEEDS
Field study	High	High	Often requires more time than some strategies listed below
Field experiment	Very high to low	High	Often requires more time than some strategies listed below; also requires an opportunity to make major change in system
Experimental simulation	Very high to low	Very high	On-line computational resources; real time operation
Laboratory experiment	Moderate	Low	Sophisticated technology for manipulation and measurement
Judgment tasks	Low	Low	Sophisticated technology for manipulation and measurement
Sample surveys	High	Moderate to low	Broad sampling base
Computer simulation	Very high	Very low	Vast and efficient (but not on-line) computer capacity
Formal theory	Moderate	Low	Empirical knowledge and creative insight

the problem rather than follow from it, seem an inevitable consequence of the amounts and kinds of resources required by the various strategies.

No one strategy is devoid of serious weaknesses and none of them is lacking in important advantages. And there is no optimal strategy in the *general* case—though we hope the investigator can approximate an optimal strategy in each particular case. Too much has been said in the literature and in the classroom about the reasons one strategy is weak or about the reasons one strategy is better than others. It is far more important, we believe, to study how each of the various strategies *differs from and is complementary to all the others*—to see what one gains and loses by choosing any one and giving up some others. They are all alternative strategies for trying to find out and understand what some portion of the real world is all about. Each "violates" the real world in its own ways, but each also can give us some leverage on understanding that world. The trick is not to search for the "right" strategy but to pick the strategy that is best *for your purposes and circumstances* and then to use all the strengths of that strategy and do whatever can be done to limit or offset its inherent weaknesses. Accordingly, the next several chapters will deal with the range of techniques available for implementing a study design of whatever type and with some crucial problems in the application of those techniques.

4-10. Further Reading

For some examples of productively designed and executed field studies, see Guetzkow and Gyr (1954); Festinger and others (1950); Kahn and others (1964); Barker and Wright (1955); Barker and Gump (1964); and J. G. Kelly (1969). For some examples of field experiments, see Morse and Reimer (1956); Newcomb (1961); Schmuck, Runkel, and Langmeyer (1969); and Sherif and others (1961). The experiment by Sherif and others could also be considered an instance of experimental simulation. More important, it is one of the extremely rare experiments in social science in which a predicted effect was not only successfully produced but was then successfully *reversed*.

Examples of experimental simulations appear in the Cooper, Leavitt, and Shelly (1964) readings; see also those reported by Guetzkow and others (1963) and Rome and Rome's (1964) Leviathan. The use of games in simulation has been described in a detailed and extensive catalog compiled by Zuckerman and Horn (1970); applications to psychology, sociology, political science, economics, business, education, industrial engineering, and military operations can be found in the collection by Guetzkow (1962); and Stoll (1969) has compiled an annotated bibliography.

The researcher can influence behavior—especially, but not exclusively, when using the laboratory-experiment strategy—in subtle ways he does not intend and may not recognize. A large literature about unintended effects of experimental arrangements has grown up in very recent years. For general discussions, see Edwards (1961), McGuigan (1963), Orne (1962), Rosenthal (1967), and Webb and others (1966); for an example of converting an experimenter's role into a natural one, see Breger and Ruiz (1966). Some of these potential effects will be discussed in Chapters 7 and 8.

Introductions to computer simulation appear in Green (1963) and in Luce, Bush, and Galanter (1963); applications to cognitive processes, language behavior, thinking, nerve nets, large business organizations, and diplomacy are included in the book edited by Borko (1962); papers on the computer simulation of personality have been collected by Tomkins and Messick (1963); Uhr (1966) includes a section on computer simulations in the study of pattern recognition; and Krasnow and Merikallio (1964) deal with general simulation language. Abelson (1968) has recounted work in the computer simulation of social behavior; and Stoll (1969) included references to computer simulation in her bibliography.

Some explanations and examples of survey research can be found in Glock (1967). For discussions of studies in different types of settings, see also Riley (1963, 1964) and Suchman (1967).

CHAPTER 5
Planning a Study: Sampling

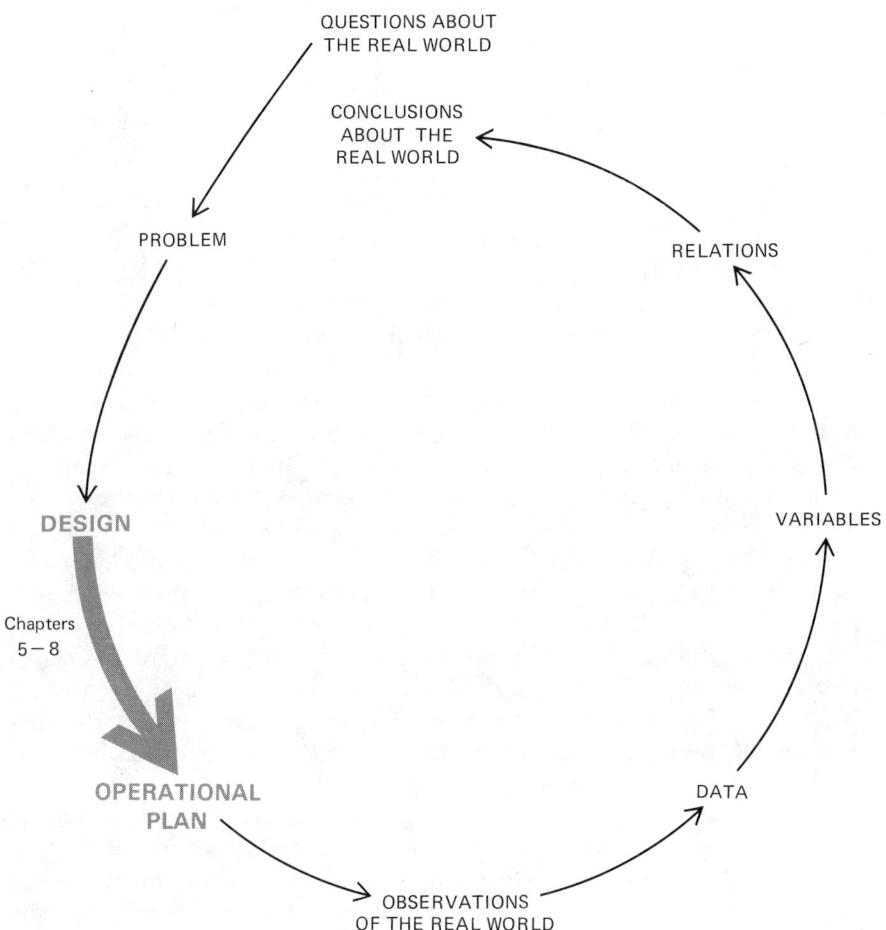

Sometimes a researcher has compelling reasons for studying a very large number of actors. For example, he might want to compare (on some relevant dimension) the voters in a national election in France in a given year with the voters in Italy in that year. When the actors to be observed are numerous and are difficult to reach, then the cost of observing the collection of actors can become very high, running to thousands or even millions of dollars.[1] Obviously, researchers seek some way of reducing this cost, and one way to do this is to observe fewer than all the actors in the collection. The reasoning behind this tactic is that some actors are very similar to one another in respect to the one or more characteristics to be observed. For example, if we are interested in proportions of an electorate voting for candidates X and Y, all those voting for candidate X are substantially identical for our purposes. Thus, it seems a waste to interview a million voters if we can somehow get a close estimate of the proportions in the electorates by interviewing a smaller number of them.

Why should a researcher *ever* want to observe all the actors in some conceivable classification? We will consider some ramifications of this question before turning to the more specific topic of the choices offered by sampling problems.

5-1. Generalizing

In Chapter 2, we discussed actors as living systems and said a few things about the strategy of trying to learn about *systems* versus trying to learn about *variables.* In Chapter 3, we described the uses of dividing actors into *partitions* and pointed out how proper partitioning increases the confidence the researcher can put in the conclusions he would like to draw from his observations. In Chapter 4, we argued that research in different *settings* is a sort of partitioning, collecting together actors alike in some respects and different in others. The research setting, in fact, selects among similarities and differences not only with respect to actors but also with respect to behaviors toward objects and with respect to contexts. In this chapter, we shall carry further the discussion of the uses of observing one or more actors, or behaviors toward objects or contexts, *with respect to other actors, behaviors, or contexts one might have observed but did not observe.* The logic of coming to some sort of conclusion about something one did *not* observe as an inference from something one did observe is called, in empirical science, *generalization.*

In Chapter 2, we pointed out that one sometimes seeks information about only one actor (or object or setting) and sometimes about more than one. When studying one particular person (one's wife, let us say), one can do so to learn more about that one particular person; we often find it valuable to learn more about one person or one group or one organization, and so forth. Information about one's own wife or one's own bowling team or one's own employing company or one's own city is often useful information. When we study only one living system because of our interest in that one particular system, we do not encounter the question of generalization in the traditional sense—that is, the question of the similarity of one living system to another. But even when

[1]In 1966, the cost of interviewing a random citizen in the United States for an hour or less was about ten dollars. This cost did not include processing the data.

we are observing a single system we can encounter the question of generalization. We can ask, if we wish, about the similarity of this particular living system *at this moment* to itself at another moment.

There seem to be three cases in which one would consider observing a person, group, or other living system at a series of moments. In one case, we assume that a characteristic never changes. For example, when we ascertain that an actor is a male, we do not usually think we need to check the next day to see whether the actor is still in the same category. When we assume that a characteristic is unchanging, we naturally do not think it necessary to make an observation of the characteristic more than once. In the second case, we conceive the behavior or characteristic to remain about the same in nature or quality, but to occur only intermittently. Consequently, the characteristic cannot be satisfactorily assessed at the researcher's convenience, as can sex or eye color. An example is determining the customary schedule a family follows in going out to purchase groceries. One must first assume that there is some recurrent pattern that can be discovered. One can then get an estimate of the pattern by making a series of observations of the shopping sallies of the members of the family. The observations might be periodic or they might be timed randomly.

The third case arises when we assume that a characteristic of the actor or a quality of behavior is undergoing continuous change—or practically continuous change. Under this assumption, the researcher would not intend to seek an average level over occasions, as in the second case, but would seek a trend. Instead of observing an actor continuously to plot changes (as one might by attaching an electronic sensor to a human body and connecting it to an automatic recorder), a researcher often observes the actor at brief periods separated by periods without observation. Observing during discrete periods is customarily called *time sampling*. Observations for the purpose of plotting change, however, have a logic different from that of observations made to estimate some characteristic of a population. We shall have more to say about assessment of change in section 13-3, but, in general, the complexities of measuring changes accurately go beyond the scope of this book. Readers who wish to learn more about sampling time periods will find discussions of the topic accompanying discussions of methods of research in special fields. Weick (1968), for example, offered some brief comments on time sampling when making direct observations of social interaction. Wright (1960) has discussed time sampling in studying the behavior of children, and Morrison (1969) has discussed some special problems of time sampling from existing records.

We said earlier that, to be valuable, information need not be generalizable beyond the single case, because a single case such as a wife or a city is often valuable in its own right. There is another case, too, in which information about many members of a population is irrelevant; this is when one is searching for *possibilities*. One may want to know whether it is *possible* for a living system of a certain sort to exist. Can a human exist more or less normally with the heart on the right side? If we can find one man sixty years of age, say, with his heart on the right side, our question is answered. Can a research organization decide by consensus on programs of research rather than, for example, by decisions of the director? If we can find one research organization that has decided upon some arbitrary number of research programs by consensus, and has carried them to completion, the answer is affirmative. Such questions of possibility are often important, because they lead to the further question: If it happened in this living system, what will enable it to happen in other living systems? But many research questions arise that require observations of more than one actor (or behavior, object, or setting); the *estimation* question is one kind, the *relation* question is another.[2]

We often want to *estimate a statistic* where the statistic represents in some way a population or a subset of actors. We might want to know, for example, the mean age of people in a class, or the proportion of women living in St. Louis who are married, or the range of typing speed covered by 80 percent of the applicants for clerical employment at the Little Wonder Clothespin Company, or the proportion of residents of the United States having incomes last year of more than $3000 who say they will purchase a refrigerator next year. Obviously, if we let the age of one person in the class represent the average in the class, we might be very far off the mark. Ascertaining the age of one person in the class gives us very accurate information about one age *that it is possible to find* in the class; it tells us very little, however, about what the mean might be.

The straightforward way to ascertain the mean is to find out the age of everyone in the class, add the ages, and divide by the number of persons. But, as we said earlier, the class or population sometimes gets very large, and taking an observation from every member of the population can become prohibitively expensive. In this case, it is more efficient to take observations from some fraction of the population. When we observe fewer than all members of a population (or subset), the question immediately arises of how we can assess the accuracy with which a description of the sample is a description of the whole. We shall discuss this question at more length later; at this point, we limit ourselves to saying that we must observe more than one actor (or object, behavior, or context) in a population if we want to make a reasonably accurate estimate of some statistic describing the population (such as the mean) and if we want to be able to compute *an estimate of the accuracy* of that statistical estimate.

The other occasion requiring observations of more than one actor is the case when we wish to examine the relation between two variables. Almost everyone is familiar with the fallacy in reaching a conclusion about a relation from a single instance. Knowing a man who smokes and who has cancer is not sufficient evidence to conclude that all people who smoke will be found to have cancer (or even most of them) or that all people who have cancer will

---

[2]Compare our classification of hypotheses in the discussion of types of hypotheses in section 2-7.

be found to smoke (or even most of them). If we want to ascertain the extent to which cancer goes with smoking,[3] we must allow persons who smoke and do *not* have cancer to come to our attention as easily as do persons who smoke and *do* have cancer. This means that we must make observations of persons who smoke both among those who do have cancer and among those who do not, if any exist.

Suppose we find that persons with and without cancer are distributed 50-50 among persons who smoke. Does this show there is no relation between smoking and cancer? Of course not. The percentage of persons with cancer among those who do *not* smoke instead of being 50 percent might be much less. In brief, to detect this relation reliably we need to observe both those with and without cancer *and* those who do and do not smoke. Actors must be sampled so that they cover an appropriate *range* on both variables. In brief, a number of actors must be observed who differ on both variables if we are properly to conclude that we have had the opportunity to ascertain the nature of a relation between the two variables.

In summary, there are two cases when we could be interested in a single instance of actor, behavior, object or context: (1) when we have an intrinsic interest in that one instance, as when a physician ascertains the temperature of a patient, and (2) when we want to know only what is *possible*, not what is typical or unusual. There are also two cases when we need more than one observation: (1) when we want to ascertain a statistic to represent a population or subset, and (2) when we want to estimate a relation between two (or more) variables. The selection of instances to be observed in these last two cases is properly known as *sampling*, and these cases differ from the first two because in the latter cases we want to *generalize* from instances we *do* observe to instances we do *not* observe. That is, we want to be able to deduce something about the entire population after observing only a portion of it.

We now turn to consider some features of sampling actors, objects, behaviors, and contexts. Actually, some of the matters to be discussed are pertinent to all these facets, but they will be easier to discuss when seen in specific applications.

5-2. Sampling Actors

It will help in understanding the ways a sample can be useful if one keeps in mind one thing a sample *cannot* do. A sample can never give any information *with certainty* about the remainder of the population. By looking at one apple from a barrel, or a dozen or a dozen dozen, one can tell nothing about the next apple that is going to come to hand. One can never be sure the next apple will not have a worm in it until he inspects it. What one *can* learn from a sample

[3]The researchable question here, as with most human questions, is not whether it does or it does not, but rather *how much*, or the *extent to which* the one variable goes with the other.

is some *probabilities* about the rest of the population. The kind of question that is answerable about a sample and its population is: If we have in hand a sample with characteristic x_1, how probable is it that we could have obtained this sample from a population having characteristic x_2? For example, suppose we want to ascertain the mean number of children per family in Venezuela. We can inspect some families in Venezuela and then ask, "Given the fact that the mean number of children in the families in my sample is, say, 3.1, how probable is it that we could have obtained such a sample from a population of families (the unobserved total population of families in Venezuela) in which the mean number of children was 3.2 or 3.7 or 5.0 or 2.0?" Given certain conditions and assumptions, such a question can be answered precisely.

Before going further with the above "standard question" about sampling, we should make sure that certain points about probability are clear. By a *probability* we mean a number we can associate with some unambiguously specifiable *event*. For example, we might say that the probability of "heads" appearing at the next toss of a coin is 0.5. Or we might assert that the probability is 0.95 that our sample has been drawn from a population of families with a mean number of children lying between 2.8 and 3.4. Note that the event is unambiguously specified. That is, it is possible, in principle, to ascertain the mean number of children in all families in Venezuela at some moment and conclude without doubt whether the mean is between 2.8 and 3.4. The concept of probability demands that the event under consideration be absolutely separable from all other events under any conceivable circumstance. For other examples, see an introduction to inferential statistics such as Hays (1963) or a book on theory of probability such as Feller (1950); the first part of the collection by Messick (1968) is an excellent introduction to probability for beginners. By a probability we also mean a number *lying between zero and one* such that the numbers assigned to all conceivable events will sum to 1.0. For example, if the probability that our sample came from a population having a children-mean lying between 2.8 and 3.4 is 0.95, then the probability of the sample having come from a population with any other mean must be 0.05. Finally, it is customary to interpret a probability as observable in the relative frequency with which events of a certain class occur. For example, if we assert the probability of heads appearing at the toss of a "fair coin" to be 0.5, then we would interpret the appearance of 501 coins out of 1000 tosses to be very good evidence that a coin was "fair." We would interpret the appearance of 500 or 499 heads similarly. In the case of sampling families from a population, one interprets a probability number by imagining a long series of samples being selected from the population of families and imagining what the mean number of children would be in each sample.

We return now to what a sample can tell about a population. We said earlier that the answerable question about a sample and its population has this form: Given this sample with a mean (or other characteristic) of x, what is the probability that a population with a mean (or other characteristic) lying somewhere between $x - a$ and $x + b$ could have produced it? Such a question

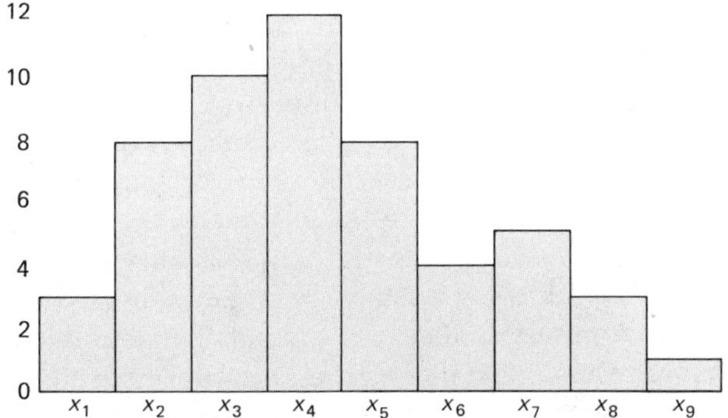

Figure 5-1. Distribution of a hypothetical population.

can be answered through the mathematics of probability. The theory of sampling begins by postulating a *population* of things or elements that differ one from another in some measurable way. The population has a *distribution;* that is, there are so many elements (such as men) of whom the measure (such as inches of height) is x_1 (such as 70.3 inches), so many of whom the measure is x_2, so many measuring x_3, and so forth. We could draw a histogram (a bar graph) in which each vertical bar represents the men of a certain height and the upward extent of the bar represents the number of men of that certain height, as in Figure 5-1.

The figure shows a distribution of 54 elements. To estimate some statistic characterizing the elements of this population (such as their mean height), we could draw a sample containing some number of elements fewer than all 54 in the population. For example, we might draw a sample of 10. There are a great many different sets of 10 that could be selected from among the 54. But—and this is very important—the mean of all the means of the samples of 10 (or any other sample size) is the mean of the population itself. Furthermore, the shape of the distribution of the sample means approximates that of the normal curve; and when the samples are large, this approximation to the normal curve becomes very close.[4] The normal curve is a bell-shaped curve of which the highest point, indicating the greatest probability, occurs at the mean value.

These facts about the distribution of the characteristic in the samples have

---

[4]For those who prefer a more technical statement, we offer that by Hays (1963):

> . . . the central limit theorem . . . can be given an approximate statement as follows:
>
> If a population has a finite variance of σ^2 and mean μ then the distribution of sample means from samples of N independent observations approaches a normal distribution with variance σ^2/N and mean μ as sample N increases. When N is very large, the sampling distribution of M is approximately normal.
>
> Absolutely nothing is said in this theorem about the form of the population distribution. Regardless of the population distribution, if a sample size N is large enough, the normal distribution is a good approximation to the sampling distribution of the mean (pp. 238–239).

important consequences. One is that the most probable sample is the one with a mean very close to that of the population. However, a second consequence is that a sample *at least somewhat different* in mean from the population is very much more probable than the sample with a mean extremely close to that of the population. For example, suppose the mean of some characteristic in a population is 7, and 99 percent of the population ranges between 3 and 11. Then drawing a sample having a mean of 7.3 or greater would have a much greater probability than drawing a sample with a mean lying between 7.0 and 7.3. In other words, samples similar to the population are more probable and samples dissimilar to the population are less probable, but the probability is overwhelming (approaching 1.0) that the sample's mean will be to some extent, however tiny an extent, different from the exact mean of the population. A third consequence of the relation between the sample and its parent population is that the sample is just as likely to have a mean smaller than that of the population as it is to have one larger. A randomly drawn sample is as likely to be "biased" in one direction as the other.[5]

We can say in another way the things we have just been saying. First, a sample, no matter how properly drawn, cannot be counted on to have the same mean (or other characteristic) as its population. Given random sampling (see section 5-3), one can compute the *probability* of the sample mean deviating from the population mean by any given amount, but one's knowledge of the relation of any particular sample to its population remains forever probabilistic, never certain. Second, samples whose means are very different from the mean of the population are very rare; computing the probability of these rare samples enables the researcher to estimate the risk he is taking in counting on his sample to be approximately accurate. Finally, in making bets, so to speak, on one's sample, one can be confident that he will be wrong in one direction as often as in the other, in the long run.

5-3. Random Sampling

All the statements we made about the relation of a sample to its population in the previous section required that a sample be drawn in a special way; namely, that it be drawn *randomly*. This technical term indicates that the sample is picked in such a way that each element of the population has an equal chance of entering the sample. The only way the probability of an element of the population entering the sample can be known is for the researcher to have a complete list of all the elements of the population (or be able to make such a list) so that each element is identifiable. He can then pick his sample in such a way that no element of the population is overlooked by the procedure. For

[5] In fact, when a way of computing a mean or other statistic characterizing a sample preserves this equal probability of obtaining sample statistics larger or smaller than the population statistic, the manner of computing the statistic is said to be *unbiased*.

example, if the employees of a particular commercial company are to be sampled, the researcher would begin by obtaining a list of all the employees. Then, if the researcher wanted to take a sample consisting of one quarter of the employees, he might spin a pointer on a wheel marked off in four sectors. Using the number indicated by the pointer as it stopped, he could then count off that many names (three, for example) to find his beginning point in the list of names. Beginning with that name, he could then select every fourth name in the list. Of course, the list of names should be thoroughly shuffled before this procedure is begun. Actual practice in carrying out random selection of elements rarely turns to spinning pointers and shuffling file cards. Common practice is to use a table of random numbers.[6]

5-4. Simple Random Sampling, Stratified Sampling, and Cluster Sampling

Slonim (1957) has provided an astonishingly brief and lucid exposition of the central concepts of sampling. We reprint here excerpts from his descriptions of some common variations of sampling strategy. Slonim (1957, pp. 147–152) says:

> Essentially, sampling consists of obtaining information from a portion of a larger group or "universe." This universe represents the entire lot on which some item or items of information are desired. The universe we desire to sample may be a large kettle of small fish; all the apes who have wandered into apiaries by mistake in 1954; or the number of USAF troops wearing 15 EEEE shoes. . . .
>
> *Simple Random Sampling*
>
> A candy manufacturer has a crate of assorted nuts weighing 500 pounds and wants to know how many nuts there are to the pound before he dabs on the chocolate coating. He could, of course, hire several small boys with heartburn to count the mountain of nuts and then divide the total number by 500 to obtain the number per pound. Or, he could select a few hundred nuts at random from the crate, count them, weigh them and divide the number by the weight in pounds. If the nuts were thoroughly mixed before each selection the sample would likely yield an acceptable result. The important thing to remember is that every nut should have the same chance of being selected in the sample. That is the prime requirement for simple random sampling.
>
> To see how this would operate on a small scale, let us draw a simple random sample of 6 nuts out of a universe of 18—the 18 consisting of 3 walnuts, 6 filberts and 9 peanuts. Let us number the 18 nuts and assign hypothetical weights (in milligrams) to each.

[6]For the manner of using random numbers, see Kish (1965, pp. 29, 33). For tables of random numbers, see Rand (1955) and Kendall and Smith (1954).

WALNUTS		FILBERTS		PEANUTS	
Nut Number	*Weight (in Mg.)*	*Nut Number*	*Weight (in Mg.)*	*Nut Number*	*Weight (in Mg.)*
1	55	4	27	10	8
2	67	5	32	11	12
3	43	6	24	12	8
		7	28	13	11
		8	31	14	7
		9	26	15	9
				16	7
				17	10
				18	9
Total	163		168		81
Average	55		28		9

Grand Total Weight (18 Nuts)—414 Mg.
Average Weight — 23 Mg.

To make a random selection of 6 out of 18 nuts we shall use the following table of random numbers and select the first six numbers between 01 and 18.

LIST OF RANDOM NUMBERS

22	57	53	93
19	48	40	21
16	61	02	95
78	36	95	97
03	18	35	69
93	88	16	04
78	09	77	61
23	12	46	85
15	85	37	21
38	38	61	15

Note: If the reader has occasion to use random numbers, we suggest that he resort to published lists rather than attempt to pick numbers haphazardly out of his own head. Lists of random numbers are not quite that easy to prepare and must satisfy a number of mathematical tests before they can qualify as truly random.

SIMPLE RANDOM SAMPLE

Nut Number	*Weight (in Mg.)*
16	7
3	43
15	9
18	9
9	26
12	8
Total	102
Average	17 (compared with 23 for all 18 nuts)

This is just one sample out of 18,564 possible different samples of 6 each from the universe of 18 nuts. All possible samples of 6 nuts could be arranged systematically in some such manner as the following:

1 2 3 4 5 6	2 3 4 5 6 7	. . . . .	11 13 14 15 16 17
1 2 3 4 5 7	2 3 4 5 6 8	. . . . .	11 13 14 15 16 18
. . . . . .	. . . . . .	. . . . .	. . . . . .
. . . . . .	. . . . . .	. . . . .	11 14 15 16 17 18
1 3 4 5 6 7	2 4 5 6 7 8	. . . . .	12 13 14 15 16 17
. . . . . .	. . . . . .	. . . . .	. . . . . .
1 14 15 16 17 18	2 14 15 16 17 18	. . . . .	13 14 15 16 17 18

It can be proved mathematically that the average weight of the 18,564 random sample averages amounts to 23 Mg., the same as the average of the original 18 nuts in our universe.

An undesirable feature of simple random samples is that every so often we may select one whose average is pretty far off the true average. Thus, instead of the sample we actually drew (average weight 17 Mg.) we might have come up with either one of the following two samples:

SAMPLE A

Nut Number	*Weight (in Mg.)*
1	55
2	67
3	43
5	32
7	28
8	31
Total	258
Average	$42\frac{2}{3}$

SAMPLE B

Nut Number	*Weight (in Mg.)*
10	8
12	8
14	7
15	9
16	7
18	9
Total	48
Average	8

Clearly, the estimates of the average weight of our universe of 18 nuts as obtained from either of these two samples are pretty poor. While the risk of selecting such a very poor sample is small, there is available a sampling technique that automatically precludes the selection of such lop-sided samples. This technique, called "Stratified Sampling," will be described [below].

Stratified Sampling

One way of improving the estimate obtained through simple random sampling . . . would be to arrange our universe of 18 nuts into strata, or layers. A fairly obvious method of stratification would be to group the nuts into their separate varieties—walnuts, filberts and peanuts. We can then take a random sample from each stratum.

Proportional Sampling

To obtain a sample of six, we would select one of the three walnuts; two of the six filberts; and three of the nine peanuts (i.e. one-third of the nuts in each stratum). We shall use the short list of random numbers [above] to select the first number between 01 and 03; the first two between 04 and 09; and the first three between 10 and 18.

STRATIFIED SAMPLE—"PROPORTIONAL"

Stratum	*Nut Number*	*Weight (in Mg.)*
Walnuts	3	43
Filberts	9	26
	4	27
Peanuts	16	7
	15	9
	18	9
Total		121
Average		$20\frac{1}{6}$ (compared with 23 for all 18 nuts)

Since each nut had the same chance of selection in our sample (one in three), it is unnecessary to weight the separate strata results to obtain the average weight of the six nuts.

One would intuitively expect a better estimate (in general) from the above stratified sample than from a simple random sample of six nuts. This is because we are certain to have nuts of each variety in our stratified sample, thereby avoiding such "wild" samples as six peanuts. In the stratified sampling method above, there are 3,780 possible samples of six each, compared with the 18,564 samples of six each possible in simple random sampling. . . .

Cluster Sampling

Another way of selecting a sample of six nuts from the 18 in our lilliputian universe would be to group the 18 into non-homogeneous clusters or piles. We can do this by making up three clusters, each containing one walnut, two filberts and three peanuts.

CLUSTER I			CLUSTER II			CLUSTER III		
Nut Number	*Variety*	*Weight (in Mg.)*	*Nut Number*	*Variety*	*Weight (in Mg.)*	*Nut Number*	*Variety*	*Weight (in Mg.)*
1	Walnut	55	2	Walnut	67	3	Walnut	43
4	Filbert	27	6	Filbert	24	8	Filbert	31
5	Filbert	32	7	Filbert	28	9	Filbert	26
10	Peanut	8	13	Peanut	11	16	Peanut	7
11	Peanut	12	14	Peanut	7	17	Peanut	10
12	Peanut	8	15	Peanut	9	18	Peanut	9
Total		142			140			126
Average		$23\frac{2}{3}$			$23\frac{1}{3}$			21

Again using the short list of random numbers (Which was printed [above]), the first number between 01 and 03 turns out to be 03; hence Cluster III is selected for our sample. The average weight of nuts in this sample is 21 Mg, compared with the Universe average of 23.

In general, the most precise results under cluster sampling will be obtained when each cluster contains as varied a mixture as possible, while one cluster is as nearly alike another as possible. The reason our cluster sample estimate above was so good is that the nuts in each cluster were "all mixed up" while each of the three clusters resembled the others closely (each had the same number of walnuts, filberts, and peanuts).

We noted [above] that the criteria for effective stratified sampling are just the reverse—strata as homogeneous as possible internally with the strata differing from one another as much as possible. Our example met these criteria nicely; each stratum comprised a separate variety of nuts, and the three varieties were quite different from one another (with regard to the average weights).

While stratification, if performed with a modicum of judgment will almost always yield a more precise estimate than a simple random sample, cluster sampling generally gives a less precise estimate than a simple random sample of the same size. The reason is that in most practical situations one must accept the clusters as they exist and often each is relatively homogeneous, while differing from all other clusters. As a matter of fact, the use of cluster sampling is generally dictated by cost and administrative considerations.

Suppose, for example, that the Double-Jointed Peanut Company wanted to know the average annual consumption of that delicacy per household in Washington, D.C. If a list of all households in the city were available it could select a sample of, say, 2,000 households at random and obtain the average consumption figure from this sample. It would be much simpler and cheaper, however, to select at random some 100 city blocks averaging 40 households each, and enumerate these blocks completely.

In general, the households in a single block are fairly homogeneous with respect to income (compared with a block in another part of town) and the block residents may well be similar in their performance as goober gourmands. Thus, our clusters would be homogeneous. Nevertheless, the sample of 100 blocks containing 4.000 households might readily provide as accurate a result as the widely dispersed random sample of 2,000 households, and at a lower total cost. While the random sample is more *precise,* size for size in the above example, the larger cluster is more *efficient,* dollar for dollar.

In actual practice sampling entire clusters is not too common. More frequently the sample is selected in two or more steps or stages. In two-stage sampling, clusters are selected at random and a subsample is drawn at random from each cluster. The clusters in such a sample design are termed primary sampling units (or p.s.u's) while the subsample elements are called elementary units. As an example, we might select 100 one-pound bags of assorted nuts from a universe of 1,000 such bags and then select 25 nuts from each of the 100 bags. The bags or clusters are the p.s.u's and the nuts are the elementary units.

Cluster sampling is often feasible in preparing sample estimates from data contained in a large volume of punch cards. If the cards are stored in a number of drawers, each drawer can be considered a cluster. Then several drawers can be picked at random and either all or a designated fraction of the cards from each drawer can be selected for the final sample.

There are many variations on the three strategies of actor sampling described above, and many difficulties in maximizing the degree to which the actors actually selected meet the specifications of the theoretically ideal sample. For these matters, consult any of the works on sampling mentioned earlier. To recapitulate, some important points to remember about random sampling are these:

1. In any kind of sampling, the characteristic of the sample will inevitably differ to some degree, however small, from the characteristic of the population. But when random sampling is used, the chances of the error occurring in one direction are known to be equal to the chances of its occurring in the other direction. And random sampling is the only method by which the probability of some specified amount of error can be estimated.

2. Random sampling permits accurate probability computations only if the actual sampling is carried out very faithfully according to the prescriptions given in the standard texts.

3. Random sampling varies greatly in the cost of reaching an individual element. Stratification increases the precision of a given size of any sample over that typical of simple random sampling. Cluster sampling usually reduces the cost per respondent to such an extent that an increase in sample size can achieve better precision than a simple random sample of the same overall cost.

5-5. Homogeneous Populations

In the previous section, Slonim gave examples of homogeneous strata and heterogeneous clusters. When a few elements are taken from each homogeneous stratum, the over-all sample is likely to be more accurate than is the case with simple random sampling. In other words, a few cases will represent a stratum or a population more accurately than the same number will represent a more heterogeneous stratum or population, on the average.

When some characteristic of the actors in a population varies over a great range, samples of those actors can have very different means (or other statistics). But if the actors are all very similar, then every sample must be very similar to the population as a whole. If the heights of ten men are 61, 62, 63, . . ., 70 inches, respectively, then the mean height in this population of ten men is 65.5 inches. But the lowest sample of three men has a mean of 62 and the highest sample of three has a mean of 69. On the other hand, consider a population of ten men of whom 9 are 65.5 inches high and one is 64.5 inches high. Any sample of three from this population that contains the one shortest man has a mean of 65.167 inches; any other sample has a mean of 65.5 inches. Clearly, samples of the second population have means differing very little from the mean of the population; the researcher will get a good estimate of the population mean no matter how carelessly he draws his sample. Working with the heterogeneous sample, the researcher will maximize his chances of getting a close estimate of the population mean only if he draws a careful random sample (though he still cannot *guarantee* himself any particular degree of accuracy). Careful attention to the procedures of random sampling becomes less important as the *homogeneity* of the population increases in respect to the relevant variables.

In some realms of human behavior, populations turn out to be very homogeneous in respect to the relevant variables. For example, humans interpret the wave frequencies of sounds very closely the same way in respect to "pitch." Consequently, in psychophysical studies such as one charting the relation between the frequency of sound vibration and perceived pitch, only a few subjects, chosen arbitrarily (that is, nonrandomly), are necessary. Sampling can be very crude in psychophysical studies.

Sometimes living systems are homogeneous in displaying the same processes, though the processes act at different levels or involve different components in different particular actors. For example, all living systems composed of groups of human individuals show the processes of role-taking, though just how this is done, how well-defined, how stable, and so forth, differs from group to group. To get a fair idea of various manners in which roles are exhibited in groups and organizations, a number of groups or organizations chosen arbitrarily to be different in some intuitive respects will serve very well. At the same time, an arbitrary sample of groups (as distinguished from a random sample) *cannot* yield an unbiased estimate of the pervasiveness of some characteristic of role-taking in the population, such as the mean number of distinguishable roles exhibited among members of the group or the variability in the rate of change in the number of persons involved in decision-making. We are saying only that the researcher can build up a useful catalog of *types* of role-taking, exhibiting some ways in which role-taking can differ, from an arbitrary sample chosen to include groups differing in a number of arbitrary respects. This point is analogous to the point we made in section 5-1 about searching for what is *possible*. This sort of information can be very useful in preparing the researcher for what he might meet next—that is, in providing him with new hypotheses—even though the researcher cannot know to what extent the information "represents" some unspecified "population."

5-6. Unlistable Populations

We emphasized earlier that random sampling cannot be done unless a list can be made (at least in principle) of the elements of the population. If the researcher cannot tell how to find every member of the population, he cannot tell himself how to assure every member of the population an equal chance of entering the sample; and this, we said, is the essence of random sampling. But we often find ourselves interested in some type of living system that can be well enough identified so that we can point out numerous instances of it, but cannot be well enough delimited so that we can tell how to find every last instance to be listed. Indeed, almost any sort of human individual or group is an example, to a greater or lesser degree, of an unspecifiable population.

As a relatively uncomplicated example, consider some of the problems in listing all the humans living within the boundaries of a nation. To begin, we must enable those who go out to find the humans, and list them, to recognize *humans* and to recognize whether they are *living within the boundaries of* the nation, unambiguously. How do we recognize a human? Do we omit those with severe mental deficiencies, who cannot communicate or maintain elementary functions unaided? Some are born without arms or eyes. Some are born with bridges of flesh to a twin, or even depending entirely on the other's heart or lungs. Do we count such twins as two or as one? *When* shall we list those living within the boundaries of the nation? If we define "now" as meaning whenever we come upon them, we shall get a different list depending upon where we start listing, for the order in which we list people will cause us to encounter different newborn babies and different men and women not quite at their last breaths. If we define "now" as a certain moment in the past, then we must depend on records and memories to tell us who was then not yet born and who was not yet dead; we cannot make these observations ourselves. How shall we define "living within the boundary?" How shall we count a man who has not set foot inside the legal boundary of the nation for five years but is legally a citizen of the nation? How shall we count a man who is not legally a citizen but spends half of each year inside the boundaries? Or a man who spends most of his time in a satellite circling the earth a thousand miles from the surface?

These are all questions that must be answered one way or another if a population is to be listed. The manner of answering them can be adapted to the problem at hand, but answered they must be, and advantages and disadvantages go with whatever answer is chosen. Furthermore, the answers *define* the population and thereby the scope of the results of the study being made. But, although some answers result in more expense than others, these questions and others like them can be answered by choosing a suitable definition of one's population.

Some other kinds of questions pose more serious problems, no matter how much money may be at the disposal of the experimenter. How does one catch the traveling salesman? the gypsy? the fugitive? If one is seeking attitudes toward the police, he may be eager to include the attitudes of persons who are being actively sought by the police. But most such persons are no doubt going to great trouble to avoid being identified and listed by researchers or anyone else. To find and list this segment of the population may be beyond any reasonable budget or beyond professional ethics.

A similar problem arises when a population can be found and listed only by making promises of action. Turning now to a new example, let us suppose we are consultants in school administration and have developed a training program for establishing new patterns of interpersonal collaboration within the school staff. And suppose, also, that the training program is designed for use with school staffs that voluntarily and knowingly invite the consultants to come and work with them for this purpose. That is, suppose the training program is *not* expected to be effective if set in motion without the willingness of the staff. Then the appropriate population within which the new training technique should undergo experimental testing is the set of schools containing staffs that voluntarily and knowingly invite the consultants to work with them. But how would we find and list such a population? We would have no way of finding with certainty those schools that would be willing to enter into training unless we carried out negotiations with each school in turn until we had reached a firm agreement, or had failed to reach an agreement, to undertake training with each school. For practical reasons, we would then have to break our promises to all but a very few. To intend this from the outset would be highly unethical, in our view. These pitfalls make the whole enterprise impractical. There seems to us no practicable way to list such a population as this.

SHIFTING THE POPULATION

We have given a few examples of populations difficult or impossible to list. When a population seems impossible to list, must we then forgo the advantages of a random sample and fall back upon the uncertainties of an arbitrary sample? Here again the researcher must balance the advantages and disadvantages of the choices. Let us be more specific about the nature of the choices.

The choices the researcher faces, when he finds that he cannot obtain a list of the population he had in mind, is not merely whether to accept an arbitrary sample or give up the study. A third alternative is to consider redefining the population somewhat. For example, if the researcher finds that transients and fugitives are beyond his budget or his ethics, he might ask himself whether he would be satisfied to learn something about a population that does not include those groups. For many research questions, a small shift in the boundaries of the population will lose little in the usefulness of the population to which the results can generalize, but will gain the important advantages of random sampling within that population.

AN ANALOGY TO CLUSTER SAMPLING

Another way of coping with an unlistable population is analogous to cluster sampling. To explain this, let us go directly to an example. Suppose the researcher wishes to study the behavior of work groups in industry. He might first select randomly a sample of industrial firms, perhaps from those listed in *Thomas' Register*. Within each firm in the sample, the researcher might list all the work groups, and either sample them or plan to work with all of them. At this point, however, the researcher might encounter some difficulty. Some firms would be those in rapidly changing technologies like electronics, computing, enzyme applications, or whatever. Correspondingly, the method of organizing and using work teams in those industries might also change very rapidly. As a consequence, the researcher might make a list of all the work teams in his sample of firms only to find, when he selected a sample of teams, that some of them were no longer in existence and some others had come into being since he made his initial list. Moreover, the actuality would have changed even more by the time he went out to study the selected work groups. In brief, the population of work groups in this example is unlistable because the actuality changes faster than the researcher's ability to make his list and get to all the selected work groups to study them. This is a kind of difficulty that is growing more common as our society's way of organizing for work and our social structure in general becomes more fluid.

To meet this difficulty, the researcher might reason that, if he does not have the capacity among himself and his helpers to study all the work teams rapidly enough, perhaps he can study one cluster of them, then another, and so on. Following this logic, he selects one firm from his sample of firms. At this point he adds a specification (mode *K*) to his definition of his population; he asks the management of the firm to designate those work teams they think will be likely to last at least as long as his study. (That is, the researcher shifts his definition of his population a little.) Then the researcher studies the work groups (or a sample of them) in this first firm. Next, he goes to another firm and repeats this process, and so on, until he has studied the work groups in his sample of firms. This strategy is one of breaking down the original population into manageable clusters. In essence, this is the strategy used in some long-term programs of research; Fiedler's (1967) studies of leadership and of performance in work groups is an example.

The strategy of "divide and conquer" has an obvious drawback. All those work teams existing in all the firms at one particular moment do *not* have an equal chance of getting into the sample of work teams. In essence, the experimenter has taken each firm as a separate population within which he can sample randomly. If he is to pool data from different firms, he must assume that each firm remains constant as an environment for work groups during the time it took to get from the first firm to that firm. Researchers often make such an assumption as a way of stretching their resources.

But there is still another complication. If these work groups are part of a rapidly changing population of work groups, then the list of existing groups when the researcher finishes analyzing his data will be considerably different from the composite of the lists with which he entered the firms. In other words, the researcher will have learned something about a population that no longer exists. We shall say more about this shortly as we consider "The Case of the Disappearing Population."

AN ANALOGY TO STRATIFIED SAMPLING

Still a further way of coping with an unlistable population is analogous to stratified sampling. That is, the researcher might specify relatively homogeneous subpopulations and study each in turn. Let us return to the example of the study of industrial work groups. The researcher could begin by choosing, with the help of some convenient theory, some facets (variables) by which work groups can be distinguished from one another; these facets could then be used to specify strata or subpopulations. Suppose the researcher were to choose the facets of size, manner of decision-making, and type of task of the work group. Further, suppose he chose elements for the three facets as follows:

Size
- s_1 two to three members
- s_2 four to seven members
- s_3 eight or more members

Manner of decision-making
- d_1 hierarchical
- d_2 collaborative

Type of task
- t_1 sequential (assembly line)
- t_2 aggregative
- t_3 inventive

Presumably, characteristics such as these could be ascertained quickly from the records of the firms, and each work group could be categorized on each of the three facets. This categorization would divide the total population into 3 times 2 times 3, or 18 parts. As in the previous example, the researcher could then select a sample and carry out the study in one subpopulation (a stratum, in this example) and proceed similarly, one by one, through all 18 subpopulations.

As before, this is essentially a technique of taking each stratum as a separate population. Some work teams existing in stratum 12 (let us say) while the researcher was at work in stratum 2 would no longer be there by the time the researcher got to stratum 12. Again, the researcher would need to assume, or take it on faith, that no significant variable was changing as he went from stratum to stratum. However, this strategy has an advantage over the strategy of the clustering analogy. The use of the facet design itself provides a check on the validity of the outcome.[7] If the results of the study fit the pattern predicted by the facet design, this is reasonable evidence that the unrandomized variables (left to mode Z between strata) were of little importance. If the results

[7] See the examples in Chapter 12.

do not fit, then the data can be rearranged, using the order in which the strata were studied as an additional facet or partition. The subsequent analysis might then display hints for redesigning the total study.

THE CASE OF THE DISAPPEARING POPULATION

We set forth the techniques just described as ways of dealing with rapidly changing populations when one's resources are inadequate to cope with the rate of change in simpler ways. Researchers meet changing populations in a variety of guises. One example is the population of families in the study by Bronfenbrenner (1958) that we recounted in section 2-2. Another example is studying the scholastic performance of a particular age group. Another is assessing the developing skill of a population of politicians. In all these examples, the researcher is always analyzing data that describe the population as it *was,* not as it now stands. Consequently, he cannot generalize his findings to any existing population. And he cannot, therefore, check to see whether the generalizations hold up—but this statement is true only if we mean generalizing to the unobserved members of the population that did exist at the time of the sampling and observing. What the researcher can do, of course, is exactly what Bronfenbrenner did—he can *extrapolate* from the trend shown by a series of shifting populations that *did* exist to a population that *will* exist and be ready to check his extrapolation with that oncoming population.

Despite the techniques we have described, there will remain some populations the researcher wants to study but can find no way to list—wholly, in pieces, or to a reasonable approximation—and that are not sufficiently homogeneous to sample arbitrarily without prohibitive risk. When faced with this contingency, the researcher can only accept the risks of an arbitrary sample or give up his study. Researchers who work in natural settings (as in field studies and field experiments) typically accept the risks of nonrandom samples.

5-7. Sampling Objects

Often we do not think of an object as unique and in a class by itself but rather as a member of a class or family—as a member of a "population" of objects. We often want to know how an actor behaves within that population of objects. A familiar example is the arithmetic test in school. The teacher does not usually include certain problems on a test (13 + 271, for example) because he thinks it is more important for the pupils to be able to solve those problems than others he might have chosen. Rather, the teacher chooses particular items as *examples* of a large class of arithmetic problems.

With a suitably specified population, random sampling of arithmetic items is easy. As an illustration, let us design a sample to be taken from the population of all addition problems that contain three numbers, two having two digits each and one having three digits. The manner of making a list of all such problems is obvious, but it is unnecessary actually to make the list. To construct any desired number of problems randomly composed from among all those possible, one can go directly to a table of random numbers and begin reading off digits. The first two digits encountered become the two digits of the first number; the next two comprise the next number; the next three compirse the three-digit number in this problem. The eighth and ninth digits encountered become the digits of the first number of the second problem, and so forth. If zero is encountered as the first digit of any number, one ignores that selection and goes on to the next digit. After selecting a sample of problems in this manner, one may then wish to arrange the two-digit and three-digit numbers in random order within problems. There are three ways the three numbers can be arranged: (1) 2-2-3, (2) 2-3-2, and (3) 3-2-2. Letting the digits 1, 2, and 3 stand for the three arrangements, respectively, one can again turn to the table of random numbers, ignore all digits except 1, 2, and 3, and let each of these digits, as encountered in the table, tell the arrangement of numbers in the next problem.

It is not difficult to think of some other "populations" of objects capable of being listed and from which random samples can be taken; we list some below.

All the main entries in a particular dictionary.

All the bolts produced by a particular bolt factory during a particular day.

All the memoranda sent via "in baskets" in a particular office building during a particular week.

All TV programs capable of being viewed by a particular receiving set (at a particular location) during a particular week.

All the women to whom any one or a particular group of men speaks during a particular week.

For another illustration, we turn to Attneave and Arnoult (1956), who showed how random samples could be taken of geometric figures such as can be drawn with a pencil. In one of their methods of constructing random shapes, they proceeded by plotting points randomly and then connecting the points with straight lines. The points were plotted by letting each point be designated by a pair of numbers used as coordinates (as in a graph); the numbers were selected randomly. Figure 5-2 shows one of the figures constructed by this method. We refer the reader to the article by Attneave and Arnoult (1956) for a number of inventive methods of constructing random figures, both of straight and curved lines. The rules are easy to put into a computer.

There remain a multitude—even an infinity—of populations of objects that are unlistable. In contrast to arithmetical items, for example, it is obviously impossible to list all conceivable items for a history test or all possible historical questions about Rome or even all conceivable questions about Rome as it existed between A.D. 1000 and 1001. In studying verbal persuasion, it is not

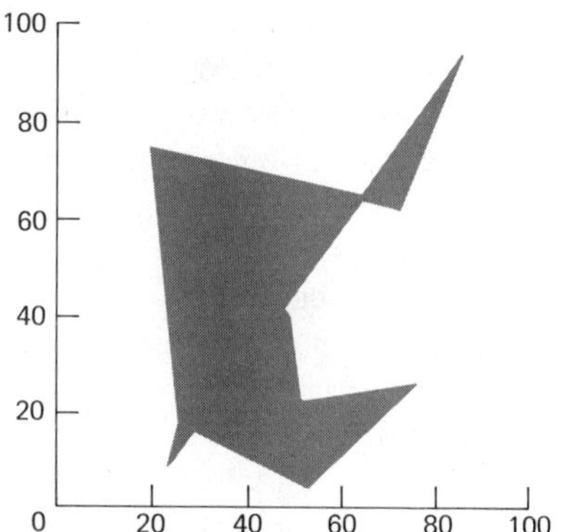

Figure 5-2. Example of a random shape constructed by one of the methods of Attneave and Arnoult (1956).

possible to list all the possible speeches that might be used in attempting to change attitudes concerning suitable foods to serve for supper. In studying esthetic categories, no researcher can list all the paintings that an actor might encounter during the next five years. These examples illustrate an option the researcher often comes upon; namely, whether to think of the population as some existing set of objects or as some conceivable set of objects, regardless of whether they now exist. The schemes of Attneave and Arnoult, for example, produce samples from populations that are conceivable but nonexistent. The researcher will usually choose the one sort of population or the other according to the application he envisions for his findings. Presumably, the teacher of mountaineering is chiefly interested in teaching his students to climb mountains that do exist. But presumably the teacher of the design of dams is chiefly interested in teaching his students how to design dams that *might conceivably* exist. The professor of social sciences often worries about the rapidity of social change and tries to prepare his students to cope with situations unlike those he himself (or perhaps anyone) has ever met. When, either for practical or conceptual reasons, a population of objects cannot be listed, the goal of "representativeness" must be sought by some other means than by random selection. At the risk of being repetitious, we emphasize that random selection does not guarantee that a sample will contain elements from all segments of the population. Random selection makes a balanced, representative sample *more probable* than an unbalanced, unrepresentative sample, and it does so without bias; error in one direction is as probable as error in another. Nevertheless, every actual random sample is unrepresentative to some degree, no matter how small. The great advantage of a random sample is that the probability of any given degree of error can be computed. But for some purposes, such as testing an idea against a wide range of conditions, a widely representative sample will serve more surely than an unbiased one. And, where listing the population is impossible, the researcher must perforce fall back on the idea of a representative sample instead of a random one.

Still, a representative sample need not be wholly arbitrary and intuitive.

To select a representative sample, we can employ the concept of facet. If the researcher has designed his study with thought to the nature of the "objects" with which his actors deal, he can usually specify some features, or facets, by which he can describe how the objects differ among themselves. For an example, let us turn to the realm of test-making. Here the idea of sampling arises in connection with selecting items for a test. Suppose we wish to construct an examination for a course in physical science. One way of specifying portions of the course in physical science is by topics or units of "content." The labels of columns in Table 5-1 show one way of partitioning the content of such a course. We can think of each topic as an element of the content facet. And there is at least one other facet by which the examination maker can distinguish items. The second facet distinguishes the kind of intellectual skill most challenged by the item. These skills label the rows in Table 5-1. Some items, for example, require knowledge of the meanings of certain terms (row IA); others require ability to interpret graphs (row IIF). The elements labeling the rows in this table were chosen to conform to the taxonomy of Bloom (1956).

These two facets define a matrix of cells; obviously, more than one item can be written to the specifications of any one cell. Table 5-1 shows the number of items written to satisfy each cell for a hypothetical examination. The number of items were chosen to parallel the "emphasis" put on the various topics, as suggested by the amount of time spent on the topics during the course. Such a table is commonly called a *table of specifications*. Remmers, Gage, and Rummel (1960) remark on some advantages of making use of facet design in test-building as follows:

> In short, the table of specifications *interacts* with the process of writing the questions; each influences the other. The table of specifications keeps the teacher aware of the emphasis he is building into his test. By tallying each item, as it is prepared, in the appropriate subdivision in the table of specifications, the teacher can keep the distribution of the items in agreement with the emphasis determined by the statement of objectives (pp. 217–219).

Notice that the teacher is not interested in an unbiased selection of items; quite the contrary—the teacher wishes to "keep the distribution of items in agreement with the . . . objectives." Consequently, the teacher lays out the facets and their elements he wants the items to span and then sees to it that they do so. And so a researcher might construct a test for assessing some sort of performance. Another example is the psychophysicist studying responses to sound frequencies.

When the researcher is considering the strategy of using systematic sampling through the use of facets as in an engineering handbook, it is important for him to keep two considerations in mind. First, one cannot use a facet design unless he has a theory or at least some hunches that suggest to him some facets, but randomization can be used even in a state of unrelieved ignorance. Second, if the researcher's primary need is to assign actors or objects to treatments in an unbiased manner, systematic sampling of them will not

Table 5-1. *Table of Specifications for a Physical Science Examination*

OBJECTIVES	CONTENT				CONTENT								
	The Universe and Solar System, Scientific Method	*Origin and Composition of Earth, Rocks—Minerals*	*Atmospheric Movements, Clouds, Weather*	*Atomic and Kinetic Theory, Gas Laws, Heat*	*Mathematics, Variations, Functions, Right Triangles*	*Weathering, Erosional Agents, Deposition of Sediments, Field Trip*	*Mechanical Energy, Gravitation, Forces and Motion*	*Electrical Energy, Statics, Magnetism, Electrical Effects*	*Chemical Energy and Changes, Acids—Bases*	*Earth Movements, Diastrophism, Vulcanism, Isostasy*	*Wave Motion, Light, Sound, Electromagnetic Radiation*	*Metals, Non-Metals, Fuels, Carbon Compounds, Periodic Chart*	*Total Number of Items*
Number of lectures	4	5	3	6	5	3	3	6	5	3	5	5	—
Number of laboratory periods	1	4	1	3	4	1	3	2	5	0	1	1	—
Total time in each area	5	9	4	9	9	4	6	8	10	3	10	6	
I. Knowledge and understanding of													
A. Scientific facts and terminology	5	12	3	4	2	6	3	6	8	2	8	4	63
B. Principles, laws, and theories	2	3	2	4	2	4	3	3	4	2	4	3	36
C. The mathematical treatment of physical concepts	1	—	1	2	—	—	2	2	2	—	2	2	14
D. Theoretical assumptions and valid experimentation	1	1	—	4	—	—	2	2	3	—	3	2	18
E. Definitions and generalizations	2	4	2	2	2	2	2	2	3	2	3	2	28

II. Skills and abilities in													
A. The solution of mathematical problems	1	—	—	4	6	—	3	4	4	—	4	—	26
B. The application of principles to familiar problem situations	2	4	1	3	2	2	3	2	2	2	4	3	30
C. The application of principles to new problem situations	1	2	1	4	2	2	2	2	4	1	2	1	24
D. Laboratory procedures and techniques	—	2	—	1	—	—	1	2	3	—	1	1	11
E. The formulation of generalizations from specific facts	2	2	1	2	—	2	2	1	2	—	3	—	17
F. The interpretation and use of data, tables, and pictorial material	1	3	3	3	4	2	2	2	3	2	4	4	33
Totals	18	33	14	33	20	20	25	28	38	11	38	22	300

From Remmers, Gage, and Rummel, 1960, pp. 218–219; after Paul L. Dressel and others as the Board of Examiners of the State College of Agriculture and Applied Science. *Comprehensive examinations in a program of general education.* East Lansing, Mich.: the College, 1949.

do it, regardless of whether the researcher makes use of facets. Systematic sampling (which, without a list, is much more systematic through the use of facets) is profitable when the researcher's primary purpose is *not* unbiased assignment to treatments but is that of mapping values over a domain, as in the case, for example, of ascertaining the scholastic achievement of pupils over a domain specified by topics and skills.

In summary, selecting actors randomly increases the probability that the next actor (not previously observed) will behave toward the same set of objects in the same way as actors already observed. Selecting objects randomly increases the probability that the actor will behave toward the next object (not yet observed in interaction with the actor) in the same way he behaved toward the sample of objects studied. Selecting both actors and objects randomly increases the researcher's confidence in his generalizations in both realms. The researcher must often choose whether lack of bias or experiencing a range of conditions is more important to him. Random sampling does not guarantee a range of conditions, but it guarantees lack of bias (that is, equal probabilities of different directions of error) in estimating a statistic in the population. Facet design does not guarantee unbiased estimates, but it guarantees the presence of every specifiable condition in each specifiable facet. For more detail on the use of facets, see sections 2-4, 12-5, and 12-6. As we mentioned before and shall mention again, no tactic of research opens the gates of heaven to the researcher, not even randomization. The researcher must choose the tactic that maximizes the advantages he believes will best advance his study and minimizes the disadvantages that will most weaken his study.

5-8. Sampling Behaviors

A behavior, of course, is an *interaction* between an actor and an object in a context. The exact form of the behavior depends on actor, object, and context. A man and a corporation (different actors) do not behave in the same way toward a bottle of beer. A family reacts differently to a bottle of beer and a bottle of milk (different objects). A man acts differently toward a bottle of milk when he is at home at breakfast time and when he is at work in a dairy (different contexts). The myriad ways a woman can say "Come here" to a man is a serious matter in schools of dramatic art—for the actress must be able to adapt her verbal behavior to role, object, and context.

But although the exact forms of behaviors are legion, even infinite, evidence is accumulating that certain types of interactions between actors and objects are ubiquitous. In the realm of interpersonal behavior, for example, Foa (1961), among others, has argued that two kinds of behavior account for a great many of the orientations that can exist between persons; namely, dominance-submission and love-hate. Schutz (1958) earlier described two similar factors: control and affection. He also proposed interaction rate as an important characteristic of interpersonal behavior. In conceiving objects of all sorts, Osgood, Suci, and Tannenbaum (1957) proposed factors that seem to overlap a good deal with those already mentioned; namely, potency, evaluation, and activity.

If particular forms of behavior are predominantly manifestations of a few recurring orientations (as is suggested by the research cited above), then the idea of listing some few facets of behavior with elements chosen to suit the particular context being studied does not seem farfetched. This strategy would require the use of objects and contexts that would elicit orientations of the types chosen to be basic. Actually, in raising the question of sampling behaviors, we have uncovered what many researchers take to be their central problem. The study of behavior, many would say, consists precisely in discovering how to reduce the myriad observable *particular* behaviors to a manageable number of ways of distinguishing among them. These ways of distinguishing particular behaviors have been called, at different times and by different researchers, instincts, motives, predispositions, sentiments, attitudes, orientations, schema, factors, and the like. The strategy of many researchers is to use arrays of actors, objects, and contexts to try to find a relatively small number of behavior types (factors? schema?) that recur in many combinations of actors, objects, and contexts. Behaviors, in this strategy, are not to be sampled at the outset but are to be produced or observed. In the language of section 3-3, the behaviors under this strategy comprise an observed partition, mode Y.

Another strategy can also be used; namely, mode X. Sometimes the researcher wishes to postulate some realms or facets of behavior at the outset. He might adopt this strategy for one of two reasons: (1) he wishes to compare actors, objects, or contexts and is using the behavioral factors as a basis, or (2) he wishes to see how much behavior he can fit to his postulated factors; that is, he wants to test a hypothesis about the adequacy of his postulated behavioral factors. Some samples of objects and contexts chosen to carry out this sort of strategy have been described by Foa (1961, 1962) and by Guttman (1966).

Neither in mode Y nor in mode X are behaviors sampled randomly. In fact, it seems obvious to us that behaviors cannot be sampled randomly in actuality, since they cannot be listed before they occur. The producers of behavior—actors, objects, and contexts—can be sampled randomly, but behaviors cannot. We might remind the reader, however, that anything can be done in imagination, and a researcher might find some reason to select behaviors randomly in preparing a computer simulation.

5-9. Sampling Contexts

Contexts can be conceived as the environments of which objects are special parts. In this vein, the logic we applied to objects seems to us to apply to contexts also.[8] It would not be easy in most natural situations to specify

[8]Brunswik (1956) was one of the first to point out the importance of carefully sampling contexts and objects as well as people.

a population of contexts, though a sufficiently restrictive definition might enable one to do so. On the other hand, facet design can be used with contexts just as with any other feature of the "stuff" to be studied, thus extending the range of situations to which the study might be generalized. Where a population of contexts cannot be listed, the researcher might resort to the analogy with stratified sampling (see section 5-6). For example, a researcher studying political behavior in the United States might wish to sample some sociopolitical environments as contexts within which to study the behavior of actors. He might choose three facets to specify the domain of contexts: (1) region of the country, (2) size of the community, and (3) whether the community had a history of one-party politics or two-party politics. The researcher might then sample actors within the various cells: rural-one-party-southern; urban-one-party-prairie-states; rural-two-party-northeast; and so forth. In this way, he would guarantee that the study had reference to the population of contexts specified by the facets and their elements, just as the table of specifications for a physical science examination displayed in section 5-7 guarantees representation of all types of items specified by the facets of that table. Sampling natural settings within the specifications of a facet design meets the intentions of Brunswik (1956), who argued that variables be studied as they are embedded in the matrix of the other variables at work in the natural range of natural settings. (For a brief discussion of Brunswik's point of view, see Selltiz, Jahoda, Deutsch, and Cook, 1959, pp. 125–127.)

Sampling at different times (occasions) within the same behavior setting is another kind of context sampling. Some comments about time sampling and some references to literature on it were presented in section 5-1. As indicated there, a full treatment of the problem of selecting discrete, sequential times at which to make observations is beyond the scope of this book.

5-10. Summary

In any kind of sampling, any characteristic of the sample will differ more or less from that of the population. Under random sampling, however, the probability of the sample erring in one direction is equal to the probability of it erring in any other. A sample is random if the researcher gives every element of the population an equal chance of being picked for the sample. Random samples vary greatly in the cost of reaching an individual element. Stratification increases precision over an equal size of simple random sample. Cluster sampling often reduces the cost per element to such an extent that the size of the sample can be increased to achieve the desired precision while still realizing a saving in cost over simple random sampling.

When a population of actors is highly homogeneous in its behavior in any one situation compared to the differences in behavior produced by different stimulus situations, careful random sampling is less important than in heterogeneous populations, because almost any sample from the homogeneous population will be representative.

When a population is unlistable and therefore not capable of random sampling, it is often possible to shift specifications so as not to hurt significantly the purposes of the study but so as to define a listable population. When shifting the boundaries of the population is not feasible, the population can sometimes be divided into parts that are separately listable. When this strategem is used, however, the parts can be put back together only by making an assumption that nothing significant was lost between the parts. Some populations cannot be listed wholly, in parts, or to any acceptable approximation by any strategem. In the latter case, the researcher can only accept the risks of relegating some variables to mode *Z*.

The logic of sampling objects and contexts is similar to that used in sampling actors. In sampling objects, the researcher is sometimes less interested in generalizing in an unbiased manner to a population of objects than he is in studying the responses of actors to a densely arranged pattern of objects that, though a restricted part of an obviously larger population, has a practical or intrinsic interest for the researcher; an example is a multiple-item test of performance over a domain of behavior of practical value. In such a case, the researcher often uses a systematic or purposeful sample of objects.

In Chapter 6, we turn to some problems in gathering evidence that remain after partitions have been chosen, settings for the study have been selected, and the sample designed.

5-11. Further Reading

Many texts have been written on the technical details of sampling. Some of the more recent are Kish (1965), Kendall and Stuart (1966, Chapters 39 and 40), Slonim (1960), and Yamane (1967).

CHAPTER 6

Planning to Gather Evidence: Validity, Reliability, and Generalizability

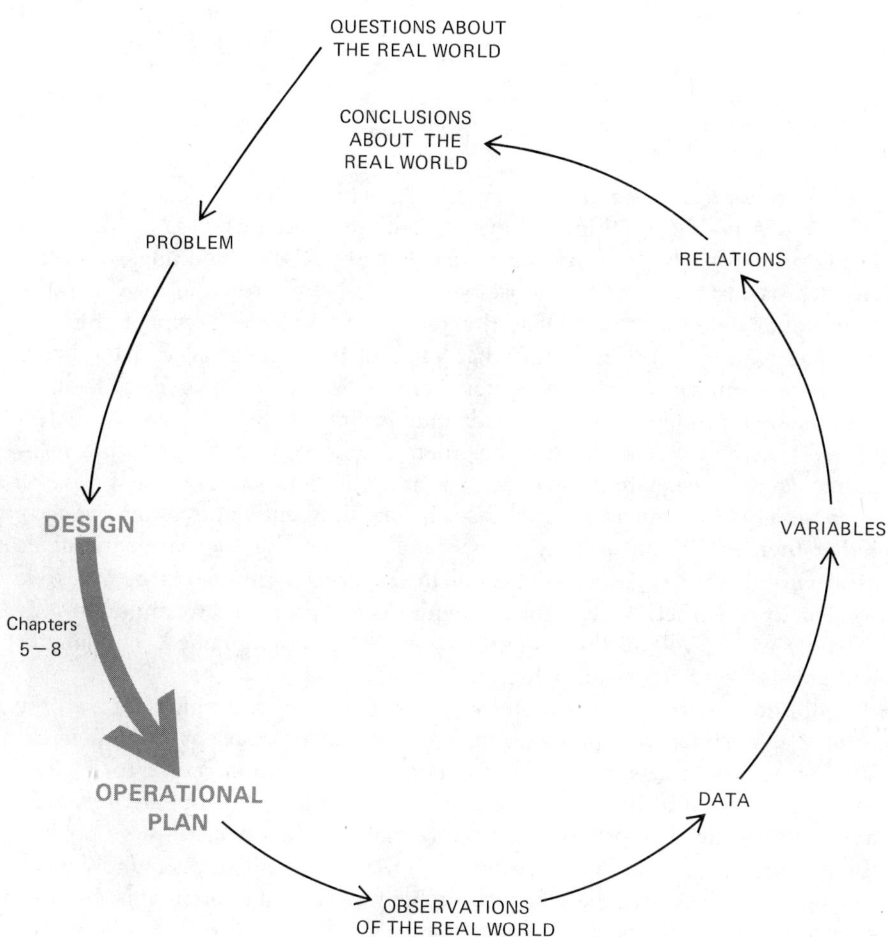

Most of our ways of thinking about behavior are highly inferential, not direct. We do not often satisfy ourselves with saying that a man moved quickly or spoke slowly, even though such actions are directly observable, open to the eye and ear of anyone. We usually prefer to say, for example, that the man moved hurriedly and spoke thoughtfully. But one cannot directly observe a hurry or a thought. One must infer these conditions from manifest signs such as quick motions and slow speech. In the social sciences, just as in everyday life, we must often work with concepts describing unobservables such as cooperation, dissonance, authoritarianism, and anomie. When working with such insensibles, researchers must choose something observable to "stand for" the unobservable thing if they are to collect empirical data.

When one selects a specific, observable thing as an indicator of a general, unobservable concept, numerous complications ensue. This chapter presents some of those complications.

6-1. Operational Definitions of Properties

To observe a property systematically, it is necessary to select one or more specific observable conditions or events to be taken as instances or indicators of the property. The technical term for a class of observable things or events selected as instances of an unobservable concept is *operational definition*. The operational definition tells what the researcher will do (accept a thing or precipitate an event) to find out what value of the conceptual variable exists in a given empirical instance. Whenever we decide to observe, control, or manipulate a property, we must find some technique by which we can detect its presence at a certain value rather than at other values. With such a technique, we can designate those cases that have different values of the property; alternatively, if we must construct cases having different values of the property rather than find them as they occur naturally, we use such a technique to ascertain whether we were successful in constructing the sorts of cases we wanted to construct. To control or manipulate a property, we must be able to know what levels of the property we have actually obtained. This matter will be discussed further in Chapter 8.

Often the property we wish to measure, control, or manipulate is in the form of an abstract concept. Consider, for example, the concept of intelligence. The *concept* of intelligence may or may not have a precise meaning for a given investigator—ability to solve problems, ability to adapt to the environment, ability to handle a lot of information, or whatever. In any case, these phrases do not in themselves tell the investigator how to go about assessing how much intelligence a given actor has. The researcher must fasten upon (that is, assume) a correspondence between the concept and one or more operations before he can assess the intelligence of actual actors. For example, he might decide to let amount of intelligence correspond to the number of right answers given to a set of questions on a certain test. A score on the test would be his operational definition of intelligence. He might use one of a number of existing tests for this, or he might decide to build a new intelligence test. Alternatively, he might define intelligence as the speed of solving certain problems, the level of performance on a particular memory task, or the like.

We emphasize the point that the researcher's observations or manipulations reflect his *operational* definition of a property, not the conceptual one.[1] His concrete observations, such as the scores on a particular test, are whatever they are, regardless of the conceptual label he may give to the property. The test scores would be the same for each case whether the investigator considered them indexes of "intelligence," "arithmetic ability," "mathematical aptitude," or simply "property 3."

The point that observations refer *only* to the operations by which they were made may seem self-evident and may seem to create problems only when we deal with "fuzzy" concepts like intelligence, personality traits, and the like. This is not the case. The point holds and needs to be recognized for any concept, however straightforward and directly observable it may seem. Consider, for example, the sex of the actor. What quality could be more straightforward and unequivocal? Certainly the standard operational definition of sex—presence of male or female genitalia—seems straightforward enough. But for many of the behavioral properties to which we might want to relate sex of actor, the crucial aspects of sex may very well be unrelated to genitalia. We might be better off dealing with some measure of masculine versus feminine attitudes or behavior styles. We find even more interesting the 1967 decision by officials of the Olympic games that the sex of apparently female athletes shall be corroborated no longer by inspection of genitalia but by analysis of chromosomes. At least one ostensible woman was found to have the chromosomes of a male, and the Olympic officials preferred the latter operational definition of sex for the purposes of enforcing the Olympic rules.

Any one of these three operational definitions—psychological, anatomical, or genetic—is a reasonable mapping of the concept of sex of actor. But the definitions are not equivalent, because the scores obtained for a set of cases vary according to the definition used. Each is only partly, not entirely, predictable from each of the others. And if they do not correlate perfectly with each other, chances are they will correlate differently with different behavior properties we might wish to examine in connection with sex of actor. If this is so for such a comparatively clear-cut concept, imagine how much more pertinent this problem is for the many concepts in behavioral science that are admittedly much more "fuzzy."

Obviously, there are many different classes of potential operational definitions for any one concept, especially for the many relatively abstract and imprecise concepts of the behavioral sciences. The potential multiplicity of operational definitions of a concept is a strong advantage up to a point (as we shall see in later discussions of convergent validity), but can lead to confusion within a a body of literature unless steps are taken to establish the *empirical* relations between alternate definitions of the same concept. The procedures for doing this are discussed later in the section dealing with validity.

[1]There has been much controversy in the behavioral sciences on use of operational and conceptual definitions. Underwood (1957) has an especially useful discussion on this topic. Construct validity and convergent validity also bear on this issue; see "Validity as Fit in a Network of Related Concepts" in section 6-3.

The question of validity is the queston of goodness of mapping (correspondence) between concept and operation. The validity question asks, in effect, whether the measure used in the operational definition is "truly" a measure of the corresponding property as conceptually defined. The related question of reliability asks whether the measure used as the operational definition can be depended upon to yield the same value in repeated independent assessments of the same actor or object. A valid measure can be erratic and a reliable measure invalid. One archer might send his arrows into the target so that their average position is at the center of the bull's-eye even though no one arrow is actually there. This archer's performance is valid in the sense that his performance tells exactly where the center of the target is; it is unreliable in the sense that no arrow tells very closely where the next arrow will fall. Another archer might be reliable in the sense that all his arrows fall within the span of a half-dollar, but invalid in the sense that the half-dollar is two feet off the target. These two topics—reliability and validity—are the subjects of the next sections of this chapter.[2]

As we have suggested, validity and reliability of measures are inextricable parts of the bridge between operational and conceptual definitions. Furthermore, they bear a close relation to some other concepts with which we have already dealt—replication versus partitioning, internal and external validity of study designs, and standardization of research setting versus generality of results. All these matters will be brought together in the final section of this chapter.

6-2. The Concept of Reliability

When we measure the length of a series of objects with some standard device for measuring length such as a yardstick or tape measure, we usually work on the premise that the resulting set of recorded values show "true" values of the length of the measured objects. Actually, even an obvious measure such as length is subject to several kinds of error.

1. We might have used the instrument irregularly, marking beginning and end points carelessly. Presumably, such error would be distributed randomly—increasing the recorded values of some objects, decreasing others. If we were then to repeat the measurement with the same instrument and same

[2] There is a large literature on validity and on reliability, and we will not deal with those concepts in depth here. Also, there is a relatively new view of these matters, exemplified in the work of Cronbach (see Cronbach, Gleser, and Rajaratnam 1963; Gleser, Cronbach, and Rajaratnam, 1965), which focuses on the concept of *generalizability* and subsumes most of the concepts in the reliability and validity areas within that concept. We find the Cronbach generalizability theory a powerful approach to these issues, one that is much more helpful in tying this area to other aspects of research design than the more traditional approaches to validity and reliability. We treat generalizability in section 6-4. But first, in sections 6-2 and 6-3, we examine the more traditional concepts.

procedures, we should expect such random imperfections to cancel out, more or less. In any case, we could ask, "To what extent do we get *different* values for a given object when we measure these objects twice, independently, with the same measuring procedures?" This is one kind of meaning of reliability—the *repeatability* of a measured value.

2. We might also have used an instrument that changed over time; for example, the tape measure might stretch with wear. This is an instance of *instrument decay,* discussed in Chapter 3. This could lead to systematic errors of measurement rather than random errors. That is, all *later* measures would be underestimates of "true" length. To detect this, we should have to measure the objects again with an alternative measuring instrument—a ruler, or a different tape measure.

3. We might also have done our measuring with an instrument having a systematic and constant error (for example, a yardstick with an end worn away) or with a constant error in our application procedure (for example, we might have sighted from one side rather than from straight above). To find out about these errors would require new measurements, this time with a different instrument or a different observer, as the case might be.

The seriousness of error depends on our purposes—on what we are going to do with the observations. For one thing, the seriousness depends on the accuracy with which we wish to make the measurements. If the random or systematic errors in measurement are of the order of a millimeter, but we are recording measurements to the nearest centimeter, then they will make very little difference. Furthermore, the seriousness of measurement error depends on the size of error relative to the *critical differences* among the set of objects being measured. If the errors are of the order of a centimeter, and the objects being measured differ from each other by several meters, then even if we are recording to the nearest centimeter, measurement error will not affect the *relative* lengths of the set of objects our measurements specify—although, of course, they will still reflect small errors of absolute length. If one city lies five miles from a certain point and another lies five miles one foot from that point, we may wish to treat the cities as being at the same distance, even if we can measure their distances accurately enough to differentiate them.

Thus, the import of error of measurement depends on the interrelation of three components:

1. The size of the errors
2. The size of the smallest unit to which we want our measurements to be "exact"
3. The smallest difference we want to be able to differentiate among the set of objects being measured.

Whatever the source of error, the general method for detecting errors of measurement is to measure the same objects a second time, independently—changing either the instrument, type of instrument, observer, observation procedures, or time of measurement (later, for example).

Ideally, to find out the reliability of a *measure,* we would like to measure the *same* objects a second time, with the same measure (treating the instrument and observer as a unit now), independently. But for reasons pointed out in Chapter 3, it is not possible to have an exact replication of an observation. At least the time of observation (hence any changes occurring in time) will have changed; the instrument itself, its user, the procedures of using it, or all of these will also have changed. Besides, if we suspect a *systematic* error (like the worn yardstick or the observer sighting off center), we would want deliberately to change that suspected aspect of the measuring procedure, because we want our results to be more general than one particular man with one particular ruler on one particular occasion.

This latter point introduces another basic dilemma in empirical research, one that applies to manipulation of a property as well as to measurement of it. The dilemma is that we want both *reliability* in the sense of repeatability, which is to be obtained by precise *standardization* of all aspects of the measurement process, and *generalizability* in the sense of applicability over a range of conditions, which is to be obtained by *variation* among cases treated alike on properties other than the one we are trying to measure or manipulate.

Let us elaborate the point about generality. It would do us very little good to have a measure of a behavioral property, however repeatable, if the obtained measurements changed for each user or for Tuesday versus Wednesday or when changing from a 7-point to a 5-point scale for recording observations. At best, differences measured with such a scale would have to be treated as differences due to an interaction of the object-property with the nature of the measuring tool, complicating greatly the interpretation of results. At worst, such varying outcomes of a measurement would indicate that the obtained effects were largely due to the measurement operations themselves rather than to the phenomena we were hoping to study.

Because it is not possible to obtain observations that are replications of one another in every way, operations to check the reliability of a measure usually take one of three forms:

1. *Test-retest reliability,* in which the same measure is applied a second time to the same set of objects under conditions as similar as the investigator can make them
2. *Alternate-forms reliability,* in which the same objects are measured by each of two instruments designed to be as similar as possible
3. *Split-half reliability* (as on a test or questionnaire or on a measure involving multiple trials), in which the investigator takes results obtained from one half of his items and checks them against the results from the other half of the items applied to the same objects.

A test-retest reliability procedure poses two problems for the investigator.

First, if the measure is reactive, its initial application may affect the subsequent measure of the same object. This problem was discussed in Chapter 3 as the confounding effects of testing. Second, if there is a change in the phenomenon between the first and second measure (whether due to testing, instrument decay, history, maturation, or some shift in conditions), the investigator has no way to distinguish between change and unreliability. (See "Change and Uncertainty of Response" in section 13-3 for further discussion of this problem.) Consequently, if the investigator obtains an indication of high reliability of his measure by a test-retest procedure, all is well and good; but if he does not, he may be unable to tell the reason.

The alternate-forms procedure for assessing reliability of a measure also presents some difficulties. If one form is modeled after the other, both may show high repeatability, but each may contain the same systematic error. Let us return to the example of measuring length. If we were to use a yardstick with a part of the end broken off and then build a second yardstick to match the first, measures made with the two instruments presumably would show high agreement (reliability), but both sets of measurements would be systematically wrong. For a test or personality inventory, we could encounter the same problem. As another example, we might train two observers to use identical observation techniques and their results would presumably show high repeatability, but both might include systematic errors.

Furthermore, it may often be difficult to develop an alternate but substantially equivalent form of a test or measure, and it may be even more difficult to be sure that we have succeeded in doing so. If alternate forms of a measure show poor reliability, the investigator has no way of telling whether the measure has intrinsically low reliability or whether the particular alternate form has failed, after all, to be equivalent.

The split-half technique is a logical extension of the alternate-forms technique, but can be applied only with measures containing multiple items (as on a test) or multiple trials. Here, the investigator considers his single test as containing two or more equivalent subsets of items and asks the repeatability question by correlating results for two subsets of items. To do this, he usually divides his items in some way such as odd-numbered items versus even-numbered items or half the items drawn at random versus the other half. He would not, ordinarily, take the first half versus the second half, because many respondents might not have time to complete later items or might approach them differently after having answered the first half.

The split-half procedure avoids the problem of finding additional equivalent measures and partially removes the problem of systematic shifts between forms by using randomization. Here, results showing low reliability are fairly unequivocal; they simply mean that all of the items in the test do *not* represent close replications one of another.

The split-half technique (as well as to some extent the alternate-forms technique) involves the assumption that each item of a test (or each trial) is essentially a replication of every other item in the test. This assumption leads to an additional technique for determining the reliability of a test or measure: internal consistency. In the internal-consistency procedure, answers to each item are compared with the answers to each other item. (See also section 11-7.) Each item is taken as an alternate form, so to speak. Some over-all index (average interitem correlation, for example) may be used as an estimate of reliability. Examining sets of relations of a given item to each of the others can also indicate which items are *not* closely correlated with the others; these items can be dropped from the test to increase its reliability. (See also the discussion of constructing unidimensional scales in Chapter 11.)

Note that the meaning of reliability has now shifted from agreement of the *same* measure applied twice (or repeatability) to agreement among different items (which implies homogeneity of content and unidimensionality of the measure). If a test is measuring a multidimensional concept such as mathematical ability, some items may reflect one aspect more than another, such as computational skill more than understanding of mathematical concepts. In such an instance, the set of items is likely to show low internal consistency even if each item would have shown high repeatability under test-retest procedures.

The notion of internal consistency among items as a type of reliability is related to three additional topics. One is unidimensionality, which is treated in Chapter 11. The second is validity; procedures based on internal consistency are sometimes conceptualized as tests of validity rather than reliability.[3] Various concepts of validity are discussed later in this chapter. The third topic is stability. The concepts of repeatability and homogeneity suggest a third way of conceptualizing reliability; namely, the stability of a measure over time. Let us turn to a few further ideas concerning stability.

STABILITY

When we measure the length or weight of an object, we often wish to assume that there is an existentially "true" value of length or weight for that object, and that the object retains the same value on that property over time unless some specific condition changes. We often wish to make the same kind of assumption about properties like intelligence, a personality trait, relations of authority in a group, work roles in an organization, and so on. It is true that most researchers would be less apt to make the assumption of sameness over time for processes such as rate of interaction, blood pressure, or reaction time. Nevertheless, the researcher will inevitably wish to generalize his results

[3]We have found that some readers object to our treatment of internal consistency under reliability, insisting that it has to do with validity. Other readers have objected to our treatment of internal consistency under validity (see "Validity as Internal Consistency" in section 6-3), insisting that it has to do with reliability. Our purpose here is to show that the concepts of reliability and validity are closely related, and internal consistency is one of the bridges between them. Internal consistency among items is a limiting case of convergent validity and also a limiting case of alternate-forms (or split-half) reliability. See Figure 6-2. For approaches that subsume and relate these concepts, see "The Multitrait-Multimethod Paradigm" and "Reliability as Generalizability" in section 6-4.

beyond the specific occasion. To do so, he must have some basis for estimating how stable the *behavior* is over time—how much it shows either systematic or random shifts from one occasion to another.

When observations are made for unreplicated samples of behavior, temporally spaced, the investigator has no way to distinguish to what extent each of four factors contributed to any differences between samples:

1. Systematic differences between samples due to *biases in the measurement operations* such as instrument decay or testing
2. Random differences due to *random errors in the measurement operations*
3. Systematic differences from one temporal occasion to another due to *behavioral changes* such as those due to history or maturation
4. Random differences from one temporal occasion to another due to *behavioral instability.*

In dealing with factor (1), an investigator attempts to detect (but not in this way to eliminate) systematic biases in measurement by changing the aspect of the measurement procedure he suspects of introducing the bias (such as the damaged yardstick or the lazy observer). He attempts to eliminate (but not detect) systematic bias in measurement by randomizing the assignment of the measuring devices (for example, by randomly splitting test items into subsets or by randomly assigning observers to cases). Using these devices requires the researcher to assume that the property remains relatively stable while he applies his various measurements procedures. In the case of factor (2), the researcher attempts to eliminate random errors of measurement by increasing the standardization of his measurement operations (though thereby decreasing the generality of his results). He attempts to eliminate the *effects* of random errors of measurement by increasing the number of replicated observations of the same behavior so that he can "average out" the random errors to obtain a resulting estimate approaching the "true" value of the property. In using the latter technique, the researcher treats as alike observations differing in temporal occasion, instrument, observer, and so forth, assuming that such differences as do occur will be small and unbiased. Furthermore, as in factor (1), the researcher must assume that the underlying property remains relatively stable if he is to cope with random errors and their effects.

In dealing with factors (3) and (4), the investigator can only estimate systematic behavior change or random behavior fluctuation if he assumes that his measurement operations are free from error and not reactive upon the behavior. The problem of distinguishing (3) from (4) within data is discussed in section 13-3.

OTHER RELATED CONCEPTS

There are several more ideas closely related to the concept of reliability. One is *consistency,* as used in Chapter 11; this has to do with the repeatability of an order relation between two points or two distances. For example, if one is asked his preferences between two candidates on each of five occasions, one's behavior or the measure of it is consistent if he prefers candidate A to B on all occasions. Another related notion, also to be dealt with in Chapter 11, is *transitivity*. Transitivity refers to the logical noncircularity of the order relation on three or more points (or distances). For example, if one prefers candidate A to B and B to C, but also prefers C to A, then one's preferences for the three objects are *not* transitive. These concepts are different from the notions of reliability discussed here, because they deal with the repeatability or predictability of an order relation between two points rather than with the ascertaining or estimating of an absolute value. This is somewhat related to the distinction between reliability as applied to an estimate of a value of a property (its stability or repeatability) and reliability as applied to a measurement procedure, which has already been discussed.

There is also the notion of the reliability of estimating a *relation* between two or more properties. One aspect of this has to do with the stabilty of the behavior and the reliability of the measures of the related properties. Another aspect has to do with the stability or change of the relation itself between the two properties in respect to the conditions under which the properties are measured. This is similar to *internal validity,* discussed in Chapter 3. Hand in hand with the latter question is the question of whether the relation would be repeatable among other samples of observations; that is, the question of the range over which the relation might generalize—and this characteristic is related to the notion of *external validity,* discussed in Chapter 3.

Finally, the idea that some underlying property can be measured with the same results by a number of different procedures is similar to the concept of *concurrent* or *convergent* validity, to be discussed in a later section.

It should be clear from the many forward references within this discussion that the concept of reliability touches in many ways upon the concept of validity. We turn now to a discussion of validity.

6-3. The Concept of Validity

The question of the validity of a measure has to do with whether that measure (an operational definition of a property) does indeed measure the conceptually defined property it is intended to measure.

If each concept had only one operational definition, then the question of validity would never arise. That operational definition could be taken as the one necessary and sufficient manifestation of the concept. It is precisely because we often wish our concepts to have meaning more general than any specific operation, and because we want to permit alternative operational definitions of any given concept, that the validity of a given operational definition becomes a problem. For example, *length* has a more general meaning than just the markings and procedures for application of a yardstick. Tape measures, calipers, odometers, and other variants of the yardstick can measure length.

Certain operations with a transit or range finder, which are not just a variant of the yardstick, are also operational definitions of length. The concept *length* is all of these things.

The question then arises: which is the "true" measure of length? For length, the answer is clear; the *all* are. But what if we were to invent a new set of operations and claim that they measure length? How would one decide the validity of our measure? Again, the answer is obvious in the case of a well-established concept like length. Before we could reasonably claim that our new operational procedures measure length, we would have to demonstrate that measuring the length of a set of objects with our procedures yields substantially the same results as measuring these objects with the standard procedures. Indeed, it is such a concordance of results that makes us willing to accept the traditional yardstick, tape measure, and transit as equally valid alternative instruments for measuring length. This rationale is sometimes referred to as *concurrent validity*.

But what about a concept for which there is not an already established operational definition? We could not determine the validity of an operation for such a new concept by checking it against another set of operations known to be valid, since the standard procedure would not yet exist. What we must do, in such a case, is to establish the concordance of several alternative operational definitions designed to be measures of the same concept. Before discussing this notion of concordance or concurrent validity further, however, let us consider some of the other traditional approaches that have been used in behavioral science to ascertain the validity of a measure.

VALIDITY AS PREDICTION

One of the traditional views about validity is that measure *a* is a measure of concept *A* if it *predicts* (that is, correlates with) another property *B* that logically or theoretically should be associated with property *A*. For example, this view would consider a particular test (*a*) a good measure of intelligence (*A*) if the test were to predict differences in academic achievement (*B*) which the researcher had taken theoretically to be the consequences of differences in intelligence.

There are several weaknesses in this conception of validity. First, its manifestation depends on the validity, in turn, of the operational definition of the behavioral property *B* to be predicted (in the example, the operational definition of academic achievement *B* might be school grades *b*). The inferred validity from *a* to *A* can be no better than the validity from *b* to *B*. Second, predictive validity is confounded with a test of the validity of the *theoretical* relation between *A* and *B* (for example, between intelligence and academic achievement). Third, even if *A* and *B* are equivalent and the mapping from *b* to *B* is valid, establishing the validity of the link between *a* and *A* through the link from *a* to *b* depends on the absence of *other factors* influencing *B* and therefore influencing *b*. In the example, to the extent that factors other than

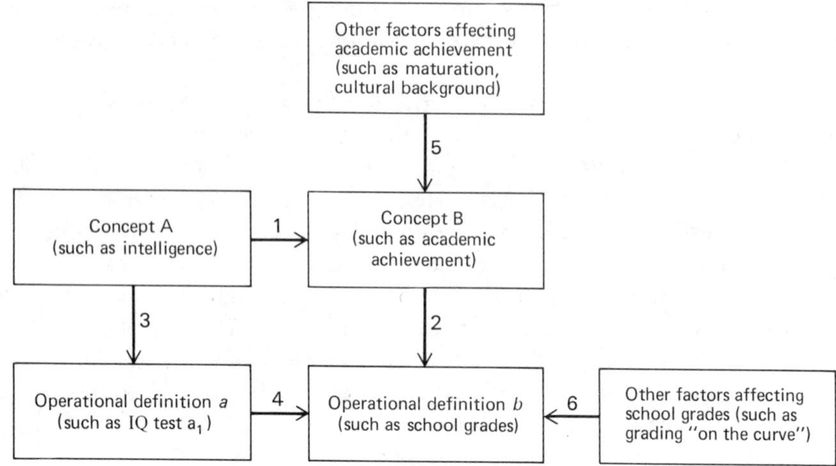

Figure 6-1. The rationale for predictive validity.

intelligence *A* also affect academic achievement *B*, and hence school grades *b*, to this extent their effects will tend to obscure the relation between the intelligence test *a* and school grades *b*. The other factors influencing *B*, in short, will reduce the *apparent* validity of the test as a measure of intelligence. The bearing of these three problems on assessing validity is diagramed in Figure 6-1.

The technique of predictive validity is an attempt to confirm link 3 by assessing link 4. It is affected by link 2 (validity of the operational definition *b* of the criterion behavior *B*), by link 1 (validity of the theoretical relation of intelligence *A* to academic achievement *B*), and by links 5 and 6 (effects of other factors on academic achievement *B* and on grades *b*).

Actually, this same paradigm is the usual one for trying to test the validity of a hypothesized theoretical relation between two conceptual properties. In that use, the investigator attempts to confirm link 1 by assessing link 4. Here, he *assumes* the validity of links 2 and 3. He also assumes the absence of effects of other factors (links 5 and 6) or does something to reckon with them, a matter we discussed in Chapter 3.

This discussion points up, once again, one of our recurrent themes. The investigator gains information about some things only by assuming he already knows some other things. He gains information about the *a*-to-*A* link by assuming that the *A*-to-*B* and *b*-to-*B* links are strong. Or he gains information about the *A*-to-*B* link by assuming that the *a*-to-*A* and *b*-to-*B* links are strong. In the same vein, we noted in the previous section that the investigator can learn about reliability of measures only by assuming stability of the measured properties; or he can learn about behavior change or instability only by assuming reliability of his measure. But he cannot learn about everything at once; he cannot learn anything without making some assumptions about some other things. And, of course, the information he gains is true only to the extent that his assumptions are true.

Returning to the problem of predictive validity, we repeat that its rationale assumes the validity of link 1, *A* to *B*, and link 3, *b* to *B*, and the inconsequentiality of other factors, links 5 and 6. Furthermore, it assumes in effect that *b* (school grades) is a better mapping of *A* (intelligence) than is *a* (an intelligence test). We say this because if the *a*-to-*b* empirical relation is low, the rationale for predictive validity rejects *a* as a measure of *A* because it does not predict *b*, which presumably mirrors *B*, which reflects *A*. Thus, to *use* the predictive-validity rationale requires already having a valid operational definition of the concept *A* in question; namely, the operation *b* used to assess the criterion concept *B*. Note that it would be just as logical to reject *b* as a measure of *B* (assuming *A*-to-*B* and *a*-to-*A* strong) on the grounds that *b* fails to be predicted by a valid measure *a* of a concept *A* which predicts the concept *B* that *b* is supposed to measure.

Thus, the predictive validity concept can be taken to be a special form of the idea of validity as concurrence or concordance of operational definitions. Before pursuing that idea further, let us explore a somewhat different notion of validity.

VALIDITY AS INTERNAL CONSISTENCY

Another way of assessing the validity of a measure is to ask whether the different parts, pieces, trials, or items of our measure give the same results. If they do, then at least we know that, whatever we are measuring, all parts of our instrument are measuring the same thing (or highly correlated things). If they do not, then we know that we are either measuring more than one thing or that the thing we are measuring has multiple dimensions. The internal consistency rationale is a direct extension of the notion that validity can be assessed in terms of the concordance of results of *different* operations used to measure the same thing. It simply takes each item (or trial) to be an alternative operational definition of the concept in question and asks about the degree to which they result in concordant measurements.

This rationale is, of course, identical to the internal-consistency technique discussed in an earlier section as a method for assessing *reliability* of a measure. There, the set of interitem correlations was taken to be an indication of reliability in the sense of internal consistency. This was seen to be a logical extension of the basic notion of reliability as repeatability, assessed by correlation between two different forms (or halves, or applications) of the *same measure*. Here, we are talking about internal consistency as a method for assessing the validity (in the sense of homogeneity or unidimensionality) of a measure. And here internal consistency is being viewed as a logical extension of the basic notion of validity as concordance or convergence of different measures of the "same thing." We can now see a direct connection between the reliability and validity concepts. That connection is shown in Figure 6-2, and the implications of this connection will be the central theme of the first two subsections of section 6-4.

TRADITIONAL LABEL	TECHNIQUES	UNDERLYING CONCEPT
Reliability	Concordance of *same* (repeated) measures of same thing at same time, independently	Repeatability
Reliability	Test-retest Alternate-forms Split-half	
Reliability / Validity	Interitem consistency	Homogeneity
Validity	Construct validity Predictive validity Concurrent validity Convergent and discriminant validity	
Validity	Concordance of *different* measures of same thing at same time, independently	Convergence

Figure 6-2. Relations between reliability and validity.

VALIDITY AS FIT IN A NETWORK OF RELATED CONCEPTS

Another conception of the validity of a measure is the degree to which it ties into a network of related concepts. If concept A (and a measure of it a_1) is known to be related to concept B (and its measure b) and also to concept C (and measure c), then we can assess the validity of another operational definition of A, namely a_2, by assessing its relations with b and c as well as with a_1. This rationale is sometimes referred to as the *construct validity* of a measure.

Obviously, this rationale is an extension of the notion of predictive validity. It requires the prior establishment of a network of relations among a set of operational measures which are presumed to be valid measures of certain related conceptual properties. It then says, in effect, that an operational measure is a valid measure of a construct (or concept) if it relates in the way that concept "should" to measures of other related concepts. This is similar to the predictive-validity rationale, but does not make the assumption of the single-criterion concept (and its associated measure) taken to be valid by definition. Construct validity depends upon a more elaborate set of relations than a single relation between one predictor and one criterion.

The construct-validity rationale is also related to the convergence or concordance notion of validity. The greater the extent that two measures correlate with each other, the more likely it is that they will correlate in the same way with other concepts. The *convergent* and discriminant-validity rationale (Campbell and Fiske, 1959), which will be treated in section 6-4 in the discussion of the multitrait-multimethod paradigm, is a combination of the construct-validity and concordance notions along with the additional notion of trait discriminability.

6-4. Validity, Reliability, and Generalizability

We have already suggested that validity and reliability are closely related concepts. Here we shall attempt to make that relation more explicit and to move the concepts of reliability and validity into a broader context. We shall do this by drawing on two excellent discussions of these questions. The first, by Campbell and Fiske (1959; see also Humphreys, 1960), presents the concepts of convergent and discriminant validity and relates them to each other and to the concept of reliability in a systematic framework called the *multitrait-multimethod matrix*. The second, by Cronbach, Rajaratnam, and Gleser (1963), provides a theoretical and mathematical rationale for relating validity and reliability to each other as special cases of the broader concept of *generalizability*.

THE MULTITRAIT-MULTIMETHOD PARADIGM

Variations among a set of observed values obtained from the use of any operational measure on any set of objects can be viewed as having at least three components:

1. Variation[4] mirroring differences in the property the operation is meant to measure
2. Variations added to the obtained measure by the biases of the operations employed
3. Variations due to random error of measurement, at least from the investigator's point of view.

If we measure a set of objects once, we have no way of separating these components. Hence, we do not have any indication of the validity (component 1) or the reliability (component 3). If we measure the set of objects twice, with the same or "equivalent" measures, we can separate out the third component (by getting an estimate of reliability), but we still have no way of separating the first, in which we usually are most interested, from the second, which is the effect of the method of measurement.

Consider, now, that we wish to apply a given method of measurement (say a questionnaire) to measure each of several *different* properties or traits (say several personality traits). Suppose that the method of measurement is such that respondents tend to adopt a certain response set when responding

[4]Books on statistics, experimental psychology, and works of similar technical precision would use the term *variance* here.

to it; for example, some respond positively to all items or some use extreme response while others use moderate ones for all items. If we then correlated the scores on the three traits, they would correlate very highly. We might interpret this as indicating a "true" relation between the traits (between the conceptual properties, that is, of which our measures are the operational definitions). Or we might interpret this result as indicating that the three measures are alternative definitions of the same trait and show convergence (hence concurrent validity) or repeatability (hence reliability) of the trait. The latter interpretations would have to assume that the three sets of scores were obtained independently, which of course they were not, since our hypothetical example deliberately put the cause of their correlation in the questionnaire common to their measurement. In fact, it may well be that a measure of *any* property obtained within such a questionnaire would correlate with *any other* property measured within the same or similar form of questionnaire. And if it were found by other operational procedures (for example, by observations or by projective techniques) that certain of these properties are independent (that is, do not correlate with one another when using the new measures), we would have to conclude that the correlation obtained among the questionnaire measures of them was an artifact of the questionnaire method. Campbell and Fiske (1959) put these two sets of considerations together and proposed a generalized paradigm for establishing the validity and reliability of a set of measures of traits. This is the multitrait-multimethod matrix.

Suppose there are several traits we wish to measure. Suppose, further, that for each trait we wish to measure, we have available a number of different types of measures. As a concrete example, let us consider three personality traits: (1) introversion, (2) neuroticism, and (3) dominance. And let us assume we have a potential measure of each of these in three forms: (a) questionnaire, (b) peer rating, and (c) direct observation of behavior in some group setting. Let us assume that we use each of these three methods to measure each of the three traits for a number of actors or respondents and that we then compute correlation coefficients[5] within every pair of these nine types of measurements—three methods for each of three traits. We can then array the correlation coefficients in a matrix, as in Figure 6-3.

The cells along the main northwest-to-southeast diagonal of the matrix (marked R in Figure 6-3.) are correlations between a given measure of a given trait and the same measure of the same trait (the two measurements presumably done independently). The R symbol indicates reliability, in the sense of repeatability. Cells below and to the left of the R diagonal are blank, since the matrix is symmetrical and entries below the diagonal could only repeat their symmetrical entries above the diagonal.

Within the small blocks involving two different methods (method *a* with *b*, *a* with *c*, and *b* with *c*), entries in the diagonals of the small blocks are labeled

[5] A correlation coefficient is an index of the degree of linear relation between two measures; see "Some Facets of Relations" in section 13-2.

		METHOD *a*			METHOD *b*			METHOD *c*		
		TRAITS			TRAITS			TRAITS		
		T_1	T_2	T_3	T_1	T_2	T_3	T_1	T_2	T_3
Method *a*	T_1	R	M	M	C	H	H	C	H	H
	T_2		R	M	H	C	H	H	C	H
	T_3			R	H	H	C	H	H	C
Method *b*	T_1				R	M	M	C	H	H
	T_2					R	M	H	C	H
	T_3						R	H	H	C
Method *c*	T_1							R	M	M
	T_2								R	M
	T_3									R

Key
R Reliability, repeatability (same method, same trait)
M Method variance (same method, different traits)
C Trait convergence (same trait, different methods)
H Hetero-trait hetero-method correlations

Figure 6-3. The Multitrait-Multimethod Matrix (adapted from Campbell & Fiske, 1959).

C to indicate what Campbell and Fiske call *convergent validity.* These are the correlations between two *different methods of* measuring the same trait. They reflect the degree of concordance between two operational definitions of one trait.[6]

In the small blocks involving only one method (method *a* with *a*, *b* with *b*, and *c* with *c*), the off-diagonal entries are labeled M, referring to *method variance.* These correlations indicate the extent to which there is concordance when the same method is used to measure *two different* traits.

The off-diagonal entries in the two-method small blocks are labeled H and show hetero-trait and hetero-method correlations; that is, a measure of one trait correlated with a different measure of another trait.

Campbell and Fiske insist that establishing convergent validity is not an adequate assessment of validity of a trait or of its measures. They urge us to interpret the entire pattern of correlations in this matrix—the relative sizes of different sorts of correlations, R, C, M, and H. First, the R correlations—same method, same trait—set the upper limit for the matrix. (A measure of a trait must correlate at least as highly with itself as it does with any other measure.) Given high R correlations, the size of the C correlations (different methods, same trait) indicate the degree of *convergence.* But the M correlations (same method, different traits) indicate the extent to which correlations among measures in the matrix are artifacts of a particular measuring instrument. The

[6]For cogent discussions of the sometimes powerful differences between measurement operations, see Willems and Willems (1965) and Bauer (1967), among others.

differences between the C correlations and the M correlations are indications of the *divergent validity* of traits; that is, the extent to which methods differentiate between *different traits,* as well as converge when measuring the same trait. Looking still further in the table, we find the correlations labeled H. If the traits are independent and the methods are independent, then the set of correlations labeled H should all be approximately zero, since they have neither a trait nor a method in common. The sizes of these H correlations relative to C also reflect divergent validity.

If the M correlations are large, rising to a substantial fraction of the C correlations, then even though the alternative operational definitions of a trait may seem to show high concordance (in high C correlations), this concordance may not be accepted as evidence of validity for that trait, because the methods give largely the same result (high M correlations) no matter to which of the supposedly different traits they are applied. We can consider that traits are distinct and have concurrent validity not attributable to the artifacts of any particular method of measurement only when two conditions are satisfied simultaneously: (1) independent methods converge (high C correlations) for each trait, and (2) each of the methods distinguishes between different traits (that is, each shows relatively low M correlations).

The multitrait-multimethod matrix is a general and very powerful frame of reference for viewing the questions of reliability and validity. It makes clear the fact that the investigator will unavoidably decide what kinds of correspondences are to be called reliability or error of measurement and what kinds are to be called validity or the lack of it, by what he chooses to define as same and as different. It is perfectly reasonable, for example, to reverse the labeling in the previous example and take the questionnaire, peer ratings, and observations as "traits." We could say we had actors displaying three characteristics: communication through (1) questionnaires, (2) rating their peers, and (3) behaving in the presence of observers. Similarly, the three erstwhile personality characteristics could be considered as three settings or opportunities for *displaying* each trait; we could thus consider introversion, neuroticism, and dominance as methods or modes through which to exhibit the three behaviors of answering questionnaires, rating peers, and performing for observers. Using the labeling in this fashion, we would apply the same logic, but the matrix would be arranged differently, so that we would interpret specific correlations differently. For example, we would now interpret high correlations among the three personality scales (on the self-report questionnaire, for example) as evidence of *convergence* (C correlations) of multiple measures of a "self-report trait." Perhaps we would want to interpret this as "response set," perhaps as a measure of "self-esteem," or perhaps as evidence of deliberate distortion. We might interpret high correlations between self- and peer ratings on neuroticism as "method variance"—an unfortunate artifact of the particular personality scales we happened to use, but of methodological rather than substantive interest for our purpose.

It should also be apparent that if we were to measure three different personality characteristics of a sample of respondents on each of three occasions, we could treat the occasions as "methods" in the multitrait-multimethod matrix if we were interested in establishing the stability of the traits; we could equally well treat the occasions as "traits" if we were interested in establishing the distinctness of each of the occasions as different situations or behavior settings.

Note that in all of these examples the multitrait-multimethod matrix is applied to correlations between pairs of measures over a set of actors. In all but the last example, the set of observations is for a single occasion. There is no logical reason why the multitrait-multimethod matrix cannot be applied to two or more measures of two or more persons (considering the persons as "traits") for each of a *series* of occasions. For example, suppose we obtained several types of scores (such as number of errors or time to complete) for each of a series of trials on a learning task for persons 1, 2, and 3. Treating the types of scores as alternative measures of learning and the three persons as traits, we could ask whether these measures agree (have high C correlations) for each person (now "trait") over trials, and whether persons 1, 2, and 3 have discriminably different learning styles over time. We would conclude that the persons did, indeed, have different learning styles if the C correlations were high, the M correlations low, and the H correlations very low.

The reader may enjoy inventing a few more examples in which the Campbell and Fiske paradigm is applied to correlations taken over occasions or behaviors rather than over actors.

Thus, the logic of the Campbell and Fiske paradigm is quite general. It can be applied to any two facets (actor, behavior, or context properties) with correlations over the third, and with trait, method, and correlate being interchangeable. In its present development, it is designed to be used with two facets (traits and methods) at a time, correlating over a third (actors), but it can be used in three or more facet applications. The multitrait-multimethod paradigm also requires that each method be applied to each trait for each respondent (a condition which the Cronbach, Rajaratnam, and Gleser model, to be discussed next, calls *matched data*). This is often difficult to apply in practice, because not all traits are readily amenable to measurement by all methods.

Whereas Campbell and Fiske focus on validity of traits, Cronbach, Rajaratnam, and Gleser (1963) take issue with the traditional techniques for estimating *reliability*. We turn next to a consideration of their rationale.

RELIABILITY AS GENERALIZABILITY

Cronbach, Rajaratnam, and Gleser (1963), after reviewing developments in reliability theory and measurement, propose a revision in the traditional concept of reliability as well as in the techniques for estimating reliability. They prefer the notion of *generalizability*. They say that the whole purpose of reliability theory has been to answer the question, How well can we generalize from this observation (or this set of observations) to a universe of observations like it? The key question then becomes, To *what* universe of potential observations do we wish to generalize?

The idea of alternate-forms reliability—with forms having highly similar content and identical question format, time limits, instructions, and so on—suggests that the universe of potential tests to which this test is to be generalized is a very narrow area indeed. Reliability estimates from a set of observations are generalizable only within the universe of conditions (that is, test forms, content, testing conditions, occasions, actors, and so on) from which the conditions actually observed have been sampled.

The mathematical formulation of the generalizability index of Cronbach, Rajaratnam, and Gleser is too complex to present even in brief summary here. (For more detail, see the cited article, which gives not only the rationale and formulation but also a good summary of the history of reliability theory and measurement in the behavioral sciences, especially in the field of mental testing. See also Gleser, Cronbach, and Rajaratnam, 1965, for some powerful extensions of generalizability theory.) The purpose of presenting the views of Cronbach, Rajaratnam, and Gleser here is to profit from their point that what we really want to know about a set of observations is to what extent (and with respect to what properties) they are *like* other sets of observations we might have taken from a given universe of potential observations; and to what extent (and with respect to what properties) they *differ* from other observations we might have taken from that (or some other) universe of potential observations. When we ask this question in the limited sense of the likeness of the observations to another, near-identical set of observations with the same forms and conditions of measurement and the same population of respondents, we find ourselves within the bounds of the traditional reliability or repeatability concepts. But if we ask the likeness question with respect to a set of observations drawn from a universe considered as some kind of "criterion" set of potential observations, we are inclined to treat the results in the vein of traditional *validity* concepts. Finally, if we ask the likeness and difference questions with respect to a universe of potential observations broadly and heterogeneously defined (with respect to measurement forms, conditions, occasions), we are asking about the limits of generalizability of the results of our set of observations. Whether we consider a particular relation among observations to be evidence of reliability, validity, or generalizability depends on how we choose to define sameness and difference of conditions, occasions, and measures. (This point should help to connect the present discussion with the earlier one on replication and partitioning in Chapter 3. It should also help to show the logical parallels between the generalizability model and the multitrait-multimethod paradigm discussed in the previous section.) And our construction of what is same and what is different in our sets of observations depends, in turn, upon the questions that we wish to answer in our study and upon the theoretical construction that we bring with us to the investigation of the phenomena under study.

VALIDITY OF MEASURES AND VALIDITY OF DESIGNS

In Chapter 3, we introduced the concepts of internal and external validity in the context of evaluating study designs, and did so without considering the specific measures involved. In the present chapter, we have been discussing various forms of validity (and reliability) of *measures,* considered more or less independently of the study design in which they are embedded. These two sets of notions—validity of designs and validity of measures—are distinct but quite related concepts, and they are related through the concept of generalizability.

To ask about the validity and reliability of specific traits or measures of them is to ask about what trait we can presume to have measured (and how well we shall have measured it) when we use this measure in the future. When we move to the notion of generalizability of a measure (a set of observations), we are asking over how broad and diverse a population of conditions (test forms, occasions, and so on) we can expect the results abstracted from our observations to hold.

When we talk about internal validity of a design, we ask for what relation we can presume to have evidence and (by probabilistic interpretation of the statistical index of our obtained relation) how repeatable that relation is for the same variables, conditions, and actors. When we move to the notion of external validity of a design, we are asking over how broad and diverse a population of actors, conditions, and occasions we can expect the results extracted from our observations to hold.

The validity of study design concerns the soundness of interpretation of relations *between* sets of observations. The validity of measures, in principle, concerns the soundness of interpretation of a *single* set of observations. In practice, however, all of the traditional methods of assessing the reliability and validity of measures involve relations *between* sets of observations—sets considered either alike or different. Any of the potential systematic sources of unreliability or lack of validity suggested earlier in this chapter can be reconstrued as one or another of the confounding factors in study design discussed in Chapter 3. For example, unreliability due to methods of measurement can be viewed as a form of testing effect; unreliability of observers can be seen as instrument decay; unreliability from test to retest can be due to history or maturation effects. If we consider that any attempt to estimate reliability or validity of measures will be carried out within some study design as discussed in Chapter 3, then the internal validity of that study design limits the meanings of reliability and validity in the narrow sense; and the external validity of that study design limits the generalizability of the results of the set of observations in the broader sense.

6-5. Standardization versus Generalizability

Our discussions of internal and external validity of study design (Chapter 3), of treatments of variables designed to control unwanted variation by removing it (mode *K*, Chapter 3), and of the reliability and validity of measures (this chapter) all hint at one of the fundamental dilemmas of empirical research. Within a fixed number of observations, *everything we do to increase precision* (that is, reduce variability within subset) *tends to decrease generalizability* (that is, narrows the number of subsets and hence the size of the sample from the universe), *and vice versa.* We may strive to choose partitions to make as alike as possible those cases we intend to treat as alike; this increases reliability in the narrow sense of repeatability by decreasing variations within subsets. At the same time, however, this reduces the variations in the conditions over which we are taking observations and therefore reduces generalizability. Thus, when we apply control techniques in a laboratory experiment to conditions we are *not* studying but which may be related to the phenomenon we are studying (mode *K*), we are at the same time narrowing the range of combinations of conditions over which our results will be generalizable.[7] Similarly, when we choose to sample (conditions, actors, occasions) from a broad and heterogeneous universe and then randomly assign cases to experimental conditions, we are not only retaining breadth of scope (generalizability) but at the same time increasing variation within subsets, and the latter is likely to obsecure relations we are trying to detect.

Stated in stark outline, this dilemma seems simple enough, even though frustrating. Yet it is not easy, when one is involved in the actual design of a study, to stay alert to the many ways in which this dilemma colors the choices in the particular setting. The problem is worth a few more words. Consider the case of a classic experimental manipulation with a two-category design partition providing the presence or absence of some experimental manipulation, where this partition is embedded in a "true" experimental design—type 5 or 6, say. Suppose that all of the major classes of potentially confounding factors have been reckoned with; that cases have been randomized; and that the measurement of the behaviors of concern is reliable and valid. Now consider mode X. It consists of a set of research activities: constructing a setting, selecting types of tasks or situations, giving instructions, and so forth. If we perform the experiment and find a difference between experimental and control conditions, we can logically attribute that difference only to the whole package of operations that make up mode X and *not* to any one of them alone. This must

---

[7] Gleser, Cronbach, and Rajaratnam (1965) make a related point when they say: "Accuracy of generalization is a function of the sample-size on each facet. . ." (p. 416); and another when they say: "As the number of situations [categories on one facet] is increased, with fixed total length, the accuracy of generalization to each . . . [situation] . . . decreases, so that the investigator has to compromise between 'bandwidth' and 'fidelity'. . . ." (p. 417).

be so, however sophisticated our experimental design, for there are always unpartitioned and unrandomized factors left out of our design; the characteristics of real-world objects and settings are inexhaustible. Though we may have restricted or flattened the "small worlds" (for this concept, see Toda and Shuford, 1965) within mode *X*, or produced "well-mixed" partitions by randomizing certain factors, still the small worlds marked out within mode *X* remain very large worlds in terms of the number of their characteristics that conceivably can have made a difference. Inevitably, it is the whole of such small worlds or packages whose effects we observe and not just the features of them we may wish we could isolate.

Suppose, for example, that the time of day when the experimental condition is applied makes a difference, as it clearly does for many physiological indexes and probably for many psychological ones as well. To the extent that we administer the experiment for all cases at the same hour, we shall have done simultaneously several important things: (a) redefined mode *X* to include the restriction "when done at *h* hour of the day"; (b) removed, by using mode *K*, the systematic variation in the effect on the dependent observations (mode *Y*) that is associated with variations in time of day (unless time of day *interacts* with properties of the actor, in which case we shall only have obscured its effects). Thus, we increase the precision but reduce the generalizability of our results.

In some respects, these remarks recapitulate what we said about modes of treatment of variables in earlier chapters. Our purpose here, however, is not only to recapitulate those points but also to tie them to the idea of generalizability and to point up the clear dilemma inherent in trying simultaneously to maximize rigor and control on the one hand and generalizability on the other.[8]

There is no solution to this dilemma, but there are two general procedures to ameliorate its effects. The first is to increase the number of observations in a set, thereby averaging out the random errors *within* a subset while increasing the systematic differences *between* subsets—provided, of course, that the additional observations are sampled from the same universe of cases and assigned at random to experimental conditions. The larger the number of cases within a subset, the more we can afford to have random error among cases treated alike and still be able to detect systematic differences between subsets of cases treated as different.

The other general strategy by which we can circumvent the standardization-versus-generalizability dilemma is to run a series of related studies in which conditions controlled by mode *K* within one study are varied systematically by mode *X* or varied randomly by mode *R* in the next; in this way, we discover the limits of the combinations of conditions over which relations hold and how those relations change for conditions beyond those limits. This

---

[8]This dilemma is discussed from another perspective in Chapter 9.

requires a prior theoretical postulation of the nature of the phenomena being studied and of the conditions that might substantially alter these phenomena. Both these procedures are costly.

6-6. Further Reading

The central idea of convergent and divergent validity is presented in Campbell and Fiske (1959). The theory of generalizability is laid out in Cronbach, Rajaratnam, and Gleser (1963), and a general model for use of that theory is elaborated in Gleser, Cronbach, and Rajaratnam (1965). Each of these also contains helpful reviews of the history of reliability theory and measurement.

CHAPTER 7

Planning to Gather Evidence: Techniques for Observing and Recording Behavior

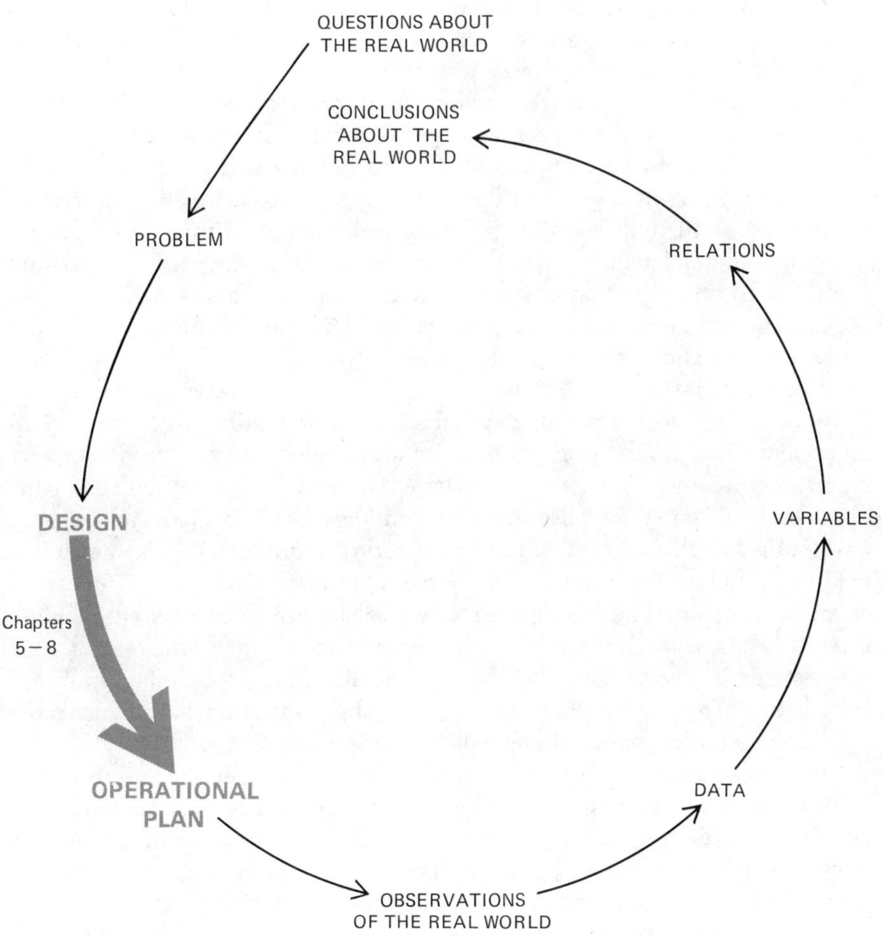

The process of generating data in an empirical science has several stages. A datum, as we shall use the term here, is an *interpretation* of a recorded observation of a behavior. *Behavior* is shorthand for "behavior of actor toward object in context." We shall give a more precise definition of data in Chapter 10. The important points here are (1) that behavior is not the same thing as data, and

(2) that a record of observed behavior is not data either until a meaning or interpretation has been imposed on it.

The data-generating process, of course, begins with *behavior*. Observing the behavior, the researcher can make a *recorded observation* which he can then or later convert into a datum suitable for analysis in combination with other data. By behavior we mean a real-world event involving overt or covert response by one or more actors (who are the referents of the study) to a task and situation,[1] self-generated or imposed. By a recorded observation we mean any symbolic record on paper, film, or any other medium specifying a category, amount, or quantity of one or more properties of an observed event; the record may be made by a human (researcher, agent, or actor) or by an instrument he employs. By converting recorded observations into data we mean imposing scoring rules and other assumptions that yield an interpretation of the meaning of the event in a sense we shall develop as we go along. But this anticipates Chapter 10; until then, we can get along well enough with the less precise meaning common language gives the term. Nevertheless, the point that a datum is always an interpretation of an observation will help us to make clear the uses of the different sources of observations (empirical evidence) to be described in this chapter.

Behavior is always done by an actor (that is, the referent of a study). By an actor, we mean any living system: individual, family, ship's crew, community, and so on. *Observing* and *recording* may be done by an actor (subjective report), by the investigator or an instrument he employs, or by someone who, in the past, generated the observation record for reasons unrelated to the study (archival records). Interpreting the observations to produce the form of information we call *data* is always done by the investigator or his agent. In earlier chapters, we sometimes mentioned *data-collection*. We must now speak more carefully and use the term *observation collection* instead. We use the term *observation* very generally to cover any method whatsoever of obtaining empirical information. The present chapter focuses on observing and recording. Making data from recorded observations will be the topic of Chapter 10.

Many ways of collecting observations (that is, of observing and recording behavior of actors in context) have been used in the behavioral sciences. Most authors have discussed these under historically honored headings such as questionnaires, tests, ratings, direct observation, biographical information, and content analysis. These techniques are the topic of the present chapter, but we shall try to present them systematically, within a framework that permits us to relate them to what has gone before (design and strategy, Chapters 3 and 4) and to what will come later (data construction and analysis, Chapters 10–13). Toward this end, we shall introduce two schema or frames of reference for classifying methods of observing and recording. One has to do with the *source* of the observation-record and the conditions under which it was gener-

[1] We use the term *task* in a very general sense to mean any impending sequence of acts guided by a goal. For further comments on task, see Runkel (1963).

ated. The other has to do with the *form* of the observation-record; that is, *how* the values or categories of one or more properties of the behavioral event are specified in the record. The first schema is important because a number of potential kinds of errors or distortions are more or less likely depending on the source of the evidence and the conditions under which the observations were generated. The second schema is important because the form of the record limits the kinds of data into which that record can be translated; hence it limits the kinds of analyses that can be performed and the kinds of conclusions that can be developed. These two schema—the sources and forms of observation-records—are the topics of the two main sections of this chapter.

7-1. Sources of Empirical Evidence

The classic situation for observing and recording is one in which an actor (individual, group, and so on) exhibits one or more of a set of alternative possible behaviors toward objects in a behavior setting or context. We can think of the behavior as occurring in response to a *performance task;* that is, a set of requirements, demands, or instructions implicit or explicit in the situation. The performance task may come from the situation or context. For example, John's boss may tell him to do some job. Or he may be faced by a stimulus situation such as quitting time that "demands" an action from him; John might perceive his choices to be to leave or to stay late. On the other hand, the performance task may be self-imposed by the actor. Or it may be deliberately imposed by the investigator: "Fill out this questionnaire," "Solve this problem," "Run 100 yards."

Empirical evidence starts when someone observes and records the one response among several alternative responses to a performance task that actually occurred. Some observation and record of the behavioral event are necessary before we can have empirical evidence about that behavior. Recording requires a structuring act by a human agent or by an instrument such as a stopwatch or counter that has been devised to help him. By a structuring act we mean an act that specifies the value the observed behavioral event has on some property or properties.

We can think of the task of observing and recording as being performed by one of three classes of agents: (1) by the actor who is the referent of the study's data; (2) by the researcher or an assistant or a recording device he employs; or (3) by a person who observed and recorded the event in the past, without any connection with the present research (as in documents compiled and preserved for other purposes).

The kind of agent who carries out the observing-and-recording task for a given set of observations is a very important matter, since each of these sources is especially vulnerable to certain weaknesses and each has its particular strengths. In each case, however, it is also important to distinguish whether the observation-record was obtained under conditions where the actor whose behavior is the subject of the records did or did not know that his behavior was being observed and recorded.

Consider the case of observation records where the actor himself records the behavior. Here we can distinguish between those cases in which he was fully aware of his participation in a research study[2] and those cases where his behavior leaves a "trace" detectable later by an investigator (for example, consuming one rather than another food, building a structure, or making a piece of pottery). The former we shall call *subjective reports;* the latter we shall call *traces,* following Webb and others (1966).

We find a similar differentiation in observation records gathered by the investigator in direct observation of the behavioral event. There are cases where the actor is aware that his behavior is the subject of observation and study; we shall call this situation *visible observation.* There are also cases where an observer or an observation instrument is present but unknown to the behaving actor; we shall call this situation *hidden observation.* Finally, among those observation records developed by persons unrelated to the research (neither actors nor investigators)—which Webb and his co-authors (1966) call archival records or secondary records—we can distinguish two sorts. In the one, the actor is aware that his behavior is to be observed and recorded, as in the case of public speeches by political figures; from occasions like this we get *records of public behavior.* In the other, the behavior is performed in situations that ordinarily draw no special attention, as in the case of purchases that result in sales records; we shall call such records merely *archival records.*

It is important to distinguish between observation records made when the actor was aware of the recording process and those made when he was not, because the former are subject to a whole set of potential biases or distortions that can arise from the effects of the observation-recording process itself on the actor's behavior. We shall refer to these effects as the *reactive effects* of observational situations to indicate that they are effects due to the reaction of the actor to the researcher's activities of observation, measurement, manipulation, control, and so on.

Subjective-report measures refer to all those methods that call upon an actor to respond to a set of questions; the category includes questionnaires, interviews, and tests. Direct observation refers to all those methods where an observer (the investigator or someone assisting him or an instrument) notes and records behavior of an actor in a setting, natural or contrived. The observer's presence and activity may be known to the actors (visible observation) or unknown to them (hidden observation). Content may include physical behavior such as hopscotch or opening a door, verbal behavior, expressive movements such as body positions and gestures, spatial locations, temporal patterns, and many others.

---

[2] Indeed, actors sometimes engage in some behavior only because they are aware that the person requesting it is conducting research.

Archival records, or secondary records, refer to past behavior, reported neither by the actor nor by the investigator but by some third party. Though the recorder is not aware of the subsequent research use to be made of his records, he may very well introduce other "reactive" biases; for example, administrators' records may be distorted for political reasons. But no doubt many archival records such as sales records, census data, membership lists, and group voting results are minimally reactive.

Trace measures are physical evidences of the past behavior of actors. Webb and others (1966) use the geological terms "outcroppings," "erosion," and "accretion." Traces are like subjective reports in that they are records made directly by the actor without intervening distortions either by the investigator or by others, but they are generally not reactive. Trace measures differ from observations in that the latter deal with contemporaneous behavior while the former deal with past behavior. Trace measures differ from archival records in that trace records are the direct result of the actor's behavior, whereas archival records are screened through an intermediary.

These six sources of evidence are displayed in Table 7-1. They constitute the universe of *sources* of potential empirical evidence, classified by two properties of the conditions under which the evidence was generated. The first property is the awareness on the part of the actor that his behavior is the subject of study and is being recorded. The second is the relation of the recording agent to the research investigation. The six sources of evidence generated by these two classifying properties differ in their vulnerability to various potential sources of error or distortion. None is without weakness; none is without its own particular strengths. And, as explained in Chapter 6, it is necessary to use *more than one* indicator or measure (or partition or operational definition) to establish firmly the usefulness of the conceptual property of concern. Therefore, an inventory of the weaknesses and strengths of various methods of observation and recording is valuable as an aid in selecting a set of methods that best complement one another's strengths and compensate one another's

Table 7-1. *Sources of Empirical Evidence*

(1) WHO PERFORMS THE BEHAVIOR UNDER STUDY? ALWAYS THE ACTOR.

(2) WHO OBSERVES AND RECORDS THE BEHAVIOR?	(3) IS THE ACTOR AWARE THAT HIS BEHAVIOR IS BEING RECORDED FOR RESEARCH? *Yes: Observation May Be Reactive*	*No: Observation is Nonreactive*
Actor	Subjective reports	Traces
Researcher	Visible observer	Hidden observer
Recorder in the past	Records of public behavior	Archival records

(4) WHO TRANSLATES RECORDS INTO DATA? ALWAYS THE RESEARCHER.

weaknesses. Let us first, then, consider some of the major sources of potential error—or, in the terms of Webb and others (1966), sources of invalidity of measures.

SOURCES OF INVALIDITY OF MEASURES

Webb and others (1966) (in what is, in our opinion, the most readable book ever published on methods in social science) present a thorough treatment of "reactive effects" and list twelve common sources of error or invalidity of measures as well as three additional desiderata of such measures. These fifteen properties provide a good working list for considering the relative strengths and weaknesses of different sources of evidence.

The first four are sources of invalidity or error that arise from the *actor* whose behavior is under study. These are the reactive effects mentioned before. They include: (1) the "guinea pig" effect from awareness of being tested; (2) role selection, resulting from the actor's perception of the demands and norms of the research setting; (3) actual changes in behavior resulting from the measurement process itself (called "testing" effects in Chapter 3); and (4) stylistic response sets such as right-turn preference, yes-answer preference, and the like, that interact with the particular measurement method. The first three are especially likely to occur in all those reactive settings in which the actor is aware of his participation in a research activity (subjective reports and visible observations) or his exposure to the public eye (records of public behavior). The fourth, response sets, may occur for the nonreactive methods as well and can best be overcome by use of multiple methods of measurement.

The second set of sources of invalidity of measures consists of two that arise from the *investigator's role* as observer and recorder of behavior. These are (5) effects stemming from the interviewer or observer, including age, sex, and other personal attributes as well as characteristics of his behavior vis-à-vis the actor such as the social reinforcement he provides; and (6) instrument decay (see section 3-1), including both improvement and degradation in the observing and recording techniques as time goes on. Effects of interviewer or observer are most likely, of course, in the more reactive settings for observing and recording. Possible changes in the instrument are an ever-present danger for any study in which the critical events are not all observed and recorded at once. Changes in the instrument can best be guarded against by allowing practice or warm-up prior to the observations that will be taken for data and by counterbalancing different observers and observational instruments with respect to times and subpopulations.

The third set of sources of invalidity of measures arises from *population sampling*. The question of sampling actors, behaviors, and occasions for inclusion in a study was discussed more fully in Chapter 5; the related question of random assignment of actors, behaviors, and occasions to study conditions was discussed in Chapters 3 and 4. In the present chapter, we repeat the three main biases that Webb and his co-authors point out can affect the selection of elements for the sample. These three sources of invalidity are: (7) population restrictions that arise from the method of sampling used and limit the kinds of actor-behavior-occasions included; (8) instability of population over time; and (9) instability of population over area, that is, over subpopulations, locations, or cultures. To illustrate how choice of method affects these sources of error, consider trying to obtain evidence by eavesdropping on conversations. By selecting only public, downtown gatherings as the locale, an investigator might very well exclude certain age, sex, and social class groups differentially and thus have a case of population restriction. By doing his eavesdropping at night, he would certainly have a different population than he would have at noon and thus have a case illustrating instability over time. If he made his observations exclusively on buses in Tupolo, Mississippi, and Portland, Maine, he would be tapping different populations and thus have a case illustrating instability over area.

All three of these sources of error (7, 8, and 9) place limits on external validity; that is, on the population to which one can generalize. The last two also threaten internal validity[3] if one is trying to compare certain behaviors within sets of observations differing in time or area. For example, imagine comparing the interest in National League baseball teams between New York and Los Angeles by eavesdropping on conversations on buses in the two cities. Differences might reflect not so much differences in interest between the populations of the two cities as differences in the populations selected for study in the two cities. There might be just as much vocal interest in the Dodgers as in the Mets, but a smaller proportion of Dodger fans than Met fans might ordinarily be bus riders—or vice versa. Conversations sampled at bars, offices, or drive-ins in the two cities might show quite different results.

The fourth set of sources of invalidity is composed of restrictions that methods place on the *content* of behaviors to which they can be applied. Again, there are three: (10) restriction on content to be included—for example, only subjective reports can get *direct* measurements of inner states such as feelings or desires; (11) stability of content over time; and (12) stability of content over areas. Instability of content over time would be exemplified by behaviors occurring cyclically through time of day, week, or year: eating, sleeping, going to work, going to church, taking a vacation. Instability of content over areas would be illustrated by behaviors that have higher base rates in some localities than in others: drinking, smoking, wearing clothes, driving cars. The remedy for content restrictions, as with population restrictions, is broader and more balanced sampling of actors, times, and locations.

Webb and his colleagues list three additional characteristics of ways of taking observations that do not affect their validity but can affect their utility for the researcher in other respects. One is (13) *dross rate,* or the proportion of observations (or observation time) resulting in unusable data; that is, data

[3]By internal validity we mean, of course, making valid conclusions about the sets of observations within one's design (see Chapter 3).

carrying little information about the property of interest. For example, observation of auto accidents at randomly selected intersections is a procedure with a high dross rate. Another example would be interviewing a random sample of the population to locate and study medical doctors. The latter aim might better be served through use of archival records such as medical directories, city directories, or phone books.

Webb and his colleagues also suggest a generalized cost criterion broader than the dross rate, though without listing it as such. Some methods with a low dross rate require such a high total cost per observation that they may be, over-all, more costly than an alternative method with a higher dross rate but lower cost per unit of observation. Methods that rely on electronic instrumentation, for example, are likely to be high cost, although they often can be used under conditions that greatly reduce the dross rate. For example, if we wanted to know the time distribution of arrivals and departures from a grocery store, we could install an electronic device such as an electric eye for counting entries and exits. We could actuate the device only for the times, or during a sample of the times, when the store was open. The cost of construction, installation, and use might, however, be much higher than simply posting an observer at the door with a stopwatch and counter. Of course, if we want to count simultaneously at many stores, or for a saturation sample of times, we might need so many human observers that the relative costs would shift. This example, incidentally, can be used to illustrate one advantage of human observer over hardware. The human could detect instances when one person triggered the counter more than once or failed to trigger it. He could also get additional information such as sex and estimated age about each actor. And he could detect some "mistakes," such as children who run in and out but are not truly customers. This flexible use of judgment is, at one and the same time, a strong advantage and a major weakness of human observers.

Another desirable feature of measurement methods is (14) the degree to which they give access to *additional descriptive cases*—supplementary data beyond observation of a specific behavioral property. The human observer at the grocery store could not only count entering customers but he could also note sex, probable age, and numerous other characteristics of the customers. This capacity for noting a wide range of properties is another superiority of human observation over observation by hardware. Webb and co-authors (1966) note that human observers "are low-fidelity observation instruments . . ." (p. 142). They might have added, in the same jargon, that humans are *broad-band* instruments, capable of observing and recording—albeit with low fidelity and high variability—a far greater range of properties of events than any preprogrammed hardware device.

The final property of methods of collecting observations considered by Webb and colleagues is (15) *feasibility of replication*. This means the extent to which a method of observation permits the investigator to gather a new and independent set of observations of the same properties on the same or a comparable population of events. This possibility is strongly connected to the matter of reliability (see Chapter 6) and can also become important when there is a need to cross-validate a hypothesis derived from an initial analysis of a set of observations.[4] With subjective reports, and with certain other classes of observations, the investigator can usually get a new set of observations on a comparable, sometimes even the same, population. With archival records or trace measures, though, there is often no possibility of doing so. The first analysis is the only one that can be made; no new sample of observations can be obtained. In a sense, "the materials may be completely consumed methodologically . . ." (Webb and others 1966, p. 34.)

SOURCES OF INVALIDITY AS RIVAL HYPOTHESES

All of the sources of invalidity of measures considered here are potentially present for any set of observations. There is no single, "best," or "magic" method of taking observations, just as there is no best design or strategy—nor, as we shall see in Chapters 10–13—any best method of analyzing data. Some methods incur greater threats from some of those sources than do other methods. We should keep in mind, therefore, the different effects from different sources of invalidity, choosing one observational method to strengthen another whenever feasible.

We can make further use of these twelve sources of invalidity by considering them to be *plausible alternative hypotheses* which might account for results instead of the hypotheses we want to investigate. As an example, response sets offer the alternative hypothesis that systematic differences between respondents in some "irrelevant" response tendency (such as tendency to agree rather than disagree with questionnaire statements) account for the obtained response patterns to a greater degree than do the properties or conditions a study was intended to explore. Similarly, the question of the stability of the population over areas offers the alternative hypothesis that differences in the incidence of conversations about baseball in buses in New York and Los Angeles (to refer to an earlier example) arose because the two cities differ in terms of *who rides buses* rather than because they differ in terms of how much interest there is in the local baseball team.

All of these alternative hypotheses are available for any method. The question is one of the plausibility or likelihood of each of the rival hypotheses. Let us borrow an illustration from Webb and co-authors: the rates of wear of floor tiles in front of various museum exhibits as an index of the relative

[4] Analysis of a body of data may show some feature or relation within the data that is very persuasive to the researcher; he may be convinced that such a feature or relation would be very likely to be found in other samples of data from the same population. However, if he did not predict the feature or relation before examining his present data, he has not yet tested the prediction; he must collect a second set of data and see whether the feature or relation appears in that second set of data if he wishes to make a test of his new hypothesis. Making a test of a hypothesis suggested by the nature of one set of data by looking into a second set of data is called *cross-validating* the hypothesis.

interest in those exhibits. It is conceivable that some or all of the museum goers felt watched and therefore adopted a particular role such as that of a "cultured person" that led them to view certain exhibits longer; or even that they were induced by previous wear to spend more time on the worn tiles. But either of these two hypotheses seems much less likely, on the face of it, than the possibility that the same museum goers distorted questionnaire responses to make themselves appear in a favorable light (for example, by remembering a great many exhibits) or to say in an interview what they thought the interviewer wanted them to say (for example, that they liked a great many exhibits). The same example can be used to illustrate the potential operation of response sets even in nonreactive methods. The possibility of response sets (for example, tendency to agree) in questionnaire or interview items is clear enough.[5] But we are fortunate that the example of the museum exhibit illustrates some *nonverbal* response sets. Melton (1936) has shown that museum goers have a right-turn tendency and that they spend differential amounts of time on exhibits near and far from exits independently of what is exhibited at those locations. Thus, the differential attractiveness of different exhibits as measured by tile wear is now threatened by the rival hypothesis of response sets, unless the study is so designed that it neutralizes this threat, perhaps by counter-balancing types of exhibits over locations. Changes in the research instrument would be a potential threat in the tile-wear case if tiles of different materials, differentially erosive, were used near different exhibits or if the tiles eroded differentially in cool areas compared to warm or in bright areas compared to dark. If we were to switch from the trace measure of tile wear to a related archival measure taken from records of dates when tiles were replaced, we might encounter another kind of threat: tiles in front areas may have been replaced when less worn than those in rear areas—just as the living room carpet in many homes is kept in better condition than the carpet in a child's bedroom.

The central point here is that none of these threats to validity can be eliminated with certainty in respect to any observational technique. And a method that minimizes the plausibility of some of these rival hypotheses frequently leaves itself more vulnerable to others. It is important to examine each method for its special vulnerabilities; it is also highly desirable, even necessary, to use *multiple* methods of measurement and to select the set of measures so as best to reduce the plausibility of *all* of these rival hypotheses. In this light, we shall examine each of the six sources of empirical evidence in turn.

[5] But there is good evidence that sets toward dealing with aspects of printed material, aside from its meaning content, usually have little effect on the response the actor makes to printed questioning. Rorer (1965, p. 129) says: "Response styles (for example, 'yeasaying') must be distinguished from response sets [proper] (for example, 'dissimulation'). When this is done, and when those designs which permit inferences concerning response styles are distinguished from those which do not, the data accumulated to date must be interpreted as indicating that response styles are of no more than trivial importance in determining responses to personality, interest, and attitude inventories . . . ."

SUBJECTIVE REPORTS

Subjective reports—all those measures that rely on the actor's own testimony for observing and recording behavior—probably form the largest single class of methods in behavioral science for obtaining observations. There are three main types, although there are many varieties within each: (1) questionnaires, (2) interviews, and (3) tests.

Questionnaires refer to all those written, preformulated sets of questions to which the respondent is instructed to record his own answers, usually within rather closely delineated alternatives. Interviews refer to the same kinds of questions and frames for answering, but the interviewer, rather than the respondent, records the answer.

Some forms of questions put comparatively severe restrictions upon the type of response the respondent is permitted. The classic example—facetious of course—is, "Have you stopped beating your wife? Answer yes or no." A more common type asks the respondent the extent to which he agrees with a statement by asking him to pick one of a very few phrases indicating degrees of agreement. For example:

Silas Marner was a bad man.
( ) strongly agree
( ) agree
( ) undecided
( ) disagree
( ) strongly disagree

Other questions put relatively little restriction on the respondent, such as, "How do you feel about the coming elections?" The first kind of question is commonly called *structured* or *closed*, and the second, *unstructured* or *open*.

The forms of the questions in a questionnaire, whether they be open or closed, are uniform from respondent to respondent because they are written on paper (though they can vary in their effects because of misreading or unfamiliarity with style of language). In the interview, however, the interviewer (being a human being) can deviate to some degree from a prescribed wording. Some designs for data collection require the interviewer to hold strictly to a prescribed script, while other designs allow the interviewer to paraphrase or even insert questions or remarks on his own initiative. From the viewpoint of the researcher asking the questions, then, the *asking* of the questions is always structured on the questionnaire, but the asking can be structured or unstructured when an interview is used.

As the questionnaire, and especially the interview, increase in openness, the method begins to resemble the visible-observer method, in which the interviewer-observer, rather than the actor, makes the record of behavior, all the while enforcing his selective perception and interpretation upon the behavior. Indeed, sometimes the interviewer-observer is instructed to record observations not only of the language behavior of the respondent but also observations of physical signs of nervousness, hesitation, and so on. At this point, the interviewer can be considered to be a visible observer. The interview, now, is still subject to the reactive sources of error because the respondent is aware that his behavior is the subject of someone's study, but it is additionally subject to effects arising from the interviewer—effects that would have been lessened in the questionnaire because the questionnaire involves less interaction between respondent and investigator.

Tests are special forms of questionnaires (or of interviews in the case of oral tests). A test is a set of questions the respondent is instructed to answer, and the questions are typically put to the subject as a challenge to his ability in some domain of competence. Tests are subject to the reactive biases to which other questionnaires are subject, but they attempt to make capital of what is often a disadvantage. Thus, they often stress to the respondent that he is in a "testing" situation, attempting thereby to induce him to select a *particular* role; that is, the tester hopes to motivate the respondent to do his best.[6] The results are usually interpreted on that basis—not as absence of reactive effects but as presence of a particular reactive posture, uniform for all test takers. The interpretation of test responses as data differ from those often placed on questionnaire and interview responses (see Chapter 10), but they are similar to questionnaires in source, reactivity, and other attributes discussed here.

All forms of subjective report are highly susceptible to reactive biases. The respondent knows he is the focus of research. We must assume—that is, it is highly plausible in the absence of contrary evidence—that respondents will select roles they feel are appropriate. Furthermore, these roles may differ among respondents. One role might have a flavor of, "I'm nobody's fool!" In such a role, the actor may try to divine the experimenter's purpose and sabotage it. Another role might have the character of devoted helpfulness. In such a role, the actor may try to do everything he thinks the experimenter would like his subjects to do (but, of course, such a subject is often wrong in what he supposes the experimenter most wants!). Another reactive effect occurs when the respondent changes in the attribute being measured because of the measurement. (Indeed, "learning" in the subject matter is often one of the purposes a teacher avows for giving a test in an academic setting. Similar kinds of learning undoubtedly occur when respondents answer attitude questionnaires.) Too, subjective reports are highly vulnerable to certain types of response sets such as biases toward socially acceptable responses—and these too differ among respondents. Subjective reports become more vulnerable to effects of inter-

---

[6]When the respondent is motivated to do his best during a test (or other period when undergoing observation) without special instructions to do so, the effect is often called the Hawthorne effect; see Chapter 9 for further details. The literature has not yet given a name to those cases when the respondent is countermotivated by the test.

viewing and observing when the reports are gathered under conditions where there is substantial interaction between respondent and interviewer or observer, as in the open-ended interview, noted above. But even the questionnaire administered under the most standardized conditions with an absolute minimum of contact between respondent and investigator can be biased as a function of attributes of the interviewer or the observer, such as age, sex, race, social status, and many others. (See Chapter 9 for further discussion of these effects.)

Changes in the research instrument over time pose two different problems for the subjective report. One is potential change in the behavior of the observer or interviewer (such as his manner of presenting oral instructions, for example) from one respondent or interviewing situation to the next. The other is potential change over time *within* the period of response to the questionnaire, interview, or test, such as practice or fatigue effects, learning, boredom, reactions to time pressure, and other like effects. Both types of change threaten validity of the measure.

Sources of invalidity of subjective reports arising from sampling have to do largely with language. Populations differ not only with respect to the language they use but also with respect to the degree to which that language is expressive for specific content and the fluency they demonstrate in the use of language. It is a fact often noted with disdain that a very large proportion of evidence about behavior is gleaned from subjective reports of college students, often on instruments using language that would not be feasible with other populations such as children, mental health patients, industrial workers, or military personnel. The "college sophomore" tradition in behavioral science is encouraged not only by the physical and administrative availability of students but also because students share with the investigator a high level of linguistic sophistication, making them "good" respondents for use with subjective reports.

In terms of content restrictions, subjective reports are probably the most flexible. As with the human observer, a human respondent is a very broad-band observation and recording instrument, though often one of low fidelity. Indeed, direct evidence on certain contents appropriate to the behavioral sciences can be obtained only through respondents' reports; examples are, "How do you *feel* about X?" "What do you *expect* to happen?" "Whom do you *like* best?" It is true that many ingenious methods have been devised for assessing feelings and attitudes by inferring their existence from overt behavior or from questions that do not directly or obviously ask about the intrapersonal orientation itself (this is called "indirect" assessment); but it also remains true that the actor is the only reporter who can look inside himself. Any other person must either ask the actor to tell him (the other) what his (the actor's) interior feelings are, or he (the other) must be content to make guesses from indirect evidence. This is not to deny (1) that the actor may be an inaccurate observer of his own processes or (2) that he may be reluctant to expose his interior state to an outside observer; but it still remains the case that he, and only he, can (if he will) give testimony about his interior state.

Subjective reports are also notable for providing a very low dross rate, a generally low cost per observation, a broad capacity for addition of secondary evidence, and high flexibility for replication.

The problem of reactivity—of the actor responding to the fact of research instead of the "natural" features of the situation—has worried researchers for a long time. One important cause of reactivity is a desire on the part of the actor to react to the purpose of the experimenter—that is, to react to what he (the actor) *believes* to be the purpose of the experimenter, and to react either to help or hinder the researcher's supposed purpose. Many researchers have felt they could render this urge unbiased, even if they could not eradicate it, by disguising the nature of their observation techniques. Some *disguised techniques* deliberately mislead the actor; most attempt merely to give no clues recognizable by the uninitiated. An example of a disguised instrument is the famous Rorschach series of inkblots; the actor is asked to tell what shapes or feelings the irregular blots suggest to him, and the diagnostician makes data from a record of the respondent's replies by translating them into personality traits. Presumably, the respondent has so little understanding of the rules for translating replies into data that he cannot succeed in giving replies that will cause the diagnostician's interpretation to go the way he might preplan it. If two respondents try to influence the diagnosis in preplanned directions, one will presumably be wrong in one direction and the other wrong in another direction; over a series of actors, the users of the test hope that the average of all the distortions will not be far from what it would have been had all the respondents been honest. Note that disguising a test does not prevent a respondent from falsifying his answers; it only prevents him (if he is not knowledgeable about the rationale of the test) from producing a particular systematic error by his falsification. Many psychological tests have been developed that are valid and useful in ascertaining averages among thirty or a hundred actors. But there is no test that the individual actor cannot make invalid, more or less, in his own case. Possibly tests using physiological indicators are the most difficult to falsify for most people, but even these are not proof against a knowledgeable and determined effort.[7]

Another famous example of a disguised test is the Thematic Apperception Test (TAT). The actor is presented with pictures in which human figures are at the center of attention. The experimenter asks the actor to tell what he thinks the people in that picture might have been doing and what they might do next. The TAT has been used extensively in studying the motive to set goals and achieve them (see, for example, Atkinson and Feather, 1965, and Harris and McClelland, 1971). For other disguised techniques, see Murstein (1965).

Webb and his colleagues (1966), in their book devoted to alternatives to subjective reports, argue that subjective reports are the most useful *single*

[7] Because the actor whose physiological responses are being measured is not giving a subjective report but is aware that his responses are being recorded, we classify this source of observation as one using a *visible observer*.

method because of great flexibility as to population and content. But they stress the vulnerability of subjective reports to reactive biases; and their central theme is that *no single method,* taken alone, is adequate to yield valid measures; multiple methods are necessary. We agree strongly with all three of these points: (1) subjective reports represent the most versatile and efficient single method for gathering evidence; (2) they are highly vulnerable to reactive effects; and (3) *no* single method, alone, is adequate to ward off all of the threats to invalidity. We concur strongly with the chief recommendation made by Webb and his co-authors: use multiple, convergent methods for all observation and measurement operations; and select in each case a *set* of methods that counterbalance, so to speak, as much as possible all the threats to invalidity we have described. It is partly because subjective reports are so broad band and convenient that behavioral scientists have tended to underuse and underdevelop other, less reactive methods. We turn now to those other methods to consider their special strengths and vulnerabilities.

TRACE RECORDS

Webb and others make a strong case for more imaginative use of trace records in behavioral science research. While highly subject to content restrictions, and somewhat vulnerable to population restrictions, they are relatively free of reactive and observer effects.

Trace measures refer to physical evidences of past behaviors. The example already mentioned of differential tile wear in front of various museum exhibits is an excellent illustration of this category of measure. A similar measure is wear on library books. The importance people give to various social functions could be measured by the amount of artistry (decoration, polish, hand-coloring, and the like) devoted to the clothing, pottery, rooms, or other artifacts used for those functions. The adulation accorded to paraded heroes could be measured in terms of the tons of confetti thrown. Noting the settings of radios in automobiles brought into repair shops could yield a measure of the drivers' preferences for various stations in the area.

Trace measures avoid or reduce reactivity threats because the actor is unaware of the subsequent research use of the traces of his behavior. At the same time, trace measures avoid deliberate or unwitting distortion by an intermediary (such as an agency keeping administrative records) and also avoid most of the biases that come from use of a human observer.

Trace records, however, may suffer from other forms of distortion. Certain kinds of traces, both erosions and accretions, may be recorded differentially. Changes in factors irrelevant to the property being measured may alter the trace record through time; examples are changes in museum waxing policy or in type of tile used. Traces may be recorded differentially by different segments of a population. Children's books may show more "use" than adult detective stories because detective buffs do not eat as many jelly sandwiches while reading as do children.

The possibility of response sets—systematic for some or all actors but irrelevant to the property being measured—have already been illustrated by right-turn and other positional biases of museum goers as they affect measures such as tile wear. All types of measures, of whatever source, are potentially vulnerable to response sets. Response sets are really interactions between actors (either as a whole or differentially) and properties of the measurement method—properties intrinsic to the method but irrelevant to the critical behaviors being measured. Sometimes response sets such as acquiescence on questionnaire items are themselves the focus of study. In such instances they are themselves the traits being measured, and the *content* of the items now becomes the irrelevant property against which we need to guard. See Chapter 6 on the multitrait-multimethod paradigm.

Threats to validity from response sets can be reduced by experimental or statistical controls. For example, one can counterbalance the position of exhibits. Or the investigator can remove the effect of position by statistical procedures such as handicapping. Counterbalancing cancels the effect; statistical analysis assigns compensatory weights. Both, though, can be done only when the investigator knows, or assumes he knows, what factors produce the response set. For example, he might be assuming (or banking on the idea without preliminary test) that position of an exhibit in relation to the entrance to the museum was the effective factor rather than the amount of open space near the exhibit. It is impossible to foresee and control for *all possible* irrelevant factors that might introduce response sets. The ever-present threat of response sets is one strong reason that Webb and his co-authors argue for multiple, overlapping operations for taking observations.

The trace methods are vulnerable, above all, to *content* restrictions. They can be used only to measure behaviors that leave traces. This seems to cut away their use from whole realms of interesting behavior—inner states and feelings, verbal and nonverbal expressive behavior—that leave no enduring discernible mark. The question of restriction of content for trace measures, though, may be overcome in many cases by the investigator's ingenuity. Webb and co-authors suggest a fascinating array of "oddball," but useful, trace measures, illustrating what can be done when human ingenuity is applied with vigor by investigators who let the problem guide the choice of method rather than the other way around.

DIRECT OBSERVATION

We use the label direct observation when the investigator (or someone assisting him or an instrument) observes and records the actor's behavior. This may be done with the presence and activity of the observer known to the actor (in which case we speak of a *visible* observer), and this is a potentially reactive situation. It may also be done with the actor unaware that observation and recording is taking place (the case of the *hidden* observer), and this avoids the first three potential reactive sources of bias; namely, guinea pig effect, role selection, and change due to measurement. The actor's behavior is, of course, still subject to response sets.

It is not always clear when an observer is "hidden." For one thing, an observer hidden to the eye but known to be there (or even one suspected of being there, whether actually present or not) is probably as reactive as a visible one. On the other hand, an observer who is literally visible to the actor may be psychologically hidden if his presence is a normal and natural part of the situation and if his observation activities are not such as to set him apart from others; an example would be the participant-observer who samples conversations in a bus or in a crowded lobby. Another example is the liaison observer, so to speak, described by Sherif and Sherif (1964). The question is not really one of literal visibility but of psychological visibility; that is, of awareness or suspicion on the part of the actors that they are being watched. Both visible and hidden observations are subject to observer biases and to instrument changes through time. These can be reduced, but not eliminated, by training the observer and by counterbalancing observers over conditions and times. Hidden-observer methods may incur some limitations on population and on content. The example used previously, of conversation sampling on public transportation, illustrates this point well. Observation is a fairly broad-band technique. Webb and others list five kinds of content that can be observed: physical actions such as hitting, verbal behavior such as conversation, expressive behavior such as smiling, spatial location, and temporal patterns.

In general, observation methods have a high dross rate. Conversation sampling for incidence of a particular topic may mean 100–to–1 or even higher rates if the topic is a low-frequency one in some populations, times, or areas. Using an observing and recording instrument, while not really reducing the dross rate, nevertheless can reduce costs. For example, putting a timer and counter on an entrance or exit may be more efficient than having a human observer posted near it. This would be especially true if the entry rate per minute were either very low (producing boredom and wasted time for an observer) or very high (at or beyond the observer's limits). However, as pointed out before, blind recording by an instrument reduces access to secondary information such as the sex or age of the entering person and may be subject to particular errors such as the same person stepping back and forth several times through the beam that counts entrances.

Instruments also may be able to detect properties the unaided human observer cannot. For example, infrared photography can take pictures of activity in the dark; appropriate apparatus can measure electrical resistance of the skin. At the same time, any one instrument is a narrow-band observer, and hardware instruments as a class are fairly restricted in content and especially restricted in access to secondary information. Finally, both hardware devices and the human observer offer opportunity for replication. While hardware often has relatively high initial cost, it usually has rapidly decreasing cost per additional case, an advantage not accruing to human observation. Hence, use of hardware instruments tends to encourage replication of observations.

ARCHIVES

Archives contain a rich lode of recorded observations in the form of political, administrative, and industrial records of many sorts. These documents yield observations of human behavior even though neither the actor nor the investigator made or recorded the observations and even though the information may have been compiled for reasons quite unrelated to social research. Broadly speaking, archives consist of (1) running records found in such public sources as vital statistics, court reports, and the like and (2) episodic records found in such private and institutional sources as sales reports, personnel files, hospital records, correspondence, speeches, diaries, and so on.

Archival records cannot be considered free of reactive biases or biases of observer or interviewer just because neither the actor nor the investigator participated in the recording or observing process. The actor may, in fact, have been completely aware of the public nature of his performance (though not of the subsequent research uses to be made of it), as is certainly true in the case of political speeches and presumably true for private letters of public figures. This awareness may produce reactive effects. Moreover, a person who is compiling accounting records, or a biographer, may introduce his own biases in the form of perceptual distortions due to his personal involvement in the events he is recording. Furthermore, the record-keeping activities may change over time (an instance of instrument change). Some archival records have major population restrictions (IQ scores, for example) and population instability over time and area. Census data, tax records, crime records, all are subject to age, race, sex, social class, and other population biases. Archival records have some content restrictions, but in general are broad-band instruments with a high dross rate. Despite the high dross rate, however, they tend to be relatively low in cost. They also have high access to secondary information; they vary greatly in how much opportunity they provide for replication.

COMPARISON OF SOURCES

Table 7-2 lists twelve sources of potential invalidity of measures (that is, twelve plausible rival hypotheses) as well as three additional desirable attributes of measures, and crosses the sources of invalidity with the six methods of observing and recording we have been discussing. The entries in the table are summary indications of the vulnerability of each type of method to each of the sources of invalidity. An "H" means that the type of method is highly vulnerable to the bias indicated; that is, the rival hypothesis represented by that source of invalidity is likely to be highly plausible for observations gathered by that method. An "M" means a moderate level of vulnerability, and a blank means a low level.

The table must classify types of methods generally or on the average; not all methods within a type will be equally vulnerable to a particular rival

Table 7-2. *Vulnerabilities of Methods of Observing and Recording*

	METHODS OF OBSERVING AND RECORDING					
	Actor's Records		*Researcher's Records*		*Previous Records*	
Sources of Invalidity of Methods; That Is, Plausible Rival Hypotheses	*Subjective Reports*	*Trace Measures*	*Visible Observer*	*Hidden Observer*	*Public Behavior*	*Archival Records*
Biases associated with the actor						
1. Guinea pig effect	H		H		M	
2. Role selection	H		H		M	
3. Measurement as change agent	H		H		M	
4. Response sets	H	M	H	M	M	M
Biases associated with the investigator						
5. Effects of interviewer or observer			H	H	M	M
6. Instrument change	H	M	H	H	M	M
Biases associated with the population						
7. Population restrictions	H	H	M	M	M	M
8. Population instability over time	M		M		M	M
9. Population instability among areas	H				M	M
Biases associated with content						
10. Content restrictions		H			M	M
11. Content instability over time		M			H	H
12. Content instability over areas		M			H	H
Other characteristics of methods						
13. Dross rate		H	M	M	M	M
14. Difficulty of access to secondary data		H				
15. Difficulty of replication		H				

KEY: H: High vulnerability to the bias or rival hypothesis.
M: Moderate vulnerability.
Absence of a symbol indicates low vulnerability.

Adapted from Webb and others, 1966.

hypothesis. We pointed out before, for example, that observation by hardware instruments was likely to be more content restricted, but less subject to interviewer biases, than observation by a human observer. Note, also, that these assessments assume normal rigor of design and procedure. *Every* method of measurement is highly vulnerable to error if improperly or carelessly applied. Note, too, that there are usually ways to reduce the bias characteristic of a method. For example, broad sampling of time and area as well as population can reduce some of the biases associated with population and content. Counterbalancing the assignments of observers, the direction and sequencing of items, the locations of stimuli, and the like, can help offset effects of response set, observer biases, and instrument changes.

Table 7-1 should make clear, however, along with the forgoing discussion, that *no one class of methods* is, or can be made to be, free from all sources of invalidity. Nor is any one class of methods clearly best in all respects; each offers some special advantages that others do not. For the most part, the methods offer complementary advantages, which, when properly combined, can cancel or offset their disadvantages taken singly.

For these reasons, we repeat our recommendations of *multiple complementary methods of measurement*. Any one method of measurement is necessarily vulnerable to some sources of invalidity. We should be reluctant to rest upon only one method as a source of evidence. Multiple sources of evidence are needed. And this does not mean two questionnaires nor two tests; it means a questionnaire and a trace, or archival data with direct observation, and so forth. The cumulative value of two or more sources of evidence depends directly on how independent each is of the other—in other words, how free each one is of the biases the other contains. It is easy to imagine a high correlation between two questionnaire measures arising from common sources of bias such as response sets or role selection with the correlation having little to do with the critical behavior intended to be measured. On the other hand, it is much harder to defend the plausibility of a claim that bias due to similarity of method could account for a high correlation between a trace measure and a subjective report or a sales record and a set of observations or a personality measure and a set of election outcomes.

In this section we have considered observational records in terms of their source and reactivity. We have also described the relative vulnerabilities of each sort of observational record to a series of potential sources of invalidity. In the next section we will consider observational records from the point of view of the kinds of choices, comparisons, or possibilities of alternative response there are for each recorded observation. We shall be describing some ways of soliciting information from actors which are essential to our discussion in Chapters 10–12 of the types of data into which records can be translated, the assumptions involved in the translations, and the techniques of analysis that enable the investigator to construct useful interpretations from the records.

7-2. *A Framework for Actors' Tasks and Researchers' Observations: The Searchingness Structure*

From the point of view of translating observations into data, there are three broad classes of *recording task* we can impose on the observing and recording agents. These can be differentiated as follows:

1. Pick any of n alternative objects
2. Pick k of n objects, where k is a specified number less than n
3. Order k of n objects, where k is a specified number less than n.

A simple example can illustrate these three classes of recording task. Suppose we present an actor with a list of political candidates. We want to know how the actor favors the candidates. Letting the actor act as his own recorder, we could ask him to do any of the three classes of tasks:

1. Pick any: "Put a check mark by all of the candidates in the list that you like."

2. Pick k of n: "Pick the two (or three, . . . up to $k \leqq n - 1$) candidates that you most prefer."

3. Order k of n: "Put a 1 by the candidate you most prefer, a 2 by the candidate who is your next most preferred, and so on (for $k \leqq n$).

Anyone who has read some reports of empirical research in the social sciences, particularly research in which observations are taken from individual humans, will recognize these three recording tasks. One or another of these instructions is inevitably given the observer.[8] This is true whether the observer is also the actor, whether the observer is the investigator or his agent, or whether the observer is reinterpreting records made by other observers in the past. The importance of this observational facet is that it, like the facets of other chapters, shows one more way in which the relation the researcher establishes between himself and the actor affects the information he can get from the actor. In earlier chapters, we dealt with the researcher's relation to sample and population and to subparts of these. Now, as we move toward the smaller detail in the research cycle (in the sense of Figure 1-1), toward the irreducible quantum of tallying a particular act of a particular actor, we shall pay more attention to the choices among which the researcher conceives the actor to be operating. The three recording tasks comprise a manifest level on which choice possibilities can be classified.

Furthermore, this classification of recording tasks enables us to be somewhat more specific concerning what we mean by a *datum* than we were at the beginning of the chapter.[9] When an actor chooses some particular object (such

---

[8] Sometimes an observer approaches actors without any preconceived plan for using these observing tasks. An example is the anthropologist entering a social group to observe the natural course of events in that group. Typically, he would not want to use an intrusive, reactive method such as posing choice tasks for the members of the group, especially not at first acquaintance. But does this nonintrusive method leave the observer outside the three tasks we have set forth? We think not. Inevitably, it seems to us, the anthropologist must note whether actors choose to do some things (pick any) and not other things; who else an actor picks to go in a canoe with him that holds 4 (pick 3 of n); what alternatives actors seek first, which next, which last (order k or n); and the like. We think there is no human action that we cannot describe to the satisfaction of the reader with one or more of these recording tasks.

[9] We shall give a more technical definition in Chapter 10.

as a candidate), though he was at liberty not to choose it, he shows the investigator a relation between himself and the object that he expressed by his choice; if the investigator has made a list of actors and objects (presumably interacting with at least some degree of freedom), he can make a tally to indicate that choice by that actor. It is this tally, indicating a relation between actor and object, that we call a *datum*.

Notice, again, that the meaning the investigator sees in a datum is more or less a result of some arbitrary assumptions on his part. That is, the observer cannot, in assessing any one variable, interpret actions of the actor in all possible ways; he must select only one interpretation. For example, the researcher might be observing an engineer struggling with a problem in designing a smog precipitator. The researcher might want to find out the extent to which the actor (and others in the population) call upon colleagues for consultation. If so, he might conceive mode Y as partitioned dichotomously and tally whether (or not) the actor sought help from a colleague with his problem. But there are more ways than this of conceiving the response potentialities of the engineer. The researcher might postulate that the engineer could (1) continue struggling with the problem on his own, (2) confer with colleagues, (3) set the problem aside for a specified time and come back to it later, (4) take a course of instruction in matters related to the problem, or (5) give up the whole thing as a failure. Depending on his purposes, the researcher might choose (1) which methods engineers choose before giving up (pick any), (2) which methods engineers pick as the first two (pick 2 of 5), or (3) the order in which the engineers choose these methods (order k of 5). The researcher cannot pick all of these interpretations at once, however. He can try out the different interpretations sequentially, but he cannot come to a specific answer to any *one* of the questions without sticking to that question. We shall explain more of the logic of dealing with mixed and unmixed types of data in Chapters 10 and 11.

To a greater or lesser degree, the recording task the researcher chooses for himself must be arbitrary. In the above example, note that the researcher could decide quite without conferring with the actor that he would interpret the actor's situation through one or another of the recording tasks. As a matter of fact, some social scientists (for example, G. A. Kelly, 1965, and Willems and Willems, 1965) have criticized current methods of research for too frequently interpreting the actor's behavior according to the researcher's perception of the available alternatives when the actor's perception may be very different from the researcher's.

The function of the last part of this chapter will be to display a set of facets that enable the researcher to be systematic about choosing the recording task through which he will establish a relation between his viewpoint and that of the actor. But before displaying that set of facets—the searchingness structure—it will be helpful to give a few more examples of how observations can be interpreted through one recording task or another.

Suppose we ask someone (or he asks himself) to run 100 yards as fast as he can, and suppose we are going to determine his time to the nearest .01 second with a stopwatch. The recording task of the timer can be viewed as, "Pick *1* of the 1/100th-second intervals (as displayed on a stopwatch) that best fits the time it takes the runner to go from starting line to finish line." This is pick k of n, where $k = 1$ and n is the set of integers representing 1/100ths of a second. Alternatively, we could construe this recording task as, "Pick any of the ordered set of 1/100th-second intervals that 'dominate' the runner (that is, that occur before he finishes)." Again, imagine that we are observing a five-man race and that it is our task to determine the winner (someone else is timing, perhaps). Here, we might use a camera, an electric eye, or whatnot as the recorder. The recording task is pick 1 of n participants or order 1 of n participants. (Pick 1 and order 1 are identical; but pick and order are different for $k > 1$.)

We might, as another example, assign an actor a task such as, "Mark the right answer to each question on this test." The recording task for the actor is pick k of n where $k = 1$ and n is the number of alternatives on a question. (Here, again order 1 of n is the same as pick 1 of n.) As yet another example, we might give a person or a group the following instructions: "Try to solve this problem; you have five minutes." (The problem could be to build a certain object, to escape from a maze, or whatever.) Here, the recording task (for us, for our assistants, or for our instruments) would be pick 1 of 2 if we wanted only to record whether each performer completed the problem, or got it right in the five minutes. If, instead, we wanted to record how long it took each actor to complete the task (say in seconds), then we would have a case similar to the time score in the earlier example: pick 1 of n, where n is 301 (300 seconds in five minutes along with the 301st category for "did not finish").

Now suppose the recording task is to observe each error that occurs, such as each wrong turn in a maze. If we want an error score instead of a time score or right-wrong score, the recording task can take either of two forms: (1) *pick any of n*, where n is the set of turns observed, some of which are to be called errors according to some criteria; (2) *pick 1 of 2* at each turn, where the $n = 2$ alternatives are right and wrong. In the last instance, the "unit of performance" we are recording has shifted from getting out of a maze to making the ith turn. The matter of combining observations of all turns in the maze, just as combining all items in a paper and pencil list, requires additional assumptions.

MOLAR AND MOLECULAR UNITS IN RECORDING OBSERVATIONS

Note that whenever the actor faces a multiitem or multitrial task—that is, one that can be divided into subunits such as turns in a maze, items in a test, or trials on a learning problem—the researcher is always faced with a choice having two related components. He can choose to view the entire performance task as a single unit, or he can focus on each item or subtask as a unit (perhaps later combining scores for all the items into a single score by making additional assumptions). If the researcher takes the entire task as a unit, he will often interpret his task of recording the actor's behavior as one of the *pick any* sort. Following are some examples of instructions the researcher might choose to work under: pick any trials on which an error occurred, pick any potential turns at which an error was made, pick any test items that were answered correctly, or pick any political candidates that were chosen. On the other hand, if the researcher takes each item or subtask as a unit, each subtask becomes pick k or n where $k = 1$ and n is the number of response alternatives (usually small) that are available for that item. For example, considered one item at a time, a test is a pick 1 of 2 (right or wrong) type of task. A potential turn in a maze is pick 1 of 2 (correct versus not correct). In general, we can always convert a "pick any" task, which necessarily has multiple parts, into a series of tasks of the type pick 1 (or order 1) of n where n represents the alternative responses to an *item*. Items often offer only two response alternatives: choose-not-choose, correct-incorrect. Notice that when we shift our focus from total task (pick any of n objects, items, turns, and so on) to subtask (pick 1 of n alternative responses to an object, item, turn, and so on) we also shift the set of things counted as n from a *set of objects* among which to choose to a *set of response alternatives* (right-left, correct-incorrect, choose-not-choose) applicable to each object, item, turn, or the like.

Several points in the forgoing discussion will be useful later on. First, it is clear that the nature of a recording task is partly a matter of how the investigator wishes to construe it. The choice is arbitrary but important, because it affects the kind of information extractable from a set of observations, as we shall see in Chapters 10 and 11. Second, the investigator usually has a choice as to what size of "chunk" of time or of behavior he will take as a basic unit for recording observations—test or item, maze or turn, molar or molecular. This choice will affect how the recording task can be conceptualized. Furthermore, if the molecular choice is made, the investigator will eventually have the further problem of whether, and how, he will combine the recorded observations of the subtasks or items. To do so, he will have to make some assumptions about how the subparts are related to one another. When he chooses to record only the *molar* performance in the first place, he is implicitly making similar assumptions about how the "parts" fit together. We shall discuss this point at greater length in Chapter 11. Third, it is always possible to shift from "pick any" to "pick k of n" by shifting from molar to molecular.

Coombs (1964) has connected all the methods for picking k of n objects and ordering k of n objects in a faceted scheme he calls the searchingness structure. This scheme enables the researcher to select in a systematic way a recording task that will maximize the kind of information he wants to extract from his observations.

THE SEARCHINGNESS STRUCTURE

The searchingness structure interrelates all of the "pick *k*" and "order *k*" forms of observation record but not "pick any." Some of the methods set forth in this structure are more searching or differentiating among classes of stimuli[10] or individuals than are others.

The searchingness structure is built upon four facets:

1. The total number of stimuli being studied: n
2. The number of stimuli presented at one time: p
3. The number of stimuli the respondent (or recorder) is asked to pick or order: k
4. Whether he is asked to *pick* k stimuli or to *order* k stimuli.

The number of stimuli being dealt with, n, can range from 2 to any positive integer. The number of stimuli presented for judgment at any one time, p, can range from 2 to n. (Both n and p start at 2 rather than 1 because it is not reasonable to ask someone to pick 1 of 1 or to order 1 of 1.) The number of stimuli to be picked or ordered, k, can range from one (of two or more) up to $p - 1$ (and therefore up to $n - 1$ when $p = n$). To order $n - 1$ is equivalent to ordering n.

Figure 7-1 is a schematic diagram of the methods encompassed by the searchingness structure. The rows are order and pick methods for various values of k, ranging from order $n - 1$ through order 1 or pick 1 to pick $n - 1$. The columns represent values of p (number of stimuli presented together) in relation to n (total number of stimuli being studied). The value of p ranges from 2 to n. For any fixed n, the whole structure can be presented; there are $(n - 1)^2$ cells. For example, we can present any five stimuli 2, 3, 4, or 5 at a time. For $p = 2$, we can have for k only pick-order 1. For $p = 3$, we can have p as pick-order 1, order 2, or pick 2. For $p = 4$, we can have these three and also order 3 or pick 3. For $p = 5$, we can have order 4, 3, or 2, pick-order 1, or pick 2, 3, or 4. For $n = 5$, in sum, there are $(5 - 1)^2 = 16$ ways of presenting the stimuli.

One advantage of thinking about the forms of observation records in these terms is that the searchingness structure interrelates not only many common methods of data collection but many other potential methods that are rarely, if ever, used. Only four of the cells in the searchingness structure have been used very much in research. These are marked by a, b, c, and d in Figure 7-1. Cell a is pick 1 (or order 1) for $p = n$ stimuli. Many of the methods of single stimulus, much used in behavioral science research, are varieties of this case. In many applications, $n = 2$ and observations take dichotomous forms such

[10] We now use the term *stimulus* as synonymous with *object* to follow Coombs' usage and make the transition easier for the reader who wishes to consult Coombs' book.

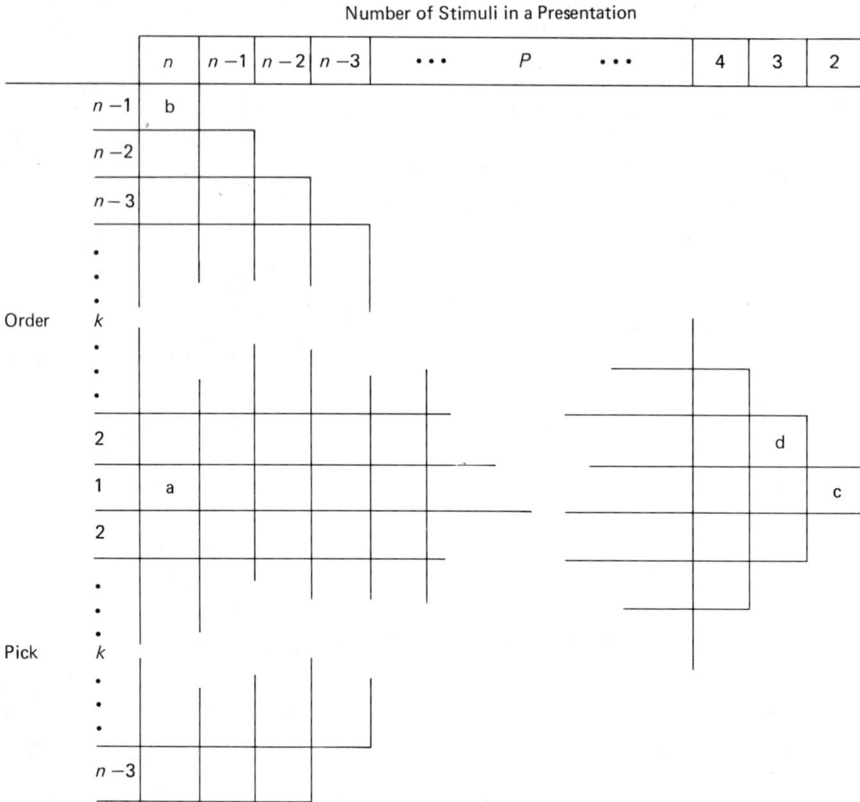

Figure 7-1. The Searchingness Structure (after Coombs, 1964).

as, "I see it, I don't see it," or, "I like it, I don't like it." Many other forms of question or observation record also fit cell a, though they might not ordinarily be considered single-stimulus methods. For example: "Which of these *n* candidates do you most prefer?" "What is your favorite brand of toothpaste?" "Who is the prettiest girl in town?" "What is your favorite color?" "Who is your best friend?"

Other kinds of questions involving a quantitative score rather than a dichotomous or multialternative choice can also be construed as pick 1 of *n*. Time scores are an example. "What was the winning runner's time, in seconds?" can be construed as, "Pick the one of the ordered 1-second intevals, from zero to infinity, that matches the number of seconds elapsing from the start of the race to the winner's finish." Quantitative intensity or magnitude measures (of pressure, of size, of value) can all be viewed in the same way, as pick 1 of *n*, where *n* is the number of available values in a scale of measurement. Many of the single-stimulus methods of psychophysics are of this type.

Cell b, at the top of the left-hand column of the searchingness structure, is the familiar method of rank order: order $n - 1$ (which is equivalent to order n). It is exemplified by the instruction: "Rank-order all of these n stimuli, giving a 1 to your most preferred, 2 to the next most preferred, and so on." Of course, the cells between a and b—rank 2 of n, 3 of n, 4 of n, up to rank $n - 2$ of n—all are used to some extent in research and in practical affairs. For example, we sometimes ask others to state their first, second, and third preferences among a set of stimuli with $n = 4$. The polls to determine ten best high school or college football or basketball teams often ask the judge to order 10 of a very large n. Researchers and others also sometimes use the cells below a in the first column—pick 2, 3, or more of n—as when a restaurant asks its customers to pick two of five or six vegetables to go with the chosen main dish.

Cell c in Figure 7-1 is the much-used method of paired comparisons. It is pick 1 (or order 1) where $p = 2$ and where n usually is much larger than 2. In paired comparisons, n stimuli are presented two at a time, usually in all combinations, and the respondent is asked to choose or pick the one of the two which has "more" of something—which is longer, which is bigger, which is more pleasant, which is greener, which is preferred. This is an especially searching method because it yields a detailed record of comparisons among the stimuli, but it is also quite costly and cumbersome, because as n increases the number of judgments (n things presented two at a time) increases very rapidly. There are three paired comparisons for three stimuli (A with B, A with C, and B with C); six for four stimuli; ten for five stimuli; and so on. There are $n(n - 1)/2$ combinations of n things taken two at a time. Of course, this method can be used even though the researcher may not choose to present all the possible pairs of n objects to the actor, but he gets proportionately less information when he does so.

Cell d—order 2 of 3, with $n > p$—is a method of relatively high frequency of use, though probably not as frequent as rank order or paired comparisons. It is usually called the method of triads. It asks the respondent to order two of three objects (equivalent to ordering all three) with sets of three objects from among the n being presented to the actor in rotation. A variation of this instruction is to ask the respondent to pick the *most* and the *least* of the three stimuli on some dimension—which is also equivalent to ordering all three.

But let us see what a couple of other methods might look like. Suppose we consider a pick method where $n = 6$, $p = 4$, and $k = 2$. The instruction to the respondent might be, "Pick the two most suitable from among these four," and all the fifteen possible subsets of four could be presented with that instruction, one subset after another. Such a technique could serve a number of purposes. For one thing, paired comparisons would be repeated, and this would provide a check on that sort of reliability. For another, the things being judged might be very complex, such as policy statements, and asking the respondent to judge four at a time might be feasible, while asking him to judge all six at once might increase the refusal rate beyond acceptability. Another purpose this technique could serve would be to check on whether the judgments of several persons about six things could fit together in a single order while asking each person only about four things only two or three times. For example, person 1 might be asked to choose the best two from A, B, C, and D, then from C, D, E, and F, and then from A, B, E, and F; person 2 might be asked to choose the best two from B, C, D, and E, then from A, D, E, and F, and then from A, B, C, and F; and so on. A disadvantage of methods containing replicated comparisons is that they ask more work from the respondent than methods in which each comparison is asked only once. We shall discuss these topics further in Chapter 11.

As a final example consider $n = 35$, $p = 7$, and order 3. The respondent would be presented with successive subsets of seven objects and asked to order, among the seven, the three objects that were greatest in some sense or that he most preferred. The uses of this information would be like the uses given in the previous example, but the amount of information obtained per presentation is different. Discussion of amounts of information gained by different methods can be found in Coombs (1964).

CARTWHEELS: A SEARCHINGNESS STRUCTURE FOR DISTANCES

There is a relatively new set of data-collection methods, mostly developed and used by Coombs (1964) and his associates, called "cartwheels." The reason for the name will be apparent when they have been described. The method of cartwheels is not a single method but a set of methods fitting any of a number of cells in the searchingness structure. It is a procedure for getting observational records that are direct judgments of the relative sizes of psychological *distances*. The cartwheel procedures are, in effect, a set of methods parallel to those in the searchingness structure, but for distances between stimuli rather than for the stimuli themselves.

The cartwheel procedure asks the respondent to compare sizes (distances) by picking or ordering some of the distances among a set of stimuli. For example, there are six possible pairs (distances) for four stimuli, as diagrammed below:

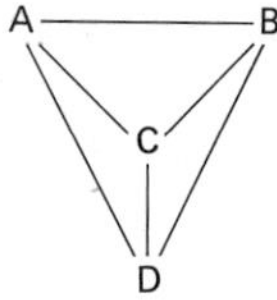

This is a cartwheel which, though it contains four stimuli, presents six distances or pair comparisons—presenting both "spokes" (AC, BC, DC) and "rims" (AD, BD, AB). We might ask the respondent to rank order all six distances (for example, "Put a 1 on the line connecting the two that are most alike, a 2 on the line of the two next most alike, and so on"). Or we might ask, "Which

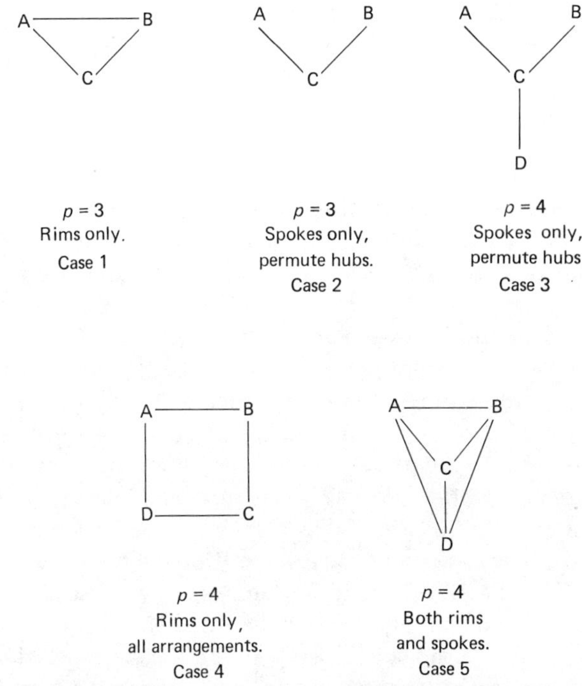

Figure 7-2. Some convenient cartwheels (after Coombs, 1964).

two are most alike?" (pick 1 of 6.) Or we might ask the question in a paired comparison form: "Which distance is the lesser, AD or BC?"

Since the number of possible pairs goes up rapidly as p increases, and the number in the set of cartwheels needed to have a full set of comparisons goes up very rapidly when n is larger than p, the number and complexity of cartwheel judgments sets a limit on the kinds of cartwheel patterns that are feasible. Only five cartwheel patterns, involving p of 3 and 4, have been much used as yet (see Figure 7-2).

COMPARISON OF SEARCHINGNESS OF METHODS

The searchingness structure provides a framework for comparing the array of pick k and order k methods in terms of a number of properties that affect their usefulness in data collection. One property, already mentioned, is the *number of presentations necessary* for comparisons of all stimuli in all combinations.[11] The number of presentations depends on p and n. The total number of paired comparisons ($p = 2$) among n objects is $n(n - 1)/2$. The total number of presentations of n objects (such as is used in the method of rank order) is one.

[11]The experimenter need not present all possible combinations of n objects p at a time. If he does not, he usually prefers to use a *balanced* subset of the possible presentations; this means a subset in which every stimulus appears for comparison with others an equal number of times. Selecting such a subset becomes mathematically complicated; see Coombs (1964).

Another property of the methods in the searchingness structure is the extent to which they test *consistency* in the responses of the actor; that is, replicability or stability of his choices. Still another property is the extent to which the methods test *transitivity* in the responses of the actor. We shall present more detail in Chapter 11 on how these methods test these properties. Finally, these methods differ in *discriminability;* that is, the number of categories into which the information in the responses can partition the stimuli and the actors when the stimuli are scaled. We shall elaborate on this, too, in Chapter 11.

Both major sections of this chapter dealt with the relations between the researcher, the observer, and the actor. In the first section, we were concerned with how the information the researcher could get would be affected when the researcher was phenomenally present to the actor. We were concerned for the same reason with the agent who makes the record—the actor, the researcher, or someone not a part of the study making the record for some other purpose. Each of these relations between researcher and actor yields somewhat different kinds of information because of the different kinds of rival hypotheses to which each is vulnerable (see Table 7-1). In the second section, we dealt with the kinds of choice situations the researcher might offer the actor or might conceive the actor to be experiencing. We showed how these choice situations could be conceived to fall among three classes we called the observer's repertoire of *recording tasks*. We showed how two of these recording tasks each has a family of variations, each variation giving the researcher a different sort of information.

Chapters 8 and 9 will also deal with the relations between researcher and actor. Chapter 8 will discuss the kinds of information that can be obtained from selecting certain classes of actors or situations to be observed, on the one hand, and intervening in the lives of the actors, on the other. Chapter 9 will discuss some of the practical considerations in establishing actual working relations with actors.

7-3. Further Reading

The effects of the actor's knowing that he is being observed have been discussed systematically by Campbell and Stanley (1963), Friedman (1967), Rosenthal (1967), and Webb and others (1966). Also useful are the papers of McGuigan (1963) and Orne (1962).

A special situation in which the actor knows he is being observed is the interview—the researcher or his agent asking the actor questions, face-to-face. Because of the strong effects the behavior, manner, and appearance of the interviewer can have on the responses of the actor, a large lore and technology of interviewing have come into being. Some recent items from that literature are Dexter (1964), Gorden (1969), Richardson, Dohrenwend, and Klein (1965), and Sherwood and Nataupsky (1968). Not so recent but still classic is the text by Kahn and Cannell (1958).

For descriptions of various existing self-report instruments and lists of sources, see Bonjean, Hill, and McLemore (1962), Buros (1965), Cronbach (1970), Glennon, Albright, and Owens (1966), Miller (1964), and Shaw and Wright (1967). Most of the books just cited give some discussion of problems and technicalities in using various types of instruments, including the self-report types. Further help of this more technical sort is available from American Psychological Association and others (1966), Cannel and Kahn (1968), Fishbein (1967), E. L. Kelly (1967), Kerlinger (1964), Sjoberg and Nett (1968), and Tyler (1971). Problems of using the method of subjective report in psychophysics are reviewed in Stevens (1951), among other places. The special cluster of techniques called *survey research* has been described by Backstrom and Hursh (1963), Glock (1967), and Young (1966), among others. Special problems in recording observations taken from bulky productions of verbal material have been discussed by Bucher, Fritz, and Quarantelli (1956a and b), Holsti, Loomba, and North (1968), and Stone and others (1966), to name only a very few.

As with subjective reports, there is a considerable literature on methods of observation, though less on hardware than on the use of human observers. For further information on this class of method, see Webb and others (1966), Amidon and Hough (1967), Boyd and DeVault (1966), Barker and Barker (1961), Flanders (1970), U.S. Office of Strategic Services (1948), Simon and Boyer (1967), Weick (1968), and Wright (1960).

Webb and others (1966) make a plea for broader and more imaginative use of nonreactive archival records and illustrate a number of such uses. The use of archival records, also called *documents* and *available materials* by some authors, has also been discussed by Kerlinger (1964, Chapter 30) and Selltiz and others (1959, Chapter 9), among others. Special applications have been reported by Anderson and others (1966), Campbell (1963, 1969), Deutsch and Madow (1961), Hackman, Jones, and McGrath (1967), and Moore (1961), as examples. Some actual sources of archival records have been listed by the U.S. National Referral Center for Science and Technology (1965), and Gurr and Panofsky (1964) have edited a collection of papers on retrieving information. Various methods of content analysis are suitable for use with archival records; see Holsti, Loomba, and North (1968) and Stone and others (1966), for example.

CHAPTER 8

Planning to Gather Evidence: Techniques for Manipulation and Control of Relevant Variables

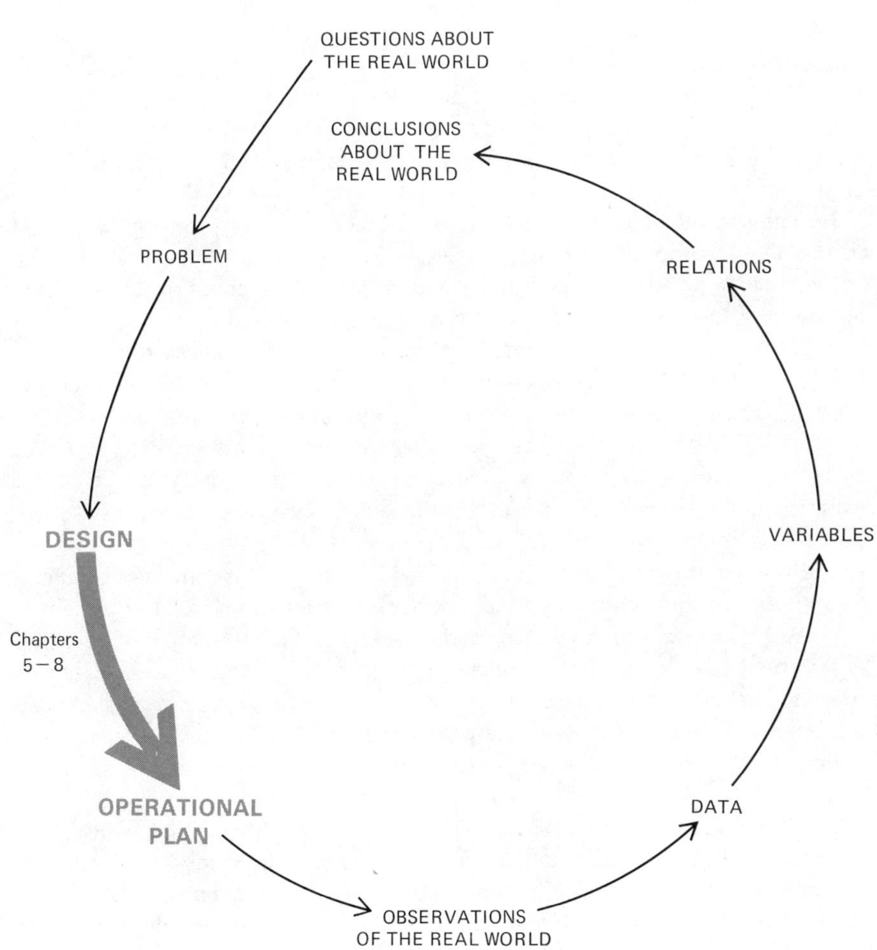

There are many techniques by means of which behavioral scientists can manipulate or control a particular property—that is, ways they can use the property as a design partition (X) or a design constant (K), as discussed in Chapter 3. While the particulars of manipulation and control differ somewhat from property to property, there are certain underlying facets that will simplify our discussion of the advantages and limitations of the techniques.

The first basis for distinguishing among the array of techniques for manipulation (X) and control (K) of properties has to do with the *inferred locus* of the property. Certain relevant properties are conceptualized as being associated with or "in" the actor, such as age, sex, intelligence, and personality traits generally. Other properties are construed as being "in" the stimulus or task—for example, complexity of stimulus. Still others are attributed to the broader situation or behavior setting, as in the case of pressure toward conformity. Finally, some properties are construed as relations lying (1) between two or more actors, as in the case of popularity or leadership; (2) between an actor and a task, as in the case of knowledge of prior results; or (3) between an actor and the behavior setting, as in the case of the kind and degree of reward available to the actor. The inferred locus of the property has a great influence on the kinds of techniques suitable for manipulating or controlling that property.

The second distinction has to do with whether the property is *inherent* in the actor, stimulus, or behavior setting at the outset of the investigation or whether it is *imposed* upon the actor, stimulus, or situation by research activities of the investigator. When the property is inherent, the investigator merely identifies the property and partitions by aggregating cases so that they will be alike on that property within each subset but will differ between subsets on that property. (If the researcher is controlling rather than manipulating the variable, then he selects all cases to have the same value on the property.) When the investigator imposes a particular level of a property, artificially or experimentally, he modifies the actor, stimulus, or behavior setting. These two facets—(1) inherent versus imposed property and (2) inferred locus of the property—are the framework for Table 8-1, which indicates in rather general terms some of the techniques used for manipulation and control of variables.

A third dimension important in the control and manipulation of variables is the manner in which the researcher goes about assuring himself, when he has undertaken to produce some condition at some locus, that he has actually succeeded in doing so. This is the problem of the validity of the operational definition. We shall discuss this problem in the next section before returning to the two facets shown in Table 8-1.

These three facets pretty well lay out the possibilities. When setting out to establish the conditions under which one wishes to study a collection of actors, one can either seek the conditions ready-made or one can undertake to produce them himself. If the conditions are to be observable, they must be observable as a feature of *something*—and we have chosen the elements of our basic unit of actor behaving toward an object in a context as the elements for specifying the loci for the manifestations of the conditions. Finally, if one undertakes to produce the desired conditions, he will usually look for evidence that he has been successful. This framework provides us an orderly way to discuss the benefits and costs of various techniques for establishing partitions. We begin with the difficulties in being sure of properties that are not directly observable.

Table 8-1. *A Two-Facet Classification of Techniques for Manipulation and Control of Variables*

	ORIGIN OF PROPERTY	
Locus of Design Property	*Inherent*	*Imposed*
In actor	Selection of actors	Practice or training
In task or stimulus	Selecting a task condition	Producing a task condition
In behavior setting, context, or situation	Selecting a situation	Producing a situation
In relation of actor to other actors	Selecting a group or organization with a particular structure	Producing a group or organization with a particular structure
In relation of actor to task	Selecting a work role; finding natural perceptions and feedback	Producing a work role; inducing perceptions and providing feedback from outside
In relation of actor to behavior setting	Selecting a setting containing certain contingencies	Producing certain contingencies

8-1. Operational Definition, Manipulation, and Control of Properties

If we consider a variable to be defined directly by the operation we use to make the variable manifest, then we shall almost always be certain we have produced the values of the variable we want, no matter what technique we are using. But we very often wish our manipulative operations to stand for a conceptually defined property, just as we wish our operationally defined measurement operations to stand for a conceptually broader property than, for example, "these check marks on these questions." And manipulative techniques differ in the degree to which the operations are close, so to speak, to the conceptual properties for which they stand. For example, if we wish to manipulate a property such as group size, and if we do it by varying the number of members in different groups, our operational definition is pretty close to the conceptualized property of interest. In contrast, if we wish to manipulate group cohesiveness, and if we do so by instructing some groups (but not others) in a way intended to make the members like one another, our operational definition (the specific instructions, as delivered) is rather far from the conceptual property (group cohesiveness) that we wish to study. Not only may there be aspects to group cohesiveness other than the liking of members one for another but there is also always a question as to whether our instructions *did* lead to increased liking among the members.

The mapping (or correspondence) a researcher may assert between cohesiveness and liking among group members is a conceptual mapping done within theoretical discourse; neither term, *liking* or *cohesiveness,* itself labels an empirical operation. The researcher moves from the concept of cohesiveness to the concept of liking because the step to an operation from the latter seems much more likely to elicit consensus from the researcher's colleagues than the step from the former. That is, if we want to find out about the distribution and intensity of liking in a group, it will probably seem reasonable to most researchers, or surely to many, to ask the members of the group about their liking for one another; to the best of our knowledge, however, no researcher has yet found a direct measure of group cohesiveness that attracts consensual acceptance from his colleagues.

Some operational definitions are virtually co-extensive with the conceptual definitions they are intended to realize, as in the example of number of members and group size. Other operational definitions stand in a many-to-one relation to the conceptual properties to which they are mapped; there are two cases: (1) where the conceptual property is a *combination* of two or more operationally defined properties (for example, task success might be assessed by a combination of productivity per time unit and by cost per time unit, each of these being independently assessed operational measures), or (2) where the operational definition is *one* of a number of indicators, *each* of which is independently symptomatic of the presence of a property (as example, a particular test item might be taken as an indicator of intelligence and a particular symptom as an indicator of a disease).

There is still another way in which an operational definition can be related to the underlying property, a way frequently used in behavioral science. The operational procedures used to manipulate a variable may be presumed to arouse or increase some process which *in turn* leads to the conceptually defined property of interest. For example, certain research activities may be intended to produce *practice* by an actor on a task, and that practice may be presumed to lead to learning and increased facility on the task. Most manipulations involving *training*—which is something the investigator *does to* the participant—really imply that there has been *learning,* which is something that goes on inside the participant himself. Here, the problem is compounded; there are two links, both of which have to hold for the manipulation to be successful. (1) The researcher's activities have to lead to practice or certain exposures called training, and (2) that practice or exposure has to lead to learning or a change in the actor's performance capability. If either of these links fails to hold, the intended manipulation is not attained. Some kinds of links are such that the experimenter can be highly confident that they have actually been accomplished. Basically, these are the kinds that depend on something the researcher himself does or does not do, or which depend on generating some overt (and therefore observable) behavior by the actors. But other kinds of links leave the investigator in considerable uncertainty as to whether he has achieved his intended effect. The latter are those manipulations that depend on change in an internal state of the actor—his perceptions, his feelings, and so forth—or in some ongoing process (such as attention) which is more or less observable.

All of this implies that the investigator must in some manner observe (mode *Y*) any property that he manipulates (mode *X*) or controls at a single value (mode *K*) if he is to verify the success of his treatment (that is, if he is to make sure that he has indeed brought that property to the intended value for each case). Indeed, we made this same assertion during our earlier discussion of operational definitions in section 6-1. To manipulate or control a property implies the prior capability of observing or measuring that property. And the investigator can know he has successfully controlled or manipulated a property only if he measures the property after he applies the operational procedures designed to manipulate or control it. It is perhaps trivial to point out that if one wants to study groups of sizes two, three, and four, one must make sure by counting members that every group one calls size two has two and only two members, and so on. But it is not trivial to point out that if one wishes to manipulate cohesiveness defined as members' liking for one another and to do so by instructions intended to increase liking, then one must apply some independent measure of degree of liking to find out if, in fact, liking among members became higher in groups receiving that instructional treatment than in groups not receiving that treatment. If it was higher, then one knows that the first link in his definitional chain held; the second link (liking being equivalent to cohesiveness) is definitional. But if one's instructions do *not* actually change liking, then whatever results one gets are *not* consequences of liking (hence cohesiveness), and failure to get differences (between high and low "cohesiveness" conditions) on a dependent variable must be interpreted as failure to implement the design partition (cohesiveness) rather than as evidence disconfirming the hypothesis involving the dependent variable. Such a check on the success of one's design partition (or design constant) is an essential step in *all* cases, though its implementation is so straightforward in instances such as number of members or sex of members that it is often done without realizing its significance.

If a manipulation succeeds for all cases, or for none, the consequences are clear-cut. If it succeeds for some but not all cases, then one has several possible alternative actions. If one ignores the fact that some of the cases manipulated to become higher on an *X* variable failed to become higher, then one weakens any comparison he makes between *X* and non-*X* subsets on other measured properties. If one removes the cases where the *X* manipulation did not succeed and compares the remaining cases of the *X* condition subset with the non-*X* subset, then one's design is vulnerable to the mortality factor or to a selection-by-treatment interaction (as discussed in Chapter 3 on study design). Still another alternative is to partition one's cases into three subsets for comparison:

1. Cases given *X*-treatment in which the treatment succeeded
2. Cases given *X*-treatment in which the treatment did not succeed
3. Cases given non-*X* treatment

There is the possibility of a fourth subset—cases given the non-X treatment but that turned out to be high on X anyway. For example, though we might have given one subset of groups instructions *not* meant to engender high liking among members, *some* of those groups might have turned out to have high liking among members anyway. Hence, we would really now have cases partitioned on two separate two-category design properties—one deliberately manipulated beforehand, the other observed (Y) and converted into a design partition (X) later. Appropriate comparisons of these four subsets of cases may give us some evidence about the effects (on some other, measured property) of liking with and without the instructional manipulation, and of the instructions with and without subsequent increases in liking among members. This procedure could indeed give us more information than our original design, but it poses two difficulties. First, we now have fewer cases within each subset and, hence, less reliable estimates of mean values. Furthermore, some of the subsets are likely to have very few cases; the better our experimental procedures, the more this will be true for the condition given the liking instruction without success and the condition given no instruction but nevertheless displaying high liking. Second, we do not have a "true experiment" with respect to our four conditions, because we did not randomize assignment of cases over those four conditions. Hence, all sorts of other properties may be varying between the subsets successfully and unsuccessfully manipulated, and one or more of these confounding properties, rather than either of our design variables, may be responsible for any systematic differences we might obtain between subsets.

The moral is obvious. First, one ought to do all he can to make sure that his operational procedures for manipulation will have their intended effect. One way to do so is to try out those procedures in a pretest and modify them until they *do* work. (See Chapter 9 on pretests.) Second, one *must* assess the success of one's manipulation procedures lest he have a confounded design and not know it. Third, if some cases do and others do not show a successful manipulation, one can use that information to partition further subsets and extract all the information one can from comparisons; but one should beware of the potential confounding of that information.[1]

8-2. Inherent versus Imposed Properties, or Selection versus Intervention

There are two general classes of techniques for manipulating and otherwise controlling properties. One is to locate cases having the desired values of the property and to include those cases in one's set of observations. This

[1] A quite different methodological orientation to this problem is presented by Aronson and Carlsmith (1968). They argue that the experimenter should strive for uniformity of effects, even if this requires nonuniformity in application of manipulation operations. We strongly disagree, for reasons that should be apparent from discussion in Chapter 3 and in Chapter 9. For a considered treatment of the two positions, see Kiesler, Collins, and Miller (1969, Chapter 2).

procedure is often called *selection* when applied to properties of actors, but the same logic can be applied to properties of tasks or of behavior settings or to properties that lie in the interaction between actors and situations. That is, one can select tasks for study, or select actors with certain relations to a setting, just as one can select actors for *their* properties. For example, a researcher interested in industrial settings might select actors according to job or function officially assigned them, such as assembly-line worker, machinist, pattern-maker, designer, foreman, office-systems expert, bookkeeper, and so forth. Alternatively, he might select tasks having several different characters, such as carrying out routine work, checking for accuracy, taking adaptive steps upon breakdown of routine, responding to a nonroutine request from another worker in the same crew, and so forth. Alternatively, the researcher might observe these actors and tasks while a new factory was being started up or while an existing factory was tooling up for a new model or while a product was being routinely produced or while a model or department or factory was being closed out. (Some problems associated with selecting samples were discussed in Chapter 5.)

The other general procedure is to *put* the desired different levels of a property into different subsets by deliberate manipulations. When applied to properties of actors, we often refer to such imposition as "practice" or "training." Modifying tasks or behavior settings is also widely done. We often seek to modify relations between actors and tasks or between actors and situations by inducing changes in perceptions of the actor or in the information the actor gets from his interactions within the setting. Perhaps the best general term for this deliberate manipulation, as distinct from *selection* techniques, is *intervention*. Whereas selection implies choosing cases for inclusion on the basis of some preexisting property (of actor, task, or setting), intervention implies deliberately generating specific levels of some property (of actor, task, or situation) for each case.

One of the two primary facets we used in Chapter 4 to elucidate the relation between the design of a study and its setting was exactly the facet we are now discussing again—the intrusiveness of modes X (and K), or selection versus intervention. Researchers sometimes conceive problems as most susceptible to the strengths of selection methods and sometimes as most susceptible to the strengths of interventionist methods. And since there is a certain amount of custom involved in matters such as this, bodies of lore grow up in connection with the study types laid out in Chapter 4. There is nothing sacred, however, about these various strategies; the researcher should choose the partitioning method best suited to the logic of his research question and let the study types fall where they may.

SELECTION TECHNIQUES

Two disadvantages of selection techniques are the potentially confounding effects of regression and selection (see Chapter 3). A crucial weakness is that partitioning by selection does not permit cases to be randomized over conditions; there may be any number of other properties associated with the property used for the design partition. (See the discussion of "unknown sampling bias" in section 3-3.) These other properties will be intrinsically confounded with the design partition; that is, using the concommitant properties to partition the cases would give nearly the same sorting of cases as was obtained by using the property actually used. The results, consequently, can be attributed just as logically to any one of these ignored and unknown variables, or to a combination of them, as to the originally intended design partition. For example, say we select actors on some personality trait (perhaps neuroticism), using some personality questionnaire to do so. Suppose that high versus low neuroticism happens to be highly correlated with high versus low intelligence within the population from which we sampled—but we do not know this, because we did not measure intelligence. Suppose, further, that intelligence *is* related to some performance which is the observed partition of our study, but that neuroticism, independent of intelligence, is not related to that performance. Our results will indicate a relation between neuroticism and the performance in question—and they will be systematically wrong. Selection techniques that do not include random assignment to conditions always run an unknown risk of this sort, and a larger risk, than do techniques using random selection.

Advantages of selection are (1) it is often less costly than intervention, (2) it is often less reactive, and (3) it usually preserves the naturalness of the setting to a greater degree than does an intervention. For further comments, see sections 4-1 and 4-2.

INTERVENTION TECHNIQUES

Intervention techniques frequently (but not always) can be accompanied by randomization of cases to treatment, thus reducing the likelihood of confounding from regression and selection effects, provided an otherwise adequate design is used. Also a very important advantage is the added confidence the intervention technique (mode X) gives the researcher that the causation does not move from the dependent variable to the independent—a point we discussed in sections 3-2 and 4-6.

Intervention techniques can avoid or minimize some of the weaknesses of selection techniques, but they are vulnerable to their own sort. For one, if the intervention is applied to different cases separately (for example, when an experiment is conducted over a period of time, with each case being observed separately on different days), then the intervention procedures may be vulnerable to "instrument decay"—that is, to *systematic* change over time (or between experimenters) in particular manipulation techniques.

An even more crucial weakness is one already discussed; namely, the investigator needs to devise some way to insure that the *intended* effect of his manipulation did in fact "take." In selection, this question is usually less crucial.[2] In selection, while the researcher must still worry about the adequacy of his choice of operational definition as a mapping of his conceptual definition, he can usually be sure that the operational definition holds for each case, because it is on the basis of his observation of this operationally defined property that he assigns each case to its appropriate subset. Thus, for example, if he measures intelligence for each case by some intelligence test and divides cases into high-, middle-, and low-intelligence groups, he "knows" that each high case did in fact have a high score on his test (though, of course, he still must be concerned about whether his test as an operational measure is an adequate one to map his *concept* of intelligence). When using intervention techniques, however, the researcher often cannot be sure that his manipulative activities had the operational result he intended, aside from the question of the adequacy of these operational results as mapped to a conceptual property. Two examples given earlier illustrate this problem: time on task as an indication of increased practice or learning and instructions as an indicator of increased liking of others which the instructions are meant to bring about.

There is a third potential weakness of intervention techniques, and perhaps the most crucial one. It is reflected in Campbell and Stanley's (1963) *testing* factor (see Chapter 3), or the term *sensitization,* or the broader term *reactive effects* (see Webb and others, 1966, and Chapter 7 of this book). The third weakness lies in the effects of the researcher's activities on the phenomena he wishes to study. This idea entered into our consideration of research designs (see testing effects, Chapter 3), our discussions of research strategies (see Chapter 4), and our discussion of the reactivity or obtrusiveness of sources of empirical evidence (see section 7-1). It is a very important part of our discussion of techniques for observation of properties, and it is crucial here, too, in our discussion of techniques for manipulation and control of properties. It is a fundamental fact of the behavioral sciences that whenever an investigator does something to assess the presence or level of a property in a given case (as in observation, mode *Y*), he risks altering that case on the property he is measuring and on some other properties. When he does something to *create* a particular level of a property in a given case, or to change the level of a property for that case, he runs an even greater risk that he will *unwittingly change other properties* at the same time.

The famous Hawthorne studies[3] represent a classic example of this problem. The investigators, attempting to study the effects of a variety of working conditions on industrial productivity, chose to put the subjects of their study in a special room where they were separated from other workers; the purpose was to isolate these workers and thus insure constancy of a number of properties the researchers wished to control (flow of materials, temperature,

---

[2]Although this is not always the case. One of the classic problems in operational definition is selecting respondents by social class. See, for example, Moore (1969).

[3]For a brief account of these studies, see Homans (1958); for further comment, see Chapter 9.

humidity, and the like) and to facilitate precise measurement of output. By their special treatment of the experimental group, however, the investigators created a very strong and favorable social climate whose effects on productivity far outweighed the effects of the design-partition variables (work-rest cycles, lighting, noise, and the like). Such *unintended consequences* are always a potential threat to the internal and external validity of a study. (See Argyris, 1968, for a discussion of this and other unintended consequences of the desire for precision and control in behavioral research.)

In brief, whenever an investigator employs an intervention technique, he runs serious risks if he does not insure (1) *that he did, in fact, change what he intended to change* by that technique; and (2) *that he did not change other things that he did not intend to change* by its use.

The problem of reactive effects of a manipulation (or control) technique is also related to the problem of variability in the dependent variable due to method, a problem introduced in our discussion of concepts of reliability and validity in Chapter 6. The effect obtained by applying any experimental manipulation is always composed of some combination of (1) a component resulting from change in the property the manipulation is intended to change, (2) a component resulting from unintended effects of that particular manipulation on one or more properties, and (3) a component resulting from unreliabilities in applying the manipulation procedures, such as those due to instrument variation. The multitrait-multimethod logic, as applied to observation of variables (mode *Y*), is also applicable to manipulation of variables (mode *X*). To establish the validity—or generalizability—of a manipulation, it is necessary to show (1) that the essential effects of the manipulation are repeatable for a population of actors and occasions, (2) that the manipulation gives the same results as other kinds of operations designed to manipulate the same property, and (3) that it gives discriminably different results than operations designed to manipulate different properties.

Let us consider as an example a study designed to compare (1) a particular training regimen that is intended to increase a leader's ability to show consideration for his group members with (2) a similar training regimen intended to increase the leader's ability to exert firm control over the group's performance of tasks. If one were to employ only the first regimen—perhaps in comparison to a condition in which the leader were given no training at all—and if one were to find that groups with trained leaders had superior performance, he might be tempted to conclude that consideration by the leader was functionally related to the effectiveness with which groups performed tasks. But suppose one also used some other method of manipulation, perhaps based on selection by a questionnaire measure of the considerateness of the leader; and suppose one also used a similar measure of the degree of control exerted by the leader. If, then, one were to apply both manipulation procedures (selection based on questionnaire, and training) for both properties (consideration and control), one might find that leaders trained in consideration had better performing groups, but that so did leaders trained in strict control. Hence, one would have to conclude that results were due to training, as such, rather than to the particular property dealt with in the training (perhaps because of the special attention involved, as in the Hawthorne studies). Perhaps, indeed, one could get similarly favorable results with *any* kind of training. Similarly, one might find that while training in consideration gave favorable results, *selection* on consideration did not. In this case, one would entertain some doubt as to which of the operational definitions of consideration, if either, was an adequate mapping of the concept—and, indeed, as to whether consideration were the crucial conceptual property involved in the improvement of performance.

Only when the researcher can show that multiple operations for manipulating or measuring the same property have similar effects, (that is, have convergent validity) and that those same kinds of operations applied to manipulate or measure another different property have different effects (that is, have discriminate validity), can he logically consider attributing those effects to the level of the particular property (such as consideration) rather than to unintended effects of the operational procedures themselves (such as the effects of training).

Selection and intervention techniques share one major weakness. Studies using selection techniques are vulnerable to confounding because the selection techniques may have partitioned cases on a cluster of properties that happen to be associated with the property on which the selection was actually based. Studies using intervention techniques are vulnerable to confounding because those techniques may also have manipulated a cluster of other properties along with the property purposely manipulated. In both cases, the investigator's desire to attribute effects to the manipulated differences on the intended property must be tempered by his awareness that the differences may have arisen because of unintended differences in other properties. The only cure for this problem is a massive checking for systematic differences in other properties that might account for the obtained differences. The further checking can be done, of course, either as supplementary analysis in the same study or as the deliberate focus of subsequent studies in a program of studies.

8-3. Inferred Locus of a Property

There are some differences in the applicability and efficiency of selection and intervention techniques that arise from the locus and substantive nature of the property to be manipulated. Consider, first, properties presumed to be inherent in the actors. Some of these, such as intelligence and other personality traits, are usually conceptualized as relatively stable and enduring states of the organism. For such variables, the possibility of manipulation by intervention is limited, if not ruled out by definition. Selection in some form would seem the only alternative. Some other properties, while also considered to inhere in the actor, are, nevertheless, conceptualized as readily modifiable, such as knowledge or level of some skill. Still others are properties that, although based on relatively permanent underlying dispositions, actually operate only when aroused by circumstances; examples are achievement striving, hunger, situationally based anxiety, and aggression. For such variables, intervention techniques may serve to create the conditions for various degrees of arousal or to produce changes in level of the property. But even here, the conception usually is that individual actors differ in the amount of the property when aroused. Hence, the investigator must consider the property as an *interaction* of actor and conditions—requiring both selection and intervention techniques.

Let us emphasize the point that the locus of a property is not something determined in heaven; it is a conception in the mind of an investigator. The concept of locus of a property is useful because it helps us to think about how we can observe the property. When we want to observe a property, we seek its locus; it is there that we shall be able to observe it. The property—so we are in the habit of thinking—exists in connection with some thing—actor, object, context, or some interaction of these.

But the allocation of locus is arbitrary, or at least largely so. In the Middle Ages, what we now believe to be culturally acquired modes of behavior were believed by almost everyone to be inborn; serfs and nobility were considered to be more disparate than different races. In our own time, we have come to relinquish the belief that the locus of leadership lies in the individuals we call leaders; we now locate leadership in the interaction between members of the group displaying different but interdependent roles. The choice of locus the researcher makes for a property is made manifest when the researcher establishes an operational definition (that is, his manipulation or measurement procedures) and again when he processes and analyzes his data.

The degree to which the investigator's conceptualizations affect the locus of a property can be illustrated by a training procedure—for example, repeatedly exposing actors to certain sets of stimulus materials. If the stimulus or task materials are considered homogeneous replications, the investigator may search for differences among individuals in learning abilities or rates; that is, he may conceive learning rate to be located in the actor. But in another case, the researcher may be interested in differential persuasibility and may consider this quality to be an interaction between actor and stimulus or actor and context. In still another case, if the investigator views the actors as more or less interchangeable replications, he may search for systematic differences in subsets of stimulus materials and may allocate to them properties such as simple versus complex or easy versus difficult or persuasive versus unpersuasive. Alternatively, the researcher may search for interaction effects between actor and stimulus such as differential reactions to neutral and arousing stimuli by actors "possessing" high and low anxiety. Another example would be the concept of aggression. In some cases, aggression appears to be considered a relatively stable property of an actor. In other cases, aggression is treated as a relation of an actor to a situation. In still others, aggression seems to be considered a relation of an actor to one or more other actors.

On the side of data analysis, relations between two or more properties are likely to show quite different patterns (even when the same operational definitions are used) when those relations are generated by pooling stimuli or situations and correlating across actors (that is, treating stimuli as replications and actors as a design partition) than when relations are computed by pooling actors and correlating across stimuli or situations (that is, treating actors as replications and stimuli as a design partition).[4] The idea that outcomes of empirical research depend on investigator's choices as well as on the investigated phenomena is a recurrent theme of this book; it will be brought out again in later chapters.

It is not possible to list exhaustively, within any reasonable space, all of the specific techniques that have been used to manipulate variables in the behavioral sciences. Even a limited exposure to the research literature will verify the wide range of techniques (and the considerable ingenuity) employed.

ESTABLISHING THE LOCI OF PROPERTIES BY SELECTION

On the selection side, there are literally as many potential techniques for manipulation and control as there are observable properties and ways of observing them. There are many tests of intelligence, abilities, personality traits, attitudes, values, and motivations. Any of these—indeed, any trait of actors for which the investigator can devise a measure—can be used as the basis for a design partition by selection. The same is true of any stimulus, task, or situational property. While far less has been done with stimulus, task, or situational properties than with properties of actors, there are, nevertheless, described in the literature many instances of partitioning these by selection as well. These range all the way from molecular properties of specific stimuli (such as degrees of illumination, frequency of sounds, curvature of lines) to molar properties and even constellations of properties by which two or more different, entire cultures can be distinguished. Again, any property or constellation of properties, different values of which can be distinguished, can be used in this way.

The ways of distinguishing or observing properties of stimuli, tasks, and situations vary widely. Sometimes, especially for the more molecular properties such as frequencies of sounds, the observation can be made with highly reliable and sensitive instruments. Sometimes variations in stimulus or task properties are established by a consensus of observers' judgments (see, for example, Fiedler, 1967; Shaw and Blum, 1966; Hackman, Jones, and McGrath, 1967). Sometimes differences among molar stimulus complexes are established on the basis of the investigator's own observation, or on grounds that the differences are self-evident (for example, comparing reactions of men in combat and men in rear areas).

[4]For an explanation of this phenomenon, see the section on relations among three or more variables in Chapter 13.

ESTABLISHING THE LOCI OF PROPERTIES BY INTERVENTION

Manipulation techniques involving intervention are also highly varied. Interventions regarding properties of the actor usually take the form of practice, exposure, and training. Those involving properties of the task or stimulus usually involve imposing a particular task experimentally or varying parameters of the task experimentally (for example, speeding up information input, adding complexity, adding ambiguity). Interventions regarding situation or setting may involve manipulation of physical parameters such as crowding or physical danger or social parameters such as isolation versus the company of others.

Perhaps the more difficult manipulations are those that involve relations between the actor and the task or the setting (including other actors). Here, three special classes of techniques have been widely used—and as widely criticized: instructions, feedback, and the use of confederates.

Instructions

One class of techniques is the use of verbal instructions to *induce* changes in actor perceptions. Perhaps the classic example is Back's (1951) use of verbal instructions to induce group cohesiveness (attraction of members for one another). Essentially, Back instructed members of his group-to-be that they had been selected for compatibility and would probably like one another. A subsequent measure of the members' attraction toward the group showed that these instructions did, in fact, achieve the desired result for most actors. The use of instructions to induce a desired level of a property has been used as the case in point for many of the problems in interventions described earlier in this chapter.

Feedback

Another class of manipulation techniques designed to alter perceptions of actors involves presenting feedback to the actor—false feedback is often used—about his own prior task performance or about others' feelings toward him. Feedback about task performance sometimes takes the form of alleged "performance norms" that purport to show that the actor's own performance has been poor (or good). Sometimes the feedback is a direct assertion by the experimenter that the actor has failed (or succeeded) on the task. Feedback about interpersonal relations often asserts that co-workers dislike the subject (or like him) or that he has been rejected (or preferred) for some group role on a vote.

Aside from the difficulties involved in all manipulations involving perceptions of actors, the use of false feedback raises two further questions. One is tactical: will the manipulation be believed? If it is not, the investigator loses his credibility, and subsequent responses from the actor may be confounded by the effects of his perceptions of the investigator and the study. The other question is ethical: does the investigator, in pursuit of "truth", have the right deliberately to deceive cooperating participants? This question has been the focus of much consideration and debate among behavioral scientists in recent years. A number of scholars (for example, Kelman, 1966; Milgram, 1964), some professional societies (see, for example, American Psychological Association, 1967), and government agencies (see, for example, U.S. Surgeon General's Office, 1967) have published thoughtful treatments of the topic and have taken positions on it. It is our judgment that ethical questions such as this one, while exceedingly important for behavioral scientists, are properly to be decided on moral or value criteria rather than on scientific or logical criteria; hence, they are personal and idiosyncratic. On the other hand, the question whether a certain type of norm concerning interpersonal behavior (such as deceiving others when it advances one's own purpose) encourages members of a society to collaborate in social-scientific studies, or discourages them from doing so, is an empirical matter. Along with others, we believe the evidence is growing that participants who have been deceived by experimenters grow significantly more suspicious and guarded toward subsequent experimenters and often pass this attitude along to otherwise naïve subjects. Even aside from this consideration, the tactical risks involved in *any* deceptive manipulation (over and above the moral risks involved) are sufficiently great that a behavioral scientist is foolish (whether or not he is "bad") to use deception if other means are available for him to accomplish the same purpose. (We shall discuss further the relation between investigator and actor and its *ethical* aspects in Chapter 9.)

Confederates

A third class of techniques intended to modify perceptions of actors is the use of confederates ("stooges," "plants"), who act as if they are ordinary participants in the study but who are actually in league with the investigator. Some of the most dramatic studies in the behavioral sciences (for example, Asch, 1956; Schacter, 1951; Milgram, 1963; Rosenthal and Cofer, 1948) have used this procedure. Use of confederates can have far more impact than instructions and can appear far more credible than feedback mediated by the investigator. Yet there remains the risk of not being believed, together with the ethical problems of deception. There is also an additional problem concerning rigor; namely, insuring that the confederate implements the intended variation in the property or properties of concern (and not in other properties) and does so in the same way, or to the same degree, for all cases. (This is the problem of instrument decay discussed in Chapter 3.)

A researcher often uses live confederates rather than instructions or false feedback because he believes that the confederate can make appropriate variations in his specific responses as the interaction proceeds, and thereby make the situation more credible than could unchanging instructions or feedback. If the investigator wants an exact, specific stimulus at each point in time regardless of the actor's particular behaviors, he may be able to obtain this without using a confederate. It is because he wants stimuli with a certain *meaning* for the participant in relation to the latter's particular behavior that he uses a live, cooperating confederate. But this very desire for flexibility invites variability over which the investigator has little control (and which he often must go to great pains to measure). The degree to which this is a problem, of course, depends on the specific properties that the confederate is trying to manipulate, on the nature of the setting, on the confederate's acting skill, and so forth. But use of confederates is always relatively vulnerable to the plausible alternative hypothesis of instrument decay, as well as to the other weaknesses of manipulations involving interventions.

8-4. Concluding Comments

At this point, the reader may feel somewhat discouraged by the constraints and limitations we have discussed. We are not, however, trying to present either complexity or difficulty for its own sake but rather to make clear the view that there is no ideal research design. Every design must in the end be accepted by its maker as less than he would wish. If there were one royal road to research, one "Open, Sesame!" it would have been discovered long ago and by now would surely have been standardized. The fact is that knowledge about the empirical world is always bought at a price, though the researcher always has some degree of choice about what he will buy and what he will pay. We have pointed out certain choices of this sort in each chapter. The fact that these choices exist only reflects the relation between man and his universe—that he can look at the world from many points of view, that he can learn something new every time, and that he will never reach the point of view that is the final, correct point of view. Every research problem will always remain open to a new onslaught of ingenuity.

We hope the designer of empirical studies, once he thoroughly understands that every design must mix weaknesses with strengths, will not display his designs to his colleagues in a spirit of apology for their weaknesses, but rather in a spirit of pride in the way he has maximized those strengths most vital to a fruitful investigation of his specific research questions. When an investigator chooses to manipulate or control a particular variable (to gain the potential advantages of doing so, as described here and in Chapter 3), he has necessarily incurred several further choices as to how he will carry out that manipulation and check on its effectiveness; and each of those choices in turn offers advantages and poses difficulties. This theme—the need to choose between alternatives, each of which offers mixed blessings—has been implicit in previous chapters and will recur again in later chapters.

8-5. Further Reading

There is little in the literature that slices the topics of this chapter in just the way we have done. Nevertheless, this chapter owes much of its content to certain authors we have already mentioned in the body of the chapter; we repeat them here for convenience: Campbell and Stanley (1963), Webb and others (1966), and Argyris (1968).

CHAPTER 9

Conduct of the Study

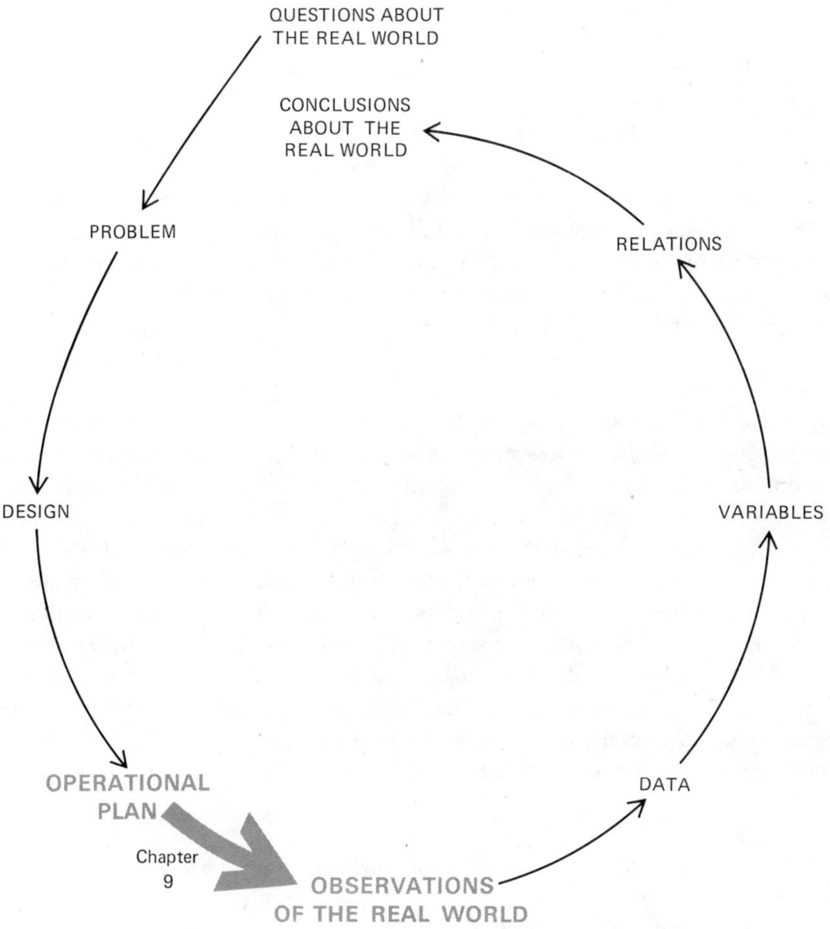

In this chapter, we take the big step from *planning* to *doing* a research study. Up to this point, we have dealt exclusively with choices involved in planning. In the chapters that follow we shall be concerned with processing, analyzing, and interpreting empirical information after it has been gathered. We are concerned in this chapter with the choices and problems that arise in actually gathering the empirical information—in implementing the plan.

This middle stage of the research process, when the plan is brought into contact with the portion of the empirical world to be studied, differs from both the prior planning stages and the subsequent analysis and interpretation stages. It is less conceptual or abstract and more concrete than earlier or later stages. Consequently, our consideration of this information-gathering stage will be less systematic and will call upon more lore and art than our discussions of earlier or later stages.

For convenience, we shall divide the chapter into four sections. The first section deals with some of the problems that arise because the empirical observations of a study are always taken from some *particular behavior setting,* whereas the investigator usually wants to draw conclusions from his data concerning a broader class of behavior settings. In other words, we shall be concerned with some of the unintended effects or constraints of the research setting itself. In some ways, this section is an elaboration of certain of the problems of study design raised in Chapters 3 and 4. The second section deals with problems concerning relations between the investigating team and the persons who participate in the study. We have already discussed some problems of a scientific or technical nature coming under this heading, such as the problems of sampling discussed in Chapter 5; but in this chapter we shall go on to some practical problems and some important ethical concerns.

The third section deals with the conduct of pilot studies and pretests—tryouts of equipment, arrangements, and procedures conducted before collecting the body of information to be included in the "main" study. Here we shall be concerned with the uses the pilot studies or pretests can serve and with the kinds of modifications of the study plan to which they can lead. We shall also discuss the question of when to stop pretesting and begin the main study. The fourth section deals with problems encountered in actually running the study. This includes matters of scheduling and timing; minor fluctuations in procedures, arrangements, and cases; and the like. These problems center around the conflicting needs for standardization and generalizability. While these are largely practical problems, the solution chosen for each of them can have major consequences on the results obtained and their interpretation.

9-1. The Information-Gathering Setting as a Behavior Setting

There are essentially three forms of behavior settings in which one can gather empirical information (see quadrants I, II, and III in Figure 4-1). First, one can make observations of behavior in existing settings (*natural* or *real-life* settings) without intervention (the field study strategy) or with relatively minor intervention (the field experiment strategy). Second, one can bring participants into a contrived setting—either a setting closely modeled after a class of natural settings (the experimental simulation strategy) or a setting modeled in terms of some abstracted set of variables, properties, or processes of real settings (the laboratory experimental strategy). Third, one can deal with the participants as "judges" or "respondents" *as if* their responses were uninfluenced by, or somehow transcended, the particular setting (doorstep interview, classroom questionnaire, and the like) in which those responses are actually made (the judgment-task strategy and the sample survey strategy). Researchers sometimes seem to forget the important fact that behavior in contrived settings or in settings the investigator wishes to ignore or mute is nonetheless behavior in a behavior setting. It is true, of course, that behavior in an experimentally contrived setting may not be affected by the same aspects of that setting, or affected in the same way, as would analogous behavior in a natural setting. Indeed, this potential difference in effect of the setting is precisely the reason that results from contrived settings often are not directly generalizeable. The important point is, however, that the behavior setting of the study, be it real, contrived, or muted, *will have effects* on the behavior providing the empirical information of the study. Some of these effects may be unintended, unrecognized, and lead to confounding unless preventive steps are taken.

SOME EFFECTS OF EXPERIMENTAL SETTINGS

When we talked about design in Chapter 3, we dealt mainly with design partitions (that is, division of cases into two or more categories) and control groups (that is, sets of cases which did and which did not receive a certain experimental treatment). But the idea of a control group is complex. Often we need what amounts to a spectrum of control groups, each "controlling" or providing a comparison with respect to some aspects, but not others, of the total experiment in a behavior setting.

Before discussing some varieties of control conditions that can yield useful comparisons, we shall consider some of the special problems which can arise because the information-gathering setting is, itself, a behavior setting; these are the problems giving rise to the need for multiple comparisons.

Effects of the Experimenter's Expectations

Research on humans, done by humans, is subject to many kinds of "human" errors. One kind stems from the fact that the experimenter himself has certain expectations (even hopes) about the outcome of his study. The research literature of psychology and social psychology is replete with studies demonstrating that the expectations of persons who are participants in studies alter and distort their perceptions of events. It should come as no surprise, therefore, that the perceptions of persons who are investigators of studies are also influenced by their expectations about outcomes. In recent years, a sizable body of research literature has developed around the idea that experimenters' expectations can affect research results.

Rosenthal (1967) has shown that results of studies of learning on animals, as well as social psychological studies of human subjects, can be affected by the investigator, *unwittingly*, in the direction favoring his hypothesis. Such effects apparently come about through small and subtle differences in the investigator's behavior toward actors in different experimental treatments. In the case of animal studies, for example, differences in the investigator's handling and fondling of animals in different treatment conditions can affect performance of experimental tasks. In the case of studies involving humans, there is ample room for subtle differences in the experimenter's behavior toward subjects—in tone of voice, facial expression, various mannerisms—which may affect the actors' later performance.

Effects of Experimental Demand

Orne and co-workers (Orne, 1962) have been concerned with a broader class of problems (which includes the experimenter's expectations) they call the "experimental demands" of the research setting. This work is built on the premise that actors enter the experimental setting with certain sets of expectations about what will happen and with certain motivations—to do well, to help science, to appear as a nice person, and the like. Once in the situation, actors seem to operate as if their main task is to find out what the experimenter wants of them and behave accordingly. The correctness of the actor's hypothesis about the experimenter's hypothesis, then, will determine whether the experiment supports or fails to support the hypotheses of the study.

Pursuing this line of reasoning, Orne has used a group of "simulating subjects" as a comparison condition. The simulating subject is told what has happened to other actors in the experimental treatment and is asked to behave *as if* he had received the real experimental treatment. To the extent that simulating actors can fool the experimenter or his agent (who does not know which actors are real and which are simulators), there is evidence that results seemingly due to the experimental treatment are confounded with effects stemming from the demands felt by the actors.

Another similar device to control for experimental demand is the case of "hypothetical" actors. Here, a separate group of actors is given a description of the experimental treatment and is asked how they think most actors would behave under such conditions. Again, to the extent that actors who are only hypothetically in the experimental treatment can predict accurately how actors in the real experimental treatment do, in fact, behave, we have reason to question the extent to which the experimental results are to be attributed to the experimental treatment itself.

EFFECTS OF THE SETTING IN NON-LABORATORY STUDIES

It is easy to get the impression from the forgoing discussion that expectations of actors and investigators, and experimental demand in general, take place only in studies done in laboratory settings. But a technical term known to all social scientists—the *Hawthorne effect*—testifies to similar effects in field studies and field experiments.

During the 1930's, a group of American behavioral scientists (see Roethlisberger and Dickson, 1939, or the brief description of their work by Homans,

1965) were attempting to find out how various working conditions (time of rest periods, lighting, noise, and so on) affected productivity. The studies were done in the Hawthorne plant of the Western Electric Company and have since been known as the Hawthorne studies. They selected a group of female workers to be tested and placed them in a separate work room. There the experimenters could control and manipulate features of the work environment and get accurate measures of each individual's work output. The investigators found that productivity increased when various favorable conditions (better lighting, more rest periods, and the like) were tried. They also found, however, that productivity increased when presumably detrimental conditions (long work periods, more noise, and the like) were tried. Indeed, they eventually concluded that variations in the work conditions themselves had little to do with the rises in productivity they found. Rather, the increased productivity seemed to come from the dramatic changes in the social conditions the investigators had unwittingly created. The research procedures had made the persons in the experimental group *feel as if they were special persons* because they were getting a great deal of special attention from the researchers and from the management. Moreover, the workers had been put into a set of conditions under which different patterns of informal social relations (closer interpersonal ties) could develop in the job setting. These influences—receiving special attention and acting within changed social relations—produced effects that far outweighed the effects of the experimental treatments the investigators had planned to study. The effects on actors of being singled out to receive the special attention of being treated as experimental subjects has become known as the *Hawthorne effect*. This is an instance of an effect similar to experimental demand such as studied by Orne, but one occurring in a field experiment rather than in a laboratory study.

Argyris (1968) has also commented on the effects of the social structure enclosing the investigator (and his agents) and the actors being studied. He points out that the usual procedures used to carry out rigorous research designs of the highly controlled sort often place the subjects of the study in a relation to the investigator that is similar to the position of lower-level employees in a hierarchical organization. This can result in certain reactions of actors in a study similar to those of lower-level employees in work organizations—such as developing dependence upon the researchers, withdrawal, aggression toward the researchers, and eventual banding together to protect their interests.

It is important to note that the Hawthorne effect can work both ways; special attention may spur actors to behave according to the researcher's hypothesis or contrary to it. Children under friendly attention often "show off" in ways for which their parents have punished them in the past. Some students perform well under the eye of the teacher, but others do poorly or deliberately slow their work rate. Workers in experimental programs do not always increase their productivity; many cases of deliberate "slowdowns" are on record. How the actor will respond to new input from the environment—whether from the researcher or from some other attention-giver—is a matter to be predicted from the theory the researcher has chosen as applicable to the particular research setting. Finally, as Sommer (1968) points out, the Hawthorne effect can be treated as a competing hypothesis and a nuisance, or it can be studied as an interesting and potentially useful effect in its own right. Some investigators who have studied the expectations in the experimental setting as interesting in their own right are Dulany (1967) and Bem (1970).

A SPECTRUM OF CONTROL AND QUASI-CONTROL CONDITIONS FOR ASSESSING EFFECTS OF RESEARCH SETTINGS

All of the potential effects of experimental settings discussed in the previous section are instances of alternative hypotheses. The task of experimental design is to render those rival hypotheses implausible, or at least to generate information by which their plausibility can be estimated. It was mentioned earlier in this chapter that the idea of a "control group" is relatively complex and that there is actually a spectrum of "control conditions" which can provide useful comparisons. These comparisons serve primarily to help assess whether certain aspects of the experimental arrangements have led to unintended effects and spurious conclusions; they extend the discussion of experimental conditions given in Chapters 3 and 4. Table 9-1 lists some of the more frequently used control and quasi-control conditions, and Table 9-2 indicates the kinds of spurious effects that can be identified by various comparisons among the conditions. Many of the conditions and comparisons displayed in the tables have to do with degrees of knowledge of members of the study population about the experimental treatments they have undergone and their guesses concerning the experimenter's expectations. These conditions are related to the broad class of experimental demands studied by Orne (1962). But another related class of problems has to do with unintended effects of the knowledge an experimenter (or observer) has about the study's hypotheses and about the

Table 9-1. *A Spectrum of Experimental, Quasi-Control, and Control Conditions for Assessing the Effects of the Experimental Setting*

Experimental treatment (X): Actor is subjected to the full experimental treatment.

Placebo condition: Actor is subjected to everything in X except the hypothesized "active ingredient." Actor thinks he is receiving the experimental treatment.

Simulating subjects: Actor (subject) is subjected to everything in X except the hypothesized "active ingredient." Actor knows he is not receiving all of X but is instructed to act as if he were.

The "everything but" control condition: Actor is subjected to everything except x and receives no special instructions.

Hypothetical condition: Actor is told about the experiment and the treatment X and is *asked* how he would respond if he were in that setting and had received treatment X.

The "no treatment" control condition: None of the procedures of other conditions are used, but dependent variables are measured.

Table 9-2. *Information Given by Some Comparisons among Experimental, Quasi-Control, and Control Conditions*

COMPARISON	INFORMATION GIVEN
X versus placebo	Effect of the "active ingredient."
X versus "everything but" control; also placebo versus "everything but" control	Effects of actor's expectations.
X versus simulating subjects	Effects of "experimental demand." Also effects of experimenter's expectations if experimenter is blind to treatments.
X versus hypothetical condition	Effects of unintended constraints or of actor's common sense, normative expectations, or implicit theory about the experiment.
"Everything but" control versus "no treatment" control	Effects of the experimental setting in relation to the "natural" base rate of the dependent variable.

experimental treatments. Some of the kinds of conditions of the observer's knowledge and the nature of the effects they may have are given in Table 9-3.

The implications of Tables 9-1 and 9-3 for experimental design may seem devastating. One premise of the experimental method as discussed in Chapter 4 is that a study needs to be designed so as to eliminate, or at least assess, *all* plausible rival hypotheses. If there is a need for four or five control conditions for a given experimental treatment, as in Table 9-1 (and, of course, a multiplication of these if more than one experimental treatment is under consideration), and if there is a need for having observers in each of various states of knowledge about the study, as in Table 9-3, as well as the need for kinds of experimental arrangements discussed in Chapters 3 and 4, then an adequate test of the effect of even a single experimental treatment, X, at a single

Table 9-3. *Effects of Knowledge on the Part of the Observer about the Study Conditions*

OBSERVER'S KNOWLEDGE ABOUT THE HYPOTHESES	OBSERVER'S KNOWLEDGE OF THE EXPERIMENTAL TREATMENTS: *Informed*	*Blind*
Informed	Observer's own expectations can systematically bias the results in favor of the investigator's hypotheses.	Observer's own hypotheses can confound the results of the study.
Blind	Observer's own hypotheses can confound the results of the study.	Observer's own hypotheses affect the study only randomly.

Note: If the investigator systematically *misinforms* the observer about treatments or hypotheses, the consequences are the same in *type* as in the table but opposite in direction of effect on the results of the study.

value X_1—not to mention multiple treatments at multiple levels—becomes virtually impossible to carry out within a single feasible study.

This depressing conclusion is, in fact, correct. Its devastating implications for the viability of scientific behavioral research are mitigated by two considerations, however:

1. It is *not* necessary, and often not useful, to employ *all* forms of control conditions within a given study.
2. It is *not* necessary, and indeed not possible, to do everything in one study; research can (in fact, must) be done so that findings are cumulative.

In regard to the first consideration, the more a study uses obtrusive manipulations or measurements, the more urgent it is that the investigator assure himself that various effects of experimental arrangements are not producing his results. It is when the actors are aware of being in an experiment, and when they have some knowledge (accurate or otherwise) of the experimental treatment and of its hypothesized effects, that one needs placebo, simulating subjects, and hypothetical conditions. When the observation is unobtrusive, the need for any but a baseline control group can often be slight. The same is true of the varieties of observers' states of knowledge. Unless one wishes deliberately to study the effects of observers' expectations, the "double-blind" condition (observers not knowing the treatment received nor the hypotheses) can often be used as a single observing condition. But often a double-blind arrangement is not possible. In such cases, it is important that the investigator understand the kinds of unwanted effects he is potentially introducing and try to devise ways to assess or minimize them.

As to the second consideration (that is, the need to design research so as to be cumulative), it has been a major theme of this book that *all* research should strive to be cumulative. For research to be cumulative, the researcher must not only have a broad knowledge of relevant prior research and theory but he must also attempt to build upon it, to elaborate and test it, and to make it possible for others to do the same with respect to his work. For example, to permit comparison of findings and interpretations of a new study with an earlier one, researchers often include control comparisons in their studies with procedures previously used by another researcher in the same problem area. We shall discuss further the characteristics of cumulative research in Chapter 14.

In any case, no one study can "prove" a hypothesis.[1] Nor can any one study rule out *all* possible rival hypotheses. The guide for good design is to rule out, by study design, the *most plausible* rival hypotheses (as many as one can afford to deal with) and at the same time to use all procedures possible (such as randomization, multiple observers, multiple measures, and counter-

---

[1] Strictly speaking, results of a study cannot even "support" a hypothesis. A study can only provide an opportunity for the hypothesis to be disconfirmed, and then *fail to disconfirm it.*

balanced sequences) to try to prevent still other factors (which are not to be dealt with in the study design) from having *systematic* biasing effects on study results. Given the limits of inductive logic, as well as limitations of time, money, and resources, that is the most any investigator can do—and the least he should set out to do.

9-2. The Information-Gathering Setting as a Relation between Research Team and Study Population

The information-gathering situation is a relation between the investigator (along with his research team) and the population whose behavior is to be studied. This fact poses a series of problems with which the investigator must grapple, some ethical, some scientific or technical, and some practical. The ethical problems arise because humans should have the right (we believe) *not* to be observed, *not* to be a participant in the investigator's study; and if they do participate in his study, they have the right to humane and decent treatment throughout. The scientific problems arise because of sampling problems and reactive effects that occur when a set of "informed volunteers" serves as study participants and the equally difficult sampling problems that arise when the study participants are people whose behavior is observed without their knowledge. The practical problems arise because of the difficulty of actually getting into communication with members of the intended study population and gaining their cooperation or gaining access to settings within which unobtrusive observations are to be made. These three sets of problems interlock; often the most practical solution or the best one from a scientific point of view raises disturbing ethical questions, and conversely. The problems are not limited to laboratory studies, though much more has been written about them in that context than in others; the problems present themselves in somewhat different guises in survey and field studies than in the laboratory. The ethical, scientific, and practical aspects of relations between study population and research team will be discussed together in this section, with the topic divided on the basis of problems that arise before the study starts (getting access to study populations and obtaining cooperation from them), problems involved during the course of the study (freedom to disengage, use of deception, irreversible effects on participants), and problems to be dealt with after the study is over (debriefing, treating data confidentially).

GAINING ACCESS TO STUDY POPULATIONS

Somehow, the investigator must gain access to some portion of the behavior of some portion of the population upon which his study is to be based. How he does this will determine (1) the relation between himself and the participants in his study; (2) the specific forms of the ethical, scientific, and practical questions he must resolve during and after his study; and (3) the specific opportunities and limitations placed upon him in his procedures for control, manipulation, and measurement of variables, and, hence, the limitations upon the questions his study can ask and answer. One important aspect of the investigator's means of gaining access to a study population is the relation of the study's participants to the study in terms of their knowledge that they are being studied and in terms of their willingness to participate. Let us consider first the case of the person who knows his behavior is to be made the subject of a research study.

Research in Which Participants Are Aware of Their Roles

There are four general ways in which an investigator can gain access to behaviors of a study population. First, he can seek out, or be sought out by, key persons who control access to the behavior of a population appropriate for study. Many studies have been done, for example, with the investigator working in a relation of consultant to client (key persons in an industrial setting, military setting, or educational setting) where members of the study population of interest were made available to him because they, or the settings they were in, were more or less under the control of the "client." Second, many studies have been carried out using as participants individuals who themselves were clients (or patients) of the investigator in clinical, counseling, or similar situations. Here the subjects themselves sought the services of the investigator.

Note that while both of these kinds of studies have in common the feature that some "client" of the investigator made access to the study population possible, they differ in the degree to which the subjects of study themselves freely volunteered to participate. In the case of studies on clients or patients, the subject of study himself sought the relation with the investigator and, hence, presumably expected to gain some benefit from the procedures comprising the study. In the cases where the client merely made available access to a population of actors who were in behavior settings more or less under the client's control, there is no basis for supposing (without explicit evidence) that individuals whose behavior thus became the subject of study were freely giving their consent or anticipated any benefit from the study.

The third and fourth major routes for access to study populations are through recruitment by the investigator. Recruitment can take either of two forms; these two forms, like the two described above, differ in the willingness of the subjects to participate. One form occurs when the investigator recruits volunteers to participate in his study, perhaps with monetary inducements, and self-selected individuals volunteer to do so. The other form occurs when the investigator recruits participants for his study by exerting influence on persons with whom he already has some influential relation—students in his classes, his friends, players on the Little League team of which he is manager, and the like. In the latter case, while the participant knows he is the subject of research, and while he may have technically given his consent, it is not reasonable to assume that his willingness is as complete as that of freely volunteering subjects. The chief difference between these two methods of inducement lies in whether the actor is offered some pleasure in participating

Table 9-4. *Relation of Participants to the Research When They Know They Are Participating*

	AGENT WHO RECRUITS PARTICIPANT	
WILLINGNESS OF PARTICIPATION	*Investigator*	*Client*
Self-selected volunteers	Willing volunteers	Clients
Semicoerced volunteers	Semicoerced volunteers	Populations controlled by clients

or is threatened (if only implicitly) with some potential unpleasantness for not participating.

We can represent these four methods of gaining access to a study population in a two-by-two diagram (Table 9-4), with one axis of the diagram labeled with respect to whether the investigator or a client establishes access to the study population and the other with respect to whether it is reasonable to presume willing consent. Note that all four cases are subject to problems of sampling, as discussed in Chapter 5, and to reactive effects, as discussed in Chapters 3 and 7. In the two cases where there is willing consent—the client and the volunteer subject—the sampling is a matter of self-selection and the resulting study population is not a randomly selected sample of any coherently specifiable population. In the two cases where there is some degree of non-willingness, the respective populations are selected on the basis of coercibility and again do not represent a random sample of a clearly specifiable population. Thus all four of these cases compromise the external validity of a study. All four cases also invite reactive effects. Self-selected volunteers presumably represent populations that have some stake in contributing to the "success" of the study and, hence, are likely to be influenced by the kinds of experimental demands described by Orne and discussed earlier in this chapter. The semi-coerced actors are very likely to resent being used as study participants; they may very well represent biases opposite in direction to those postulated by Orne. The nonvolunteer cases, of course, also raise serious problems of an ethical nature—under what conditions, if any, is it appropriate for individuals to be coerced, either by the investigator or by a client, into having their behavior become the subject of a research study when they are not free to refuse? This and related questions of ethics will be discussed under "The Ethical Issues of Informed Consent" later in this section.

Some Roles of Investigators

Behavioral scientists have become accustomed to referring to the persons whose behavior they are studying as *subjects*. Originally, this word was used, as in the *subject* of a sentence, to denote the unit of study. Unfortunately, the word *subject* also has a social-status meaning—as in *subject of the crown*—which denotes one of subservient status. Even more unfortunately, the term as used in behavioral science research too often seems to carry the flavor of subjugation, at least in the minds of potential study participants—if not, indeed, for some investigators as well. We have avoided use of the term *subject* in this book. Instead, we have used *actor,* which itself has certain unfortunate connotations. It is not really very important which word is used in reference to study participants. What matters is the investigator's attitude toward participants in his study and their attitude toward him.

When speaking of attitudes between the investigator and the people he is studying, we mean, of course, the readiness the investigator has to act toward the actors in certain preferred ways, and vice versa. There is hardly any assertion more honored by the literature of social science and by common experience than the assertion that the possibilities for interaction between humans are circumscribed by the expectations for reciprocal role behavior that exist at the onset of the interaction. The expectations with which the researcher approaches the participants and the expectations with which they approach him will have a great influence on the ensuing behavior. As we mentioned in section 9-1, Argyris (1968) has described in detail the effects of a role relation in which the researcher and actors accept the role of the researcher as *authority* or "boss." There are other kinds of role relations a researcher can have with participants. He can be called in by participants to ferret out information about them that they are unable to conceive or elicit themselves; in this role, the researcher might be viewed as an *expert*—much as one considers an auditor or a pest exterminator. For example, industrial organizations often call in applied social scientists to study the functioning of the organization and make prognoses or recommendations about steps that will produce desirable changes.

Another role for the researcher is that of *facilitator;* in this role, he joins more intimately with the actors in their day-to-day work and helps them learn how to conduct research sequences that will enhance their problem-solving. A geologist, for example, might participate with members of a construction firm in assessing the load-bearing characteristics of terrain and soils where some new buildings were planned; in the process, the builders would learn how to carry on certain parts of this kind of research by themselves. As another example, a policy committee might appoint one of its members to collect information periodically (by questionnaire, immediate oral report, pressing signal buttons, or whatever) concerning the effectiveness of its own deliberations and decision-making. Upon considering the facilitator's report, the committee could design new procedures to improve its processes. In both these last examples, the facilitator is an active member of the actual work group.

Perhaps some other styles of interaction will be developed in the future. It is desirable, of course, to find a relation in which both the investigators and the participants stand to gain from their joint activities. While the investigator needs access to appropriate settings and behavior to obtain research data, he should try to develop ways to give participants some feedback that will be valuable to them in some way. He should do this not only because such an exchange is decent and equitable but also because it is under such circumstances that participants are most likely to be willing to participate and be cooperative throughout the study.

When a researcher from a university or government agency enters a school or a business firm to collect data primarily for his own purposes, it is difficult for the participants to see him in any other role than that of an authority wielding arbitrary power. As a result, they are likely to react defensively and keep to themselves information they think might put them in an undesirable light. This is a disadvantage. On the other hand, people will reveal certain kinds of information to an outsider that they will not tell to an insider. It is difficult to specify the kinds of information that are more easily elicited by insiders and outsiders, but one example may help. We have found that members of school organizations are reluctant to name names to outsiders before a confidential relation has been established. But members would be equally reluctant to tell an insider their feelings about relations inside the organization even without naming names, because it is too easy for the insider to deduce whom the respondent is talking about.

When a researcher is a member of the organization he is studying, the participants are more likely to feel that the study could have effects on their own welfare. As a result, they will often reveal more relevant information than they would to an outsider who has no personal stake in their organization. This is an advantage. On the other hand, the very investment some individuals have in the present shape of things can cause them to withhold information from the inside researcher or even try to mislead him. Again, multiple methods can bring more confidence in final conclusions than any single method.

Unobtrusive Studies

Much was made in Chapter 7 of the relative advantages of using unobtrusive measurement and manipulation procedures, following the line of reasoning of Webb and others (1966). Those authors argue for the advantages of using measures taken in such a way that the actor whose behavior is the subject of study is not aware that his behavior is to be researched. These methods include observation carried out by hidden observers, the use of traces of past behavior, and the use of archival records of past behavior. It is possible to think not merely of *measures* as being unobtrusive but of entire *studies* as being unobtrusive. This can be achieved by selecting *settings* to study (as has been done by Barker and Gump, 1964, Kelly, 1969, and Gump, 1969, among others) rather than *actors*. The investigator then seeks behavior settings in which a self-selected population will be (or have been) carrying out certain classes of behavior. Rather than asking himself, "What kinds of actor populations will be most advantageous for my study and how can I get access to those people or groups?" the investigator can ask himself, "What kinds of behavior settings will be most advantageous for my study and how can I gain access to them?" The primary sampling emphasis has shifted from actors to settings (contexts).

We can further divide such unobtrusive studies into those dealing with behavior in settings that are essentially public—speeches, public accounts or records, behavior in public places such as streets and buses—and those dealing with behavior intended to be private—diaries, confidential correspondence, behavior in homes or offices, behavior in cars along lovers' lane.

The distinction between public and private has both scientific and ethical implications. Webb and his co-authors (1966) have pointed out that certain archival records where the behavior was produced with the intention of being public (speeches by political figures, official correspondence, accounting records, and the like) may suffer from effects similar to the reactive effects involved in subjective reports. The actor, being aware that his behavior is to be observed and noted by others (even though not for research purposes), may therefore modify his behavior so that it presents the kind of public image he wishes those others to have of him. One must interpret the meaning of archival records of public behavior with this qualification in mind. The same line of reasoning can be extended to the direct though unobtrusive observation of public behavior. People behave in public places with the expectation that others may be watching, and, in a manner analogous to the politician polishing his public image, modify their behavior to conform with the presentation of themselves they wish to make.[2] The argument is more tenuous when extended to trace measures.

Behavior measured unobtrusively and intended to be private is not as likely to have been altered to fit a public image as is public behavior. The unobtrusive measurement of inherently private behavior by observation, trace measures, or archival records, however, raises some ethical questions even more severe, it seems to us, than those raised by the use of semicoerced subjects. Now, the question is, under what conditions, if any, does a researcher have the right to obtain and use records of private behavior of individuals who do not know their behavior was being observed or used for research purposes, and who presumably might not be willing to permit their behavior to be so recorded and used? It is one thing to observe (and even record and quantify) behavior of people in lobbies, on streets, in buses. It is quite another thing to eavesdrop on living room, office, or bedroom, or to make use of private letters, or the like, without the persons whose behavior is being studied knowing that such is the case. So, while the unobtrusive recording of private behavior removes many of the problems of image management and reactive measures for the investigator, in comparison to other strategies for obtaining empirical evidence, it places upon him an enormous burden of ethical problems.

In fact, there seems a general relation between reactivity and willing

[2] There are social scientists (for example, Goffman, 1959) who take such "self presentation" effects as phenomena worthy of study in themselves rather than as unwanted artifact of method, and legitimately so. Our point is only that one must be aware how the situation (natural or laboratory) may modify behavior if one is to interpret the resulting behavior sensibly. Thus, one must take into account the "publicness" of behavior measured unobtrusively as well as the reactive effects of the participant's knowing he is being systematically observed, if one is sensibly to construe the meaning of the resulting measurements.

consent. The ways of gaining access to behavior that involve the greatest degree of willing and informed consent and hence raise the fewest ethical problems are usually those most subject to sampling biases and reactive effects. Conversely, those ways of gaining access to behavior that partially solve the sampling and reactive problems by decreasing either the degree of the participant's knowledge or the willingness of his consent, or both, make their technical gains at the cost of very serious ethical risks.

The Ethical Issues of Informed Consent[3]

One crucial issue has already been posed in relation to the problems of gaining access to study populations. The issue can be stated as follows: under what conditions, if any, does a researcher have the right to record, analyze, and report data based on the behavior of persons who have not given their *willing and informed consent?* The issue takes two forms. One form is in relation to cases where individuals are participants in a study, know that this is the case, but are involved because of some degree of coercion, not having given their own individual willing consent. Such cases include many studies where a population or sample is put at the disposal of an investigator through some agent. The principal makes the students' time available for research; the colonel makes the enlisted men's time available; the supervisor makes the workmen's time available; and the like. Such cases also include studies where the researcher himself is the source of the coercion—he carries out the study within his own classroom, he uses subjects who are fulfilling a course requirement, and so forth. It is our contention that, at the *most,* a researcher should use such nonvolunteer interactions as *opportunities to initiate communication with potential study participants,* whose *willing* cooperation he then seeks to obtain through permission rather than coercion. It seems perfectly reasonable to us for an investigator to work through principals or supervisors to gain access to potential study participants. However, to proceed then as if those potential participants *must* participate in the study seems presumptuous. Moveover, to proceed as if such participants were *motivated* to participate seems a foolish and misleading assumption. Rather, the investigator should use the opportunity opened by the superior to try to persuade those individuals under his control to give their willing and informed consent to participation. But he should do so under conditions where they are substantially free *not* to participate.

The other form of this same ethical issue arises in those studies where behavior (or traces of it) is to be measured unobtrusively, with actors not aware of being participants in a study. Here, the crucial distinction seems to us to be whether the behavior in question is essentially public or private. It seems to us perfectly reasonable for a researcher to observe and record systematically any behavior taking place in behavior settings where he and others would have normally been in a position to observe that behavior had no research been

[3] In this section, we present our own values; we believe it is as much the duty of social scientists to proclaim their values as to describe their assumptions, theories, and findings.

involved, and to do so without seeking permission of the actors. This category might include observations in theaters, ball parks, classrooms, libraries, cafeterias, museums, hotel lobbies, streets, and playgrounds. It includes content analysis of television performances, public speeches, printed articles, and the like.

On the other hand, it seems to us a serious invasion of privacy to obtain and use, even if only for the purest of scientific purposes, records of behavior the actor intended to be private and had every reason to expect to be private. This category includes records of private behavior obtained by hidden cameras, electronic devices, and the like, as well as by peeping through keyholes and reading private correspondence or diaries. In all these cases, where the observer would not normally have had access to the behavior as it occurred in its natural settings, there seems to us no ethical justification for violating the actor's right of privacy, unbeknownst to him, no matter how important the study nor how vital to its success the unobtrusive measure might seem to be.

So, in regard to the ethics of gaining access to observations of behavior, we propose two guides:

1. If the actor is to knowingly participate in the study, his willing consent, given freely rather than under coercive conditions, must be obtained.
2. If behavior is to be observed unobtrusively, without the actors being consciously in the study but rather behaving in natural settings, then observation for research purposes should be limited to behavior intended to be public and should not include behavior intended to be private even if the researcher can find clever devices to obtain records of the private behavior.[4]

These same issues of informal consent and privacy will arise again, in slightly different forms, in our discussion of later stages of the relation between investigator and participant.

TREATMENT OF PARTICIPANTS DURING THE STUDY

The effects of the relation of the participants to the study carry throughout the conduct of the study, as do the scientific and ethical problems involved. For studies in which actors are knowing participants, three key problems arise: (1) the right of the individual to withdraw or cease participation at any time throughout the study; (2) the use of deception, which involves the right of the individual to know the *true* purpose and nature of the study if he is to give

[4] Another view is that the crucial feature of unobtrusive data collection, from an ethical point of view, is the anonymity and confidentiality of treatment of the data. In our view, confidentiality is a necessary guarantee for study participants under any conditions of data collection, but is not a *sufficient* condition to absolve the investigator of the ethical burden of obtaining *informed consent*.

informed consent; and (3) the possibility of effecting more or less irreversible changes in the person, group, or organization.

The first of these problems is simply an extension of that of the individual's right not to participate unless he has willingly given consent. It is easy for a researcher to design his laboratory situation so that continuing participation is easy and discontinuing participation is difficult, awkward, embarrassing, or threatening. But even though the investigator has a stake in obtaining participants' cooperation to completion, it seems to us he has the ethical burden of insuring that each participant is psychologically free to cease participation whenever he wishes to do so.

The issue of deception poses a very complex set of problems. It is useful to distinguish between deception by withholding of information and deception by use of misinformation. The former includes a spectrum of omissions, from not telling participants all the hypotheses one is interested in nor all the ways one is going to analyze the data to withholding knowledge about the true purpose of the study or about some stressful or painful events one has planned for him. The active forms of deception include false feedback (telling the participant that something is true of him or of his performance or of other participants that is not, in fact, true); use of confederates who pretend to be fellow-participants but who are preprogrammed to carry out certain behavior; and misrepresentation of study purposes, of the nature of task materials, or of other aspects of the situation. Rubin (1970) has collected into one paper some descriptions of actual examples of some of these types of deceptions.

Many social scientists argue that certain kinds of deception are necessary for a study to be meaningful. Certainly if the participants are aware of the hypotheses of a study, then the experimental demand effects discussed earlier are more likely to operate. If participants are aware of all aspects of the experimental situation, their behavior is more likely to be affected by (reactive to) that knowledge. Furthermore, some argue, many of these so-called deceptions are relatively innocuous, do not harm the participant in any way, and his temporary misinformation can be corrected by telling him the true situation and the reasons for deceiving him in a careful debriefing at the end of the study.

This indeed often appears to be the case. By and large, the deceptions (of omission or commission) used in most social psychological studies involve rather unimportant features. But this is not *always* the case. A few studies have been done in which the participants were subjected to highly stressful conditions[5] involving substantial emotional and psychological disturbance. If, indeed, participants in these studies were seriously disturbed as a result of deceptions, then it does not really matter whether the deceptions were "necessary" in the eyes of the investigator. What matters is the question, Under what conditions, if any, does a researcher have the right to induce painful emotional situations

[5] See, for example, Milgram (1963) and Lazarus (1966).

by deception and, hence, without the possibility of informed consent on the part of the participant? *Our* answer to that question is, *There are no such conditions.*[6] If a researcher should intend to carry out deceptive practices, it seems to us that a heavy ethical burden of proof as to the innocuousness of the matter is on him. Certainly he must plan to conduct a thorough and careful debriefing. But even if he does, there remains the risk that the debriefing may not remove the emotional distress of the deceived participant.

Aside from the ethical questions involved in the use of deception, there are some further technical and practical questions. If a study hinges on participants believing false feedback or misleading instructions, then the investigator must concern himself with two new problems. First, some participants may not believe what they are told. When investigators lie to participants, they may do so with more or less skill. If deception is complex, participants may well see through the subterfuge. When this occurs, the entire experimental procedure is likely to lose its credibility. Second, since all actors cannot participate simultaneously, there is always a substantial possibility that some participants will come to the study fully aware of certain deceptions because they have talked with participants from earlier sessions who were properly debriefed. Lichtenstein (1970) and Wuebben (1967), among others, have published data showing that the percentage of participants who reveal a deception after being asked not to do so can be very high. Indeed, there has been so much use of deception in psychological studies that there is the considerable probability that many participants come to experiments *with the expectation* that the investigator will try to dupe them in some way, thus affecting the credibility of studies that do not use deception as well as those that do. We argue for reducing severely the frequency and degree of deception in social science experiments; we further suggest that if researchers would put the time and ingenuity now directed toward concocting clever subterfuges into an effort to develop alternate, nondeceptive designs and procedures, the results might solve or obviate some of the technical problems and do so in an ethically satisfactory manner.

An additional word needs to be said about the use of confederates. The usual justification for use of a confederate is that he can implement a set of experimental conditions (for example, rejection of another participant or disagreement on an issue) throughout an interaction, while instructions or feedback from the experimenter can be given only at limited times. Furthermore, the confederate can tailor the specifics of his behavior to the actions of the participant, thus increasing credibility. The problem here is twofold. To the extent that the confederate does enact his role flexibly, there is the risk that different cases which were to be considered replications actually received different conditions. To the extent that the confederate enacts his role by

[6] This is an *ethical,* not a scientific, question; Thus, its answer is a matter for each to determine for himself; and there is room for disagreement among men of good will. Other researchers, whom we respect both scientifically and ethically, reach different conclusions on this question. We here present merely our conclusion.

sticking rigidly to a script—thus insuring standardization—one loses the very flexibility and "realness" which is the main justification for using the confederate. Ethical questions of deception aside, using confederates to implement experimental conditions should be done only when the practice offers some clear methodological gains, and then must be done with great care to insure that the *same* conditions are produced in all cases assigned to a given experimental treatment.

The third issue has to do with *changing* the participants. Let us first turn to those instances in which participants enter the study *for the purpose of bringing about changes in themselves* or their environment. We might call these participants clients or patients and consider the changes resulting from the study as therapeutic changes. They are, presumably, beneficial to the client, at least in his judgment.

But consider now those cases where the participants are recruited for the study. Here, the burden of insuring that the person is *not changed* by the study—or that he is changed in ways that *he* would judge desirable—is on the investigator. While it almost goes without saying that no sensible and humane experimenter would contemplate a study that might do physical harm to his subjects, there are numerous instances in which there does seem to be some risk of undesirable psychological change. Studies practicing deception that lead the individual to do things that may shatter his self-esteem—however thorough the debriefing—seem to us to be unjustifiable breeches of ethics. Furthermore, studies designed to produce changes in attitudes or values may well be similar breeches. Even though the investigator may think that such attitude changes are for the better, it does not give him the right to impose his own values on the participants. As with coercion to participate and deceptive practices, a question of experimental ethics should never be resolved on grounds of whether it is "necessary" or convenient in a particular study. Even if a particular study seemingly cannot be done without procedures that represent coercion or deception or unasked-for changes in participants, that is not a sufficient ethical justification for using those procedures. Perhaps it is better, under such conditions, that the study *not* be done.

POSTSTUDY RELATIONS WITH PARTICIPANTS

When the study is completed, the investigator has three remaining responsibilities to his participants: (1) to tell them all they wish to know about the study, to help them understand their own experience in the study, and to give them any information he may have obtained about themselves which may be of value to them; (2) to treat confidentially all data given in confidence; and (3) to report study results in such a manner that it will not embarrass or harm the participants. Little needs to be said about the last two points. A brief comment is needed about debriefing.

It is customary for experimenters to conduct a postsession debriefing in which the subject is given any information that has been withheld up to that time. Often, the debriefing is also used as a medium for eliciting and discussing any emotions that may have been aroused by the operations of the study and in general to alleviate any residual anxieties. This is an essential practice (even if no deceptions have been carried out) and requires care and skill on the part of the experimenter. It is also a potentially valuable source of information and insight for the investigator.

In all of this, perhaps the overall guiding principle can best be stated as honoring, in all stages of the study, the participants' right to be treated with decency, human respect, and dignity. The investigator needs always to think through how the procedures of his study are likely to be viewed by the study participant. He must then avoid doing things that he himself would see as malevolent or unreasonable or as violations of his rights if he were in the position of participant. Too often, we have found, neophyte social scientists seem to feel that in order to do a "good" study they must find some clever ways to deceive their participants. At times, it seems as if they believe deception to be a requirement for conducting a "real" study. In our view, deception raises serious ethical problems and has many technical disadvantages as well. Social scientists should be encouraged to extend their creative efforts toward study designs that do not require deceptions but that still provide the comparisons necessary for testing worthwhile and interesting hypotheses. If this is impossible, we hope social scientists will find it possible to put a higher value on the rights of the individual than on an immediate test of a hypothesis.

9-3. Pilot Studies and Pretests

We strongly recommend the common practice of trying out all aspects of a study plan before launching the main study. This can sometimes be done by trying, separately, each piece of apparatus, each questionnaire, each set of instruments, and each observation task. Sometimes it can be done better, however, by running a "miniature study"—that is, a study like the main study in all respects except that only a few cases are run.

There are a number of reasons for conducting pilot tests or trial runs. Members of the research team need *practice* in all aspects of their roles, and the investigator needs to be assured that each person knows how to do his assigned tasks and when to do them. He also needs to be sure that each instrument—hardware or verbal—will work accurately under the conditions in which it will be used in the study. For example, if one is going to use a camera to record behavior, he must be sure that the room has sufficient light for clear photographic results and that there is sufficient depth and width of field to capture on film the behavior to be recorded. If the investigator is going to use a questionnaire, he needs to ascertain that the respondents actually understand and can answer the questions. If the study involves observation of behavior, then observers probably will need extensive training and practice. Sometimes such practice can be done in settings other than the study setting, but sometimes observation tasks can be practiced only in what amounts to a trial run of the situation.

Another reason for running a small-scale pilot study is to obtain gross information about some substantive aspects of the study. For example, for a study designed to test relations between two variables—for example, attitudes toward school and school achievement—it might be worthwhile to determine in advance whether or not there is considerable variation among students in their attitudes toward school (or, for that matter, in school achievement). If there are no differences among students in attitudes—if all the students in the study population hate school, or all love it—then there is no possibility that differences in achievement (or anything else) are associated with such attitudinal differences.

Another kind of substantive effect that might be worth exploring in a pilot study is the case where a certain set of experimental conditions is expected to produce a certain effect, and that effect, in turn, is hypothesized to lead to a subsequent effect (see Chapter 8 for discussion of such indirect experimental manipulations). For example, small-group studies have sometimes used instructions to induce interpersonal attraction (see, for example, Back, 1951) and have then studied the effects of attraction differences on other aspects of group process and performance. Such a study stands or falls on the extent to which the instructional manipulation *actually produces* the intended degree of interpersonal attraction. In such a case, it would seem well worth the cost and effort to run a pilot study to see if, in fact, the instructions tend to produce the desired effect. One can extend this idea one step further, of course, and decide to do a pilot study to determine whether the main hypothesis of the study seems likely to be supported. In the above example, this could mean a pilot study to see if instructions induce attraction differences *and* if attraction differences lead to differences in performance. At some point, of course, one is no longer doing a pilot study but has begun the main study, although perhaps on a small scale.

Just what needs to be tested before one starts, and how thoroughly that testing needs to be done, depends on several features of the study:

1. How uncertain is it that a feature of the study will work as planned? How new is it, how untried, how complex, how many ways can it fail?

2. How crucial is the feature to the study? Is it the only measure, or one of several measures, of a given variable?

3. How costly will the main study be in time and manpower and in other ways? How costly might a pilot test be?

4. How irreversible will be a decision to forgo further pilot testing and start the main study? Will it still be possible to make changes as the main study goes along? Could it be decided, on the basis of early cases, to stop the

study and redesign it without an enormous cost in wasted resources? Once the study is started, has the available population been forever contaminated or used up?

The decision to stop pretesting and start the main study must be made in terms of the particular situation. Perhaps one good general rule is that one should continue to pretest as long as new information is being obtained but that the main study should be started (or cancelled) when one is no longer gaining information from pretests or when one cannot afford for some other reason to delay further.

The matter of gaining new information from pretesting deserves further comment. Beginning researchers often seem to react to results of pretests categorically—either "it works" and we go ahead with the study or "it doesn't work" and we abandon the study. But results of most pilot studies actually warrant intermediate conclusions: some aspects of the study are fine and should be left alone; other aspects need revision. It is appropriate for an investigator to have the expectation that he will probably make changes in his study plan, but not abandon it, as a result of pilot testing. If he is committed unequivocally to his study plan as it is and will not contemplate any changes in it, then he might as well not do any pilot testing because no benefit will be derived from it. Pilot testing is useful only if one is ready to make use of the results to modify the study plan.

What kinds of things can be learned from pilot testing? Certain outcomes can provide clear-cut information. For example, a questionnaire may turn out to take 45 minutes rather than the 10 minutes planned for it; instructions may be unclear to respondents or be rejected (or even laughed at) by them; or an investigator may find out that respondents take entirely different meanings from his instructions or questions than he had intended. All of these results indicate that changes need to be made, although they do not necessarily tell what changes to make. But most pilot results will be less clear-cut. It may be possible to conclude only that certain aspects of the study apparently did not fail to work. An investigator is less likely to be confident that they *did* work; and he almost surely will not be in a position to conclude that they will work in the main study (since he probably pretested only on a few cases and under conditions somewhat different from those of the main study). Thus, it is primarily negative information that can be gleaned from pilot testing. But this is very valuable information indeed: to identify the major flaws in a study plan before starting the main study.

One of the best sources of potential information from pilot testing lies in the experiences and reactions of the respondents. Often, it is useful to interview pilot study participants informally but in detail. The investigator will want to find out how they interpreted various aspects of the study procedures and how they felt about them. It is often fruitful, as well, to ask respondents for ideas about how to modify the study, especially those aspects of it that seem to be creating difficulties or confusion for them. The investigator, of course, will have to decide in the light of the purposes of his study whether the participants' suggestions are useful, but this source of insights and ideas is often very valuable and should not be overlooked.

9-4. Some Procedural Problems Affecting Standardization and Generalizability

When the investigator gets down to the actual conduct of his study, he encounters an array of procedural variables that, although they may have little or no conceptual importance in his substantive problem, can affect the outcome of the study. While it is not possible to anticipate all procedural problems that might appear in an empirical study, we shall describe certain problems of procedure that are frequently met. In describing these procedural choices, we shall illustrate once again how the investigator arranges the conditions within which he takes his observations so as to put more weight to the one side or the other in the ever-present choice between standardization and generalizability (see also section 6-5).

There is always a choice of logistics in arranging the interaction between the observer (investigator or his agent) and the actor-behavior-context. For example, the investigator must decide whether to observe all cases simultaneously, or in batches of certain numbers, or one at a time. If he observes all cases at once or in batches, he must then contend with the effects of grouping and possibly with effects of multiple observers. If he observes batches of actors in sequences or single actors in sequence, he must somehow distribute cases with respect to time—both *sequence* (which cases he runs first, which next, and so on) and *spacing* (how much calendar time between observations).

Now, the investigator may suspect that the time a case is observed may affect his results; for example, cases drawn from a college population observed late on Friday afternoon are likely to differ from those observed on Tuesday morning, or cases observed just before midterm exams differ from those observed afterwards, or cases observed late in the sequence of cases may have heard rumors about the study or have meanwhile been involved in other seemingly similar studies. If the investigator entertains such suspicions, he may choose one of two sorts of design: (1) observe *all* cases at a given time of day or day of week, or even observe all cases at one single moment—that is, hold time of observation constant; or (2) *counterbalance* time over treatment conditions (that is, among the categories of his design partitions) so that each hour or day is equally represented in each condition, or so that each condition has equal numbers of cases observed early and late in the sequence. If the investigator does not see a need for control or counterbalancing with respect to time, then he may elect to let time of observation be randomized. Notice that counterbalancing permits the investigator later to remove or assess the effects of the variable handled by that method as if it were another design partition in his study (although he may expect that it will not produce important differences). Randomization of times over all conditions does not permit such assessment of the effect of the randomized variable. Of course, since counterbalancing operates like a design partition, it has costs: it multiplies the number of subsets of cases and reduces the number of cases per subset proportionally to the number of categories involved in the counterbalancing partition.

We give here an example to illustrate the sort of complexity sometimes necessary in scheduling observers. Runkel and others (1971) have reported a study of the stages of group development as exhibited by small work groups, each assigned to complete an empirical investigation as part of a university course. These task-oriented groups, composed mostly of strangers, had to form themselves from larger sections into work groups of four or more individuals each, choose a task, pursue the investigation, and present the work in written form at the completion of the project. These work groups were observed by students who had been through the course the previous year. The basic framework for the observations was Tuckman's (1965) model proposing four developmental phases. Special features were required in the design of this study because of the fact that the observers were also helpers (group facilitators) in class sections where they did *not* observe, and

> it was not possible to keep the observers innocent of the purpose of the experiment. Consequently, great care was taken to reduce the ability of the observers to influence the sections and groups in their development, and to reduce the possibility that observers might be more ready to see happening what they thought Tuckman or Runkel might "want" to have happen. Toward these ends, we worked out a complicated schedule for assigning observers. Although each observer also acted as an active consultant to one section, he or she was permitted to observe only in the other two sections. To reduce the opportunity for an observer to perceive trends (or to imagine they were perceiving them) in the development of any particular group, observers were rotated frequently in observing any one section or work group. About nine or ten observers shared the work of observing one section, and no observer ever observed a run of consecutive meetings of a section longer than two. Usually, there were two observers present at a meeting. Finally, Runkel made it plain at the outset that Tuckman's article *did not specify the length of time* each stage could be expected to take. Consequently, the observers could not expect any particular stage to arrive at any particular time.

Still another aspect of the problem of scheduling is the differential effect on actors of concomitant events. If a large number of actors or other cases are to be observed, then to observe them one at a time has the effect of prolonging the calendar time between the beginning and completion of the observational (empirical) stage of the study. In the case of a study of students, for example, a long calendar would multiply the opportunities for holidays, examinations, elections, and even fires and riots to affect some (but not other) actors. At the other extreme, observing all cases simultaneously often requires costly multiplication of experimental personnel and facilities, and the danger arises of differential effects from differences among observers, among experimental rooms, and the like. Between these extremes, investigators sometimes choose to observe several batches of cases, each batch containing a number of cases. For example, 100 cases might be divided into five batches of 20 cases each. This reduces time-based extraneous effects by shortening the time from the first case until the last. But it requires sufficient staff to observe 20 cases at once. Furthermore, care must be taken to randomize cases among batches and to randomize and counterbalance conditions (experimenters, rooms, and the like) within each batch. This is often difficult to arrange. To recapitulate, if the investigator chooses to randomize a procedural factor, then he is gambling that that factor will not add sufficient variability among cases *within* subsets to obscure the differences he is trying to detect between subsets. If the relation he is searching for is robust enough, that gamble will work. If it is not—if, in fact, it is a small difference or a weak relation—then the variation among cases within a subset, due to effects of variables handled by randomization, will obscure that small difference and the investigator will be misled in the conclusions he draws.

If the investigator chooses to hold constant a particular procedural condition such as time, he will have solved one problem while incurring another. He will have guaranteed that his cases treated alike will be alike on that procedural variable, so that variations will not obscure his results. But now his findings will be limited to that one particular value of the variable in question—say two o'clock on Tuesday, May 27. He does not know, from results of that study, whether his findings would hold for 3 o'clock Tuesday or 2 o'clock Wednesday or 2 o'clock Tuesday on June 15. In other words, he has seriously delimited the external validity or generalizability of his results. If he had randomized with respect to that variable and had still found the relation (that is, if the relation were robust enough not to be obscured by minor but unbiased variations among cases in that variable), then he would have had a much broader basis for generalizing his results.

There are a large number of such procedural variables which operate in the conduct of any study and which require the investigator to make choices—randomization, counterbalancing, holding constant, or ignoring. Those choices affect the precision, cost, and generalizability of results. These include, in addition to the time factors discussed above, such procedural matters as sex, age, status, and various palpable attributes of the experimenter in relation to the actors; the degree to which experimental instructions are to be delivered verbatim or extemporaneously, and, hence, the degree to which they will be constant or vary over cases; and the degree to which the features of the physical environment (light, temperature, wall color, space, chair comfort, and so on) are to be exactly constant for all cases, substantially the same, or varied over cases.

To the extent that the investigator *ignores* such procedural variables (which are usually *not* of substantive interest to him), he invites both systematic and random error. If he handles procedures by counterbalancing (for example, distributing male and female experimenters equally over conditions and trials), then he incurs sizable costs by increasing the number of cases needed to insure a given number of cases per condition. If the experimenter randomizes procedural variables, he reduces the probability of systematic bias due to these factors, but he does not curtail the introduction of random error that can obscure his results unless the relations he seeks are sufficiently robust. If he deals with procedural factors by standardizing procedures so as to make all of those aspects identical for all cases, he avoids both systematic bias and random error, but he greatly restricts the generality of his results.

As a final illustration of the choices that can be encountered in the empirical conduct of research, consider the matter of delivering instructions to participants. Often very important features of the experimental procedures are conveyed through instructions (see Chapter 8). If instructions are not communicated effectively, the value of the study may be seriously impaired. There is an advantage, in terms of standardization, in having instructions identical for all cases in a given condition. On the other hand, there is often an advantage to delivering instructions in a natural and unstilted manner. If the investigator or his assistants read instructions, the procedure may seem impersonal to participants. (The impersonality is often increased further when tape-recorded instructions are used.) If assistants memorize instructions and say them by rote, the procedure may seem stilted. But if they extemporize, they will certainly introduce at least minor variations in timing, manner, and content from case to case. Then again, one can argue that a study is not very robust or useful if its results can be expected to appear only when certain specific verbal instructions are delivered in a certain way. Once again, the researcher must balance, as best suits his purposes, the opposed requirements of standardization and generalizability.

The direct opposition of the need for standardization and the need for generalizability is a dilemma that can never be resolved in a completely satisfactory way. Some researchers have argued for the utmost emphasis on standardization, even at a serious cost in scope or generalizability. They would suggest doing multiple, related studies, each highly standardized and narrow but designed so that they provide mutually overlapping and supporting information. This strategy is costly, admittedly, requiring a lengthy series of studies before the results can produce information of reasonable scope. Other investigators have sought a resolution to the dilemma in the opposite way, arguing (given our present stage of knowledge) that we ought to aim to identify large and robust effects and hence allow cases to vary randomly with respect to all those procedural variables that are conceptually unimportant so that results can be built on a broader and more generalizable base. In doing this, of course, there is the risk of allowing important but nonrobust relations to be obscured, and therefore of wasting the resources used for the study (if relations truly existing were obscured by error variance and therefore overlooked).

Each of these solutions has its merits under appropriate circumstances.

Neither provides a general and satisfactory resolution of the dilemma. Whether standardization or heterogeneity of procedures is more appropriate with respect to various sets of procedural variables (timing, instructions, assignment of experimenters to cases, and so on) depends on the particular procedures and the particular study in which they are embedded. The investigator must choose the form and degree to which his study emphasizes one or the other of these strategies. He should do whatever he does in this regard purposefully and thoughtfully. To resolve the dilemma by ignoring it—either because of lack of forethought or because no easy resolution is available—is to risk picking the least suitable strategy by default.

9-5. Further Reading

Argyris (1968) has dealt at some length with the status relations between researcher and actor, treating the matter of rapport in a manner more sophisticated than most. Brock and Becker (1966) have discussed some of the difficulties of the experimenter who attempts to explain a deception to his subjects.

Rosenthal (1967) has dealt with the research setting as a behavior setting. Hackman (1968) has discussed the effects of the characteristics of the experimental task on the possible products of a group's work. Willems and Raush (1969) have collected very useful papers on behavior settings in the field. Blum (1952) wrote about the difficulties an outsider encounters in soliciting information from insiders.

Kelman (1967) has expressed a point of view concerning the treatment of experimental subjects that is very similar to ours. Several other writers have been concerned with the ethical issues we have raised in this chapter; for example, Benne (1965), King and Spector (1963), Reissman (1967), and Ruebhausen and Brim (1966). Sanford (1965) has described his hopes that psychologists will be able to apply their work to pressing human problems.

CHAPTER 10

Analyzing Empirical Evidence: Translating Observations into Data

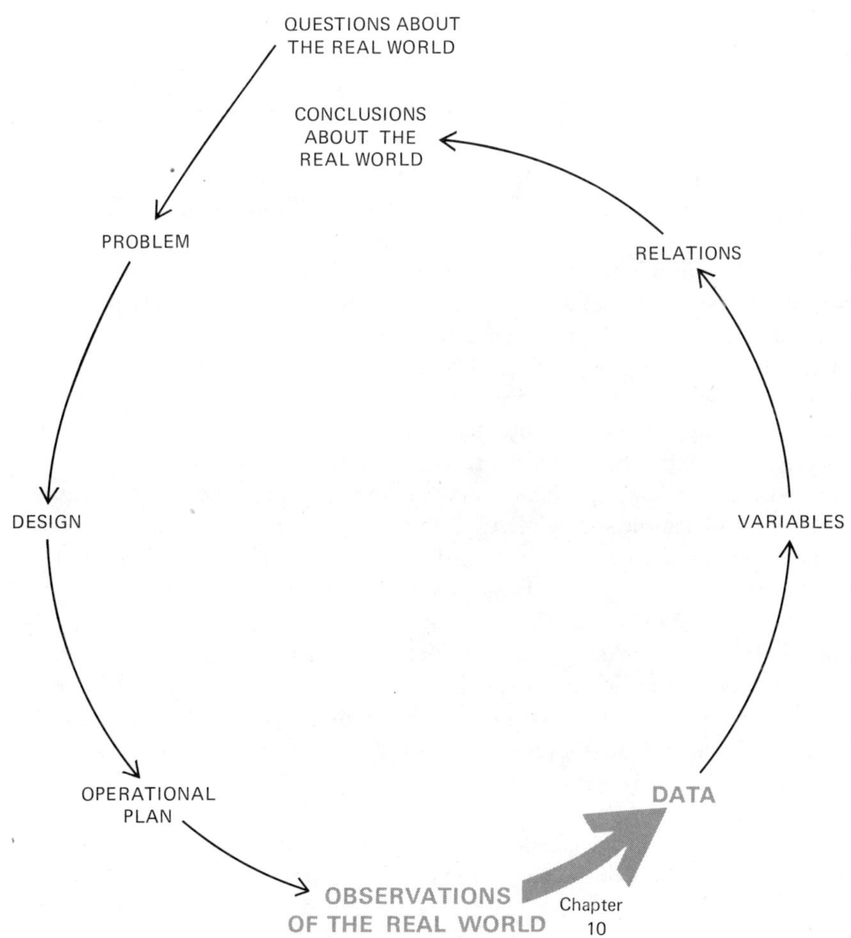

Throughout this chapter we emphasize that the researcher *must* make certain choices about how he will extract information from the set of observations he has recorded. When the researcher looks at the neat record of his observations, the first set of choices he faces deals with *what kinds of information he will assume those observations contain.* The observations do not tell him what they mean; he must *impose* structure upon them and view them from one or another perspective in deciding what they mean—that is, what questions he will try to answer with them. This chapter focuses on the first step in the process of extracting information and meaning from observations, the process we shall call mapping observations into data. Later steps—combining data into scales or variables, relating variables to each other, and testing hypotheses—will be treated in later chapters.

The reader may not at first see the point of devoting a chapter to mapping observations into data. In the everyday language and in the informal conversation of many scientists, records of observations *are* the data. Here, however, we are using the term *data* in a particular technical way, following the usage of C. H. Coombs (1964). By a datum we mean a logical form into which raw observations are classified. The logical form gives us a systematic way, no matter what the actual content of the data, of (1) combining, organizing, and summarizing large numbers of observations and (2) extracting meaning from them.

As an example of how the same observations can mean different things, imagine that you have asked a number of actors to make some judgments about a set of political candidates. What do these observations mean? Part of the answer to that question depends on just what kind of judgment you asked them to make. Another very important part of the answer depends on your purposes. Suppose you had the actors consider each pair of candidates and judge which of the two they preferred. Combining all judgments in certain ways would permit you to make some statements about the *relative preferability* of the various candidates: Greene is indicated by the actors to be preferable to the other of the pair more frequently than is Brown, Brown more frequently than White, and so on. On the other hand, you could construe these same data as telling you some things about the political attitudes *of the judging individuals:* actor A usually finds the conservative candidates more preferable than the liberal candidates, while actor B shows the contrary preference.

Suppose, in addition, you had individuals judge each pair of candidates in terms of certain attributes—for example, their maturity, their leadership ability, or their stands on certain issues. You could then combine the observations in such a way as to make statements about the judged attributes or policies or public images *of the candidates,* each alone or comparatively. Conversely, you could combine the same observations to make statements about the political perceptions *of the judging population;* and you could also make statements comparing the perceptions of different actors or of different subpopulations. Whenever A reacts to B, one can always choose whether he will take this as a measure of A or of B. He can choose to say that B is the kind of thing that would draw that reaction from A (or a set of As), or he can choose to say that A is the kind of person who would react like that to a B (or a set of Bs).

These examples may seem obvious and trivial, but the underlying point is crucial. Any given set of observations can be viewed in different ways, and the kind of information that can be extracted from them depends on which of these alternative views is accepted. Another way of stating this point is to say that the concrete observations limit but do not fully determine the information and conclusions that can be drawn from them. Still another way of stating the point is to say that the *researcher must decide what kind of data he will make out of his observations.*

This decision as to what kind of data to make out of a given set of observations has two important sets of consequences for the investigator. First, it determines what kinds of conclusions he can draw from his results—what questions can be answered—because different types of data contain different information. Second, the decision as to type of data determines what kinds of tools or procedures (the formal term is *models*) he can draw upon from the very extensive theory and technology of data analysis to help him combine, order, and interpret the data he generates. Which models he uses, in turn, will affect the time and cost of data processing; they will also affect the kind of conclusion he can draw from the results of that data processing.

Accordingly, the objective of this chapter is to describe systematically the various types of datum it is possible to make out of observations; the kinds of observations that can be mapped into each of the various data types; and the consequences of mapping observations into one rather than another datum type, in terms of both the kinds of information that can be extracted from the different types of data and the kinds of data-processing models that are available for combining and ordering data of the different types.

While the business of working with data derived from behavioral observations has been written about for many years, it has been only very recently that a *systematic* treatment of the ways of mapping observations into data and combining data into variables has been developed; namely, Coombs' "theory of data" (1964). In the pages to follow, we shall present Coombs' basic theory of data in those respects in which it deals with the four questions we have listed above; namely, (1) what kinds or types of data need be distinguished, (2) what kinds of observations can be mapped into each datum type, (3) what kinds of information can be extracted from each type of datum, and (4) what kinds of models are available for extracting this information from each type of datum. We shall present the theory of data using Coombs' abstract terms, but avoiding as best we can many formal and mathematical complexities that would take us beyond the scope and purpose of this book. We shall also point out some correspondences between terms we have introduced earlier in the book (for example, actor, behavior, and context) and terms in Coombs' theory of data (for example, individuals and stimuli).

10-1. Coombs' Theory of Data

Coombs has proposed some facets that seem to be encountered whenever we convert observations into data and whenever we convert data into variables, and these facets enable us to compare, one with another, the great variety of methods now in existence. Furthermore, Coombs' theory of data systematizes the field in such a way that we can use it to tell ourselves how to invent new methods of converting records into data and how to choose appropriate methods for analyzing data gathered by old or new methods.

The theory of data begins by looking at things two at a time. It looks at two elements (to be explained in more detail as we go along) drawn from actors, behaviors with objects, and contexts and deals with the relation between the two elements. More exactly, the theory of data lets a mathematical point represent each of the elements drawn from the real world and deals with the possible relations between two points. The researcher is free to assign any kind of element he wishes to the two points. His choice will depend on the kind of question he wants to ask of his data. The table lists some examples of ways elements might be drawn from the real world and put into correspondence with the two points.

QUESTION		1ST POINT	2D POINT
Is John rejected by Rutgers?		John	Rutgers
Does firm A or firm B do the larger business?		Firm A	Firm B
Which motivation yields the higher productivity?		Motivation A	Motivation B
Does madame find the gown acceptable?		Madame	Gown
Does the necktie go well with my suit?		Necktie	Suit
Has John become a leader in this group?		John	Group
	or:	John	Seizing leadership
	or:	Group	Conferring leadership

In Coombs' *Theory of Data* (1964) and most other discussions of data, the points are called *individuals* and *stimuli*. These labels, like our *actor, behavior,* and *context,* are arbitrary. In talking about the theory of data, we shall most often use the terms *individuals* and *stimuli*; this will help the reader to use other books alongside this one. What is construed as "individual" and what as "stimulus" depends on the investigator's purposes. For example, if we are interested in the characteristics of John, we can call John a point representing an individual and Rutgers a point representing a stimulus. We can then represent the observation that John was not admitted to Rutgers by saying the relation between the two points is that the individual point is on the "negative" side of the stimulus point. However, if we are talking about various policies at Rutgers and other colleges, we might call Rutgers the individual and each policy a stimulus.

The theory of data is built on three principal facets, each one of which contains only two elements. The first facet asks whether the datum is to be represented by (1) a relation of *dominance* between the two points or (2) a relation of *proximity*. The second facet asks whether the datum is to be represented by (1) both points from *one set* or (2) points from two *different sets*. The third facet asks whether the datum to be represented is (1) a pair of *points* or (2) a pair of *distances,* each distance, of course, being bounded in turn by a pair of points.

DOMINANCE AND PROXIMITY

When we speak of the *dominance* relation, we have in mind examples such as John being rejected by Rutgers, firm A doing a larger business than firm B, Robert passing a test, one test item being more difficult than another, and Amy being taller than Ruth or bigger than a breadbox. In each of these examples, we can conceive one point dominating or surpassing the other in some sense. Examples of relations of *proximity* would be madame finding the gown acceptable (that is, sufficiently close to her taste), the necktie going well with my suit, John being considered a member of the club, and the like. In these examples, we can conceive one point approaching the other point sufficiently closely in respect to some quality.

Note that these classifications are arbitrary. The necktie going well with my suit, to take one case, could be viewed as proximity, in the sense that the necktie is similar in style to my suit; the styles are close or proximate. On the other hand, one could consider this a dominance relation by asking the question whether the necktie passes (dominates) the criterion of style set by my suit. The interpretation is arbitrary but important. If we were more interested in similarities of various styles, we would be interested in the proximity question. If we were more interested in what "measures up" to, or exceeds, standards set by other things, we would be interested in the dominance question.

SAME SET AND DIFFERENT SETS

When we speak of points being from the *same set,* we have in mind examples such as firm A doing a larger business than firm B. One might be considering both firms to be members of a set of firms, all considered from the same point of view. If we were interested in the relative behaviors of firms, we would consider both firms to be drawn from the set of actors. If we were considering the firms to be undergoing influences or treatments or evaluation by some outside actor, then we might think of them as objects (stimuli) being compared by the outside actor. In either case, we would be considering the firms to be from the same set, either from the set of individuals or the set of stimuli.

An example of the points being from *different sets* would be John being rejected by Rutgers. If we were interested in how John reacted to Rutgers, we would probably call John the actor or individual and Rutgers the stimulus. If we were interested in how Rutgers reacted to John, we would probably reverse labels. Other examples of points from different sets could be madame finding the gown acceptable, John becoming a leader of the group, Robert passing a

Table 10-1. *Data Classified by Two Facets*

DIFFERENT SETS: BOTH INDIVIDUALS AND STIMULI	
Dominance: John exceeds Rutgers. For example, John passes Rutgers' requirements.	*Proximity:* John is closer to Rutgers (from either direction) than some criterion distance. For example, John's ability is close to the average at Rutgers.
SAME SET: INDIVIDUALS OR STIMULI	
Dominance: Tuition at Rutgers is higher than at Harvard.	*Proximity:* Tuition at Rutgers is about the same as at Harvard.

test, and possibly the necktie going well with my suit. Table 10-1 lays out both facets discussed so far and gives examples of the four resulting types of data.

PAIRS OF POINTS AND PAIRS OF DISTANCES

We have introduced the theory of data by describing two facets: dominance versus proximity and same set versus different sets. A third facet remains: whether the datum is to represent a pair of points or a pair of distances. To describe this third facet, let us reconsider a datum represented by the proximity of two points from different sets. The example given in Table 10-1 was that John's ability is close to the average at Rutgers. Geometrically, we can represent this datum as in Figure 10-1, in which the bracket shows some criterion distance, epsilon, in either direction from the average at Rutgers, as the distance defining "close to." On the same dimension of ability, we can plot more than one datum; we can plot John's proximity to the average at a number of colleges. In Figure 10-2, we see John in relation to the epsilons for colleges A, R, and V. In this diagram, we see that John's ability is within the epsilon criterion of R; that is, it is close to R. However, it is not close to A, being too low, and not close to V, being too high.

The three data pictured above could be represented in a matrix (a two-dimensional display or table) by entering a 1 if John's ability is close to a college and a zero if otherwise:

	V	R	A	. . .
John	0	1	0	
Alfred				
. . .				

Now let us suppose that we replicate each of the three observations. For example, we might assess John's ability in relation to each of the three colleges

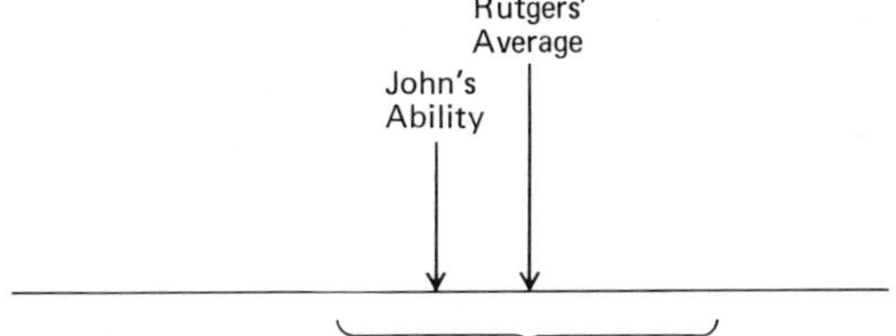

Figure 10-1.

more than once. Let us suppose we make such an assessment seven times (perhaps by administering to John seven equivalent forms of an entrance examination—if we could find a test with seven equivalent forms!). And suppose John passes one of V's seven forms, five of R's, and three of A's. We could then enter into the cells of the matrix the proportion of successes in each case:

	V	R	A	. . .
John	$1/7$	$5/7$	$3/7$	
Alfred				
. . .				

If we take the proportion of successes as a measure of the degree of dominance (as we do for baseball leagues), then we have more information in this latter matrix than we had in the earlier matrix which had only 1s and zeros. The earlier matrix told us that John was close enough to R, but not to A or V. The latter matrix also tells us that much (if we take .5, for example, to be the boundary of "close to"); it also tells us that, among the three, John is closest to R (because he passed five of R's seven tests), next closest to A (passing three of A's seven tests), and farthest from V (passing only one of V's seven tests). In other words, this matrix tells us about the dominance of one *distance* over another. It tells us that

the distance from John to R is less than from John to A;
the distance from John to R is less than from John to V; and
the distance from John to A is less than from John to V.

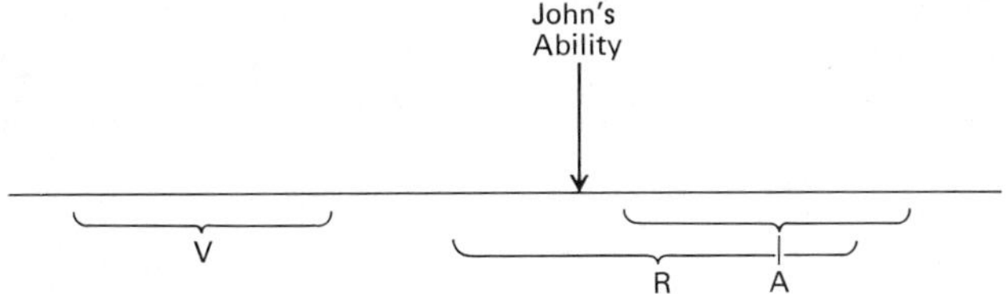

Figure 10-2.

For present purposes, let us ignore the possibility that we might make ratios from the fractions $^1/_7$, $^3/_7$, and $^5/_7$; let us note only that we are now able to *rank order the distances* from John to V, R, and A, from Alfred to V, R, and A, and so forth.

We now have a new kind of datum, one in which we have a dominance relation involving two sets (students and colleges, in this example). Instead of having a relation between points, however, we now have a *relation between distances.* The third facet we need, in brief, is one telling us whether we are interpreting an observation as a relation on a pair of points or as a relation on a pair of distances.

Perhaps *preference data* is as descriptive a term as any for the case where we interpret an observation as a dominance relation on distances between points from different sets. For example, if we observe that Alfred prefers oleomargerine to butter, we could represent this preference by a diagram in which the distance from the Alfred point to the oleomargerine point is less than the distance from the Alfred point to the butter point (see Figure 10-3). The horizontal line, of course, represents some dimension on which Alfred bases his choice of oleomargerine over butter. Alfred's preference, it is true, could be mediated by two dimensions rather than one. We shall deal only with unidimensional cases for the present, reserving multidimensional scaling for Chapter 12.

We can make the same kind of conversion to relations between distances from data that are originally proximity relations on points from the same set. The example in Table 10-1 was: the tuition at Rutgers is the same as at Harvard. Using merely capital letters instead of names, we can enter data of this sort into a matrix in which the rows represent points from the set of colleges and so also do the columns:

	R	H	A	V	. . .
R		1	0	0	
H					
. . .					

If we had replications of those relations between points, we could translate the above matrix into a matrix of proportions and then into a matrix of *distances,* as in the previous example. Note that data mapped into one data type can then be remapped into a different data type—for example, from points to distances. Such mappings are discussed in the next section.

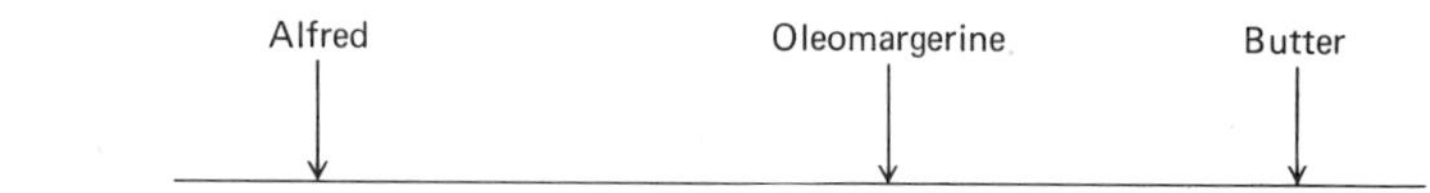

Figure 10-3.

Table 10-2. *The Data Quadrants*

DIFFERENT SETS: BOTH INDIVIDUALS AND STIMULI	
A Pair of Points	*A Pair of Distances*
Quadrant II: Single stimulus	*Quadrant I: Preference*
QIIa (dominance): John exceeds Rutgers. For example: John passes Rutgers' requirements.	QIa (dominance): The distance from John to Rutgers is less than that from John to Harvard. For example: John's preference for Rutgers is greater than his preference for Harvard.
QIIb (proximity): John is closer to Rutgers (from either direction) than some criterion distance. For example: John's ability is close to the average at Rutgers.	QIb (proximity): John shows no difference in preference between Rutgers and Harvard.
SAME SET: INDIVIDUALS OR STIMULI	
A Pair of Points	*A Pair of Distances*
Quadrant III: Stimulus comparison	*Quadrant IV: Similarities*
QIIIa (dominance): Tuition at Rutgers is higher than at Harvard.	QIVa (dominance): The difference between tuition at Rutgers and Harvard is less than the difference between Rutgers and Princeton.
QIIIb (proximity): Tuition at Rutgers is about the same as at Harvard.	QIVb (proximity): Rutgers and Harvard are as similar in standards as Georgia and Georgia Tech.

THE DATA QUADRANTS

We are now ready to display the intersections of the three basic facets on which the theory of data rests: (1) same set versus different sets, (2) dominance versus proximity, and (3) points versus distances. The result is shown in Table 10-2. A comparison of this table with Table 10-1 reveals that Table 10-2 contains Table 10-1. In Table 10-2, we have given to the quadrants the names customarily used by Coombs. The reasons for the names will become clear as we go along.

We are now ready to define a datum more formally than we have done so far. *A datum is a relation on a pair of points.* More fully, a datum is a relation on a pair of points (or a pair of distances) that serves to interpret an observation. Operationally, a datum is some sort of tally mark entered in a data matrix, accompanied by a decision to treat that entry as belonging in a particular data quadrant. The intersection of the three facets define eight classes of data. In the next main division of this chapter, we shall describe in more detail the data in each quadrant.

We mentioned at the outset that observations are not automatically data—that the researcher must select the aspects of events he wants to know about and must interpret his observations according to what kind of knowledge he is seeking. As an example, we used judgments about some political candidates. We have now illustrated some ways that observations can be interpreted as, or mapped into, eight different types of data.

We emphasize that mapping observations into data octants is an arbitrary business. Two different onlookers can get rather different information out of observing the same event. Given the observation that Mary said, "What a hateful thing to say!" to John, one observer might be interested in the fact that Mary rejected John's verbal offering. He might map this observation into QIIb as a negative datum: John's utterance (the stimulus) is not within the acceptance range (epsilon) of Mary (the individual). Alternatively, the observer might map his observation into QIIIb: Mary and John do not match, or belong to the same opinion class. Another observer, on the other hand, might be interested in the fact that Mary did not ignore John but rather paid close attention to him. This observer might interpret Mary's statement as meaning that Mary valued John's opinion. This observer might map his observation into QIIa: John (the individual) passes Mary's requirement (the stimulus) for being an interesting person.

The point is that the researcher must always remember that *no event has an intrinsic meaning* that will be the same to every onlooker. Researchers are not immune to the rule that humans see those features of events they have alerted themselves to see. Selective perception is an inevitable characteristic of observation, and we need to design our own research and profit from the research of others while keeping in mind that the translation of observations into data is not a matter of what is obvious (because what is obvious to you is not to me), nor of what is best (because different interpretations of observations serve different purposes), nor of what is right (because the kinds of data to be made out of an observation are arbitrary). Rather, it is a matter of what purposes the researcher has in mind.

A NOTE ON DATA MATRICES

The fact that in the theory of data a datum is defined as a relation on two points (or distances) makes it convenient to display a set of data in a two-dimensional table or matrix. We have already used this device in our examples. Displaying a set of data in a matrix makes it easier to search for patterns in that set. In a data matrix, each column often stands for a point from one set and each row for a point from the same set (QIII or IV) or from a second set (QI or II). Each cell in the matrix represents a *relation* of the row point to the column point—that is, the cell represents a datum.

Different types of data lead to different types of data matrices. For example, data defined on points (QII and III) need a point designating each row and each column, while data defined on distances (QI and IV) need data matrices where each row and each column is designated by a distance (a *pair* of points), each cell representing a relation between the row distance and the column distance.

When the points are from a single set (QIII and IV), then for every column of the data matrix there will be a row with the same label. Such matrices we

Table 10-3.

	R	H	V	A	I	. . .
John	1	1	0	0	1	. . .
Henry	0	1	1	0	1	
Alfred	1	0	0	1	1	
. . .						

shall call square or *intact*. If, however, the points are from different sets, as in QI and II, the column labels will be different from the row labels. For example, the columns may be a set of stimuli (perhaps colleges) and the rows a set of actors (perhaps students), as in Table 10-3. For certain purposes, we may want to consider such a matrix as a *part* of a square and intact matrix, where colleges *and* students are used as columns, and both also as rows. Table 10-4 illustrates this possibility. The matrix of Table 10-3 showing stimuli (colleges) crossed with individuals (students) is seen to be embedded in the upper right-hand *off-diagonal portion* of the larger intact matrix displayed as Table 10-4. In the example we have been using, the larger matrix is ludicrous, since we would normally not make observations about John being admitted by Alfred or about Harvard being admitted by Rutgers. However, we shall need the distinction between intact and off-diagonal matrices later.

Some intact data matrices have the property of *symmetry*, which means that the cell entries in the triangular portion above and to the right of the main diagonal constitute a mirror image of the lower-left triangular portion. For

Table 10-4.

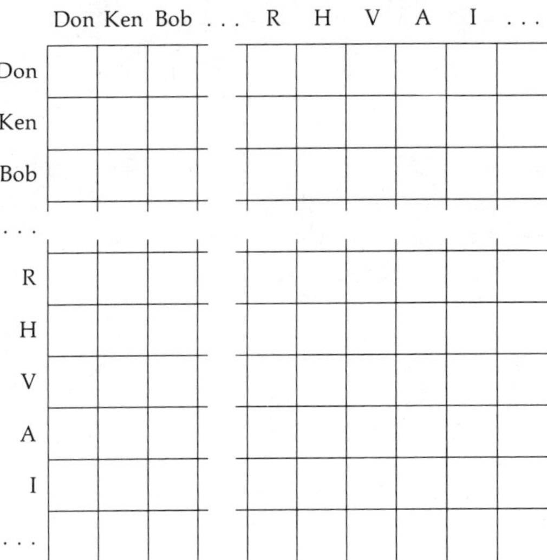

	Don	Ken	Bob	. . .	R	H	V	A	I	. . .
Don										
Ken										
Bob										
. . .										
R										
H										
V										
A										
I										
. . .										

example, if Rutgers has the same tuition as Harvard (represented by a 1 in the R row and H column of a matrix), then Harvard has the same tuition as Rutgers (represented by a 1 in the H row and R column of that same matrix). Dominance data are never symmetrical. Some proximity matrices are symmetrical, but some are not. For example, we might ask each of a set of people to choose his best friend and interpret choices as proximity data (QIIIb). If John chooses Henry, Henry may or may not choose John. Such data would yield a non-symmetric data matrix, with a 1 (for chooses) in the John row and Henry column, but perhaps with a zero in the Henry row and John column. Such a matrix is called conditional, because the meaning of a datum depends on which of the points (John or Henry) is taken as the point of reference (row) and which as the comparison (column). We will use the distinction between symmetrical and conditional matrices later.

The entry in the cell of a data matrix may be *dichotomous* (zero or 1), representing presence or absence of either dominance or proximity. But some kinds of observation records can provide quantitative variations beyond a simple *yes* or *no*. One of these cases, mentioned in an earlier example, occurs when there are replications of the observations for a given pair of points. When we have more than one comparison of A with B, we can make a *nondichotomous* entry in the A-B cell by entering the proportion of times A dominates B (or is proximal to B). Another way to get nondichotomous entries in a data matrix is by using observations already expressed in quantitative forms, such as test scores or time delays. Thus, perhaps John beat Henry by three minutes and Alfred by seven minutes. We can think of test scores as reflecting something like a proportion of a series of replicated items.

The availability of nondichotomous entries makes it possible for us to do two things. First, it permits us to convert a proximity on points QIIb or IIIb to dominance on distances QIa or IVa, a procedure we have already briefly discussed. Second, it permits us to extract stronger information about distances than their rank order, as we shall see in the next chapter.

10-2. Information in the Data Quadrants

We shall now describe the "meanings" of the data represented by the several quadrants. That is, we shall look at the kind of information we can carry forward into our analyses after having mapped an observation into a particular quadrant. Because it can be explained most simply, we begin with QII.

QUADRANT IIA: SINGLE-STIMULUS DOMINANCE DATA

In QIIa, a datum is a relation between an individual (actor) and a stimulus (object), showing whether one dominates the other.

Let the horizontal line in Figure 10-4 represent some relevant dimension, the direction to the right being positive in some sense. Then Actor 1 does not surpass or dominate the stimulus; a *zero* would be entered in the cell of a data

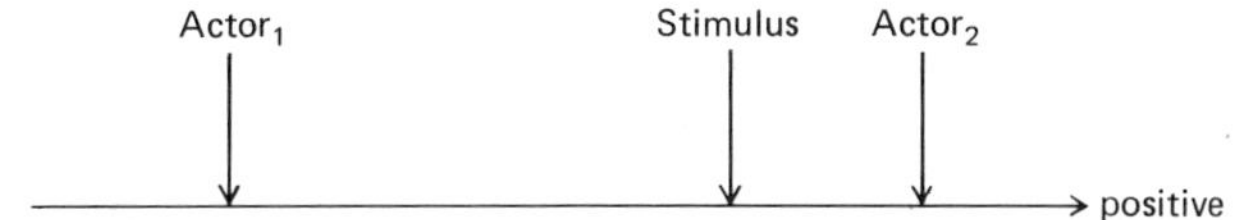

Figure 10-4.

matrix representing the interaction of this actor with this stimulus. Actor 2 does surpass or dominate the stimulus; a *1* would be entered in the corresponding cell of a data matrix.

It will now be clearer what we mean in this book by behavior toward an object. We mean an interaction between an actor and his immediate world that generates data. By context, in turn, we mean any feature of the interaction setting that the experimenter does *not* map directly into a datum. That is, context contains those characteristics of the situation, no matter how effective they may be in shaping behavior, that are *not* used by the experimenter as dimensions, points, distances, and directions when he constructs data from observations.

Coombs (1964) gave the label *single stimulus* to QII to remind us of the traditional method of collecting data in which a subject is asked to respond to a single stimulus at a time. His response is recorded in a yes-no fashion; either he saw the stimulus, or heard it, or recognized it, or liked it, or accepted it, or he did not. In this method of collecting data, the actor is not asked to compare things nor to assess their similarities. He is asked only, "Do you (something) the stimulus, or not? Yes or no." Another convenient name for observations interpreted according to the model of this quadrant is yes-no data.

To make QIIa seem more familiar, we give below some examples of observations that can easily be mapped into this quadrant. They are all examples of what we mean by an actor *dominating* or being dominated by a stimulus.

John says that he saw a flash of light.

John reports that the letters are now large enough for him to read them.

John says, "Ouch!" in response to the pressure on his skin.

The rat reaches some criterion indicating his having learned to turn right.

The rat leaps off the electrified grill.

The candidate wins the election.

The lobbyist persuades the legislator.

The dancer chooses a partner.

John says he is over 33 years old.

The jury pronounces the prisoner guilty.

John coughs up some vile-tasting food.

The athlete fails to clear the bar.

The citizen votes for candidate X.

John responds to dust by sneezing.

The throat responds to the foreign body with peristalsis.

Customers respond to the cost-benefit ratio by purchasing.

John gets a test item right.

John gets a test item wrong.

Of course, we do not deal with data one at a time. We deal with them many at a time. Typically, in collecting data that we intend to interpret as being of the QIIa type, we present a lot of actors with a lot of stimuli. (Equivalently, we present a lot of stimuli with a lot of actors.) Typically, then, our record of observations consists of yesses and noes—or more usually 1s and zeros—entered into a matrix in which the actors are represented by rows and the stimuli by columns, and a cell tells whether the actor surpassed (dominated) the stimulus:

	Stimuli							
	1	2	3	4	5	6	7	. . .
John	1	1	0	0	0	1	0	. . .
George	0	1	0	1	0	0	1	. . .
Don	0	1	1	1	1	1	0	. . .
Ken	0	0	1	1	1	0	0	. . .
. . .								

Having obtained a matrix full of data, the researcher must then try to reduce that bewildering splash of data to some reasonably simple picture. We shall take up the topic of data reduction in the next chapter. For now, we continue to consider the kind of information that is contained in QIIa data.

QIIa designates the datum type in which a point from one set exceeds a point from another set. The stimulus point either surpasses the individual point or it does not. The datum tells us, therefore, whether the stimulus comes up to the individual's standard—whether he passes it, fails it, overcomes it, and so on. Data of this sort do *not* tell us whether the individual prefers one stimulus over another, whether one stimulus has more of some specified quality than another, or whether two stimuli are alike in some respect. It would not be a correct deduction, for example, to observe that a nation (the "individual") found two immigrants (the "stimuli") both healthy enough to be admitted and then conclude that the two immigrants are equally healthy.

QUADRANT IIB: SINGLE-STIMULUS PROXIMITY DATA

In QIIb, a datum is a relation between an individual (actor) and a stimulus (object) showing whether the actor point and the stimulus point come within some criterion degree of proximity we call *epsilon*. The distance, epsilon, is not some absolute distance specified beforehand. We postulate this "leeway" because we know, for example, that red does not have to be "just so" before most people are willing to call it red. In Figure 10-5, the actor is sufficiently close or proximal in some sense to stimulus 1 to draw a "positive" response, but not sufficiently close to stimulus 2. An example might be whether the actor

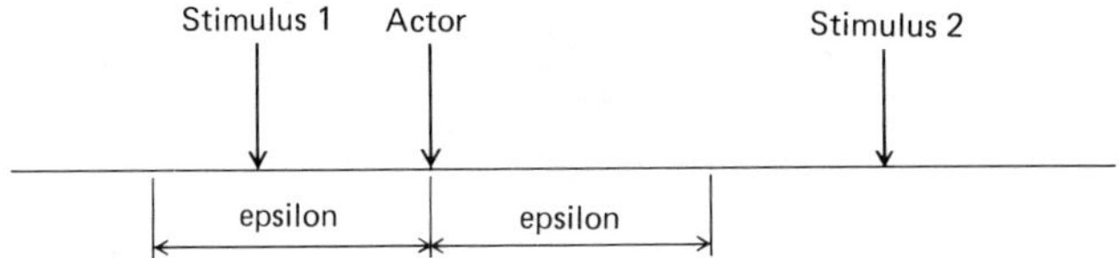

Figure 10-5.

endorses certain political statements; in such a case, the dimension might represent conservatism to liberalism. If liberalism is to the left of the figure, then the actor endorses stimulus 1 because it is not *too* liberal (that is, not too far to the left), but he rejects stimulus 2 because it is too conservative. The range along the dimension extending from one epsilon on one side to one epsilon on the other side of the actor's point can be called the actor's *latitude of acceptance,* a term put forward by Hovland, Harvey, and Sherif (1957).

The following are some examples of observations that would be likely candidates for QIIb:

John says the coffee has the right amount of cream in it.

I'd call him an inspiring leader.

The water is tepid; that is, this water comes within the epsilon range of the word *tepid* (from a set of words like cold, cool, warm, hot).

He belongs to the middle class.

He is of average intelligence.

I call it spinach.

John says the girl is the right height to dance with (not too tall, not too short).

John says the problem is difficult (not easy, but not impossible).

The Republicans were in the middle of the road.

That color is red.

His red corpuscle count is normal.

His name is John.

QIIb designates the datum in which a point from one set does or does not come within epsilon distance of a point from another set. The datum tells us whether the individual finds the stimulus acceptable in some sense—whether he eats it, likes it, understands it, flies it on his flagstaff, and so on. Data of this sort do *not* tell us whether the stimulus is *above* or *below* a standard—only that the stimulus is within the range of acceptability. For example, if the subject says, "That's about the amount of sugar I like in my coffee," we know that the amount of sugar is close enough to his ideal amount so that he finds it acceptable. We do not know whether the amount is a little less or a little more than his ideal amount. Furthermore, a single QIIb datum cannot tell us whether the individual prefers one stimulus to another nor whether one stimulus has more of some quality than another. Knowing that the subject finds a certain amount of sugar to be acceptable in his coffee tells us nothing about whether he will also find a little less or a little more sugar also acceptable.

QUADRANT IIIA: STIMULUS-COMPARISON DOMINANCE DATA

In QIIIa, a datum is a relation between two points, either both from the set of individuals or both from the set of stimuli, showing which dominates the other. A matrix of QIIIa data is always square, since the rows represent the same things as the columns. In Figure 10-6, stimulus 2 surpasses or dominates stimulus 1; perhaps we have observed that one cabbage is heavier than another.

Figure 10-6.

It is easy to see why this quadrant is called the quadrant for stimulus comparison. In the data matrix, we would enter a 1 in the row for stimulus 2 and the column for stimulus 1 to show that the row stimulus dominates the column stimulus. We would enter a zero in the column for stimulus 2 and the row for stimulus 1. The following are some examples of observations that would seem easily mapped into QIIIa:

You are heavier than I am.

This car costs more than that one.

Apple 1 tastes better than apple 2.

He wins out over her.

The trumpet is louder than the violin.

He is farther along in his work than you are.

QIIIa designates data in which a point from one set exceeds a point from the same set. The datum tells us whether one object has more of some quality than another—whether one object is heavier than another, more aggressive than another, greener than another, and so on. Data of this sort do *not* tell us whether an individual prefers one of the objects to the other, nor whether one object is much like the other, nor whether an individual finds either one acceptable.

QUADRANT IIIB: STIMULUS-COMPARISON PROXIMITY DATA

In QIIIb, a datum is a relation between two points, both from the same set, showing whether one is within epsilon proximity of the other. In Figure 10-7, stimulus 2 is within epsilon of stimulus 1; stimulus 3 is not. The following observations can easily be mapped into QIIIb:

Two peas from the same pod (or two peas from different pods).

They are sisters (or not).

The two are equal in ability (or not).

Both men are Armenians (or one or none is Armenian).

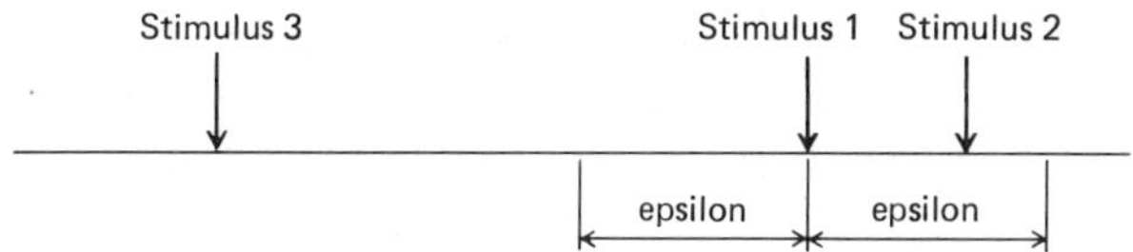

Figure 10-7.

QIIIb designates data in which a point from one set does or does not match, in some respect, another point from the same set. The datum tells us whether two stimuli are or are not alike. Data of this sort do *not* tell us whether one object has more of some quality than the other, whether an individual prefers one to the other, or whether an individual finds either one acceptable.

QUADRANT IA: PREFERENCE DATA

In QIa, a datum is a relation between two distances, and the points bounding the distances come from different sets; the datum shows which distance dominates or is smaller than the other. In Figures 10-8 through 10-11, stimulus 1 is closer to the actor than stimulus 2. A corresponding observation might be that John prefers food 1 to food 2.

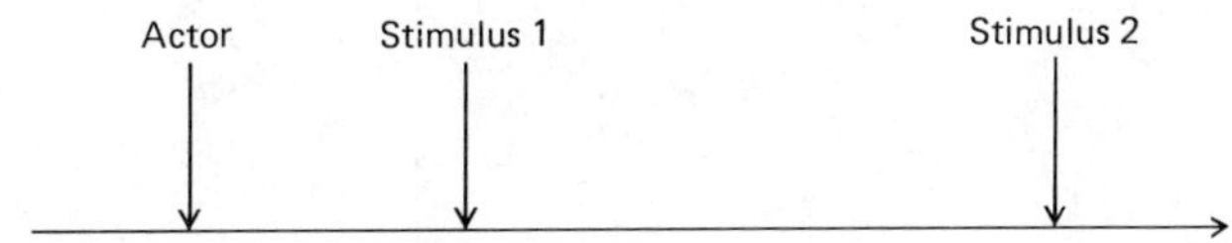

Figure 10-8.

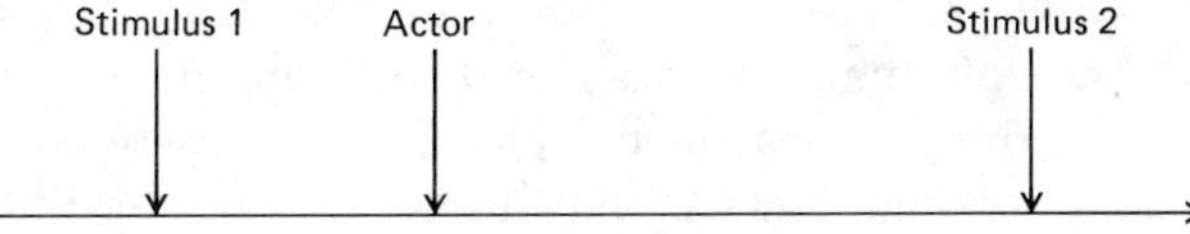

Figure 10-9.

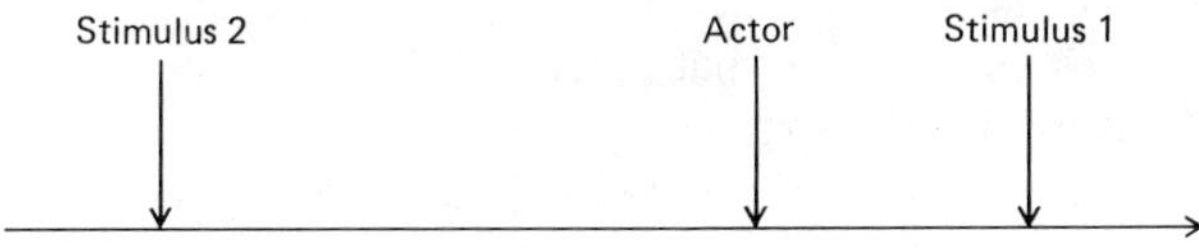

Figure 10-10.

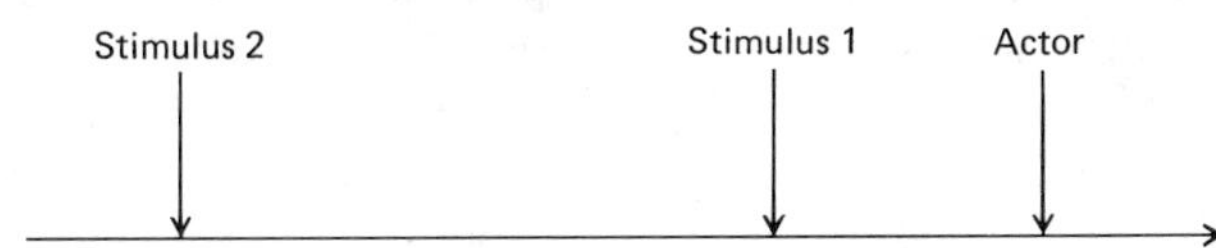

Figure 10-11.

The kind of QIa data with which we are most familiar is the kind after which the quadrant is named—preference data. The example we just used is of this kind. Most of the QIa data reported in the social scientific literature are this subvariety of QIa datum. Formally, this subvariety is distinguished by the fact that the distances being compared have a common terminus. In our example, we are comparing the distance from *John* to food 1 with the distance from *John* to food 2. As another example, let us return to the example pictured in Figure 10-2, in which we portrayed John's proximity to three colleges. In presenting that example, we showed how replications of observations could yield measures of *relative distances* from John to the three colleges. We saw how the data in the matrix could be taken for a ranking of the distances from John to the colleges. Now let us extend that example and suppose that we have a number of students and a number of colleges. The corresponding matrix looks like this:

Colleges:

	V	R	A	H	. . .
John					
George					
Nancy					
Florence					

Every cell in the above matrix, of course, represents a *distance* between a student and a college. When we put measures of *relative* distances into the cells (whether by replicating observations or by some direct measurement), we can then make comparisons among cells. The subvariety of data we have been discussing so far (John prefers food 1 to food 2; John's qualities are closer to Rutgers' requirements than to Harvard's) are taken only from comparisons among cells in the same row; the terminus of any distance being compared with any other is the row individual.

Data are also conceivable that correspond to comparing two cells *not* in the same row. Suppose John chooses Rutgers and George chooses Harvard. Who has made the better choice? The question to which we point here is not which college is the better one but rather which student made the better choice of a college suited to *him;* the question is one of compatibility or suitability. Formally, is the distance from John to Rutgers smaller than the distance from George to Harvard? As another example, consider a mother with two children, one of whom beseeches her for a bicycle and the other for a guitar. If she has money for only one of these desiderata, she may make her choice on the basis of which child would be the more disappointed to be deprived. She may have to make the complex judgment that Amy wants the bicycle with a greater (or lesser) yearning than Maybelle wants the guitar. As a third example, compare changes in scores. Let one set of points be the scores of a set of persons at time 1; let the other set be their scores at time 2. A datum in QIa would tell whether John's change exceeded (or did not exceed) George's.

QIa designates data in which a point from one set is nearer to a point from a second set than is the first point (or some other point) of the first set from another point of the second set. The datum tells us whether the distance from an individual to one stimulus is less, or not less, than the distance from that individual (or another individual) to another stimulus. It tells us whether, for example, an individual prefers one stimulus to another. Data of this sort do *not* tell us whether the individual finds either stimulus acceptable or whether one stimulus has more of some quality than the other.

It is common in the social sciences for an investigator to present two or more stimuli to a study participant, observe which one he chooses, and then conclude that the individual *likes* that one, or finds it acceptable in some sense. In the logic of the datum, such a conclusion is, of course, incorrect. In Figure 10-12, the individual prefers stimulus 1 to stimulus 2, but likes both—that is, both are within his latitude of acceptance. He prefers stimulus 2 to stimulus 3, likes 2, and dislikes 3. He prefers stimulus 3 to stimulus 4 and dislikes both.

Even though it is common for an individual to dislike a stimulus while still preferring it to another—he may merely dislike it with a lesser intensity than the other—social scientists often do collect data of the preferential form and then interpret the data as if they were of the epsilon sort. For example, the Kuder Preference Record (Kuder, 1956) presents three phrases describing activities and asks which the respondent likes best and which least. The interpretation is then made that the respondent will actively enjoy occupations that require activities similar to those chosen as liked best. (This is a considerable simplification of the logic used in constructing the Kuder Preference Record, but we believe it does not distort the logic enough to hurt the example.) Another example is apparent in the way people vote in presidential elections in the United States. Most voters probably consider third party candidates beneath contempt or beyond possible election and respond primarily to the candidates of the two major parties. The winner of the election usually seems to believe that he has the support of those who voted for him. Yet many people may vote for a candidate because it hurts them less than voting for his opponent. Even though the conclusions we have just displayed in these two examples are illogical, nevertheless both methods of data collection seem to be useful—the Kuder Preference Record and the political election. How can this be?

When a respondent chooses a most-liked activity described in the Kuder

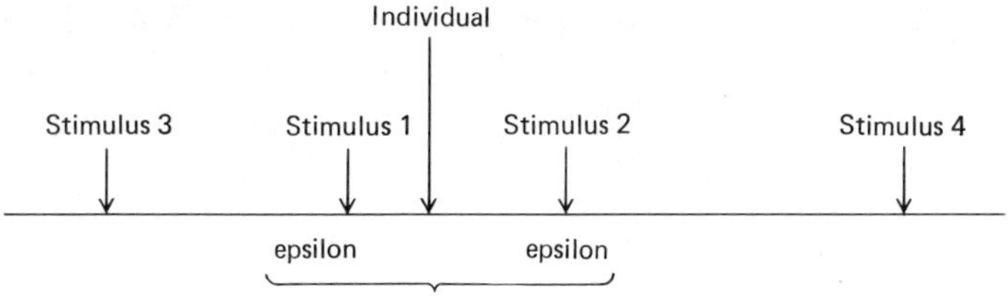

Figure 10-12.

Preference Record, he may or may not like it. But, in fact, there is a circumstance that makes it likely that he *will* like it. The circumstance is the shared culture between the respondent and the early respondents whose likes and dislikes helped construct the test. The activities described in the Kuder Preference Record were chosen to be activities liked by people comfortable in some occupations and disliked by people comfortable in other occupations. Consequently, when today's respondents express a preference for one activity over another, it is very likely that a majority of them will also actually *like* that activity, because today's respondent shares the same core U.S. culture with the people on whose preferences the test was originally constructed. It is not because of the logic of the data collection method that we can conclude that the respondents like the activities they choose as most preferred. Rather, we can conclude that *most* respondents (not all) will like the activities they choose as most preferred because the thousands of people on whose tastes the test was built liked some of the activities described in the test. Similarly, most people will surely like something about the candidate they vote for because of the common culture shared by the people who nominate him and the people who vote for him. Granted that the candidate is never the ideal of very many people, still he must be reasonably acceptable to the bulk of his "supporters" because of shared values and goals. Regardless of this argument, however, the researcher needs to be wary, for common culture will not always save him from logical mistakes of this sort.

QUADRANT IVA: SIMILARITIES DATA

In QIVa, a datum is a relation between two distances, with the points bounding the distances all coming from the same set, either individuals or stimuli; the data show which distance dominates, or is smaller than, the other. We interpret data of this sort to tell us which similarity between stimuli (or individuals) is the greater (that is, which distance is the smaller)—the similarity between A and B or that between C and D. A convenient label for this quadrant, consequently, is *similarities.*

In Figure 10-13, stimuli 3 and 4 are more similar than 1 and 2. Stimuli 2 and 3 are more similar than 1 and 4, stimuli 1 and 2 are more similar than 1 and 3, and so forth.

The data matrix for QIVa is built by letting a row represent a distance between two particular stimuli (or individuals); a corresponding column also represents the distance between the same two stimuli. The matrix is square, of course, and an entry in a cell tells whether the row distance is smaller than the

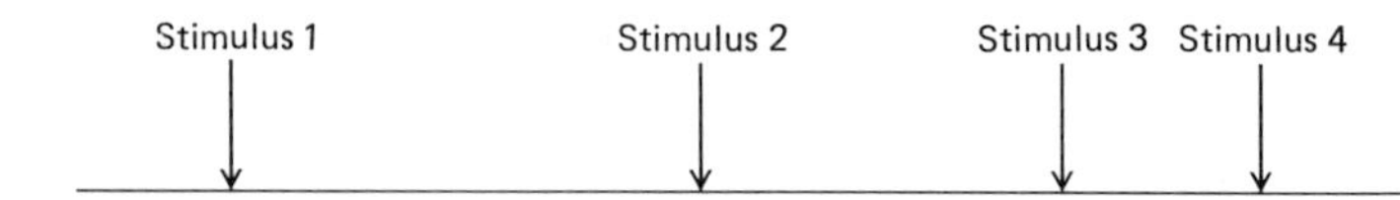

Figure 10-13.

column distance. As explained earlier, this matrix can originate from an intact dominance or proximity matrix in which the rows and columns stand for points (QIIIa and b) if the entries in the cells of the point matrix are other than 1 and zero so that cells can be compared for magnitude. If the cells of a QIIIa or QIIIb point matrix can be compared for magnitude (for example, by frequency of dominance in replicated observations), then a new QIVa matrix can be built with rows and columns corresponding to the cells of the point matrix; the cells of the new QIVa distance matrix tell whether the row distance dominates, or is smaller than, the column distance.

Let us recall the QIIIb matrix. A common form of the QIIIb matrix is the correlation matrix, in which a cell tells the proximity of one stimulus to another. In this case, the stimuli are tests or other measures on which correlations can be computed, and the proximities are the correlation coefficients. Such a matrix is easily converted into a QIVa matrix, since rows and columns can represent pairs of tests and the cell can tell whether one correlation between two tests is higher than another. The higher correlation, of course, expresses a closer similarity.

QIVa designates data in which two points from a set are closer together than two other points from that set. The datum tells us whether one distance is shorter than the other; that is, whether two objects are more similar than another two. Data of this sort do *not* tell us whether an individual finds any of the stimuli acceptable or preferable or whether one stimulus has more of some quality than another. Neither do they tell us whether the members of either pair of stimuli are alike (to some epsilon criterion of being alike). If John and Mary are better suited to each other than are Cal and Carol, it does not mean that some further person would like any of the four or prefer any one to any other. Nor does it mean that John is more husbandly than Cal or Mary more loving than Carol.

QUADRANTS IB AND IVB: PROXIMITY DATA ON DISTANCES

In QIb, a datum is a relation between two distances, showing whether the two are proximate or not—that is, whether they match in length. This kind of datum is often sought in ordinary life. The cashier asks, "Do you care if I give you five dimes instead of a half dollar?" The automobile salesman asks, "Do you have a preference about the color of the upholstery?" At the beginning of a ceremony, someone asks, "Do you care who goes first?"

In research work, however, asking whether an actor has a preference usually seems to be an inefficient way to go about things. It seems to take little or no more effort to discover *what* the preference of the actor may be. Instead of asking, "Do you have a preference between A and B?" the researcher almost always asks, "Which do you prefer, A or B?" In psychological work, especially in studying cognitive structure, researchers almost never seem to want to allow the actor to have *no* preference. In fact, instructions to the actor often go something like, "Please choose one in every case even though it is sometimes difficult to do so." Though such a technique may introduce error into the results (in those instances where the actor really has no preference), it avoids the awkwardness of finding oneself with two types of data on one's hands: QIa and QIb. It is awkward to try to simplify a data matrix containing more than one type of datum, because, as we have seen in previous sections, we choose different types of data precisely because they carry different kinds of information. It is difficult to make some kind of combined sense from one actor's information that he prefers candidate A to candidate B (QIa) and another actor's information that he has no preference between them. Sometimes, it is true, an actor's lack of preference might mean that he believes A and B to be equivalent and not to be put in *either* order. Two or more types of data can be combined in the same analysis only by adopting some sort of simplifying assumption.

Nevertheless, questionnaires written by behavioral scientists do sometimes contain items such as this:

Which do you prefer, A or B?
( ) A
( ) B
( ) Have no preference for one over the other.

If the results of putting such an item (or series of them) to a number of respondents are totaled and presented merely as the percentages of respondents giving each answer, no difficulty is encountered. But if scaling is to be done, then such an item becomes an embarrassment precisely because it delivers *both* QIa and QIb data. This is not to say that one should not sometimes live with such embarrassment. It would be too bad for a company to invest thousands of dollars in some product, after looking at the tally of preferences, only to discover too late that the questionnaire-maker had omitted the choice, "I have no preference" or, "I couldn't care less."

Presenting two choices to an actor without affording him the opportunity to indicate a lack of preference (that is, without giving him an opportunity to decline the choice) is often called a forced-choice technique. This is a misleading term, because not only data-collection methods for QIa but many other data-collection methods force some kind of limited choice upon the actor. In QIIa, if we ask a subject to tell us when he sees an "L" upon a screen, he might (if we let him) give us all these responses:

I see an E.

I see half an L.

I'm sleepy.

I hear an auto honking.

When you walk by, I smell sweat.

I see some vague thing on the screen, I don't know what, but I'll call it an "L" to hurry things along.

Typically, the experimenter would pay no "official" attention to any of the above statements, considering them all equivalent to, "No, I do not see an 'L.'" In brief, the experimenter in this situation will not listen to anything the actor may freely choose to tell him; the actor is "forced" into only one of two replies, "Yes, I see it" or, "No, I don't see it." That is, the experimenter interprets whatever the actor says as equivalent either to "yes" or "no." Similarly, when the actor is presented with an arithmetic item on a test, the tester limits the actor to two classes of answers: (1) the "right" answer and (2) all others, the "wrong" ones. The tester usually ignores such responses as:

> This is a difficult problem.
>
> If you mean ____, the answer is 7, but if you mean ____, the answer is $3\frac{1}{3}$.

It would be easy to point out how data-collection methods associated with other quadrants also limit the choices of the actor, at least insofar as the researcher will pay attention to them. The point is that the term *forced-choice* puts a misleading emphasis on the forcing of choices in QIa.

The fact of forced-choice techniques shows up once again a dilemma we have seen in many guises: shall the researcher leave the actor completely free to tell him how he (the actor) perceives the world about him, or shall the researcher describe the possible worlds and merely allow the actor to choose among them? If he gives the actor complete freedom, he may end with no more than a catalog of personal, idiosyncratic perceptions. If he offers the actor a limited choice, he may fail to offer an alternative that comes close to the way the actor actually perceives things. As with other dilemmas in research, the investigator must decide which risk carries the lesser penalties and the greater gains for his purposes.

To summarize our remarks about the nature of data interpreted according to QIb, we have said that although we are sometimes interested in discovering in daily life whether people are indifferent to paired alternatives, researchers do not often interpret observations as this kind of datum. Even more rarely do they compile data of this type unaccompanied by data from other quadrants. Furthermore, at this writing, we know of only one scheme for analyzing QIb data, that of Lingoes (1963, 1968a, 1968b), and it requires a large-scale computer. Since QIb data are rarely collected and discussion of Lingoes' model would unduly lengthen later chapters, we shall pay no more attention to QIb data in this book.

In QIVb, a datum is a relation between two distances, and the points bounding the distances all come from the same set. The datum shows whether the two distances are proximate—that is, whether they match in length. As matters stand at this writing, QIVb data are in much the same limbo as QIb data, and we shall not mention this sort of data again.

SUMMARY OF DATA QUADRANTS AND MATRICES

Ignoring QIb and QIVb for practical purposes, we shall deal with only six data types. We summarize them below.

- QIa — Dominance relations between distances bounded by points from different sets (preference data). (The datum asks, Does the distance from individual A to stimulus 1 exceed the distance from individual B—or A—to stimulus 2?)
- QIIa — Dominance relations between points of different sets (single-stimulus data). (The datum asks, Does the individual surpass the stimulus in some sense—or does the stimulus surpass the individual?)
- QIIb — Proximity on relations between points of different sets (single-stimulus data). (The datum asks, Does individual A belong with, match, or have the property denoted by stimulus 1?)
- QIIIa — Dominance relations between points of the same set (stimulus comparison). (The datum asks, Does stimulus 1 exceed stimulus 2 in some specified property? Does individual A exceed individual B in some specified property?)
- QIIIb — Proximity relations between points of the same set (stimulus comparison). (The datum asks, Do stimuli 1 and 2 belong in the same class? Do individuals A and B belong in the same class?)
- QIVa — Dominance relations between distances bounded by points from the same set, with or without a common terminus (similarities data). (The datum asks, Does the distance from stimulus 1 to stimulus 2 exceed the distance from stimulus 3 to stimulus 4? Does the distance from individual A to individual B exceed the distance from individual C to individual D?)

For purposes of data analysis, in two of these six types (IIb and IIIb) data usually get mapped into other quadrants (Ia and IVa, respectively). We shall give more detail about mapping from one quadrant to another below, and the idea of analytic methods resting on the assumptions of a particular quadrant will come clear in Chapter 11. As a summary of this chapter so far, we review some distinctions (or facets) among types of data matrices.

First, the data matrix can be *dichotomous*—that is, it can have a yes or no, or a one or zero, in each cell. It can also be *nondichotomous* and include numerical entries that vary in more degrees than two. Nondichotomous data can always be generated by replication of dichotomous data, as in several examples given earlier in this chapter. Nondichotomous data can also be collected directly, in terms such as number of score points by which one team dominates another, number of communications from one actor to another, time to complete a task, and so on. A matrix containing nondichotomous data on points can always be translated into a dominance matrix on distances. That is, nondichotomous data of QIIa (dominance) or IIb (proximity) can be translated into a matrix of dominance relations on distances—type Ia. Similarly, nondichotomous data of QIIIa or IIIb can be translated into a matrix of dominance relations on distances IVa.

Second, when the data points (or distances) are drawn from the same set (as symbolized by III and IV), the data matrix consists of a row for each stimulus (or individual) and a column for each stimulus (or individual). Thus, the data matrix is always square, or *intact*. When the data consist of points (or distances) from two sets (as in QII and I), there is a row for each individual and a column for each stimulus (or vice versa), but the same reference points do not appear in both rows and columns. We can, however, consider such a matrix *as if* it were drawn from a larger intact matrix, in which there is a row for each stimulus *and* each individual and a column for each stimulus *and* each individual. In effect, then, an individuals-by-stimuli matrix is an *off-diagonal submatrix* of a larger (stimuli-plus-individuals by stimuli-plus-individuals) intact matrix. The data matrices representing data in QIIa, IIb, and Ia are *off-diagonal* matrices, while those representing data in QIIIa, IIIb, and IVa are *intact* matrices.

Third, some data matrices are *symmetrical*—the row 1 column 2 entry is identical to the column 1 row 2 entry—and some are not. When a matrix is not symmetrical, it may or may not be complementary. (To be complementary, for example, the row 1 column 2 entry and the row 2 column 1 entry might be fractions adding to 1, or might be positive and negative entries adding to zero.) Dominance matrices on points or distances are *not* symmetric. Often, they are complementary (if A dominates B, then B is dominated by A), but they do not have to be complementary. Intact proximity matrices are often symmetrical (if A is in the same class with B, then B is in the same class with A). Off-diagonal matrices cannot be symmetrical in themselves, since they are not necessarily square; but they can be symmetrical within the total intact matrix (if John is suitable to Rutgers, then Rutgers is suitable to John). We can call the nonsymmetric case a *conditional* proximity matrix.

Recall that we decided to drop further consideration of the two data types defined by proximity on distances (Ib and IVb) because such data are seldom collected and because so far only one analysis model (Lingoes, 1968b) is available. Note also that the two proximity-on-points data quadrants (IIb and IIIb), if the data are nondichotomous, can be (and usually are) mapped into *dominance-on-distance* matrices (Ia and IVa) for analysis. Consequently, the four types of data most frequently used in research and their corresponding matrices are the following:

Quadrant IIa	Off-diagonal, dichotomous or nondichotomous dominance on points.
Quadrant Ia	Off-diagonal, dichotomous or nondichotomous dominance on distances.
Quadrant IIIa	Intact, dichotomous or nondichotomous dominance on points.
Quadrant IVa	Intact, dichotomous or nondichotomous dominance on distances.

However, some models are available for analysis of proximity on points without translating them into dominance on distances; we shall occasionally mention proximities on points:

Quadrant IIb	Off-diagonal, dichotomous or nondichotomous, symmetric or conditional proximity on points.
Quadrant IIIb	Intact, dichotomous or nondichotomous, symmetric or conditional proximity on points.

The several types of data matrices and their connections with the data quadrants are presented in Figure 10-14.

Various models for analyzing data will be discussed in the next two chapters; each is specialized for use with one, or at most a few, but not for all of the data types we have described. To understand how various analytic models can be applied to a particular set of data, it is necessary to understand the conditions or assumptions by which the researcher *makes* one type of datum rather than another. These assumptions are the topic of the next section. While the investigator will very likely find it difficult to imagine how a particular observation can be interpreted in all eight of the octants, he will usually find it easy to imagine how he could map the observation into more than one of the octants. The investigator must *decide* what kind of data he will make from his observations. *And having thus decided, he will have limited* (1) *the kinds of questions*

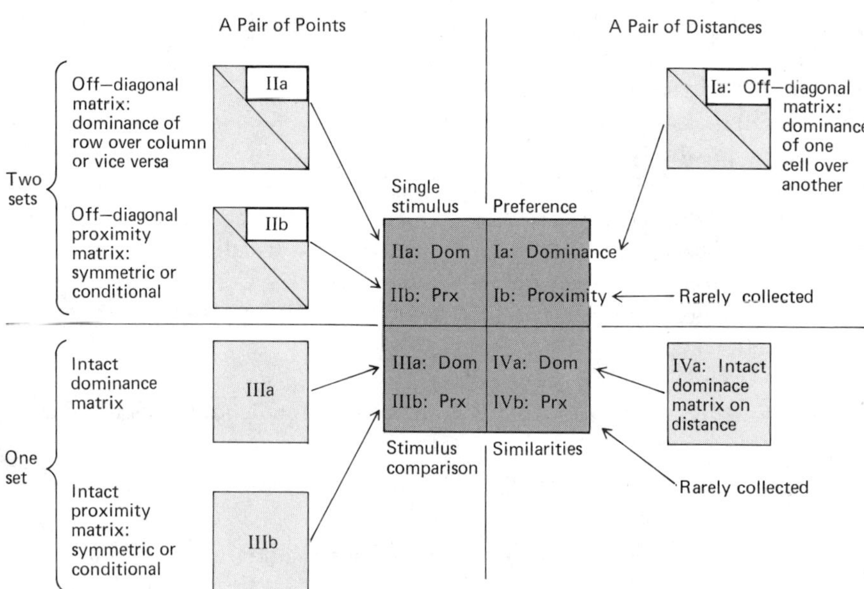

Figure 10-14. Data matrices and data quadrants.

he can answer, (2) *the kinds of analysis models he can use, and hence* (3) *the kinds of answers to those questions he can obtain.* Thus, the mapping of observations into data is a crucial choice point greatly affecting the outcome of a research study.

10-3. Assumptions Required for Translating Observations into Data

A recurrent theme in this book has been the principle that one must assume something to learn something. This is true at every stage of the research process, including the stages of mapping observation records into data and of applying analytic models to those data. As we shall use the term, an *assumption* is an assertion we take to be true during a particular study without testing whether it is true. (We shall not use the term *assumption* synonymously with *hypothesis,* as is often done in informal conversation.)

This chapter demonstrates how the researcher can gain empirical information from a set of recorded observations. This involves translating observation records into *data* (remembering that a datum is a relation of dominance or proximity on a pair of points or a pair of distances). Chapters 11 and 12 will discuss the state of organizing sets of data into arrays so as (1) to determine what pattern they have or (2) to test whether in fact they have a hypothesized pattern. Finally, Chapter 13 will turn to the matter of relating two or more patterned arrays of data to one another. Many alternatives are available at each of these stages, depending on the choices made in previous stages. Each alternative involves making *different sets of assumptions* about the nature or meaning of the data.

We turn now to some of the kinds of assumptions behavioral scientists make (implicitly or explicitly) in generating data from observation records and in analyzing those data. Some of the assumptions are necessary to map observations into one or another of the data quadrants. Others are needed to apply certain analytic models. The latter are included in Appendix I, but will also be discussed in Chapters 11 and 12.

BASIC ASSUMPTIONS UNDERLYING THE DATA MODELS

Three assumptions underlie every kind of datum. The first assumption is that *a datum represents a relation on a pair of points*—an "individual" and a "stimulus" by arbitrary convention. Alternatively, and with formal equivalence, a datum can be constructed of two distances having individuals or stimuli as end points. The second assumption is that *there is at least one dimension* (or attribute or respect or aspect) along which both elements (points or distances) may be arrayed; that is, there is some respect in which one element can be said to dominate the other or to be more or less proximate to it. This assumption puts the two points or distances into a common space within which the relations of dominance and proximity can be defined. (For some analysis models later on we shall need a stronger assumption—unidimensionality—which says that there is one and only one dimension on which the points in a datum are compared; but for other analysis models—multidimensional ones—we need assume only that there is one *or more* such dimension.)

The third assumption is that of *excluded indifference.* This simply means that we will not "permit" an indeterminate case to occur. One stimulus either dominates another or it does not; one stimulus is either proximate to another or it is not. Perhaps a good example of the assumption of excluded indifference occurs when we flip a coin to decide something. We do not "permit" the coin to land on its edge and thus show neither heads nor tails. This outcome, of course, logically *can* occur, and at very rare times it undoubtedly does. But it is not a "permissible" outcome from the point of view of the coin flippers; it does not provide a decision. Hence, they would most often disregard that outcome and flip again. An alternative resolution, incidentally, would be to decide the outcomes are to be heads versus not-heads (rather than heads versus tails). With this partition, on-edge is no longer indeterminate; it is not-heads. In a similar vein, we have said that one stimulus either dominates or does not dominate another. We tried not to say that a stimulus either dominates or is dominated by another; such a case could, logically, leave exact ties in the area of indifference or indeterminancy.

These three assumptions permit us to form data of the proximity type. These assumptions seem innocuous; they seem to do no violence to our notions of reality. Yet it is important to have them explicit. One of the ways scientific thinking advances is through challenges to assumptions, and it may be that one day someone will show one of these assumptions to be pernicious.

ASSUMPTIONS UNDERLYING DOMINANCE DATA

In addition to the basic assumptions required for all data within Coombs' quadrants, two further assumptions are needed for all data arrays that are to be interpreted as dominance data (QIa, IIa, IIIa, IVa). One (our fourth) is the assumption of *positive direction.* This simply means that the researcher must assume he knows, or must decide arbitrarily, which response is the "right" response or is to be treated as the response exhibiting more of the assumed underlying dimension than other possible responses. If runner A has a *lower* time score than runner B, we would usually consider A to dominate B on the assumption that faster is in some sense better or more appropriate under the circumstances. There are, of course, many items or stimuli or sets of item alternatives for which there is no clear-cut natural or right direction. If stimulus A is west of B, then B is east of A. To treat this as a dominance datum, the investigator must decide that *one* of the directions (east or west, it often makes no difference which) is the "positive" direction. He then has to stay with that decision for all comparisons (A with B, A with D, B with C, and so on) that he wishes to put into a common array for analysis. If A is west of B and west of C but east of D, we would *not* want to say that A dominates B, C, *and* D on this dimension. Rather, we might choose west, arbitrarily, as the "positive" direction and then say that A dominates B and C while D dominates A. Thus, the assumption of positive direction permits a uniform directionality for all items to be compared.

A related assumption (our fifth) for all analytic models of dominance data is called *monotonicity*. The key idea of monotonicity is that a trend, once it is begun, never reverses itself. To say that a datum is monotonic is to say that the nature of the underlying property is such that if an actor surpasses a stimulus in some respect, the actor can never exhibit so much more of the relevant property that he somehow fails to surpass the stimulus. In the dominance model, an actor fails to surpass or says *no* to a stimulus as long as the stimulus point is in the positive direction from the actor point (as in the relation between Actor 1 and the stimulus in Figure 10-4); when the actor point is in the positive direction from the stimulus point (as in the relation between Actor 2 and the stimulus in Figure 10-4) the actor surpasses the stimulus or says *yes*. In other words, as an actor point overtakes the stimulus point and surpasses it, the response changes *only once* from *no* to *yes*. This contrasts with proximity data, with which the response is *no* when, for example, the coffee has too little sugar, *yes* when the coffee has about the right amount, and *no* again when the coffee has too much sugar.

For dominance data, it is necessary to assume monotonicity of the relation between the underlying dimension and the direction of the response (that is, positive or negative). If a man clears a hurdle by one inch, he dominates it; if he clears it by a foot, he still dominates it, and there is no higher clearance at which he fails to dominate it. If it takes a certain amount of arithmetic ability to pass (dominate) a test item, then persons with that amount *or any greater amount* will pass the item.

The five assumptions we have described so far illustrate how researchers must make assumptions (that go untested except in methodological studies) even at the very foundations of data gathering—that is, at the level of the meaning of the individual datum itself. In the next section, we shall point out some of the practical uses of knowing about the assumptions in one's data.

Further assumptions necessary in constructing various analytic models are given in Appendix I; they include the interchangeability of identical response patterns, unidimensionality or multidimensionality, deterministic or probabilistic location of points, local independence, random error distribution, interchangeability of positive responses, and equal intervals among alternatives.

10-4. Uses of Chapter 10

In what ways can one make use of his knowledge of datum models and assumptions about data? First, when we adopt a particular data model as our interpretation of an observation, the specifications for data in that quadrant make explicit the kind of inference that is logically warranted and the kind that is not. In section 10-2 we gave the example of the Kuder Preference Record—Vocational, in which *preferences* (matching the QIa model) were elicited but then interpreted as *acceptances* (having the acceptance-and-rejection form of QIIb). Thinking in terms of the data models made it immediately clear that the Kuder Preference Record was making a further assumption—that actors who express preferences in the multiple choices offered also actively *like* the activities they choose.

Another example is given by Hays (1960), who points out that a researcher is often interested in coming to a decision whether the actors have agreed with each other merely by chance or because of some influence the researcher is studying. In the case of rank ordering objects, one might, upon first thought, begin by ascertaining the likelihood of obtaining by sheer chance the rank order upon which the actors seem to have agreed. In the case of rank ordering five objects, for example, there are $5! = 120$ orders in which the five things can be placed. But can one say that the chance of a particular order turning up is 1 in 120? Hays points out that an actor can be influenced or uninfluenced only in respect to those things in his behavioral repertoire (and therefore available to him as a response). A clue to the maximum limits of this repertoire can be obtained, in the case of rank orders, by looking at the number of orders given by the population as a whole. If certain sectors of the 120 rankings (in the case of five objects) are systematically omitted, then it may be that the culture of the actors, or their heredity, or their definition of the situation, has reduced the probability of those orders to near zero, and they should not be considered in computing the likelihood that two actors will agree on the same rank order. Now, it can be shown (as we shall do in Chapter 11) that when five objects are arranged in one dimension, say, there are many fewer preference orders an actor can deliver (using the model QIa) than when the objects are arranged in more dimensions. Thinking in this fashion and raising the question of the dimensionality assumption, one finds that it becomes immediately pertinent to make a correction in the current way of thinking about agreements on rank orders among actors.

A second use of the concepts in this chapter is to insure that the researcher is collecting observations that will satisfy him that he is making sense when he interprets them as the same type of datum. When we enter data into a tabulation from which to analyze them—that is, a tabulation from which to put actors or stimuli, or both, into scales on the basis of the pattern in the data—all the data must be of the same form; there is no analytic model yet produced (except very complex computer programs embodying their own lists of assumptions) that will work any other way. This means that we must have some concepts for classifying data according to the requirements of analytic models that now exist or that might conceivably be built. There is more than one set of concepts that will serve this purpose, but it seems to us that Coombs' quadrants perform this service most simply. The simplicity is symbolized in the two figures in Appendix I.

Third, we need to have a convenient way of explaining to ourselves how to reinterpret observations. We have seen that the researcher can interpret an observation in more than one way, choosing one or another formal model to represent the feature of the relation between actor and stimulus that best suits his purpose. Furthermore, he can convert data of one sort into data of another sort through reinterpretations. An example could go as follows: Give a man a rifle and ask him to fire at a target. Assign numbers to the various rings in the target and let these numbers be a rating scale (QIIb) by which a numerical rating can be given to the actor according to the circle his bullet strikes. Give him several other numerical ratings having to do with soldiering. Add up the ratings. If his total score (QIIa—as with a "test") exceeds a certain level, give him a prize or a medal. Then compare his score this month with his score next month. If it stays within a certain degree of change (QIIIb), ignore it; otherwise call him in to compliment him or scold him. But we might be interested in comparative stabilities between military life and civilian life. So we might collect similar summated ratings on a group of civilians as well as on a group of soldiers. Pairing soldier to civilian, we might note whether the change by one exceeded the change by the other (QIa or QIIa). We could then consider each soldier-to-civilian comparison to be a distance and take them all as a population of distances to be compared with one another (QIVa). An analysis using an appropriate model could be made at any or all of these stages. An always-applicable classification scheme that is related to analytic models, such as Coombs' quadrants, makes charting these transformations easier to conceive.

Fourth, being explicit about assumptions in a fairly formal way enables one to avoid misleading labels such as forced choice, deterministic versus probabilistic,[1] and others. Finally, a thread that has run through all four of these claims is that a simple language that can deal with any situation one might meet is helpful in dealing with the local languages one also encounters in those situations. Coombs' data quadrants provide such a *lingua Franca,* running from the collection of observations of any sort to the construction of scales and spaces of any sort.

A final word on assumptions. The more assumptions or the stronger assumptions one makes, the more one insures that his analysis will yield clear-cut and interpretable results; at the same time, the *researcher,* more than the empirical observations records, is determining these results. For example, if an investigator uses an error-tolerant unidimensional model, the provisions for dealing with error will *guarantee* a unidimensional array, but may mask evidences of multidimensionality, inconsistency, and intransitivity. Thus, the assumptions the researcher makes in choosing the data quadrant within which he will interpret his observation records and in choosing an analytic model by which he will array them or organize them into a patterned set—these

[1] The assumptions contained in so-called deterministic and probabilistic models are discussed in connection with Assumption 8 in Appendix I.

assumptions affect the kind and amount of information he can reap from his analysis of the data. We shall discuss more of these matters in the next two chapters.

10-5. Further Reading

See Coombs (1964).

CHAPTER 11
Analyzing Empirical Evidence: Arranging Data into Unidimensional Patterns

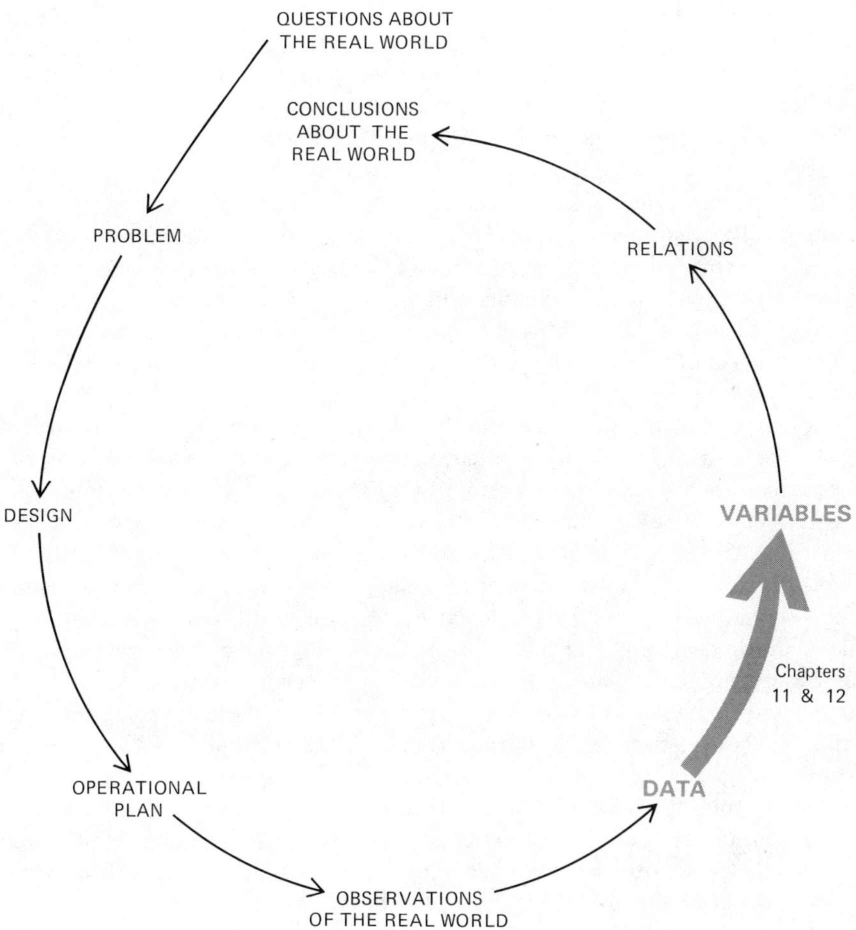

This chapter opens our discussion of the reduction of data. Let us suppose the investigator has made the various choices described in earlier chapters, has made some observations, and has filled in a data matrix. At this point, he must choose an analytic model with which to simplify the spread of his data.

11-1. Reasons for Reduction of Data

Why is the researcher not satisfied to cease his work once he has filled in his data matrix? Why must he do something further with his data beyond looking at them and seeing what they mean? In essence, the answer is very simple. The researcher will usually want to rearrange his data because in all likelihood his data matrix will be too complex for him to understand by merely looking at it. He will inevitably begin moving things around, hoping he can find a pattern in what at first appears utter confusion. If the data matrix is very simple, the researcher may well draw his conclusions immediately. If three friends, for example, tell one another which of three movies they would like to attend, they are not likely to get out pencil and paper, much less a computer, to digest the information. But a data matrix does not have to be much larger than that before the possibilities for interpretation become sufficiently complicated to justify all we say in Chapters 11 and 12 and all that is said in the literature we refer to. To consider this question of searching for a pattern in more detail, let us divide it into two parts: (1) Why should the researcher want to seek a pattern in his observations? (2) What kinds of patterns might he seek?

Turning to the first question, let us expand upon the brief answer we just gave; namely, until the researcher finds some pattern in a set of observations, or somehow imposes a pattern upon them, he will not usually feel that he has made sense of the observations. Each observation is a record of a particular property of a particular event. Each record of observation is now a datum, translated into an entry in a data matrix. If each datum remains a representation of a unique, particular event unrelated to others in that set of data, the investigator will have accomplished nothing beyond making a list of observations. To gain useful information from his empirical activities, he must find some way to describe a set of observations in compact, efficient, and economical terms. The purpose of inquiry is to search out and present some unifying *organization* among disparate objects or events—not necessarily a very simple organization but an order or a pattern that is at least simpler than the total set of objects or events. If it takes ten separate unifying principles to explain or account for ten observations, then those principles are merely restatements of the initial observations. But if the ten observations can be explained in terms of *one* underlying principle, then we are making progress toward a unifying principle in a useful sense. This goal of finding concepts that simplify our understanding of experience is commonly called the principle of parsimony or, Occam's razor.

The second step in our search for a pattern deals with the kinds of patterns to be sought. The data do not tell us, by themselves, what pattern best describes them. To organize data into a pattern, the researcher must have in mind some pattern or some rules that any acceptable pattern must follow; he can then ask how well the data can be arranged to fit the pattern or the

Table 11-1. *A Hypothetical Data Matrix*

		ITEMS							
		a	*b*	*c*	*d*	*e*	*f*	*g*	*h*
Actor	1	1	1	0	0	1	1	0	0
	2	0	0	0	0	1	0	1	0
	3	0	1	0	0	0	0	1	1
	4	0	1	0	1	1	1	1	0
	5	1	0	1	1	0	0	0	1
	6	1	1	1	0	1	0	1	0
	7	0	0	0	0	1	0	1	0
	8	1	1	1	0	1	0	1	1
	9	0	0	1	0	1	0	1	1
	10	0	0	1	0	1	0	1	1

rules without violating any of the assumptions he has already chosen to make about the data. This chapter will display some models for seeking patterns in data. Each model can be considered a systematic procedure for asking a series of questions of a set of data to see how well they fit some particular *kind* of pattern.

We can take some steps to simplify a data matrix by using only those assumptions underlying *every* method of analyzing data. To make it easier to visualize what we are discussing, we shall refer to Table 11-1; let this matrix contain data interpreted as QIIa—let us say test items represented by columns and test-takers by rows. An entry of 1 could indicate our interpretation that the row actor had passed the column item; an entry of 0 could mean the actor had failed the item. Let us now begin the process of data reduction by asking, Are *all* the data the same or do they differ? If every test-taker passed every item, all entries in the matrix would be 1. If this turns out to be the case, there is no further question to ask; the pattern is one of invariance. We would not know whether some of the people had more of the tested ability than other people. We would not know whether some of the items required more of the tested ability than other items. But it is not quite true that a test matrix containing all 1s will always be unprofitable. If the matrix is different from what we predicted, we have learned something. An example would be the case of a teacher who is not sure his students know the answers to the items in a test. If it turns out that every student answers every item correctly, the information is very profitable. Knowledge is knowledge of differences; if the data matrix is to convey information to the researcher, it must contain differences within it or be different from what the researcher predicted or be different from something conceivable beforehand such as a random array. If some of the entries in the data matrix are different from others, we shall find that some people passed some items but not others and that some items were passed by some people but not by others. We can then ask a series of questions:

1. For each item: Which actors pass it; which fail it?
2. For each person: Which items does he pass; which does he fail?
3. Can we find a set of actors who all pass the same set of items and fail the rest?

By answering this last question, we can group all the data into identical response classes; that is, we can reduce the number of rows in the data matrix by treating as alike (and interchangeable) all actors who had the same pattern of responses over items, such as the pair of actors 2 and 7 in Table 11-1 and also the pair 9 and 10. (In doing this we are making the interchangeability assumption given as number 6 in Appendix I.) Next, we can pose the obverse question:

4. Can we find a set of items which are all passed by the same set of actors and failed by all the rest?

With this question we can further reduce the matrix by grouping together all columns (items) having identical patterns of response over rows (there are no identical columns in Table 11-1). Combining columns requires a new assumption:[1]

Assumption 15: Interchangeability of items: columns (representing items, stimuli, or objects) bearing identical patterns of response in the data-matrix are identical psychologically and can be interchanged without significant effect.

These combinations of rows with identical response patterns over items and of columns with identical response patterns over actors can reduce the complexity of the data matrix considerably. We have remaining a matrix with each row representing a set of actors with a particular response pattern over items, and each column representing a set of one or more items with a particular response pattern over actors.

In sum, the following patterns can be simplified using only a few assumptions about *data* and adopting no analytic model:

1. All entries alike (invariance)
2. Actors sharing a response pattern over items
3. Items sharing a response pattern over actors
4. Various mixtures of (2) and (3).

[1] Assumptions 6 through 14 are given in Appendix I.

Up to this point, the steps we are describing would be appropriate for *all* types of data; we help ourselves to study patterns of variability when we reduce the data matrix by combining identical response patterns over persons and over items. At this juncture, however, there are alternative next steps, depending on the types of data we are working with and what our purposes are. In this chapter and the next, we shall discuss how to lace data together into strings and into higher-dimensional arrays. We shall describe a number of conceptions, or "models," for fitting together the data in orderly ways. To fit together the data, we shall have to make use of the assumptions underlying analytic models that we mentioned near the end of Chapter 10 and in Appendix I. We shall call the problem of fitting the data together into ordered arrays or scales the problem of the *external validity of data.* The choice facing the researcher who has a matrix of data and wants to establish a simpler order among his data is a choice among alternative sets of assumptions. If the researcher can accept no further assumption, he cannot further simplify the data.

11-2. Internal and External Validity of Data[2]

Two fundamental problems occur in drawing conclusions from data. The first has to do with what kinds of statements one can logically make from a datum. Assumptions 1 through 5 (discussed in section 10-3) make the validity of our conclusions always less than certain. Assumption 1, for example, claims a common dimension connecting the actor point and the stimulus point, but the fact that we seem to observe a response to the stimulus may be misleading. As researchers, we may be interested in the effects on B of what actor A is saying. But when B suddenly leaves the room, it may not be primarily a response to what A is saying; it may be primarily a response to a full bladder. As another example, we could be wrong about assumption 5 concerning monotonicity; as the magnitude of stimuli increases in respect to the property mediating the response, the responses of the actor may, contrary to our expectations, be first negative, then positive, and then negative again. For example, we usually take it for granted that one cannot have *too much* arithmetic ability to pass an arithmetic item. But there is room for doubt, and if we were to discover we were wrong about this, the nature of testing and test-making would change radically. These are matters that affect what we can logically conclude from a single datum—matters that affect what we might call the *internal validity of the datum.*

We must also deal with the *external validity of the datum.* Even when the actor is indeed responding on the dimension we hope he will, even when he is stable in his relation to the stimulus, even when we are right about mono-

[2]See Chapters 3 and 6 for discussions of internal and external validity in the context of study design and measurement. The discussion here is of internal and external validity in the context of a single datum.

tonicity or nonmonotonicity, even when assumptions 1 through 5 and any other relevant assumptions are felicitous, there remains nevertheless the further question whether any features of the datum have generality. If the observed relation, or more properly the *interpreted* relation, between actor and stimulus holds only for this one actor at this one time (perhaps in this one data matrix), then we would surely doubt the generalizability of our observation. (When we see a rabbit lifted from the hat of only one man, and then during his performance on the stage, we do not expect to fit this observation into our other observations of the habits of rabbits.) Similarly, one would doubt an observation that seemed to hold for only one stimulus, uniquely. Again, if the actor found a particular dimension relevant only when he was in the presence of one particular stimulus, the phenomenon would not draw the interest of very many people except as an oddity. In fact, the unique stimulus sometimes signals pathology; an example is the behavior of the person who can become sexually aroused only in the presence of a particular undergarment.

Suppose, for example, we have observed the reaction of a male 20-year-old native of Montana in the presence of a written question asking, "Do you have strong confidence in the general capabilities of the present administration?" Suppose his response was to check a written alternative reading, "Complete lack of confidence." Let us interpret this observation as QIIb data, and let us suppose that we have high confidence in the internal validity of this datum. Can we now find any other male 20-year-old native of Montana who also will check, "Complete lack of confidence?" If so, can we find that these actors endorse also some statements indicating a desire to disassociate themselves from patterns of American life overlapping the present administration's policies? Can we find that these actors choose answers indicating, too, some lack of confidence when we ask other similar, but somewhat different, questions about the administration? If the answer to all of these questions is *no,* then the datum has little interest other than as a curio. The problem we raise here is one of *generality* among data; more precisely, the problem is whether we can somehow combine data so as to draw conclusions from a *body* of data (such as the body of data in a data matrix) instead of having to draw as many conclusions from our observations as we have data.

We must concern ourselves with generality in three forms. First, there is the matter of the behavior toward the stimulus. By this phrase we mean to indicate the *relation* between the actor and the stimulus. In the example just given, we mean translating into the QIIb model the observed behavior of checking "Complete lack of confidence." The relation between actor and stimulus is that the actor finds the opinion represented by the stem of the question together with the chosen alternative to be sufficiently acceptable to him that he can indicate agreement with it; in terms of the abstract model, the alternative is within *epsilon.* If this datum is to have any usefulness in combination with other data, checking "Complete lack of confidence" in answer to the stem of the item must have much the same meaning whenever it is checked and by whomever it is checked. It must *not* be the case that three actors who check "Complete lack of confidence" have in mind such disparate meanings as the following:

> What I value in political life is boldness, enthusiasm, and surprise. I don't know whether the present administration has much "capability" in the ordinary, stodgy meaning of the term, and I don't care. I have a complete lack of confidence in my ability to predict what they are going to do, or whether the so-called experts would consider their actions competent, but I think the men in the administration are bold and enthusiastic, and that's what I want them to be.
>
> I have a complete lack of confidence in the capability of any administration. No one gets in power because he knows anything about the problems of the rest of us. He gets in power because that's what he wants. You can't vote for an administration on the basis of competence. You have to vote for them on the basis of whether their getting what *they* want will get you what *you* want.
>
> I have a complete lack of confidence in this administration. We need to get them out of there at the earliest possible moment and get some guys in who know what they're doing.

What we are saying here is that the general "direction" and the general pointing of the dimension mediating the responses must be approximately alike for different actors at slightly different times and places responding to the same stimulus. Another way of saying this is that a 1 entered in a particular item column of a data matrix must have about the same meaning in any row. Still another way to say this is that we are putting forth a sort of "local-continuity" assumption when we propound assumption 6 on the interchangeability of response patterns. We cannot cope with a world in which each response of each actor to each stimulus at each time and each place is unique. We must assume that two *yesses* given by actors closely of the same sort at moments close together in very similar circumstances in response to very similar stimuli differ only negligibly in "meaning." This is what we mean by generality in respect to behavior toward the stimulus.

Second, there is the matter of generality over actors. We must assume that there is enough similarity among humans that some of what we learn from one actor can be applied at least to some other actors. In terms of drawing a conclusion from a body of data, we must assume that there is some group of actors within which a datum taken from observing one actor is equivalent to the same form (positive or negative) of datum taken from any other actor (assumption 6 again).

Finally, we must assume, when there is no evidence in the data to the contrary, that actors are in fact responding on the basis of the *same* dimension. These three kinds of generality among data are the same three domains of generality we have mentioned before: (1) actors, (2) behaving toward objects, (3) in a context. When we make the assumptions that enable us to draw conclusions from a *body* of data (such as one finds in a data matrix) instead of from each datum separately, we are in a position to study actors behaving toward objects in a context. When we are concerned about being able to put together data in this way, we are concerned with *interdata validity,* that is, the external validity of data.

How do we establish interdata validity? Any single design for scaling, even the most grandly planned, can provide empirical evidence for only a limited portion of its structure. In the end, every analytic model must rest heavily upon assumptions, as we tried to make clear in Chapter 10. One can search for evidence that subgroups of actors do *not* order the objects of their experiences in the same way or that they do *not* put the same meaning on their relations with the objects or that they do *not* mean substantially the same thing when they say *yes* to a question. But in the absence of evidence that must break a group of actors into two or more parts or must divide a group of behaviors toward objects or must decompose a group of situations, we must assume that data can be fitted together in one or another manner such as will be described in this chapter and in Chapter 12. In brief, it is customary to take interdata validity as established if a fairly complex data matrix fails to display contrary evidence.

The logic of interdata validity is reminiscent of the logic of the multi-trait-multimethod matrix discussed in section 6-4. Just as a single trait measured by a single method yields a result of dubious meaning, so does a single response of an actor to a single stimulus. We become more confident of all the data when we can compare many responses of many actors to many stimuli.

11-3. Purposes and Facets for Arraying Data

At this point, we need to distinguish between the sorts of arrays we shall discuss in this chapter and the sorts we will consider in later chapters. The first distinction we need to make is that between a distribution and a relation. Let us divide the purposes of the investigator into two classes: (1) to study the pattern within one array of data—that is, to study the *distribution* of some data; and (2) to study the *relation* between two or more arrays of data—that is, to study the pattern in the way changes or differences in one array are accompanied by changes or differences in the other.[3] An example of a pattern within one set of observations is the number of persons voting for candidate A, the number voting for B, and the number voting for C. Another example is the frequency of actors receiving various scores on a test of clerical aptitude. A third example is the number of runners successfully leaping hurdle 1, the number leaping hurdles 1 and 2, the number leaping hurdles 1, 2, and 3, and so forth. An example of a relation is the distribution of scores on a test of clerical aptitude made by males contrasted with the distribution made by

[3]These purposes are not logically distinct. A bivariate distribution shows a relation; so can a study of the patterning of distances among objects. But the distinction is useful heuristically.

females. Here we have two sets of observations, two partitions: one is sex and the other is score on the test of clerical aptitude. As each actor is observed, both his sex and his aptitude score are recorded. In the analysis, we can note how the differences among persons in aptitude score are different for the different sexes. We discuss patterns within single arrays of data in this chapter and the next, reserving the matter of relations between arrays for Chapter 13.

The next important distinction is that between unidimensionality and multidimensionality. When we think about a property (or an aspect or a characteristic), we commonly think about it as ranging from less to more, with every object having an amount of the property less than, more than, or equal to the amount belonging to every other object. Examples would be blueness, height, loudness, and the like. Values or quantities of such a property can be arrayed along a single line. If we are ready to take instances of a property as being related to each other in the same way as points on a line or beads on a string, we call the property *unidimensional.*

Let us be more formal about this. Points or elements are arrayed unidimensionally if three conditions are satisfied. (1) One is that of asymmetry: if we have two points that are not actually the same point, then we require either that one is farther along the dimension than the other or the reverse. In briefer symbols, let a and b be the points and let the symbol $>$ indicate the relation in which we are interested, whether more than, farther along than, exceeding, dominating, or whatever. The first condition can then be expressed by saying that for any two points such that $a \neq b$, either $a > b$ or $b > a$ is required to hold, but not both.[4] (2) Another condition is that of irreflexivity: $a > a$ is not permitted. No element in the dimension will be said (for example) to be greater than itself or to have more of some property than it has itself. (These examples would sound less strange if we did not use relations such as greater than and more than, but these terms carry the connotation we want terms such as *dimension* and *property* to carry). (3) The last condition is that of transitivity: if $a > b$ and $b > c$, then $a > c$. If objects are arrayed so as to satisfy these three conditions, they are said to be arrayed in a *chain* or *simple order*—and this is what we mean, minimally, by their being arrayed unidimensionally.

The researcher often seeks a pattern within a set of data that will satisfy the requirements of unidimensionality. For example, U.S. public schools have been using tests to measure "intelligence" of pupils for some decades. Teachers and others have come to think of intelligence as unidimensional. Following this conception, researchers have put a great amount of effort into trying to develop "pure" or highly unidimensional intelligence tests. But researchers sometimes seek patterns having more than one dimension. For example, human mental functioning has been conceived as multidimensional. Probably the first coupling of this idea with sophisticated measurement was done by Thurstone (1938). A recent multidimensional study of intelligence based on a multi-

[4] Alternatively expressed, $a > b$ implies $a \not< b$.

dimensional definition of intelligence has been done by Louis Guttman (1965); we shall describe this study in section 12-5.

The third distinction we need to make for dealing with arrays of data is that between two purposes of *scaling*, that is, of seeking ordered patterns among data. The two purposes are:

1. *Seeking* a pattern: What pattern best describes the data?
2. *Testing* a pattern: Do the data fit (or how well do they fit) some pattern chosen at the outset?

For example, we might (1) seek maximum closeness of fit, regardless of whether the solution requires one, two, three, or however many dimensions. Alternatively, we might (2) test how good a fit to the data a unidimensional array of points may be.

11-4. Deterministic Models for Dominance Data

Of all the scaling models, it seems to us that scalogram analysis exhibits most simply the intimate connections among the data model, the logic through which a unidimensional pattern is sought, and the information that becomes evident in the unidimensional array. Moreover, the assumptions needed for this model are minimal. For these reasons, we shall begin our exposition of analytic models with a detailed explanation of scalogram analysis.

In the literature of the social sciences, it is true, scalogram analysis is not the most frequently used technique of converting a data matrix into a unidimensional array of points. At this writing, in most branches of social science the probabilistic models are used more frequently than the deterministic ones. But it is not our purpose to apportion amount of detail to frequency of current use; rather, it is to set forth choice points with clarity.[5] The scalogram technique exemplifies the general strategy of converting a data matrix to a simpler form.

SCALOGRAM ANALYSIS[6]

Consider how a particular ordering of stimuli on an underlying dimension might generate a matrix of obtained data. Imagine that actors respond to some stimuli as if the stimuli differed from one another in such a way that they could be laid out along a line, and their ordering and spacing along the line would correspond to the way they differed. We do not mean that actors must

[5] Furthermore, the preference for probabilistic models may not remain as strong as it now is. Among studies using multidimensional scaling, recent literature has shown an increased frequency of studies using deterministic models—in the sense of models that do not accept every datum, but seek goodness of fit to certain criteria.

[6] Scalogram analysis was first set forth by Guttman (1944, 1950).

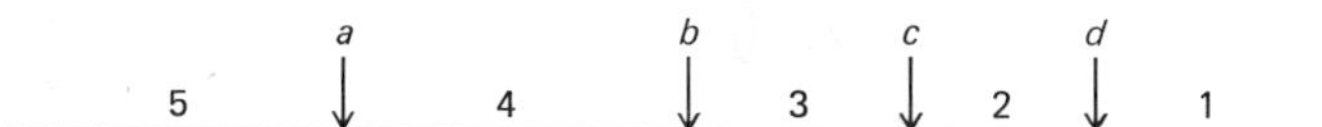

Figure 11-1.

be able to *say* this about the stimuli; we ask only that they be able to make choices and discriminations that reflect this pattern in the stimuli. Now, let each actor be represented by a point on the same dimension. If the dimension were arithmetic ability, the actor point would represent the arithmetic ability of the actor and a stimulus point would represent the amount of arithmetic ability required by, let us say, an item in addition. If the dimension were sensitivity to acrid odors, the actor point would represent the olfactory threshold of the actor for this sort of odor.

When we speak of generating a data matrix, we mean imagining a dimension that bears stimulus points and actor points and then reading off, for each actor point, the responses the actor would give if he were located at that particular psychological "place" among the stimuli and if he were responding according to a specified data model. Let us proceed with such an exercise. Imagine a dimension (considerateness, arithmetic ability, or whatever) with the positive direction to the right, upon which we represent four stimuli. Between the stimuli lie regions we can number from 1 to 5, as in Figure 11-1. If we imagine an actor point to the left of stimulus *a* in region 5, we would have a datum represented by the relation between this actor point and stimulus *a*. With positive to the right, we would interpret the relation to be one in which the actor would "fail" item *a*. Speaking generally, the item *a* would dominate the actor. Similarly, this actor point would say *no* to items *b*, *c*, and *d*.

An actor point between items *a* and *b* in region 4 would say *yes* to *a* and *no* to *b*, *c*, and *d*. Actors in region 3 would say *yes* to items *a* and *b* and *no* to *c* and *d*. And so forth. Letting the actors be represented by numbers and the stimuli by letters, as above, we see that the data matrix would look like Table 11-2.

If actors and stimuli are arrayed as in Figure 11-1, it is clear that one can construct a corresponding matrix bearing the triangular pattern shown in Table 11-2. Conversely, if data are gathered into a matrix that can be arranged to have the triangular pattern of the table, it must be possible to draw a corresponding diagram similar to Figure 11-1 for which the triangular table

Table 11-2.

	A	B	C	D		A	B	C	D
1	yes	yes	yes	yes	*or*	1	1	1	1
2	yes	yes	yes	no		1	1	1	0
3	yes	yes	no	no		1	1	0	0
4	yes	no	no	no		1	0	0	0
5	no	no	no	no		0	0	0	0

Table 11-3.

OAK	GUM	ELM	FIR
no	no	yes	no
yes	yes	yes	no
yes	yes	yes	yes
yes	no	yes	no
no	no	no	no

tells us the order of labeling for the actors (regions) and the stimuli.[7] This pattern typifies QIIa.

So far, however, our explanation is not very helpful to the researcher who, data in hand, sits staring at a data matrix (such as Table 11-1), but who still has to discover whether a scale such as that pictured in Figure 11-1 is possible (or how closely it can be approximated) with the obtained data. How does the researcher begin his analysis?

In actual practice, our problem would begin when we had obtained a matrix of data. Suppose we had presented the items *oak, gum, elm,* and *fir* to a collection of actors and had asked them to answer *yes* or *no* to each. (The question might be directed to entomologists and be concerned with the susceptibility of certain trees, over the next few years, to infestation.) Whatever the number of actors, let us suppose they give us back five *patterns* of response, as in Table 11-3.

We shall not lose any information from the matrix, nor add any to it, if we rearrange the rows in a hunt for a triangular arrangement, placing the row containing four *yesses* first, the row containing three *yesses* next, and so on, as in Table 11-4.

Table 11-4.

OAK	GUM	ELM	FIR
yes	yes	yes	yes
yes	yes	yes	no
yes	no	yes	no
no	no	yes	no
no	no	no	no

Table 11-5.

ELM	OAK	GUM	FIR
yes	yes	yes	yes
yes	yes	yes	no
yes	yes	no	no
yes	no	no	no
no	no	no	no

Likewise, we shall lose no information, nor add any, if we now rearrange the columns as in Table 11-5.

[7] It does not follow that the data in a triangular matrix *must* have been generated from an array ordered by some one dimension, as in Figure 11-1. Conceivably, actors 1 and 2 might respond on the basis of one dimension to stimuli *a* and *b* and on the basis of a different dimension to stimuli *c* and *d,* but with a dominance pattern that happens to fit equally well the unidimensional explanation. Furthermore, actor 2 might respond to all stimuli on one dimension and actor 3 on another, but in such a manner that they both fit into the triangular pattern. This illustrates the necessity (if we are to accept scalogram analysis as a unidimensional explanation) for the assumptions of common dimension across actors and across stimuli set forth in section 10-3.

Table 11-6.

	ELM	OAK	GUM	FIR
1	yes	yes	yes	yes
2	yes	yes	yes	no
3	yes	no	no	yes
4	yes	no	no	no
5	no	no	no	no

Here we have the same triangular pattern we had in the first example, a pattern that could have been generated from an array like that shown in Figure 11-1.

Scalogram analysis is suitable for use with any deterministic, dichotomous, dominance matrix; such a matrix results from interpreting observations as QIIa. Essentially, scalogram analysis consists of our rearranging first rows (or columns) and then columns (or rows) until the triangular pattern appears—if it can. Further detail on this method is given by Coombs (1964, Chapters 11 and 17).

Obviously, it is not always possible to obtain a perfect triangular pattern from actual data. For example, no matter how we arrange rows and columns, we cannot fit the response patterns in Table 11-6 into a triangular array.

Goodness of Fit

When the triangular pattern is violated, we can adopt one or more of the following interpretations:

1. One or more of the assumptions listed in section 10-3 is invalid.
2. The "response space" mediating the responses is not unidimensional; the actors require more than one dimension in forming their reactions.
3. The nonfitting cells of the matrix contain error.

As an example of (1), we might entertain the possibility that actors 1, 2, 4, and 5 in Table 11-6 responded according to one particular dimension and actor 3 according to another; although all actors would have been responding unidimensionally, they would have been responding according to different dimensions, and the resulting matrix would therefore show a multidimensional (that is, nontriangular) pattern. When data do not fit a hypothesized pattern, it is always worthwhile to examine one's assumptions; this approach sometimes produces useful new hypotheses.

If one's purpose in analysis is to *test* whether the response space is unidimensional and the data matrix is impervious to scalogram analysis, one would conclude that the response space is *not* unidimensional. This is an example of (2). If one's purpose is to *seek* an error-free pattern in this data matrix and triangular analysis failed to produce a triangle, one would then go on to seek a multidimensional pattern.

Finally, one might have good reason to believe that one's actors are behaving in a predominantly unidimensional manner. One might feel that his understanding of the domain of behavior could best be enhanced by pursuing the unidimensional hypothesis farther, accepting some number of nonfitting data as "error"—that is, as unpredictable in direction or nature, as non-understandable, and as worthy of being neglected if they do not occur too often. This would be the third alternative a researcher might use to cope with an outcropping of nonfitting data.

Actually, as we said in section 10-3, the strategy of accepting some number of nonfitting data as "error" and of establishing a criterion for the number of data to be accepted as error is ancient[8] and contains some techniques figuring importantly in the current practice of researchers in the behavioral sciences. One important application of this idea is the *coefficient of reproducibility;* this index is often used with scalogram analysis and will be explained shortly. Another application is in culling items through the process called *item analysis,* a process we will consider in the section on probabilistic models. A third application is to be found in looking at the *rank ordering of distances* among actors or stimuli (or both) contained in the data and comparing that rank ordering with the rank ordering permitted by a particular analytic model. We shall discuss this application in section 12-5. Before turning to the particular application called the coefficient of reproducibility, it will be helpful to examine the patterns in which nonfitting data can occur and the relations between these patterns and the assumptions and hypotheses the researcher is making about the shape of the data.

Fitting the Populations of Actors and Stimuli. When error crops up in a data matrix, it must occur in a row and in a column. Hence, there are three possible sources of the error: (1) the actor represented by the row, (2) the stimulus represented by the column, and (3) the interaction of the two represented by the cell in which the nonfitting datum occurs. In turn, we shall consider the tactics of (1) rejecting the actor, (2) jettisoning this stimulus, and (3) ignoring the cell.

Ruling out Actors. The capital letters that label columns in Table 11-7 stand for stimuli, items, or other aspects of the situation to which the researcher is giving his attention; we shall arbitrarily use the term *item* in this section. Each numeral labeling a row stands for the one or more actors who gave that response pattern.

Our hypothetical matrix is almost triangular in pattern. Regardless of whether a researcher were testing the data for unidimensionality or seeking an ordering for individuals and stimuli, he would be likely to feel disappointed that he had come so close but had not quite achieved a complete, perfect solution. He would be reluctant to say, "These data are not unidimensional," or "I must seek elsewhere for a scale." Table 11-7 comes very close to satisfying the required triangular pattern. In fact, if those actors giving pattern 4 had felt differently for the moment about stimuli *B* or *C*, pattern 4 would have

[8] It is at least as old as the first mother who, when embarrassed in the presence of visitors by the behavior of her child, explained, "He's not really himself today."

Table 11-7. *A Hypothetical QIIa Data Matrix with Error*

	A	B	C	D	E	F
Pattern 1	0	0	0	0	0	0
2	1	0	0	0	0	0
3	1	1	0	0	0	0
4	1	0	1	0	0	0
5	1	1	1	0	0	0
6	1	1	1	1	0	0
7	1	1	1	1	1	0
8	1	1	1	1	1	1

been identical with 3 or 5 and the total pattern would have been perfect. One way to accept this matrix as indicating a unidimensional pattern would be to declare the respondents of pattern 4 not to be members of the population of actors we are interested in studying. That is, we might argue that all the other actors give evidence that we were right in predicting that their responses could be encompassed within a unidimensional pattern; consequently, the few actors who do not fit are actors who somehow got into our study by mistake. Those actors who do not fit the pattern of the rest, we could argue, are actually not enough like the others to be considered part of the same population. We might, for example, be studying the behavior of people who differ on authoritarianism; if we find a few actors who do not fit the triangular pattern in their responses to our questions, we might conclude that they were not judging the situation in respect to authoritarianism. And if the dimension of authoritarianism were not relevant for these deviant actors, then their behavior could not help us in our study of the relation between degrees of authoritarianism and other variables.

Ruling Out Stimuli. There is another tactic by which a researcher might manage to accept a data matrix such as Table 11-7 as reliable. Instead of disqualifying an actor, he might disqualify a stimulus. The triangular pattern would be perfect if he were to drop item B and then combine response patterns 2 and 3 (which would then be identical) as well as patterns 4 and 5. Alternatively, he could drop item C and then combine response patterns 2 and 4 as well as 3 and 5. Using this tactic would be equivalent to claiming that the dropped item does not belong to the domain of stimuli (or behavior toward object) he wishes to study. In particular, since we are interested here in a unidimensional array, using this tactic would permit the researcher to argue that he had inadvertently picked an item that belonged on some dimension *other* than the one he was attempting to assess with his other items.

The technique of dropping nonfitting items is very commonly used in building mental tests. The test builders may begin with many times the number of items they wish to include in the test and gradually eliminate those that do not "perform" according to their criteria when administered to trial groups of participants. See, for example, Cronbach (1970), Nunnally (1964), or

Remmers, Gage, and Rummel (1960). We shall mention this point again in the section on test theory.

A note of caution needs to be sounded here. It is always possible, if one eliminates enough subjects or stimuli, or both, to achieve a perfect pattern, if only with two actors and two stimuli! Consequently, a final solution can never be accepted confidently until it is tried out again with another group of participants to be sure the same pattern will occur in another matrix of actual data. The trial with the second group of subjects is called a *cross validation.* When one has obtained a matrix having about the same degree of reproducibility as that computed after last dropping an actor or a stimulus, one can have confidence in using the items as a completed instrument. One cannot have confidence in the pattern a set of stimuli will produce until he has administered *that* set, no more and no less, to a group of actors and has observed the result.

Ruling Out the Interaction. Finally, the researcher may find insufficient reason to jettison either the actor or the item, but may want to ignore just the intersection of the two. Researchers often do decide to ignore nonfitting cells, provided there are not too many of them.

In deciding whether to accept the nonfitting cells as error, it is useful to have some measure of the *goodness of fit* of the obtained data to the analytic model. For example, the matrix of Table 11-7 would conform perfectly to the triangular model if only one cell were changed; in other words, the triangular pattern would reproduce correctly all the cells except for B in pattern 4. We might express this as a percentage. Here, however, the concept begins to take on complications, and we refer the reader to the more sophisticated measures available in the literature. Applied to scalogram analysis, these measures are called *coefficients of reproducibility* because they indicate the degree to which the obtained matrix is successfully reproduced by the triangular matrix. For some particular coefficients and discussions of their characteristics, see Guttman (1944), Willis (1954), Milholland (1955), White and Saltz (1957), Torgerson (1958, pp. 307–331), L. A. Goodman (1959), and Sagi (1959). For a multidimensional index, see Kruskal (1964). Note, finally, that the coefficient of reproducibility, like any index of goodness of fit, implies a probability assumption. It implies that any entry in the data matrix has a probability less than one of being nonerror. As we say in Appendix I (in the discussion of Assumption 8), researchers almost always use some sort of probabilistic assumption when they seek to interpret data through a model, even when they use so-called deterministic models.

Purposes and Choices. The researcher, as we have said, can make a variety of choices when he meets nonfitting cases in a matrix of obtained data. To summarize, he can

1. Conclude that one or more of his assumptions about the nature of the data (see section 10-3) are invalid[9]

[9] When the researcher begins to suspect the validity of one of his assumptions, he is then, of course, no longer treating the assertion as an assumption but as a hypothesis.

2. Conclude that some feature of the analytic model (such as unidimensionality) is invalid
3. Conclude that the data matrix contains a mistake, in which case he can
   - 3a. Conclude that some actors not members of the proper population have somehow crept into his study
   - 3b. Conclude that some stimuli not members of the proper population have somehow crept into his study
   - 3c. Conclude that some entries in cells of the data matrix are unpredictable error, not understandable, and worthy only to be ignored.

Each choice suits some purposes better than others. If the researcher were studying the effects of using various data models, he might prefer to choose conclusion (1); he might prefer this choice also if he were interested in the validity of translating certain types of observed events into certain types of data. If the researcher were studying the validity (empirical fit) of the analytic model, he would perhaps choose (2), but he might prefer to work with *degrees* of fit to the model and therefore choose (3c). Conclusion (3a) would probably be chosen by a researcher who wanted to select members of a population that suit the specifications of a particular analytic model. This conclusion might also be chosen by a researcher studying the nature of a subpopulation of actors.[10] Similarly, conclusion (3b) might be chosen when selecting items or when studying subsets of items. Finally, a researcher might be interested primarily in comparing the positions of actors or items on one dimension with their positions on another dimension; he might be willing to accept some amount of error (3c) to keep actors and items in his comparisons. As we have mentioned in other contexts, there is no single best choice for researchers to make when they meet a matrix containing nonfitting data. The best choice depends on the researcher's purpose.

The Skewed Hourglass

We now turn to a method of triangular analysis that, though somewhat more subtle in concept than the scalogram, is often easier to use in practice. Scalogram analysis requires the researcher to assume beforehand the positive response to each item. In other words, the researcher must know whether to enter a 1 or a 0 in the matrix to correspond to the actor's response. For example, suppose we had an item like this in a questionnaire written to assess the consideration given by a leader to his followers: "He treats members as being beneath him." The positive answer to such an item would be a *no* because a *no* would indicate *more* consideration than a *yes*. But many items are not as obvious as this. Is it a mark of general good health to have sickle-cell anemia? Perhaps not in Quebec; but in countries with malaria-carrying mosquitoes, people with sickle-cell anemia seem rarely to come down with malaria (see

[10] An analytic model can be taken either as a set of assumptions or as a set of hypotheses.

Dobzhansky, 1962, pp. 150–154). Consequently, in countries with uncontrolled malaria-bearing mosquitoes, having sickle-cell anemia might be a positive item in an inventory of healthful assets.

Strictly speaking, however, it is not really necessary for the researcher to designate the positive directions for all items before he makes his observations. For an example, let us return to Table 11-5; we supposed in that hypothetical example that the item *gum* had received *yes* answers by two actors who also gave *yes* answers to most of the other items. But suppose we had interpreted the positive response to the item *gum* in the direction opposite to the example of Table 11-5. That is, suppose we had interpreted *yes* as negative and *no* as positive, as in the example of consideration just above. With this alternative interpretation, Table 11-5 would have looked like Table 11-8.

With such an outcome, it would be obvious that a perfect triangle could be achieved by reversing the interpretation of item *gum*; that is, by interchanging *yes* and *no* under *gum*. It would accord entirely with scientific logic to accept the responses of the actors as the facts and adapt our interpretation of the meaning of *yes* and *no* to the facts. We should properly give up any preconceived choice of positive direction and adopt instead the direction pointed by the pattern in the obtained data.

In accepting the direction pointed by the data, notice that we are accepting the direction pointed by the entries in the majority of columns. In fact, the particular choice of direction for each item can be made by referring to the *majority response* to the item. This possibility has been demonstrated by Dawes, Brown, and Kaplan (1965); these authors provide us with a modification of triangular analysis they have called *the skewed hourglass.* We recommend this method not only because it automatically copes with the problem of positive direction but because it makes the job of looking for promising rearrangements of rows and columns much easier.

The method of the skewed hourglass proceeds by converting a data matrix to a matrix of "dissenting" responses. That is, the minority response in each column is called a *dissenting response* and a new matrix is made showing dissenting and nondissenting responses. Note that *dissenting* does not necessarily mean a response of *no;* it means a response other than the response given by the majority. When we enter a *d* for each dissenting or minority response in Table 11-8, the new matrix appears as in Table 11-9. This new table is

Table 11-8.

ELM	OAK	GUM	FIR
yes	yes	no	yes
yes	yes	no	no
yes	yes	yes	no
yes	no	yes	no
no	no	yes	no

Table 11-9.

ELM	OAK	GUM	FIR
0	0	d	d
0	0	d	0
0	0	0	0
0	d	0	0
d	d	0	0

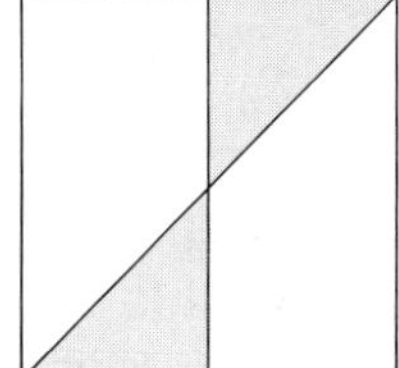

Figure 11-2.

equivalent to the triangular pattern; using dissenting responses, however, gives a pattern like that of Figure 11-2—the skewed hourglass. Table 11-9 has a vertical and a diagonal line drawn in it to accentuate the pattern.

After converting a data matrix to a matrix of dissenting responses, the data analyst permutes rows and columns to arrive at a pattern of d-entries forming a skewed hourglass. The rows with the most dissenting responses will go at top and bottom; the row with the fewest or none will go in the middle. The columns with the fewest dissenting responses will go at the outside; the columns with the most will go in the middle.

The assumption of positive direction (assumption 4 of section 10-3) is not really circumvented by the method of the skewed hourglass. The researcher who uses the skewed hourglass, instead of making a direct attempt himself to define the positive direction of the items, is assuming that the actors, collectively, can tell him the positive direction of each item for each actor. That they are correct about it is still an assumption. But this assumption is no shakier—probably in most cases it is firmer—than the assumption that the researcher can guess right beforehand.

So far, we have been discussing only dichotomous items. A popular type of verbal item, however, is the multiple-choice item in which a number of alternatives are offered the actor with instructions to pick one. Such items are called Likert items because their scalability was first discussed by Rensis Likert (1932).[11] For example:

Presbyterians should be shipped back to the country they came from.
( ) strongly agree
( ) agree
( ) undecided
( ) disagree
( ) strongly disagree

This type of item, too, is suited to scalogram analysis or to analysis by the skewed hourglass. Coombs (1964, pp. 229–236) calls the triangular procedure for this type of item *disorderly interlocking* and explains the analytic procedure.

[11]For a brief discussion of the use of Likert items in attitude work, see Shaw and Wright (1967, pp. 24–25).

UNFOLDING

In this section we continue to discuss methods of analysis for deterministic dominance data; so far, we have dealt with matrices in which rows and columns are taken to represent *points*—QIIa or QIIIa. We now turn to matrices that deal directly with distances; that is, to matrices of QIa and QIVa data. Analyzing data of the QIa variety is the topic of this section.

At this writing, there exist only two methods of analyzing QIa data: one is the *unfolding method* of Coombs (1964); the other is the method of *nonmetric multidimensional scaling,* to be described in Chapter 12. As a matter of fact, since the nonmetric methods are built on the concept of constructing a configuration of points that maintains the *relative distances* among the points implied in the original data, these methods are built on the same basic concept as the unfolding technique.

Unfolding analysis becomes possible whenever observations are interpreted so as to yield data that compare distances having a common terminus. By distances having a common terminus, we mean the distances from A to B, from A to C, from A to D, and so on. Such distances, also known as *conjoint* distances, are symbolized by the lines in Figure 11-3. We sometimes form questions conforming to the QIa model that require comparing two distances that do *not* have a common terminus. Consider, for example, two actors, François and Fujube, and two "stimuli," the two native lands of the actors. We might then seek observations to translate into data that answer the question, "Who loves his country more, François or Fujube?" That is, who is closer to his country in this sense? More formally, which distance dominates the other, the distance from François to his country, or the distance from Fujube to his? Another example is asking which pair of lovers is more devoted—assuming that four different people are involved. At this writing, however, only the nonmetric multidimensional methods will handle these latter kinds of data. The unfolding technique requires data that compare conjoint distances. Figure 11-3, which displays some conjoint distances, is drawn in two dimensions. In one dimension, of course, distances are collinear, and a diagram of an arrangement of points,

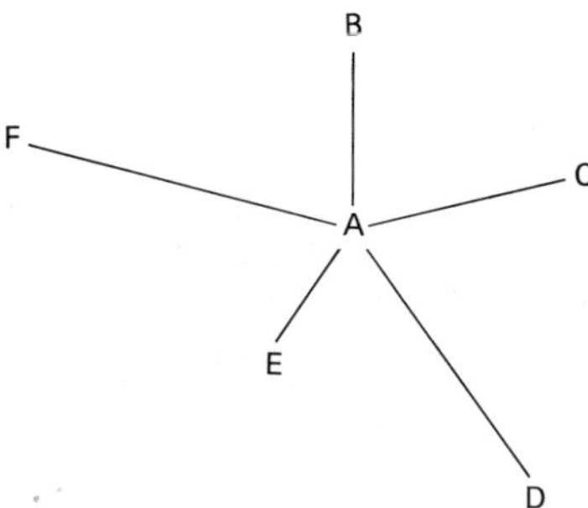

Figure 11-3.

C B A E D F

Figure 11-4.

Figure 11-4, looks like others we have used in this chapter. The distances (in actual inches on the paper) from A to the other points are the same in Figures 11-3 and 11-4.

The unfolding technique, as we said earlier, makes use of information about conjoint distances. This fact singles out the point serving as the end point of several distances for special attention. A datum in QI to be used in unfolding analysis always compares the distance from an individual to stimulus 1 with the distance from that same individual to stimulus 2. Asking actors to put objects in order of preference delivers responses easily interpretable as QIa data. In many studies, data have been obtained in the form of rank orders or partial rank orders, that is, by method *order k*. One might compose a rank order from actors' responses when the actors have been instructed to *order k* among p, where $p < n$, the stimuli having been presented to the actors p at a time until all n have been presented. (This terminology was presented in section 7-2.)

When an actor gives us a rank ordering of stimuli according to his preferences among them and we interpret them according to the data model of QIa, we then take the observations to mean that the actor has told us the relative distances of all the stimuli from a point representing the actor himself. In an ordinary data matrix, we can record information of this sort by entering in each cell a numeral showing the rank position given the column stimulus by the row actor. A briefer notation simply places the labels of the stimuli in a row as preferred by a particular actor, with the most-preferred stimulus at the left. Table 11-10 shows hypothetical preference orders of 16 actors among six stimuli.

Table 11-10.

1.	C	A	D	B	E	F
2.	C	A	D	E	B	F
3.	A	C	B	D	E	F
4.	D	C	E	A	F	B
5.	C	D	E	A	F	B
6.	E	F	D	C	A	B
7.	D	E	F	C	A	B
8.	F	E	D	C	A	B
9.	C	D	A	E	B	F
10.	A	C	D	B	E	F
11.	C	D	A	E	F	B
12.	B	A	C	D	E	F
13.	D	E	C	A	F	B
14.	A	B	C	D	E	F
15.	D	E	C	F	A	B
16.	E	D	F	C	A	B

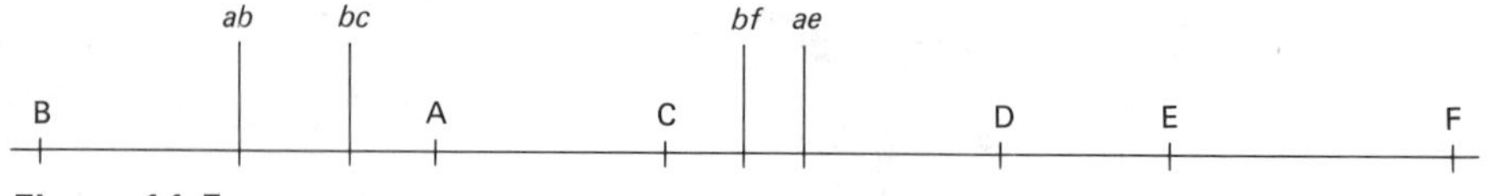

Figure 11-5.

If the 16 rank orders shown in Table 11-10 are to be interpreted as having been generated by actors all perceiving the stimuli according to the same dimension, we must be able to show how the stimuli can be ordered and spaced, and how the actors can be placed among them, so that the relative distances from each actor to the stimuli are those recorded in Table 11-10. As it happens, an arrangement of stimuli as in Figure 11-5 could generate the rank orders of Table 11-10. To aid the illustration, we have marked four of the 15 midpoints on the figure; the midpoint between stimuli A and B is marked by the vertical line *ab*, and so on. Now points on the dimension to the left of midpoint *ab* are points closest to B, next closest to A, then to C, and so on; accordingly, the region to the left of midpoint *ab* contains the points representing actors all of whom have the preference order BACDEF. Similarly, the region between midpoints *ab* and *bc* represents actors with the preference order ABCDEF. The region between the midpoints *bf* and *ae* represents the order CDAEFB. The fifteen midpoints divide the unidimensional continuum into 16 regions; the preference orders corresponding to the regions are listed below, not in the arbitrary order we gave them in Table 11-10, but in the order they would fall, left to right, were we to draw in all the midpoints in Figure 11-5.

BACDEF
ABCDEF
ACBDEF
ACDBEF
CADBEF
CADEBF
CDAEBF
CDAEFB
CDEAFB
DCEAFB
DECAFB
DECFAB
DEFCAB
EDFCAB
EFDCAB
FEDCAB

The unfolding technique consists, substantially, of reordering the preference orders given by the actors, as in the illustration above, to test whether they can all be generated from a common underlying order of stimuli, as illustrated by Figure 11-5. The process is called *unfolding* for the reason that the underlying ordering of stimuli, if they are diagramed on a strip of paper, can actually be folded at appropriate points so as to fold into every one of the preference orders in turn. For example, we might fold the page at some point between *bf* and *ae* in Figure 11-5 so that one arm of the horizontal line falls over on the other arm. Looking at the page against a sufficiently bright light, we would see the letters, beginning at the fold, in the order CDAEFB. Similarly, folding the page in each of the other regions would yield all the other preference orders in turn.

Unfolding analysis comes in three forms. The original form (and the name) is due to Coombs (1964), and he gives details of the procedure. The skewed hourglass (Dawes, Brown, and Kaplan, 1965) is easily adapted to perform unfolding. Finally, if the actor's responses will fit a unidimensional space, some techniques of nonmetric multidimensional scaling will do the same job; see Chapter 12. For further elaborations, see Greenberg (1963) and Ramanujacharyulu (1964).

OTHER QUADRANTS

We have devoted our illustrations of triangular analysis to QIIa data and our illustrations of unfolding to QIa data. We have said nothing about dominance data in QIIIa and QIVa.

A form of analysis very similar to the scalogram method can be applied usefully to QIIIa data; see Coombs (1964, Chapter 17). However, QIIIa data are rarely analyzed by this method. QIIIa interprets observed events as the comparison of one stimulus with another in terms of one surpassing the other in some respect. Much of the time, when a researcher is interested in how humans (and their institutions) make such comparisons, the researcher already has in mind a dimension or attribute in respect to which he wants to observe the comparison. After all, a researcher would have to be almost unbelievably unsophisticated to phrase a research question such as, "I wonder whether people generally feel that baseball is more than football." Surely, the first actor queried would retort, "More *what*?" Having in mind some dimension at the outset, researchers very often ask actors to respond within that dimension. "Is this object *heavier* than that?" "Does baseball *draw more spectators* per year than football?" "Is having three children around the house more *fulfilling to you as a mother* than having only two?" Thus, the researcher assumes a dimension and knows that actors differ in respect to it. Often (as in the case of the sensation of heaviness) he even knows the *order* in which the actors will place the stimuli, and what he wants the data to tell him is the spacing along the dimension—the amounts of difference between pairs of objects, or their ratios in respect to the property being studied.

To study psychological distances along a dimension, there are more powerful methods available in QI and IV than the variant of scalogram analysis; consequently, when faced with a problem that could be phrased in terms of

QIIIa data, researchers often use one of the methods from the searchingness structure (section 7-2) that yields replications of comparisons and then they interpret the observations as QIa or QIV data, thus availing themselves of the analytic models built for those types of data. We have discussed the unfolding technique for QIa above. We shall discuss QIVa a little later.

Another strategy researchers use with QIIIa data is to adopt a probabilistic model to be used with a dimension taken as known at the outset. This has been the typical strategy of researchers in the field of psychophysics; that is, in studying such domains as the psychological counterparts of differences in pitches or intensities of sound, in saturations of visual color, in weights of objects, in separation of tactual stimuli on the skin, and so forth. See, for example, Stevens (1951). We shall discuss a few of these methods later in this chapter in the sections on probabilistic methods.

QIV data compare distances, the termini of the distances being objects all belonging to the same set. Such data are very rich in distance comparisons, and the data are vulnerable to relations in the data that imply multidimensionality. Consequently, researchers interpreting behavior as QIVa data usually turn immediately to the multidimensional models (see section 12-5). However, a few reports of studies using QIVa data in one dimension do exist. An especially elegant example is that of Goldberg and Coombs (1963) concerning mothers' preferences for different numbers of children.

11-5. Types of Information in Replicated Data

In working with humans, one often wonders how stable the response of the actor may be. The researcher would like to question the actor again, perhaps many times, to see what proportion of the actor's responses remain the same. This sort of replication of observations (and thence of data) is easily done in domains of behavior where the actor is uncertain about what he is doing. An example is the study of sensory thresholds where the actor is told to respond as soon as he senses, no matter how slightly, a sound, a light, or a difference of some sensory sort. Since he is rarely sure he experiences anything at all, he is even less sure whether the stimulus he doubtfully perceives at this moment is a replication of some stimulus he met earlier.

When we deal with more clearly identifiable stimuli, however, we experience practical difficulties. If we ask an actor, "Do you prefer candidate A to candidate B?" and then ask him the same question, even some time later, we are likely not to get the sort of answer we seek, but something like, "What's the matter, you hard of hearing?"

A number of studies have shown, however, that just such queries as the one above can be repeated without causing the actor serious frustration if the query is embedded in a more complicated array of queries, such as can be built using the designs on the "inside" of the searchingness structure (see section 7-2). For example, we might present the actor with the names of three candidates, asking him to tell us which of the three he likes most and which least. (This is equivalent to asking him to rank order the three.) We might present him then with three more names with the same instruction, and so on until all combinations[12] of three have been presented. Candidates A and B would be presented together with candidate C, then later in another presentation with candidate D, then again with E, and so on. This is the method of triads, *order 2 of 3* (see section 7-2). For many kinds of judgments or choices, the changing triads seem for all practical purposes to be experimentally independent situations; actors typically do not always give the same response to a pair of stimuli when the pair reappears in new triads (or other sizes of presentations).

Then, too, some "actors" have very short memories. We might be interested in assessing the relative pulling power of a city among immigrants from various sections of the country, and we might collect data on the proportions of immigrants coming to the city from those sections during each of a series of weeks. We could use the magnitudes of the proportions as a way of assigning ranks in *order k of p*, where p is the number of sections sending more than zero immigrants, and $k = p - l$. The act of getting this information from the city would probably have little effect on any week's immigration.[13]

Since pair comparisons can often be replicated in methods of observation-collection from the inside of the searchingness structure with minimal reactivity, certain kinds of information are available from those replicated comparisons. We shall briefly describe information relevant to consistency, transitivity, and reliability.

CONSISTENCY

In social science usage, the word *consistency* is used in a number of ways. Many writers use it to mean "consistent with a rule or practice in which I am particularly interested." For example, many writers use the term *consistent* to mean *transitive*. In this meaning, a writer might explain that if we start with the knowledge that A comes before B and B comes before C, then it is "inconsistent" to say that C comes before A. But, of course, it is *not illogical* to say that C comes before A. For example, twelve o'clock comes before four o'clock, four o'clock before eight o'clock, and eight o'clock before twelve o'clock. On a trip around the world, New York comes before Damascus, Damascus before Tokyo, and Tokyo before New York.[14]

We use *consistent* here to mean noncontradictory in the mathematical

[12] In many applications, it is not necessary to present all possible combinations; see Coombs (1964, pp. 42–43).

[13] The problem we are setting forth here is the same as that of testing effect (see Chapter 3) or reactivity of measures (see Chapter 7), except that here we are giving special attention to the effect of asking an actor to respond more than once to the same pair comparison of objects.

[14] For a study of consistent and predictable intransitivities in human judgment, see Tversky (1969).

sense. Following the common rule of logic called the law of the excluded middle, we know that a thing cannot at the same time be a member of X and of not-X. A thing A cannot at the same time be smaller than B and not smaller than B. A cannot both dominate B and not dominate B. And so forth. Translating this logic into the data models, we can give an example within QIIb by pointing out that it is *inconsistent* for an actor both to accept a stimulus and not accept it.

An example of inconsistency in QIIIa would occur if we asked an actor to compare the cleverness of various persons. We might use the method *order 2 of 3,* presenting identifications (such as names of persons known to the actor) and asking the actor to order the persons represented by the identifications in respect to cleverness. For example, one item (presentation) might be arranged like this:

> Place an "M" beside the name of the cleverest person and an "L" beside the name of the least clever among these three:
>
> Cathy
>
> Clyde Cal

Another item with the same instruction might look like this:

> Clyde
>
> John Cathy

In response to the first item, the actor might indicate Cathy to be cleverer than Clyde, but in response to the second he might indicate the reverse.

There are two assumptions one must make if one is to ascertain consistency and inconsistency in this way. One is that the reversed choices are not changes but are contradictions. We could take the view that the actor had "changed his mind." If we do not, but instead call the reversed choice inconsistency, we must assume that the actor is in substantially the same psychological situation at the two presentations. The following are the two types of interpretation of such a reversed choice: (1) the responses were probable responses from a repertoire or distribution of possible responses, the apparently contradictory responses showing that the underlying distances involved are very similar, or (2) the two presentations are being judged from different points of view; and regardless of whether we make the probability assumption, the actor is judging the relation of the two stimuli in one presentation according to one criterion or dimension, and in the other presentation according to a different criterion or dimension. In short, the total situation spanning the presentations is multidimensional.

The other assumption one must make to use a method of presenting more than two stimuli at a time (but then examining replicated pairs for consistency) is that the presentations are experimentally independent. By this we mean that the actor is not constrained in his reaction to one presentation by his reaction to an earlier presentation; to put it in other words, the presentations are not reactive.

Since the more "searching" methods of observation-collection (see section 7-2) do provide us with replications of pair comparisons, these methods offer us a way to ascertain the consistency of the actors in their choices. Consistency, in turn, might sometimes be a useful index of reliability; we shall make more comments about this below.

TRANSITIVITY

If relations among stimuli turn out to be intransitive, then we know that the judgments or choices or actions of the actor (or actors) cannot be well encompassed in an explanation that tries to array the stimuli on only one dimension. For example, if we are interested in a relation like "comes before," then we must at least go round in a closed loop, using at least two dimensions to express an intransitivity:

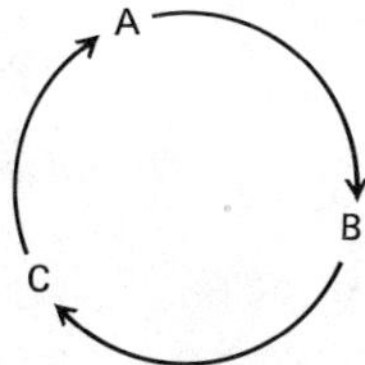

The more "interior" of the searchingness methods enable us to ascertain the existence of intransitivity separately from inconsistency. For example, let us suppose we are using the method *order 2 of 3*, $n = 7$, to collect some data of the QIa model. Perhaps we are asking the actors their preferences among cities in the United States as places to rear a family. We might want to know how clear the opinions of the actors are and whether each actor does, in fact, perceive the cities to be ordered in a linear array. We could present the names of the cities (perhaps accompanied by some additional information) three at a time and ask the actor to order them. One particular way to do this would be to instruct the actor to "mark with a *B* the city you believe best among these three for raising a family and with a *P* the city you believe poorest among these three."

We could (though there is no magical virtue in doing so) present to the actor all possible combinations of the names of the seven cities three at a time. If we presented all possible triads, each *pair* of cities would be presented to each actor five times. If the actor preferred city A to city B in some of those presentations but not all, he would be more or less *inconsistent*. But inconsistent or not, he might still behave transitively or intransitively. To test the actor's responses for *transitivity*, we look beyond the one pair comparison. If the actor prefers city A to city B (in most or all of the five presentations containing those two), and prefers B to C (in most or all presentations), and A to C, then we can conclude that the actor is (at least most of the time) transitive in his preferences. In this kind of presentation of task to actor, consistency and transitivity can be ascertained independently.

RELIABILITY

Consistency is akin to *reliability*. When the data given by an individual are highly inconsistent, then the "votes" within each paired comparison are very close, and the change of one or a few tallies could make changes in the rank order one deduces from the paired comparisons. One has the feeling that the actor might easily yield data we would have to interpret as a different rank order if the actor were to give us a new set of data. In brief, consistency can be taken as an internal index of reliability (see Chapter 6 on reliability as repeatability). If much inconsistency occurs, it is sometimes interpreted as a lack of clear cognitive structure within the individual. Inconsistency is often used, too, together with the probability assumption, to index confusion or proximity of stimuli in the perception of the individual.

11-6. Probabilistic Models for Dominance Data

Data that fit the requirements of a scale perfectly are rare. Consequently, if we are to construct scales useful with actual data, we often must be willing to accept some proportion of nonfitting data, or "error." The discussion of "Goodness of Fit" in section 11-4 explained how the technique can be used to accomplish this. Another technique rests on the assumption of probabilistic position (assumption 9 in Appendix I); this technique endows every datum with error and at the same time provides a way of fitting every datum to the model, regardless of the amount of error that may be lurking in it. This section will describe various applications of the latter assumption.

CLASSICAL TEST THEORY (QIIA)

When we use the word *test*, we usually think of putting some questions before an actor who answers them by writing or making some kind of mark; then his answers are compared with the "right" answers, and he is assigned a "score." Examples are the usual kinds of printed intelligence tests, academic aptitude tests, personality and interest inventories that yield scores, and the like. Some tests, often called *performance tests*, may present an actor with nonverbal situations, usually, however, accompanied by verbal instructions. Tests of digital dexterity may ask the test-taker to insert some small objects into holes of various sizes and shapes. Tests of visual acuity may ask the participant to adjust objects or images to achieve some specified sort of matching. Tests of certain kinds of mental functioning may present some various-shaped objects and ask the individual to assemble them in some specified way, in the manner of a puzzle.

Two obvious characteristics of what we mean by a test score are that there are *right answers* for the component items and a *score* for the total pattern of answers. Another way to say this is that the researcher divides all conceivable responses of the actor into two categories and labels one *right* and the other *wrong*. For example, an item on an arithmetic test might ask the test-taker to add 3 and 11. The researcher might decide to call any legibly written representation of the number 14 right and anything else wrong, including skipping the item and the note, "We didn't have this lesson yet," written beside it.[15] As another example, the test might ask the actor to find the peg that fits a W-shaped hole. To categorize the actor's response as right, the tester might require that the actor insert a W-shaped peg in the hole and leave it there until he (the actor) gives some signal of satisfaction or completion such as saying, "There!" or answering "Yes," to the tester's question, "Have you finished?" The tester might call any other response wrong.

Dividing responses into two classes and thinking of them as right and wrong is formally the same as thinking of responses in one of the classes as dominating the stimulus and of responses in the other as not dominating it. In other words, the test item of classical test theory fits the model of the QIIa datum—a dominance relation between two points, one representing an actor and the other an item or stimulus. The relation is monotonic; if the actor has enough ability to pass an item, he cannot have so much of that same ability that he fails the item.

To deal with data of this sort by using classical test theory, we need to add some further assumptions. One is assumption 12 of Appendix I: that items are interchangeable. This assumption enables us to count the number of "right" items without regard to which items we are counting. Next, the theory can become a probabilistic theory if we add assumptions 9b, 10b, and 11a of Appendix I; namely, the assumptions that every test score has two components, the true score and the error component; that errors are distributed normally about the true score; and that consecutive errors are independent of one another. These assumptions,[16] along with others for the data-model of QIIa, permit a very elaborate theory of test scores.

Since numerous helpful expositions of test theory are given in books on measurement in the social sciences as well as in a number of books devoted entirely to the subject, not to speak of the voluminous literature in the professional journals, we shall not go into the technical details of constructing or

[15] Sometimes a tester chooses not to count skipped items as wrong, categorizing as right or wrong only those items the test-taker attempts and scoring the test as the percentage right among the items attempted. One way to interpret this practice would be to say that the tester decides, after each test-taker has finished, which items will be in the test for that test-taker and then applies the right-wrong categorization to those items.

[16] The descriptions of assumptions underlying test theory given in the paragraphs above follow Hays (1967, pp. 66–67).

analyzing tests in this book. The reader who wishes to construct a test, or use one available commercially, should consult the available literature. For the beginner, a good way to become acquainted with some of the problems involved is to look at the technical standards set forth by the APA, AERA, and NCME (1966) and to browse through the criticisms compiled by Buros (1961, 1965).

Homogeneity and Discriminability

Despite limitations of space, we touch upon two further concepts useful to test builders and ubiquitous in the literature: (1) the homogeneity of a test and (2) the discriminability of an item. These concepts are related to each other, and both are related to reliability (see sections 6-2, 6-4, and the discussion of "Reliability" in section 11-5). Within test theory, these concepts become complex; we describe them only briefly for two purposes. The first is to show that the user of test theory has a number of choices to make concerning the characteristics of the test he will use to collect observations, since not all types of tests serve different purposes equally well. The second is to show in more detail the two contrasting ways of dealing with nonfitting data, the deterministic and the probabilistic.

Deterministic Concepts. To discuss deterministic concepts of homogeneity and discriminability we shall begin with the hypothetical example of Table 11-11, showing QIIa data that fit perfectly into a scalogram, indicating unidimensionality. In this table, for simplicity we let each row represent the response of one actor, but our discussion would not be altered in principle were some rows to represent more than one actor or were some row patterns to be given by no actor.

We can say that the items represented in Table 11-11 are homogeneous, not in the sense that they are all alike but in the sense that they all fit the same pattern—in this case, the scalogram pattern. Each item does its bit, so to speak, in building the unidimensional scale. We might use still another metaphor in talking about the sort of homogeneity we see in Table 11-11; we

Table 11-11. *Unidimensional Pattern for QIIa Deterministic Data*

		ITEMS							TOTAL
	ACTOR	1	2	3	4	5	6	7	SCORE
	1	1	1	1	1	1	1	1	7
	2	1	1	1	1	1	1	0	6
	3	1	1	1	1	1	0	0	5
	4	1	1	1	1	0	0	0	4
	5	1	1	1	0	0	0	0	3
	6	1	1	0	0	0	0	0	2
	7	1	0	0	0	0	0	0	1
	8	0	0	0	0	0	0	0	0
Proportion of actors failing:		$\frac{1}{8}$	$\frac{2}{8}$	$\frac{3}{8}$	$\frac{4}{8}$	$\frac{5}{8}$	$\frac{6}{8}$	$\frac{7}{8}$	

Table 11-12. *Item Discriminability of Items 4 and 5*

	TOTAL SCORE		
Score on item 4	Low	High	
1	0	4	Phi = 1.000
0	4	0	
Score on item 5	Low	High	
1	0	3	Phi = .774
0	4	1	

might say that every item works toward the same end—that of discriminating actors whose positions on the scale are more negative from those whose positions are more positive. We saw the geometry of this in the discussion of "Scalogram Analysis" in section 11-4.

Another way to portray homogeneity of items is to compare how an item discriminates actors (that is, divides them into groups) with the way the total score does so. For example, look at item 4 in Table 11-11. The actors who pass item 4 (passing is indicated by the numeral 1) all get higher total scores than the actors who fail item 4. The item points in the same direction as the total score; the item is homogeneous with the over-all pattern. We can quantify the way the item fits the over-all pattern by using a contingency table that shows how many of the eight actors passed and failed the item and at the same time how many got high and low total scores. Calling a score of four or more "high," we have constructed Table 11-12, which shows this sort of information for items 4 and 5 as illustrative.

There are several ways to compute indexes from tables such as those of Table 11-12 that will reflect the extent to which the item divides the actors in the same way as does the total score. One such index is called the phi coefficient;[17] its values for the two illustrations are included in Table 11-12. Item 4, clearly, is the only item of Table 11-11 that can have a phi coefficient of 1.00. All other items will have lower coefficients, the lowest being .378 for items 1 and 7.

In the case of a single item, we speak of its *discriminability* instead of its homogeneity. Turning again to the illustration of the contingency tables, we

[17]The formula for the phi coefficient is

$$\text{phi} = \frac{p_{ij} - p_i p_j}{(p_i q_i p_j q_j)^{1/2}}$$

where p_i is the proportion of positive cases according to one categorization, p_j the proportion of positive cases in the other, p_{ij} the proportion of cases simultaneously positive in both categorizations, $q_i = 1 - p_i$, and $q_j = 1 - p_j$. In the example of item 5, $p_i = 3/8$, $q_i = 5/8$, $p_j = 4/8$, $q_j = 4/8$, and $p_{ij} = 3/8$.

Table 11-13. *Homogeneous Pattern for QIIa Probabilistic Data*

	ITEMS							
ACTOR	1	2	3	4	5	6	7	TOTAL SCORES
1	1	1	1	1	1	1	1	7
2	1	1	1	1	1	1	0	6
3	1	1	1	1	0	0	1	5
4	1	0	0	0	1	1	1	4
5	0	1	0	0	1	0	1	3
6	0	0	1	0	0	1	0	2
7	0	0	0	1	0	0	0	1
8	0	0	0	0	0	0	0	0
Difficulty	4/8	4/8	4/8	4/8	4/8	4/8	4/8	

see that they tell us how well each item *discriminates* the high-scoring actors (in terms of total score) from the low-scoring actors. The phi coefficient is one index of discriminability of the item. Looking at the discriminability of items is commonly called *item analysis.*

Probabilistic Concepts. Table 11-13 shows a hypothetical data matrix for QIIa data in which the items are very homogeneous in the sense of the phi coefficient; no item has a phi coefficient less than .500. Note that the items will not fit a scalogram pattern. Nevertheless, all items have good discriminability and, as a group, are therefore highly homogeneous. The probabilistic assumption enables a test to be homogeneous without the triangular scalogram pattern; in Table 11-13, an actor's score depends only on the number of items he passes and not at all on his pattern of response among the items.

A concept frequently used in characterizing an item is its *difficulty*. If many actors pass the item, it is said to be less difficult, and more difficult if few pass it. Items fitting the triangular pattern must necessarily extend over a range of difficulty, as in Table 11-11. If items are all to be high in discriminability, however, their difficulties must be much more alike, as in Table 11-13. Nevertheless, if a test-maker wishes to use the probabilistic assumption and build a test with items of varying difficulty, he can do so.

When a test contains items all near .5 in difficulty and the respondent is asked to respond correctly to as many of these items of equal difficulty as he can in a given period of time, the test is called a *speed test*. When a test is composed of items of varying difficulty and the respondent is asked to respond correctly to as many as he can without time limit, the test is called a *power test*. In a speed test, few actors will answer all items correctly because of the time limit. In the power test, few will answer all correctly because of the range of difficulty.

The relations among data under the probabilistic assumption can become exceedingly complex, some of the relations remaining mysteries even to the most devoted students. As an example, we quote Horst (1966):

> Suppose we have a perfectly homogeneous set of items, hence perfectly scalable in the Guttman [scalogram] sense, and we get the intercorrelations of these items in terms of the Pearson product-moment correlations. These correlations would be phi coefficients, of course, because they come from binary scores. Then since the items all measure the same thing, we might expect that a factor analysis would reveal only one factor. But this is not the case. A factor analysis reveals as many different factors as there are different degrees of difficulty among the items. . . . This phenomenon presents a dilemma which psychological measurement specialists have tried, so far unsuccessfully, to deal with (p. 162).

The deterministic assumptions serve a purpose somewhat different from that of the probabilistic assumptions. Scalogram analysis permits some response patterns *not to fit;* consequently, this technique enables the researcher to *test* whether the data fit a unidimensional pattern. The probabilistic assumption of interchangeable items enables *every* response pattern to be given a score; consequently, that technique enables the researcher to keep every actor in the study and still find a place for his score among all others.[18] Typically, the researcher using a deterministic analysis must either drop out actors or items, or both, or must accept either error or multidimensionality in the data, or both, because data perfectly scalable by the triangular technique are not easy to find. The probabilistic assumption has the advantage that items can be dropped after item analysis without the danger of dropping actors. The disadvantages of the probabilistic model are that (1) some researchers worry about every added assumption in a scaling model, and (2) some researchers find the probabilistic model more difficult than the deterministic model to understand for reasons of which Horst's, mentioned above, is an example. Whether either of these perplexities is serious depends on both the study and the researcher.

Multiple-Alternative Items

Many verbal tests contain items that present more than two alternatives among which the respondent is to choose an answer. In tests, it is typical for one of these answers to be "correct" and all the others to be "wrong." In such a case, the item is formally a dichotomous item such as we have been discussing in this chapter so far. There are other types of assessment, however, where multiple-alternative items are not interpreted as dichotomous. A common technique of assessment in which all alternatives are taken as having differentiable meanings is the *Likert technique.* Likert (1932) developed his technique within the context of attitude scaling, but the technique is, of course, equally applicable to any kind of observation gathering in which the researcher can offer the respondent more than two *ordered* alternatives. Suppose, for example, we were employing a "test" containing items that offered ordered alternatives such as:

---

[18] For more detailed comments comparing the assumptions of deterministic and probabilistic models, see the discussion in Appendix I following Assumption 8.

Our high school should teach social dancing.
( ) strongly approve
( ) approve
( ) undecided
( ) disapprove
( ) strongly disapprove

One way to go about scaling the items on such a test would be to make use of the technique of *disorderly interlocking,* mentioned at the end of the discussion of the skewed hourglass in section 11-4. A second would be to dichotomize the array of alternatives between two adjacent alternatives, arbitrarily chosen, and then to make use of any of the methods we have discussed as suitable for QIIa data. A third approach would be to employ the Likert technique.

One way to use the Likert technique with this item would be to assign the most favorable alternative a weight of 5, and so on, assigning the least favorable a weight of 1. Or we might assign any other arbitrary set of weights. Instead of merely counting the number of items "right" to obtain a score, then, we would *add the weights* indicated by the actor's choice in each item. This technique adds assumptions beyond those of mental test theory. First, it assumes that the intervals between adjacent alternatives are equal (or spaced as indicated by the weights given the alternative). That is, it assumes that choosing an alternative weighted 3 contributes the same increment to the score over an alternative weighted 2—namely, an increment of one—as an alternative assigned a 2 contributes over an alternative assigned a 1. Second, the method assumes equal intervals *across* items, since an increment of one more positive step if one item contributes exactly as much and no more to the total score as does one step in any other item. (Any other set of assigned weights would require corresponding assumptions about intervals and across items.) It is difficult to show evidence for equal intervals on a psychological scale between the alternatives of a Likert item; in fact, most researchers who use this Likert technique do not bother to try. Nevertheless, this technique has been used fruitfully to assess attitudes in a great many studies. One can find examples in any collection of social-psychological studies. A convenient collection is that of Fishbein (1967), which also reprints Likert's original contribution.

In requiring the researcher to be able to put ordered weights on the alternatives of every item, the Likert technique also requires him to know or assume at the outset the positive direction of each item. But this requirement does not limit the Likert technique to attitude assessment; it can be used whereever the researcher can designate a "right" or positive direction to all the items at the outset. The Likert technique applies to items of many formats; it requires only that an item be interpretable as presenting ordered alternatives to which the researcher can assign weights.

Let us look at another example. A teacher might be giving a test in astronomy and might want to assess the "feel" the students had acquired for proportions in the solar system. Accordingly, one item might be this:

> If the orbits of Earth and Mars are at the distance shown, about where would the Moon's orbit pass? Circle the number you believe comes closest to where the Moon's orbit would pass.

Earth	7	6	5	4	3	2	1	Mars

If the teacher feels that picking the number nearest Earth is the most correct answer and picking numbers farther away is progressively farther away from the right answer, he could weight the nearest mark most heavily and the successive marks successively less. Clearly, this item is formally a Likert item turned on its side; the choices are mutually exclusive, exhaustive, and ordered. In its horizontal layout, this type of format has become widely known through its use by Osgood, Suci, and Tannebaum (1957) in their *semantic differential* instruments. It has also been used, of course, by many other researchers. For a collection of studies, see Snider and Osgood (1968). For a concise explanation of the semantic differential and its use, see Kerlinger (1964, Chapter 32).

This book does not contain a separate section on assessing attitudes, since neither the techniques not the logic of gathering observations concerning attitudes is unique to attitude assessment. The datum model of any quadrant can be used for attitude assessment. For example, the QIIa item can be considered a Likert-type item with two alternatives instead of five. As a matter of fact, all of the techniques set forth in Chapters 11 and 12 are available to the ingenuity of the attitude measurer.

MODELS FOR STIMULUS-COMPARISON DATA (QIIIA)

At the present writing, data of the QIIIa form seem to be analyzed most often by Thurstone's (1927a, b, 1928) "law" of comparative judgment or by methods of direct estimate such as Stevens' (1958) method of ratio estimation. We shall say a few words here about Thurstone's model of comparative judgment to show how a scale bearing numbers that quantify intervals along the scale can be obtained by using appropriate assumptions.

A frequently used method of collecting observations is that of paired comparisons. Two objects are presented to the actor and he is asked to pick one, or say which one exceeds the other in some specified respect. If each pair is presented only once, this method produces a dichotomous, conditional, one-set matrix for QIIIa. If each pair is presented to more than one actor (with actors considered interchangeable), or more than once to one actor, we can enter proportions into the cells of the matrix, obtaining a nondichotomous matrix. A nondichotomous or probabilistic matrix is the beginning point for the law of comparative judgment.

Table 11-14. *Proportions of Times That the Column Stimulus Was Judged Heavier Than the Row Stimulus*

	A	B	C	D	E
A	.50	.81	.23	.47	.61
B	.19	.50	.06	.17	.28
C	.77	.94	.50	.74	.85
D	.53	.83	.26	.50	.64
E	.39	.72	.15	.36	.50

After obtaining a sizable number of judgments on each paired comparison, one can construct a data matrix, as in Table 11-14 (reproduced from Hays, 1967, p. 30 Table 1), which we might take to represent the outcome of comparing objects as to their heaviness. In the table, each cell shows the proportion of times the column object was judged heavier than the row object. For example, B was judged heavier than C 94 percent of the time. Arbitrarily, we insert .50 in the cells of the diagonal to indicate our belief that an actor, if required to say which of two identical objects was heavier, would choose each about half the time.[19]

To use Thurstone's model, we next assume that each object has a "true scale position" as to perceived weight. Any object i will have some "true" scale value x_i.[20] A further part of this assumption is that at any particular moment t there is a certain amount of "error" or deviation e_{it} from the true position, and consequently the behavior we observe is behavior reflecting the true value combined with the variable error, $x_i + e_{it}$. Thurstone next adopted the assumption that the errors about the true value of any object or item are normally distributed[21] and consequently that the manifest or behavioral values $(x_i + e_{it})$ are normally distributed also, and that the *differences* between behavioral values, too, are normally distributed. It follows from the mathematical characteristics of the normal distribution that the mean difference between a behavioral value $(x_i + e_{it})$ for an object i and a behavioral value $(x_j + e_{jt})$ for an object j will be just $x_i - x_j$, on the average. That is, the "true" difference between the heavinesses of objects i and j can be taken, on the average, to be equal to the difference between the mean of a great number of observations of the manifest scale value of object i and the mean of a great number of observations of the manifest scale value of object j. And, indeed, the cell values in Table

[19] To remove visual cues, experiments with weights typically use weights that are all identical except in weight; they are the same in size, material, shape, color, and so forth. Consequently, a pair of the weights can be presented repeatedly to an actor without his being sure when this is happening.

[20] The symbol T is usually reserved to stand for the "true score" on a *test*. Hence, we use x_i here to stand for the "true" scale position of an object or item. We do not use t, because we use t to denote a moment in time.

[21] See Hays (1963) or any book on statistics for the concept of the normal distribution.

11-14 give us just this sort of information. A cell value in this table tells us how often, proportionally, the manifest scale value $(x_j + e_{jt})$ turns out to be larger than the manifest scale value $(x_i + e_{it})$ over the many moments t when the pair (i, j) is presented to the actor or actors. However, Table 11-14 does not tell us the scale values of individual objects. So far, we have only proportions of "dominance" from which we wish to infer units of difference between stimuli. How can we transform proportions of difference judgments within *pairs* of stimuli into scale values for each stimulus singly?

Thurstone overcame this problem and made the law of comparative judgment available for practical use by adding two more assumptions: (1) that the variance[22] of the difference distribution $(x_j - x_i)$ for one pair of stimuli is equal to that of the distribution for every other pair; and (2) that this variance is equal to one. These assumptions, together with the mathematical characteristics of the normal distribution, enable the researcher to convert the information in Table 11-14 into scale values for the objects. For details of computation, see Hays (1967, pp. 30–34), among others.

The result of this series of assumptions is a model that delivers an *interval scale*[23] of values for the objects. An interval scale has no natural zero point; nevertheless, the numbers on the scale enable predictions to be made about behavior. For example, if the difference in behavioral response to objects at scale values of 2 and 3 is known, a similar difference can be predicted to appear between the scale values of 3 and 4, between 4 and 5, and so on. This is a very powerful result, especially if the judgments of large numbers of people do correspond in their relations to the real numbers in the scale. At the same time, this power is bought at the cost of making a rather large series of assumptions, and the entire edifice may fall if only one of the assumptions is wrong. Furthermore, beyond the assumptions listed in this section, there are still further weaknesses in the Thurstone model; for a discussion of them, see Coombs (1964, pp. 410–417 and Chapter 23). Again, in this example of Thurstone's model of comparative judgment, we see that we must assume we already know something if we are to learn something, but what we learn is valid only insofar as our assumptions are valid.

OTHER QUADRANTS

We described a deterministic model for analyzing distance comparisons in the discussion of "Unfolding" in section 11-4. A probabilistic analytic model suitable for unidimensional solutions of data matrices containing QIa data is that of Greenberg (1963). Probabilistic *multidimensional* analytic models are available that cope efficiently with QIa and QIVa data and deliver unidimensional solutions when the nature of the data permits. We shall describe these models in Chapter 12.

---

[22] See Hays (1963) or any introductory book on statistics for a definition of *variance*.

[23] See Chapter 8 of Dawes (1972) for an exposition of interval scales and other types of scales.

11-7. Deterministic Models for Proximity Data (QIIb)

We cannot describe any practical analytic models for QIIIb, because at this writing no practical unidimensional model exists. However, we can describe some deterministic and probabilistic models for QIIb data.

Any observation interpreted as QIIb data can be likened to the use of a rating scale. We follow Coombs (1964) in welcoming rather more types of observations under the label-rating scale than do most authors. A set of labels an actor can apply to a set of objects can be called a rating scale. Sometimes the labels merely identify categories or types; in other cases the labels are numbers that quantify positions along the scale. We can interpret labeling behavior as QIIb data.

1. Name a dish you'd like to have for dinner.
2. Name some political candidates you'd say have the right degree of doggedness.
3. How many grams would you say each of these objects weighs?

NOMINAL CATEGORIES

Consider the first illustrative instruction above. This instruction to actors provides us with two sets of points, a set of dishes on the one hand and a set of actors exhibiting preferences toward objects on the other. But, in terms of the searchingness structure, this is a *pick-one* method. Consequently, no scaling in a nontrivial sense is possible. We can only categorize the actors according to the dish each picked and label them with the name of the picked dish: here are the "steak men," we might say, and here are the "halibut men," the "macaroni men," and so forth.

PICK ANY

When using the second instruction given above, we have the political candidates as a set of objects and some imaginary "right" points on a scale of doggedness as a set of labels. In using this instruction, we allow each actor to pick more than one object; we allow him to *pick any* number from zero upwards. Because different actors pick different numbers of objects as acceptable, comparisons between actors are typically ambiguous. No generally satisfactory analytic model exists for data collected in this form.[24]

DIRECT MEASUREMENT

The third illustrative item provides the actor, on the one hand, with all the

[24] For applications where a unique ordering of actors and objects is not vital, Coombs (1964, Chapter 4) has suggested the use of parallelogram analysis.

natural numbers and their fractions as a set of labels to represent number of grams. On the other hand, the actor confronts a series of objects. The instructions tell him to label each set of objects with one of the numbers. In this case, the elements of the set of labels are also elements of a *measure set*. Knowing something about the characteristics of the measure set, we also know something about the objects measured—if the measurement was valid. For example, if we are told that one object has a weight of 2 ounces, another a weight of 4, and a third a weight of 6, we deduce from our knowledge of arithmetic that $2 + 4 = 6$ and also that together the first and second objects will balance the third.[25]

Suppose we ask the actor to estimate, by calling out numerical weights in grams, the weights of a series of objects. Since the measure in this example is applied directly to the object, through the agency of the actor, we call this an illustration of *direct measurement*. The analytic model, in this case, is almost nonexistent. In the case of one actor, we can only take his responses at face value. In the case of multiple actors rating the same weights, we might go so far as to take the mean of the actor's judgments concerning each object.

The methods of direct measurement have been used predominately in the realm of psychophysics—the study of how psychological quantities (loudness, for example) correspond to physical quantities (pressure of airwaves on the eardrum). There are many methods of collecting psychophysical observations, which need not be catalogued here. After considering the bulk of indirect and logically complex scaling techniques described earlier in this chapter, however, we may have a more balanced perspective if we look at a few more types of direct measurement. Again, we follow Torgerson (1958), who says that "a subject is capable of directly perceiving and reporting the magnitude of a sense-ratio; i.e., the ratio between two subjective magnitudes," though this assumption is "subject to tests of internal consistency" (p. 94). Torgerson distinguishes two types of *fractionation* methods: direct-estimate methods and prescribed-ratio methods.

In the direct-estimate method, the "subject is presented with two stimuli and instructed to report the subjective ratio between them with respect to the designated attribute" (p. 94). For example, we can present two sounds and ask for the ratio of the second to the first in loudness. We can also present one stimulus as a standard and let others be compared with it. If the pair of stimuli is considered to correspond to a point in one set and the ratio a point in a label set, then the interpretation is in QIIb. If the estimate of the ratio is interpreted to tell which stimulus exceeds the other (and perhaps with what

[25] Dawes (1972, Chapter 2; see also Coombs, Dawes, and Tversky, 1970, pp. 17–19) points out that in cases like this, a manipulation or computation of the labels (numbers) results in a testable prediction about observations that can be made (in this case, the 2-ounce weight and the 4-ounce weight, together, balancing the 6-ounce weight) and that not all labeling has this potential. Dawes reserves the term *measure* for the more stringent correspondence between labels and observable quantities, suggesting that we use some other term for the weaker sort of labeling. In a personal communication, he has suggested *indicator* for the weaker sort of label.

probability), then the interpretation is in QIIIa. In the method of prescribed ratio, Torgerson says:

> The subject's task is to report when two stimuli stand in a prescribed ratio. One stimulus (the standard) is kept fixed, and the other (the variable) is adjusted.
>
> In either form [direct-estimate or prescribed-ratio] it is easy to see that the problem concerned with obtaining a linear scale which is referred to a rational origin, i.e., a ratio scale, are solved. . . . We are thus free to assign the value of one stimulus arbitrarily (to specify the unit), and the values of the remaining stimuli are then determined. As an illustration, assume that the following relations are known among stimuli *a*, *b*, *c*, *d*, and *e*:
>
> $$\frac{a}{b} = \frac{1}{2}, \quad \frac{b}{c} = \frac{1}{2}, \quad \frac{c}{d} = \frac{1}{2}, \quad \frac{d}{e} = \frac{1}{2}$$
>
> For the purpose of illustration, let $a = 1$. Any other positive value assigned to this or any other of the stimuli would serve as well. Given $a = 1$, then $b = 2$, $c = 4$, $d = 8$, and $e = 16$ follow immediately (Torgerson, 1958, pp. 95–96).

11-8. Probabilistic Models for Proximity Data (QIIb)

When we obtain more than one response to one object, regardless of whether all the responses are taken from one actor or from a number of actors considered as interchangeable, we are faced with the problem of what to do with disagreements among responses. There are only four alternatives open: (1) the disagreements can be interpreted as evidence of change over time on the part of one or more actors; (2) they can be interpreted as evidence of change on the part of one or more stimuli; (3) they can be considered perceptual differences among actors; or (4) they can be taken as evidence of error. In the last case, the assumption of probabilistic position must be invoked.

We saw in section 11-7 that analytic models to be used in connection with rating scales need not be complex or subtle. In certain cases—such as labeling with nominal categories—the "analytic" procedure is so direct and simple as to be almost unrecognizable as a "procedure" at all.[26] Since labeling methods are so direct and intuitively uncomplicated, it seems not surprising that there are few practicable indirect unidimensional analytic models for QIIb data. The latent-class analysis and latent-structure analysis of Lazarsfeld (1959) have been little used; perhaps the computational difficulties are deterring. A model that has seen a good deal of use, especially in the study of attitudes, is the *method of equal-appearing intervals;* we shall describe this method briefly.

The name equal-appearing intervals is given both to a method of collecting observations and to some methods of analysis applicable to data obtained

---

[26]See also Coombs (1964, pp. 318–319) on this point.

through the corresponding observational method. To collect observations by this method, we present the actor with a collection of objects or stimuli and ask him to sort them into piles so that the psychological "distances" between the piles seem to him equal in some sense. This method differs from the method of using a rating scale with equal intervals in it. In the rating-scale case the experimenter gives the actor a scale already labeled and asks the subject to match the stimuli one at a time to the points marked off on the scale. In the method of equal-appearing intervals, however, the actor "labels" his own scale point, so to speak, by choosing a particular subset of stimuli to pile onto that imaginary point. Typically, the actor following the method of equal-appearing intervals is encouraged to rearrange the stimuli as much as he wishes until he feels satisfied that the distances between successive piles are equal. The experimenter may then assign successive integers, every stimulus in any one pile receiving the same integer as its scale value. When more than one actor has sorted the stimuli, the calculation of scale values is still straightforward: the scale value of any one stimulus is obtained by taking the average of the scale values attached to it by all the actors.

11-9. Summary of Unidimensional Analytic Models

Table 11-15 summarizes the analytic models described in this chapter. The table shows the types of data (by quadrant label) needed by the model.

Table 11-15. *Summary of Unidimensional Analytic Models Described in This Chapter*

MODEL	QUAD[a]	SEARCH[b]	SECTION[c]
Deterministic models for dominance data			
Scalogram analysis	IIa[d]	Pick 1	11-4
Unfolding technique	Ia[e]	All except pick 1	11-4
Probabilistic models for dominance data			
Test theory	IIa	Pick 1	11-6
Thurstone's law of comparative judgment	IIIa	All except pick 1	11-6
Deterministic model for proximity data			
Rating scales	IIb	Pick k	11-7
Probabilistic model for proximity data			
Method of equal-appearing intervals	IIb	Pick k	11-8

Note: No practicable unidimensional deterministic model exists for IIIb data. No practicable unidimensional probabilistic model exists for IIIb or IVa data.

[a] Types of data required by the model, as categorized in Chapter 10 by quadrants.
[b] Methods by which observations can be collected, as described in section 7-3, and from which to obtain data.
[c] Section where model is described in this chapter.
[d] Also IIIa, but rarely used there in practice.
[e] Also IVa, but rarely used there in practice.

It also shows the kinds of observational designs (in terms of the searchingness structure displayed in section 7-2) that most directly produce observations interpretable as the types of data needed. The last column refers the reader to the section of the chapter where the model is described.

Table 11-15 comprises a partial facet design. It contains, of course, the three basic facets of Coombs' theory of data. It also contains the so-called deterministic-probabilistic dichotomy and two facets from the searchingness structure. Obviously, if all possible cells provided by six dichotomous facets were to contain at least one corresponding analytic model, we would have 64 names of models in the table. Just as obviously, the table lists far fewer, and in the text of the chapter we have mentioned and referred to fewer than 64 analytic models. But by the time this book is published, the table will surely be out of date, both because new conceptualizations will have appeared in the literature and because new computer programs will make old models more easily applicable.

11-10. Further Reading

For more detail on most of the topics of this chapter, see Torgerson (1958), Coombs (1964), and Dawes (1972).

Scalogram analysis was first set forth by Guttman (1944, 1950); see also Chapters 2, 3, 6, 8, and 9 in Stouffer and others (1950). More up-to-date accounts will be found in Chapter 12 of Torgerson (1958) and in Chapter 11 of Coombs (1964). A brief account within the context of attitude measurement appears in Shaw and Wright (1967, pp. 25–26). The latter authors also exhibit the application of the unfolding technique to attitude measurement.

For studies interpreting inconsistency as lack of clear cognitive structure, see Dodd and Svalastoga (1952), Fiske and Maddi (1961), Fiske and Rice (1955), Glaser (1952), and Runkel (1958). For a significance test for consistency among replicated pairs of stimuli, see Miller and Madow (1963) and Cronholm (1963).

For discussions of testing of the sort where a score is taken from a number of items, each interpretable as right or wrong, see Anastasi (1968), Cronbach (1970), Ebel (1965), Findley (1968), Ghiselli (1964), Guilford (1954), Gulliksen (1950), Hase and Goldberg (1967), Hays (1967), Horst (1966), APA, AERA, and NCME Joint Committee (1966), Jackson and Messick (1968), E. L. Kelly (1967), Lord and Novick (1968), Magnuson (1967), Millman, Bishop, and Ebel (1965), Novick (1966), Nunnally (1964, 1967), Remmers, Gage, and Rummel (1960), Rasch (1960), Rorer (1965), Stern, Stein, and Bloom (1956), Thorndike and Hagen (1961), and Tyler (1971). For an exhaustive listing of mental tests of all sorts, see Buros (1961, 1965).

For descriptions of some tests that go beyond pencil-and-paper forms, see Atkinson (1958), Bechtoldt (1951), Fitts (1951), Fitts and Posner (1967), Porteus (1950), and Seashore (1951), among many others. Goslin (1963) has discussed at length the use of formal tests for economic and social purposes and has set forth some of the ethical problems that arise.

There are other kinds of structured tasks that deliver useful information to the researcher, but for which he may not choose to designate a right answer. Examples are given by Guetzkow (1962), Moore and Anderson (1954), Morris (1965), Murstein (1965), U.S. Office of Strategic Services (1948), Rechtschaffen and Mednick (1955), Royce and others (1966), Shubik (1964), and Zajonc (1965a).

For various types and methods of item analysis, see Ebel (1965, Chapter 11), Hays (1967, pp. 63–64), Horst (1966, pp. 241–242 and Chapter 24), and Nunnally (1964, pp. 135–136), among others. For more detail on homogeneity, discriminability, power tests, and speed tests, see Ebel (1965, Chapters 9 and 11), Hays (1967, pp. 61–64), and Horst (1966, Chapters 14, 24, and 25), among others.

For discussions of applications of unidimensional scaling to attitude measurement, see, for example, Darnell (1966), Dawes (1972), Fishbein (1967), Oppenheim (1966), Scott (1968), Shaw and Wright (1967), and Upshaw (1968).

For a brief description of the law of comparative judgment, see Coombs (1964, pp. 363–364); for an extended discussion, see Torgerson (1958, Chapter 9); both discussions are rather technical. For a somewhat less technical exposition, though precise, see Hays (1967, pp. 30–34). For other descriptions of the method of ratio estimation, see Coombs (1964, pp. 371–374) and Torgerson (1958, pp. 97–112). Other probabilistic models available for QIIIa data have been described by Coombs (1964, pp. 359–368) and still others by Stevens (1958), Thurstone and Jones (1957), and Siegel (1956). Multidimensional models are available for QIIIa data; see Chapter 12.

For further information about methods of collecting psychophysical observations, see Torgerson (1958, especially Chapter 4), Guilford (1954), Luce and Galanter (1963), Manning and Rosenstock (1968), Poulton (1968), Stevens (1951), or Underwood (1957), among others.

For a discussion of the complexities of the method of equal-appearing intervals, see Torgerson (1958, pp. 67–87), Shaw and Wright (1967, pp. 21–22), and Upshaw (1962). The method acquired its early fame through its use by Thurstone and Chave (1929) to construct *master scales* for assessing attitudes. Agreeing with Torgerson that Thurstone and Chave assumed that "the probability that a subject will endorse an item decreases as the distance (amount of difference) between his own attitude and that reflected by the item increases" (Torgerson, 1958, p. 89), Coombs (1964, pp. 107–118 and Chapter 23) has pointed out that this assumed monotonicity between probability of endorsement and distance to the stimulus may sometimes be a mistaken assumption. Coombs (1964, Chapter 23) has discussed this difficulty under the heading *laterality effects*.

CHAPTER 12

Analyzing Empirical Evidence: Arranging Data into Multidimensional Patterns

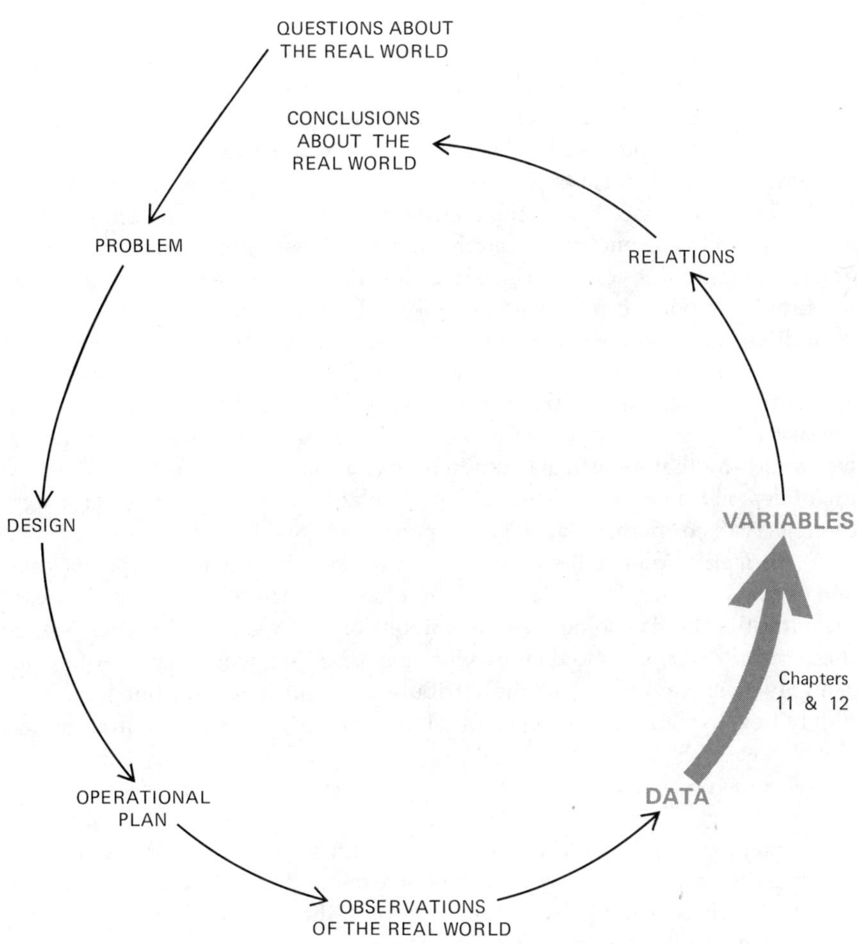

What choices are open to the researcher when, in the course of analyzing his empirical evidence, he finds his data will not fit into one dimension? He has three options. First, he can conclude that his design for data collection was faulty; he can redesign the study, collect new data, and try again for a unidimensional solution. Second, he can maintain a unidimensional solution by adopting the probability assumption and accepting the nonfitting data as "error." Finally, if the proportion of nonfitting data seems excessive, the researcher can seek a multidimensional solution instead of a unidimensional one. This chapter is devoted to some multidimensional models for arraying data.

12-1. Some Terminology

We need, at the outset, to define certain terms that will appear throughout our discussion of multidimensionality—especially since not all authors whose works are cited, and not all teachers, use these terms in the same way.

Dimension. Some authors seem to use *dimension* to mean merely mode of classification. Our use of the term is stronger than this; we explicitly mean that a dimension specifies a single criterion (aggressiveness, length, subordination, warmth, frequency of interaction, intelligence, exasperation, number of residents, salinity, conservatism, lasciviousness, or whatever) by which actors or stimuli, or both, can at least be *ordered.* We mean for the term to have a very direct geometrical representation, such as an array of points or a line.

Quantity, Value, Amount, Degree, Extent, Scale point. We use these terms as alternative ways of speaking of the place or point along a dimension that "measures" some object or actor. When we speak of a dimension of length, we would say that a particular umbrella has a *value* or *extent* of 32 inches. We might describe a particular actor, at a particular moment, as having a *high degree* of conservatism, perhaps at the 89th percentile.

Attribute. Some writers use the term *attribute* the way we use *quality, value,* and so on. They say, for example, "Albert has the attribute of acquisitiveness," meaning that he has some positive amount of that quality. However, we use the term *attribute* as synonymous with *dimension.* We would say, "Albert has a highly positive amount of the attribute of acquisitiveness, but Joan has a highly negative amount." Torgerson (1958) uses attribute in the multidimensional sense.

Continuum. Many social scientists use the term *continuum* as synonymous with our term *dimension.* They use it to indicate a unidimensional array and sometimes merely an ordered array. The term is borrowed, of course, from mathematics, where it is used to mean an array of points in which every point is in the "neighborhood" of some other point; there are no "gaps"; no region is separate or discontinuous from its neighbor; the entire space is *continuous.* A continuum, mathematically, need not be unidimensional; it can have any dimensionality. (In physics, the continuum customarily has four dimensions.) We shall use the term as mathematicians use it.

Measurement. The operation we call measurement provides a method or rule for picking out a particular number from an array of numbers. For example, in using a yardstick one follows a specified procedure: one lays the "zero" end of the yardstick precisely at one end of the thing being measured; then the number to pick is the number matching the other end of the thing being measured. The important point is that the measuring rule or device provides *one and only one* number to correspond to the property being measured.[1] However, this statement is a little too strict to be quite correct. We need not assign a *number;* we can assign some other sort of symbol as long as we assign *one and only one* symbol out of the set of symbols to one particular object; even assigning first prize, second prize, and so on, is a sort of measurement, however primitive.

Variable. Ascertaining a measure of some aspect of an object does not tell us much about the object. The important thing about a measurement is that we find out not only which element in the measure corresponds to the object but also what elements *do not* correspond to the object. We learn something useful when we learn that some particular object corresponds to *this* element in the measure set while other objects correspond to *other* elements in the set. More precisely, a particular rule for measurement (much as the yardstick, the balance, or the scoring system in football) will *vary* in the number or symbol it assigns to objects subjected to it. The number or symbol the rule "emits" depends on the particular object brought to it; in brief, the number or symbol *varies* with the object being measured. Consequently, we speak of a particular measure set as a *variable.* In somewhat more mathematical language, let X be any element of a measure set that might be chosen by a measurement operation performed on some object; then X is a variable. Other terms will be defined as they are used in subsequent sections.

12-2. Order in More Than One Dimension

Order in one dimension has a quick intuitive meaning. We think of people standing in line, or of a series of moments, or of any sequence of events or objects to which the natural numbers can be matched, one to one. In more than one dimension, however, the notion of order becomes more complex. In what sense, for example, are the points in Figure 12-1 ordered?

Obviously, we have our choice of more than one criterion by which we might declare an order to exist among the points in Figure 12-1. To answer the question whether one point stands farther than another, some criteria we might use are: lower on the page, farther to the northeast, or closer to point D. Just as we must have a criterion for ordering points in one dimension such as dominance or proximity, so in multidimensional space we must have a criterion by which to say whether one stimulus is more positive than another. Let us now leave abstract geometry and turn to a more down-to-earth example.

---

[1]Dawes (1972, Chapter 2; see also Coombs, Dawes, and Tversky, 1970, pp. 17–19) puts another restriction on the definition of *measurement.* He requires that the relations among the numbers correspond (be homeomorphic) to the relations among the objects being measured. For example, if object A balances a two-pound weight and object B a three-pound weight, then both together should balance a five-pound weight, just as in the arithmetic relation two plus three equals five. In a personal communication, Dawes has suggested the term *indicator* (instead of *measure*) for a number assigned to an object from an array of numbers among which relations are implied that do not hold among the objects.

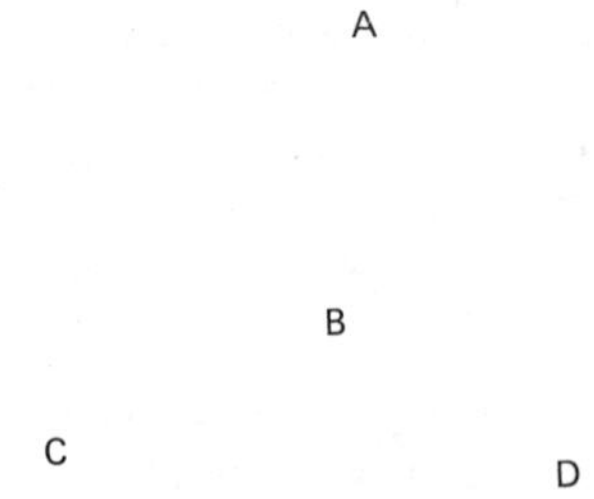

A

B

C D

Figure 12-1.

Four questionnaire items used by John Hemphill (1955) to assess perceptions of a leader by group members are:

1. He looks out for the personal welfare of individual members.
2. He treats all members as his equal.
3. He puts suggestions by the group into operation.
4. He gets group approval on important matters before going ahead.

Responses to these items could readily be interpreted as QIIa data: dichotomous, monotonic, dominance relations between an actor point and an item point. Let 1 indicate a response to any item indicating more consideration on the part of the leader toward group members. We can then indicate the responses of any actor to the four items by a series of four 1's or zeros. If an actor said *yes* to 3 and *no* to the other items, we would write:

0 0 1 0

Consider now the following two of the many possible response patterns to these four items:

0 1 0 0
0 0 1 0

Which of these two patterns indicates the more consideration on the part of the group leader? The first actor indicates more consideration in respect to item 2, but the second actor indicates more in respect to item 3. Coombs (1964, pp. 245–246) expresses the problem this way:

> The crux of the problem resides in the choice of what is called a *composition axiom*. A point in a space of r dimensions may be though of as a vector or an r-tuple, the r-tuple being the set of r ordered numbers representing the coordinates of the point in the r corresponding dimensions. The interpretation of the behavior has induced an order relation on two such points, two r-tuples. How, in the model, shall it be decided which r-tuple is to dominate another? The model must make such a decision for every pair of points, because any individual may take any item and will either pass or fail. Now if all the elements of one r-tuple are at least as great as the corresponding elements of another r-tuple, an order relation on them is intuitively acceptable. If there are two r-tuples such that each

> exceeds the other on at least one dimension, however, there is no intuitively compelling order relation on them. Nevertheless, one must be defined, and the model must contain a "composition axiom" to do this.

When Coombs speaks of an *r*-tuple in the passage above, he means a series of numbers such as we gave earlier: 0 0 1 0. The numbers are ordered to correspond to the items to which they indicate the responses. Since all the numbers in (0 0 1 1) are as great or greater than the corresponding numbers in (0 0 1 0), we can intuitively accept the former as greater than (or dominating) the latter. But what kind of *composition axiom* can we adopt to decide whether (0 0 1 0) is greater than (0 1 0 0)? As we state in Appendix I, one kind of composition axiom widely used assumes items to be interchangeable (assumption 12). This axiom implies that all points in the space will collapse into a single dimension in which patterns yielding higher scores are greater than those with lower scores, and patterns having the same scores are equivalent. When dealing with items such as those of Hemphill describing the consideration a leader gives to group members, counting items as equivalent has an intuitive appeal; we often feel that a leader who cannot be considerate in one way might very well make up for it by being considerate in another way. In contrast, however, consider these questions about cities:

1. Does the city have an honest government?
2. Do the schools draw out the capabilities of the students?
3. Do the citizens give adequate support to public health measures?
4. Do the police protect the civil rights of all segments of the citizenry?

With items such as these, and with actors choosing a city in which to live, different actors might differ violently about the substituting of a *yes* on one item for a *yes* on another. Consequently, telling someone that a city scored 3 on the above test might give him insufficient information. He might ask, "What *kind* of a 3 is that?"

But, asking these questions of hundreds of cities, we might not find that we obtain all possible response patterns. That is, the cities might not differ from each other in all possible respects. There are 16 ways in which *yes* and *no* answers to four items can be patterned, but we might not find as many as 16 types of cities being perceived by the actors. When we find fewer than all possible response patterns, it is worth seeking a simpler explanation of the outcome than "anything can happen" even if the explanation cannot be as simple as the unidimensional one.

12-3. Rules for Dominance among Points

Dominance among points in multidimensional space can be defined by the conjuctive rule, the disjunctive, or the compensatory. Other rules have been proposed, but these three are by far the most commonly used.

CONJUNCTIVE COMPOSITION

One way of putting together response patterns that exceed the possibilities for unidimensional meshing is to use the conjunctive composition rule. This rule states that one stimulus point or actor point is more positive than another only if it exceeds the other in respect to *all* the dimensions of the multidimensional space. As well as being conceived as a point, each stimulus can be characterized by the boundary formed by lines running out from the point and running parallel to the dimensions of the space. In Figure 12-2, for example, point P is represented by the L-shaped boundaries running parallel to the two dimensions indicated by the lines tipped with arrows. In three dimensions, of course, the boundary would be formed by planes, not by lines. The boundary would look like the corner of a box. In Figure 12-2, an actor point will exceed point P only if it lies within the "L"—that is, only if it lies to the northeast of the boundary lines. In the northeast sector, a point lies more positively than P both in the horizontal *and* in the vertical direction.

In Figure 12-3, any point (actor or stimulus) in the area labeled 1000 passes point A but no others. A point in the area labeled 0100 passes point B but no others. In area 0110, points pass B and C but not A or D; and so on. Points in area 1000 are more positive than those in 0000; in 1010, more positive than in 0010; in 0011, more positive than in 0010; in 1111, more positive than in any other area. In general, each area is more positively placed than areas that lie to the left of it, below, or both.

Reading from left to right in Figure 12-3, we find that any row of 4-tuples would yield a perfect solution to scalogram analysis (see "Scalogram Analysis" in section 11-4). This is also true of any vertical series of 4-tuples in the figure. Conjunctive composition cannot, however, give us a simple order on all pairs of response patterns; in Figure 12-3, we cannot tell which is the most positive of the three patterns 1000, 0010, and 0100. Nor can we tell the most positive of the three 1010, 0011, and 0110; nor of the two 1011 and 0111. Nevertheless, even though these triples and pair of patterns are unorderable, note that enough patterns are ordered so that every region in the figure is fixed in its place by its relation to others. It is not true, for example, that we could interchange

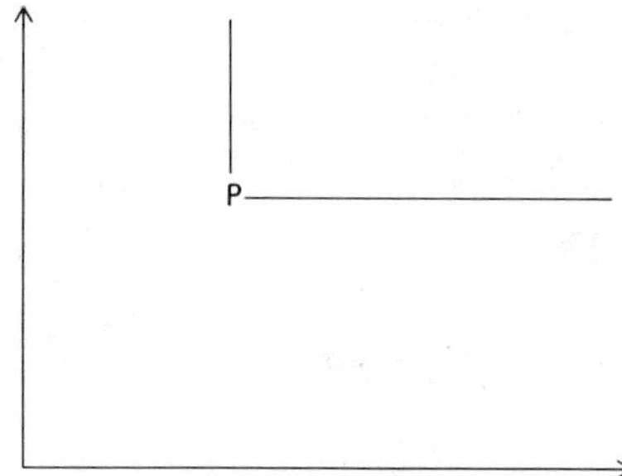

Figure 12-2.

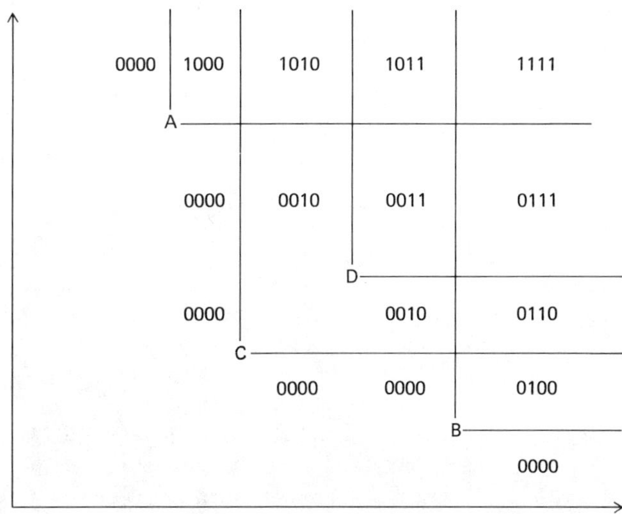

Figure 12-3.

the positions of regions 1000 and 0010, despite the fact that they are incomparable in respect to each other, and still maintain the orders in the rows, columns, and radiating diagonals. Since the simuli and response patterns are fixed in relation to each other in a geometrical sense, we say that we have ordered, or scaled, four stimuli and ten response patterns (classes of actors) in two dimensions using the conjunctive composition rule. If the four stimuli were arrayed in one dimension, only five response patterns could be encompassed.

The conjunctive composition is a very useful concept even when a scaling procedure is not applied, as is illustrated below with a study by Dawes. Coombs (1964, Chapter 12) gives details concerning analysis.

DISJUNCTIVE COMPOSITION

The disjunctive rule states that one stimulus dominates another if it exceeds the other *in at least one underlying dimension*. Suppose we are dealing with four stimuli and we again use a 4-tuple to tell us whether actors dominate the stimuli. Analogously to Figure 12-3, Figure 12-4 shows the regions of relative dominance in a two-dimensional array. Note that actors now dominate a stimulus if they exceed it in respect to *either one* of the underlying dimensions. The relation between the conjunctive and the disjunctive models is one of complementarity.

An instructive illustration contrasting the uses of conjunctive and disjunctive models has been given by Dawes (1964a). We reproduce excerpts from Dawes' article below.

> Kemeny (1962) has suggested that well-rounded colleges are more desirable than well-rounded students. What he proposes is essentially a

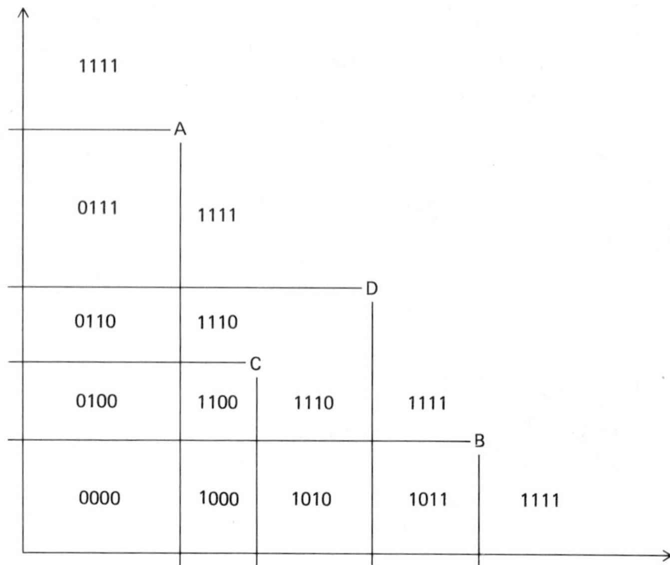

Figure 12-4.

disjunctive selection procedure for college students, rather than a conjunctive one. Let us compare these two procedures by means of a hypothetical example.

Suppose a college evaluates applicants for admissions on each of four attributes—for example, intellectual ability, academic ability, extracurricular activities, and character—and that it has applicants' scores on each of these attributes (that is, it is aware of the applicants' talents). Assume, moreover, that these attributes are independent and that the college considers them all equally important. (These assumptions are made for mathematical convenience and are not critical to the following argument and conclusions.)

Suppose the college wishes to accept one third of its applicants.

If the college uses a conjunctive procedure for selection, it will accept only applicants who scored above certain cutting scores on all the attributes it considers. Let P_1 be the probability that a randomly chosen applicant scores above the cutting score on the first attribute, P_2 be the probability that he scores above the cutting score on the second attribute, and so on. The college wishes to determine cutting scores such that $P_1 \times P_2 \times P_3 \times P_4 = 1/3$. If, as we have assumed, the college considers all attributes equally important, $P_1 = P_2 = P_3 = P_4 = P$, and so $P^4 = 1/3$, or $P = .76$. Hence, the college must choose a cutting score for each attributute such that 76% of its applicants will place above this score. We shall term such a cutting score a *conjunctive cutting score,* and we shall term P $(= .76)$ the *conjunctive probability.*

If the college uses a disjunctive procedure, it will accept any applicant who scores above the cutting score on any attribute. Let p (lower case) be the probability that a randomly chosen applicant places above the cutting score on any particular attribute; we see that $(1 - p)^4$, the probability of scoring below the cutting score on all four attributes, must equal $2/3$, or p

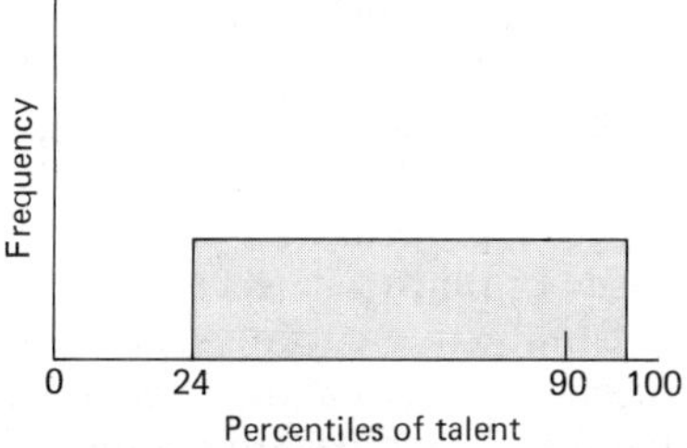

Figure 12-5. Distributions of talent resulting from a conjunctive procedure.

(the *disjunctive probability*) equals .10. Hence, the *disjunctive cutting score* for each attribute will be one such that 10% of the applicants score above it—a contrast to the conjunctive cutting score.

Consider the distributions of talents determined by each procedure. If the college uses a conjunctive procedure, then each applicant accepted will have a score above the cutting score on each attribute i. Using percentiles as units of talent, we see that an applicant selected by the conjunctive procedure will have an attribute score (that is, a talent) above the twenty-fourth percentile and that, moreover, he is equally likely to have any score lying between the twenty-fourth and one-hundredth percentiles. Hence, the distribution of each talent will be rectangular from the twenty-fourth to the one-hundredth percentile, as illustrated in Figure 12-5.

Suppose on the other hand, the college uses a disjunctive procedure. Again consider talents in terms of percentiles. A randomly chosen accepted applicant has a probability of $\frac{1}{4}$ of having been accepted for his amount of a particular attribute i—in which case he has an equal probability of lying anywhere between the ninetieth and one-hundredth percentiles. With probability $\frac{3}{4}$, he was not chosen for his amount of attribute i—in which case he has an equal probability of lying anywhere from the first percentile to the one-hundredth. The distribution of each talent will thus be the sum of a rectangular distribution from the ninetieth to the one-hundredth percentiles and a rectangular distribution from the first to the one-hundredth percentiles, as illustrated in Figure 12-6.

The proportion of overlap in the student body acceptable to *both* procedures may be calculated as follows. A randomly chosen applicant selected by the conjunctive procedure has a probability of 10/76 of having

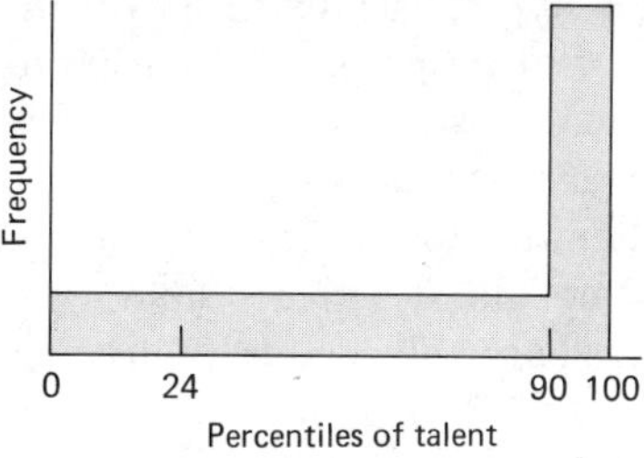

Figure 12-6. Distributions of talent resulting from a disjunctive procedure.

scored above the disjunctive cutting score on a particular attribute i (for he may be anywhere from the twenty-fourth to the one-hundredth percentile, and he scores above the disjunctive cutting score if he is above the ninetieth). Thus, the probability such an applicant would have been chosen according to the disjunctive procedure is $1 - (66/76)^4 = .44$.

A randomly chosen applicant selected by the disjunctive procedure has a score above the conjunctive cutting score on the attribute for which he was selected. His probability of having been selected by the conjunctive procedure is his probability of scoring above the conjunctive cutting score on the remaining three attributes, which is $(.76)^3 = .44$. Thus, 56% of the student body selected by each procedure would not have been selected by the other.

COMPENSATORY COMPOSITION

The most commonly used way of combining two or more attributes so that one stimulus can be ordered in respect to another is by the compensatory rule. For example, the requirement that a student have a certain grade-point *average* to graduate from college is a compensatory rule. If the student does poorly in one subject, this can be *compensated* by his doing well in another subject. No single subject (so far as the grade-point average is concerned) is specified in which he must do well; he must do well enough only in a sufficient number. As another example, when a score on a test is computed by counting the number of "right" answers, or by adding weighted answers, the compensatory rule is being followed, since getting one item right compensates for getting another wrong without regard to which items are involved.

Most models for multidimensional scaling make use of the compensatory rule somewhere in their design. Factor analysis, for example, makes use of the linear hypothesis—meaning that a score is assumed to be composed of a number of components to be added together, and the total score can be high even though one component is low if another component is sufficiently high. A measurement z_j (such as one obtained from a test) is assumed to be composed of additive parts, as indicated by the formula[2]

$$z_j = a_j z_a + b_j z_b + s_j z_{sj} + e_j z_{ej}$$

We shall explain this formula later; the point now is merely to exhibit the typical form of the linear hypothesis, which postulates a score (here z_j) to be compounded of a number of terms or components to be added together.

The compensatory composition rule is so popular, common, useful, and important that almost everyone who writes about analytic models devotes all or almost all of his attention to it. At this writing, except for the multidimensional scalogram models of Lingoes (1963, 1966c, 1967c, 1968c), the compensatory rule is the only rule within which the very powerful models

[2]Baggaley's (1964) notation.

such as nonmetric multidimensional scaling[3] and factor analysis have been developed. The remaining examples in this chapter employ the compensatory rule.

We presented brief descriptions of the conjunctive and disjunctive rules to make it clear that other rules besides the compensatory are possible—indeed, that they are being developed. We wanted to make clear, also, that the compensatory rule has its own special composition axiom and that all researchers may not be convinced that all observations in the real world conform to this axiom. One woman may feel, perhaps, that irascibility in a husband can be compensated if he has a great deal of money. Another may feel that a good husband must have both a sweet temper and a great deal of money—the conjunctive rule. Still a third may feel that either money or a sweet temper makes a man marriageable—the disjunctive rule. One reason researchers use the compensatory rule, of course, is that it is powerful in the sense that it can order any data the researcher obtains. The conjunctive and disjunctive rules leave some pairs of points incomparable because they contain no assumption (composition axiom) for reaching a decision when a pair of points is ordered one way in respect to one dimension and the other way in respect to another. The compensatory composition axiom is *strong* in the sense that it offers a rule by which any pair of points can be ordered. Factor analysis, to be described in the next section, is a model that makes use of the compensatory composition axiom; it makes use of all obtained data in reaching a multidimensional ordering of points.

12-4. Factor Analysis: A Probabilistic Model for Proximities among Points

The necessary input to a factor analysis is a matrix of intercorrelations;[4] and in most applications to date, the rows and columns of the input matrix have represented tests of some sort. Customarily, we interpret a high correlation between two tests to mean that they demand very much the same kind of ability or performance from the actors responding to them. A high correlation, in other words, indicates a high similarity between the two tests. Consequently, it is easy to interpret a matrix of intercorrelations among tests as a matrix of similarities (or proximities) among points representing the tests. This interpretation corresponds to QIIIb: stimulus-comparison proximity data.

It is true that the correlations themselves are usually obtained by beginning with tests in which a set of items is presented to a set of actors to ascertain

[3]The model (in the sense of this section) of nonmetric multidimensional scaling is not a simple or single thing; in fact, the computer programs are typically built so that the operator must exercise some points of choice in the application of the compensatory composition axiom. But this is too technical a point for this book.

[4]If the reader has not himself actually calculated a correlation coefficient, he can find a short statement of the nature of the correlation statistic in Chapter 13.

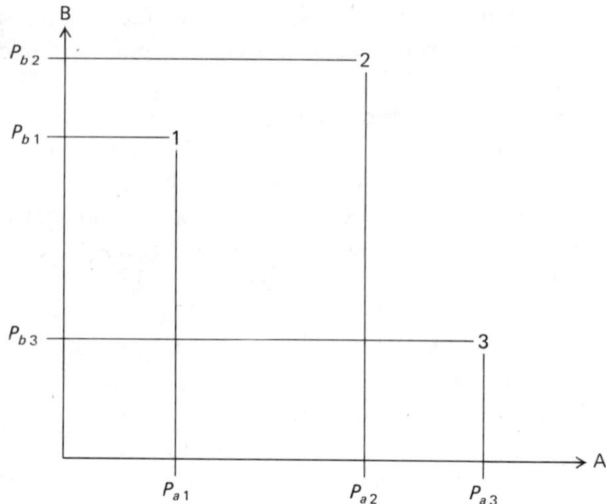

Figure 12-7.

whether the actors dominate the items, and this situation can be interpreted most easily as producing QIIa data. However, there is always more than one way to obtain the entries for the cells in a data matrix. The important point here is that factor analysis must begin with a matrix of correlations, and the factor-analytic routine cares not by what prior process the correlations were obtained. The computational procedure requires only a symmetrical matrix filled with numbers ranging between -1 and $+1$.[5] This reasoning leads us to classify factor analysis, for the purposes of this book, as a model built for nondichotomous symmetrical proximities among points; that is, for nondichotomous symmetrical QIIIb data.

The conception with which factor analysis begins is simply that of Cartesian coordinates. Every stimulus is represented by a point, and every point has a projection, or position, on every dimension or "reference vector." In two dimensions, the point i has the projections p_{ai} and p_{bi} on the dimensions A and B; in three dimensions, the point i has the projections p_{ai}, p_{bi}, and p_{ci} on dimensions A, B, and C; and so forth. Figure 12-7 shows three points (typically representing scorable stimuli such as tests) lying in a two-space[6] of dimensions A and B. The projection of point 2 on dimension A is p_{a2}. Factor-analytic models require explicit use of axes of reference vectors in the space. Factor analysis represents stimulus points (tests, for example) as vectors (that is, directed lines) and seeks a reduced set of vectors spanning a space in which the original vectors can be embedded. In factor analysis, consequently, the search for axes or reference vectors is explicit, and the choice of an efficient set of axes is a central problem. This is not so in some other models for multidimensional scaling

[5]This does not deny that the manner of obtaining the correlations will reflect the nature of the observations, consequently the patterning of the correlations, and consequently the final configuration of points yielded by the factor analysis.

[6]Short for "two-dimensional space."

such as those of Guttman and Lingoes (see, for example, Guttman, 1968), Kruskal (1964a and b), Shepard (1962), Torgerson (1965), and Young (1968). We now turn to a more detailed description of factor analysis, following Baggaley (1964).

THE MODEL

The input matrix for factor analysis is a nondichotomous, symmetrical, proximity matrix, QIIIb, containing correlation coefficients in the cells. Typically, though not always, these coefficients are correlations between tests. When the correlations are computed between tests, they rest on the assumptions necessary to obtain scores for actors on at least an interval scale. Because factor analysis is so frequently used with correlations between scores, we shall continue to speak of the rows and columns of the input matrix as representing tests; the reader should understand, however, that the rows and columns can also represent actors or occasions. See, for example, Cattell (1965), Fruchter (1954), Harman (1967), Harris (1962), Stephenson (1953), and Tucker (1960, 1962, 1965).

The original tests might or might not be highly unidimensional within themselves. Sometimes factor analysis is used with tests before they are highly refined for the express purpose of finding out how to design them so they will be unidimensional within themselves and will at the same time be relatively independent of one another.

We must now assume that the tests "overlap" to some degree; that is, we must assume that getting a high score on one test is due in at least some degree to an ability or quality that helps one to get a high score on another test. We must assume, in other words, that there are more tests in our list than there are factors that enable actors to achieve high scores on the tests. This is almost inevitably a safe assumption. (For an insightful discussion of this point in relation to intelligence testing, see Wesman, 1968). We can maximize parsimony, then, to the extent that we can find a few factors (or vectors in the space containing the tests as vectors) that, among them, represent a great many of the ways in which the actor can achieve a high score on any test included in the analysis.

We next *assume* the linear hypothesis. That is, we assume that an obtained score on a test results from components that act in an additive way, not a multiplicative way or still some other way. For simplicity, let us suppose that a test score z_j is composed only of two common factors as well as a factor elicited only by the test j and an error component. The linear hypothesis for this case has the form

$$z_j = a_j z_a + b_j z_b + s_j z_{sj} + e_j z_{ej}$$

where:

z_j is the test score in standard form,
z_a is the score (if one could know it) on factor A, such as spatial ability,

z_b is the score (if one could know it) on factor B, such as verbal ability,
z_{sj} is the score (if one could know it) on whatever is measured specifically by this test and by no other, and
z_{ej} is the contribution of error to the score.

Furthermore, the linear hypothesis *assumes* "that the common factors, the specific factors, and the error factors are independent and therefore uncorrelated with each other" (Baggaley, 1964, p. 98). The coefficients a_j, b_j, s_j, and e_j are "factor loadings" telling how much each factor or component contributes to the obtained score. These assumptions lead to the *fundamental theorem*

$$r_{jk} = a_j a_k + b_j b_k$$

That is, the correlation between any two tests is equal to the "inner product" of their common factor loadings. This theorem can be expressed similarly for any number of common factors. For four common factors, for example,

$$r_{jk} = a_j a_k + b_j b_k + c_j c_k + d_j d_k$$

Now, correlations, factors, and factor loadings can be represented by the geometry of vectors, as in Figure 12-8. A vector is a line with direction and length. We can represent a vector by an arrow, with its length drawn to some scale and the head of the arrow indicating direction. Figure 12-8 shows vectors 1 and 2. The figure shows only those components of the total score z_j due to the common factors A and B; the remainder of the score (the quantity $s_j z_{sj} + e_j z_{ej}$) is implied by the gap between the end of the vector j and the unit circle. For simplicity, only two vectors (tests) are shown in the figure. Factors A and B are represented by the reference vectors labeled A and B. The figure

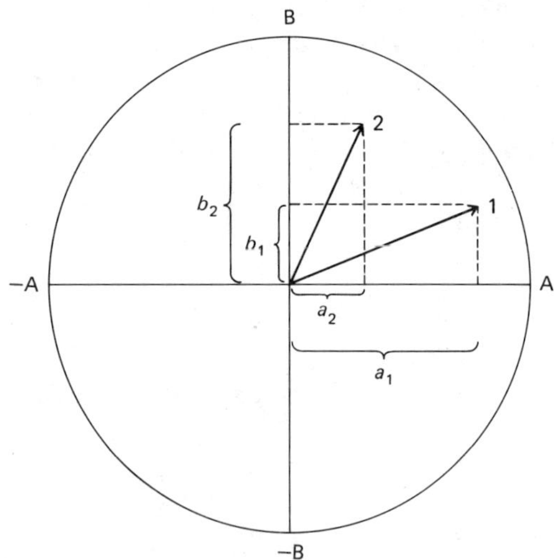

Figure 12-8. Test vectors in a two-space (reproduced from Baggaley, 1964, p. 112).

represents "normalized" scores, which means that the maximum length of any vector is 1.

If a line is drawn from the tip of vector 1 to the reference vector A in such a way that it is perpendicular (that is, at right angles) to the vector A, the distance a_1 thereby marked off on A is the *projection* of vector 1 on factor A; using factor-analytic language, a_1 is the *loading* of test 1 on factor A. Similarly, b_1 is the projection or loading of test 1 on factor B.

Using the Pythagorean theorem, we find the length of vector 1

$$h_1 = (a_1^2 + b_1^2)^{1/2}$$

and the length of vector 2 to be

$$h_2 = (a_2^2 + b_2^2)^{1/2}, \qquad \text{and so on}$$

In the language of factor analysis, h_j is called the *communality* of the test; that is, the component of the score due only to common factors. Parsimony is high when communalities are high. For dimensionalities greater than two,

$$h_j = (a_j^2 + b_j^2 + c_j^2 + \cdots + f_j^2)^{1/2}$$

Now by trigonometry,

$$r_{jk} = h_j h_k \cos \theta_{jk}$$

Thus, the correlation between two tests can be represented by a function of (1) the angle between the vectors and (2) their lengths. If we think of correlations as angles, it is easy to see how the computations of factor analysis can ascertain the number of dimensions required to contain the test vectors and the angles between them. If we have tests such that the sum of the angle θ_{12} between vectors 1 and 2 and the angle θ_{23} between vectors 2 and 3 exactly equal the angle θ_{13} between vectors 1 and 3, in brief $\theta_{12} + \theta_{23} = \theta_{13}$, then two dimensions are sufficient to represent the correlations among the three tests. However, if $\theta_{12} + \theta_{23} > \theta_{13}$, then three dimensions are required. If the angles among the vectors radiating from the origin spread those vectors farther apart than is possible in the spherical space surrounding the origin, then four dimensions are necessary; and so forth. The result of a factor analysis can be represented by drawing some reference vectors and some points determined by their loadings or projections on the reference vectors.

There are many technicalities to factor analysis. One of the more important ones is known as the *rotation* problem. Since a researcher typically begins a factor analysis without a facet structure within which to interpret the results, it is usually an important matter, unresolved before the factor analysis is begun, to find appealing ways to describe the differences and similarities among the tests that went into the analysis. This amounts to finding reference vectors that yield arrays of loadings that "make sense" to the researcher. Often the first set of factors obtained in an analysis is not a set that makes the best sense. Consequently, researchers usually *rotate* the factors first found to positions that give a more useful array of loadings. See Kaiser (1965), Fruchter (1954), and Harman (1967) for explanations and examples.

FURTHER COMPLEXITIES

It is possible, nowadays, to hire a factor analysis done. Many varieties of factor analysis are programmed for computers. It is entirely possible for the reader, after reading no more about factor analysis than is given here, to pick six dozen tests from the nearest test file, administer them to 500 actors, go to the nearest commercial or academic computer installation, purchase the processing of the data according to some available factor-analysis routine, and go home with a table of factor loadings and communalities. This would be a mistake.

Factor analysis uses a complex mathematical model, and there is a variety of submodels. There is nothing in the nature of multidimensional scaling that makes one model "better" than another. The researcher must choose a submodel according to his purposes. To make this choice effectively, he must know more about factor analysis than we have space to explain here. As a good start, we suggest an introduction such as that by Baggaley (1964). An example of a factor analysis used to test a hypothesis—a rarity in the literature—is the work by Rokeach and Fruchter (1956), which has been described concisely by Kerlinger (1964).

12-5. Deterministic Models of Dominance among Distances

"The purpose of nonmetric multidimensional scaling is to represent stimuli or individuals as a configuration of points in a space in such a way that some or all of the interpoint distances are monotonically related to measures of proximity among the stimuli or individuals" (Gleason, 1967, p. 2). In this statement, Gleason is speaking of arranging points in a geometric space in such a way that if the observed *behavioral* dissimilarity between stimuli A and B is greater than that between C and D, then the *geometric* distance (on paper, if you wish) between the corresponding points A and B will be greater than that between points C and D. We deal with data here, in other words, that compare the magnitudes of distances—QIa or QIVa.

The term *general nonmetric* has come to be widely used to signify models for dominance relations among distances. Thus, Gleason (1967) speaks of a "general model for nonmetric multidimensional scaling," and Guttman (1968) of a "general nonmetric technique . . . for a configuration of points." Work in this realm of model building has opened new views of the possibilities of multidimensional scaling and its interpretations. Lingoes (1966b) has said:

> The impact of the nonmetric breakthrough has had at least five significant consequences. First, in addition to the stimulation the computational breakthrough has had for the nonmetric formulation and reformulation of

> older and better established techniques, new methods, having no metric counterpart, have evolved. . . . Second, the movement has served as an impetus for establishing new theorems. . . . Third, it has now become possible to integrate factor analysis as a special case of a more general solution, having important implications for both order theory . . . and the perennial problem of communalities. . . . Fourth, the urgency of taking another critical look at the psychological problem of similarity (or its converse, distance) vis-à-vis its geometrical representation in the various nonmetric solutions, becomes apparent. . . . And fifth, as these methods become more widely used, an increasing need will be felt for theoretical guides and interpretive aids for both specifying the kind of solution desired and for helping us look at multidimensional spaces. This need might in part be met by, for example, Guttman's facet theory . . . , serving in some respects the function of Thurstone's concept of simple structure in linear factor analysis. This last requirement would seem to be particularly critical, since, in general, arbitrary coordinate systems are singularly uninformative psychologically. . . .

Speaking, then, of current models built for dominance relations among distances, the chief feature the model maker tries to preserve when seeking a configuration of points is the ordering of the relative similarities observed among the objects (or actors). In the model, correspondingly, emphasis is put on the relative distances among the points. In Figure 12-9, for example, we draw attention to the distance represented by the lines connecting the points (black balls) and consider the axes in the background to be there only to help the eye conceive the space; the axes are not an essential part of the conception. Correspondingly, the primary criterion of this sort of model is the monotonicity criterion we quoted earlier from Gleason; namely, that the rank order of dissimilarities among pairs of stimuli or actors should agree with the rank order of distances among the points (black balls) in the final configuration produced by the model. When interpreting the final configuration, the researcher seeks clusterings of one sort or another among the points. A rudimentary example of clustering is to be seen even in Figure 12-9; there are three "clusters" of points in the figure—one containing three points, one containing two points, and one trivial cluster containing one point.

THE GENERAL MODEL

Let us now become somewhat more precise. Using Gleason's (1967) notation for the moment, let s_{ij} represent an observed behavioral dissimilarity between two objects (stimuli or actors), i and j. Let d_{ij} represent the distance between the corresponding points in the geometric model. Given any two behavioral dissimilarities $s_{gh} < s_{ij}$, the goal of general nonmetric multidimensional scaling—or scaling using dominance on distances—is to find points x_g, x_h, x_i, and x_j such that $d_{gh} < d_{ij}$ for any objects g, h, i, or j.

Reverting now to our usual notation, consider four arbitrary points A,

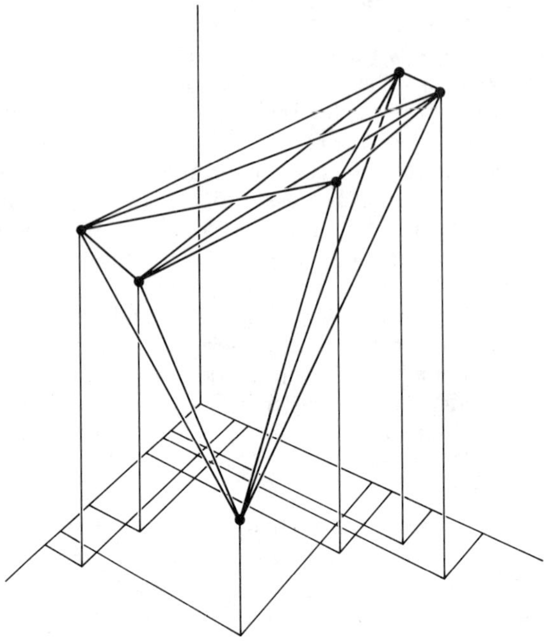

Figure 12-9.

B, C, and D and the six distances among them. Suppose that psychological proximities have been observed and the observations have been interpreted as dominances among dissimilarities, as shown in Table 12-1, in which a 1 means that the row dissimilarity is larger than the column dissimilarity. The symbols AB, AC, and the like, have the same meaning as Gleason's s_{ij}.

Table 12-1.

	AB	AC	AD	BC	BD	CD
AB	—	1	1	0	1	1
AC	0	—	1	0	0	1
AD	0	0	—	0	0	1
BC	1	1	1	—	1	1
BD	0	1	1	0	—	1
CD	0	0	0	0	0	—

Just to make sure the actors have not burdened us with a distance intransitivity, we can rearrange rows and columns in a triangular analysis of dissimilarities. Successfully achieving a triangle, as shown in Table 12-2, we can conclude that distances corresponding to the dissimilarities can be encompassed in ordinary Euclidean space.

Figure 12-10 shows a geometric figure (one of many possible) satisfying the relations specified by Table 12-2. This figure lies in two dimensions. A

Table 12-2.

	BC	AB	BD	AC	AD	CD
BC	—	1	1	1	1	1
AB	0	—	1	1	1	1
BD	0	0	—	1	1	1
AC	0	0	0	—	1	1
AD	0	0	0	0	—	1
CD	0	0	0	0	0	—

figure maintaining the same ordering of distances could be drawn in three dimensions, of course, but three or more dimensions are not necessary. Conversely, this distance ordering cannot be encompassed in one dimension, as can readily be proved. According to Table 12-2, B and C must be farther apart than any other pair of points; in one dimension, this would require that all other points fall between B and C. Table 12-2 also specifies that AC must be a longer distance than CD; that is, D must fall closer to C than does A. But AB is specified larger than BD; this means that D must fall closer to B than does A. In one dimension, however, it is impossible for D to be closer to *both* ends of a line segment than A. Therefore, the configuration implicit in Table 12-1 cannot be encompassed in one dimension.

In brief, some patterns of dominance among distances will require more dimensions than will others if we are to maintain the same ordering of distances in the solution as we found among the original observations. It is obvious, too, that we can reach a solution in fewer dimensions if we are willing to accept a goodness of fit that is less than perfect. For example, we could represent in a configuration of one dimension *most* of the relations among dissimilarities shown in Table 12-1. We usually want to maintain all the relations observed among the similarities when we construct a configuration; not to do so is to throw away or even contradict some of the information collected through observation. On the other hand, we usually seek a configuration in as few dimensions as possible. Fewer dimensions give us a configuration easier to understand; this is the direction of parsimony. Often, however, we cannot maximize both these criteria. All nonmetric multidimensional scaling models incorporate some means of exchanging one of these criteria for the other; specifying some index of fit less than perfect will reduce the dimensionality

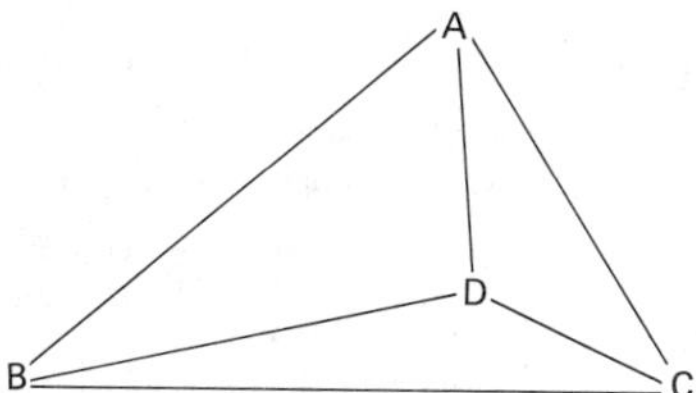

Figure 12-10.

of the final configuration. Some further features of the general model for nonmetric multidimensional scaling are described in technical language in Appendix II.

SMALLEST-SPACE ANALYSIS

Modern developments in nonmetric multidimensional scaling rest in large part upon the logic put forward by Shepard (1962). The concepts and criteria proposed by Shepard enabled others to develop a variety of computing programs that have made nonmetric multidimensional scaling feasible for use with bodies of data of many sorts.

In turn, the development of computing programs has helped to illuminate the assumptions of the models. A computer can do only what it is instructed to do and can make decisions only if the criteria for the decisions are explicitly given it. Consequently, examining the decision criteria embedded in a computer program makes very clear the assumptions on which the model rests. In other words, the program displays in a systematic way the choices the researcher is making between what he will assume he knows about the final configuration and what he will allow the model to propose in the way of a solution. The crucial choices were made clear by Shepard (1962) and have since been illuminated in papers by Shepard and Carroll (1966), Guttman (1966a and b, 1967, 1968), Lingoes (1966a and b), Gleason (1967), Young (1968), and Beals, Krantz, and Tversky (1968). At present writing, the Guttman-Lingoes series of programs for smallest-space analysis constitutes the most elaborated nonmetric multidimensional model in terms of the amount of literature available concerning its theory and practice and in terms of the varieties of computer programs available for use. To display more of the choices the researcher must make, implicitly or explicitly, when he chooses a multidimensional model with which to array his data, we shall devote the present section to a quick survey of the features of smallest-space analysis.

Smallest-space analysis falls under the heading of nonmetric multidimensional scaling. The basic rationale is very simple, and its simplicity is best seen in an example that does not require elaborate computational procedures. We shall give the flavor of smallest-space analysis with a small example of our own and one of Guttman's.

A Hand-drawn Example

Some time ago, the senior author undertook to do an opinion survey of a psychology department. The department had been carrying on long discussions of policy and eventually appointed a committee to survey opinions in the department about policy matters. The paragraphs below report one portion of the outcomes of that survey.

From the arguments that had been taking place in the department, the researcher chose four facets with which to design a questionnaire; under each facet, he specified two or more elements from which to compound items in the questionnaire. The facets and elements are listed below (these are *not* items from the questionnaire but are the "raw materials" from which the items were built, as will be explained immediately):

Facet *a*: In regard to the various fields of the curriculum (learning, perception, social, and so on),
Element 1: We should distribute our resources to get a reasonably even balance among whatever fields we have.
Element 2: We should choose a limited number of fields to receive the major part of our resources.

Facet *b*: The department should
Element 1: Stay about the size it is now.
Element 2: Grow to a limited degree as occasioned by specified goals.
Element 3: Grow freely.

Facet *c*: When hiring new people for our psychology faculty, and granting that a candidate is a desirable one,
Element 1: We should pay no higher salaries than those of our present members having comparable rank and years of experience.
Element 2: We should pay as much as our people in the next higher rank are getting (or proportionally for full professors) if it will get a commitment from the man we want.
Element 3: We should be ready to pay whatever is the persuasive amount more than others are offering who are competing with us for a man, regardless of the comparison with our own salary schedule.

Facet *d*: In encouraging one orientation or another in our department toward psychology as a discipline,
Element 1: The greater portion of our efforts should focus on the basic science aspects of psychology.
Element 2: The greater portion of our efforts should focus on the uses of psychological approaches by the nonpsychologist—on ways psychology can help with practical problems.

The investigator wrote a number of questionnaire items by selecting, for each item, one element from each of the four facets and writing an item describing a policy characterized by those four elements. For example, he wrote the following item to portray the combination of policies in element 1 of facet *a*, 1 of facet *b*, 1 of *c*, and 2 of *d:*

1112: The department should continue at least for some time at about the size it is now, replacing people who leave in such a way as to maintain good balance among salaries and among the customary fields within the department; but within this framework we should find more people who are interested in applications to the current problems of our society.

The following item was written to the specification of the elements 2 of facet *a*, 3 of *b*, 3 of *c*, and 1 of *d:*

> *2331:* Salary levels and additional faculty should be used as techniques for achieving important goals. Whatever the size of department or salary levels needed, we should pick a limited number of curricular areas in which to reach toward eminence and put our emphasis on the basic science aspects of those fields, using new people and highly attractive salary levels to move quickly in these directions.

Since there were two elements in facet *a*, three in *b*, three in *c*, and two in *d*, it would have been possible to write $2 \times 3 \times 3 \times 2 = 36$ items of this sort for the questionnaire. However, the investigator judged that 36 would be too many of this frustrating type to put before the respondents involved. Consequently, he selected 13 from the 36 in a systematic manner. The specifications (in the manner above) for the 13 items were:

1 1 1 2	2 1 2 2
1 1 2 1	2 2 2 1
1 2 1 1	2 2 3 1
1 2 1 2	2 2 3 2
1 3 2 1	2 3 2 2
1 3 2 2	2 3 3 1
2 1 2 1	

Subjects were asked to express agreement or disagreement with each of the 13 items. Correlations were then computed between pairs of faculty members over the 13 items. The correlations are shown in Table 12-3. The capital letters represent faculty members. The table shows a trend toward the pattern

Table 12-3.

	B	C	D	E	F	G	H	I	J	K	L	M	N	O	P
A	78	78	46	−23	−23	−40	−40	−40	−27	−34	−18	−23	−18	−27	−12
B		57	59	13	13	−14	−14	−51	−35	−43	−23	−30	−23	−47	−16
C			59	13	13	−14	−14	−14	−35	−43	−23	−30	−23	−47	−16
D				59	59	07	07	−24	−59	−73	−40	−51	−40	−29	−27
E					57	23	23	−14	−35	−43	−23	−30	−23	−47	−16
F						59	59	23	−35	−43	−23	−30	−23	−23	−16
G							69	69	32	22	46	23	46	30	31
H								69	51	22	46	−14	02	−20	21
I									69	54	46	23	46	20	31
J										81	74	30	49	12	50
K											54	69	54	20	37
L												27	41	27	68
M													78	47	53
N														54	68
O															37

that Louis Guttman calls a *circumplex* pattern (see section 12-6, "Circumplex"). That is, the numbers along the diagonal are generally higher than the numbers near the middle of row or column, and so are the numbers at the upper right-hand corner. In other words, the lowest numbers are usually found neither at the diagonal nor at the upper right-hand corner of the matrix. When the correlations are interpreted as proximities and translated into distances, with the higher correlations corresponding to the shorter distances and conversely, a circumplex gives an array of the actors (faculty members, in this case) that is circular. Since Table 12-3 is not a perfect circumplex, we shall not expect the faculty members to fall in a perfect circle.

The next step was to translate the correlation figures into distances on paper. The researcher drew a line and marked off correlation values along it, like this:

100 80 60 40 20 0 −20 −40 −60 −80

Scale of correlations

He then put one point of a compass at 100 and the other point at the value of the correlation he wanted to translate into a distance. In this way, he began laying off distances between faculty members, as specified by Table 12-3. However, no attempt was made to maintain all the distances exactly as they came from the scale of correlations. What the investigator did was to strive to maintain *orders* of distances. For example, if the correlation was greater between faculty members F and H than between D and K, he strove to maintain the distance D to K larger than F to H on the paper. Maintaining the monotonicity between correlations and distances on paper was possible for almost every pair of distances. The results of this kind of translation is Figure 12-11, which shows the relative distances among the 16 faculty who answered the questionnaire. We find, in this solution, that the points representing faculty

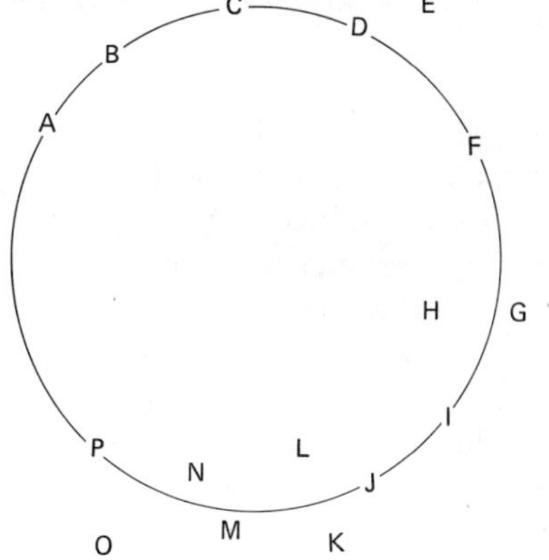

Figure 12-11. Plot of similarities (correlations) among members of a faculty concerning items of policy.

did indeed fall roughly in a circular array. (The circle drawn in Figure 12-11 has no purpose other than to persuade you that the array of points is more circular than hodgepodge.)

Although we began with four facets, we found it possible to maintain almost all the distance relations among the faculty in only two dimensions. The roughly circular arrangement of actors should be paralleled, of course, by a rotating series of response patterns characterizing the actors. To give a brief example, a typical item receiving approval in the region of person A (to the northwest in Figure 12-11) was 1111; that is, persons in the region of A expressed agreement relatively often with items containing elements labeled 1 in the listing we gave earlier. The typical item receiving approval in the region of person D was 2221; in the region of H, 2332; and in the region of N, 1322. Tabulating these patterns, and adding a hypothetical pattern (in parentheses) to typify some hypothetical actor between A and P, we have

A: 1 1 1 1
D: 2 2 2 1
H: 2 3 3 2
N: 1 3 2 2
(1 2 2 2)
A: 1 1 1 1

In each column (each column represents a facet) note that the elements rotate as one goes round the circle; in each column of digits, that is, the numbers rise and then return again to one.

In a more customary design, the investigator might have written each item to display a facet and its elements, as for example:

The department should
( ) Stay about the size it is now.
( ) Grow to a limited degree as occasioned by specified goals.
( ) Grow freely.

The respondent could have been asked to pick one alternative in each item. The investigator would have found, of course, that each alternative was chosen by an important fraction of the subjects in every one of the four items. Each item would have suggested a polarity of opinion in the faculty. Indeed, it was widely believed at the time of this research that there was a strong, polarized division of opinion about policy in the department.

This example of attitudes concerning departmental policy is one in which the several aspects of policy turn out to be not at all separate (even though orthogonal) but serve to spread the faculty in small steps round a circle. In this circle, each person differs only a very little in his views on policy from those persons near to him on the circle, but he differs a great deal from the persons across the circle from him. It is as if the faculty were sitting round a large table, each person with his friends at his elbows and his opponents sitting across from him. It is no wonder that discussions were frustrating that year, since everyone always found that he had both supporters and opponents (and this felt like a polarity); yet his supporters and opponents often changed as different facets of policy came into discussion.

The pattern of Figure 12-11 shows an opinion structure in a group that is not unidimensional, but instead circular. There are no "extremes" of attitude here in the usual sense of a two-ended polarity; there are innumerable extremes. Above all, there were not two camps. Finally, no one was equally distant from the rest or indifferent; there was no one in the middle of the "table"; no one was a neutral. By conceiving the possibility of an opinion structure beyond the unidimensional and by using a matrix of similarities, it was possible to learn about a subtle pattern of viewpoints in this department that would have been hidden by the use of more traditional methods.

Structure among Intelligence Tests

Guttman (1965a) has recently proposed a faceted definition of intelligence. The words in parentheses indicate (though not one for one) the postulated facets:

> An act of a subject is *intelligent* to the (extent) to which it is classified by a (tester) as (demonstrating) a *correct* perception of an unexhibited *logical* (aspect) of a (relation) intended by the tester, on the basis of another (exhibited) logical (aspect) of that relation that is correctly perceived by the subject (p. 26).

This definition led Guttman (1965b) to examine some previously published tabulations of intercorrelations among intelligence tests. Among these sources was the monograph by L. L. Thurstone (1938) on *Primary Mental Abilities*. Inspecting the tests used by Thurstone, Guttman hypothesized that some of the tests could be distinguished from others according to (1) the kind of performance required from the test-taker and (2) the sort of language mediating the communication between tester and test-taker. Guttman divided kind of performance into two elements: (1) analytical ability, such as deducing the rule in an analogy and (2) achievement, such as applying a presumably known rule in adding 17 and 36. He divided the testing language into three elements: (1) those items couched in words only, (2) those using mathematical or other abstract symbols, and (3) those expressing relations through pictures.

After selecting tests that he could classify according to these two facets, Guttman (1965b) subjected the intercorrelations among the tests to analysis by means of a computer program for smallest-space analysis written by James Lingoes (1965). The resulting plot of points (each point representing a test) is shown in Figure 12-12.

The figure distinguishes the tests in exactly the clusters Guttman hypothesized. The numerical, verbal, and geometric tests separate themselves into

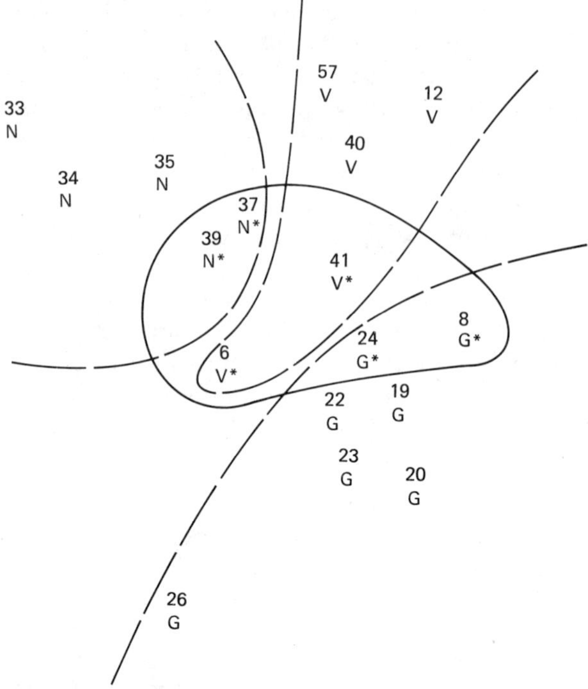

Figure 12-12. Relative similarities of analytical, achievement, numerical, verbal, and geometric tests of primary mental abilities (adapted from Guttman, 1965b, Figure 2).

three separate sectors of the space. Furthermore, the analytical tests occupy the center of the space, leaving the periphery to the achievement tests. (The lines in the figure are there only to draw the eye to the regions just mentioned. The numbers are Thurstone's labels for the tests.) Concerning this outcome, Guttman says:

> What are the basic implications of this kind of structural analysis of interrelations? First of all, . . . considering diagrams such as Figure 12-12, I think we can realize that perhaps one should not look at concepts like "numerical," "geometrical," "verbal," and so forth, as names of factors, but rather as *elements of rules for item construction*. We can give detailed instructions to item constructors on how to make up types of items we want, by using these and elements of other facets which are implied in the general definition of intelligence above. . . .
>
> A second important implication is for the problem of prediction. If there are external criteria we wish to predict—such as success in college or success on the job—having a simple map such as [Figure 12-12] enables us to deduce what the most parsimonious way may be for accomplishing this. The ideal thing would be to have a map of the set of criteria as well as of the predictors, and to see what the joint map is. The combined space will

usually be larger than that for each set alone, since the criteria and the predictors will differ usually on some facet which is constant within each set separately.

That point in the predictor space closest to a criterion in the combined space can be called the *image* of that criterion. In general, a good way of predicting a criterion is to use the tests which most closely surround its image in the predictor space. For example, if a criterion's image happens to be amidst [points 19, 20, 22, and 23 in Figure 12-12], then a good choice of a small set of predictors is the corresponding four tests . . . (1965b, pp. 35–36).

The Models for SSA and SSAR

As we have seen, the underlying logic for smallest-space analysis (as also for factor analysis) is reasonably simple. Working out an algorithm,[7] however, can become very complex. As we saw when looking at Figure 12-10, there is almost always more than one final configuration of points that can maintain, either completely or to some specified approximation, the rank ordering of distances specified in the input matrix. Since it is convenient to have an algorithm that produces one *and only one* solution when operating on a particular input matrix, the algorithm must contain within itself criteria for making choices so as to produce, in the end, one particular configuration and only one.

It is important to note that no researcher would worry through the complexities of smallest-space analysis, or factor analysis, or any other mode of analysis if he were willing to accept his data just as they appear in his data matrix. Furthermore, it is always possible to make a plot of points in a geometric space, with the configuration fitting perfectly any criteria one cares to name, if one plots the points in a space having a large enough number of dimensions. If one is considering only two points, it is always possible to locate them on a line, no matter how close together or far apart they may be. If one is dealing with three points, it is always possible to represent them on a flat, two-dimensional sheet of paper and maintain their relative distances from one another. If one is dealing with four points, one can always plot them in three-space, and so forth. In general, n points can be plotted in a space of $n - 1$ dimensions, no matter what features of the original interpoint relations one wishes to maintain. However, thinking of a space of four or five dimensions, not to speak of ten or twenty dimensions, stretches the imagination of most of us. Parsimony and communicability press us to accept less than a perfect fit if some features of the input matrix can reasonably be charged to "error" and if we can achieve a gain in simplicity of conception and interpretation by accepting some error.

Any algorithm for probabilistic multidimensional scaling must contain a process for assessing degree or goodness of fit of the solution to the original data. In smallest-space analysis, goodness of fit takes the form, roughly, of

[7] An objectively specified series of steps for moving from given information to a problem solution satisfying stated criteria is called an *algorithm*.

a rank-order agreement between the magnitudes of the dissimilarities in the input matrix and the distances among the points of the configuration produced as a solution. More exactly, the Guttman-Lingoes programs make use of a "coefficient of alienation from monotonicity" between the two rank orders.

A different sort of criterion for accepting placements of points in the solution has been proposed by Shepard and Carroll (1966); namely, a criterion of continuity or "smoothness" in the array of points. This criterion promises to be especially helpful in reducing dimensionality where reducing the dimensionality of a configuration will not seriously distort distance comparisons in local regions; an example would be unrolling a spiral-shaped array.

All algorithms for multidimensional analysis employ an iterative process of satisfying the criteria specified in the program. That is, beginning with the input data and some arbitrary levels of certain parameters, the computer computes a solution. The characteristics of this first solution (such as goodness of fit) are then compared with criterial levels; if the criteria are not met, the computer moves to specified new values of the parameters and computes a new solution. The iteration continues until the requisite criteria are met. This process requires (1) a specification for an initial trial configuration, (2) a way of specifying how the parameters should change in value for the next trial configuration, and (3) a design for the algorithm that assures that the iterated solutions will "converge"—that is, that the improvement in goodness of fit will become smaller at every new iteration and will vanish when the fit is perfect.

Algorithms often contain other features such as ways of coping with tied distance magnitudes, with empty cells in the input matrix (that is, missing data), and with inconsistent or conflicting data. Discussions of these features of an algorithm for smallest-space analysis can be found in Guttman (1968). The researcher can achieve optimum answers to his questions about his data if he becomes familiar with the choices and alterations that are available in the programs and the way they can affect the information in the final configuration.

To offer the researcher a choice of algorithms for smallest-space analysis, some offering some advantages and some others, Lingoes has written eight computer programs, four to accept a symmetrical input matrix (the SSA series) and four to accept an asymmetrical input matrix (the SSAR series). Some characteristics of these are summarized in Table 12-4.

Table 12-4 indicates similarities and differences among the SSA and SSAR programs in acceptable input, in procedure, and in output. While the programs make differing assumptions about the nature of the input data, nevertheless, every one of them proceeds by constructing a matrix of comparisons among distances corresponding to psychological dissimilarities (if the input matrix is not already in that form). Hence, we can say that the "basic" data for Guttman-Lingoes SSA and SSAR programs are those of QIa and QIVa, although the programs are built to accept other forms of data and reinterpret them as Ia and IVa.

Certain features are common to all Guttman-Lingoes smallest-space programs. For one thing, all the Guttman-Lingoes programs are constructed so that the user can instruct the computer to maximize certain criteria at the

Table 12-4. *Features of Guttman-Lingoes SSA and SSAR Programs*

	SSA				SSAR			
Features	*1*	*2*	*3*	*4*	*1*	*2*	*3*	*4*
Input matrix must be square	x	x	x	x				x
Input matrix may be rectangular					x	x	x	
Accepts symmetrical input matrix	x	x	x	x				
Accepts asymmetrical input matrix		x			x	x	x	x
Accepts off-diagonal input submatrix (that is, rows and columns represent different sets)					x	x	x	
Assumptions of QIIIb match assumptions of program about entry in cell of input matrix when entry is dichotomous; program will not violate assumptions of QIIIa	x		x	x				
Assumptions of QIVa match assumptions of program about comparisons between any two cells in input matrix when entries in cells are probabilistic	x		x	x	x			
Assumptions of QIIb match assumptions of program about entry in cell of input matrix when entry is dichotomous; program will not violate assumptions of QIIa		x			x	x	x	x
Assumptions of QIa match assumptions of program about comparisons between cells in the same row (or column) when entries in cells of input matrix are probabilistic	x					x	x	x
Interprets data as similarities or dissimilarities to be ordered	x	x			x	x	x	x
Interprets data as correlation coefficients or covariances			x	x				
Proceeds by ordering all cells of input matrix	x		x	x	x			
Proceeds by ordering cells within rows (and/or columns) only		x				x	x	x
Solves for unknown diagonal elements			x	x				x

expense of others and to carry its iterations to a point satisfying one or another criterion at a certain level. For example, the researcher can instruct the computer to produce the best possible fit within a certain maximum number of dimensions, or he can instruct the machine to produce a solution in the smallest number of dimensions that can achieve a specified goodness of fit. This is one of the choices the researcher must make when he selects a model for multidimensional scaling.

Another common feature of the Guttman-Lingoes programs is that they use the rules of Euclidean space, the distinguishing feature of which is the triangle inequality; that is, the sum of the distances from A to B and from B to C must be equal to or greater than the distance from A to C. However, the programs can be modified to accept a family of "semimetrics" (see Guttman, 1968, pp. 5–6). All programs, too, interpret tied distances so as to minimize the dimensionality of the solution, and all accommodate missing data. Finally, all programs include geometric plots of points as part of the output.

Other Models

The model for Guttman-Lingoes smallest-space analysis is not in itself a completely general model. Other models for nonmetric and nonlinear multidimensional scaling and discrimination are available both in descriptive form and in the form of computer programs. We have presented the Guttman-Lingoes programs here because they illustrate very well the problems and advantages of nonmetric multidimensional scaling, because the programs themselves are becoming widely available, and because there is a considerable body of literature describing the theory and application of these programs. In our opinion, one of the major advances in the methodology of the social sciences in recent years has been the development of methods for studying the simultaneous operation of many variables. In this thrust, the nonmetric and nonlinear multidimensional models comprise the most general and most adaptable modes. The combination of these models with facet design offers researchers an analytical tool of a power never before available.

FACETS VERSUS FACTORS

Social scientists have carried on a long controversy[8] concerning the substantive meaning that might be given to factors. We see no important profit in trying to make some sort of "thing" of a factor or even a precisely defined direction of variability that would be useful as a reference vector in a large number of behavioral domains; we think it more profitable, in most applications, to postulate modes of variability in the manner of facet design. The postulation can then be tested by the relative proximities among the specified subsets of the points in the configuration.

Humphreys (1962) recommends using factor analysis chiefly as an aid in forming hypotheses and urges the use of facet design in designing multivariate studies. In contrast to the method of factor analysis, Foa (1968) writes of facet design and nonmetric analysis as follows:

> Facet theory . . . attempts to avoid [the previously described] problems by proceeding from the definition of the set of variables to hypotheses about their structure and, from here, to empirical testing. Accordingly, this theory can be seen as made up of three interrelated parts following one another in the given order:
>
> 1. Facet design for the systematic generation of a set of variables.
> 2. Metahypotheses for the prediction of the order of interrelationship of the variables.
> 3. Empirical testing of the predicted order.

Shepard and Carroll (1966) describe an experiment by Boynton and

[8] A recent contribution to this controversy is that of Coan (1964).

Gordon (1965) in which subjects were presented with color patches; the problem was to compute a configuration among points standing for the color patches that would reproduce the ordering of similarities in the perceptions of the subjects. Shepard and Carroll say about this problem:

> The possibility . . . of achieving a reduction from the four measured variables [i.e., frequency of use of the four color-names] to just one underlying dimension depends upon the existence of strong interdependencies among the measures. Even in the original, unordered set of profiles . . . , a hint of the existence of such interdependencies could have been gleaned from the absence of whole classes of possible patterns. . . . The standard method of linear factor analysis . . . , however, is unable to take full advantage of these strong interdependencies, for they are also strongly nonlinear. An analysis of these same 23 profiles into principal components, for example, yielded three significant dimensions instead of the single one recovered . . . here (p. 569).

Perhaps by now the reader will have perceived a quality we believe we see in the comments of the authors who offer the new nonmetric and nonlinear analytic techniques. The older writings about factor analysis often seemed to suggest that "underlying" or "genotypic" vectors could be "found" in any particular domain of behavior—vectors that would reliably and repeatedly reveal themselves to investigators skilled in the factor-analytic technique. The writings on the new techniques of nonmetric analysis, on the contrary, make no promise that truth lies merely camouflaged by the show of things. Rather, the "new look" invites us to put our own construction on events. Facet design, for example, is a tool available to any designer of research, no matter how arbitrary or idiosyncratic may be his views on the reasons the events in the world cluster the way they do and no matter how unconventional may be the domain he wishes to investigate. He need not strive to reinterpret factors resulting from his analysis. He need only make sure that his facets define, to his own satisfaction, the domain in which he is interested and that the elements within each facet are exhaustive and mutually exclusive: if the points in his solution then cluster as specified in his design, he is vindicated.

Vindication in empirical test, of course, does not make the investigator's facets any more "real" than anyone else's. There is no special merit in "finding" a factor. The merit lies in choosing the facets for each domain that produce useful differences. And the generalizability of a facet becomes known as skillful theorists and researchers find ways of making use of it in new domains; we do not seek to "discover" it emerging on its own, so to speak, from random mountains of data. In brief, the view of the inventors and users of nonmetric analysis is that science makes headway when it discovers ways of specifying useful differences among events. Followers of this view (with whom we are included) do not believe that it makes sense to try to find empirical "truth." What one must do is seek useful ways of conceiving experience (including scientific observations). The world is always, until the end of time, only partially known. A theory always describes only partial aspects or views of reality; no theory can ever encompass all, and no series of theoretical statements can ever be demonstrated to approach the ultimate truth. What we can do is learn to cope more and more effectively with our environment. But this does not mean that we thereby come closer to understanding its "ultimate nature."

We have seen that the basic idea of nonmetric multidimensional scaling is simple—that the distances among the points in the solution should maintain as closely as possible the same order among themselves that existed among the corresponding psychological dissimilarities indicated by the responses. We have also seen that carrying out this criterion in practice can get complicated. As these models are put to wider use and methodologists have time to scrutinize both the outcomes of their use and the assumptions of the models themselves, further complexities will surely appear. Given such a simple basic requirement, it seems at first thought very unlikely, for example, that procedures such as those we have cited could violate any geometrical rules; yet this is just the specter that has been raised in an article by Beals, Krantz, and Tversky (1968), in which they discuss "the qualitative properties that must be satisfied if an ordering of dissimilarities is to be representable by an ordering of distances in any one of a wide variety (Euclidean, etc.) of distance geometries . . ." (p. 127). We urge the beginning researcher to seek expert help when he believes a model is suitable for his data, especially if that model requires that the data be processed by a computer.

12-6. Configurations in Proximity Space

We have mentioned that techniques of multidimensional analysis become prohibitively cumbersome when large input matrices are necessary unless a computer is available. It is true, however, that small matrices can be examined without a computer. Furthermore, much useful information can be extracted from fairly large matrices if they happen to show certain relatively simple patterns. We describe below three patterns that occur fairly often in matrices of similarity (proximity) measures; when these patterns appear they can help the investigator to uncover a large portion of the relations in the data without the help of a computer. Guttman (1954, 1957) has applied the terms *simplex*, *circumplex*, and *radex* to the three patterns.

SIMPLEX

The simplex pattern in a matrix corresponds to a set of objects having degrees of similarity and dissimilarity with one another in such a way that they can be arranged in a line and each object will be more like an object immediately beside it than like any object farther away in the line. The objects at the ends of the line will be the pair least alike. In Figure 12-13, the simplex pattern is exemplified if C is more like B and D than like A or E, and more like

A B C D E F

Figure 12-13. Objects arranged by similarities within pairs, corresponding to a simplex of similarity measures.

E than F, and if A and F are less alike than are any other pair. In a matrix corresponding to this arrangement, rows and columns can be permuted so that the similarity measures (perhaps correlations) will be highest along the diagonal and lowest in the upper-right and lower-left corners. (The matrix will be symmetrical about the diagonal.) Figure 12-14 shows the pattern of the entries of the cells in the matrix.

CIRCUMPLEX

The chart in Chapter 1 showing stages of research (Figure 1-1) and the one in Chapter 4 showing relations among eight types of research settings (Figure 4-1) both exhibit the circumplex pattern. An example of attitudes taking the circumplex pattern among members of a faculty was given in section 5 in the discussion "A Hand-drawn Example." Elsewhere, some very instructive circumplexes have been displayed by Foa (1961, 1962, 1966). In an input matrix containing a circumplex, rows and columns can be permuted so that the values in the cells are highest along the diagonal *and* at the opposite corners and lowest in some band lying between the diagonal and the corner, as shown in Figure 12-15.

RADEX

The radex is the most general of Guttman's three patterns for describing relations among points; the simplex and circumplex are special cases. A cone is the prototype shape in which the points of a radex are distributed. If points

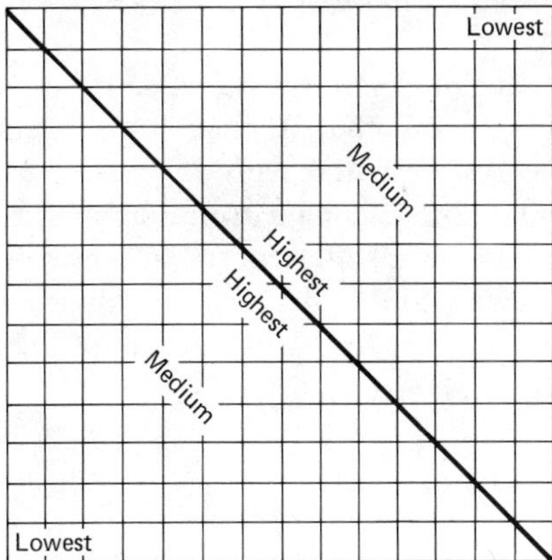

Figure 12-14. The simplex pattern in an input matrix.

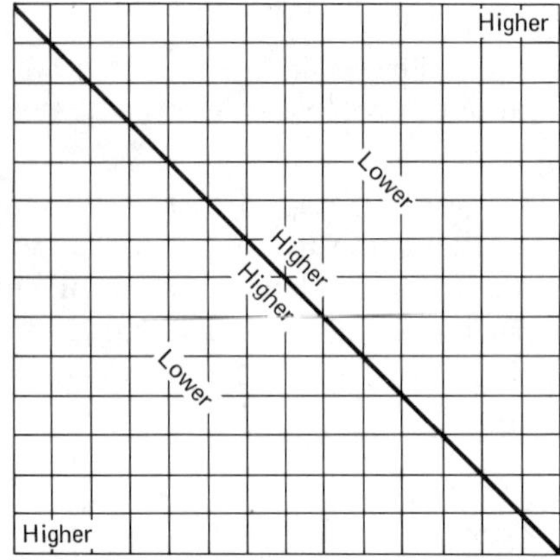

Figure 12-15. The circumplex pattern in an input matrix.

lie on the surface of a cone and the cone becomes so wide that the angle through the apex becomes 180 degrees, points are then distributed in two dimensions, with similarities radiating from a center. Such an array of points is shown in Figure 12-12. If the cone of the radex becomes so wide that it doubles back on itself, points fill the space in all directions. If the cone gets narrower and narrower until the "sides" meet, a geometric line and a simplex is formed. If a cone of points is hollow, so that points lie only on the surface of the cone, and if a cross section is taken at some distance from the apex of the cone, the points appear in a circular arrangement—a circumplex.

A full radex is not easily seen in a table of similarities. It is available to the researcher chiefly through the use of a computer program. Nevertheless, it is worth mentioning here because of its generality. Detailed discussions of the radex can be found in Guttman (1954, 1957).

12-7. Non-Cartesian Models

All the multidimensional models we have described so far have been embedded in Cartesian space—that is, they have required one distance (of whatever definition) to be compared with another, and they have depended on an explicit statement of dimensionality (number of dimensions within which distances were being computed). It is possible, however, to present data to oneself and others without referring to an explicit dimensionality. It is possible to array data in ways that aid the search for meaning in the data without resorting to a Cartesian framework.

GRAPHS

One way to treat a data matrix is simply not to treat it at all; that is, merely to present it as it stands. We do this frequently in everyday life. For example, a committee may be conferring on possible plans of action. At one point, the

Table 12-5.

	A	B	C
Joe	1	1	0
Phil	0	1	1
Al	0	0	1
Tom	1	1	1

chairman may review the discussion thus: "Joe is willing to go along with plans A and B; Phil will accept B or C; Al will accept only plan C; and Tom will go along with any of the plans." This statement is equivalent to reading off a rectangular matrix such as Table 12-5.

Of course, a matrix is not the only way to put data on paper. A graph[9] can be made to represent the data without adding any information to that contained in the matrix or subtracting any from it. In the graph, each pair of elements—such as a committee member and a plan—corresponds (in this example) to a cell in the matrix. An arrow between two elements corresponds to a 1 entry in a cell. We could use a graph to represent the statement of the chairman of the committee, as in Figure 12-16.

Probably the field that has made the most use of graphs for the presentation of data has been the field of *sociometry*. This term has been used by most writers to denote the study of interpersonal relations by means of data of the QIIIa and QIIIb types. In a data matrix for a sociometric study, the rows represent persons, the columns represent the same persons, and an entry in a cell tells whether the row person chooses the column person, dominates him, matches him, and so on. For example, we might ask six people, "Whom would you like to marry?" and we might obtain the matrix given in Table 12-6. In graphical form, this would appear as in Figure 12-17.

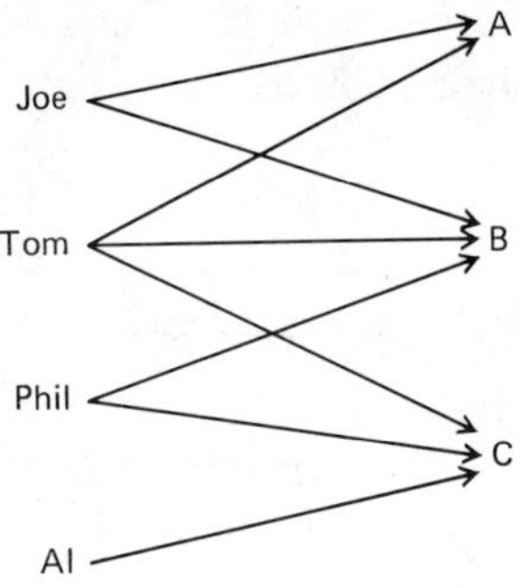

Figure 12-16.

In earlier years, analysis of sociometric data was largely limited to graphical portrayal. Frequently, an author would draw a diagram that combined information from more than one matrix. For example, an author might ask

[9]For comprehensive discussions of the use of graphs in data analysis, see Harary, Norman, and Cartwright (1965) and Flament (1963).

Table 12-6.

	MARY	JOHN	MAY	JULES	MAUD	JUDD
Mary	—	1	0	0	0	0
John	0	—	1	0	0	0
May	0	0	—	1	0	0
Jules	0	0	0	—	1	0
Maud	0	0	0	0	—	1
Judd	1	0	0	0	0	—

actors to name their first choices of a person with whom to go on a picnic, then their second and third choices, and also their first, second, and third choices of persons with whom they would not want to go to a picnic. Using solid lines for choosing positively, dashed lines for rejecting, and numbering the first, second, and third choices, we might find that a portion of the sociogram might appear as in Figure 12-18.

Clearly, whatever the number of persons being studied or the kinds of links involved, one can go on drawing sociographs of the sort illustrated in Figure 12-18 as long as one has a sheet of paper large enough. Clearly, too, the concept of dimensionality has no obvious application in such a diagram. The complexity of the relations may make for a messy diagram, but drawing one is not impossible in principle.

Free as it may be from mathematical restrictions, a diagram such as that of Figure 12-18 can become very confusing to anyone trying to find a pattern in it. Worse, the draughtsman's efforts to keep the lines reasonably distinguishable can lead the eye to miss patterns that actually exist among the relations. This kind of consideration has led researchers to seek more systematic ways, usually algebraic ways, of studying interpersonal relations. An excellent survey of early efforts to use algebraic manipulations in sociometry, along with illustrative applications, was given by Glanzer and Glaser (1959, 1961).

To recapitulate, we have pointed out that sociometric data are often intrinsically interesting, as in the case of who wants to marry whom. When numbers are small and the nature of the relation important to individuals, we often prefer our data in the raw state, unprocessed and unsummarized. When numbers multiply, however, even the liveliest of relations becomes repetitive

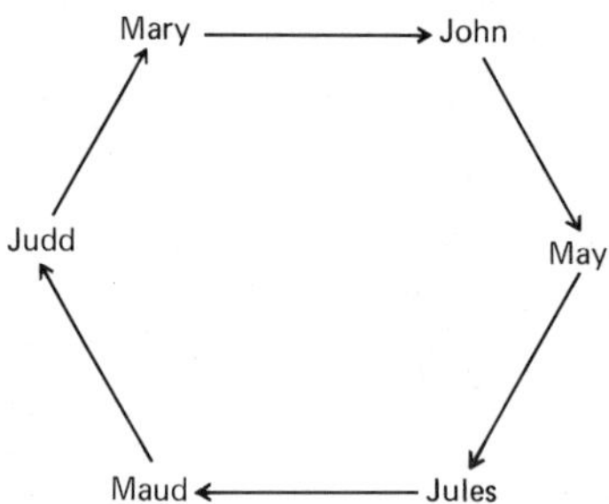

Figure 12-17.

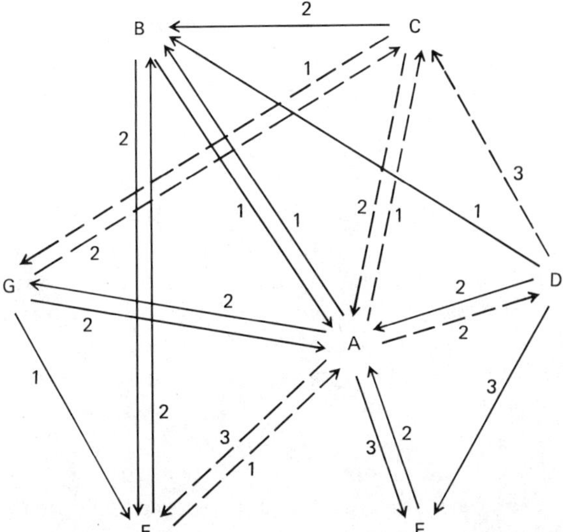

Figure 12-18.

and dull—as in the Book of Genesis (46:8–28). When the number of actors becomes large and we are interested in clusters rather than each pairing, we then seek some procedure for processing and summarizing the data.

We have exhibited some techniques in this chapter that could be used for sociometric analysis. Traditionally, researchers have used the term sociometry when they were thinking of asking persons directly about one another. In the case of the academic department described in section 12-5 in the discussion "A Hand-drawn Example," we might have asked each person, concerning each other, "Would you vote with him on policy X?" Again, an index of similarity could have been computed over a series of policies for each pair of persons. (The measure of similarity actually used was the correlation between the two individuals over policy questions.) The analysis would then proceed as before. Since any sociometric relation can be interpreted as a proximity, any model built to analyze proximities can be used with sociometric data.

We see, incidentally, that the realm of sociometry has been given rather arbitrary boundaries in the past. On the one hand, there are many ways of obtaining information about relations between persons without asking them questions directly about one another. On the other hand, there are no distinctly "sociometric methods" for analyzing data—any model will do if it deals with one set of elements (that is, actors) and the similarities or proximities among them.

CONTENT ANALYSIS

The term *content analysis* is customarily applied to the task of extracting data from natural language, obtained either in written or oral form. This kind of task often arises when the researcher is dealing with documents containing discursive prose that does not contain direct answers to questions which he might have wished to put to the subjects. Sometimes the researcher finds himself dealing with newspapers, committee minutes, or other historical records and must extract what evidences he can of the occurrence of the phenomena he seeks. At other times, he may ask the subject to tell him a story as in Murray's (1938) Thematic Apperception Test (for the use of which see also McClelland and others, 1953, and Atkinson, 1964) and may seek evidence in the story for sensitivities of which the subject may be largely unaware.

Basically, the task of content analysis consists of finding (1) units or "mentions" to count and (2) variables. As long as the researcher is satisfied with a list of classifications it is again clear that the question of dimensionality does not arise. And for many purposes, a simple list of categories will suffice. When the data become complicated, however, the same considerations arise that we have already discussed in this chapter.

Because of space limitations, we shall not explain the special problems of content analysis any further here. General treatments of the subject have been given by Berelson (1954), Cartwright (1953), McGranahan (1951), and North and others (1963).

Sometimes the researcher wishes to classify events as they occur rather than on the basis of a verbal report of them. In such a case we speak of making "direct observations," and we are faced with the problem of finding some way to record the facts that are relevant to our research, selecting from the natural, unlabeled universe. We do this by preparing, in advance, a coding scheme that will enable our coders to classify readily anything that happens—or so we hope. Since we must train our observers through language, this domain of work, too, approaches the problems of content analysis. Weick (1968) has written a recent survey of problems of direct observation.

12-8. Summary

Order in more than one dimension consists of establishing the relative proximities of each point uniquely in respect to others, though not necessarily all others. But if one point is to be considered to be "beyond" another in some sense, some arbitrary rule must be used to "compose" the dimensions of the space so as to yield the decision whether the one point is beyond the other. The composition rule most frequently used in multidimensional analytic models is the compensatory, according to which a longer distance on any dimension "compensates" for a shorter distance on any other. Factor analysis and all current versions of nonmetric multidimensional scaling employ the compensatory rule.

The most general model for multidimensional analysis is what is currently known as *general nonmetric multidimensional scaling.* This technique seeks a configuration of points in geometric space such that if the responses of actors are interpreted to put more dissimilarity between objects A and B than between objects C and D, then the distance in the solution between A and B will be greater than that between C and D, and this will be true for a maximum number of pairs of pairs of psychological objects and geometric points. A subclass of the general model, the Guttman-Lingoes smallest-space model, is a nonmetric multidimensional model relatively well represented by the amount of literature available concerning its theory and practice and by the varieties of computing programs available for use.

The computer programs built to carry out smallest-space analyses proceed by first constructing a matrix of comparisons among distances—if the input matrix is not already in that form. It is not unreasonable, therefore, to say that the "basic" data for the smallest-space analysis is of the form QIa or QIVa, though programs are available that accept other forms of data and reinterpret them as QIa or QIVa. Features of various computer programs available for smallest-space analysis are shown in Table 12-5.

Computers are not always necessary in analyzing data under the assumption of multidimensionality. Sometimes certain patterns can be discerned in the input data matrix that can simplify the analysis. We described the patterns called simplex, circumplex, and radex and pointed to examples given in various places in the book.

We also mentioned certain non-Cartesian models for analysis of data: graphs and content analysis. Graphs can be translated into matrices, but content analysis proceeds, at base, by using the logic of classes.

Finding the configuration of points in a space, when the dimensions of the space are specified and named, has some similarities of form to finding relations among variables. Chapter 13 is devoted to this latter topic.

12-9. Further Reading

For further discussion of conjunctive, disjunctive, and compensatory rules, see Coombs (1964, Chapters 9 and 12), Dawes (1964a and b), Farnsworth (1966), Gleason (1967), Gulliksen and Messick (1960), and Hyman and Well (1967). Other composition rules are being developed; see Coombs (1964, Chapters 9 and 12).

As an introduction to factor analysis, we have already suggested Baggaley (1964). For an example of a factor analysis that begins with similarities between people instead of correlations between tests, see Wright and Evitts (1961). The reader who wishes to explore the subtleties might go on to a text such as that by Harman (1967), the short treatise on computer method by Fruchter and Jennings (1962), the article on reliability by Armstrong and Soelberg (1968), and the forward-looking commentary by Kaiser (1965). For help in understanding the algebraic manipulation of matrices, see Horst (1963). For a new and more general factor-analytical model which deals with three modes (three facets: individuals, tests, and occasions) rather than only two modes and which in principle can be carried to four or more modes, see Tucker (1965).

Applications of facet design and analysis are increasing as we write. For citations to the literature, see section 2-9.

For descriptions of the SSA and SSAR computer programs, see Lingoes (1966a and b, 1968e), Lingoes and Vandenberg (1966), Guttman (1966a, 1967, 1968), and Lingoes and Guttman (1967). Although we have used the Guttman-Lingoes models in this chapter to illustrate multidimensional scaling beyond factor analysis, a number of authors have put forward other particular models; they include Richardson (1938), Klingberg (1941), Attneave (1950), Osgood and Suci (1952), Torgerson (1952, 1965), Messick (1956), Shepard (1962), Kruskal (1964a and b), Shepard and Carroll (1966), Lingoes (1966c, 1967a, b, and c, 1968a, b, c, and d), and Young (1968). Jones (1968) has contrasted this general type of analytic model with factor analysis and with *multidimensional distribution resolution,* the last being the main topic of the article.

For examples of simplexes and circumplexes in addition to those already mentioned in this chapter, see Becker and Krug (1964), Mori (1965), and Wish (1965). The last contains a very concise outline of the steps in facet design and analysis.

Types of relations that have been studied by sociometry and some discussions of method can be found in Gronlund (1959), Kerlinger (1964, Chapter 31), Lindzey and Borgatta (1954), Lindzey and Byrne (1968), Moreno (1960), and Proctor and Loomis (1951). We have mentioned the important surveys of sociometric method by Glanzer and Glaser (1959, 1961). Bereiter (1966), Coleman (1964), Rapoport (1963), and Wright and Evitts (1963) have also given important views. In addition to the papers cited by Glanzer and Glaser (1959), papers written on special technical and theoretical points include those by Beauchamp (1965), Campbell, Kruskal, and Wallace (1966), Guttman (1964), Harary (1964), Katz and Wilson (1956), Leavitt and Knight (1963), Luce, Macy, and Tagiuri (1955), Moore and Anderson (1962), Oeser and Harary (1962), Parthasarathy (1964), Runkel, Smith, and Newcomb (1957), and White (1962). An astonishingly complex use of graphic and matrix methods, partially overlapping with sociometry, has been made by Harrison White (1963) in the study of kinship.

There is some literature helpful in converting verbal discourse and documents into data. Special lists of types of content generally called background data have been compiled and discussed by Glennon, Albright, and Owens (1966) and by Owens and Henry (1966). Turning to the problems of collecting oral discourse, Bucher, Fritz, and Quarantelli (1956a and b) have discussed the special problems of recording oral conversation, transcribing it to typescript, and processing the information. A very general computer program called the General Inquirer has been developed that will process, store, find, and classify written information. It operates in any special field through a "dictionary" developed for that field, though a dictionary can often be expeditiously adapted from a neighboring field. Useful discussions of the General Inquirer have been given by Dunphy, Stone, and Smith (1965), Holsti (1964), and Stone and others (1966). Other uses of the computer relevant to this problem have been described by Hayes (1962) and Iker and Harway (1965). Problems of analyzing special areas of content have been discussed by Dressel and Mayhew (1954) and by Hackman, Jones, and McGrath (1967).

Finding a way of constructing relevant categories into which to place ideas is a central problem in content analysis and also in filing and retrieving information. Consequently, much of the literature on information retrieval is relevant to the problems of content analysis. Some obvious instances are those of DeGrazia (1965), Gurr and Panofsky (1964), and Janda (1967).

Useful writings on problems of direct observation include those of Amidon and Flanders (1963), Amidon and Hough (1967), Bales (1970), Bales and Hare (1965), Borgatta (1963), Carter (1954), Ferraby (1953), Flanders (1964, 1969), Heyns and Lippitt (1954), Heyns and Zander (1953), Leary (1957), Longabaugh (1963), Mann (1967), Medley and Mitzel (1958, 1963), Mills (1964), Sawyer and Friedell (1965), Schoggen (1964), Schutz (1958), Simon and Boyer (1967), Waxler and Mishler (1966), Weick (1968), and Wright (1960).

CHAPTER 13
Analyzing Empirical Evidence: Relations among Sets of Data

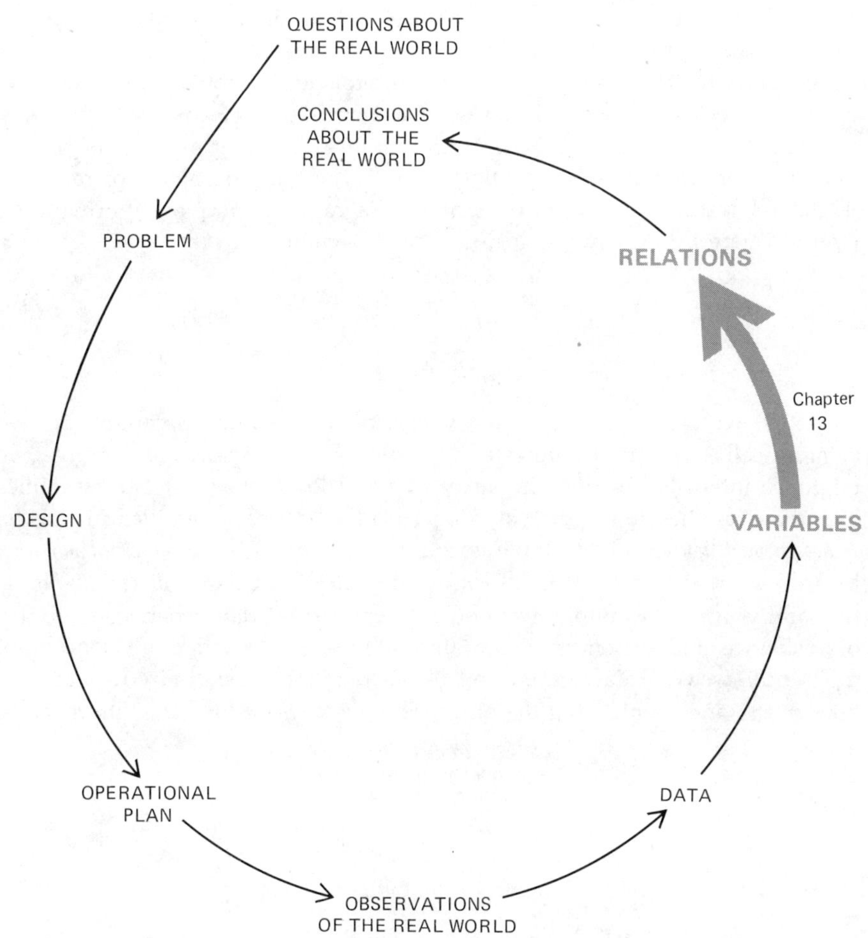

In discussing relations, we shall make use of the language of facets set forth in Chapter 2 and also the concept of partitioning described in Chapter 3. In Chapter 2, we said that facets divide a domain into mutually exclusive *cells,* each cell being labeled by a series (an *n*-tuple) of element labels, one element label drawn from each facet. A number of observable units (actors, behaviors toward objects, contexts) can be classified within each cell. Each observable unit is evaluated by some characteristic called variously the *range* or *dependent variable* or *observed partition*. We can use the language of facets and partitions to review the sorts of questions we can ask of the data—the sorts of hypotheses we can test with the data.

1. If we are interested in the range within a single cell of a conceivable domain, we say we are interested in *assessment* or *estimation*. For example, taking the amount of money spent per year on automobiles, we might be interested in that characteristic among urban families in Nigeria. Our interest might be limited to this single cell: to families, not individuals, neighborhoods, or corporations; to urban families, not rural; and to Nigeria, not any other country. We would seek our answer in terms of a distribution of amounts of money or in terms of some single statistic such as a mean or other measure of central tendency. Information about a single value is the building block for relations of all sorts; just to emphasize the point, we diagram this simplest informational assertion here by drawing a single cell with a number in it:

MEAN EXPENDITURE PER YEAR
PER NIGERIAN URBAN FAMILY
ON AUTOMOBILES

x dollars

2. If we are interested in the values of the dependent variable in two or more cells, we can be interested in a *relation*[1] or a *change*. For example, we might be interested in the amount of money spent per year for automobiles by urban families in Nigeria in comparison with urban families in France. A *design partition* in this example is country of residence; the *observed partition* is again amount of money spent for automobiles per year. A *design constant* is the family. In this example, we would ascertain the *relation* between country of residence and expenditure for automobiles. Expressed equivalently but differently, we would ascertain the *difference* between expenditure for automobiles in the one country and the other. The diagram to show the difference is:

MEAN EXPENDITURE PER YEAR
PER NIGERIAN URBAN FAMILY
ON AUTOMOBILES

France	(More dollars)
Nigeria	(Fewer dollars)

If we were to compare expenditures in two different years instead of in two different countries, we would call the comparison a *difference between years*, a *relation between time and expenditure*, or a *trend*. The corresponding diagram is:

MEAN EXPENDITURE PER YEAR
PER NIGERIAN URBAN FAMILY
ON AUTOMOBILES

Later year	(More dollars)
Earlier year	(Fewer dollars)

[1] We shall define a relation formally in Section 13-2.

The diagrams above are in a form writers (on paper and on chalkboard) often use to display numbers when they want to make comparisons among them. ("See, expenditures were larger this year than last.") This same information can be presented in another form, one favored by writers who want to emphasize the relation between different properties (such as expenditure for automobiles, country of residence, or year of expenditure) of the units being observed (families, in this case). The diagram for the difference between countries is given in Table 13-1.

Table 13-1.

	EXPENDITURE PER YEAR ON AUTOMOBILES	
	Below Median[a] Expenditure	*Above Median Expenditure*
France	(Fewer families)	(More families)
Nigeria	(More families)	(Fewer families)

[a]The median is a commonly used point at which to dichotomize, but other arbitrary points are also frequently used, depending on the hypothesis.

In Table 13-1, we entered counts of families in the cells, not dollar amounts. The amounts of expenditures show in a different way; the families, regardless of country, are partitioned according to annual expenditure. In the table, we have indicated our presumption that a greater proportion of families with the higher expenditures would be found in France than in Nigeria. This table now displays a geometric mapping of the two variables; expenditure is partitioned to the left and right and country is partitioned to the upper and lower parts. Families in France showing the greater expenditures are tallied in the northeast part of the diagram, and so on. A tabulation of this sort, in which the particular cell receiving the tally for a family is contingent upon the family's possession of one or more of the classifying properties, is called a *contingency table.* It shows an association (a primitive sort of relation) between two or more classifications (and a classification is a primitive sort of variable).

3. We might also be interested in how a *relation differs from one condition to another.* If this were our interest, we would examine the dependent variable or range within elements a_1 and a_2 of facet A under the condition of element b_1 of facet B to determine the relation between A and the dependent variable under the condition b_1; next, we would examine the dependent variable in a_1 and a_2 under the condition of b_2. We would then be able to compare the relation between A and the dependent variable under the condition b_1 with that relation under the condition b_2. In this example, at least two facets and four cells are involved; namely a_1b_1, a_2b_1, a_1b_2, and a_2b_2. In this example, if the facet B is time, then we would be comparing a relation at time 1 (that is, at b_1) with the relation at time 2 (that is, b_2); in the latter case we would say that we are studying a *change in relation.* If we were to cast information of this sort into a

contingency table, the display would have eight cells for tallies. The tally at time 1 would look like Table 13-1, and the display at time 2 would have the same form but would contain the new counts of units (families) at time 2.

In another form of this same example, four or more cells within the time facet might be involved. In such a case, we would compare the change from time 1 to time 2 with the change from time 3 to time 4; this would be a study of a *change in changes,* or in *rates of change.* As more and more cells of the facet design become involved in the comparisons that interest the researcher, more complex relations become possible. For continued discussion, see section 13-3.

We shall suggest that hypotheses about relations specify the *kind* of relation hypothesized. Before discussing this matter, however, we shall take a few paragraphs to show the connection between relations and multidimensional scaling (we discussed the latter in Chapter 12).

The relation between multidimensional scaling and the delineation of relations is intimate. It is no wonder, as researchers have come to want to understand the simultaneous relations among large numbers of variables, that they have developed various forms of multidimensional scaling as well as techniques for assessing interdependencies among clusters of many variables.[2] We demonstrate now, in a simple example (that given in the discussion "A Hand-drawn Example" in section 12-5) how multidimensional scaling and the study of relations can overlap.

In the example of section 12-5, we said that a particular 4 of the 16 faculty members subscribed to various elements of four facets of policy, as given in Table 13-2.

Table 13-2.

FACULTY MEMBERS	FACETS			
	I	*II*	*III*	*IV*
A	1	1	1	1
D	2	2	2	1
H	2	3	3	2
N	1	3	2	2

Let us pretend now, to help the argument along, that each facet was actually measured separately, as a variable, and let us examine the relations among variables I through IV. To do this, we must look to see how the remainder of the 16 actors "voted" on the variables. We recall from Figure 12-11 that the actors arranged themselves, in terms of preferences for policy, as in Figure 13-1. From Table 13-2, we note that endorsement of element 1 of variable I

[2] We have space in this book to present only some of the most general considerations in analyzing clusters of variables; see section 13-3, "Changes among Multiple Variables." For a recent and instructive example of a technique for analyzing interrelations among multiple variables, see Werts and Linn (1970) on path analysis.

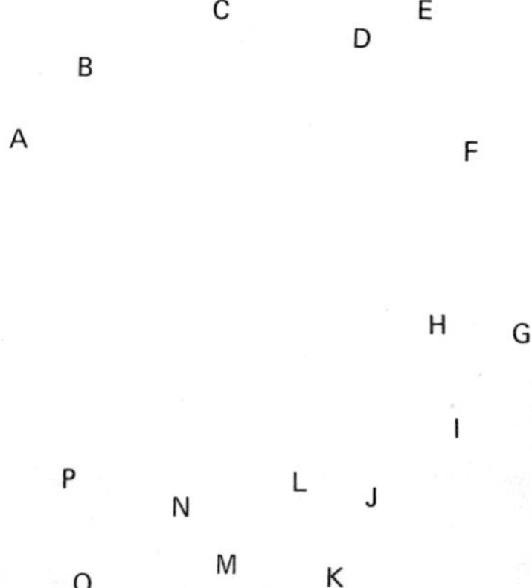

Figure 13-1. Interrelationships of 16 faculty members in terms of policies endorsed.

changes to endorsement of element 2 some place between actors A and D and back again to element 1 some place between actors H and N. Let us suppose, when we look at the questionnaires returned by the 16 actors, that we find that actors to the left of the line in Figure 13-2 are characterized by 1 on variable I and actors to the right of the line by 2. Similarly, suppose that actors choose the elements of variable II according to the sectors shown in Figure 13-3.

We can now tally the relation between variables I and II. Putting together Figures 13-2 and 13-3, we see that no faculty member endorsed element 1 of variable I at the same time as 2 of II; our tally in cell (1, 2) of the contingency table is zero. Those endorsing 1 of I along with 3 of II are actors J through P;

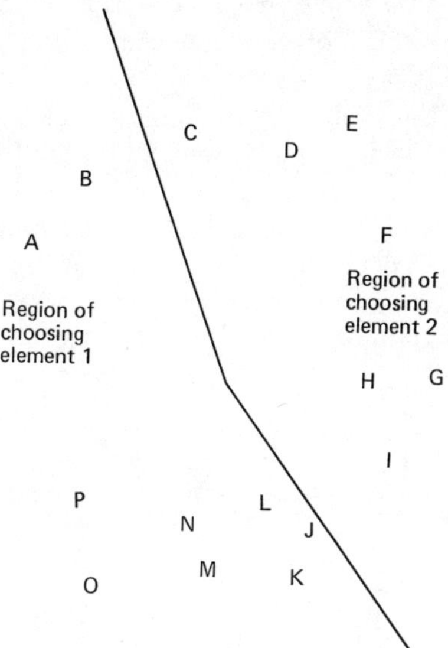

Figure 13-2. Actors choosing elements 1 and 2 on variable I.

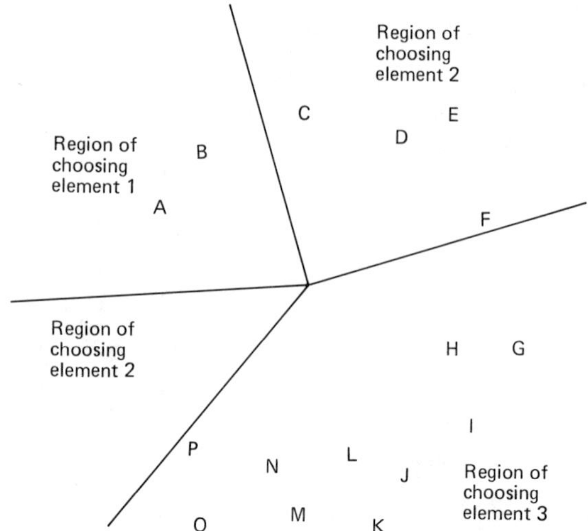

Figure 13-3. Actors choosing elements 1, 2, and 3 on variable II.

our count for cell (1, 3) is seven. Continuing in this fashion produces Table 13-3.

This table displays a relation, but so does Figure 13-1. The trouble with the figure is that it does not have the labels for variables and values. Figures 13-2 and 13-3 supply the labels, however. These two figures display all the information contained in Table 13-3 and more; they show every actor and his relation with others, while the table shows only the count of actors in six conceivable regions. On the other hand, the figures do not lay out clearly the conceivable regions—only those in which actors actually appear. The chief point here is that both the plot of nonmetric scaling and the tabulation tell us about relations.

Since we have four variables, it could require as many as four dimensions to expand Table 13-3 to show the various patterns of endorsements that are logically possible. But the plot of points for these data requires only two dimensions, substantially. This means that some possible patterns that could have been tabulated did not occur; it is possible to arrange the response patterns that did occur in a regular arrangement such as Figure 13-1 that requires fewer than four dimensions to draw. Continuing as we did in Figures 13-2 and 13-3,

Table 13-3. *Counts of Actors Endorsing Particular Elements of Variable I at the Same Time as Particular Elements of Variable II*

	II		
I	*2*	*3*	*1*
1	0	7	2
2	4	3	0

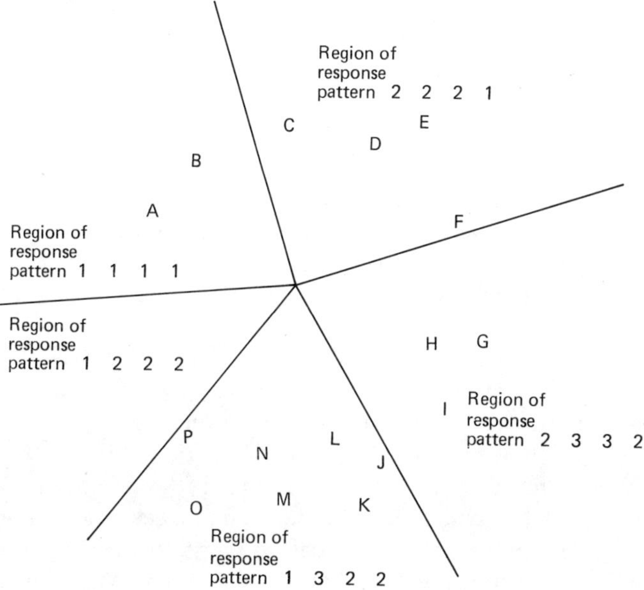

Figure 13-4. Actors choosing various combinations of elements on four variables in two dimensions.

partitioning the plot for variables III and IV, and combining the results for all four variables, we obtain merely the simple diagram of Figure 13-4. Regions corresponding to the remainder of the 13 patterns used in the study could be fitted into the same diagram.[3]

In brief, when many variables threaten to multiply to great numbers the cells that result from cross classification, researchers often turn to the analysis of dissimilarities we call multidimensional scaling. It is often found that the interrelations among the response patterns of the actors do not require a space of as many dimensions as the number of variables originally conceived. We began with four facets or variables in our example and found that the response patterns could be encompassed in two dimensions.

A contingency table can be conceived as a listing of the number of actors falling in the various regions of a proximity diagram such as Figure 13-4; the dimensions of the table, however, are not necessarily (or usually) the same as those in the diagram. The scaling model, in contrast, does not merely list the points falling in a particular region; it distinguishes and locates every point in relation to every other.

All this does not mean that the study of relations will soon be superseded by scaling techniques. We shall illustrate in this chapter many choices to be made in looking for relations that are not easily conceived within scaling models. First, however, we devote a few paragraphs to explaining that a relation is at bottom a listing of differences that go together.

[3] Though some error would result.

13-1. Knowledge Is Knowledge of Differences

We cannot know anything except in contrasts—that is, except as figure and ground; this is true of humans as researchers just as it is true of humans in any other role. If we see only a completely uniform visual field, we see nothing. If we hear a sound that continues unchanging, we soon become unaware of it. When the information we receive is not different from the information we already have, we receive no information at all. If everyone in the world likes potatoes, it is not news that the residents of Idaho like potatoes.

In formal research, we are also interested in differences. We count or estimate the number of people in a city because we know that not all cities contain the same number of inhabitants; we want to know how a particular city stands in comparison with others. When we know the base rate (perhaps the absentee rate for all wage earners in a factory) and become interested in some subgroup of the population (perhaps employees who live in a certain district of town), then we establish a design partition by comparing the subgroup with the rest of the previously known population. When we do not know the base rate, we establish a design partition by comparing one group with one or more comparison groups. We may, for example, compare the frequency of some type of behavior among high school graduates with the frequency among college graduates.

Beyond being interested in differences, we are often interested in differences among differences. Having noted that the average height of men born 60 years ago in the United States is less than the average height of men born 30 years ago, we might be interested in comparing this difference with the corresponding difference in France or Japan or Uganda. Having noted that the number of automobile accidents increases year by year, we might be interested in comparing the increases in the number of miles traveled by automobiles each year.

Comparing a rate in a subgroup to a base rate or to the rate in a comparison group is conceptually simple. As we add partitions (each new facet in the design implies a new partition) and more sequential measurements, however, the comparisons become more complex. Finding the proportion of men born to families of the middle and lower classes who remain unmarried to the age of 40 presents us with a simple comparison. But determining the proportion of men remaining unmarried when we consider not only social class origin but also the age at which each man remains unmarried, the year each reaches that age, and the region of the country each comes from is a very complex matter indeed. In the remainder of this chapter, we shall discuss some ways of conceiving relations among partitions—or, equivalently, among variables.[4]

[4] *Variable* was defined in section 12-1.

13-2. Relations and Hypotheses

In section 2-7 we put forward some types of hypotheses classified by three facets:

1. The single case versus a population
2. The characteristic versus a relation
3. One occasion versus multiple occasions.

In this section, we point to the fact that a hypothesis concerning a relation can specify one of many types of relations, and we describe some of the kinds of relations a researcher might choose to predict.

When we array data in one dimension, we have ascertained a way in which objects (or actors or contexts) are variable; we have thus ascertained and laid out *a variable*. The simplest sort of variable has only two values or categories. In such a case, it is moot whether we call the values ordered or unordered. The question needed to relate this dichotomous variable to another is simple: Does the value of an object (or actor or context) on a variable *A* have any association with the value of the object on variable *B*? Alternatively, does knowing the value of the object on variable *A* give us any information (that is, does it reduce our uncertainty) about the (probable) value of the object on variable *B*? We shall begin our discussion of relations with this simple case and will bring in further complexities as we move from case to case.

RELATIONS BETWEEN DICHOTOMOUS VARIABLES

If we can give an object only two values on a variable, we can divide all the objects into two classes accordingly; as general labels, let us call these two classes by the labels *yes* and *no*. Given two such dichotomous variables, the possible classifications into which an object can fall can be diagramed as in Table 13-4.

The relation between *A* and *B* is nonzero if knowing the *A* values of objects tells us more about their distribution in the diagram than knowing only their distribution on *B*. Suppose the base rate in *B* is 60 percent *yes* and 40 percent *no*. If this same rate in B holds for objects that are *yes* on *A* and for

Table 13-4.

		B: *No*	B: *Yes*
A	yes		
	no		

Table 13-5.

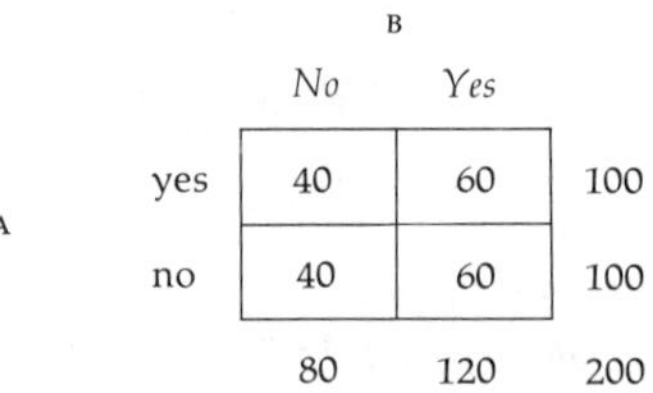

		B		
		No	*Yes*	
A	yes	40	60	100
	no	40	60	100
		80	120	200

those that are *no* on *A*, as in Table 13-5, we call this a *zero* or *null* relation. We say there is *no association* between *A* and *B*. If, however, the proportions in *B* are, say, 80–20 among *A*s that are *yes* and 40–60 among *A*s that are *no,* as in Table 13-6, then knowing the value of *A* makes a difference in the distribution we expect to find in *B*. In this case, we say there is a nonzero relation between *A* and *B*; and since the objects fall in the *yes-yes* cells or the *no-no* cells more often than in the *yes-no* or *no-yes* cells, we would be following custom to call this a *positive* relation.

There are many indexes for assessing the degree of association in the 2×2 frequency table; see Maruyama (1962) and Hays (1963, pp. 603–612). One kind of index reaches a value of one, indicating complete association, when any one cell of the table reaches zero; an example is Kendall's Q-statistic (Kendall and Stuart, 1961, pp. 538–545). If we label the cells of a 2×2 table as follows:

a	*b*
c	*d*

$$\text{then Kendall's } Q = \frac{ad - bc}{ad + bc}$$

Another sort of index reaches one, indicating complete association, only when diagonally opposite cells *both* reach zero. A well-known example is the phi coefficient (Hays, 1963, pp. 604–606):

$$\text{phi} = \frac{(ad - bc)}{[(a + b)(c + d)(a + c)(b + d)]^{1/2}}$$

Table 13-6.

		B		
		No	*Yes*	
A	yes	20	80	100
	no	60	40	100
		80	120	200

These different kinds of indexes (represented by Q and by phi) are suitable for examining different sorts of hypotheses. Suppose, for example, a researcher believes he has found a "treatment" that will reduce recidivism significantly. Among persons discharged from prison and treated by his method, then, he would want to predict a significant paucity of those returning to prison. However, he would presumably be reluctant to predict that all or most of those *not* treated by his method *would* return to prison. In brief, this researcher would expect only one cell to approach zero—the cell containing those persons treated by the researcher's method but returning subsequently to prison. He might, therefore, use Q to index the relation he finds between use of his treatment and recidivism.

On the other hand, a researcher might hypothesize that living a short distance from a movie theater would encourage people to attend it more often than more distant theaters, and conversely. The researcher could make a 2×2 table for each family and plot, for perhaps a year's time, the theaters attended by the family more often and less often and whether they were near or far. To see the extent to which distance made a difference in attendance in this sense, the researcher would want an index like phi, that would approach one only if two diagonal cells (in this case the cells for theaters far but attended more frequently and for those near but attended less frequently) *both* approached zero.

DEFINITION

A *relation* between two sets of elements is defined by mathematicians as the pairing of certain elements from one set with certain elements from the other. *Every* such list of pairs is a relation. An example is the correspondence between the number of seats in a vehicle and the number of passengers that can be accommodated in the seats. This relation is shown in Figure 13-5. In the figure, the relation consists of all those pairs of numbers—one drawn from the set of elements that makes up the variable "number accommodated" and one drawn from the set of elements that makes up the variable "number of seats"—indicated by the x's. For a concise and helpful discussion of relations, see Kerlinger (1964, Chapter 6).

Figure 13-5.

Number Accommodated						
	5					x
	4				x	x
	3			x	x	x
	2		x	x	x	x
	1	x	x	x	x	x
		1	2	3	4	5
		Number of Seats				

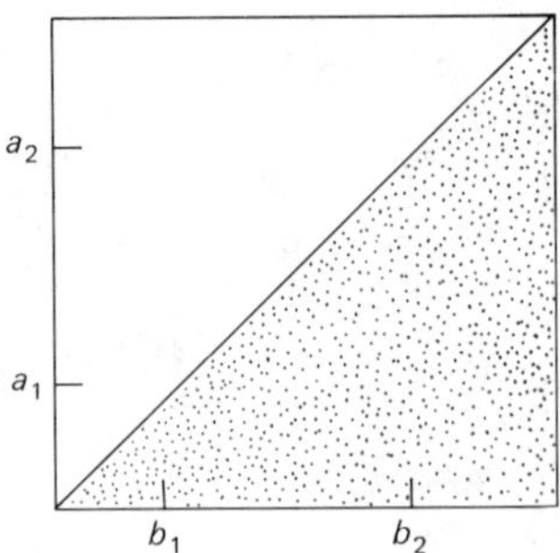

Figure 13-6.

SOME FACETS OF RELATIONS

There are several facets by which relations can be distinguished. One is whether the variables have more than two values or categories. Another is whether the relation lies among two, three, or more variables. A third is whether the points in the relation between two variables lie roughly in a triangular form, as in Figures 13-6 and 13-7, or in the form of a band, as in Figures 13-8 and 13-9. In the case of Figure 13-6, we can call the relation a *one-way implication,* since, while a low value such as b_1 must imply a low value such as a_1, the converse is not true: a low value such as a_1 implies a range very little restricted in B; the value a_1 can be associated either with low values such as b_1 or with high values such as b_2. The case of Figure 13-7 is similar. Figure 13-8 illustrates a *two-way implication;* a low value such as b_1 implies a low value such as a_1 *and the reverse.* We described the meaning of one-way and two-way implications within 2 × 2 contingency tables in the discussion of "Relations between Dichotomous Variables."

A fourth facet by which relations can be distinguished is whether the variables contain discrete values or are continuous. A fifth is whether we think of the points in the relation as approximating a curve (among which we include straight lines) or as meaningfully occupying an area. In psychophysical experiments, for example, researchers often wish to determine whether average values of perceived intensity, when plotted against values of physical energies

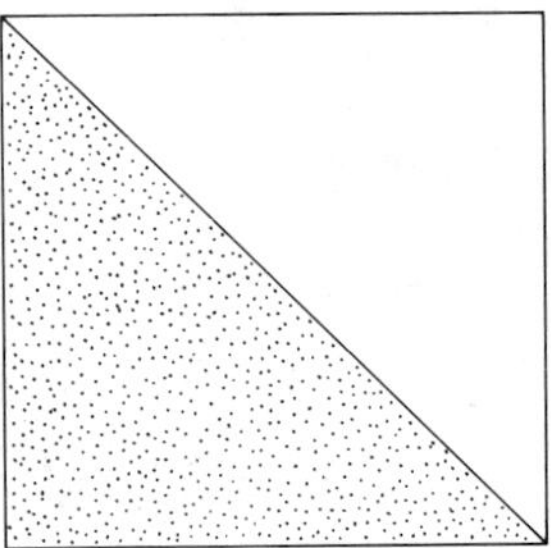

Figure 13-7.

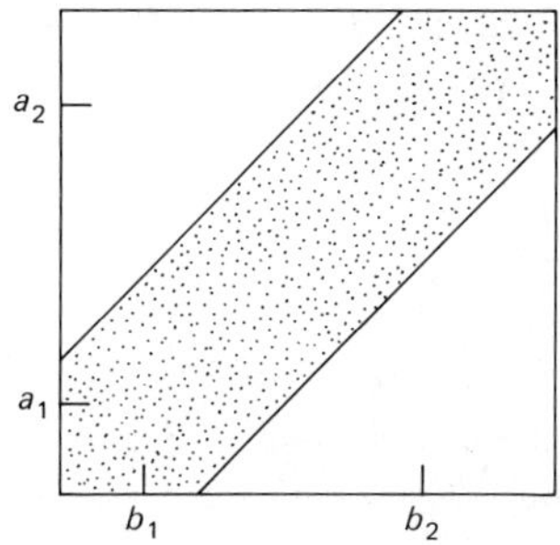

Figure 13-8.

received, will describe some simple mathematical curve. The same researchers, if studying the ranges of human ability to tell pitches, may be interested in the *spread* of frequencies subjects will accept as sounding the same as a fixed frequency; here they would be accepting the spread of points (not the central tendency) as having direct usefulness. If we think of the points *not* as approximating a curve but as having equal importance in the relation, we can divide relations into those for which a value in A can be paired with *more* than one point in B and those in which a point in A can be paired with *only* one point in B. The latter form of relation is called a *function*.

Phrasing Hypotheses

When a researcher wishes to explore how one variable is related to another, he usually has some idea of the nature of the relation. He can make his hypothesis about the relation more precise if he specifies the sort of relation he thinks most probable and the sort he thinks least probable. Sometimes the researcher's theory will not allow him to be this precise. But a hypothesis about a relation, if supported by the evidence, becomes the more powerful the more precisely the relation has been specified in advance.

Sometimes researchers phrase a hypothesis so as to predict only "a relation" between *A* and *B*. Such a prediction is meaningless, strictly speaking, since we have seen that *any* collection of points indicating pairings of elements from *A* and *B* is a relation. Even if the researcher feels able to predict only

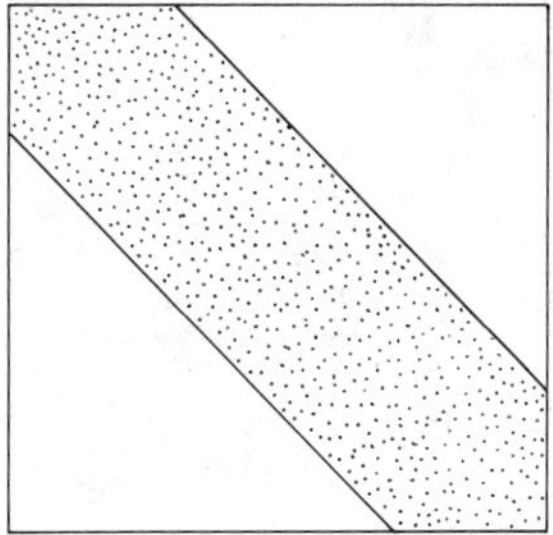

Figure 13-9.

a *nonchance* relation, the probability of the relation occurring by chance[5] cannot be computed unless the researcher specifies some specific form of relation from which the probability of chance deviations can be computed. Then again, some researchers predict only a "positive relation." This, too, is imprecise; the relations shown in Table 13-6 and Figures 13-5 and 13-8 are all positive, but the strength of the relations would be quantified by different indexes, and they would be tested against chance by different inferential statistics.

We do not say that a researcher should give up a project if he is unable to select a precise statement of the relation he wants to hypothesize. We say only that the study of a relation will gain power to the extent that the hypothesis can specify the relation precisely. Studies that break new ground must often get along with relatively inexact hypotheses; studies in fields with some history of research and theorizing can often test the more exact hypotheses.

Relations Approximating Curves

Researchers in social science use three concepts with special frequency in thinking about the shapes of relations: monotonicity, correlation, and function.

Monotonicity. One very general kind of curve is called monotonic; monotonic curves with no descending portion are called monotonically increasing; those with no ascending portion, monotonically decreasing. Figure 13-10 shows examples of monotonic curves. For a monotonic relation to be ascertainable, we must assume that the categories $a_1, a_2, \ldots$ and $b_1, b_2, \ldots$ are ordered within each variable.

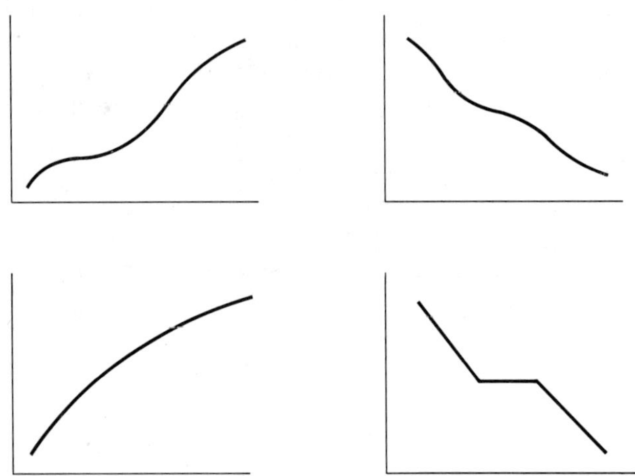

Figure 13-10.

Correlation. Figure 13-11 plots a relation between two variables, X and Y. It can be seen that the points seem to cluster upon an imaginary straight

[5]For discussion of the rival hypothesis of a chance result, see section 14-13.

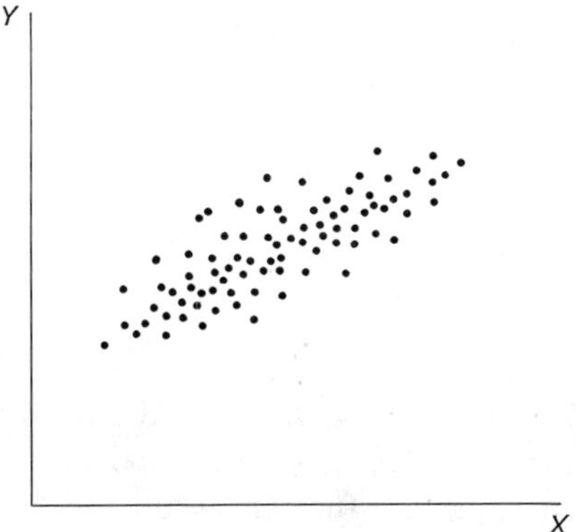

Figure 13-11.

line sloping upward from left to right. A straight-line trend is a special subclass of monotonic relation. Several indexes reflect the extent to which a cloud of points congregate and thicken about a straight line; no doubt the best-known of them is the Pearson product-moment *correlation coefficient* (see Kendall and Stuart, 1961, pp. 278–292, and Hays, 1963, pp. 490–510). The correlation coefficient requires numbers as the values of the two variables; the index is especially useful when continuous variables are assumed. A formula for *r*, the correlation coefficient, is

$$r_{XY} = \frac{N\sum_i X_iY_i - \left(\sum_i X_i\right)\left(\sum_i Y_i\right)}{\sqrt{\left[N\sum_i X_i^2 - \left(\sum_i X_i\right)^2\right]\left[N\sum_i Y_i^2 - \left(\sum_i Y_1\right)^2\right]}}$$

where N is the total number of points, X_i is a particular X value, and Y_i is a particular Y value.

The correlation coefficient r uses the *principle of least squares* in assessing the deviation of points from a straight line. (See Hays, 1963, pp. 496–498, or Kendall and Stuart, 1961, Chapter 19, among others, for an explanation of the least-squares criterion.) Another index that uses the least-squares criterion is known as the *correlation ratio* or *eta*. Unlike the Pearson coefficient, however, the eta ratio does not use a straight line as its "ideal." The eta ratio assesses only the extent to which points of any X value cluster upon one particular Y value. The line that the cloud of points may be approximating is conceived merely as a string of points, there being as many points in the line as there are different X values. A formula for eta is

$$\eta_{Y \cdot X}{}^2 = \frac{\sum_j n_j(M_{Yj} - M_Y)^2}{\sum_j \sum_i (Y_{ij} - M_Y)^2}$$

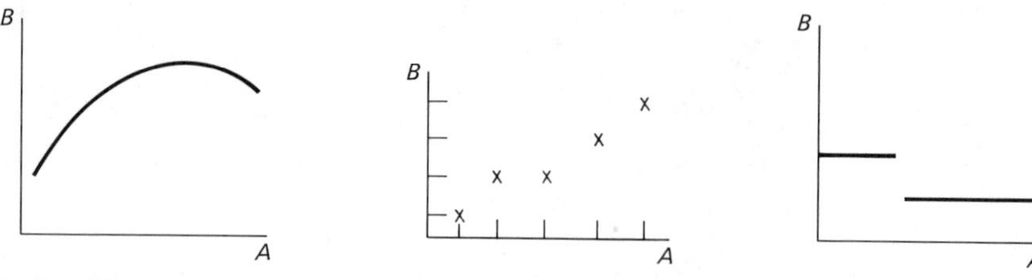

Figure 13-12.

where M_Y is the mean of all the Y values and M_{Yj} is the mean of those Y values corresponding to a particular X value, and n_j is the number of points having the particular X value. For further discussion of eta, see among others, Hays (1963, pp. 547–550) and Kendall and Stuart (1961, pp. 296–300).

Functions. Formally, a relation is a *function* if, for every value of A, there is one and only one value of B. For example, the relations in Figure 13-12 are functions, but those in Figure 13-13 are not. As empirical relations, functions occur only rarely in research in the social sciences. As aids to theorizing, however, functions can be very useful. As an example of the latter, see Ashby's (1952) use of the stepfunction.

Relations among three or more variables. The ways that three or more variables can be interrelated are very complex indeed. We hope, nevertheless, that a few brief and simple examples will encourage the reader to go on to other sources. To begin simply, we will adopt an example in which each of the three variables is dichotomous. Let us consider manufacturing companies and use as variables

A: Whether the company has only one production department or more than one
B: Whether the company employs one or more full-time counselors
C: Whether the annual loss of employees since the first employment of a full-time counselor has averaged as much as 10 percent or less than 10 percent.

Suppose we observe 200 companies and find them distributed as in Table 13-7. Among companies with only one production department, our imaginary data show a fairly strong positive relation between number of counselors and loss rate; among companies with more than one department, we see the reverse

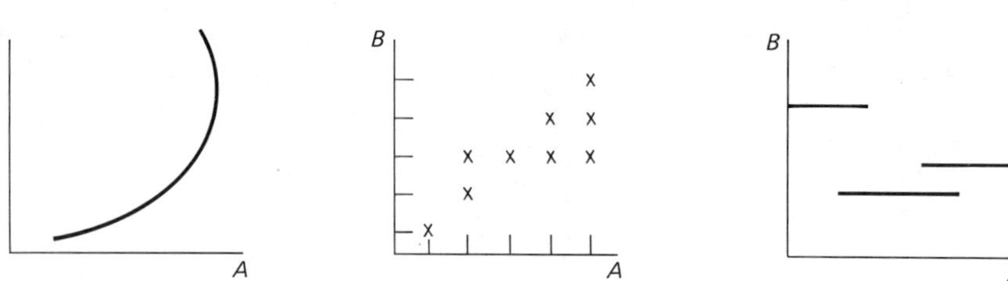

Figure 13-13.

Table 13-7.

a_1: ONE DEPARTMENT

	Loss of Employees		
Counselors	c_1: $< 10\%$	c_2: $\geq 10\%$	*Total*
b_2: ≥ 1	10	**30**	40
b_1: 0	**35**	25	60
Total	45	55	100

a_2: TWO OR MORE DEPARTMENTS

	Loss of Employees		
Counselors	c_1: $< 10\%$	c_2: $\geq 10\%$	*Total*
b_2: ≥ 1	**40**	20	60
b_1: 0	10	**30**	40
Total	50	50	100

relation.[6] If we had examined only the relation between having counselors and annual loss of employees without regard to the number of production departments in the company, we would have found only the very weak relation shown in Table 13-8. However, we see from Table 13-7 that separating the data by number of production departments uncovers a strong relation between having counselors and loss of employees.

Table 13-8.

	c_1	c_2	
b_2	50	50	100
b_1	45	55	100
	95	105	200

Contrary to Table 13-8, Table 13-7 implies that the loss of employees *is* related to having counselors, though differently among companies with one production department and those with more than one. Low losses of employees in this hypothetical example are found relatively more often in companies with one production department and no counselors *and also* in companies with two or more production departments and one or more counselors. We see in this example that one variable can make an important difference in what the researcher can discover about the relation between two other variables. The same principle can be applied with more than three variables.

Let us turn to a second example,[7] one that will carry a little further the

[6] The proportionally heavier frequencies are shown in bold type in the tables.
[7] This example is an analog of the argument given by Mandler (1959).

Table 13-9. *Hypothetical Response to Variables B and C by Three Companies in Four Contexts*

COMPANY	VARIABLE	CONTEXT			
		y_1	y_2	y_3	y_4
1	*C*	1	2	3	4
	B	4	3	2	1
2	*C*	2	3	4	5
	B	5	4	3	2
3	*C*	3	4	5	5
	B	5	5	4	3

sort of complexity exhibited in the first example. Let us again examine a hypothetical set of data for the relation between variables *B* (number of counselors) and *C* (rate of annual loss of employees). As a third variable of interest, let us look at companies operating over the years with four different chief sources of labor supply: y_1, y_2, y_3, and y_4. Let us assume no natural ordering among companies or among sources of labor supply, and let us speak of the sources of labor supply as "contexts." Suppose that variables *B* and *C* are each assessed in five ordered categories. Suppose, finally, that we obtain data as shown in Table 13-9. This table shows that Company 1 scores 1 on *C* (loss of employees) and 4 on *B* (number of counselors) when it operates with labor supply y_1; this company scores 2 on *C* and 3 on *B* when operating with y_2; and so forth.

Now let us set up a series of contingency tables, dividing the data by context. In each of the four subtables, we shall indicate by a 1 a company falling in a particular cell. This rearrangement of the data from Table 13-9 gives us Table 13-10. The table shows that the relation between *B* and *C* is everywhere positive: linear in two of the tables and monotonic in all four.

But let us not stop here. Let us now again rearrange the data from Table 13-9, this time breaking the data by company and tallying in each subtable the fall of contexts. This gives us Table 13-11.

Table 13-11 shows us that the relation between *B* and *C* is *negative* in every subtable. This outcome is opposite that of Table 13-10. What is the true nature of the relation between *B* and *C*? The question is a false one and sounds reasonable only if we forget that variables are not things. They are arbitrary aspects of things such as companies. It is the *companies* that show behavior, not the variables. Table 13-10 tells us that, *within each context,* companies are characterized by certain pairings of characteristics *B* and *C* showing positive relations. Table 13-11 tells us that, within any one company, the company is characterized by certain pairings of characteristics *B* and *C* as it moves *from context to context.* It should be no surprise that the pattern of pairings of *B* and *C* of one company over contexts can be different from the pattern of pairings of *B* and *C* for one context over companies.

Table 13-10.

CONTEXT 1

B	C: 1	2	3
5		1	1
4	1		

CONTEXT 2

B	C: 2	3	4
5			1
4		1	
3	1		

CONTEXT 3

B	C: 3	4	5
4			1
3		1	
2	1		

CONTEXT 4

B	C: 4	5
3		1
2		1
1	1	

Now let us use a third example to display three ways a relation can be discerned in contingency tables. Returning to our earlier example, but using new imaginary data, we see that Table 13-12 shows hypothetical frequencies for different rates of loss of employees in companies with and without counselors crossed with companies having one and more than one production department.

The figures in parentheses in Table 13-12 are the base rates. In this table, the base rates are separately computed in a_1 and a_2. Consider, for example, the frequency of 30 found in cell $a_1b_2c_1$: the frequency of companies having less than 10 percent loss of employees among companies with counselors and only one production department. Considering only those companies with one production department, the base rate in cell $a_1b_2c_1$ is the rate of companies with less than 10 percent loss (to wit, 55/100) applied to the number of companies with counselors (that is, 45); in brief, the rate in this cell is $45 \times 55/100 = 24.75$. The base rates for all other cells are computed similarly. For convenience to the eye, the frequencies larger than the base rates are printed in bold type. These frequencies show that, within companies with one produc-

Table 13-11.

COMPANY 1

B	C: 1	2	3	4
4	1			
3		1		
2			1	
1				1

COMPANY 2

B	C: 2	3	4	5
5	1			
4		1		
3			1	
2				1

COMPANY 3

B	C: 3	4	5
5	1	1	
4			1
3			1

Table 13-12.

a_1: ONE DEPARTMENT

	Loss of Employees		
Counselors	c_1: $<10\%$	c_2: $\geq 10\%$	*Total*
b_2: ≥ 1	**30** (24.75)	15 (20.25)	45
b_1: 0	25 (30.25)	**30** (24.75)	55
Total	55	45	100

a_2: TWO OR MORE DEPARTMENTS

	Loss of Employees		
Counselors	c_1: $<10\%$	c_2: $\geq 10\%$	*Total*
b_2: ≥ 1	**35** (32.50)	30 (32.50)	65
b_1: 0	15 (17.50)	**20** (17.50)	35
Total	50	50	100

tion department, proportionately more with counselors have low loss rates than do those without counselors; the same relation is evident among companies with two or more production departments. Notice that this way of looking at relations considers the base rates in each segment of the data separately; this is called *holding constant* the variable of number of departments while looking at the relation between other variables within each segment. The analogous technique when using correlational measures of relation is called *partial correlation*. The key idea here is that the data are partitioned according to one or more variables, leaving the relation between two remaining variables to be examined within each segment of the data. When a relation between two variables considered by themselves is weak—that is, when the frequencies are close to the base rates—holding a third variable constant often reveals the shape of relation we displayed in Table 13-7.[8]

A second kind of technique for examining relations in contingency tables consists of comparing the base rate of the dependent variable as it occurs throughout the entire body of data with the obtained rate in every possible cross category of the data. Table 13-13 shows the same data as Table 13-12 but rearranged so that the frequencies of each category of loss of employees can be easily seen within each of the four cross categories specified by number of production departments and number of counselors. Again, the base rates are shown in parentheses and the obtained frequencies that are larger than

[8] Complexities exist in determining the confidence one can put in the separateness of a relation seen in a subtable from the variable held constant. The complexities become especially subtle when one assumes that every cell can contain some actors erroneously classified there because of errors in the measures, and that this kind of error can also affect allocation of actors in the main partition (by number of departments, in this case). See Brewer, Campbell, and Crano (1970) for an explanation of these complexities.

the base rates are shown in bold type. The base rates in the top row are computed by taking 95/200 of the total frequencies in the columns. The table shows that the low rate of loss of employees (bottom row) among these hypothetical companies occurs proportionally more often among companies having counselors; number of production departments has little to do with the matter. Note that a single base rate (95/200)[9] is used for comparison in this example, while two base rates (55/100 and 50/100)[10] were used in the example of Table 13-12; correspondingly, the base rates in the two tables are somewhat different. In the earlier table, furthermore, the computations gave no information about the relation between number of departments and loss of employees; in Table 13-13, the relative loss rate can be examined within every combination of categories of the other two variables. By using this technique, the researcher can examine the way in which two or more variables, acting together, can single out the proportionally larger frequencies of a dependent variable. The analogous technique when dealing with correlational measures of relation is called *multiple correlation*.

A third technique for examining relations in contingency tables is one that uses as many base rates as there are categories in all the variables, but does not segment the data to do so. Furthermore, this technique does not designate a particular dependent variable; the base rate in each cell is computed from the total cases in every one of the categories designating that cell. The base rate for the cell $a_1b_2c_1$, for example, is computed by using the total number of cases that are a_1, the total that are b_2, and the total that are c_1. For a numerical example, see Figure 13-14; this figure shows the same data as before (but without base rates) with the eight cell frequencies arranged at the corners of a cube. As before, the cell $a_1b_1c_1$ contains an obtained frequency of 25, $a_1b_2c_1$ contains 30, and so on. The base rate for cell $a_1b_1c_1$ is computed by multiplying the number of cases that are a_1 (namely, $30 + 15 + 25 + 30 = 100$) by the

Table 13-13.

	PRODUCTION DEPARTMENTS				
	1		*≥2*		
	COUNSELORS				
LOSS OF EMPLOYEES	*0*	*≥1*	*0*	*≥1*	*Totals*
≥10%	**30** (26.125)	15 (21.375)	**20** (16.625)	30 (30.875)	95
<10%	25 (28.875)	**30** (23.625)	15 (18.375)	35 (34.125)	105
Total	55	45	35	65	200

[9] Along with its complement of 105/200.
[10] Along with their complements of 45/100 and 50/100, respectively.

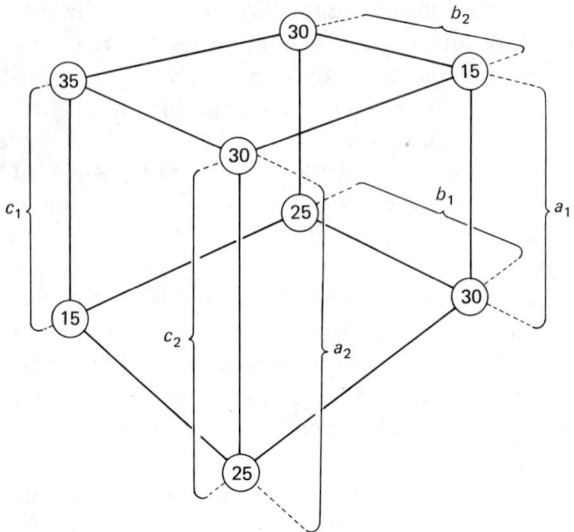

Figure 13-14.

number that are b_1 (namely, 15 + 25 + 20 + 30 = 90) by the number that are c_1 (namely, 35 + 30 + 15 + 25 = 105) and dividing by the square of the total number of cases; in brief,

$$\text{base rate for} \quad a_1b_1c_1 = \frac{(100)(90)(105)}{200^2}$$

The base rate for $a_2b_1c_2$, to take another example, is

$$\text{base rate for} \quad a_2b_1c_2 = \frac{(100)(90)(95)}{200^2}$$

and so on.

Note that each base rate is computed from a unique combination of frequencies taken each from one category of each of the three variables. The base rate in any cell can equally well be considered the number within a category of any of the variables that conforms to the rate specified by the other two variables. For example, in connection with cell $a_1b_1c_1$, the base rate for the cell can be considered to be the base rate of cases that are both a_1 and b_1; namely,

$$\frac{(100)(90)}{200}$$

multiplied by the fraction that is c_1; namely, 105/200. This gives us

$$\frac{(100)(90)}{200} \times \frac{105}{200} = 23.625$$

Equivalently, however,

$$\frac{(100)(105)}{200} \times \frac{90}{200} = \frac{(90)(105)}{200} \times \frac{100}{200} = 23.625$$

When this manner of computing base rates is used, the following cells turn out to contain larger frequencies than their respective base rates: $a_1b_1c_1$, $a_1b_1c_2$, $a_2b_2c_1$, and $a_2b_2c_2$. This set of cells is different from the set singled out by either of the two techniques we applied earlier in this section to these hypothetical data. In sum, this technique permits us to examine the way in which all three (or more) variables, acting together, single out the cells containing the proportionally larger frequencies.

We pointed out, in connection with the two techniques described earlier in this section, that there are corresponding techniques of computation using correlation coefficients called partial correlation and multiple correlation. There exists no analog in correlational computations, however, corresponding to the third technique just described.

RECAPITULATION

A hypothesis about a relation does not say much unless it specifies the *type* of relation. And relations come in many varieties: dichotomous, polychotomous, or continuous; having two, three, or more variables involved; one-way or two-way implication; approximating a curve or not; monotonic or non-monotonic; correlation; function; and others. Each type delimits the ordered pairs (or triplets, and so forth) in its own special way. Each, in its specifications, is a part of the *theory* the investigator is using. We have brushed only lightly against the domain of types of relations. Even so, a very important class of relation remains: the class containing *time* as one of the variables.

13-3. Change: Relations with Time

The "things" that social scientists study (and that this book is about) are living systems. As such, they are not forever the same; they change. Living systems are *adaptive* systems, and they change their ways of interacting with their environments—they show *morphogenesis,* to use Buckley's (1967) term. Some of these changes, if not all, are irreversible. Because change is ubiquitous in living systems, way of conceiving change and ways of charting it are important tools. We present some key concepts.

CHANGE AND UNCERTAINTY OF RESPONSE

An investigator makes an arbitrary choice when he decides whether to look at changes in one characteristic of an actor or in a complex of variables. For example, parents may chart the growth of a child by making marks on the wall showing the height of the child at various times; this information can serve many uses. However, there can be purposes for which knowledge of only this variable becomes insufficient. If the parents begin having difficulty in finding clothing that fits the child, they may examine other characteristics of the child and judge whether a revised relation between the two variables of height and weight can be established. In the end, we think it likely that the study of living systems inevitably leads to the description of complexes of variables. Upon many occasions, however, we find it useful to examine one variable at a time, such as the height of a child, gasoline consumption per mile, bushels per acre, and the like. Furthermore, thinking of changes in one variable is simpler than thinking of relations among changes in many variables.

If there is some way in which an actor can vary, the variation can occur slowly or rapidly; furthermore, the slow and rapid variations can occur simultaneously. The number of members present in a family varies diurnally as members go off to work and school and then return home again. The number also varies over the years as children are born and later leave to form their own families or die. The money acquired by a commercial firm varies in quantity from day to day, year to year, and generation to generation. An individual's blood pressure varies from systole to diastole, from activity to activity during the day, and in most cases increases with age. We often think of longer-term variations as *changes* from one state to another, but of the shorter-term variations as the unpredictable inconstancy of an uncertain world. When we are uninterested in the shorter cycles of variability or have no hypotheses about their source, we call them something like *uncertainties of response;* the point is that we want to ignore them and pay attention to the longer-term changes. But when we take an assessment at two different times and note that an actor has responded differently at two times, is the difference evidence of change, or of uncertainty of response? The problem of distinguishing between these two types of variability is an ever-present difficulty in studying change (or in studying uncertainty of response), and we shall now describe the problem in more detail.

To illustrate the mixture of change and uncertainty typically found in practice, we borrow the example used by Coleman (1964, p. 2 ff.), who in turn obtained the data from Fourt (1960). Table 13-14 shows the brands of pancake mix purchased by 987 customers at time t and at time $t + 1$. Of the 324 customers who purchased brand 1 at time t, 232 purchased brand 1 again at $t + 1$, but 55 bought brand 2 and 37 bought brand 3.

We can imagine these data to have been collected from 987 persons who had been buying pancake mix for some time before the researcher came along and continued buying it after the researcher departed. At any given time, some customers bought the same brand they had bought the previous time and some bought a different brand. If we assume that no sudden and influential event has occurred to affect the rate of changing brands, then we might feel it reasonable to take the rate of change from time t to $t + 1$ as an estimate of the rate of change from $t + 1$ to $t + 2$. Let us follow this reasoning and see

Table 13-14. *Brands of Pancake Mix Purchased at Time t and at Time t + 1*

PURCHASE AT TIME t	PURCHASE AT $t+1$			
	1	*2*	*3*	
1	232	55	37	324
2	50	213	59	322
3	32	56	253	341
Total	314	324	349	987

Adapted from Coleman (1964), p. 2.

what prediction this method would give us of the changes from t to $t + 2$; we shall later compare the estimates with actual data from Fourt (1960).

We proceed by using the data of Table 13-14 to provide estimates. The rate of transition from brand 1 to brand 2 is 55 from among 324, or 55/324; the rate of those choosing brand 2 who continue to choose brand 2 is 213/322; the rate from brand 2 to brand 3 is 59/322; and so forth. To construct a prediction matrix for changes from time t to time $t + 2$, we apply these transition rates to the appropriate frequencies. As an example of the arithmetic, let us compute the predicted frequency with which persons buying brand 1 at time t will buy brand 2 at time $t + 2$.

The persons buying brand 1 at time t and brand 2 at time $t + 2$ will be those who go from brand 1 at time t to brand 1 again at $t + 1$ and then to brand 2 at $t + 2$, also those who go from brand 1 to brand 2 and then again choose brand 2, and finally those who go from brand 1 to brand 3 and then to brand 2. Since Table 13-14 gives us the frequencies at time $t + 1$, we need only carry the computation from $t + 1$ to $t + 2$. Of those customers who chose brand 1 at time t, we are predicting that the 232 who again chose brand 1 at $t + 1$ will now change to brand 2 at the rate of 55/324; multiplying 232 by 55/324 gives 39.4 as the estimated number of persons going from brand 1 to 1 and thence to 2. The 55 customers who went from brand 1 to brand 2 at time $t + 1$ are predicted to remain with brand 2 at the rate of 213/322; this gives 36.4 as the number predicted to go from brand 1 to 2 to 2. And the number predicted to go from brand 1 to 3 to 2 is 37 multiplied by 56/341, or 6.1. Adding these three subgroups (39.4 + 36.4 + 6.1) and rounding off to the integer, we obtain 82 as the predicted number of those choosing brand 1 at time t who will be found choosing brand 2 at time $t + 2$. Proceeding in this manner yields Table 13-15, showing the entire set of predictions.

In the computations above, we have assumed that choices were *changing;* that is, that the proportion of the 987 customers choosing brand 1 would differ from time to time, and we made no allowance for the random variability of the uncertainty of response. If we were to go to the opposite extreme and assume that all the variability in Table 13-15 were only uncertainty of response,

Table 13-15. *Purchases of Brands of Pancake Mix Predicted from Time t to Time t + 2*

PURCHASE AT TIME t	PURCHASE AT $t + 2$			
	1	2	3	
1	178	82	64	324
2	74	159	89	322
3	55	84	202	341
Total	307	325	355	987

Adapted from Coleman (1964), p. 4.

we would then predict that the proportions choosing each brand would stay the same from time to time. We would interpret the differing marginal totals in Table 13-14 from time t to $t + 1$ as random fluctuations from a stable trend. Our prediction from time t to $t + 2$ would be merely a replication of Table 13-14 with the one proviso that while the diagonal frequencies would stay as they are, the other frequencies would take on symmetrical values.

We now have two estimates of purchases at time $t + 2$; Table 13-15 gives an estimate if we interpret the data of Table 13-14 as entirely due to change, and a symmetrical and stable version of Table 13-14 gives an estimate if we interpret the data as due entirely to uncertainty. Let us now compare those estimates with the actual data given by Fourt and shown in Table 13-16.

Clearly, the outcome in Table 13-16 falls between our two predictions. Using the main diagonal as a convenient basis for comparison, we find that the prediction assuming change with no uncertainty (Table 13-15) gave us values 178, 159, and 202; the prediction assuming uncertainty with no change gave us 232, 213, and 253; the actual values were 218, 186, and 252. The actual values fall between the two estimates; obviously, the most straightforward conclusion is that the actual values are due partly to change and partly to uncertainty.

Table 13-16. *Actual Purchases of Brands of Pancake Mix at Time t and at Time t + 2*

PURCHASE AT TIME t	PURCHASE AT $t + 2$			
	1	2	3	
1	218	65	41	324
2	67	186	69	322
3	33	56	252	341
Total	318	307	362	987

Adapted from Coleman (1964), p. 5.

In studying data of this sort, it is obviously impossible to separate the effects of uncertainty from the effects of change if one has no more information than that provided by measurements taken on a single group at only two times, such as is displayed in Table 13-14. Coleman reviews various methods of separating the estimates and proposes a technique that makes use of measurements at three times. The technicalities of this method would take too much space to present here; we suggest the interested reader turn to Coleman's (1964, Chapters 2 and 3) own exposition.

Beyond Coleman's technique, there are other ways of separating uncertainty from change. A time-honored method is to try to *cause* one group of actors to change while leaving another group uninfluenced. Such a partition of actors (see Chapter 3) enables the variability *within* the groups (not differentially subjected to influence) to serve as an estimate of uncertainty while the mean difference *between* the groups serves as an estimate of change. We shall return to some further considerations connected with this strategy later in this chapter.

INFERRING CAUSE OF CHANGE IN ONE VARIABLE

We return in this section to the frame of thought we used in Chapter 3, where we discussed partitions, control groups, and the like. In section 3-1, we discussed a number of difficulties in concluding that a treatment X, coming before an observation O, causes the level or manifestation of the property observed. We reviewed many experimental designs that could help rule out alternative hypotheses. As an example with which to discuss change and response uncertainty, we recall here the pretest-posttest control group design:

$$R\begin{cases} O_1 \; X \; O_2 \\ O_3 \quad\;\; O_4 \end{cases}$$

In this design, if a change is observed when one compares O_1 and O_2, but not when one compares O_3 and O_4, one explanation is that X caused the difference between O_1 and O_2—or at least was an essential part of the cause. Here we think of the difference between O_1 and O_2 as change, not uncertainty, because we observe a number of actors in the group symbolized by the top row in the diagram and a number also in the control group symbolized by the bottom row in the diagram. If there is variability within O_1 and O_2, we can compare that variability both to the mean difference between O_1 and O_2 and also to the variability within O_3 and O_4. The comparison of the variability within groups to the average difference between groups gives us a basis for deciding whether the amount of change between O_1 and O_2 is significant.

But there is another scheme for assessing the reliability of a change: this is the interrupted time series. In our discussion of the time series, we follow Campbell and Stanley (1963). The time series design can be diagramed:

$$O_1O_2O_3O_4 \quad X \quad O_5O_6O_7O_8$$

This design is typical of much work in engineering but is fairly rare in the social sciences. One reason may be the expense of making more than two observations. Another may be the loss of actors during the time series; that is, mortality. Still another may be the difficulty of obtaining scales to which numbers can meaningfully be applied, making it impossible to be sure of the slopes of the graphs in a figure such as Figure 13-15.

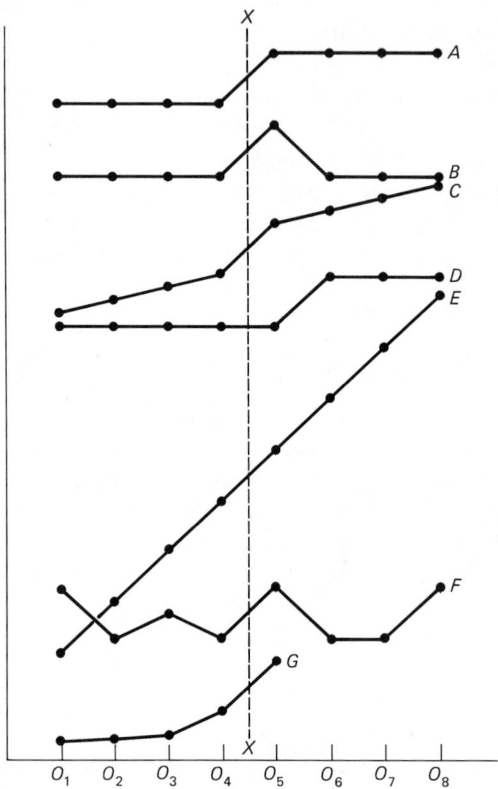

Figure 13-15. Some possible outcome patterns from the introduction of an experimental variable at point *X* into a time series of measurements, O_1–O_8. (Except for *D*, the O_4–O_5 gain is the same for all time series, while the legitimacy of inferring an effect varies widely, being strongest in *A* and *B*, and totally unjustified in *E*, *F*, and *G*.) Reproduced from Campbell and Stanley (1963, p. 38).

The figure makes the logic obvious. We can have reasonable confidence that treatment X had a causal effect on the series *A* and *B*, some confidence in the cases of C and *D*, and no confidence in the cases of *E*, *F*, and G. Where a discontinuity occurred following X and the discontinuity was greater in size than the ordinary irregularities in the series (as is *not* the case in series *F*), then we conclude that the abrupt change stands out in contrast to the rest of the series and that the immediate proximity of X is no coincidence. This design can serve well in many natural situations where a control group is not feasible. Of course, when a comparable control group is not available, special caution must be taken in the over-all design that events close to treatment X in time are not causing the discontinuity instead of the treatment X. The following techniques can help rule out alternative explanations. (1) Design the treatment X to occur abruptly at a localizable moment or date in order to distinguish the effect from that of some secular trend. (2) Introduce treatment X when the dependent variable is reasonably stable. (3) Continue observing until some stable level or trend is reached, especially if the dependent variable is subject to cycles.

CHANGES AMONG MULTIPLE VARIABLES

Under the topic of change, we have so far spoken of change in one variable. But change usually affects clusters of variables. More accurately, change affects actors or objects (that is, living systems and the objects with which they interact), and actors and objects can be characterized in numerous ways. As the aspects of actors or objects change, there can occur various kinds of patterns among the changes of properties. We make these matters more explicit in the next section.

Some Facets of Change

To begin, we can look at change in one variable or change in multiple variables. Nested within this facet (one versus more than one variable), however, are other facets.

Changes can occur within one variable in several ways. Most simply, changes can occur uniformly, or linearly, as in Figure 13-16. A way of characterizing this sort of trend is to say that the *rate of change* in any shorter interval such as from *a* to *b* is the same as in any longer interval such as from *a* to *c*.

Change in a variable can also be *monotonically changing*, as in Figure 13-17. In this illustration, the rate of change over the shorter interval from time *a* to time *b* is represented by the slope of the line *AB*, while the rate of change

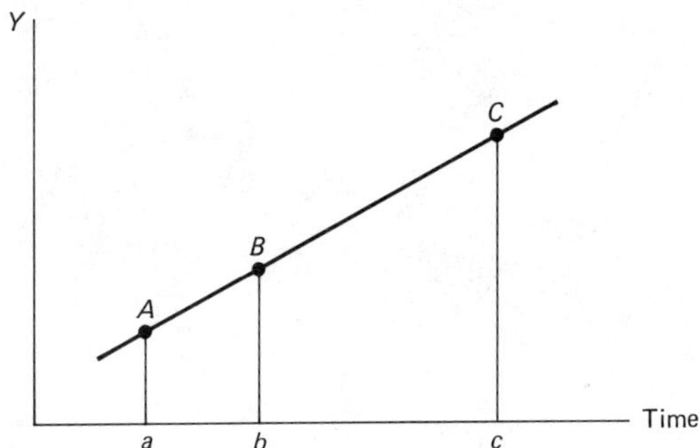

Figure 13-16. A uniform trend.

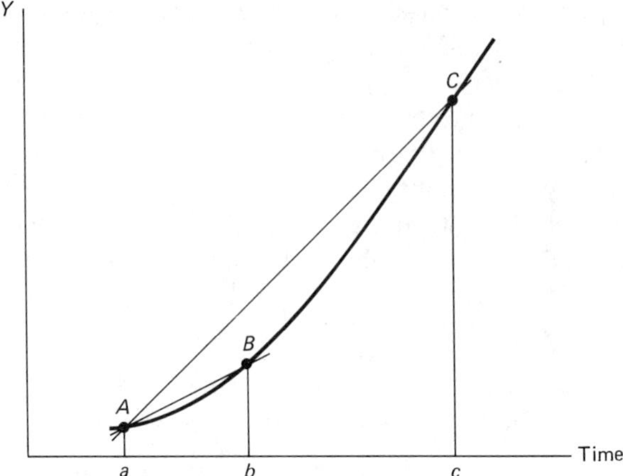

Figure 13-17. A monotonically increasing trend.

over the longer interval from *a* to *c* is the slope of *AC*. In the case of a monotonically increasing trend, the rate of change during a shorter interval is always less than or equal to the rate of change in a longer interval; in a monotonically decreasing trend, the rate in the shorter interval is always greater than or equal to the rate in the longer interval.

Change in a variable can be *nonmonotonically changing,* as in Figure 13-18. Here a rate of change in a shorter interval can be different from the rate of change in a longer interval, as in the comparison of change during the interval *a* to *b* with the change during the interval *a* to *d*. The rate of change in the shorter interval can be either smaller or greater than the rate in the longer interval, as in the comparison of the slope from *A* to *C* with that from *A* to *D*. This kind of trend typifies short-term variability overlying a secular trend.

This facet, comprising three elements differing in the way the change in a shorter interval compares with that in a longer interval, is one way of classifying type of change in one variable. Depending on whether the researcher predicts one type of change or another, he will design differently the timing of observations. Other things being equal, the uniform trend will require

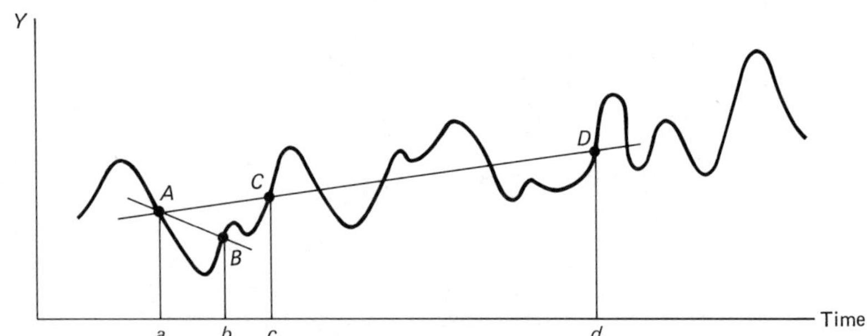

Figure 13-18. A nonmonotonic trend.

observations at the fewest points in time, and the nonmonotonic trend will require observations at the most points.

Changes among multiple variables can also occur in several patterns. We shall distinguish three, borrowing the conceptions of Foa (1968). First, there can be a change in the *central tendencies* of the cluster of dependent variables, and we can compare the amount of change in one variable with the amount of change in another. Usually, one variable changes the most, with a declining spread of effect among the other variables. Second, the *degree of relation* among the variables can generally increase or decrease, while the relative relations among the relations remain the same. The first pattern of change lies merely in a difference of value or level from one time to another. The second pattern lies in a difference of differences: since a relation is a correspondence between differences in one variable with differences in another, a change in degree of relation is a change in the reliability with which a difference in one variable corresponds to a difference in another. In this sort of pattern of change, however, the differences *among the new relations* remain relatively about the same as they had been among the old. As changes become more complex, they involve more complex differences among differences.

Third, the *order of the variables*—in the sense of simplex, circumplex, and radex (see section 12-6)—can change. In this case, we look at the ordering of differences among the relations among variables.

Change in Central Tendencies

Foa (1968) illustrates a pattern of change in central tendencies with ratings on the performance of 32 groups performing tasks of construction. In 16 of these groups, an American leader had been trained in the norms of interpersonal relations among the Thai. The American leaders of the other 16 groups had been trained in the geography of Thailand. Each group contained three members: a Thai, another Far Eastern member, and the American leader. After carrying out the construction, each team was rated on five scales (sets of items) by four persons: the three team members and an independent Thai observer. Crossing the facet of scale (five elements) with the facet of rater gives 20 variables upon which each team could receive an evaluation. That is, each of four raters could rate each team high or low on each of five sets of items. Table 13-17 indicates the five scales by listing at the left an illustrative item from each. The persons doing the rating are listed across the top. Each number in the body of the table shows the *difference* (in standard scores) between the mean rating of the teams with the leaders trained in interpersonal norms and those trained in geography. For the purposes of illustration, however, we can think of these numbers as *change scores,* as if they indicated change in rating from before to after training in interpersonal norms.

Clearly, the raters and scales could be arranged[11] to show that one variable

[11] See the original for a full explanation of the arrangement. For more detail on the entire study, see Mitchell and Foa (1969).

Table 13-17. *Changes in Performance on Construction Teams as Rated by Four Persons on Five Scales*

	RATER			
SCALE (INDICATED BY A SAMPLE ITEM FROM EACH)	*American Leader*	*Thai Observer*	*Thai Member*	*Non-Thai Member*
The group atmosphere was efficient	.00	.17	−.02	−.14
The American was efficient	.20	.67	.12	−.06
The American was tactful	.50	1.38	.55	.15
The American was interested in my ideas	.66	1.31	.28	.04
The group atmosphere was pleasant	.27	1.02	.25	.10

Adapted from Foa (1968).

exhibited the largest mean change (1.38 for behavior of leader toward group, such as "tactful") while others showed successively less effect. The numbers decrease as one moves away from the column of the Thai observer and also as one moves away from the row of the American being tactful (two exceptions: .66 in the column of the American leader and .10 in the column of the non-Thai member). This illustrates the pattern of change of means accompanied by spread of effect from the most changed variable.

Change in Degree of Relation

To illustrate change in degree of relation, Foa presents two patterns of intercorrelations among variables describing personality—one pattern for 23 students who succeeded academically and the other for 28 who failed. The interrelations among the variables for each of the two groups, and the differences between corresponding correlations, are shown in Table 13-18. (To save space, we do not describe here the nature of the personality variables measured.)

Again interpreting the differences as changes for the purposes of illustration, the bottom third of the table shows clearly that the intercorrelations in the condition of failure were uniformly weaker than those in the condition of success. The ordering of the personality variables retains the simplex pattern within each matrix, but the strength or degree of relation decreases in the failure condition.

Restructuring

In recent years, attention of social scientists has turned more and more toward complex interrelations—toward what is often called the *structure* of a system or of a sequence of behavior. A simple way to ask about structure is to ask *what goes with what,* and to what degree. In a business office, it may be that A consults with B more often than with C, and this is part of the structure of the working relations in that office. In a church, rituals of thanksgiving may be more frequent in one season of the year and rituals of supplication more frequent in another season. The association of these types of prayers with the season is part of the liturgical structure in that church. When the patterns of interrelations of variables change, we can call the change *restructuring.*

Foa (1968) illustrates restructuring with relations among variables that describe orientations between people. The labels at the left of Table 13-19 describe eight types of orientation toward self or other and give a verbal item, for each orientation, of the sort that was used in a study of relations between husbands and wives. Each correlation coefficient in the table shows the degree to which an actor's answering one of the eight types of items in a favorable direction is predictable from his answering some other type in a favorable direction. The first half of the table shows these correlations before therapy; the second half shows them after therapy. The data are taken from responses to questions about the ideal wife.

A glance at Table 13-19 reveals generally higher correlation after therapy than before among orientations toward self and other concerning giving or denying love and status. But here we want to point out not the average strength of the correlations, but the patterning of higher and lower correlations *within each* of the two matrices. In both matrices, an approximate circumplex (see section 12-6) appears. Correlations are highest along the diagonal, lowest some place between the diagonal and the corner, and then rise again as we move toward the corner. The circumplex patterns are not perfect, but these arrangements of rows and columns yield fewer violations of pattern than any other ordering of variables and fewer than attempting a simplex or radex.

As it turns out, the optimum ordering of variables (giving fewest viola-

Table 13-18. *Intercorrelations of Personality Variables for Students Who Succeeded and Those Who Failed*

CONDITION	PERSONALITY VARIABLE	2	3	4
	1	54	52	25
Success	2		73	69
	3			71
	1	25	09	05
Failure	2		64	63
	3			62
Difference	1	+29	+43	+20
between	2		+09	+06
conditions	3			+09

After Foa (1968).

Table 13-19. *Intercorrelation of Interpersonal Variables before and after Therapy*

BEFORE THERAPY

Variable	*Shortened form of item*	2	1	4	3	6	5	8	7
2. Giving love to other	Loves wife very much	—	30	02	−13	−02	28	−25	−18
1. Giving status to other	Displays respect and esteem for wife		—	−02	−05	−07	−42	−58	−53
4. Giving status to self	Esteems and relies on self			—	53	08	−20	21	−38
3. Giving love to self	Feels at peace with self				—	56	21	60	−36
6. Denying love to self	Rejects and blames self					—	27	21	−05
5. Denying status to self	Difficult to make decisions by self						—	32	20
8. Denying status to other	Thinks wife makes mistakes							—	32
7. Denying love to other	Feels angry toward wife								—

AFTER THERAPY

	1	2	3	4	5	6	7	8
1	—	65	72	52	38	26	28	41
2		—	55	66	35	25	−08	35
3			—	73	48	37	33	28
4				—	75	57	26	45
5					—	75	66	36
6						—	63	47
7							—	09
8								—

From Foa (1968).

tions of the circumplex pattern among the correlations) requires *different* ordering of variables before and after therapy. This illustrates change of the third kind—change in configuration or structuring.

To remind ourselves that we are discussing a facet wherein the elements consist of varying abstractions of differences, let us repeat what we have just said, but in the language of differences. There are differences among the relations in either matrix; in the "before" matrix, for example, the correlation of .30 between variables 1 and 2 differs from the correlation of .02 between variables 2 and 4. And there are differences among the differences in a matrix.

For example, the difference between .30 and .02 is a descending difference, while the difference between −.25 and −.18 (same row of the "before" matrix) is an ascending one. And, finally, there are differences between the differences lying in the different matrices. For example, before therapy, the correlation of .30 between variables 1 and 2 differs from the correlation of .02 between variables 2 and 4 by being larger; this is not true of the corresponding correlations after therapy: .65 for variables 1 and 2 and .66 for variables 2 and 4. It is this latter kind of difference between differences that requires a new ordering, after therapy, of rows and columns corresponding to variables if the matrix is to show a maximal approximation to the circumplex pattern. This is what Foa means by *restructuring*.

At the beginning of this chapter, we said that hypotheses could specify different types of relations. Similarly, hypotheses about change can specify one or more of the types of changes we have described in this section.

13-4. Summary

This final chapter on the analysis of empirical evidence has dealt with the relations among sets of data. We began with the comment that knowledge is knowledge of differences—that we cannot know anything except through contrasts. It is especially useful to learn the rates of one kind of action A that occur in the presence of specified rates of another kind of action B; such a series of correspondences is called a *relation*. This is not to say that research into relations is somehow more virtuous than research into base rates. The two types of investigation are complementary.

Relations between variables can differ in many facets. For one thing, implication from one variable to another can be one way or two way (see "Relations between Dichotomous Variables" and "Some Facets of Relations" in section 13-2). For another, the number of variables involved can be two, three, or any number. Each variable can have two, three, or any number of values. The variables can be discrete or continuous. The points in the relation can be conceived as approximating a curve or as covering an area. All of these characteristics are useful in phrasing hypotheses ("Some Facets of Relations," section 13-2). If a hypothesis specifies a relation, its precision is increased if it specifies the *type* of relation. Different types of relations fit different sorts of contingencies to be observed in the real world. The type of relation specified, consequently, is part of the researcher's theory about the domain of behavior he is studying.

A relation in which one variable is time is called a *change* (section 13-3). In this chapter, we have set forth some of the complexities the researcher can encounter in studying relations and changes. The logic and empirical strategy of these matters will continue to attract the attention of those thinkers who seek to improve methodology. We expect important advances to be made even while this book is in press. In studying change, the experimenter faces the perplexing question of which differences are reliable change and which are uncertainties of response ("Change and Uncertainty of Response," section 13-3). Typically, the experimenter takes the differences in which he is primarily interested as change and variabilities that are shorter or smaller than those as response uncertainties. Clearly, these two kinds of differences must be defined arbitrarily, according to the interest of the experimenter. What is important and lucrative change to the advertising researcher is faddish variability to the student of civilizations.

When the researcher is thinking about a single variable, he may want to specify merely a difference between two times. A more powerful hypothesis is the prediction of a trend. The researcher may wish to specify a uniform trend, a monotonically changing trend, or a nonmonotonically changing trend ("Some Facets of Change," section 13-3).

When the researcher is thinking about multiple variables, he may wish to specify one or more of three types of change among them, depending on his theory about their interrelation. (1) He may predict a change in central tendencies—for example, an increase in means such that the increase is largest in one particular variable and successively less in other variables. (2) He may predict an increase or decrease in the strength of the relations between variables, though the over-all pattern of interrelations remains the same. (3) He may predict changes in the strengths of the interrelations among the variables that alter the ordering of differences among the relations ("Change in Central Tendencies," "Change in Degree of Relation," and "Restructuring," section 13-3). If the researcher's theory is sufficiently sophisticated, hypotheses specifying these types of changes can provide powerful tests. Even if a hypothesis of this sort cannot be specified in advance, searching for one or more of the change patterns can be a potent source of hypotheses for later studies.

We ended the chapter, as we began it, speaking of the differences that yield knowledge.

13-5. Further Reading

A measure (gamma) of monotonicity in contingency tables has been furnished by Goodman and Kruskal (1954; this index is also described by Hays, 1963, pp. 642–656). Other indexes of monotonicity are the Spearman rank correlation coefficient (see Kendall and Stuart, 1961, pp. 476–477, and Hays, 1963, pp. 643–647) and the index commonly called Kendall's tau (Kendall and Stuart, 1961, call this index merely t on pages 477–480; see Hays, 1963, pp. 647–655).

See Maruyama (1962) for the advantages and disadvantages of various indexes of association in 2×2 contingency tables. The conclusions a researcher can reach by examining relations in contingency tables must depend, of course, on the strengths of the relations and upon their probability of being chance patterns. For discussion of these and other matters in connection with contingency tables, see Castellan (1965), Hays (1963, Chapter 17), Kastenbaum (1960), Lancaster (1949, 1951), Maxwell (1961), Mitra (1955), Smith (1966), Snedecor and Cochran (1967), and Sutcliffe (1957). For cautions in using partial and multiple correlations and their analogs in contingency tables, we have already mentioned Brewer, Campbell, and Crano (1970).

For more information on the use of the interrupted time series, see Campbell (1969) and Ross, Campbell, and Glass (1970). Also relevant to conceptualizing and analyzing changes are articles by Fisher, Rubinstein, and Freeman (1956), Gottman, McFall, and Barnett (1969), and Solomon and Lessac (1968).

The problem of choosing evidence in support of presumed change is subtle; a good introduction to these subleties is given by Bereiter (1963) in the pioneering collection of papers on methods of studying change edited by Harris (1963). A common technique of assessing change is to compare *gains* in an experimental group of actors with gains in a control group. But gain scores bring special complexities, only one of which is whether the starting place (pretest score) influences the amount of gain to be expected. A recent and sophisticated discussion of the difficulties encountered with gain scores is that of Cronbach and Furby (1970). Gain scores are similar in their logic to "dyadic" scores; problems in using these were discussed by Cronbach (1958) in an article now classic.

A recently developed technique for examining the relative strengths of relations among multiple variables and the causal directions embedded in them is called *path analysis*. This technique has been described by several authors in the volumes edited by Borgatta and Bohrnstedt (1969, 1970) as well as by Werts and Linn (1970).

CHAPTER 14
Interpreting Results

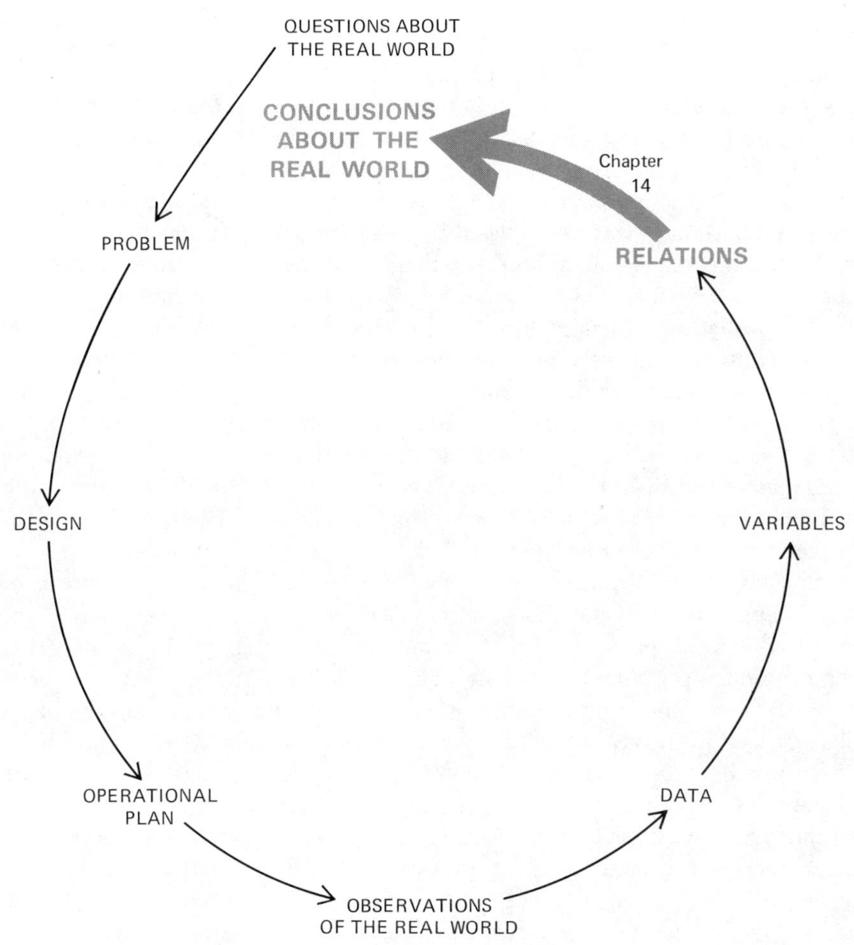

The empirical researcher begins a study with one or more hypotheses. That is, he sets out for himself certain statements for which he would like to find justification in some empirical domain. Then he seeks information from the observable world to ascertain whether factual justification is there. He converts observations into data and organizes the data. He examines the distributions of his data and—if he has more than one array of data—the relations among arrays. He must then decide whether the results are worth the trouble; that is, whether he can make certain statements more confidently (or less so) now that he has arrayed the data and judged their implications. This chapter reviews some of the complexities in judging the implications of data.

14-1. The Domain of Investigation

At the outset, simply because the world of human understanding is potentially infinite, the investigator must limit his research to a tiny part of the world about him. He is then immediately faced with the problem of how he will tell himself and others how he is ascertaining the limits of his study. He must do this if he is to be at all precise about his conclusions, for conclusions must be conclusions about *something*. Describing the limits of his domain of investigation is one way the investigator describes the *something* about which he is drawing conclusions. The researcher who reports a distribution of durations for holding the breath will not be giving very useful information unless he states whether he has included in his study one or both sexes, resting or active states, individuals immersed in water or air, immersed in a laboratory tank or in the natural ocean, moving at will or being chased by a shark, breathing natural air or diver's mixture, and so forth.

A straightforward way to delimit a realm of study is to specify its facets. Examples of facetized studies were given in Chapters 2 and 12. With facets and their elements specified, the investigator can state precisely from what portions of the domain he took observations and what portions remain to be studied empirically—either by himself or by others. He can state with precision what combinations of elements of the facets were sampled in his study and therefore in what portions of the domain other investigators might expect to come upon findings like his own. In other words, specifying a domain by facets helps the researcher think about how far he can generalize the results of his observations (in terms of the partitions he has made and observed and those he chose not to make or observe); it also helps him to be precise when communicating his conclusions to others. It is important, in a facet design, to specify all the facets one considers relevant to the domain, regardless of whether all the properties involved are to be dealt with in the immediate empirical phase of the research. The meaning of present outcomes is enriched if the outcomes are assessed in the light of facets conceived as relevant but which remain as yet unexplored. For example, if an investigator of behavior in work groups turns to the laboratory to test an idea, he keeps himself alert, and the readers of his report as well, if he specifies how the facets of his study span both the laboratory situation and the natural work group, even though none of his data will be from the latter.

Granted, the researcher cannot always feel confident in specifying facets. Some studies lie in domains so little studied that the researcher must go in with only guesses as guides. In such a case, the investigator must choose between (1) collecting data with little theory to guide him in its interpretation or (2) pausing to build theory while having few facts to give him confidence that he is building something useful. Given such a choice, most of us choose the alternative we find personally the less frustrating.

14-2. Actor, Behavior, and Context

In themselves, actors, behaviors, and contexts can be taken as facets. That is, the domain of a study can include various kinds of actors, behaviors, and contexts. More broadly, the designer of a study can take these larger facets as a checklist of types, and he can ask himself what facets of actors, what facets of behaviors toward objects, and what facets of contexts belong in his domain. In studying the game of baseball, for example, one could choose individual players as actors (What do baseball players do? How do they function as parts of the system?), or teams, or leagues. Obviously, what one takes as his system of immediate interest restricts his conclusions to that kind of system. It is illogical to conclude that all citizens of a nation that builds an empire are imperialistic or that a group composed of individually effective problem-solvers will be effective in solving problems as a group.

Behaviors, too, are limitless. Depending on the domain of interest, one might choose to observe eye movements, jumping, or protest marches. Similarly, contexts might range over the amount of noise during a concert, the distribution of opinion among the actor's friends, and the general level of welfare in the society. What one chooses as actors, behaviors, objects (stimuli), and contexts will depend heavily upon what his theory tells him are the systems, suprasystems, and subsystems (see section 2-2) he is observing. And when one has gathered and arrayed his data, what he can say with new confidence will apply within the kinds of actors, behaviors, and contexts that his facet design has specified. This remains true even when the investigator's facet design is informal and intuitive rather than explicit and systematic; for the investigator's facets are implied by his manner of choosing his sample, his design partitions, his design constants, his matching variables, and his observed partitions (see section 3-3).

A notable example of the difficulties of interpreting results that occur when facets are not specified has been given by Hovland (1959). Hovland pointed out that laboratory studies and naturalistic studies of attitude change have usually yielded patterns of results that seem inconsistent. Experimental studies in the laboratory often show large effects from attempts to change attitudes, while sample surveys in the field usually show little or no attitude change in response to influence from the mass media. In his own terms, Hovland argued that researchers, in failing to look beyond their "variables of interest," had failed to specify the facets that could have tied the characteristics of the laboratory situation to the characteristics of the field. Lacking specifications of the domain of attitude change, especially of those facets describing the different facilitating conditions to be found in the social contexts of the laboratory and the field, most researchers remained baffled by the apparently contradictory results of the two types of studies until Hovland turned his attention to this specific point. (See also sections 4-2 on field studies and 4-5 on laboratory experiments.)

14-3. Sampling

It is not often that a researcher is able to take observations on every actor in which he is interested, or on every behavior or context. Almost always, the researcher wants to observe actors of some particular type, but is prevented from observing all actors of that type by restrictions on time or money, by relatively rapid shifting by the actors from one type to another, or by some other difficulty. Hence, the researcher must usually be satisfied to make his observations on a subset of the actors he wants to learn more about. The same situation occurs with behaviors, objects, and contexts. The problem then arises how the researcher, observing only a sample of the population he wants to learn about, can be confident he has learned something about the members of the population he has *not* observed. These matters were discussed in Chapter 5.

If all members of the population are substantially alike, then sampling is no problem. That is, if the behaviors one wants to study vary more from object to object or from context to context than from actor to actor, then one can learn a great deal from any actor about the conditions under which the behavior occurs and changes. This is typically assumed to be the case in psychophysical studies; for example, whether two pricks on the upper arm are felt as one or two depends much more on how far apart the two pricks are made than upon the individual actor undergoing the experience (see also section 4-5). Similarly, in some studies one may assume that contexts are substantially alike. In survey research, the actors may be asked questions in many different contexts—at the front door or in the kitchen; when interrupted during a meal, during a nap, or during a financial discussion with a spouse; and so forth. But the differing contexts are typically assumed to have insignificant effects on the actors' answers to the questions in the survey (see also section 4-6).

Often, however, the researcher believes that different members of a population may stand differently at the outset in respect to the observed partition (the dependent variable) or in readiness to respond to a treatment that will affect the observed partition. In these cases, it is vital for the researcher to be able to have some knowledge of how his sample stands in respect to the rest of the population. Obviously, if the researcher knew at the outset the measures of his sample and the rest of the population on the dependent variable, he would not need to conduct the study. Obviously, the researcher cannot know at the outset how his sample stands in respect to the rest of the population on any variable not yet measured. What he can know, however, is the *probability* of any given difference between the sample and the population. If a sample is taken by a random method, then the greatest likelihood is that the sample will be distributed similarly to the population as a whole in respect to any characteristics not used as a design partition or design constant (see section 3-2). With random selection, one can conclude that the probability of his sample having more of some property than the population as a whole is the same as the probability of its having less of the property. Thus, random sampling makes it a good bet for the researcher to conclude that his sample is "unbiased" in respect to the population. But random selection does not make that bet a sure thing. No matter how careful his randomization, the researcher must always be prepared to meet the unhappy event that later studies will force him to conclude that one of his earlier investigations owed its outcome to a mischance of sampling and not to the relations among variables that he thought he had demonstrated at the time. But even with this uncertainty, the bets with randomization are much better than those without randomization.

Random sampling can be done only if a list of the population, or the substantial equivalent of a list, is available. Sometimes such a list is impractical to obtain. Suppose, for example, someone is investigating the bodily movements and gestures of persons in natural situations who are reacting to a feeling of being rejected or "put down" by someone whose regard they value. Clearly, the boundaries of such a population of persons reacting to a feeling of being rejected are so arbitrary as to be meaningless; to try to make a list from which to sample actors about to undergo such an experience in the natural situation would be absurd. Clearly, a sample of behaviors of this sort could not be drawn from a list of discrete possibilities, and a sample of actors showing this type of behavior would have to be an opportunistic sample.[1]

In the case of unlistable populations, however, the researcher can use a facet design to increase his confidence that his sample is not strongly biased. For example, to select a sample of actors experiencing feelings of rejection, a researcher might postulate that important facets of reactions to rejection might include (1) whether the rejector was an individual such as a sorority sister, a small group such as the local chapter of the sorority, or a large, geographically removed reference group such as the national organization of the sorority; (2) whether the actor was trained in perceiving rejection explicitly; (3) the presence of other familiar or unfamiliar persons at the event; and (4) the extent to which the context immediately preceding the reaction was such as to foster survival-oriented reactions, group-building reactions, or self-actualizing reactions. The researcher might then seek out situations characterized by the various combinations of the elements of these facets; he could then be confident that his observations included cases distributed over the conditions he postulated as important. In fact, it might be possible for the researcher to select situations randomly within some of the "cells" of such a design; if so, his design would approximate stratified sampling (see section 5-4).

---

[1]For further discussion of similar problems, see Schmuck and Runkel (1970, Appendix M).

Without random sampling or a facet design, the researcher can conclude that it is possible for the outcomes of his study to occur under the conditions of his study. With a facet design and observations in a number of cells, the researcher can conclude that different specified outcomes can occur under different specified conditions. With random sampling, the researcher can state the probabilities of the outcomes in the various conditions having been produced by chance from an undifferentiated population.

14-4. Partitions

An investigator's purpose in designing a study always is to arrange his observations and conditions so that each possible pattern of observations he might obtain will have one and only one logical interpretation. If his study is designed so that each pattern of outcome has an interpretation distinct from every other pattern of outcome, then he will be able to draw unequivocal conclusions from his study, no matter what occurs.

There are always some certain conditions (or values of independent variables) in which the researcher has a primary interest. More often than not, a researcher wants to know how the independent variables form relations with the dependent variables. Beyond the variables that are of primary interest to the researcher, however, there are always potentially present some conditions (such as history of the situation, maturation of the actors, testing effects, and so forth; "The Problem of Drawing Valid Conclusions," section 3-1) that could affect the outcome and that therefore loom as alternative hypotheses. If the researcher thinks any of these alternative effects reasonably likely, then only observations under conditions that allow these effects to show themselves separately from the design partitions can enable him to conclude against the one kind of effect and in favor of the other. The researcher must rely on his judgment whether an effect is likely enough to justify the expense of including an opportunity to observe it by providing for it in his design. No design can provide for observations to cope with every conceivable alternative hypothesis. The researcher must be willing to declare some alternative hypotheses too unlikely, in his judgment, to justify collecting data to test them against his primary hypotheses.

The observed partition or specification of possible outcomes (see "Partitioning" and "Some Guides for Partitioning" in section 3-2) can set forth two *or more* possible patterns of outcome. Unfortunately, many studies conducted by social scientists in the middle decades of the twentieth century—and especially those conducted by psychologists—have conceived only two possible outcomes: the one outcome predicted by the investigator's preferred hypothesis and the class of all other outcomes. At the same time, a mathematical theory of probability has been used to enable the researcher to attach a numerical level to his confidence that the outcome of the study justified his original hypothesis. But some methodologists have pointed out that the statistical models used for applying probability theory to the outcomes of experiments have been "violently biased against the null hypothesis" (Edwards, 1965, p. 400)—usually, that is, against the class of outcomes other than the one the investigator prefers. In view of this characteristic of most recent analyses using statistical inference, Lykken (1968, p. 151) says, "Confirmation of a single directional prediction should usually add little to one's confidence in the theory being tested." (We return to this topic in section 14-13).

Knowledge is always a knowledge of differences.[2] We learn something about the world when we partition the possibilities beforehand and specify the different ways the data might conceivably fall. Then the fall of the data gives us new knowledge to the extent that the fit of the data is closer to one of the ways we specified as conceivable than it is to any of the other ways. For example, Runkel (1962) studied the respect that teachers in high schools held for one another's judgment about guidance and counseling. He contrasted three types of pairs with one another: (1) pairs having relatively little communication, (2) pairs having relatively frequent communication, and (3) pairs having relatively frequent communication not only with each other but with mutual others. Runkel predicted that mean levels of respect would be lowest in (1), higher in (2), and highest in (3). There were six possible ways in which the data on respect could order the three groups of pairs: it was easy to see in the data whether the fit to the predicted order was better than the fit to any of the other five orders.

As another example, recall Guttman's (1965b) study of items in intelligence tests, recounted in Chapter 12. Using a geometric space in which to represent the patterns in his data, Guttman predicted that the points representing numerical items, verbal items, and geometric items would fall in a circumplex, with each sort of item clustered in its own region. Furthermore, items testing academic achievement would fall near the center of the pattern, with items requiring analytic ability falling around the achievement items. Obviously, many other patterns in which the item points might have fallen are conceivable. The fit of the data to the predicted pattern (with the one exception that the regions of the achievement items and the analytic items were reversed) was so remarkable that Guttman did not discuss many of the other patterns that could logically have occurred.

To check whether he knows something about the empirical world, the researcher, in brief,

1. Partitions some actors, behaviors toward objects, and contexts according to some selected properties
2. Conceives ways that other properties of the actors, behaviors, and contexts might be found to fall (perhaps after some intervention designed by himself)
3. Chooses one outcome (or set of outcomes) as most likely

[2] Or of similarities, since differences and similarities are obverses of one another.

4. Observes the outcome in the pattern of his data and decides whether the obtained pattern is closer to the outcome he predicted than to any other outcome he conceived.

14-5. Internal and External Validity

Internal validity was discussed under "The Problem of Drawing Valid Conclusions" in section 3-1 and external validity under "Internal and External Validity" in section 3-1. Internal validity concerns the kinds of alternative hypotheses that can be ruled out about what processes were going on among the *observed* cases. One can conclude that a particular alternative hypothesis—for example, that the outcomes were produced by administering the pretests—is untenable only if one provides for collecting comparative data by a design partition that subjects some cases to a pretest and exempts others, or if one designs the study so that *no* cases receive a pretest.

External validity asks whether processes going on among cases *not observed* but presumed to be equivalent[3] to those observed are the same processes that took place among those observed. Such a conclusion, of course, can be correct only to the extent that the cases observed are, in fact, a fair sample of the cases one would like to consider equivalent. Here careful sampling procedures—using randomization or facet design or both—are a safeguard. These matters were set forth in "Internal and External Validity," section 3-1; in "Replication," section 3-2; in Chapters 5 and 6; and in section 14-3.

14-6. Replication and Equivalence

Concepts of sample and population presuppose that a set of actors, behaviors toward objects, or contexts called a population can be ascertained such that every member of the set is in some theoretically appropriate sense the same kind of thing. Perhaps, as in the case of a political poll, the actors are all, equivalently, eligible voters. Perhaps, in the case of the study of vision, the actors are all equivalent receivers and processors of electromagnetic energy. Perhaps, in the same example, the recognition reactions (such as, "I see the light now!" or, "There it is!") are all equivalent recognitions. These matters were discussed under "Replication" in section 3-2. Of course, if one is mistaken about the substantial equivalence of members of a population, his conclusions will be as awry as if his sampling is biased. In effect, if one is wrong about the population (of actors, of behaviors, or of events) being all of one kind, the result is like getting both gnus and shrews into one's sample when one thought he was sampling only from gnus.

Still another sort of problem in replicability was recounted in section

[3]That is, belonging to the same population. See "Replication" in section 3-2 for further discussion of equivalence and replication.

11-5—that of whether choice situations in different contexts are the "same" choice situations. For example, is the actor making the same choice between objects A and B when he can also choose C as he is when asked to choose among A, B, and D? One's conclusions sometimes must depend on the assumptions that the two tasks are the same in respect to the relative attractions of A and B.

14-7. Operational Definitions

Characteristics (properties) of actors, behaviors, objects, or contexts are not always directly evident to the senses. (Optical illusions remind us that we can easily be misled even about characteristics directly evident to the senses.) Often, we must employ some "operation" or procedure to decide whether actor, behavior, object, or context has some stated amount of some conceived property; and often, the operation we choose is an arbitrary selection from a number of possibilities that seem to us equally likely to index the conceived property accurately.

There remains the question whether, indeed, the operation does reflect the conceptual property. This correspondence, of course, cannot be ascertained directly. The best strategy for establishing the correspondence is that of the multitrait-multimethod paradigm (see section 6-4). To the extent that the researcher hopes a particular operation—such as a particular verbal test, a particular physiological measurement, a particular movement of approach or avoidance—will correctly index the property he wants indexed, to that extent he risks everything on one throw. Of course, if his operation has been compared with other operations and other outcomes in other studies that have produced evidence of the validity of the operation, the researcher may be making an advantageous bet. Nevertheless, given the uncertainties of generalizing from the context of one study to the context of another, the researcher always increases the odds in his favor by employing the multitrait-multimethod paradigm in his own study.

In fact, the same logical problem exists between studies as within a study. If two studies are mutually to strengthen each other, it is not enough for the investigators conducting the two studies merely to describe the targets of their studies in the same words; it is not enough, for example, for both investigators to claim, "I studied the distribution of variable X among actors of type Q." By this we mean more than merely that different people often mean different things by the same words. We claim that even when two researchers might confidently agree that they mean theoretically the very same thing by the term *variable* X, when they both agree that the operations each used to assess variable X were appropriately conducted, and when they both agree that both were observing actors of type Q, even then one could lead himself to erroneous conclusions were he to pool the data from the two studies to obtain a single distribution of variable X over all the actors observed in the two studies. The logic here is again that of the multitrait-multimethod paradigm.

The key idea in the multitrait-multimethod paradigm is that measuring the same trait by different methods gives us confidence that the methods will respond similarly to the same trait, and that measuring a number of traits by one method tests whether the method will respond differently to different traits; consequently, only by assessing more than one trait by more than one method can we obtain direct evidence that our data give us dependable information about the traits in which we are interested. Without this crossing of measures with variables (traits, in the example), we can only hope that our results are telling us about the phenomena we most care about—that our results are telling us something about the characteristics of humans and their behavior that we set out to study.

The originators of the multitrait-multimethod paradigm, D. T. Campbell and D. W. Fiske (1959), named it in illustration of its applicability to sorting out the properties of actors one wants to learn about from their reactions to different types of measuring methods as such. The same logic can be applied to sorting out actors' reactions to different objects and to different contexts. To be complete, the paradigm should cross every class of variability with every other—actors of different sorts (traits), different methods of assessing the classes of actors, different sorts of behaviors toward objects displayed by the actors, different methods of detecting those behaviors, different kinds of contexts, and different techniques for establishing the existence of the different contexts.

Someday researchers and the agencies that give financial support to research will understand the costs of mounting a research program having the kind of deep and confident penetration into new knowledge that the expanded multitrait-multimethod paradigm and a facet design based on that logic can make possible. That time is not yet. In the meantime, a careful facet design will enable the researcher and his potential colleagues to keep themselves aware of what they conceive to be the total behavioral system or functional unity[4] within which they are working, of the sectors (or cells; see section 2-3) of that total domain from which they have collected data, and of the sectors from which data must still be collected before certain of their conclusions can be reasonably firm.

Drawing dependable conclusions from observations has many ramifications and touches in one way or another on most of the topics treated in this book. For the purpose of guiding the reader to other relevant considerations, however, we suggest that some of the more obvious connections are presented in sections 2-4. Chapter 6, section 7-1, and Chapters 8 and 10.

14-8. Sources of Observations

An especially important aspect of an operation for assessing a characteristic or property is the *source* of the evidence that the operation relies upon; that is, subjective reports, trace records, direct observation, or archival records,

[4] Or "small world," as Toda and Shuford (1965) insightfully call it.

as discussed in section 7-1. Each of these sources of observations offers its own advantages and disadvantages, as summarized in Table 7-2. Again, because some limitations are to be found in every operation for making observations, the researcher who uses evidence from only one of these sources runs the risk of having his conclusions undermined by the defects in his method. Ideally, he should choose methods that complement each other in their strengths and weaknesses.

14-9. Links among Theory, Variables, and Operations

We said in section 6-1 and again in section 14-7 that several operations, not just one, will usually seem to the investigator to be reasonable representations of the theoretical property he has in mind. To put it another way, there is usually more than one operation that will produce a state or level of an independent variable required by the experimental design. In Section 8-1 we pointed out that one's *success* in producing the required level of the independent variable was not to be taken for granted. To avoid letting every conclusion drawn from the research rest on the mere *assumption* that an operation has produced a required level of an independent variable (or design partition), it is prudent to check whether the desired level was indeed produced—at least in cases where it is possible to do so and in which there is a reasonable possibility the operation might not work. If one wishes to study the behavior of groups of five, ten, and fifteen members, one can check group size merely be counting the number of persons present before proceeding. But cases requiring training, for example, are more complex. If the researcher needs some people who can find their way on foot from the top of hill 19 to Benson's Bridge, he might give some people training in traversing the route. Since training does not always succeed, however, he would be leaving an extremely weak link in his study if he did not check the outcome of his training by a test of actual performance.

The link between the theoretical concept of a variable and its actual measurement is only one of the many links that must be forged, strongly or weakly, among parts of the research process. Another link is the theoretical reasoning that goes from the design partition (independent variable) to the observed partition (dependent variable). Perhaps a theory says that the quality and speed of producing objects through an assembly line process will be limited by the least competent member of the line, because that one person can inject poor quality or slow speed independently of the others; on the other hand, the quality and speed of performing a task such as solving a puzzle may exceed the abilities of the most competent individual working alone if the group has the skill of drawing out of every individual whatever insights he has about the puzzle. With such direct reasons or links for the predictions associated with the two types of task, it would be easy to design tests of the hypotheses, and, if the differential prediction were not borne out, the links to check for defects would be few.

In contrast, suppose a theory were to predict that men spending their working days on an assembly line, compared to men working essentially as members of problem-solving teams, would have little pride in their work and would less often associate with other members of the work group during leisure hours. Here the links of reasoning to get from the antecedent conditions to the consequent conditions are numerous (the reader might try specifying them, in observable form, himself); and, in case the prediction failed, it would be far from obvious how to begin the troubleshooting process. Both Platt (1964) and Deese (1969) have made similar points; Deese says:

> The heart of the experimental method lies in the ability to control some condition (the independent variable) upon which some other condition (the dependent variable) is said to be contingent. If the method is to be useful, the link of control over the independent variable must be simple and fairly direct. There should be no reasonable doubt that if the proper device is activated, the independent variable changes in a particular way—for example, when we move the optic wedge, the luminosity of the stimulus changes. It is equally important that the link between the independent and dependent variable be simple and direct. This aspect of experimentation is often forgotten, not only by psychologists, but by agricultural scientists and others who study problems in which there is no well-developed theoretical network for specifying the subtle and intricate links between independent and dependent variables. An indirect relation between independent and dependent variables must be supported by well-established and tested sets of intervening links, or the whole process of testing a theory becomes an exercise in futility. The traditional physical sciences, chemistry and physics, are preeminent in experimentation because of well-developed theory, not the other way around. No new series of experiments should be given the task of testing a very large and poorly specified series of intervening links, as were the learning-behavior theories of the 1940s and 1950s. . . . However, we still find experimental psychologists performing experiments to test theories of this sort as a kind of magical rite. The tedium of these exercises is only relieved by the surprise value. Observations so seldom seem to be repeatable (p. 517).

Platt (1964), on strong inference, states:

> It is like climbing a tree. At the first fork, we choose—or in this case, "nature" or the experimental outcome chooses—to go to the right branch or the left; at the next fork, to go left or right; and so on (p. 347).
>
> Surveys, taxonomy, design of equipment, systematic measurements and tables, theoretical computations—all have their proper and honored place, provided they are parts of a chain of precise induction of how nature works (p. 351).
>
> The most important thing is to keep in mind that this kind of thinking is not a lucky knack but a system that *can* be taught and learned. The second thing is to be explicit and formal and regular about it, to devote a half hour

or an hour to analytical thinking every day, writing out the logical tree and the alternatives and crucial experiments explicitly in a permanent notebook (p. 352).

. . . I will mention one severe but useful private test. . . . It consists of asking in your own mind, on hearing any scientific explanation or theory put forward, "But sir, what experiment could *dis*prove your hypothesis?"; or, on hearing a scientific experiment described, "But sir, what hypothesis does your experiment *dis*prove?" (p. 352).

14-10. Types of Data

So far, we have been reviewing the larger structure of research: the settings for data collection, the partitions of observations, and the like. In Chapter 10, we turned to the micro-structure of data. We described the three dichotomized facets proposed by Coombs (1964) and reminded the reader that the researcher must decide what kinds of data he will make out of his observations. A basic postulate in the theory of data of Coombs is that the smallest, irreducible sort of observation corresponds to a datum, and the sort of information the researcher gets from such a basic observation can always be symbolized abstractly by a relation between two points. The theory goes on to distinguish three questions we can ask about the two points, each one offering a dichotomy:

1. Will the researcher choose to interpret his observation to mean (a) that one point dominates (surpasses) the other (or does not) or (b) that the two points are in proximity to each other (or are not)?
2. Will the researcher choose to interpret his observation to mean (a) that the two points both stand for actors or both for objects or (b) that one point stands for one kind of thing and the other for another?
3. Will the researcher choose to interpret his observation to mean (a) that each point stands indeed for a value to be conceived as a point or location or (b) that each point instead stands for a value to be conceived as a distance or similarity?

These three facets, each with two elements, generate eight types of data, each carrying a certain sort of information from the observation into the formal analysis of the data. Examining the model for each of the eight types of data in turn warns us about making one kind of interpretation (mapping from observation into a particular type of data) when recording the observations and then making a different sort of interpretation when combining data or comparing different groups of actors. A simple example of this kind of error would be to interpret the act of a particular nation in admitting an immigrant to mean that the nation determined that the immigrant's health surpassed a certain standard, but then to interpret the nation's admission of two immigrants to mean that the two immigrants were equivalent in degree of health. Similarly, researchers have sometimes asked respondents to rank order goals or values from a given list—for example, "Order the goals listed below according to what you think it would be most worthwhile for the city council to undertake next year"—and have then interpreted the results to mean that two respondents who put the number 1 on a particular choice both preferred that goal above everything else, even above goals not included in the list offered them.

Data can be compared and summarized systematically, by scaling for example, only if each datum in the set is interpreted by the same model. Constructing a scale is equivalent to concluding that the data *can* be scaled—that the interrelations among the data are such that they can all mesh in a scalable way (see Chapter 11). The scale may not fairly represent behavior in the real world if interpretations of observations are muddled in moving from one phase to another. (See section 10-2 for descriptions of the data models.)

Furthermore, if contradictory assumptions are made about the data, then an unpredicted outcome of the research leaves the researcher with contradictory clues about where to start tracking down the errors of his procedures. In section 10-3 and Appendix I we listed the 14 assumptions necessary to combine sets of data into unidimensional and multidimensional arrays. From a logician's point of view, we no doubt overlooked some; those presented are only the assumptions necessary for converting observations into arrays of data. In any study, it is impossible to avoid making numerous assumptions (states of affairs taken for granted without empirical checking). When a hypothesis fails, any one or more of these assumptions may be the culprit. This is the reason many researchers prefer the weak scaling methods, or the methods that require the fewest assumptions. (Often, a researcher will analyze a body of data by two or more different scaling methods to find out what difference might appear in the outcome between, for example, a weak method and a strong one.) There is probably no best strategy in the use of methods based on different assumptions. No doubt some research questions, populations, contexts, data-collection methods, and so forth, are delicate in respect to certain assumptions and robust in respect to others, but very little is known about this matter.

14-11. Unidimensional and Multidimensional Arrays

Once the researcher has a collection of data, he may be able to speak more confidently than he could when he framed his hypothesis; that is, he may be able to tell that his data do or do not support his hypothesis merely by looking at the data matrix. For this to be possible, however, the data would ordinarily have to be few and the hypothesis simple. In most cases, the relation of the data to the hypothesis cannot be divined merely by inspecting the matrix of obtained data. The need for sophisticated analysis of the data is especially clear when the data are weak and the hypothesis strong. For example, the data might have been constructed from weak, uncalibrated judgments such as, "A_1

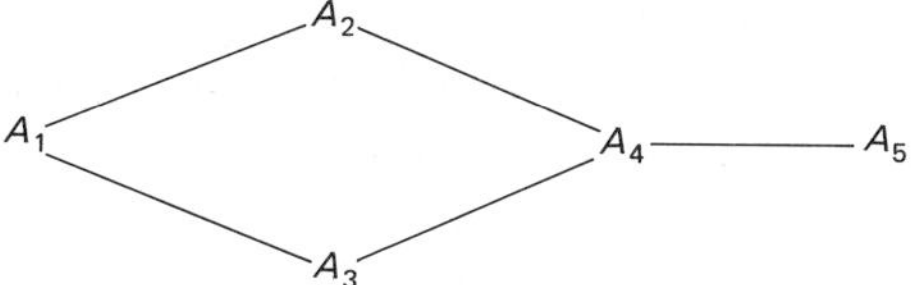

Figure 14-1.

is greater than A_2"; and actors might only partially order the objects. One actor, for example, might be unable to order A_2 and A_3 and might yield a partial order, as in Figure 14-1. Another actor might yield some other partial order. But the hypothesis might call for a monotonic relation such as, "Large As are accompanied by larger Bs than are small As." In such a case, the process of ordering all the As from small to large, given a series of judgments on pairs of As, is not necessarily straightforward; further assumptions are often required and alternative assumptions are often available. The final conclusions the investigator draws from his research are no more valid than these assumptions. These matters were discussed in Chapters 11 and 12, and they are sufficiently complex that we shall not recapitulate them here.

One assumption that permeates research in human behavior, and therefore bears repeating, is the probability assumption: given a particular situation eliciting behavior, the probability that any specific response will actually occur is greater than zero and less than one. This assumption enables the researcher to designate some data as very unlikely and therefore as error. This device makes it easier to fit data to a scale. It also opens the possibility of mistakenly designating some data as error. When the researcher adopts a conclusion that rests on assuming that part of his data are in error, he can be more confident if he can offer reasonable grounds for making this choice rather than taking the data at face value. For example, if 80 percent of the data fit a unidimensional scale but 20 percent do not, it seems reasonable to ask for some reason beyond ease of computation for counting the nonfitting 20 percent as error rather than as evidence for a second dimension in the behavior.

14-12. Inferring Relations

Knowledge is knowledge of differences. One learns something about a rate in a subset—such as the mean number of children per family in France—if it turns out differently from the base rate. An obvious next question is, What differences go together? This question is the paradigm for the study of relations. If it turns out that families having more children than others also have more annual income than those others, then we have one type of *relation* between number of children per family and annual income per family. Relations are always observed by observing two or more properties, both exhibited by each of a series of members of a population, such as families, persons, firms, or stimuli. Relations were discussed in Chapter 13.

Hypotheses often describe certain types of relations that the investigator expects to find in his data. And certain types of relations require that the constituent properties be measured with certain types of scales. A monotonic relation cannot be ascertained from data unless the categories of the observed partitions are at least ordered—that is, unless the variables are assessed on scales the elements of which are at least ordered. A correlation is interpreted as linear only with daring unless intervals of the constituent variables—such as from 5 to 6 and from 6 to 7—can be considered equal because of some evidence or as a reasonable assumption.

A difference that is related to increments in time is called a *change*. In studying changes, the investigator usually wants to distinguish two types: (1) change proper and (2) uncertainty of response (see "Change and Uncertainty of Response," section 13-3). We usually reserve the term *change* for differences that occur slowly enough and have a sufficient period of stability that we can do something interesting or useful at the different levels of the variable. If a discussion group begins in the morning with seven members and one leaves at noontime and does not return by the adjournment of the group at four in the afternoon, we are likely to say that the size of the group *decreased* from seven to six. We are likely to say so, at least, if the time from noon to four was enough time for the group to adopt new ways based on an "economy" of six instead of seven. On the other hand, if some of the seven leave on short errands and return, we are likely to speak of the group as maintaining a membership of seven even though only six are present during large fractions of the day. In brief, when an alteration is relatively slow and stable in its trend in a way that behavior can adapt to it by forming a new pattern, we are more likely to call it a *change*. But when an alteration is relatively fast in fluctuating and behavior can only adapt to the fact of fluctuation—not to separate stable states—then we are more likely to call it *variability*. When we are not only uninterested in the shorter fluctuations but see no regularity in them and have no hypothesis about their cause, we often speak of them as *random variability*.

To conclude that a difference between a level of a variable at time 1 and its level at time 2 represents a reliable change is sometimes risky; the difference may have a large component of random variability. This problem was discussed in "Change and Uncertainty of Response," section 13-3. We also discussed change and variability as inconsistency in "Consistency," section 11-5 and as unreliability in section 6-4; "Reliability," in section 11-5; and "Models for Stimulus-Comparison Data," in section 11-6.

When the investigator is studying more than one dependent variable (observed partition), the cluster of dependent variables can take on a variety of patterns. When comparing the pattern at time 1 with that at time 2, the difference between the patterns can be random or it can be one of (1) difference in level or central tendency, (2) difference in degree of relation among the variables, or (3) difference in ordering among the variables (see "Changes among Multiple Variables," section 13-3). When a study contains more than one variable, it is a waste of resources merely to look at the changes in level of each variable.

Looking at changes in the central tendencies of some dependent variables, we might find that some have increased and some have decreased. In such a case, the conclusion that changes were merely scattered might not best describe the data. If the amount of change in the variables followed an order theoretically to be expected, the pattern might be very significant. For example, suppose a middle-level executive proposes a more efficient way of doing things in an industrial organization. People at various levels might be asked to rate the value of the new idea, with the following results:

Top-level executives	1.2
The middle-level proposer himself	2.3
Lower-level executives	0.9
Supervisors	0.2
Workers	−2.3

The rating 3.0 represents "will do a terrific amount of good," zero represents "won't change anything important one way or the other," and −3.0 represents "will do a terrific amount of harm." Paying no attention to *who* gave the various ratings, the over-all rating is not impressive in this example. But if our theory predicted that people on more distant levels would give successively poorer ratings to the idea, then these results would be very impressive. We discussed in "Changes among Multiple Variables," section 13-3, examples of the ways conclusions can be drawn concerning changes in degree of relation among dependent variables and changes in ordering among the variables.

When researchers are interested in change, they are usually also interested in the causes of change. In fact, observing changes is a time-honored way of inferring causes (see Chapter 3). Sometimes the change observed is the change from the absence of some property to its presence. In such a case,[5] the researcher can have fair confidence, given proper safeguards in design (see Chapter 3), that the cause of the property A is associated with the conditions that were present when A was present and absent when A was absent. However, when we are observing changes from some nonzero quantity of a characteristic to more (or less) of that characteristic, the logic becomes more complicated. The change may not be caused to any degree at all by some experimental action on the part of the investigator; rather, it may be part of a trend due to causes quite beyond the investigator's awareness.[6] Consequently, the investigator of changes of this sort must often study trends (also called time series) before he can confidently conclude that his independent variable has a causal connection with his dependent variable (see "Inferring Cause of Change in One Variable," section 13-3).

---

[5] The case of presence or absence of a property seems to have been the paradigm considered by J. S. Mill (1891) in his famous four methods of deducing causation. See Phillips (1966) and Madge (1965) for concise presentations of Mills' methods.

[6] Actually, the simpler dichotomous case is only a special case of a trend; an absence of a property can be called a stable trend of zero quantity and slope.

14-13. The Chance Hypothesis

Some events occur by chance. By this we mean that when a number of events are possible, we cannot be sure which of them will occur. And sometimes one of the unlikely events occurs instead of the most likely. When we are testing a hypothesis that is controversial, we could be wrong in interpreting some particular outcome, even though we predicted it, as giving evidence in favor of our hypothesis—for *this* outcome might actually be the chance event. Indeed, no matter how carefully we design an experiment and carry it out, the chance event is always a rival hypothesis that challenges the hypothesis for which (or against which) we seek evidence. As we explained in sections 2-6, 14-4, and 14-9, one way to become more confident that a predicted outcome did *not* occur by chance is to arrange an experiment in which several outcomes are possible and specifiable in advance. If the investigator then calls the outcome that does, indeed, occur, he increases his confidence that the predicted outcome will again win out over competing outcomes in the future. If one carries out further similar experiments that yield the same outcome, one's confidence in one's ability to predict correctly continues to increase. For example, one might undertake to predict the mean number of persons to be found in conversational clusters in lobbies of various kinds of buildings upon certain kinds of occasions. Since these clusters might reasonably vary in size from two (or one?) to perhaps seven or eight, one might feel confident that he had discovered the right clues if he found himself picking the correct mean number (to the nearest integer, let us say) in (let us say) three such experiments out of four.

But social scientists have long used another strategem to increase their confidence that the outcome of a *single* study is not a chance event. This strategem is the statistical *significance test*. This technique proceeds as follows. First, the investigator chooses a particular quantitative outcome that he believes would be the most probable outcome if nothing but chance were affecting the outcome of his experiment. If the investigator had decided to test the hypothesis that he could produce greater high-jumping ability by a certain regimen than is produced by a traditional regimen, he would ask himself what he would predict if he were wrong about his hypothesis and only chance were going to decide whether high jumpers trained under his regimen or jumpers trained traditionally would jump higher. He might reasonably feel that if the new method of training and the old have substantially equivalent effects on the jumpers, then the most likely result would be no difference at all in mean height of jumping between the two groups, that is, the most probable mean difference in jumping would be exactly zero, even though it could also happen that the mean difference would depart to some degree from zero. In fact, it is very likely indeed that the actual difference would depart at least in some slight degree from zero; if only chance is operating to separate the groups, the probability of the difference turning out to lie between -0.0005 and $+0.0005$ of an inch, while larger than the probability of the difference lying within any other interval of 0.001 of an inch, is still very small. The probability of the difference being larger than 0.0005 (in either direction) is very large.

Continuing with this line of thought, and still supposing the actual difference between the two regimens (aside from chance effects) to be zero, we discover that the probability that the difference between two actual groups will turn out to be *at least* 0.005 of an inch (in either direction) is a little less than the probability of its being at least 0.0005, even though it is still large. And the probability of its being at least 0.05 is a little less still; and so on with 0.1 of an inch, with 0.2, 0.3, and with 1 inch. The probability that a mean difference as large as 1 inch (or larger) would occur by chance between two groups actually equivalent in high-jumping ability is surely rather small.[7] The probability of obtaining a mean difference of 10 inches purely by happenstance is surely so low as to make the outcome unbelievable. This disbelief is the next step in the strategy of statistical inference.

We stated that the researcher begins this reasoning by asking himself what he thinks the most likely outcome if nothing but chance were operating in his experiment. Then we saw that if only chance is operating, outcomes farther and farther from the most likely outcome are less and less likely. To return to the example of the high-jumping groups, if the difference that does occur is large enough to make the probability of that much difference (or more) *extremely* improbable, then it is reasonable to doubt whether the result *did* indeed occur by chance. Finally, if we reject the chance explanation and there are only two outcomes allowed, the remaining alternative is the hypothesis the researcher preferred in the first place—that the outcome was due to his experimental design. The viability of that hypothesis, of course, depends on how well the study design has ruled out alternative plausible hypotheses (as discussed in Chapter 3).

It is possible, given a few assumptions, to compute the probabilities of certain quantitative outcomes when nothing other than chance is operating (see any introductory text in statistics for social scientists, for example, Hays, 1963). Using the techniques of statistical inference, the investigator can compute these probabilities after he has chosen a particular quantitative outcome[8] to represent the most likely outcome if only chance is operating. Then, if his computation of the probability of the outcome that actually occurred is very small—say, one in a hundred—he rejects the hypothesis that it occurred in a situation in which only chance was operating and, instead, adopts the alternative that the nonchance factor he hypothesized in his design may be responsible for the outcome.

For various technical and strategic reasons, tests of hypotheses by statistical inference (called tests of significance) have come into question in recent years. For example, Bakan (1967, p. xiv) has said, "the test of significance . . .

[7] Given groups of reasonably large size.

[8] This outcome is called the *null hypothesis*.

yields little or no information in most of the instances in which it is used in psychological research." The arguments are technical and we shall not go into them here. The interested reader should consult such articles as those by Bakan (1966), Edwards (1965), Lykken (1968), Meehl (1967), and Winch and Campbell (1969). Regardless of the utility of the significance test, however, the researcher will always find the chance hypothesis competing with the hypothesis for which he is seeking evidence. Depending on the various costs involved, the researcher will want to devote some portion of his resources to features of design that will increase his confidence that the outcome of his research is not merely a happenstance.

14-14. Combining Evidence from Different Studies

Persons and groups move in many contexts and display myriad behaviors. But any one study must limit its observations and its conclusions to a small fraction of the types of persons or groups conceivable, to one or a few contexts, and to a small portion of the behaviors that might usefully be observed. How, then, can the behavior of even a limited class of living system—let us say, the middle income, midwestern, white, married, Protestant, third-or-more-generation, male, U.S. citizen—ever be exhaustively, or even adequately described? How can a collection of studies of this creature somehow be pooled and conclusions drawn from comparisons among the studies? In Chapter 3, we pointed out numerous dangers in observing different groups of actors without carefully designing the ways comparisons were to be made between the groups; but independent researchers conducting studies unknown to each other do not usually design their observations to be compared later. In section 6-4, we described the multitrait-multimethod paradigm to show how validity depends on overlapping measuring methods and behaviors; but independent researchers do not necessarily choose overlapping methods and behavior dimensions. How can separate studies yield cumulative knowledge about human behavior?

Many writers on science claim that knowledge of human behavior cumulates through accretions to "the literature," and professors tell their students that their duty as researchers is not discharged until they have published reports of their studies. But, surely, the cumulation of knowledge must mean more than the accumulation of pages of reports. Indeed, the whole purpose of theory (a special sort of "knowledge") is to describe more and more of the real world in fewer and fewer concepts and discourses. To the extent that the researcher's efforts end by merely increasing the number of reports in the library, the results are something like a row of trophies on a shelf. They are a source of pride and comfort to the winner and are interesting to his friends—but there is little to do with a collection of trophies except stand them in a row and recall with pleasure the effort that went into winning them. We claim that scientific reports will *usually* suffer this same fate unless (1) the studies are deliberately designed to dovetail in useful ways with other studies and (2) some investigator deliberately undertakes the task of comparing two or more studies and drawing new conclusions. Comparison is a human act, not something that happens by osmosis on a library shelf.

By many times, the greatest portion of the literature in the social sciences reports new data. In most of these reports, the author claims a theoretical connection to earlier studies through one or more variables common to his study and the earlier studies. Rarely, however, does the author consider in detail the differences in the measures of those variables he used in his study and the measures used in past studies. Even more rarely does the author invoke the logic of the multitrait-multimethod paradigm in making his comparisons. Rarely, too, does the author specify precisely the domain of behavior toward objects he studied in comparison to past studies, or the comparative contexts. Sometimes it is even uncertain whether an author was intending to study individuals, groups, or organizations. These same imprecisions and logical gaps characterize even the articles (few in number compared to those reporting new data) that explicitly undertake to *compare* a cluster of research reports. In fact, even many of the latter sort of article are "review" articles and do not presume to do a tightly logical job of drawing new conclusions from old studies; rather, they serve as guides to the literature for readers who might like to try drawing their own new conclusions. The article that makes the explicit attempt to compare previous studies with careful attention to theoretical and technical detail is rare. One of the most careful articles of this sort is the one by Zajonc (1965) on social facilitation; another is the one by Bronfenbrenner (1958) on social class and child rearing, mentioned in section 2-2. Bronfenbrenner describes some of the difficulties of reaching for new conclusions in a collection of old reports, given the nature of the ordinary literature in social science:

> The difficulties involved in comparing the results of more than a dozen studies conducted at different times and places for somewhat different purposes are at once formidable, delicate, and perilous (p. 405).
>
> . . . there was considerable variation in the number of social class categories employed. Thus, in the Anderson report, data were analyzed in terms of seven SES levels, the New York survey distinguished five, the second Chicago and the two Detroit studies each had four, and Klatskin used three. The majority, however, following the precedent of Havighurst and Davis, differentiated two levels only (p. 404).
>
> A source of variation perhaps not sufficiently emphasized in these and other reports is the manner in which cases were selected. As Davis and Havighurst properly pointed out in their original publication, their sample was subject to possible bias "in the direction of getting a middle-class group which had been subjected to the kind of teaching about child rearing which is prevalent among the middle-class people who send their children to nursery schools." Equally important may be the relatively high proportion in the Chicago lower-class sample of mothers coming from East European and Irish background, or the four-year discrepancy in the average ages of the mothers at the two class levels (p. 406).

> In interpreting reports of child-rearing practices it is essential to distinguish between the date at which the information was obtained and the actual period to which the information refers. This caution is particularly relevant in dealing with descriptions of infant care for children who (as in the Eugene or Detroit studies) may be as old as 12, 14, or 18 at the time of the interview. In such instances it is possible only to guess at the probable time at which the practice occurred by making due allowances for the age of the child. The problem is further complicated by the fact that none of the studies reports SES differences by age. The best one can do, therefore, is to estimate the median age of the group and from this approximate the period at which the practice may have taken place (pp. 406–407).
>
> It is clear that many factors, some known and many more unknown, may operate to produce differences in results from one sample to the next. It is hardly likely, however, that these manifold influences will operate in a consistent direction over time or space. The possibility of obtaining interpretable findings, therefore, rests on the long chance that major trends, if they exist, will be sufficiently marked to override the effects of bias arising from variations in sampling and method. This is a rash and optimistic hope, but—somewhat to our own surprise—it seems to have been realized a least in part, in [our] analyses . . . (p. 406).

There are some examples in the literature of series of studies designed to dovetail and produce conclusions beyond a mere listing from the separate studies. Almost always, such a series is directed by one man; examples are the work of Fiedler (1967) on leadership and J. R. P. French (1963) on the social environment of mental health. Sometimes a series of cumulating studies is produced by a group following the strong leadership of one or two men; an example is the program of studies on attitude change conducted at Yale (see Hovland, 1957; Hovland and Janis, 1959; Hovland, Janis, and Kelley, 1953; and Hovland and Rosenberg, 1960). These programs of work, given overlapping designs by the conceptualization of one man or of a small group of closely compatible men, make a clear contrast with the bulk of studies in the literature that connect with one another only through using a few common methods and designs in their actual execution. Investigators who want to learn a lot about some domain of behavior usually find that the existing literature fails to fit together well enough to give them confidence in drawing conclusions from it beyond those drawn in the separate reports—and this despite the fact that the literature is sometimes voluminous. For a discussion of problems in comparing observations in different cultures, societies, and political systems, see Przeworski and Teune (1970). In brief, if the cumulative effects of studies are to be maximized, those studies must be related to one another by the same tactics used within any one study—the tactics we set forth in Chapters 3 and 4.

Knowledge will cumulate more rapidly if researchers do not leave the task of comparing their studies with future studies entirely to some obliging future thinker but instead take at least the first step of this task by specifying with precision the natural system they believe they are studying, as well as the populations or domains of actor, behavior, object, and context and the methods they use to reach these systems, populations, and domains empirically. If the problem chosen makes it impossible to be precise about one or more of these matters, it will be helpful to readers of the report if the researcher says so explicitly.

14-15. A Brief Reprise

In this chapter we surveyed, in summary fashion, some of the choices facing the researcher as he goes about his work and gave special attention to a few complexities that transcend the particular phases of the research process. Throughout this book, we have emphasized that the research process involves a series of choices, each of which affects (1) the choices available in later stages of the process; (2) the kinds of questions that can be answered by the study; and (3) the range of alternative answers that can be adduced from study results. Those choices are, ultimately, arbitrary. There is no one best set of choices; what is best in a particular case depends on the problem, the state of prior knowledge, the assumptions the investigator is willing to make, the resources he has available, and, especially, his purposes, or the questions he wishes to investigate.

But although the choices are arbitrary, they are in no sense trivial. Each choice point presents a set of alternatives, each of which offers some advantages and imposes some limitations. The outcome of a study is in large measure shaped by the interdependent series of choices the investigator makes. What the study can find out, and indeed what it does find out, depends to a great extent on the alternatives chosen—and this is the case whether the investigator thinks out all of the choices carefully or makes some of the choices without being aware he has chosen.

The purpose of this book, then, has been to lay out the choice points and the alternatives offered by each; to indicate the "leverage" to be gained by each alternative and also the constraints imposed by it; and to show how choices at one stage tie into and modify the choices available at later stages of the research process. In other words, to return to an analogy used in Chapter 1, we have tried to construct a detailed and useful map of the research process. We shall recapitulate some of the major choice points here.

SOME MAJOR CHOICE POINTS IN THE RESEARCH PROCESS

Chapter 2. What questions am I pursuing? What systems are to be studied? What actors, behaviors, and contexts are involved? What form of question am I investigating (comparison, correlation, description, exploration, test of theory, or whatever)?

Chapter 3. How should I design my study? With what properties of the systems to be studied must I reckon? How shall I choose treatments?

hapter 4. In what setting and by what over-all strategy shall I gather e? What resources does this require? What amount and kinds of tion can I gain?

napter 5. How shall I select events (actors, behaviors, contexts) from among a population, and how shall I apportion them to be observed?

Chapter 6. How shall I operationalize each property of concern? How shall I know, afterwards, the usefulness of my measures and the generalizability of the information gained from their use?

Chapter 7. From what sources (subjective report, direct observation, or other) shall I seek evidence about each property which is to be measured? What comparisons among objects shall I ask of the actor?

Chapter 8. How shall I carry out manipulation and control procedures?

Chapter 9. How shall I solicit and interact with the actors while conducting the study?

Chapter 10. How shall I convert observational records into data? What types of data can I generate? What assumptions do I wish to make about the data?

Chapters 11 and 12. How shall I organize the data for analysis? What kinds of questions do I want to ask of the data? What kinds of analytic models are available for my questions, given my data and assumptions?

Chapter 13. How shall I relate sets of data to each other? What kinds of analytic models are available? Which models can I use, given my questions, my design, my data, and my assumptions?

Chapter 14. What inferences can I validly make from results of my analyses? What constraints are there on internal validity? What limitations are there on external validity? What do my results mean in terms of my initial questions? What do my results mean in relation to evidence from other studies?

SOME CLOSING COMMENTS

We have tried to be explicit and emphatic about the fact that there is no one best research design. Even for a particular researcher investigating a particular hypothesis with a particular assortment of resources and certain purposes in mind, there is not one best design. Some research designs are surely more promising than others for certain researchers, problems, populations, and purposes. Some designs will be very bad for certain purposes. But no matter how precisely we specify criteria at the outset, there will remain numerous alternatives of design that promise about equal advantages. However, whether a design is filled in by using a tossed coin or a sophisticated theory of method, the final form of the design always affects to a greater or lesser degree the conclusions that can reasonably be drawn from the outcomes. In other words, the conclusions reached must inevitably depend on the design of the research and hence upon the predilections of the designer, his values, and his purposes. A clear and concise discussion of these and related matters has been given by Madge (1965, pp. xv-xxxv).

The idiosyncrasies of the designer-researcher do not make his research less valid any more than the view of a mountain from the east is less valid than the view from the west, or a picture of the mountain taken in infrared light less valid than one taken in ultraviolet. It is important to keep in mind that wresting information from the real world is always, and inevitably, an interaction between the researcher and the empirical world. The research report is the narrative of that interaction. It is as important for the report to tell what the researcher put into the interaction—his choices, assumptions, and values—as it is to put in the record of the behavior that was observed. Of course, it is evident to the reader by now that the number of choices a researcher makes either implicitly or explicitly is very large, and to remark upon them all—even if only upon those of which the researcher is aware—would make research reports very much larger than they customarily are today. However, the researcher can maximize the chances that his work will cumulate with the work of others in a mutually illuminating way if he specifies as precisely as he can the main frames of his study: the natural system he seeks ultimately to understand, the population of these systems (actors) about which he wants to come to conclusions, the behavior he wants to encompass, the objects important to this behavior, the contexts of it, and any values or purposes he holds that will help others to understand more fully his assumptions and biases.

This is not to say that once one has made an honest effort to explain his biases that his interpretation of the facts is then bound to be as good as any other. Where empirical matters are concerned, we insist (along with almost all scientists) that goodness of fit to the observations is a crucial criterion for the "goodness" of an interpretation. The explanation that covers more facts and that includes a way of instructing people how to *test* whether a fact is covered—such an explanation should win out, in our belief, over an explanation that covers fewer facts or leaves us uncertain which facts it can encompass.

Within the structure of the facts, however, there can always be more than one way of selecting facets, more than one set of axioms with which to begin a theory, and more than one way to design an experiment—even though the facets, the theories, and the experimental designs may all seek to encompass some or all of the same set of observable facts. There is always room for a new theory, a new set of assumptions, or a new style of experimentation if it gives us a new insight for comparing observations with concepts.

Appendix I

Assumptions Underlying Analytic Models

In Chapter 10, we discussed three assumptions needed to translate observation records into any kind of datum (that is, into any data quadrant) and two further assumptions needed to map records into dominance data (QIa, IIa, IIIa, IVa). We turn now to still further assumptions needed when we analyze an array of data.[1] By analyze, we mean to seek a pattern that will enable us to describe the data more economically than by a sheer listing of them. But before proceeding, let us recapitulate briefly the first five assumptions.

The data models of QIIb and QIIIb for proximity data rest on these assumptions:

1. Datum a relation: a datum is a relation on a pair of points or a pair of distances.

2. Common dimension: there exists as least one dimension (aspect) that is psychologically common (relevant) to both real-world counterparts of the two points.

3. Excluded indifference: either a given relation or its complement connects the two points; no third category exists.

The data models of QIa, QIIa, QIIIa, and QIVa for dominance data rest on assumptions 1, 2, and 3 and also upon 4 and 5:

4. Positive direction: the researcher decides in advance which response he will arbitrarily call positive and interpret to mean that one point dominated a second, not that the second dominated the first.

5. Monotonicity: the relation between the response (positive or negative) and the order of the two points is monotonic.

[1]Neither in Chapter 10 nor here do we claim to have stated the sufficient assumptions for data-models and analytic models. We claim only to have stated some necessary and important assumptions. Some writers (for example, Suppes and Zinnes, 1963; Adams, Fagot, and Robinson, 1965) are now examining assumptions in the field of "fundamental measurement," and we hope studies of the same logical and rigorous sort will return soon to data proper.

An assumption necessary to every analysis model is the assumption that if the same form of datum is interpreted from two separate observations, then the two data are equivalent and interchangeable. The two observations could be of two actors presented with the same stimulus; for example, one actor might mark alternative b on a test item after only a little thought while another marks alternative b only after prolonged thought during which he chews a fingernail. However, once these two responses are translated into data by tally-marks in the column for alternative b of that item, the researcher then assumes the two data equivalent and interchangeable. Again, the two observations could be made of the same actor at two different times; in two separate elections, for example, the nation might elect a Republican president. One election might have had a very different quality from the other. If the researcher is examining only the party identity of the winning candidate, he translates the two observations into the same data form and treats the two data as interchangeable. We can call this assumption the assumption of the interchangeability of actors, or—more accurately—the *interchangeability of identical response patterns* (assumption 6).

Let us look at a few more aspects of this assumption. If person A says "yes" to a question, and so does person B, this assumption leads us to say that A and B have given equivalent responses—and, by implication, that they are responding to the *same* aspect or aspects of the stimulus question. By this assumption, A and B belong in the same response class, and either one is an equally good representative of it. It may be that A and B actually were responding to different aspects of the question; but unless we get further information on which they differ (for example, by asking additional questions bearing on the same matter), we must assume that we can treat the actors as the same because their responses are the same. This matter is related to the point made in Chapter 3; namely, to treat things as different, we must have some basis for specifying how they differ; and to treat things as the same, we must ignore all of the uncounted ways in which they may actually differ, on the premise that those differences do not make a significant difference for our purposes.

Chapter 11 discusses analytic models that make the assumption of *unidimensionality:* that there exists exactly one dimension—no more, no fewer—relevant to the relations among actors and stimuli (assumption 7).

Chapters 11 and 12 are subdivided to treat deterministic models in one section and probabilistic models in another. Deterministic models make the assumption of *deterministic location:* that each actor point and stimulus point, considered alone, has a location with a probability equal to one (assumption 8). That is, the researcher accepts the datum he has translated from his observation as having the meaning he puts on it—such as: the actor preferred candidate A to candidate B at the time of the observation—with no reservations. The researcher does not say to himself, "The actor probably preferred A to B; he'd probably say that most of the time if a series of people asked him."

The researcher takes the datum at face value, at least until the pattern in other portions of the data force him to reconsider. We shall say more about deterministic and probabilistic analytic models below.

Assumptions for Unidimensional Analytic Models

Our account of the assumptions necessary to the several sorts of data and to the several sorts of analytic models is becoming somewhat complex. We have said that assumptions 1, 2, and 3 lead to the data models of QIIb and QIIIb; that those assumptions together with assumptions 4 and 5 lead to the data models of QIa, IIa, IIIa, and IVa; and that further assumptions in combination with 1 through 5 lead to further delineations of analytic models. These logical relations are diagramed in Figure I-1. So far, we have described the relations between assumptions 1 through 5 and the data models (diagramed at the left side of the figure) and the necessity for assumptions 6 through 8 in building deterministic unidimensional analytic models (indicated in the upper-central portion of the diagram). In the rest of this section, we shall trace out the remainder of the relations in the diagram (each arrow means "leads to" in the logical sense), confining our attention all the while to models for one dimension.

To recapitulate, we have said that assumptions 6, 7, and 8, repeated below, lead to deterministic unidimensional models for analyzing data.

6. Interchangeability (or equivalence) of actors: response patterns identi-

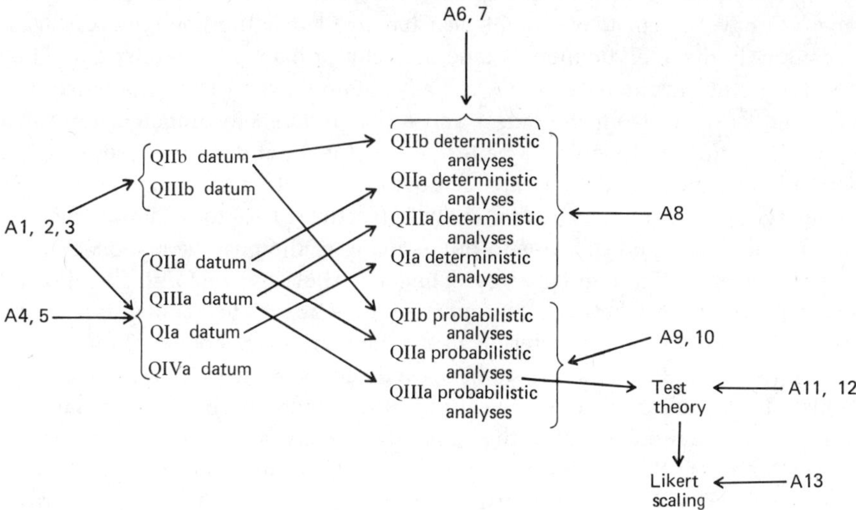

Figure I-1. Assumptions underlying unidimensional analytic models.

cal in form in the data matrix are identical psychologically and may be interchanged without significant effect.

7. Unidimensionality: there exists exactly one dimension relevant to the relations among actors and stimuli.

8. Deterministic location: each actor point and stimulus point, considered alone, has a location with probability equal to one.

Assumptions 6 and 8 deserve special comment, beginning with assumption 6. It is obvious that in some studies we shall not be willing to interchange the response of one actor for another without limit. We shall want sometimes to distinguish one category of actor from another even before establishing scale positions for the individual actors. That is, we may want to test the nature of the scale that one and another category of actor will "accept." It may be that actors in one category array themselves differently among the stimuli, or among one another, than do actors in another category.

When this sort of consideration arises, we are facing the problem of partitioning discussed in "Partitioning," section 3-2. If we decide *before* the data analysis that we want to perform the analysis separately for two or more categories of actor, we are making a *design partition*. If we *enter* the analysis to discover two or more categories of actor according to whether they cluster on one scale or another, we are then making an *observed partition*. It is, of course, at the point where the data or the scaling pattern identifies actor, behavior toward object, or context that the working connections are made between the design of the partitions in the study (Chapter 3), the design for collecting observations (Chapters 7 through 10), and the analysis of data (Chapters 11, 12, and 13).

Assumption 8 also deserves additional comment. As well as using the label we have given it, we might also have called it the goodness-of-fit assumption. Some analytic models take the actor at his word, so to speak. They take the datum in the data matrix not as containing error from the outset but as being "correct" from the outset and to be declared incompetent only if it turns out in the end to violate a pattern set by the other data. In these so-called deterministic models, the researcher does his best to arrange the data so as to satisfy the model. In scalogram analysis (section 11-4), for example, he tries to rearrange rows and columns to put as many of the positive response tallies as possible into a triangular array. Then he labels the remaining responses as error. To decide whether to accept the model as a "true" configuration, the researcher employs some criterion using the concept of goodness of fit.

One sometimes hears it said, or even sees it written, that deterministic models for analysis are not as useful as they might be because actual data so rarely fit the model; that is, the actual data rarely show the perfect pattern. But such an assertion shows poor understanding of the human spirit; humans are not often discouraged from using a good idea by a small discrepancy from reality. The fact is that deterministic models for data analysis have seen a good deal of use in recent years. Researchers manage this by using the principle of goodness of fit. If the data take a pattern that seems a sufficiently good approximation to the specifications of the model, they declare the model vindicated and the data as conforming to it—or at least those data that did indeed fall inside the specifications of the model.

In brief, researchers *do* use a concept of probability when they use deterministic models for data analysis. They assume that some of the data are not going to fit the model. They cannot tell in advance which particular observation is going to produce the recalcitrant datum. But they know that some of the data will have to be labeled error. While the probability concept in the probabilistic model says that every datum deviates to some extent from its "true" value, the probability concept in the deterministic model says that every *obtained configuration* of data deviates *in the case of a few data* from the "true" configuration.

This is not to say that a student of models must assume a probability process to *talk about* or *design* deterministic models. What we are saying is that researchers do accept error in unpredictable outcroppings when they *use* deterministic models, and accepting this error is a probabilistic process. Furthermore, the motivation to make a model useful is the same motivation that prompts the use of the probabilistic assumption in probabilistic models. Even though we have shown that the labels *deterministic* and *probabilistic* imply a difference in use that does not exist, we shall go on using the two terms because of the custom in the literature. The reader should keep in mind, nevertheless, that researchers accept unpredictable error when using both sorts of analytic models.

We give below some examples of deterministic, unidimensional, analytic models that make use of certain data models. Some of these analytic models are discussed in Chapter 11; some are not. We mention the analytic models we do in this section not because every one is easy to use or better in some sense than others, but (1) to connect our modes of classification to the existing literature for the convenience of those familiar with it and (2) to identify that literature for those who would like to become better acquainted with it. Some of the brief phrases identifying analytic models will seem cryptic to the beginner; Chapter 11 gives these phrases more meaning. Our chief purpose in this section is to provide a verbal map to go with Figure I-1.

The following analytic models require *assumptions 1, 2, 3, 6, 7, 8, and the data model of QIIb:*

Rating scales and direct measurement[2] of all sorts.

Method of subjective estimate or absolute judgment (see Torgerson, 1958, Chapter 4).

Method of prescribed ratio (see Torgerson, 1958, pp. 97–104).

[2]By direct measurement, we mean that an observer (usually the actor) assigns a number directly to an object or other experience; for example, the actor reports that one light is *twice* as bright as another.

The examples above are methods requiring only the mentioned assumptions when the actor's judgment is taken directly as the scale value. When responses of more than one actor are averaged, however, or responses at more than one time are averaged, then the assumption of probabilistic position is being called upon. This point is discussed in Chapter 11.

No practicable, deterministic, unidimensional, analytic model exists at this writing for the above assumptions and the datum model of QIIIb.

The following analytic model requires *assumptions 1 through 8 and the data model of QIIa:*

> Scalogram analysis (including the skewed hourglass and disorderly interlocking; see Chapter 11).

The following analytic models require *assumptions 1 through 8 and the data model of QIIIa:*

> Stevens' (1958) method of ratio estimation—though the assumption of probabilistic location enters when means are taken over actors or times. See also Coombs (1964, pp. 371–374) and Torgerson (1958, pp. 97–112).
>
> Triangular analysis of *distances* to obtain an ordering on distances. But analysis of configuration of points is usually carried out by comparing these distances as inputs to a method of analysis in QIa or QIVa. For discussion of the paucity of deterministic unidimensional models for QIIIa, see Coombs (1964, pp. 347–359).

The following analytic model requires *assumptions 1 through 8 and the data model of QIa:*

> Unfolding analysis (including parallelogram analysis and the skewed hourglass).

No practicable, deterministic, unidimensional, analytic model exists at this writing for the above assumptions and the datum model QIVa.

We now need two new assumptions:

9. Probabilistic location: each actor point or stimulus point has a location with a probability less than one. That is, at any moment that an actor observes a stimulus, he may find it to have a quantity that differs somewhat from what he would find at another time; and these quantities cluster about a mean that we might call the "true" quantity of that stimulus.

10. Local independence: If two actor points are "in the same locality" in respect to some property (for example, if two individuals are close to each other in spelling ability) and if both respond positively (or negatively) to a particular stimulus (for example, if both are able to spell *cantankerous*), then the response of one to a second stimulus nevertheless remains independent

of the response of the other to the second stimulus (for example, though both can spell *cantankerous,* the ability of one actor to spell *callipygian* is not connected to the ability of the other to spell it). In other words, the probability of placement of two stimulus points about one actor point is taken to have no necessary connection to the probability of the placement of those points about a second actor point when the two actor points are close together. In more technical language, "the correlation between items is due to the latent variable x, and if this is held constant or partialled out, the probability of responding positively to two or more items is the product of the probabilities of responding positively to each" (Coombs, 1964, p. 312; see also pp. 306–307).

Assumptions 6, 7, 9, and 10 lead to probabilistic unidimensional models for analyzing data. Some examples of probabilistic, unidimensional, analytic models using the several data models are mentioned below. The following analytic models require *assumptions 1, 2, 3, 6, 7, 9, and 10 and the data model of QIIb:*

Stevens' (1956) method of magnitude estimation.

Lazarsfeld's (1959) latent class analysis. See also Coombs (1964, pp. 305–309). *Note:* this model does not by itself yield an ordered scale; it yields nominal categories (classes) that may be interpreted as ordered or multidimensional according to further information about the categories.

Lazarsfeld's (1959) latent structure analysis with nonmonotonic trace line. See also Coombs (1964, pp. 312–314).

For the method of equal-appearing intervals (see Torgerson, 1958, p. 67–87), we need not only *assumptions 1, 2, 3, 6, 7, 9, and 10 and the data model of QIIb but also the three error assumptions below:*

9a. Error component: the position of an item on the scale is composed of two components: (1) the "true" position and (2) the "error" or deviation of the actually occurring position from the "true" position.

10a. Independent errors: upon repeated responses, errors occur independently of one another.

11. Random error distribution: errors are distributed randomly (or normally) around the true position.

We have numbered these as we have because it seems to us that assumption 9a implies 9 and, given 9a, that 10a is another way of stating 10. The three statements just above embody phrasing which is more common in the literature of scaling and testing than is our phrasing of 9 and 10.

No practicable, unidimensional, analytic model exists at this writing for the above assumptions and the data model of QIIIb.

The following analytic models require *assumptions 1 through 7, 9 and 10 and the data model of QIIa:*

Torgerson's (1958, Chapter 10) law of categorical judgment, along with the special cases of the methods of successive intervals of Saffir (1937), Mosier (1940), and Diederich, Messick, and Tucker (1957), as well as Attneave's (1949) method of graded dichotomies, Garner and Hake's (1951) scale of equidiscriminability, and Edwards' (1952) special case of the method of successive intervals. For comments, see Torgerson (1958, pp. 210–241) and Coombs (1964, pp. 238–242).

Lazarsfeld's (1959) latent-distance analysis.

Lazarsfeld's (1959) latent-structure analysis with monotonic trace line.

Classical test theory also makes use of the QIIa datum model within one dimension. It differs from models we have mentioned so far, however, in that it deals with *test scores* rather than with items separately. A model such as Torgerson's law of categorical judgment seeks patterns among test scores, ignoring patterns of response among items and treating them as interchangeable. Test theory requires the error assumptions, which we now restate in terms of test scores:

9b. Error component: a test score is composed of two components: (1) the "true" score and (2) the "error" or deviation of the actually occurring score from the "true" score.

10b. Independent errors: upon repeated testings, errors occur independently of one another.

11a. Random error distribution: errors are distributed randomly (or normally) around the true score.

And in addition to assumptions already mentioned, classical test theory requires yet another; namely:

12. Interchangeability of positive responses: items within a test are psychologically indistinguishable:[3] an actor's response to one is psychologically equivalent to the same direction of response to another.

Classical test theory requires *assumptions 1 through 7 and 9 through 12 as well as the model of QIIa*. The rationale of this random-error model and the assumptions involved in it will now be sketched very briefly. For further explanation, see Chapter 11.

[3] At least, items of the same *difficulty* (a technical term explained in Chapter 11) are taken as indistinguishable. Assumption 10 makes this qualification possible.

The random-error model first provides some way to combine data into a score (for example, by counting the number of items to which a "correct" response was given) and then interprets the score (X) as having two additive components: a "true score" (T), and an "error" (e); that is, $X = T + e$. Further, the error component is assumed to be small (relative to differences between true scores for different data) and randomly distributed around the value of T. The distribution of e is usually assumed to be that of the *normal curve,* a symmetrical curve describing the way many sorts of chance events do indeed distribute themselves. This interpretation assumes that any *obtained* score X is a value occurring at random from a distribution of possible X scores, with the mean of the X-score distribution equal to the T score, and with the X scores distributed "normally." On a series of repeated observations, therefore, the X scores will show some variance, but they will cluster about T. The variation may show up in inconsistency, because if X_1 and X_2 are close enough together so that their error distributions overlap, then some comparisons of them will have $X_2 > X_1$ even though most comparisons, as well as the "true" locations of X_1 and X_2 on the underlying dimension, might have $X_1 > X_2$.[4] All of this assumes that each measurement of X is independent of every other measurement (that is, one measurement neither affects nor is affected by the next)—so that the location of each observed X score in its distribution (hence, its e component) is independent of every other X score.

This packet of three assumptions—(9b) $X = T + e$, (10b) *e*s distributed randomly, and (11a) *e*s independent for repeated measurements of X—is the basis for most "error-tolerant" analytic models. The addition of assumption 12 is needed for many of the analytic models that make up test theory or mental test theory, the assumption of interchangeability of positive responses. This assumption means that if a test has 10 items, for example, and two people each answer five items correctly, they will be given the same *score* even if they answered *different* items correctly. Thus, the assumption says that to pass (dominate) any one item is equivalent to passing any other item—that it takes the same amount of the underlying attribute to pass one item as to pass any other item.

Mental test theory, employing the forgoing error assumptions and the assumption of interchangeability of items, is usually applied to tests containing dichotomous items. However, the same assumptions can be applied to data construed from observations taken through verbal items of other types. One application is to "tests" involving multiple-alternative items, where the items have more than two alternatives and some alternatives are "more correct" than others. For example, there may be a three-alternative item for which one answer is "best," another next best, and the third poorest from the point of view of the investigator's arbitrary decision about positive direction of the item. This

[4]See the law of comparative judgment model, Chapter 11, for a discussion of interpretation of confusion (inconsistency) as distance.

assumes an *ordered set* of alternatives. If it is further assumed that the alternatives are spaced at equal intervals (that is, poorest to middle is the same distance as middle to best), then the researcher might assign one point or credit for the middle alternative, two points for the best alternative, and zero points for the poorest. To say this another way, the alternatives can be weighted with numbers indicating how much the researcher guesses each alternative contributes to an over-all positive score when summed up over a collection of such items, the collection of such items itself being called a scale. Obtaining a score in this manner requires the following assumption:

13. Equal intervals among alternatives: the intervals among item alternatives are equal (or as otherwise specified) not only within an item but also between corresponding alternatives of different items.

This is the basis for many analyses of attitudes; further information can be found in Edwards (1957), Fishbein (1967), Oppenheim (1966), and Shaw and Wright (1967). We return now to our list of examples of probabilistic unidimensional analytic models. Our last set of examples dealt with those making use of QIIa data; we go now to QIIIa data.

The following analytic model requires *assumptions 1 through 7, 9, 10, and 11 and the data model of QIIIa:*

Thurstone's (1927a, b,) law of comparative judgment.

No practicable analytic model exists at this writing for those assumptions and the data models of QIa and QIVa.

We have now described all the assumptions indicated in Figure I-1. We mentioned, however, no analytic models making use of the data models of QIIIb or QIVa. The reason is that the literature contains no practicable unidimensional models of this sort. The data of QIIIb and QIVa are especially well suited to multidimensional analyses, not unidimensional; Coombs (1964, Chapters 19 and 20) has discussed this point.

The methods of data analysis most often used by social scientists up to the present—at least by those who collect observations by verbal methods—have been the unidimensional, probabilistic methods. These methods, as we saw, include test theory and Likert-type attitude scales. These will be discussed further in Chapter 11.

We now turn to multidimensional models. In doing so, it is well to note that multidimensional models do not comprise a different species from unidimensional models. Unidimensional models are obviously the special case where the number of dimensions is one. In fact, all multidimensional models contain some mechanism for testing out the suitability of different dimensionalities. Other things being equal, a multidimensional model seeks the smallest dimensionality within which the data may be encompassed while still observing the other built-in rules of the model. There are not separate models for two dimensions, for three dimensions, and so forth. Consequently, a solution to a data matrix using a multidimensional model is quite capable of producing a unidimensional solution.[5]

Assumptions for Multidimensional Analytic Models

We give below the assumption for multidimensionality and then list the assumptions and data models underlying some multidimensional analytic models. Some of these models are described in more detail in Chapter 12. The exposition in this section will follow the scheme of Figure I-2. The left side of Figure I-2 is, of course, identical with that side of Figure I-1. But the data models contribute in different proportions than in the earlier figure to the deterministic and probabilistic analytic models. And, of course, the symbol for assumption 7 (unidimensionality) has vanished from the top of the page and has been replaced by the number 14 (for multidimensionality).

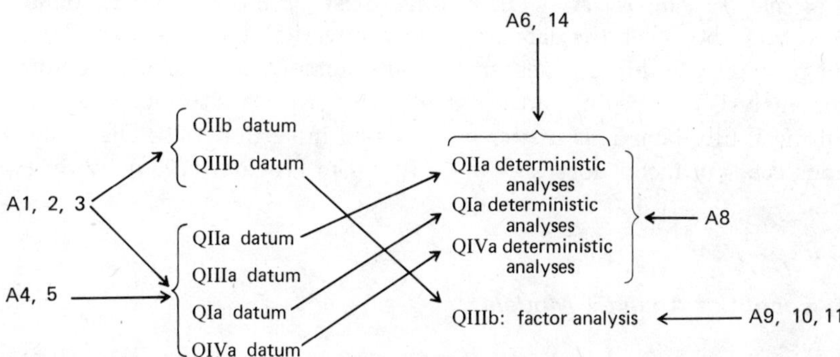

Figure I-2. Assumptions underlying multidimensional analytic models.

14. Multidimensionality: there exist one or more dimensions relevant to the relations among actors and stimuli.

Turning first to deterministic models, we find that the following requires *assumptions 1 through 6, 8 and 14 and the data model of QIIa:*

> Milholland's (see Coombs, 1964, pp. 245–259) conjunctive and disjunctive models.

The following analytic model requires *assumptions 1 through 6, 8 and 14 and the data model of QIa or IVa:*

[5] A good example of how a multidimensional model can be used to find a *unidimensional* solution that is "better" in specifiable ways than solutions achievable by unidimensional models is given by Shepard and Carroll (1966).

Hays' (see Coombs, 1964, Chapters 21 and 22) model for multidimensional unfolding of similarities.

Shepard's (1962 I, II) model for the analysis of proximities. See also Shepard and Carroll (1966).

Carroll's (1963) model with the continuity criterion. Young's (1968) program for nonmetric scaling. Guttman-Lingoes programs (see Chapter 12).

We note here that the nonmetric programs for computers are very adaptable. Although we have classified them as consumers of QIVa data, most can be adjusted to accept data from almost all quadrants. These matters are discussed in Chapter 12.

No practicable, deterministic, multidimensional, analytic model exists at this writing for the above assumptions and the data models of QIIb, QIIIa, or QIIIb.

At this writing, the only probabilistic multidimensional models existing are those of *factor analysis*. These all require *assumptions 1 through 6, 9, 11, and 14 and the data model of QIIIb*. Regardless of the manner of obtaining observations, however, the data are always converted into measures of similarity or proximity within one set (such as an intercorrelation matrix) before the factor analysis can begin, and for that reason we classify factor analysis as requiring QIIIb data. This matter is discussed in section 12-4. Discussions of various types of factor analysis can be found in Fruchter (1954) and in Horst (1965).

Facets of Analytic Models

We saw in Chapter 10 that it is possible to set forth three facets for *data models* and that at least two facets are useful in classifying *analytic models*. One such facet is that of unidimensionality (A7) versus multidimensionality (A14). The other is that of the so-called deterministic models (A8) versus the probabilistic (A9, 10, 11); we have said this latter facet would be better described as the way the probability assumption enters the analysis model.

However, there seems no obvious way to choose facets so that there is a one-to-one correspondence between the data models and the types of analytic models. This becomes especially true when we meet multipurpose computer programs. Nevertheless, there does not yet exist an analytic model or even a computer program that will accept a data matrix of any form whatsoever. It is therefore indispensable that the researcher have a way of classifying data that enables him to recognize the input requirements of the various models for analyzing data.

Appendix II

The General Model for Nonmetric Multidimensional Scaling

We follow Gleason (1967) in describing some further features of the general model for nonmetric multidimensional scaling, even though we do so very briefly.

Let x_0 and x_1 be arbitrary but fixed points in a space of unknown dimensionality. Imagine a line passing through these two points and a third point x lying on the same line. The point x can be described by the equation

$$x = x_0 + \lambda (x_1 - x_0) \qquad \text{[Eq. 1]}$$

We can interpret x_0 as a base point, the term $(x_1 - x_0)$ as a direction, and λ as a distance. If $\lambda > 0$, the x is at a distance λ in the direction of x_1 from x_0. And if $\lambda < 0$, then x is at a distance $|\lambda|$ from x_0 in the direction *away* from x_1. In other words, a new point x_i can be selected to be any specified degree closer to x_0 or farther from x_0 than x_1 by properly choosing the value of λ.

Now consider three sets of quantities:

$\{s_{ij}\}$ A collection of measures of psychological proximities. These are the data with which we begin: the recorded interpretations of the observations we have made.

$\{\delta_{ij}\}$ A set of distances among points, the distances being monotonically related to the proximities s_{ij}. Arranged according to the distances δ_{ij}, the points lie in the configuration which is the solution we are seeking. We shall call the distances δ_{ij} *appropriate distances.*

$\{d_{ij}\}$ A set of distances not among points arranged in the final configuration but arranged in some arbitrary or beginning configuration—a configuration that is an interim attempt to reach the final configuration.

Of course, if the distances d_{ij} are monotonically related to the appropriate distances δ_{ij}, then the distances d_{ij} are also monotonically related to the proximities s_{ij}, and the distances d_{ij} do themselves become appropriate distances and specify a solution for the data matrix. And if the distances d_{ij} are monotonically related to the appropriate distances δ_{ij}, it will be true in any nontrivial application that the distances d_{ij} will be very close to or even exactly the same as the appropriate distances δ_{ij}. However, with a beginning or arbitrary configuration, it will generally be true that the distances will not be monotonic with the appropriate distances, or even very close to monotonic with them, and the points of the interim configuration will have to be moved to improve the match between d_{ij} and δ_{ij}.

Now consider the ratio δ_{ij}/d_{ij}. If d_{ij} is too large (that is, if the points x_i and x_j are too far apart), then the ratio is smaller than one. But if d_{ij} is too small (that is, if the points are too close together), then the ratio is greater than one. Consequently, we can calculate a new position for the point x_i by substituting

$$1 - \frac{\delta_{ij}}{d_{ij}}$$

for λ in (Eq. 1). That is:

$$x = x_i + \left(1 - \frac{\delta_{ij}}{d_{ij}}\right)(x_j - x_i)$$

[Eq. 2]

We now quote directly from Gleason (1967):

> We have seen from the above discussion that given a point x_i, we can get an estimate of a new position for x_i by applying [Eq. 2] for each point x_j. To arrive at a new position for x_i using estimates from all the points x_j we simply take a weighted vector sum of each estimate, that is,
>
> $$x_i' = x_i + \alpha \sum_{j=1}^{p} \lambda_{ij} (x_j - x_i)$$
>
> [Eq. 3]
>
> where α is the weighting constant. Subsequently α will be called the *step size.*
>
> A general method, then, for calculating a configuration of points that satisfies a given proximity matrix consists of resolutions to the following problems: (a) selecting an appropriate initial configuration . . . , (b) estimating the appropriate distances between points from the proximity measures, that is, finding a function f such that $\delta_{ij} = f(s_{ij})$, (c) determining an appropriate constant α so that with repeated applications of [Eq. 3] the successive configurations . . . converge, and finally, (d) constructing come measure of goodness of fit of the configuration to the data. . . .

References

Abelson, R. P. Simulation of social behavior. In G. Lindzey & E. Aronson (Eds.), *Handbook of social psychology.* Vol. 2. Reading, Mass.: Addison-Wesley, 1968. Pp. 274–356.

Adams, E. W., Fagot, R. F., & Robinson, R. E. A theory of appropriate statistics. *Psychometrika,* 1965, **30,** 99–127.

Agnew, N. McK., & Pyke, S. W. *The science game: An introduction to research in the behavioral sciences.* Englewood Cliffs, N.J.: Prentice-Hall, 1969.

Altman, I. Choicepoints in the classification of scientific knowledge. In B. P. Indik & K. Berrien (Eds.), *People, groups, and organizations: An effective integration.* New York: Teachers College Press, 1968. Pp. 47–69.

American Psychological Association. Privacy and behavioral research: Preliminary summary of the report of the panel on privacy and behavioral research. *American Psychologist,* 1967, **22,** 345–349.

American Psychological Association, American Educational Research Association, & National Council on Measurement in Education (joint committee). *Standards for educational and psychological tests and manuals.* Washington, D.C.: American Psychological Association, 1966.

Amidon, E. J., & Flanders, N. *The role of the teacher in the classroom.* Minneapolis, Minn.: Paul S. Amidon and Associates, 1963.

Amidon, E. J., & Hough, J. B. (Eds.) *Interaction analysis: Theory, research, and application.* Reading, Mass.: Addison-Wesley, 1967.

Anastasi, A. *Psychological testing.* (3rd ed.) New York: Macmillan, 1968.

Anderson, B. F. *The psychology experiment: An introduction to the scientific method.* Belmont, Calif.: Wadsworth, 1966.

Anderson, L. F., and others. *Legislative roll call analysis.* Evanston, Ill.: Northwestern University Press, 1966.

Argyris, C. Some unintended consequences of rigorous research. *Psychological Bulletin,* 1968, **70,** 185–197.

Armstrong, J. S., & Soelberg, P. On the interpretation of factor analysis. *Psychological Bulletin,* 1968, **70,** 361–364.

Aronson, E., & Carlsmith, J. M. Experimentation in social psychology. In G. Lindzey and E. Aronson (Eds.), *Handbook of social psychology.* Vol. 2. Reading, Mass.: Addison-Wesley, 1968. Pp. 1–79.

Asch, S. E. Studies of independence and conformity: I. A minority of one against a unanimous majority. *Psychological Monographs,* 1956, **70,** (9, Whole No. 416).

Ashby, W. R. *Design for a brain.* New York: Wiley, 1952.

Ashby, W. R. Principles of the self-organizing system. In H. Von Foerster and G. W. Zopf (Eds.), *Principles of self-organization.* New York: Pergamon Press, 1962. Pp. 255–278. Reprinted in W. Buckley (Ed.), *Modern systems research for the behavioral scientist: A sourcebook.* Chicago: Aldine, 1968.

Atkinson, J. W. (Ed.) *Motives in fantasy, action, and society.* Princeton, N.J.: Van Nostrand, 1958.

Atkinson, J. W. *An introduction to motivation.* Princeton, N.J.: Van Nostrand, 1964.

Atkinson, J. W., & Feather, N. T. (Eds.) *A theory of achievement motivation.* New York: Wiley, 1965.

Attneave, F. A method of graded dichotomies for the scaling of judgments. *Psychological Review,* 1949, **56,** 334–340.

Attneave, F. Dimensions of similarity. *American Journal of Psychology,* 1950, **63,** 516–556.

Attneave, F., & Arnoult, M. D. The quantitative study of shape and pattern perception. *Psychological Bulletin,* 1956, **53,** 452–471.

Bachrach, A. J. *Psychological research: An introduction.* New York: Random House, 1962.

Back, K. Influence through social communication. *Journal of Abnormal and Social Psychology,* 1951, **46,** 9–23.

Backstrom, C. H., & Hursh, G. D. *Survey research.* Evanston, Ill.: Northwestern University Press, 1963.

Baggaley, A. R. *Intermediate correlational methods.* New York: Wiley, 1964.

Bakan, D. The test of significance in psychological research. *Psychological Bulletin,* 1966, **66,** 423–437. Reprinted in D. Bakan, *On method.* San Francisco: Jossey-Bass, 1967. Pp. 1–29.

Bakan, D. *On method.* San Francisco: Jossey-Bass, 1967.

Bales, R. F. *Personality and interpersonal behavior.* New York: Holt, Rinehart and Winston, 1970.

Bales, R. F., & Hare, A. P. Diagnostic use of the interaction profile. *Journal of Social Psychology,* 1965, **67,** 239–258.

Barker, R. G. On the nature of the environment. *Journal of Social Issues,* 1963, **19** (4), 17–38.

Barker, R. G. Explorations in ecological psychology. *American Psychologist,* 1965, **20,** 1–14.

Barker, R. G., & Barker, L. S. Behavior units for the comparative study of cultures. In B. Kaplan (Ed.), *Studying personality cross-culturally.* Evanston, Ill.: Row, Peterson, 1961. Pp. 457–476.

Barker, R. G., & Gump, P. *Big school, small school.* Stanford, Calif.: Stanford University Press, 1964.

Barker, R. G., & Wright, H. F. *Midwest and its children.* New York: Harper and Row, 1955.

Bauer, R. A. (Ed.) *Social indicators.* Cambridge, Mass.: MIT Press, 1967.

Beals, R., Krantz, D. H., & Tversky, A. Foundations of multidimensional scaling. *Psychological Review,* 1968, **75,** 127–142.

Beauchamp, M. A. An improved index of centrality. *Behavioral Science,* 1965, **10,** 161–163.

Bechtoldt, H. P. Selection. In S. S. Stevens (Ed.), *Handbook of experimental psychology.* New York: Wiley, 1951, Pp. 1237–1266.

Becker, W. C., & Krug, R. S. A circumplex model for social behavior in children. *Child Development,* 1964, **35,** 371–396.

Bem, D. J. *Beliefs, attitudes, and human affairs.* Belmont, Calif.: Brooks-Cole, 1970.

Benne, K. D. (Ed.) The social responsibilities of the behavioral scientist. *Journal of Social Issues,* 1965, **21** (2).

Bereiter, C. Some persisting dilemmas in the measurement of change. In C. W. Harris (Ed.), *Problems in measuring change.* Madison, Wis.: University of Wisconsin Press, 1963. Pp. 3–20.

Bereiter, C. Multivariate analysis of the behavior and structure of groups and organizations. In R. B. Cattell (Ed.), *Handbook of multivariate experimental psychology.* Chicago: Rand McNally, 1966. Pp. 753–768.

Berelson, B. Content analysis. In G. Lindzey (Ed.), *Handbook of social psychology.* Vol. 1. Cambridge, Mass.: Addison-Wesley, 1954. Pp. 488–522.

Blalock, H. M., Jr. *Theory construction: From verbal to mathematical formulations.* Engelwood Cliffs, N.J.: Prentice-Hall, 1969.

Bloom, B. S. (Ed.) *Taxonomy of educational objectives: The classification of educational goals. Handbook I: Cognitive domain.* New York: Longmans, Green, 1956.

Blum, F. H. Getting individuals to give information to the outsider. *Journal of Social Issues,* 1952, **8,** 35–42.

Bonjean, C. M., Hill, R. J., & McLemore, S. D. *Sociological measurement: An inventory of scales and indices.* San Francisco: Chandler, 1962.

Borgatta, E. F. A new systematic interaction observation system: Behavior Scores System (BSS). *Journal of Psychological Studies,* 1963, **14,** 25–44.

Borgatta, E. F., & Bohrnstedt, G. W. (Eds.) *Sociological methodology 1969.* San Francisco: Jossey-Bass, 1969.

Borgatta, E. F., & Bohrnstedt, G. W. (Eds.) *Sociological methodology 1970.* San Francisco: Jossey-Bass, 1970.

Borko, H. *Computer applications in the behavioral sciences.* Englewood Cliffs, N.J.: Prentice-Hall, 1962.

Boulding, K. E. *The image.* Ann Arbor, Mich.: University of Michigan Press, 1961.

Boyd, R. D., & DeVault, M. V. The observation and recording of behavior. *Review of Educational Research,* 1966, **36,** 529–551.

Boynton, R. M., & Gordon, J. Bezold-Brüke hue shift measured by color-naming technique. *Journal of the Optical Society of America,* 1965, **55,** 78–86.

Bradford, L. P., Gibb, J. R., & Benne, K. D. (Eds.) *T-group theory and laboratory method.* New York: Wiley, 1964.

Breger, L., & Ruiz, C. The role of ego-defense in conformity. *Journal of Social Psychology,* 1966, **69,** 73–85.

Brewer, M. B., Campbell, D. T., & Crano, W. D. Testing a single-factor model as an alternative to the misuse of partial correlations in hypothesis-testing research. *Sociometry,* 1970, **33** (1), 1–11.

Brock, T. C., & Becker, L. A. "Debriefing" and susceptibility to subsequent experimental manipulations. *Journal of Experimental Social Psychology,* 1966, **2,** 314–323.

Bronfenbrenner, U. Socialization and social class through time and space. In E. E. Maccoby, T. M. Newcomb, & E. L. Hartley (Eds.), *Readings in social psychology.* New York: Holt, Rinehart and Winston, 1958. Pp. 400–424. Condensed in H. Proshansky & B. Seidenberg (Eds.), *Basic studies in social psychology.* New York: Holt, Rinehart and Winston, 1965. Pp. 349–365.

Brunswik, E. *Perception and the representative design of psychological experiments.* Berkeley: University of California Press, 1956.

Bruyn, S. T. *The human perspective in sociology: The methodology of participant observation.* Englewood Cliffs, N.J.: Prentice-Hall, 1966.

Bucher, R., Fritz, C. E., & Quarantelli, E. L. Tape recorded research: Some field and data processing problems. *Public Opinion Quarterly,* 1956, **20,** 427–439. (a)

Bucher, R., Fritz, C. E., & Quarantelli, E. L. Tape recorded interviews in social research *American Sociological Review,* 1956, **21,** 359–364. (b)

Buckley, W. *Sociology and modern systems theory.* Englewood Cliffs, N.J.: Prentice-Hall, 1967.

Buckley, W. (Ed.) *Modern systems research for the behavioral scientist: A sourcebook.* Chicago: Aldine, 1968.

Buros, O. K. (Ed.) *Tests in print: A comprehensive bibliography of tests for use in education, psychology, and industry.* Highland Park, N.J.: Gryphon Press, 1961.

Buros, O. K. (Ed.) *The sixth mental measurements yearbook.* Highland Park, N.J.: Gryphon Press, 1965.

Campbell, D. T. From description to experimentation: Interpreting trends as quasi-experiments. In C. W. Harris (Ed.), *Problems in measuring change.* Madison, Wis.: University of Wisconsin Press, 1962. Pp. 212–242.

Campbell, D. T. Administrative experimentation, institutional records, and non-reactive measures. In B. J. Chandler and others (Eds.), *Research seminar on teacher education.* Cooperative Research Project No. G-011, ED 003 428, 1963, Evanston: Northwestern University Press. Pp. 75–120. Reprinted in J. C. Stanley (Ed.), *Improving experimental design and statistical analysis.* Chicago: Rand McNally, 1967. Pp. 257–291.

Campbell, D. T. Reforms as experiments. *American Psychologist,* 1969, **24** (4), 409–429.

Campbell, D. T., & Fiske, D. W. Convergent and discriminant validation by the multitrait-multimethod matrix. *Psychological Bulletin,* 1959, **56,** 81–105.

Campbell, D. T., & Stanley, J. C. Experimental and quasi-experimental designs for research on teaching. In N. L. Gage (Ed.), *Handbook of research on teaching.* Chicago: Rand McNally, 1963. Pp. 171–246. Reprinted separately as *Experimental and quasi-experimental designs for research.* Chicago: Rand McNally, 1966.

Campbell, D. T., Kruskal, W. H., & Wallace, W. P. Seating aggregation as an index of attitute. *Sociometry,* 1966, **29,** 1–15.

Cannel, C. F., & Kahn, R. L. Interviewing. In G. Lindzey & E. Aronson (Eds.), *Handbook of social psychology.* Vol. 2. (2nd ed.) Reading, Mass.: Addison-Wesley, 1968. Pp. 526–595.

Carroll, J. D. Functional learning: The learning of continuous functional mappings relating stimulus and response continua. *Educational Testing Service Research Bulletin RB-63-26.* Princeton, N.J., 1963.

Carter, L. F. Recording and evaluating the performance of individuals as members of small groups. *Personnel Psychology,* 1954, **7,** 477–484. Reprinted in A. P. Hare, E. F. Borgatta, & R. F. Bales (Eds.), *Small groups: Studies in social interaction.* New York: Knopf, 1955. Pp. 492–497.

Cartwright, D. P. Analysis of qualitative material. In L. Festinger & D. Katz (Eds.), *Research methods in the behavioral sciences.* New York: Dryden, 1953. Pp. 421–470.

Castellan, N. J. On the partitioning of contingency tables. *Psychological Bulletin, 1965,* **64,** 330–338.

Cattell, R. B. Factor analysis: An introduction to essentials. I. The purpose and underlying models. II. The role of factor analysis in research. *Biometrics,* 1965, **21,** 190–215, 405–435.

Coan, R. W. Facts, factors, and artifacts: The quest for psychological meaning. *Psychological Review,* 1964, **71,** 123–140.

Coleman, J. S. *Introduction to mathematical sociology.* London: Collier-Macmillan, 1964.

Coleman, J. S. *Models of change and response uncertainty.* Englewood Cliffs, N.J.: Prentice-Hall, 1964.

Coombs, C. H. *A theory of data.* New York: Wiley, 1964.

Coombs, C. H., Dawes, R. M., & Tversky, A. *Mathematical psychology: An elementary introduction.* Englewood Cliffs, N.J.: Prentice-Hall, 1970.

Coombs, C. H., Raiffa, H., & Thrall, R. M. Some views on mathematical models and measurement theory. *Psychological Review,* 1954, **61,** 131–144. Reprinted in R. M. Thrall, C. H. Coombs, & R. L. Davis (Eds.), *Decision processes.* New York: Wiley, 1954. Pp. 19–37.

Cooper, W. W., Leavitt, H. J., & Shelly, M. W., II (Eds.) *New perspectives in organizational research.* New York: Wiley, 1964.

Cronbach, L. J. Proposals leading to analytic treatment of social perception scores. In R. Tajiuri & L. Petrullo (Eds.), *Person perception and interpersonal behavior.* Stanford, Calif.: Stanford University Press, 1958. Pp. 353–379.

Cronbach, L. J. *Essentials of psychological testing.* (3rd ed.) New York: Harper and Row, 1970.

Cronbach, L. J., & Furby, L. How we should measure "change"—or should we? *Psychological Bulletin,* 1970, **74** (1), 68–80.

Cronbach, L. J., Rajaratnam, N., & Gleser, G. C. Theory of generalizability: A liberalization of reliability theory. *British Journal of Statistical Psychology,* 1963, **16** (2), 137–163.

Cronholm, J. N. A general method of obtaining exact sampling probabilities of the Shannon-Wiener measure of information H. *Psychometrika,* 1963, **28,** 405–413.

Darnell, D. K. Concept-scale interaction in the semantic differential. *Journal of Communication,* 1966, **16,** 104–114.

Dawes, R. M. Social selection based on multidimensional criteria. *Journal of Abnormal and Social Psychology,* 1964, **68,** 104–109. (a)

Dawes, R. M. Toward a general framework for evaluation. *Michigan Mathematical Psychology Program,* MMPP No. 64-7. Ann Arbor, Mich.: University of Michigan Department of Psychology, 1964. (b)

Dawes, R. M. *Attitude scaling and measurement.* New York: Wiley, 1972.

Dawes, R. M., Brown, M. E., & Kaplan, N. The skewed hourglass: A configurational approach to constructing a Guttman scale when domination is unspecified. Paper presented at the convention of the Midwestern Psychological Association, Chicago, 1965.

Deese, J. Behavior and fact. *American Psychologist,* 1969, **24,** 515–522.

DeGrazia, A. The universal reference system. *American Behavioral Scientist,* 1965, **8** (8), 3–14.

Deutsch, K. W., & Madow, W. G. A note on the appearance of wisdom in large bureaucratic organizations. *Behavioral Science,* 1961, **6,** 72–78.

Deutsch, M., & Collins, M. E. *Interracial housing: A psychological evaluation of a social experiment.* Minneapolis, Minn.: University of Minnesota Press, 1951. Adapted and condensed in G. E. Swanson, T. M. Newcomb, & E. L. Hartley (Eds.), *Readings in social psychology.* (2nd ed.) New York: Holt, Rinehart and Winston, 1952. Pp. 582–593. Also in E. E. Maccoby, T. M. Newcomb, & E. L. Hartley (Eds.), *Readings in social psychology.* (3rd ed.) New York: Holt, Rinehart and Winston, 1958. Pp. 612–623. Also in H. Proshansky & B. Seidenberg (Eds.), *Basic studies in social psychology.* New York: Holt, Rinehart and Winston, 1965. Pp. 646–657.

Dexter, L. A. The good will of important people: More on the jeopardy of the interview. *Public Opinion Quarterly,* 1964, **28,** 556–563.

Diab, L. N. Studies in social attitudes: I. Variations in latitudes of acceptance and rejection as a function of varying positions on a controversial social issue. III. Attitude assessment through the semantic-differential technique. *Journal of Social Psychology,* 1965, **67,** 283–295, 303–314.

Diederich, G. W., Messick, S. J., & Tucker, L. R. A general least squares solution for successive intervals. *Psychometrika,* 1957, **22,** 159–173.

Doby, J. T. and others (Eds.) *An introduction to social research.* New York: Appleton-Century-Crofts, 1966.

Dobzhansky, T. *Mankind evolving: The evolution of the human species.* New Haven, Conn.: Yale University Press, 1962.

Dodd, S. C., & Svalastoga, K. On estimating latent from manifest undecidedness: The "don't know" percent as a warning of instability among the knowers. *Educational and Psychological Measurement,* 1952, **12,** 467–471.

Dressel, P. L., & Mayhew, L. B. *Handbook for theme analysis.* Dubuque, Iowa: William C. Brown, 1954.

Dulaney, D. E. Awareness, rules, and propositional control: A confrontation with S-R behavior theory. In D. Horton and T. Dixon (Eds.), *Verbal behavior and S-R behavior theory.* Englewood Cliffs, N.J.: Prentice-Hall, 1967.

Dunphy, D. C., Stone, P. J., & Smith, M. S. The general inquirer: Further developments in a computer system for content analysis of verbal data in the social sciences. *Behavioral Science,* 1965, **10,** 468–480.

Ebel, R. L. *Measuring educational achievement.* Englewood Cliffs, N.J.: Prentice-Hall, 1965.

Edwards, A. L. The scaling of stimuli by the method of successive intervals. *Journal of Applied Psychology,* 1952, **36,** 118–122.

Edwards, A. L. *Techniques of attitude scale construction.* New York: Appleton-Century-Crofts, 1957.

Edwards, A. L. *Experimental design in psychological research.* (4th ed.) New York: Holt, Rinehart and Winston, 1972.

Edwards, W. Costs and payoffs are instructions. *Psychological Review,* 1961, **68,** 275–284.

Edwards, W. Tactical note on the relation between scientific and statistical hypotheses. *Psychological Bulletin,* 1965, **63,** 400–402.

Elizur, D. *A structural analysis of behavior in organizations toward the computer.* Jerusalem: Jerusalem Academic Press, 1969.

Fairweather, G. W. *Methods for experimental social innovation.* New York: Wiley, 1967.

Farnsworth, K. E. Application of scaling techniques to the evaluation of counseling outcomes. *Psychological Bulletin,* 1966, **66,** 81–93.

Feller, W. *An introduction to probability theory and its applications.* New York: Wiley, 1950.

Ferraby, J. G. Planning a mass-observation investigation. In B. Berelson and M. Janowitz (Eds.), *Public opinion and communication.* New York: Free Press, 1953. Pp. 525–534.

Festinger, L., & Katz, D. (Eds.) *Research methods in the behavioral sciences.* New York: Dryden, 1953. Pp. 136–172.

Festinger, L., Reichen, H. W., Jr., & Schachter, S. *When prophecy fails.* Minneapolis, Minn.: University of Minnesota Press, 1956. Adapted and condensed in E. E. Maccoby, T. M. Newcomb, & E. L. Hartley (Eds.), *Readings in social psychology.* New York: Holt, Rinehart and Winston, 1958. Pp. 156–163.

Festinger, L., Schacter, S., & Back, K. *Social pressures in informal groups: A study of human factors in housing.* New York: Harper and Row, 1950.

Feyerabend, P., & Maxwell, G. (Eds.) *Mind, matter, and method.* Minneapolis, Minn.: University of Minnesota Press, 1965.

Fiedler, F. E. *A theory of leadership effectiveness.* New York: McGraw-Hill, 1967.

Findley, W. G. (Ed.) Educational and psychological testing. *Review of Educational Research,* 1968, **38** (1).

Fishbein, M. (Ed.) *Readings in attitude theory and measurement.* New York: Wiley, 1967.

Fisher, S., Rubinstein, I., & Freeman, R. W. Intertrial effects of immediate self-commital in a continuous social influence situation. *Journal of Abnormal and Social Psychology,* 1956, **52,** 200–207.

Fiske, D. W., & Maddi, S. R. (Eds.) *Functions of varied experience.* Homewood, Ill.: Dorsey Press, 1961.

Fiske, D. W., & Rice, L. Intra-individual response variability. *Psychological Bulletin,* 1955, **52,** 217–250.

Fitts, P. M. Engineering psychology and equipment design. In S. S. Stevens (Ed.), *Handbook of experimental psychology.* New York: Wiley, 1951. Pp. 1287–1340.

Fitts, P. M., & Posner, M. I. *Human performance.* Belmont, Calif.: Brooks-Cole, 1967.

Flament, C. *Applications of graph theory to group structure.* Englewood Cliffs, N.J.: Prentice-Hall, 1963.

Flanders, N. A. Some relationships among teacher influence, pupil attitudes, and achievement. In B. J. Biddle and W. J. Ellena (Eds.), *Contemporary research on teacher effectiveness.* New York: Holt, Rinehart and Winston, 1964, Pp. 196–231.

Flanders, N. A. *Analyzing classroom interaction.* Reading, Mass.: Addison-Wesley, 1969.

Foa, U. G. The contiguity principle in the structure of interpersonal relations. *Human Relations,* 1958, **11,** 229–238.

Foa, U. G. Convergences in the analysis of the structure of interpersonal behavior. *Psychological Review,* 1961, **68,** 341–353.

Foa, U. G. The structure of interpersonal behavior in the dyad. In J. Criswell, H. Solomon, & P. Suppes (Eds.), *Mathematical models in small group processes.* Stanford, Calif.: Stanford University Press, 1962. Pp. 166–179.

Foa, U. G. New developments in facet design and analysis. *Psychological Review,* 1965, **72** (4), 262–274.

Foa, U. G. Perception of behavior in reciprocal roles: The ringex model. *Psychological Monographs: General and Applied,* 1966, **80** (15, Whole No. 623).

Foa, U. G. Three kinds of behavioral changes. *Psychological Bulletin,* 1968, **70,** 460–473.

Foa, U. G., Triandis, H. C., & Katz, E. W. Cross-cultural invariance in the differentiation and organization of family roles. *Journal of Personality and Social Psychology,* 1966, **4** (3), 316–327.

Fourt, L. Applying Markov chain analysis to NCP brand switching data. Mimeographed. New York: Market Research Corporation of America, 1960.

French, J. R. P. The social environment and mental health. *Journal of Social Issues,* 1963, **19** (4), 39–56.

Friedman, N. *The social nature of psychological research: The psychological experiment as a social interaction.* New York: Basic Books, 1967.

Frohock, F. M. *The nature of political inquiry.* Homewood, Ill.: Dorsey Press, 1967.

Fruchter, B. *Introduction to factor analysis.* Princeton, N.J.: Van Nostrand, 1954.

Fruchter, B., & Jennings, E. Factor analysis. In H. Borko (Ed.), *Computer applications in the behavioral sciences.* Englewood Cliffs, N.J.: Prentice-Hall, 1962. Pp. 238–263.

Gamow, G. The principle of uncertainty. *Scientific American,* 1958, **198** (1), 51–59.

Garner, W. R., & Hake, H. W. The amount of information in absolute judgements. *Psychological Review,* 1951, **58,** 446–459.

Gephart, W. J., & Ingle, R. B. (Eds.) *Educational research: Selected readings.* Columbus, Ohio: Charles E. Merrill, 1969.

Ghiselli, E. E. *Theory of psychological measurement.* N.Y.: McGraw-Hill, 1964.

Glanzer, M., & Glaser, R. Techniques for the study of group structure and behavior: I. Analysis of structure. II. Empirical studies of the effects of structure in small groups. *Psychological Bulletin,* 1959, **56,** 317–332; 1961, **58,** 1–27.

Glaser, B. G., & Strauss, A. *The discovery of grounded theory: strategies for qualitative research.* Chicago: Aldine, 1967.

Glaser, R. The reliability of inconsistency. *Educational and Psychological Measurement,* 1952, **12,** 60–64.

Gleason, T. C. A general model for nonmetric multidimensional scaling. *Michigan Mathematical Psychology Program* MMPP No. 67-3. Ann Arbor, Mich.: University of Michigan Department of Psychology, 1967.

Glennon, J. R., Albright, L. E., & Owens, W. A. *A catalog of life history items.* Greensboro, N.C.: Creativity Research Institute, Richardson Foundation, 1966.

Gleser, G. C., Cronbach, L. J., & Rajaratnam, N. Generalizability of scores influenced by multiple sources of variance. *Psychometrika,* 1965, **30** (4), 395–418.

Glock, C. Y. (Ed.) *Survey research in the social sciences.* New York: Russell Sage Foundation, 1967.

Goffman, E. *The presentation of self in everyday life.* New York: Doubleday, 1959.

Goldberg, D., & Coombs, C. H. Some applications of unfolding theory to fertility analysis. In *Emerging techniques in population research,* proceedings of the 1962 annual conference of the Milbank Memorial Fund. New York: Milbank Memorial Fund, 1963. Pp. 105–129.

Goodman, L. A. Simple statistical methods for scalogram analysis. *Psychometrika,* 1959, **24,** 29–44.

Goodman, L. A., & Kruskal, W. H. Measures of association for cross-classifications. *Journal of the American Statistical Association,* 1954, **49,** 732–764.

Gorden, R. L. *Interviewing: Strategy, technique, and tactics.* Homewood, Ill.: Dorsey Press, 1969.

Goslin, D. A. *The search for ability: Standardized testing in social perspective.* New York: Russell Sage Foundation, 1963.

Gottman, J. M., McFall, R. M., & Barnett, J. T. Design and analysis of research using time series. *Psychological Bulletin,* 1969, **72,** 299–306.

Green, B. F. *Digital computers in research: An introduction for behavioral and social scientists.* New York: McGraw-Hill, 1963.

Greenberg, M. G. *J* scale models for preference behavior. *Psychometrika,* 1963, **28,** 265–271.

Gronlund, N. *Sociometry in the classroom.* New York: Harper and Row, 1959.

Guetzkow, H. (Ed.) *Simulation in social science: Readings.* Englewood Cliffs, N.J.: Prentice-Hall, 1962.

Guetzkow, H., & Gyr, J. An analysis of conflict in decision making groups. *Human Relations,* 1954, **7,** 367–382.

Guetzkow, H., and others. *Simulation in international relations: Developments for research and teaching.* Englewood Cliffs, N.J.: Prentice-Hall, 1963.

Guilford, J. P. *Psychometric methods.* (2nd ed.) New York: McGraw-Hill, 1954.

Gulliksen, H. *Theory of mental tests.* New York: Wiley, 1950.

Gulliksen, H., & Messick, S. (Eds.) *Psychological scaling: Theory and applications.* New York: Wiley, 1960.

Gump, P. V. Intra-setting analysis. The third grade classroom as a special but instructive case. In E. P. Willems & H. L. Raush (Eds.), *Naturalistic viewpoints in psychological research.* New York: Holt, Rinehart and Winston, 1969. Pp. 200–220.

Gurr, T., & Panofsky, H. (Eds.) Information retrieval in the social sciences: Problems, programs, and proposals. *American Behavioral Scientist,* 1964, **7** (10).

Guttman, L. A basis for scaling qualitative data. *American Sociological Review,* 1944, **9,** 139–150. Reprinted in M. Fishbein (Ed.), *Readings in attitude theory and measurement.* New York: Wiley, 1967. Pp. 96–107.

Guttman, L. The basis for scalogram analysis. In S. A. Stouffer and others (Eds.), *Measurement and prediction.* Princeton, N.J.: Princeton University Press, 1950. Pp. 60–90.

Guttman, L. A new approach to factor analysis: The radex. In P. F. Lazarsfeld (Ed.), *Mathematical thinking in the social sciences.* New York: Free Press, 1954. Pp. 258–348.

Guttman, L. Empirical verification of the radex structure of mental abilities and personality traits. *Educational and Psychological Measurement,* 1957, **17,** 391–407.

Guttman, L. Introduction to facet design and analysis. In *Proceedings of the fifteenth international congress of psychology, Brussels—1957.* Amsterdam: North Holland Publishing Company, 1959. Pp. 130–132. (a)

Guttman, L. A structural theory for intergroup beliefs and action. *American Sociological Review,* 1959, **24,** 318–328. (b)

Guttman, L. A definition of dimensionality and distance for graphs. Unpublished paper, Jerusalem: Israel Institute for Applied Social Research, 1964.

Guttman, L. A faceted definition of intelligence. *Scripta Hierosolymitana,* 1965, **14,** 166–181. (a)

Guttman, L. The structure of interrelations among intelligence tests. In C. W. Harris (Ed.), *Proceedings of the 1964 invitational conference on testing problems.* Princeton, N.J.: Educational Testing Service, 1965. Pp. 25–37. (b)

Guttman, L. The nonmetric breakthrough for the behavioral sciences. In *Proceedings of the second national conference on data processing.* Jerusalem, 1966. Pp. 495–510. (a)

Guttman, L. Order analysis of correlation matrices. In R. B. Cattell (Ed.), *Handbook of multivariate experimental psychology.* Chicago: Rand McNally, 1966. Pp. 438–458. (b)

Guttman, L. The development of nonmetric space analysis: A letter to John Ross. *Multivariate Behavioral Research,* 1967, **2,** 71–82.

Guttman, L. A general nonmetric technique for finding the smallest coordinate space for a configuration of points. *Psychometrika,* 1968, **33,** 469–506.

Hackman, J. R. Effects of task characteristics on group products. *Journal of Experimental Social Psychology,* 1968, **4** (2), 162–187.

Hackman, J. R., Jones, L. E., & McGrath, J. E. A set of dimensions for describing the general properties of group-generated written passages. *Psychological Bulletin,* 1967, **67** (6), 379–390.

Hammond, P. E. *Sociologists at work: Essays on the craft of social research.* New York: Basic Books, 1964.

Handy, R., & Kurtz, P. *A current appraisal of the behavioral sciences.* Great Barrington, Mass.: Behavioral Research Council, 1963.

Hanson, N. R. *Patterns of discovery.* New York: Cambridge University Press, 1958.

Harary, F. A graph theoretic approach to similarity relations. *Psychometrika,* 1964, **29,** 143–152.

Harary, F., Norman, R. Z., & Cartwright, D. *Structural models: An introduction to the theory of directed graphs.* New York: Wiley, 1965.

Harmon, H. H. *Modern factor analysis.* (2nd ed.) Chicago: University of Chicago Press, 1967.

Harris, C. W. Canonical factor models for the description of change. In *Problems in measuring change.* Madison, Wis.: University of Wisconsin Press, 1963. Pp. 138–155. Also in R. B. Cattell (Ed.), *Handbook of multivariate experimental psychology.* Chicago: Rand McNally, 1966. Pp. 403–416.

Harris, C. W. (Ed.) *Problems in measuring change.* Madison, Wis.: University of Wisconsin Press, 1963.

Harris, T. G., & McClelland, D. C. To know why men do what they do. *Psychology Today,* 1971, **4** (8), 35–39, 70–75.

Hase, H. D., & Goldberg, L. R. The comparative validity of different strategies of constructing personality inventory scales. *Psychological Bulletin,* 1967, **67,** 231–248.

Hayes, D. G. Automatic language data processing. In H. Borko (Ed.), *Computer applications in the behavioral sciences.* Englewood Cliffs, N.J.: Prentice-Hall, 1962. Pp. 394–423.

Hays, W. L. Psychological dimensionality and the distribution of rank order agreement among judges. *Sociometry,* 1960, **23,** 262–272.

Hays, W. L. *Statistics for psychologists.* New York: Holt, Rinehart and Winston, 1963.

Hays, W. L. *Quantification in psychology.* Basic concepts in psychology series. Belmont, Calif.: Brooks-Cole, 1967.

Helmer, O. *Social technology.* New York: Basic Books, 1966.

Hemphill, J. K. Leadership behavior associated with the administrative reputation of college departments. *Journal of Educational Psychology,* 1955, **46,** 385–401. Reprinted in W. W. Charters, Jr. & N. L. Gage (Eds.), *Readings in the social psychology of education.* Boston: Allyn and Bacon, 1963. Pp. 319–326.

Heyns, R. W., & Lippitt, R. Systematic observational techniques. In G. Lindzey (Ed.), *Handbook of social psychology* Vol. 1. Cambridge, Mass.: Addison-Wesley, 1954. Pp. 370–404.

Heyns, R. W., & Zander, A. F. Observations of group behavior. In L. Festinger & D. Katz (Eds.), *Research methods in the behavioral sciences.* New York: Dryden, 1953. Pp. 381–418.

Holmberg, A. R. and others. The transformation of the political, legal, and social systems of suppressed peasant societies: The Vicos case. *American Behavioral Scientist,* 1965, **8** (7).

Holsti, O. R. An adaptation of the "General Inquirer" for the systematic analysis of political documents. *Behavioral Science,* 1964, **9,** 382–388.

Holsti, O. R., Loomba, J. K., & North, R. C. Content analysis. In G. Lindzey and E. Aronson (Eds.), *Handbook of social psychology.* Vol. 2. (2nd ed.) Reading, Mass.: Addison-Wesley, 1968. Pp. 596–692.

Homans, G. C. Group factors in worker productivity. In E. Maccoby, T. M. Newcomb, & E. Hartley (Eds.), *Readings in social psychology.* (3rd ed.) New York: Holt, Rinehart and Winston, 1958. Pp. 583–595. Reprinted in H. Proshansky & B. Seidenberg (Eds.), *Basic studies in social psychology.* New York: Holt, Rinehart and Winston, 1965. Pp. 592–604.

Horst, P. *Matrix algebra for social scientists.* New York: Holt, Rinehart and Winston, 1963.

Horst, P. *Factor analysis of data matrices.* New York: Holt, Rinehart and Winston, 1965.

Horst, P. *Psychological measurement and prediction.* Belmont, Calif.: Brooks-Cole, 1966.

Hovland, C. I. (Ed.) *Order of presentation in persuasion.* New Haven, Conn.: Yale University Press, 1957.

Hovland, C. I. Reconciling conflicting results derived from experimental and survey studies of attitude change. *American Psychologist,* 1959, **14,** 8–17. Reprinted in E. E. Sampson (Ed.), *Approaches, contexts, and problems of social psychology.* Englewood Cliffs, N.J.: Prentice-Hall, 1964. Pp. 288–298. Also reprinted in I. D. Steiner & M. Fishbein (Eds.), *Current studies in social psychology.* New York: Holt, Rinehart and Winston, 1965. Pp. 173–186.

Hovland, C. I., Harvey, O. J., & Sherif, M. Assimilation and contrast effects in reactions to communication and attitude change. *Journal of Abnormal and Social Psychology,* 1957, **55,** 244–252. Reprinted in W. E. Vinacke, W. R. Wilson, & G. M. Meridith (Eds.), *Dimensions of social psychology.* Chicago: Scott, Foresman, 1964. Pp. 306–315. Also reprinted in H. Proshansky and B. Seidenberg (Eds.), *Basic studies in social psychology.* New York: Holt, Rinehart and Winston, 1965.

Hovland, C. I., & Janis, I. L. (Eds.) *Personality and persuasibility.* New Haven, Conn.: Yale University Press, 1959.

Hovland, C. I., Janis, I. L., & Kelley, H. H. *Communication and persuasion.* New Haven, Conn.: Yale University Press, 1953.

Hovland, C. I., & Rosenberg, M. J. (Eds.) *Attitude organization and change.* New Haven, Conn.: Yale University Press, 1960.

Humphreys, L. G. Note on the multitrait-multimethod matrix. *Psychological Bulletin,* 1960, **57,** 86–88.

Humphreys, L. G. The organization of human abilities. *American Psychologist,* 1962, **17,** 475–483.

Hyman, R. *The nature of psychological inquiry.* Englewood Cliffs, N.J.: Prentice-Hall, 1964.

Hyman, R., & Well, A. Judgments of similarity and spatial models. *Perception and Psychophysics,* 1967, **2,** 233–248.

Iker, H. P., & Harway, N. I. A computer approach towards the analysis of content. *Behavioral Science,* 1965, **10,** 173–182.

Jackson, D. N., & Messick, S. *Problems of human assessment.* New York: McGraw-Hill, 1968.

Janda, K. (Ed.) Advances in information retrieval in the social sciences. *American Behavioral Scientist,* 1967, **10,** (5–6).

Jones, K. J. Problems of grouping individuals and the method of modality. *Behavioral Science,* 1968, **13** (6), 496–511.

Kahn, R. L., & Cannell, C. F. *The dynamics of interviewing: Theory, technique, and cases.* New York: Wiley, 1958.

Kahn, R. L., Wolfe, D. M., Quinn, R. P., Snoek, J. D., & Rosenthal, R. A. *Organizational stress: Studies in role conflict and ambiguity.* New York: Wiley, 1964.

Kaiser, H. F. Psychometric approaches to factor analysis. In *proceedings of the 1964 invitational conference on testing problems.* Princeton, N. J.: Educational Testing Service, 1965. Pp. 37–45.

Kaplan, A. *The conduct of inquiry: Methodology for behavioral science.* San Francisco: Chandler, 1964.

Kastenbaum, M. A. A note on the additive partitioning of chi-squares in contingency tables. *Biometrics,* 1960, **16,** 416–422.

Katz, D., & Kahn, R. L. *The social psychology of organizations.* New York: Wiley, 1966.

Katz, L., & Wilson, T. R. The variance of the number of mutual choices in sociometry. *Psychometrika,* 1956, **21,** 299–304.

Kaufmann, H. *Introduction to the study of human behavior.* Philadelphia: Saunders, 1968.

Kelly, E. L. *Assessment of human characteristics.* Belmont, Calif.: Brooks-Cole, 1967.

Kelly, G. A. *The psychology of personal constructs.* New York: Norton, 1955.

Kelly, G. A. The language of hypothesis: Man's psychological instrument. *Journal of Individual Psychology,* 1964, **20,** 137–152. Reprinted in B. Maher (Ed.), *Clinical psychology and personality: The selected papers of George Kelly.* New York: Wiley, 1969. Pp. 147–162.

Kelly, G. A. The strategy of psychological research. *Bulletin of the British Psychological Society,* 1965, **18,** 1–15. Reprinted in B. Maher (Ed.), *Clinical psychology and personality: The selected papers of George Kelly.* New York: Wiley, 1969. Pp. 114–132.

Kelly, J. G. Naturalistic observations in contrasting social environments. In E. P. Willems and H. L. Raush (Eds.), *Naturalistic viewpoints in psychological research.* New York: Holt, Rinehart and Winston, 1969. Pp. 183–199.

Kelman, H. C. Deception in social research. *Trans-Action,* 1966, **3** (5), 20–24.

Kelman, H. C. Human use of human subjects: The problem of deception in social psychological experiments. *Psychological Bulletin,* 1967, **67** (1), 1–11. Reprinted in H. C. Kelman, *A time to speak: On human values and social research.* San Francisco: Jossey-Bass, 1968.

Kemeny, J. C. Needed: Well-rounded colleges. *New York Times Magazine,* March 25, 1962. P. 31.

Kendall, M. G., & Smith, B. *Tables of random sampling numbers.* New York: Cambridge University Press, 1954.

Kendall, M. G., & Stuart, A. *The advanced theory of statistics.* Vol. 2. New York: Hafner, 1961.

Kendall, M. G., & Stuart, A. *The advanced theory of statistics.* Vol. 3. New York: Hafner, 1966.

Kerlinger, F. N. *Foundations of behavioral research.* New York: Holt, Rinehart and Winston, 1964.

Kiesler, C. A., Collins, B. E., & Miller, N. *Attitude change: A critical analysis of theoretical approaches.* New York: Wiley, 1969.

King, A. J., & Spector, A. J. Ethical and legal aspects of survey research. *American Psychologist,* 1963, **18,** 204–208.

Kirk, R. E. *Experimental design: Procedures for the behavioral sciences.* Belmont, Calif.: Brooks-Cole, 1968.

Kish, L. *Survey sampling.* New York: Wiley, 1965.

Klingberg, F. L. Studies in measurement of the relations among sovereign states. *Psychometrika,* 1941, **6,** 335–352.

Krasnow, H. S., & Merikallio, R. A. The past, present, and future of general simulation languages. *Management Science,* 1964, **11,** 236–267.

Kruskal, J. B. Multidimensional scaling by optimizing goodness of fit to a nonmetric hypothesis. *Psychometrika,* 1964, **29,** 1–28. (a)

Kruskal, J. B. Nonmetric multidimensional scaling: A numerical method. *Psychometrika,* 1964, **29,** 115–129. (b)

Kuder, G. F. *Kuder preference record—vocational.* Chicago: Science Research Associates, 1956.

Kuhn, T. S. *The structure of scientific revolutions.* Chicago: University of Chicago Press, 1962.

Lancaster, B. O. Complex contingency tables treated by the partition of chi-square. *Journal of the Royal Statistical Society,* Series B, 1951, **13,** 242–249.

Lancaster, B. O. The derivation and partition of chi-square in certain discrete distributions. *Biometrika,* 1949, **36,** 117.

Laumann, E. O., & Guttman, L. The relative associational contiguity of occupations in an urban setting. *American Sociological Review,* 1966, **31,** 169–178.

Lazarsfeld, P. F. Latent structure analysis. In S. Koch (Ed.), *Psychology: A study of a science.* Vol. 3. New York: McGraw-Hill, 1959.

Lazarsfeld, P. F. Problems in methodology. In R. K. Merton, L. Broom, & L. S. Cottrell (Eds.), *Sociology today.* New York: Basic Books, 1959. Pp. 39–80.

Lazarus, R. S. *Psychological stress and the coping process.* New York: McGraw-Hill, 1966.

Leary, T. *Interpersonal diagnosis of personality.* New York: Ronald Press, 1957.

Leavitt, H. J., & Knight, K. E. Most "efficient" solutions to communication networks. Empirical versus analytical search. *Sociometry,* 1963, **26,** 260–267.

Leavitt, H. J., & Mueller, R. A. H. Some effects of feedback on communication. *Human Relations,* 1951, **4,** 401–410.

Leavitt, H. J., & Shelly, M. W. II (Eds.) *New perspectives in organization research.* New York: Wiley, 1964. Pp. 515–532.

Lefkowitz, M., Blake, R. R., & Mouton, J. S. Status factors in pedestrian violation of traffic signals. *Journal of Abnormal and Social Psychology,* 1955, **51** (3), 704–706.

Lichtenstein, E. "Please don't talk to anyone about this experiment"; Disclosure of deception by debriefed subjects. *Psychological Reports,* 1970, **26,** 485–486.

Likert, R. A technique for the measurement of attitudes. *Archives of Psychology,* 1932, No. 140. Excerpted in M. Fishbein (ed.), *Readings in attitude theory and measurement.* New York: Wiley, 1967. Pp. 90–95.

Lindquist, E. F. *Design and analysis or experiments in psychology and education.* Boston: Houghton Mifflin, 1953.

Lindzey, G., & Aronson, E. (Eds.) *Handbook of social psychology.* Vol. 2. (2nd ed.) Reading, Mass.: Addison-Wesley, 1968.

Lindzey, G., & Borgatta, E. Sociometric measurement. In G. Lindzey (Ed.), *Handbook of social psychology.* Vol. 1. Cambridge, Mass.: Addison-Wesley, 1954. Chapter 11.

Lindzey, G., & Byrne, D. Measurement of social choice and interpersonal attractiveness. In G. Lindzey and E. Aronson (Eds.), *Handbook of social psychology* Vol. 2. (2nd ed.) Reading, Mass.: Addison-Wesley, 1968. Pp. 452–525.

Lingoes, J. C. Multiple scalogram analysis: A set-theoretic model for analyzing dichotomous items. *Educational and Psychological Measurement,* 1963, **23,** 501–524.

Lingoes, J. C. An IBM 7090 program for Guttman-Lingoes smallest space analysis: I. *Behavioral Science,* 1965, **10,** 183–184.

Lingoes, J. C. New computer developments in pattern analysis and nonmetric techniques. In *Proceedings of the IBM symposium, computers in psychological research.* Paris: Gauthier-Villars, 1966. Pp. 1–22. (a)

Lingoes, J. C. Recent computational advances in nonmetric methodology for the behavioral sciences. In *Proceedings of the international symposium on mathematical and computational methods in social sciences.* Rome: International Computation Centre, 1966. Pp. 1–38. (b)

Lingoes, J. C. An IBM 7090 program for Guttman-Lingoes multidimensional scalogram analysis: I. *Behavioral Science,* 1966, **11,** 76–78. (c)

Lingoes, J. C. An IBM 7090 program for Guttman-Lingoes configurational similarity: I. *Behavioral Science,* 1967, **12,** 502–503. (a)

Lingoes, J. C. An IBM 7090 program for Guttman-Lingoes conjoint measurement—I. *Behavioral Science,* 1967, **12,** 501–502. (b)

Lingoes, J. C. An IBM 7090 program for Guttman-Lingoes multidimensional scalogram analysis: II. *Behavioral Science,* 1967, **12,** 268–270. (c)

Lingoes, J. C. An IBM 7090 program for Guttman-Lingoes conjoint measurement: II. *Behavioral Science,* 1968, **13,** 85–87. (a)

Lingoes, J. C. An IBM 360/67 program for Guttman-Lingoes conjoint measurement: III. *Behavioral Science,* 1968, **13,** 421–422. (b)

Lingoes, J. C. An IBM 360/67 program for Guttman-Lingoes multidimensional scalogram analysis: III. *Behavioral Science,* 1968, **13,** 512–513. (c)

Lingoes, J. C. The multivariate analysis of qualitative data. *Multivariate Behavioral Research,* 1968, **3** (1), 61–94. (d)

Lingoes, J. C. The rationale of the Guttman-Lingoes nonmetric series: A letter to Doctor Philip Runkel. *Multivariate Behavioral Research,* 1968, **3** (4), 495–507. (e)

Lingoes, J. C., & Guttman, L. Nonmetric factor analysis: A rank reducing alternative to linear factor analysis. *Multivariate Behavioral Research,* 1967, **2,** 485–505.

Lingoes, J. C., & Vandenberg, S. A nonmetric analysis of twin data based on a multifaceted design. *Louisville Twin Study Research Report,* 1966, **17,** 1–17.

Longabaugh, R. A category system for coding interpersonal behavior as social exchange. *Sociometry,* 1963, **26,** 319–344.

Lord, F. M., & Novick, M. R. *Statistical theories of mental test scores.* Reading, Mass.: Addison-Wesley, 1968.

Luce, R. D., Bush, R. R., & Galanter, E. (Eds.) *Handbook of mathematical psychology.* Vol. I. New York: Wiley, 1963.

Luce, R. D., & Galanter, E. Psycholophysical scaling. In R. D. Luce, R. R. Bush, & E. Galanter (Eds.), *Handbook of mathematical psychology.* New York: Wiley, 1963. Pp. 245–308.

Luce, R. D., Macy, J., Jr., & Taguiri, R. A statistical model for relational analysis. *Psychometrika,* 1955, **20,** 319–327. Reprinted in R. D. Luce, R. R. Bush, & E. Galanter (Eds.), *Readings in mathematical psychology.* Vol. 2. New York: Wiley, 1965. Pp. 272–280.

Lykken, D. T. Statistical significance in psychological research. *Psychological Bulletin,* 1968, **70,** 151–159.

Mack, D. E. Where the black-matriarchy theorists went wrong. *Psychology Today,* 1971, **4** (8), 24, 86–87.

Madge, J. *The origin of scientific sociology.* New York: Free Press, 1962.

Madge, J. *The tools of social science.* New York: Doubleday, Anchor Books, 1965. Originally published by Longmans, Green, 1953.

Magnuson, D. *Test theory.* Reading, Mass.: Addison-Wesley, 1967.

Mandler, G. Stimulus variables and subject variables: A caution. *Psychological Review,* 1959, **66,** 145–149.

Mann, R. D. *Interpersonal styles and group development: An analysis of the member-leader relationship.* New York: Wiley, 1967.

Manning, S. A., & Rosenstock, E. *Classical psychophysics and scaling.* New York: McGraw-Hill, 1968.

Marien, M. Notes on the education complex as an emerging macro-system. In E. O. Attinger (Ed.), *Global systems dynamics.* New York: S. Karger, 1970. Pp. 225–244.

Maruyama, M. Conjunctive-disjunctive-implicational models in discrete scales. *Journal of Experimental Education,* 1962, **30,** 289–305.

Maslow, A. H. *The psychology of science: A reconnaissance.* New York: Harper and Row, 1966.

Maxwell, A. E. *Analysing qualitative data.* London: Methuen, 1961.

McClelland, D. C., Atkinson, J. W., Clark, R. W., & Lowell, E. L. *The achievement motive.* New York: Appleton-Century-Crofts, 1953.

McGranahan, D. V. Content analysis of the mass media of communication. In M. Jahoda, M. Deutsch, & S. Cook (Eds.), *Research methods in social relations.* New York: Dryden, 1951.

McGrath, J. E. Toward a "theory of method" for research on organizations. In W. Cooper, H. Leavitt, and M. Shelly II (Eds.), *New perspectives in organization research.* New York: Wiley, 1964. Pp. 533–556.

McGrath, J. E. A multi-facet approach to classification of individual, group, and organizational concepts. In B. Indik and K. Berrien (Eds.), *People, groups, and organizations: An effective integration.* New York: Teachers College Press, 1967. Pp. 191–215.

McGrath, J. E., & Altman, I. *Small-group research: A synthesis and critique of the field.* New York: Holt, Rinehart and Winston, 1966.

McGuigan, F. J. The experimenter: A neglected stimulus object. *Psychological Bulletin,* 1963, **60,** 421–428.

McGuigan, F. J. *Experimental psychology.* (2nd ed.) Englewood Cliffs, N.J.: Prentice-Hall, 1968.

Medley, D. M., & Mitzel, H. E. A technique for measuring classroom behavior. *Journal of Educational Psychology,* 1958, **49,** 46–92.

Medley, D. M., & Mitzel, H. E. Measuring classroom behavior by systematic observation. In N. L. Gage (Ed.), *Handbook of research on teaching.* Chicago: Rand McNally, 1963. Pp. 247–328.

Meehl, P. E. Theory-testing in psychology and physics: A methodological paradox. *Philosophy of Science,* 1967, **34,** 103–115.

Melton, A. W. Distribution of attention in galleries in a museum of science and industry. *Museum News,* 1936, **13** (3), 5–8.

Messick, D. M. (Ed.) *Mathematical thinking in behavioral sciences: Readings from Scientific American.* San Francisco: Freeman, 1968.

Messick, S. The perception of social attitudes. *Journal of Abnormal and Social Psychology,* 1956, **52** (1), 57–66.

Miles, M. B. *Learning to work in groups.* New York: Teachers College Press, 1959.

Milgram, S. Behavioral study of obedience. *Journal of Abnormal and Social Psychology,* 1963, **67,** 371–378.

Milgram, S. Issues in the study of obedience: A reply to Baumrind. *American Psychologist,* 1964, **19,** 848–852.

Milgram, S. The lost-letter technique. *Psychology Today,* 1969, **3** (1), 30–33, 66–68.

Miller, D. C. *Handbook of research design and social measurement.* New York: David McKay, 1964.

Miller, G. A., & Madow, W. G. On the maximum likelihood estimate of the Shannon-Wiener measure of information. In R. D. Luce, R. R. Bush, & E. Galanter (Eds.), *Readings in mathematical psychology* Vol. 1. New York: Wiley, 1963. Pp. 448–469.

Miller, J. G. Living systems: Basic concepts. *Behavioral Science,* 1965, **10,** 193–237. Structure and process, 337–379. Cross-level hypotheses, 380–411.

Millholland, J. E. Four kinds of reproducibility in scale analysis. *Educational and Psychological Measurement,* 1955, **15,** 478–482.

Mill, J. S. *A system of logic.* Vol. I. New York: Harper and Row, 1891.

Millman, J., Bishop, C. H., & Ebel, R. An analysis of test-wiseness. *Educational and Psychological Measurement,* 1965, **25,** 707–726.

Mills, T. M. *Group transformation: An analysis of a learning group.* Englewood Cliffs, N.J.: Prentice-Hall, 1964.

Mitchell, T. R., & Foa, U. G. Diffusion of the effect of cultural training of the leader in the structure of heterocultural task groups. *Australian Journal of Psychology,* 1969, **21,** 31–43.

Mitra, S. K. *Contributions to the statistical analysis of categorical data.* Chapel Hill, N.C.: University of North Carolina, Institute of Statistics, 1955. Mimeograph Series No. 142.

Moore, F. W. (Ed.) *Readings in cross-cultural methodology.* New Haven, Conn.: Human Relations Area Files Press, 1961.

Moore, O. K., & Anderson, A. R. Some puzzling aspects of social interaction. In J. H. Criswell, H. Solomon, & P. Suppes (Eds.), *Mathematical methods in small group processes.* Stanford, Calif.: Stanford University Press, 1962. Pp. 232–249.

Moore, O. K., & Anderson, S. B. Modern logic and tasks for experiments on problem solving behavior. *Journal of Psychology,* 1954, **38,** 151–160.

Moore, W. E. Social structure and behavior. In G. Lindzey and E. Aronson (Eds.), *Handbook of social psychology.* Vol. 4. (2nd ed.) Reading, Mass.: Addison-Wesley, 1969. Pp. 283–322.

Moreno, J., and others. *The sociometry reader.* New York: Free Press, 1960.

Mori, T. Structure of motivations for becoming a teacher. *Journal of Educational Psychology,* 1965, **56,** 175–183.

Morris, C. G., II. Effects of task characteristics on group process. Technical Report No. 2, July 1965, University of Illinois Department of Psychology, AFOSR 65-1519, Contract AF 49(638)-1291.

Morrison, P. A. Probabilities from longitudinal records. In E. F. Borgatta (Ed.), *Sociological methodology 1969.* San Francisco: Jossey-Bass, 1969. Pp. 286–294.

Morse, N., & Reimer, E. The experimental change of a major organizational variable. *Journal of Abnormal Social Psychology,* 1956, **52,** 120–129.

Mosier, C. I. A modification of the method of successive intervals. *Psychometrika,* 1940, **5,** 101–107.

Murray, H. A., and others. *Explorations in personality.* New York: Oxford University Press, 1938.

Murstein, B. I. (Ed.) *Handbook of projective techniques.* New York: Basic Books, 1965.

Myers, A. Team competition, success, and adjustment of group members. *Journal of Abnormal and Social Psychology,* 1962, **65,** 325–332.

Nagel, E. *The structure of science: Problems in the logic of scientific explanation.* New York: Harcourt, Brace, & Jovanovich, 1961.

Newcomb, T. M. *The acquaintance process.* New York: Holt, Rinehart and Winston, 1961.

North, R. C., and others. *Content analysis: A handbook with applications for the study of international crisis.* Evanston, Ill.: Northwestern University Press, 1963.

Novick, M. R. The axioms and principal results of classical test theory. *Journal of Mathematical Psychology,* 1966, **3,** 1–18.

Nunnally, J. C. *Educational measurement and evaluation.* New York: McGraw-Hill, 1964.

Nunnally, J. C. *Psychometric theory.* New York: McGraw-Hill, 1967.

Oeser, O. A., and Harary, F. A mathematical model for structural role theory. *Human Relations.* Pt. I: 1962, **15,** 89–109. Pt. II: 1964, **17,** 3–17.

Oppenheim, A. N. *Questionnaire design and attitude measurement.* New York: Basic Books, 1966.

Orne, M. T. On the social psychology of the psychological experiment: With particular reference to demand characteristics and their implications. *American Psychologist,* 1962, **17,** 776–783.

Osgood, C. E., & Suci, G. J. A measure of relation determined by both mean difference and profile information. *Psychological Bulletin,* 1952, **49,** 251–262.

Osgood, C. E., Suci, G. J., & Tannenbaum, P. H. *The measurement of meaning.* Urbana, Ill.: University of Illinois Press, 1957.

Owens, W. A., & Henry, E. R. *Biographical data in industrial psychology: A review and evaluation.* Greensboro, N.C.: Creativity Research Institute, Richardson Foundation, 1966.

Parthasarathy, K. R. Enumeration of paths in digraphs. *Psychometrika,* 1964, **29,** 153–166.

Peak, H. Problems of objective observation. In L. Festinger & D. Katz (Eds.), *Research methods in the behavioral sciences.* New York: Dryden, 1953. Pp. 243–299.

Peng, K. C. *The design and analysis of scientific experiments.* Reading, Mass. Addison-Wesley, 1967

Phillips, B. S. *Social research: Strategy and tactics.* New York: Macmillan, 1966.

Platt, J. R. Strong inference. *Science,* 1964, **146** (Whole No. 3642), 347–353. Reprinted in J. R. Platt, *The step to man.* New York: Wiley, 1966. Pp. 19–36.

Plutchik, R. *Foundations of experimental research.* New York: Harper and Row, 1968.

Popper, K. *The logic of scientific discovery.* New York: Basic Books, 1959.

Porteus, S. D. *The Porteus maze test and intelligence.* Palo Alto, Calif.: Pacific Books, 1950.

Poulton, E. C. The new psychophysics: Six models for magnitude estimation. *Psychological Bulletin,* 1968, **69,** 1–19.

Proctor, C., & Loomis, C. Analysis of sociometric data. In M. Jahoda, M. Deutsch, & S. Cook (Eds.), *Research methods in social relations.* Pt. II. New York: Holt, Rinehart and Winston, 1951. Chap. 17.

Przeworski, A., & Teune, H. *Logic of comparative social inquiry.* New York: Wiley, 1970.

Psychology Today (special section), 1967, **1** (7), 16–41.

Ramanujacharyulu, C. Analysis of preferential experiments. *Psychometrika,* 1964, **29,** 257–261.

Rand Corporation. *A million random digits with 100,000 normal deviates.* New York: Free Press, 1955.

Rapoport, A. Mathematical models of social interaction. In R. D. Luce, R. R. Bush, & E. Galanter (Eds.), *Handbook of mathematical psychology.* Vol. II. New York: Wiley, 1963. Pp. 493–579.

Rapoport, A. Mathematical aspects of general systems analysis. In L. von Bertalanffy & A. Rapoport (Eds.), *General systems: The yearbook of the society for general systems research.* Vol. 11. Ann Arbor, Mich.: The Society for General Systems Research, Mental Health Research Institute, 1966. Pp. 3–11.

Rasch, G. *Probabilistic models for some intelligence and attainment tests.* Copenhagen: Danish Institute for Educational Research, 1960.

Rechtschaffen, A., & Mednick, S. A. The autokinetic word technique. *Journal of Abnormal and Social Psychology,* 1955, **51,** 346.

Reissman, L. (Ed.) Ethics and social science research. *American Behavioral Scientist,* 1967, **10** (10).

Remmers, H. H., Gage, N. L., & Rummel, J. F. *A practical introduction to measurement and evaluation.* New York: Harper and Row, 1960.

Richardson, M. W. Multidimensional psychophysics. *Psychological Bulletin,* 1938, **35,** 659–660. (Abstract)

Richardson, S. A., Dohrenwend, B. S. & Klein, D. *Interviewing: Its forms and functions.* New York: Basic Books, 1965.

Riley, M. W. *Sociological research: A case approach.* New York: Harcourt, Brace, Jovanovich, 1963.

Riley, M. W. Sources and types of sociological data. In R. E. L. Faris (Ed.), *Handbook of modern sociology.* Chicago: Rand McNally, 1964. Pp. 978–1026.

Robinson, J. P., & Hefner, R. Perceptual maps of the world. *Public Opinion Quarterly,* 1968, **32,** 273–280.

Roethlisberger, F. J., & Dickson, W. J. *Management and the worker.* Cambridge, Mass.: Harvard University Press, 1939.

Rokeach, M., & Fruchter, B. A factorial study of dogmatism and related concepts. *Journal of Abnormal and Social Psychology,* 1956, **53,** 356–360.

Rome, B. K., & Rome, S. C. *Organizational growth through decision-making: A computer-based experiment in eductive method.* New York: American Elsevier, 1971.

Rorer, L. G. The great response style myth. *Psychological Bulletin,* 1965, **63,** 129–156.

Rosenthal, D., & Cofer, C. N. The effect on group performance of an indifferent and neglectful attitude shown by one group member. *Journal of Experimental Psychology,* 1948, **38,** 568–577.

Rosenthal, R. *Experimenter effects in behavioral research.* New York: Appleton-Century-Crofts, 1967.

Ross, H. L., Campbell, D. T., & Glass, G. V. Determining the social effects of a legal reform: The British "breathalyser" crackdown of 1967. *American Behavioral Scientist,* 1970, **13** (4), 493–509.

Royce, J. R., and others. The autokinetic phenomenon: A critical review. *Psychological Bulletin,* 1966, **65,** 243–260.

Rubin, Z. Jokers wild in the lab. *Psychology Today,* 1970, **4** (7), 18–24.

Ruebhausen, O. M., & Brim, O. G., Jr. Privacy and behavioral research. *American Psychologist,* 1966, **21,** 423–437.

Runkel, P. J. Some consistency effects. *Educational and Psychological Measurement,* 1958, **18,** 527–541.

Runkel, P. J. Replicated tests of the attraction-communication hypothesis in a setting of technical information flow. *American Sociological Review,* 1962, **27,** 402–408.

Runkel, P. J. Dimensionality, map-matching, and anxiety. *Psychological Reports,* 1963, **13,** 335–350.

Runkel, P. J., Smith, J. E. K., & Newcomb, T. M. Estimating interaction effects among overlapping pairs. *Psychological Bulletin,* 1957, **54,** 152–158.

Runkel, P. J., and others. Stages of group development: An empirical test of Tuckman's hypothesis. *Journal of Applied Behavioral Science,* 1971, **7** (2), 180–193.

Saffir, M. A comparative study of scales constructed by three psychophysical methods. *Psychometrika,* 1937, **2,** 179–198.

Sagi, P. C. A statistical test for the significance of a coefficient of reproducibility. *Psychometrika,* 1959, **24,** 19–28.

Sanford, N. Will psychologists study human problems? *American Psychologist,* 1965, **20,** 192–202.

Sawyer, J., & Friedell, M. F. The interaction screen: An operational model for experimentation on interpersonal behavior. *Behavioral Science,* 1965, **10,** 446–460.

Schachter, S. Deviation, rejection, and communication. *Journal of Abnormal and Social Psychology,* 1951, **46,** 190–207.

Schmuck, R. A., & Runkel, P. J. *Organizational training for a school faculty.* Eugene, Oreg.: Center for the Advanced Study of Educational Administration, University of Oregon, 1970.

Schmuck, R. A., Runkel, P. J. & Langmeyer, D. Improving organizational problem-solving in a school faculty. *Journal of Applied Behavioral Science,* 1969, **5,** 455–482. Reprinted in *ISR Journal,* 1970, **2** (2), 69–93. Also reprinted in R. A. Schmuck & M. B. Miles (Eds.), *Organization development in schools.* Palo Alto, Calif.: National Press Books, 1971. Pp. 51–69.

Schoggen, P. Mechanical aids for making specimen records of behavior. *Child Development,* 1964, **35,** 985–988.

Schutz, W. C. *FIRO: A three-dimensional theory of interpersonal behavior.* New York: Holt, Rinehart and Winston, 1958.

Scott, W. A. Attitude measurement. In G. Lindzey & E. Aronson (Eds.), *Handbook of social psychology.* Vol. 2. (2nd ed.) Reading, Mass.: Addison-Wesley, 1968. Pp. 204–273.

Scott, W. A., & Wertheimer, M. *Introduction to psychological research.* New York: Wiley, 1962.

Seashore, R. H. Work and motor performance. In S. S. Stevens (Ed.), *Handbook of experimental psychology.* New York: Wiley, 1951.

Sells, S. B. Toward a taxonomy of organizations. In W. W. Cooper, H. J. Leavitt, & M. W. Shelly II (Eds.), *New perspectives in organizational research.* New York: Wiley, 1964. Pp. 515–532.

Selltiz, C., and others. *Research methods in social relations.* (Rev. ed.) New York: Holt, Rinehart and Winston, 1959.

Shaw, M. E., & Blum, J. M. Effects of leadership style upon group performance as a function of task structure. *Journal of Personality and Social Psychology,* 1966, **3,** 238–242.

Shaw, M. E., & Wright, J. M. *Scales for the treatment of attitudes.* New York: McGraw-Hill, 1967.

Shepard, R. N. The analysis of proximities: Multidimensional scaling with an unknown distance function. *Psychometrika,* I: 1962, **27,** 125–139 (a), II: 1962, **27,** 219–246. (b)

Shepard, R. N., & Carroll, J. D. Parametric representation of nonlinear data structures. In P. R. Krishnaiah (Ed.), *Multivariate analysis: International symposium on multivariate analysis.* New York: Academic Press, 1966. Pp. 561–592.

Sherif, M., & Sherif, C. W. *Reference groups: Exploration into conformity and deviation of adolescents.* New York: Harper and Row, 1964.

Sherif, M., and others. *Intergroup conflict and cooperation: The Robbers Cave experiment.* Norman, Okla.: The Institute of Group Relations, University of Oklahoma, 1961.

Sherwood, J. J., & Nataupsky, M. Predicting the conclusions of Negro-white intelligence research from biographical characteristics of the investigator. *Journal of Personality and Social Psychology,* 1968, **8,** 53–58.

Shubik, M. (Ed.) *Game theory and related approaches to social behavior.* New York: Wiley, 1964.

Siegel, S. A method for obtaining an ordered metric scale. *Psychometrika,* 1956, **21,** 207–216.

Simon, A., & Boyer, E. G. (Eds.) *Mirrors for behavior: An anthology of classroom observation instruments.* Philadelphia: Research for Better Schools (a Regional Education Laboratory) and the Center for the Study of Teaching at Temple University. 1967. 15 vols.

Simon, J. L. *Basic research methods in social science: The art of empirical investigation.* New York: Random House, 1968.

Sjoberg, G., & Nett, R. *A methodology for social research.* New York: Harper and Row, 1968.

Slonim, M. J. Sampling in a nutshell. *American Statistical Association Journal,* 1957, **52,** 143–161.

Slonim, M. J. *Sampling in a nutshell.* New York: Simon and Schuster, 1960.

Smith, J. E. K. Posterior comparisons in contingency tables. *Michigan Mathematical Psychology Program,* MMPP No. 66-4. Ann Arbor, Mich.: University of Michigan Department of Psychology, 1966.

Snedecor, G. W., & Cochran, W. G. *Statistical methods.* (6th ed.) Ames, Iowa: Iowa State University Press, 1967.

Snider, J. G., & Osgood, C. E. (Eds.) *Semantic differential technique: A sourcebook.* Chicago: Aldine, 1968.

Solomon, R. L., & Lessac, M. S. A control group design for experimental studies of developmental processes. *Psychological Bulletin,* 1968, **70,** 145–150.

Sommer, R. Hawthorne dogma. *Psychological Bulletin,* 1968, **70,** 592–595.

Stanley, J. C. A common class of pseudo-experiments. *American Educational Research Journal,* 1966, **3,** 79–87.

Stanley, J. C. (Ed.) *Improving experimental design and statistical analysis.* Chicago: Rand McNally, 1967.

Stephenson, W. *The study of behavior.* Chicago: University of Chicago Press, 1953.

Stern, G. G., Stein, M. I., & Bloom, B. S. *Methods in personality assessment.* New York: Free Press, 1956.

Stevens, S. S. Mathematics, measurement, and psychophysics. In *Handbook of experimental psychology.* New York: Wiley, 1951. Pp. 1–49.

Stevens, S. S. (Ed.) *Handbook of experimental psychology.* New York: Wiley, 1951.

Stevens, S. S. The direct estimate of sensory magnitudes—loudness. *American Journal of Psychology,* 1956, **69,** 1–25.

Stevens, S. S. Problems and methods of psychophysics. *Psychological Bulletin,* 1958, **55,** 177–196.

Stoll, C. S. Introduction to simulation: An annotated bibliography. *American Behavioral Scientist,* 1969, **12** (6), 47.

Stone, P. J., Dunphy, D. C., Smith, M. S., & Ogilvie, D. M. *The general inquirer: A computer approach to content analysis.* Cambridge, Mass.: MIT Press, 1966.

Stouffer, S. A., and others. *Measurement and prediction.* Vol. 4. *Studies in social psychology in World War II.* Princeton, N.J.: Princeton University Press, 1950.

Suchman, E. A. *Evaluative research.* New York: Russell Sage Foundation, 1967.

Suppes, P., & Zinnes, J. L. Basic measurement theory. In R. D. Luce, R. R. Bush, & E. Galanter (Eds.), *Handbook of mathematical psychology.* Vol. 1. New York: Wiley, 1963. Pp. 1–76.

Sutcliffe, J. P. A general method of analysis of frequency data for multiple classification designs. *Psychological Bulletin,* 1957, **54,** 134–137.

Thorndike, R. L., & Hagen, E. *Measurement and evaluation in psychology and education.* (2nd ed.) New York: Wiley, 1961.

Thurstone, L. L. A law of comparative judgment. *Psychological Review,* 1927, **34,** 273–286. (a)

Thurstone, L. L. The method of paired comparisons for social values. *Journal of Abnormal and Social Psychology,* 1927, **21,** 384–400. (b)

Thurstone, L. L. Attitudes can be measured. *American Journal of Sociology,* 1928, **33,** 529–554. Reprinted in M. Fishbein (Ed.), *Readings in attitude theory and measurement.* New York: Wiley, 1967. Pp. 77–89.

Thurstone, L. L. *Primary mental abilities.* Chicago: University of Chicago Press, 1938.

Thurstone, L. L., & Chave, E. J. *The measurement of attitude.* Chicago: University of Chicago Press, 1929.

Thurstone, L. L., & Jones, L. V. The rational origin for measuring subjective values. *Journal of the American Statistical Association,* 1957, **52,** 458–471.

Toda, M. About the notions of communication and structure: A perspective. In L. Thayer (Ed.), *Communication: Concepts and perspectives.* Washington, D.C.: Spartan Books, 1967. Pp. 25–52.

Toda, M. & Shuford, E., Jr. Utility, induced utilities, and small worlds. *Behavioral Science,* 1965, **10,** 238–254.

Tompkins, S. S., & Messick, S. (Eds.) *Computer simulation of personality: Frontier of psychological theory.* New York: Wiley, 1963.

Torgerson, W. S. Multidimensional scaling: I. Theory and method. *Psychometrika,* 1952, **17,** 401–419.

Torgerson, W. S. *Theory and methods of scaling.* New York: Wiley, 1958.

Torgerson, W. S. Multidimensional scaling of similarity. *Psychometrika,* 1965, **30,** 379–393.

Travers, R. M. W. An introduction to educational research. (2nd ed.) New York: Macmillan, 1964.

Tucker, L. R. Intra-individual and inter-individual multidimensionality. In H. Gulliksen and S. Messick (Eds.), *Psychological scaling: Theory and applications.* New York: Wiley, 1960. Pp. 155–167.

Tucker, L. R. Implications of factor analysis of three-way matrices for measurement of change. In C. W. Harris (Ed.), *Problems in measuring change.* Madison, Wis.: University of Wisconsin Press, 1963. Pp. 122–137.

Tucker, L. R. Experiments in multi-mode factor analysis. In C. W. Harris (Ed.), *Proceedings of the 1964 invitational conference on testing problems.* Princeton, N.J.: Educational Testing Service, 1965. Pp. 46–57.

Tuckman, B. W. Developmental sequence in small groups. *Psychological Bulletin,* 1965, **63,** 384–399.

Turk, H. Instrumental and expressive ratings reconsidered. *Sociometry,* 1961, **24,** 76–81.

Turner, M. B. *Philosophy and the science of behavior.* New York: Appleton-Century-Crofts, 1965.

Tversky, A. Intransitivity of preferences. *Psychological Review,* 1969, **76,** 31–48.

Tyler, L. E. *Tests and measurements.* (3rd ed.) Englewood Cliffs, N.J.: Prentice-Hall, 1971.

Uhr, L. (Ed.) *Pattern recognition: Theory, experiment, computer simulations, and dynamic models of form perception and discovery.* New York: Wiley, 1966.

Underwood, B. J. *Psychological research.* New York: Appleton-Century-Crofts, 1957.

U.S. National Referral Center for Science and Technology. *A directory of information resources in the United States: Social sciences.* Washington, D.C.: Government Printing Office, 1965.

U.S. Office of Strategic Services. *Assessment of men.* New York: Holt, Rinehart and Winston, 1948.

U.S. Surgeon General's Office. Surgeon General's directives on human experimentation. *American Psychologist,* 1967, **22,** 350–355.

Upshaw, H. S. Own attitude as an anchor in equal-appearing intervals. *Journal of Abnormal and Social Psychology,* 1962, **64,** 85–96.

Upshaw, H. S. Attitude measurement. In H. M. Blalock and A. B. Blalock (Eds.), *Methodology in social research.* New York: McGraw-Hill, 1968. Pp. 60–111.

Waxler, N. W., & Mishler, E. G. Scoring and reliability problems in interaction process analysis: A methodological note. *Sociometry,* 1966, **29,** 28–40.

Webb, E. J., and others. *Unobtrusive measures: Nonreactive research in the social sciences.* Chicago: Rand McNally, 1966.

Weick, K. E. Systematic observational methods. In G. Lindzey & E. Aronson (Eds.), *Handbook of social psychology.* Vol. 2. (2nd ed.) Reading, Mass.: Addison-Wesley, 1968. Pp. 357–451.

Werts, C. E., & Linn, R. L. Path analysis: Psychological examples. *Psychological Bulletin,* 1970, **74** (3), 193–212.

Wesman, A. G. Intelligence testing. *American Psychologist,* 1968, **23,** 267–276.

White, B. W., & Saltz, E. Measurement of reproducibility. *Psychological Bulletin,* 1957, **54,** 81–99.

White, H. C. Chance models of systems of casual groups. *Sociometry,* 1962, **25,** 153–172.

White, H. C. *An anatomy of kinship.* Englewood Cliffs, N.J.: Prentice-Hall, 1963.

Wiggins, J. A. Hypothesis validity and experimental laboratory methods. In H. M. Blalock & A. B. Blalock (Eds.), *Methodology in social research.* New York: McGraw-Hill, 1968. Pp. 390–427.

Willems, E. P., & Raush, H. L. (Eds.) *Naturalistic viewpoints in psychological research.* New York: Holt, Rinehart and Winston, 1969.

Willems, E. P., & Willems, G. J. Comparative validity of data yielded by three methods. *Merrill-Palmer Quarterly,* 1965, **11,** 65–71.

Willis, R. H. Estimating the scalability of a series of items—an application of information theory. *Psychological Bulletin,* 1954, **51,** 511–516.

Winch, R. F., & Campbell, D. T. Proof? No. Evidence? Yes. The significance of tests of significance. *American Sociologist,* 1969, **4** (2), 140–143.

Wish, M. A facet-theoretic approach for Morse code and related signals. *Michigan Mathematical Psychology Program,* MMPP No. 65-6, Ann Arbor, Mich.: University of Michigan Department of Psychology, 1965.

Wolman, B. B., & Nagel, E. (Eds.) *Scientific psychology: Principles and approaches.* New York: Basic Books, 1965.

Woodger, J. H. The technique of theory construction. *International encyclopedia of unified science.* Vol. 2, No. 5. Chicago: University of Chicago Press, 1929.

Wright, B., & Evitts, M. S. Direct factor analysis in sociometry. *Sociometry,* 1961, **24,** 82–98.

Wright, B., & Evitts, M. S. Multiple regression in the explanation of social structure. *Journal of Social Psychology,* 1963, **61,** 87–98.

Wright, H. F. Observational child study. In P. H. Mussen (Ed.), *Handbook of research methods in child development.* New York: Wiley, 1960. Pp. 71–139.

Wuebben, P. L. Honesty of subjects and birth order. *Journal of Personality and Social Psychology,* 1967, **5,** 350–352.

Yamane, T. *Elementary sampling theory.* Englewood Cliffs, N.J.: Prentice-Hall, 1967.

Yee, A. H., & Runkel, P. J. Simplicial structures of middle-class and lower-class pupils' attitudes toward teachers. *Developmental Psychology,* 1969, **1,** 646–652.

Young, F. W. *A FORTRAN IV program for nonmetric multidimensional scaling.* Chapel Hill, N.C.: L. L. Thurstone Psychometric Laboratory Report No. 56, March, 1968.

Young, P. V. *Scientific social surveys and research.* (4th ed.) Englewood Cliffs, N.J.: Prentice-Hall, 1966.

Zajonc, R. B. The requirements and design of a standard group task. *Journal of Experimental Social Psychology,* 1965, **1,** 71–88. (a)

Zajonc, R. B. Social facilitation. *Science,* 1965, **149** (Whole No. 3681), 269–274. (b)

Zetterberg, H. L. *On theory and verification in sociology.* (2nd ed.) Totowa, N.J.: Bedminister Press, 1963.

Zuckerman, D. W., & Horn, R. E. *The guide to simulation games for education and training.* Cambridge, Mass.: Information Resources, 1970.

Index to Authors

A

B

C

D

E

F

G

H

I

J

K

L

M

S

T

U

V

W

Y

Z

Index to Subjects

A

B

C

D

H

I

O

P

S

T

U

V

W